Küng in Conflict

Küng in Conflict

EDITED
WITH TRANSLATION AND COMMENTARY

by Leonard Swidler

IMAGE BOOKS
A DIVISION OF DOUBLEDAY & COMPANY, INC.
GARDEN CITY, NEW YORK
1981

ISBN: 0-385-17552-3
Library of Congress Catalog Card Number: 80–2878

Contents

WORLD PROTEST

Europe

CONTENTS

Introduction

On December 18, 1979, the Vatican announced that Hans Küng could no longer be considered a Catholic theologian; the German Bishops' Conference simultaneously announced that it agreed. A broad spectrum of Catholic theologians around the world quickly responded publicly that Hans Küng is indeed a Catholic theologian. All the news media were immediately full of statements, counterstatements, protests, and counterprotests. Eventually, in April 1980, a compromise solution was arrived at that removed Küng from the Catholic Theology Faculty of the University of Tübingen—sort of—but left him professor of ecumenical theology and able to chair committees for the two doctorates in theology in the Catholic Theology Faculty at Tübingen. What happened in between? In the years before that led to the explosion? Who was "right"? Who was "wrong"?

The German Bishops' Conference issued an extensive *Documentation* on December 18, 1979, which they felt would help justify their concerted action with the Vatican against Küng. In book form the English translation of the *Documentation* (*The Küng Dialogue*, Washington, D.C.: U. S. Catholic Conference, 1980) ran to somewhat more than 200 pages, covering the period from the late sixties to the end of 1979 (a supplement ran from December 18 to 30, 1979). A colleague of Küng's, Professor Walter Jens, had edited the documentation concerning the debate centering on Küng's *On Being a Christian* from 1973 to 1978 in a book of just under 400 pages (*Um Nichts als die Wahrheit,* Munich: Piper Verlag, 1978). Then Professors Norbert Greinacher and Herbert Haag edited a 546-page book (*Der Fall Küng,* Munich: Piper Verlag, 1980) with the documentation from where Jens left off till April 1980.

Of the almost 1,000 pages of documentation involved in these latter two volumes, less than 200 pages have been translated into English. Perhaps the optimum would be to make all of the 1,000 pages available in English, but that would be prohibitively expensive. On the other hand, the translation of *The Küng Dialogue,* helpful as it is, still leaves out much very important material, including world reaction to the long affair. Hence, a compromise seemed in order, one that would provide close to three times as much as the Bishops' *Documentation,* just over half of Küng's colleagues' two books, in the setting of a spare narrative which would provide both the context for the texts and a continuity between the important documents, thereby eliminating the need to reproduce the less important documents. With the original sources in a contextual setting, the reader is enabled to understand just what was going on and why, and also to decide which claim or counterclaim is warranted.

However, a good deal more is provided in these documents than the ability to decide who is "right" and who is "wrong." Well over 200 of these pages were written by Küng himself, practically none of which has ever appeared before in English. They not only provide a valuable insight into an extremely important train of events but also in many instances expound important elements of Küng's Catholic thought. One can trace here the dramatic shift from theology "from above," as in, e.g., *Menschwerdung Gottes,* to theology "from below," as in, e.g., *On Being a Christian.* Küng's method in doing theology "from below" is spelled out in great detail—in an extended attempt to make it both understandable and acceptable to various Church authorities. Küng deals at length with truth, its standards, and who decides about it. Hence, anyone wanting to understand the principles underlying Küng's whole theology will find them clearly enunciated, explained, and argued in the following documents. To learn them will provide a key insight into the development of much of contemporary—and future—Catholic theology, for one of Küng's great virtues is his ability to sense the questions that are bothering contemporary opinion-makers and provide answers in a language that speaks to them effectively. The proof of this is not only his tremendous popularity, as evidenced by the sale of hundreds of thousands of his books, but most concretely the massive resistance he has called forth from the Catholic Church authorities, as evidenced in the documents of this book.

The narrative and documents that follow are basically in chronological order. The essential information about each document is given in the narrative immediately preceding it, that is, date, origin, addressee, etc. The vast majority of the documents are published in their original language (almost always German) in the two books mentioned above, edited by Jens and Greinacher and Haag, or in a few instances of documents earlier than 1973, in the German Bishop's *Documentation*. The main exception to this rule comes toward the end of this book where a number of American reactions to Küng's censure are provided.

Each document is numbered sequentially and is also thus listed in a "table of contents" with the origin and addressee of the document provided so that a quick overview can be had as well as the location of a particular document in this volume.

Küng in Conflict

Background

In 1957, the year he received his doctorate in theology from the Institut Catholique in Paris, Hans Küng's dossier 399/57/i was, as he later remarked in a letter to the Vatican, "to judge by the number, already started by the Index" Department of the Holy Office in Rome. He was then twenty-eight years old, and from that time forward he frequently, at times constantly, had to defend himself vis-à-vis the Vatican and/or the German Bishops.

It was not always that way. As a young boy Küng was convinced he had a vocation to the priesthood. He had been born March 19, 1928, into a devout Catholic family at Sursee near Lucerne, Switzerland, and although he attended a coeducational Gymnasium in Lucerne and absorbed the culture and freedom-loving heritage of the Swiss, he eagerly went off to seven years of strict seminary discipline and study in Rome in 1948. It was, as Küng later related, "an education in the strict Tridentine spirit—during seven whole years in which I would be allowed to travel home once, at most twice. . . . I wanted above all an intense scholarly schooling, which the Papal Gregorian University with six semesters of philosophy and eight semesters of theology appeared to guarantee. I wanted the strict inner and outer discipline of the Papal Collegium Germanicum, which like the Gregorian was run by Jesuits" (see Hermann Häring and Karl-Josef

Kuschel, *Hans Küng / His Work and His Way,* Garden City, N.Y.:
Doubleday Image Books, 1980, p. 131).
The years 1948–55 were "great years in Rome. . . . Pius XII
at that time stood at the height of his power and prestige. . . .
the triumphalistic definition of the Assumption of Mary into
heaven and so forth. . . . Yes, in the beginning I accepted all of
that unreservedly. . . . And in conversation with students from
German universities I criticized at that time the 'pride' and
'hypercriticism' of the screaming rationalistic German theology
professors who had their doubts about this matter" (*ibid.,* p. 132).

However, this uncritical enthusiasm for the Church authority
position began to change to a more mature, differentiating attitude and led to what Küng calls a "critical loyalty." Küng attended lectures by the outstanding Bible exegete Stanislas Lyon-
net (who was silenced and banned by the Holy Office in 1961).
He also came to know in a small study circle Yves Congar, the
great Catholic "reform" theologian, who had been silenced and
exiled—he came to Rome! Küng also chaired a study circle on
dialectical materialism for the rector of the Papal Collegium Rus-
sicum, Gustav A. Wetter, and also another study circle on sociology for the papal adviser Gustav Gundlach. At the same time a
crisis in Church leadership was occurring, with the suppression of
ecumenism, especially in Germany (*Monitum,* 1948; *Instructio,*
1949), the crushing of the "New Theology" in France (*Humani
generis,* 1950), and the suppression of the French worker priests
(1953). According to Küng, there was a "constant inflation of
magisterial declarations by addresses and encyclicals of a pope
who memorized, and ultimately only read, what others—whom I
knew only too well—had written. The daily—if you will—look
behind the scenery of this pontificate had led to a 'demythologisa-
tion' of this pope whom we had all before idealized" (*ibid.,* p.
133).

Then Küng noted that the promises of neo-scholastic theology
did not materialize. In another study circle the theology of the supernatural and the "two-tier" grace theory were debated (Henri
de Lubac, who had tried to overcome this dualism in his *Surna-
turel,* 1946, had been silenced and exiled). Further, more and

more college disciplinary rules began to be perceived as unreasonable and uncreative. Then, toward the end of his Roman study period, as a young priest, he was made chaplain of the Italian workers at the Collegium Germanicum; he took the responsibility seriously and worked for the improvement of their social and financial situation—which brought him into conflict with the Collegium administration and provided him an insight into the practical need of reform even at that level in the Church.

In 1951, Küng wrote a thesis for his Licentiate in Philosophy on the atheistic humanism of Jean-Paul Sartre and in 1955 a thesis for his Licentiate in Theology on the doctrine of justification in Karl Barth, a fellow Swiss and the most influential Protestant theologian alive. In this latter work he was supported by his professors at Rome and by another Swiss, a well-known Catholic theologian, Hans Urs von Balthasar (also an expert on Barth's theology), who urged Küng to expand his work on Barth into a doctoral dissertation. This Küng did during his year and a half at the Sorbonne and the Institut Catholique in Paris (1955–57), with the title "Justification, La doctrine de Karl Barth et une réflexion catholique," under Louis Bouyer. The dissertation appeared simultaneously as a German book, published by von Balthasar in Switzerland (1957). The book, which argued that Barth's doctrine of justification and the Council of Trent's were fundamentally the same, caused a sensation in Protestant and Catholic theological worlds. (I can recall a seminar being offered on it by Heinrich Diem of the Protestant faculty at the University of Tübingen the summer semester of 1958.) After all, the disagreement on the doctrine of justification was one of the key theological reasons for the sixteenth-century Protestant-Catholic split.

It was precisely this bridging of the presumably unbridgeable that brought immediate and manifold delations (technical term for tattling) to Rome. At the time Küng judged the chances of the book's being placed on the Index of Forbidden Books about fifty-fifty. However, the support of his teachers, especially Sebastian Tromp, Franz Hürth, Louis Bouyer, and Guy de Broglie, fended off that effort. But that move started his dossier 399/57/i—and it has been active ever since.

Küng at that point spent a year and a half in pastoral work in Switzerland, and then, following the urging of Heinrich Fries (whose successor he beame in 1960 at the University of Tübingen), Hermann Volk (whose assistant he became in 1959 at the University of Münster and who later became the Cardinal Archbishop of Mainz), and Karl Rahner, the most renowned living Catholic theologian, opted for the academic life in Germany. In 1960, he was called to the Catholic Theology Faculty of Tübingen and in the same year published another "sensational" book, *The Council, Reform and Reunion* (over the strong doubts of Professor Volk and Cardinal Döpfner of Munich, but with an introduction by Cardinal Koenig of Vienna), which urged a whole battery of reforms in the spirit of Pope John XXIII's "aggiornamento."

Under the influence of the newly announced Council (in January 1959 by John XXIII) and the encouragement of his Church-history colleague Karl August Fink, Küng began an intensive study of the whole conciliar tradition, which resulted in the publication in 1962, the year Vatican II began, of *Structures of the Church*. All of the seemingly settled problems of authority, decision making, etc., were laid open again in the simple presenting of the historical evidence. This apparently made the Vatican so uneasy that Küng was called to a proceedings against the book. It took place in 1963, during the second session of the Council (Küng was an "expert" appointed to the Council by the Pope), at the temporary Roman residence of Bishop Leiprecht of Rottenburg (in which diocese Tübingen lay). Fortunately for Küng the great ecumenist Cardinal Augustin Bea (who, despite his name, came from Swabia—Tübingen's province) was put in charge of the proceedings. Küng later recalled, "Well, it was the period of the Council, and so I was forgiven a certain amount. At all events a solemn session took place in Rome with Cardinal Bea in the chair along with the Bishop of Basel [Küng's home diocese] as well as professors from the Gregorian. I had to answer various questions that had been drawn up by the Holy Office. Later I had to repeat my answers in writing in Latin. Without a doubt it was thanks to Cardinal Bea, whom I had got to know during my first years in Rome when he was Visitator at the German College in the days when he was a simple Jesuit priest and Pius XII's confessor, that the proceedings came to a happy conclusion and were terminated without any obligation of any kind being laid upon me" (*ibid.*, p. 160).

Earlier that same year, 1963, Küng made the first of what might be described as his "triumphal tours" through the United States. But again restrictions by Church authorities—this time episcopal rather than papal—played a significant role. It all started with the so-called Catholic University affair.

A list of possible speakers for a Lenten series of lectures to be sponsored by the university was submitted by the appropriate committee of graduate students—chaired by a woman student newly come from Duquesne University. The rector of the university then struck from the list the names of Gustave Weigel, John Courtney Murray, Godfrey Diekmann, and Hans Küng, the first three some of the most respected theologians of the American Catholic Church (Küng of course had suddenly become widely known in the United States through the wide distribution of his book *The Council, Reform and Reunion*). This was all to remain private—in the usual fashion. But it didn't. The former Duquesne student protested and went to the student newspaper, which published its protest. *Time* magazine picked up the story, and so did a few Catholic diocesan newspapers. In the past such a situation would probably never have developed even that far. But if it had, the most that would have been forthcoming would have been a few scattered remarks and then silence. But the old days were gone. Dozens of Catholic newspapers carried the story week after week. Many of them criticized the administration of the Catholic University—whose board of trustees was composed of all the American cardinals, a number of bishops, and a few laymen. Several of the faculties of the Catholic University, including the Theology Faculty and the Canon Law Faculty, publicly censured the administration for its actions. Other Catholic University faculties also raised objections. As the protests spread and grew, evidence of a practice of past suppression came out. Monsignor John Tracy Ellis, the most highly respected American Catholic Church historian, stated openly that similar suppression had been going on for at least the past ten years—with specifics given. An article was published by a Pittsburgh priest in the Steubenville, Ohio, Catholic newspaper (whose editor, Monsignor Francis Brown, was no longer a monsignor by the end of that year), criticizing openly the Apostolic Delegate, Archbishop Vagnozzi, in Washington, D.C., for having manipulated the whole suppression.

In the midst of all this Küng arrived in the United States for his previously scheduled lecture tour. Several other places had forbidden him to speak (his lecture was on freedom and unfreedom in the Church), notably Philadelphia, Los Angeles, San Diego, and St. Paul. But wherever he did speak, the hall was jammed to overflowing; his audiences ran as high as five and six thousand. When he arrived at Duquesne University in Pittsburgh, for example, he was to speak in an auditorium which normally held 1,000 persons. Additional chairs were put everywhere, including 200 on the stage, so that 1,600 could be packed in. For days ahead of time it was announced on the radio, etc., that people were not to come if they didn't have tickets. Still, there came an additional 200 who had to sit in the cafeteria to hear Küng by loudspeaker. Hans Küng had suddenly become the symbol of the new freedom of the Catholic Church. Without the first session of Vatican II— with its "revolt of the cardinals" against the Curia, which revolt was supported by Pope John XXIII (who unfortunately died in the spring of 1963)—all this would have been impossible. But since it happened, the Catholic Church could never be the same again.

That year, 1963, was filled with high and low points for Küng. Although he was appointed a *peritus* to the Council by John XXIII that year, Küng also saw the death of his patron Pope. Although he also met and became an avid admirer of John F. Kennedy while in America that spring (he did nevertheless visit Washington), that fall President Kennedy was assassinated. Although he was enthusiastically feted in many cities in America, he was banned in others. Although he was very active in that session of the Council and was even recommended by Karl Rahner for a position on the Doctrinal Commission of the Council, because of blockages he perceived there (the extremely conservative head of the Holy Office, Cardinal Alfredo Ottaviani, chaired the Commission), he decided not to pursue the possibility.

Years later he remarked: "During the second session I drafted an assessment that was concerned particularly with the election of a fresh Doctrinal Commission and the replacement of Cardinal Ottaviani by a president to be elected by the Council. This assessment was handed over to Paul VI personally by the Melkite Patriarch Maximos IV Saigh. The result of this and many similar initiatives was merely that a few more members were elected onto the Commission, a second secretary was appointed, and other steps were taken along these lines. For the rest, however, everything stayed as it was. This made it clear that there could be no thought of recasting the fundamental conciliar Constitution on the Church to place it on a more solid biblical basis. In particular, no decisive change would be possible in what is now the third chapter on the Church's hierarchical structure, which confirmed Vatican I with its problematical definitions of papal primacy and infallibility without introducing any differentiation and even partly extended this to the episcopate. This was the reason why I was not ready to take part in the work of this Commission, whose First Secretary, incidentally, was my old teacher the Dutchman Sebastian Tromp. Likewise my often expressed demand to put more competent and critical exegetes on this Commission remained unfulfilled. Critical German exegesis was *de facto* not present in the Council" (*ibid.*, pp. 170–71).

When Küng was asked whether he had not missed a chance to influence the thinking of the Council by not going onto the Commission, he replied: "Naturally I could have accomplished something within the Theological Commission, and I was indeed also of the opinion that others—some friends among them—should work on this Commission. But I could not have changed anything decisive in this situation. And therefore other things appeared more important to me. And I nevertheless still always had possibilities, directly or indirectly, of bringing about important changes, for example in the Constitution on the Church insofar as I drew up various important Council speeches of bishops: for example on the charismatic dimension of the Church, on the significance of the local Church, on the sinful Church and the necessity of continual reform, on the three-fold offices of ordination and other similar matters. It was likewise possible to exercise influence through public statements in the world press: my timely orientation of the large newspapers in reference to the curial maneuvers to set aside the Declaration on the Jews as well as the Declaration on Religious Freedom put the brakes on these maneuvers. Short and clear: I was present in the Council even if I was not present on the Theological Commission. The decisive thing was something else: at the beginning of the second session —after a careful study of the revised schema of the Constitution on the Church—I decided after days of reflection to begin my book *The Church*. I had intended in later decades to dedicate myself to the writing of something like a *Spirit of Catholicism* (the German title is the "Essence," *Wesen*, of Catholicism) according to the model of my great predecessor in dogmatics at Tübingen, Karl Adam. But now seemed to be the time to write a book on the essence of the Church—in a very different manner of course. And inwardly I entered into a competition with the Theological Commission to finish my book at about the same time. A year after the close of the Council the manuscript was after endless effort finished and in 1967 it was published" (*ibid.*, pp. 171–72).

The Attack
on *The Church*

It was in April of that year, 1967, that the German edition of *The Church* came, and the Dutch shortly thereafter. The Holy Office, which had its name changed to the Congregation for the Doctrine of the Faith, was still headed by Cardinal Ottaviani; they were displeased enough with the book to reprimand the diocese of Rottenburg for having given the book an *Imprimatur* and to order that further distribution and translation of the book be halted until after the author had had a discussion with representatives to be named by the Doctrinal Congregation. This was communicated to the Bishop of Rottenburg on December 19, 1967, and was sent from there to Küng (by special-delivery letter to both Tübingen and his Swiss family home in Sursee). It reached him two days after Christmas.

From the perspective of later years it would seem that that time of the year, Christmas vacation time, and the middle of the summer vacation time are favorite periods for the Vatican to issue its restrictions, condemnations, etc. Küng then called his publishers in Paris, London, and New York and arranged to have at least the latter two editions dated 1967, although they actually appeared only in early 1968. The French also appeared in 1968, as did the Spanish; the Italian and Portuguese came out in 1969. However, through the Nunciature the Vatican was able to stop a Korean edition from appearing. But Christmas 1967 was just the

beginning of what was to become an eight-year-long struggle and
negotiation between Küng and the Vatican, apparently being terminated in 1975, but then suddenly being revived again by the
Vatican—at Christmas time 1979.

In the spring of 1968 Küng received a letter from the Doctrinal
Congregation telling him that he had to appear in Rome in nine
days at 9:30 A.M. in the Palace of the Holy Office for a "discussion." It was rather risky, to say the least, to depend on the Italian
mail service to get the letter to Germany on time. They were for-
tunate: it arrived on Saturday, May 4. It was of course the middle
of a university semester, and it was the following Wednesday that
Küng was to appear in Rome. The brief letter, dated April 30, was
as follows:

(1)

Dear Professor Küng,
    The Congregation for the Doctrine of the Faith is examin-
ing your book *The Church*.
    According to the norms of the motu proprio *Integrae ser-
vandae,* a discussion with the author should be held. I ask
you, dear Professor Küng, to come to this discussion on
Thursday, May 9, at 9:30 A.M., in the Palazzo del S. Uffizio
in Rome.
Respectfully,

For a number of reasons Küng felt he could not drop everything and go unprepared and uniformed to a "discussion" at the
Palace of the Holy Office. Hence, on May 8 he sent a telegram
stating: "Unfortunately prevented, letter follows. Küng." Later
that month he did send a lengthy letter explaining why he could
not come then. One reason he did not explicitly name but which
may well have played a role was the concern about the sort of
treatment he might have received at that Vatican "discussion."
Just a few days after Küng wrote his letter, in June 1968, Monsignor Ivan Illich was summoned to Rome for a "discussion," the
later description of which read like a gothic novel, with dark
rooms in the basement of the Palace, isolation, an eighty-five-

point questionnaire with such extraordinary questions as: "What do you say about those who say you arc 'petulant, adventurous, imprudent, fanatical and hypnotizing, a rebel to any authority, disposed to accept and recognize only that of the Bishop of Cuernavaca [where Illich was the founder and director of the Intercultural Center of Documentation, which started out to train North American priests and religious for work in Latin America]'?" The result was that a few months later the Doctrinal Congregation forbade priests and religious to go to the Center.

In any case, after Küng outlined why he did not come to the "discussion," he added five conditions which he felt were essential if a fair discussion were to be held: (1) access to the documents in his Vatican dossier; (2) a written statement of the problem areas ahead of time from the Congregation; (3) because of the scholarly nature of his book, the Congregation's discussants should be competent experts in exegesis, history, and dogmatics, and Küng should be informed who they would be; (4) the discussion would be in his native tongue, German; (5) Küng would be financially reimbursed for the expenses involved.

A point that is extremely important to notice, in light of subsequent—and present—accusations that Küng refused to go to Rome for a discussion, is that before Küng listed the conditions essential to a fair discussion, even before he explained why he could not keep the May 9 date, he stated clearly and in an extremely friendly tone that he was "in principle . . . prepared to participate in a discussion," that he looked upon "the invitation to a discussion as significant progress compared to the procedure customary in the past. . . . You can be assured of my cooperation."

On May 30, 1968, then, Küng wrote to Archbishop Paolo Philippe, O.P., Secretary of the Doctrinal Congregation, as follows:

(2)

Dear Archbishop:
As I indicated to you by telegram on May 8, I was unfortunately prevented from appearing at the discussion sched-

uled for May 9. In the meantime, I have taken care to reflect carefully on my answer to your letter and to discuss it with other competent professors and ecclesiastics.

From the beginning I would like to state that, in principle, I am prepared to participate in a discussion. I consider the invitation to a discussion as significant progress compared to the procedure customary in the past. I am persuaded that through an open and congenial exchange of views future difficulties and ambiguities can be entirely clarified. In the post-conciliar era dialogue among Catholics is at least as important as dialogue with other Christian churches and with the modern world. You can be assured of my cooperation.

At the same time, I cannot conceal my surprise at the way in which this invitation has been issued to me. In view of the fact that the date for a discussion ought to be arranged by mutual agreement, I cannot understand how this invitation could have been issued on such short notice. I do not know whether this has been reckoned with in your Congregation. Your letter is dated April 30. It was handed to me on Saturday, May 4. To be present at the discussion in Rome on May 9, I would have had to leave May 8. In my opinion, this was a serious imposition. Apparently, people are hardly aware of the work load of a university professor. Precisely because of my work load, I was even forced at that same time to decline the invitation of a Catholic university in the U.S.A. to receive an honorary doctorate. You will, therefore, understand that an unplanned journey to Rome is out of the question during the semester at the University of Tübingen. Besides, it must be your concern as well as mine that the conditions for a fruitful and successful discussion be agreed upon before my departure. In this connection, the following appear to be essential.

1. In your letter of April 30, 1968, as well as in earlier letters of the Congregation, there is a reference to your dossier 399/57/i, which clearly concerns me. If I am to participate intelligently in a discussion, it is indispensable that I should have unrestricted access to the official documents and free perusal of my dossier, which, judging by the number,

was already started by the Index. In my view, the discussion cannot be fair unless I am fully aware of the official documents that concern me and free to use them without restrictions of any kind. I hardly need to mention that in all civilized states of the West even criminals are guaranteed complete access to the dossiers that pertain to them. I therefore request written assurance that I shall be allowed unhindered access to the official documents relative to me.

2. The letter of your Congregation to the Bishop of Rottenburg of December 19, 1967, No. 399/57, already deals with me and my book *The Church*. In this letter it is stated that the examination of my book by your Congregation had been concluded and had led to the publication of a decree on November 29, which, however, has not been made public in the meantime. Your latest letter of April 30, 1968, says, on the contrary, that the Congregation for the Doctrine of the Faith "is" still "examining" my book. If so, the earlier statement must be regarded as immaterial. Likewise, the "authoritative invitation" mentioned at that time to renounce my right to further disseminate my book, would as a consequence likewise be immaterial since the proceedings are obviously still in progress and the examination continues. I am glad to be able to take part in your discussion free from this burden, which incidentally, contrary to the motu proprio of Pope Paul VI, *Integrae servandae,* of December 7, 1965, was imposed without the author and the local Ordinary being heard. The discussion will hopefully show that the Bishop of Rottenburg did not grant the *Imprimatur* irresponsibly, as has been alleged, but rather in keeping with canonical norms.

3. Your Congregation, I presume, is interested in specific points in my book. You will no doubt understand that it is important for me to be informed beforehand about the questions to be discussed, and the ambiguities you find difficult to understand. This is what *Integrae servandae* stipulates. In this way I can prepare my answers, which in turn will make for a pointed and fruitful discussion. I therefore ask you to provide me with a written statement of your position on the matter.

4. Since my book is not a piece of popularization but a scholarly, technical, and theological treatise, I can expect that the discussion will take place with competent experts. An expert judgment on the book *The Church* presupposes specialized and precise exegetical, historical, and dogmatic knowledge. As I know from prior experience, it makes little sense to discuss exegetical, historical, and dogmatic questions with a canon lawyer who is not well informed in such matters. I therefore ask you to let me know in writing the names of my partners in the discussion.

5. The motu proprio of Pope Paul VI *Pro comperto sane* of August 6, 1967, stipulated that the Curia may now conduct business in modern languages. I wish to make use of this right. Since this discussion concerns a German book of an author who speaks German, I wish to use my mother tongue, that is, German. I ask you to advise me whether you agree to this request.

6. For the sake of this discussion, I am being required to travel to Rome. You will understand, no doubt, that I regard as inequitable the expenses entailed. I therefore ask to be assured in writing that all the expenses in connection with this discussion will be reimbursed to me by the Congregation for the Doctrine of the Faith. Should this solution be unacceptable, the conversation could certainly take place in Tübingen. My house would be at your disposal.

It seems to me that it would be an advantage to everyone concerned if this matter could be disposed of without causing a public scene; otherwise, harm would come to the Church, which my whole theological work intends to serve. Assuring you once more that I am willing to cooperate, I send you my greetings.

Most respectfully,
Hans Küng

cc: Dr. Carl Joseph Leiprecht, Bishop of Rottenburg
      Prof. Dr. Joseph Ratzinger, Dean of the Catholic Theology Faculty, University of Tübingen

On July 8, 1968, Archbishop Philippe responded to Küng, granting his least significant point, financial reimbursement, explicitly refusing his most important, access to his dossier, and implicitly accepting Küng's reasons for not making the May 9 date. However, his language revealed something the duplication of which three years hence would deeply disturb Küng (see documents 18 and 21), that is, the issuance of a decree without any discussion with or informing of the author, a practice so common then that it apparently did not occur to Archbishop Philippe to avoid referring to it. His letter stated:

(3)

Dear Professor Küng:

In response to your letter of May 30, 1968, be advised that in a decree issued July 3, 1968, their Eminences the Cardinals of the Congregation for the Doctrine of the Faith have decided the following:

1. The Congregation for the Doctrine of the Faith requests that you submit dates on which you would be able to come to Rome.

2. This Congregation intends to reimburse you for travel expenses, etc.

3. We are here not dealing with a *trial* but with a *discussion* on some of the theses advocated in your book *The Church,* as provided for by the norms of the motu proprio *Integrae servandae.* Access to the dossier 399/57/i, to which you refer, is not necessary. The dossier is not pertinent to the matter at hand.

Respectfully,
Paolo Philippe
Secretary

Küng rather quickly responded to Archbishop Philippe, starting immediately with a reaffirmation of his willingness to come to Rome for a discussion, and stressing, as he had in his previous letter, the importance within the Church of dialogue on doctrinal matters, which Küng and many other Catholic theologians regard as being the most apt, most human, most Christian way to arrive at the best understanding of the truth. Küng noted that the Congregation had made a concession on one of his points, and so he made one in return—on language. He gently but firmly pressed again the matter of the background and names of his interlocutors and also for a list of the problematic theses from his book ahead of time. In connection with that matter he added another dimension, asking for a copy of the order of procedure the Congregation followed—he wanted to know the rules by which he should operate. On the final condition mentioned earlier, access to his dossier, he surprisingly did not press the matter, but offered to postpone negotiations over it until after the other points had been settled. He also added a complaint and request about what he considered defamatory attacks on him stemming from Rome. On July 27, 1968, he wrote:

(4)

Dear Archbishop:
   Having received your letter of July 8, I wish to confirm that I am willing to come to Rome and to participate in the discussion you require.
   After a conversation with you in Rome, Archbishop Clarizio, Apostolic Delegate to Canada, wrote me that my letter of May 30 has given a polemical impression. It was not my intention to cause such an impression. My concern was to provide an objective answer to an objective letter. Before the Council I had emphasized what a curse it was that for centuries on end Catholics and Protestants should meet only to argue. After the Council I have pointed out time and again how important it is now for Catholics to understand each other. The inner Church dialogue is of basic importance if we are to overcome today's difficulties. I do not need to stress that I am no friend of "psychological" or similar schisms. On the contrary. I have often and publicly branded the "private excommunication" handed out to those who

think differently in the same Church as a basic evil of Protestantism. I have advocated a further "catholicizing" of the Roman Curia (nationalities *and* mentalities). Thus, I number myself among those who would never let themselves be guided by an anti-Roman sentiment but have sought in various ways to conduct a dialogue with Roman authorities. May I here remark in all modesty that in my theology I have advocated the necessity and usefulness of a Petrine office in today's world more effectively perhaps than all the apologists of another sort to whom no one listens anymore. I would therefore plead with you to understand that, as I wrote in my letter, my one and only concern was to make certain that a *genuine* discussion should come about, that is, a discussion from which all the marks of the Inquisition trials are removed.

Therefore I am truly glad that on various points agreement has already been reached. I thank you for kindly taking into account the difficulties connected with my schedule. I am gladly prepared to indicate the times when I can come to Rome, and am grateful for your willingness to cover my travel expenses.

For my part, I would also like to show good will where I have the opportunity of doing so. If it proves difficult to find appropriate discussion partners with a command of the German language, I am prepared to conduct the discussion in other modern languages (English, French, Spanish, and Italian). I am also persuaded that agreement is attainable with regard to the remaining points. In this connection allow me to come back to what I have already stated.

In my letter to you, I had asked that you give me the names of my eventual discussion partners. In your letter you made no mention of this request. I repeat my request. Would you let me know *with which experts* the discussion will take place? I emphasize again that competence in exegesis and history is particularly important.

It is also important to know ahead of time precisely *what* is to be discussed. I do not need to repeat that only if this condition is fulfilled can a meaningful and fruitful discussion take place, sufficient preparation be made, and the discussion be conducted without waste of time. In your letter you restrict yourself to noting that the discussion is to deal with "some" theses from my book *The Church.* From your earlier letter I already had to assume that this would be so. However, it would be simple for the Congregation for the Doctrine of the Faith to delimit precisely which are the theses from my book which cause difficulties for you and why. For the sake of the matter at hand, I therefore ask you again not to deny me this.

I would also be grateful if you would send me the order of procedure of your Congregation as worked out on the basis of *Integrae servandae.*

You emphasize in your letter that you regard access to the documents of your Congregation pertaining to me as "unnecessary." Not to make this letter too burdensome, I will at this stage of the preparations for the planned discussion put off my request in this matter until mutual understanding has been achieved on the matters above.

In the last month, the Italian press of the extreme right has been spreading false allegations against me. The Roman newspaper *Il Tempo* has asserted, in connection with the first meeting of the Cardinals of the Curia, that I had offended the Pope, and that therefore the Pope himself had ordered the Cardinals to take measures against me (cf. *Il Tempo,* June 12, 1968). The Vatican correspondent "Lo Svizzero" of *Il Borghese* (July 4, 1968) said that the Vatican was proceeding against me because of an alleged "heretical attitude." Since *Il Tempo* and Lo Svizzero of *Il Borghese* are said to be closely connected with certain circles in the Curia, the serious allegations against me were taken up by the German press (cf., for example, the *Frankfurter Allgemeine Zeitung,* June 13–14; *Der Spiegel,* June 24). I had to enter a vigorous protest against these reports. I would have been grateful if the press office of your Congregation had intervened in an appropriate manner against these offensive actions. However, since no official démenti or anything like it appeared in Rome, I as the injured party was forced to make clear in the press what was false and what was correct in these press reports.

Despite this publicity campaign originating in Rome, I will not permit myself to become bitter. I will do whatever may help the cause and make possible the discussion you wish. As once again I assure you of my readiness, I send my greetings to you.

Respectfully,
Hans Küng

Real progress seemed to be in the making, for the Congregation quickly replied (August 31) with the names of the three interlocutors: Dhanis (a Belgian and one of the fiercest of critics of the liberal *Dutch Catechism*), Witte (a Gregorian University professor specializing in Protestant and ecumenical theology), and Ahern (a mild-mannered, open American biblical exegete)—a more than balanced selection. The order of procedure was said to be only experimental and therefore not available for distribution —a rather questionable legal stance. The topics for discussion were promised; the dossier matter was not mentioned. It would seem that agreement was almost attained and that a perhaps not uncreative discussion was in the offing.

However, it did not take place, for it was almost three years before the problem topics from *The Church* were sent to Küng, and then he was no longer asked to come to a discussion—at least not for another two years—but rather to respond in writing. Why the three-year gap? It is difficult to know unless one was privy to the deliberations of the Doctrinal Congregation and other Vatican agencies. One consideration was that the Doctrinal Congregation became very busy in the late sixties and early seventies with restrictions against various theologians. Then too, in the summer of 1968 Paul VI issued his encyclical *Humanae vitae* against birth control (one wag referred to it as "Paul's Epistle to the Fallopians"), which elicited a vast storm of protest from all over the Catholic world, including even many national episcopal confer-

ences; it was that encyclical which precipitated the book that
caused Küng—and the Vatican—the greatest difficulty: *Infallible? An Inquiry*. Perhaps the Congregation simply did not want
to move any further against Küng until it had firmly established
its order of procedure, which in 1968 it had said was only experimental. But perhaps it was the other way around: Küng's book
Infallible?, striking at the heart of the old authority structure as it
did, appeared in July 1970. Was it a major cause in the new
order of procedure (it had been ordered by Paul VI back in
1965), now rather suddenly appearing in January 1971? Cardinal
Franjo Šeper of Yugoslavia, by then the new Prefect of the Doctrinal Congregation, would have said no, that they were concerned that Küng have the new order of procedure so that everything would be fair. He mentioned this in a letter to Küng in
January 1970 when he remarked that the printing of the new
order of procedure "is to be done soon." However the "soon"
turned into a year (January 1971) and then there were another
four months to pass before it was sent on to Küng (May 6,
1971—see document 14).

Cardinal Šeper's letter to Küng of January 24, 1970—which
was occasioned by the arranging of a meeting between the Congregation and members of Concilium, the international theological
publishing group that Küng, Congar, Rahner, Metz, and Schillebeeckx had organized after the Council—made a point very
clearly that is important to keep in mind in light of later developments and accusations: the fact that it was not Küng's fault that
the discussion between him and the Congregation did not take
place over all those years and that the Congregation in no way
held him responsible. Cardinal Šeper wrote:

(5)

399/57/i   January 24, 1970
Dear Professor Küng:
    The Congregation for the Doctrine of the Faith has re-
ceived a copy of your letter of December 6, 1969, to Mr. van
den Boogaard, president of the Foundation Concilium. Mr.

van den Boogaard had sent your letter to the Secretariat of State, where preparations are proceeding for an eventual meeting of representatives of the Holy See with representatives of the Foundation Concilium.

In the letters concerning this meeting some misunderstandings have clearly arisen. Because of this and in order to inform you about the inquiry being conducted here into your book *The Church* I give you the following information:

The Congregation for the Doctrine of the Faith has circulated no reports of any sort about the inquiry now in progress on your book *The Church,* or about you yourself. The Congregation is also not responsible for what has been revealed concerning you in the press in and outside Rome.

The Congregation required of you neither directly nor indirectly a "good will gesture." Because the date for the discussion on your book *The Church* had first been set on short notice, you were prevented by your schedule from attending the meeting. The Congregation did not, however, regard this fact as a refusal on your part to come and participate in any discussion. The Congregation only had reservations about some of your proposals concerning the discussion and rejected these; others it accepted. Thus, the names of the three discussion partners were sent to you, and you were promised that you would be informed about the items to be discussed.

True, the discussion has not yet taken place and indeed, for reasons for which you are not responsible. Perhaps you know that one of the participants is not living in Europe. He happened to be staying in Rome on May 9, 1968. This was why on April 30, 1968, an invitation was sent to you on short notice. Moreover, we intended to send you the order of procedure, as you wished. However, this could not be done until the order of procedure, which was being employed experimentally, was printed. This is to be done soon.

As you see, the Congregation for the Doctrine of the Faith considers it important that you be acquainted with the order of procedure before the discussion takes place, and that you be persuaded that the Congregation will proceed with loy-

alty, equity, and without arbitrariness. The preceding shows
that you are mistaken in your assumption that the examination of your book has been terminated.

After the *Modus procedendi in examine doctrinali* is published, you will receive another communication about the
matters still pending.

The Congregation for the Doctrine of the Faith asks you
to share this letter with the persons to whom you wrote in
your letter of December 6, 1969, that is, Mr. van den
Boogaard, Fathers Congar, Rahner, and Schillebeeckx, so
that they too may be persuaded that the intentions of this
Congregation are loyal.

With the expression of my singular respect,

Devotedly yours,
Card. Franjo Šeper

A few months later Küng replied to Šeper, gratefully acknowledging his generous, "benevolent" letter and again professing his
willingness to participate in a discussion. This letter, along with
Šeper's previous one, are important documentary evidence of the
open, concessionary, and even friendly atmosphere that existed at
that time between Küng and the Doctrinal Congregation. Küng
wrote on June 1, 1970, to Cardinal Šeper as follows:

(6)

Dear Cardinal:

After a lengthy stay in Belgium, Holland, England, and
the United States, I returned to Tübingen at the beginning of
the summer semester. I can now answer your friendly letter.
I am sorry not to have been able to answer it earlier.

You have addressed the misunderstandings which have
arisen in connection with the future discussion with your
Congregation in such a clear, objective, and benevolent way.
For this I am truly grateful. I happily acknowledge that
your Congregation is not responsible for the indiscretions
and rumors circulated in the press about me. I am also happy

to learn that your Congregation has not asked of me, directly or indirectly, "a good will gesture." In particular, it is very important for me that you unambiguously state that the Congregation has never regarded the fact that I was prevented by my schedule from participating in the proposed discussion (in fact, I have repeated many times over that I was prepared to take part) as a refusal and that I am not responsible for the postponement of the discussion.

There is no need to stress that I have, with the greatest satisfaction, noted the statement that, to use your own words, the Congregation will proceed with loyalty, equity, and without arbitrariness, and that the order of procedure of the Congregation is to be made public before the discussion and made available to me. Doubtless I may assume that in formulating this order of procedure attention will be paid to the constructive proposals which were worked out by various theologians connected with the publication *Concilium* and endorsed by 1,360 professors of theology all over the world.

A termination of the proceedings would have been welcome nevertheless. The book *The Church* is entirely orthodox. I am convinced of this now even more than three years ago when the book was published. The book takes a middle position between a legalistic institutionalism and a fanaticism that rebels in principle against anything institutional, a fanaticism which is being advocated today within the Church by way of a somewhat understandable overreaction. The reason I would have welcomed the termination of the proceedings is that I worry that the resumption of the proceedings will inflict still more harm on the Church, and further injure the credibility of the Roman authorities. Wherever I go in Europe and elsewhere in the world people ask me about these proceedings. We cannot ignore the fact that the proposed discussion is connected with earlier decisions of the Congregation on the same book for which you, my dear Cardinal, are not responsible but which, contrary to the present intention of the Congregation, were not loyal, equitable, and free from arbitrariness. These I had to regard as quite inquisitorial and discriminatory. It is true that at present the Inquisition is being repudiated in Rome (your letter is a valuable confirmation of this); yet I am certainly entitled to sympathetic understanding if I insist again on the conditions for a discussion as set forth in the first letter I wrote to the Congregation about this matter.

For this reason, then, I still would welcome the termination of the proceedings, which were initiated under an unlucky star. The discussion could still take place independently of these proceedings, unburdened by the events of the past, and in the new spirit of loyalty, equity, and mutual understanding to which you refer.

However, I have no intentions of giving the Congregation for the Doctrine of the Faith orders about how it should conduct its business. Regardless of how it all turns out, I am grateful that your letter has brought about a basic clarification. What comes of it, as particularly important for the negotiations between the Foundation Concilium and the Secretariat of State, is this: There is no reason why on my account a meeting between representatives of the Holy See and of the Foundation Concilium should not occur.

I have not desired this meeting myself, but neither have I opposed it. In view of what has happened, I would have had enough grounds for doing so. Rather, from the beginning I have explicitly agreed to it, which could be construed as "a good will gesture" on my part. Such a meeting could perhaps bring about a better understanding at a time when, more than in the past, the Church needs the unity of all people of good will, and especially friendly relations between the Curia and theologians in the Church. It is true that, on the basis of the Christian message itself, and together with many others, I hold the view that I must stand up for a broader and deeper understanding of what the papacy should be. And yet, as my book *The Church* shows, I am deeply convinced that a renewed Petrine office is the source of many blessings in the Church. In this connection, if I may say this again with all modesty, I am also convinced that, through the critical and constructive theological positions I have taken in the book *The Church* and other publications, I have rendered the Pope a greater service among Catholics and non-Catholics than the numerous superficial defenders and comfortable eulogizers of the Pope. I do not partake of that basic anti-Roman sentiment which, because of various Roman interventions, is widespread in our Church. My concern was not and is not subversion and revolution, but thorough reform and renewal in the spirit of the Gospel of Jesus Christ. Regardless of how sharp my criticism of Rome had to be and, I am sorry to say, still has to be, whatever comes from Rome in the spirit of the Gospel can always reckon with my cheerful support. My criticisms may now and then sound harsh indeed and lacking in compassion (they come from the "periphery" and from a younger generation), especially in Rome. Because of the plight of so many, measures which are by far too short and the slow pace of post-conciliar renewal have put my patience to a hard test. I ask, if not for approval, at least for some understanding. It is important to me that even in the Congregation for the Doctrine of the Faith there should not be any doubt about my basic attitude toward the Church. With God's grace, I hope forever to remain loyal to the Church. Moreover, I do not regard myself as infallible. I submit all my theological views to public criticism in the Church. These criticisms, which I intend to ponder over, will help me not to grow rigid as I push forward, but to remain always, even as a teacher of theology, a learner of theology.

If I may summarize my letter: I sincerely thank you, my dear Cardinal, for your clarifying and friendly letter. I conclude from it that you have never held the view that I had refused to participate in a discussion with the Congregation for the Doctrine of the Faith, and that I had not been responsible for the postponement of the discussion. Now as before, I am ready to participate in a fair discussion. But I do suggest that the discussion should be separated from the proceedings which apparently are still in progress against me. For various reasons I am of the opinion that these proceedings, begun two years ago, should be terminated. The discussion could take place apart from these. Unburdened by these proceedings, the discussion would turn out to be all the more fruitful. Finally, I thank you that my case is being completely separated from the discussion being planned between the representatives of the Foundation Concilium and those of the Holy See. I have clearly said that I renounce personally taking part in this discussion if my person should prove to be an obstacle to the project. I would not want anyone to use me as an excuse to cancel this meeting. I am grateful to you for having clearly said that the idea of making me look like the stumbling block cannot be attributed to you.

In keeping with your wishes I immediately shared your benevolent letter with the members of the Foundation Concilium you mentioned. I will also share this letter with them. With the expression of my singular esteem, I send you my greetings.

Devotedly yours,
Hans Küng

An important international document that has a significant bearing on the relationship between Church authorities and theologians came out in 1968. It was a declaration by 1,360 Catholic theologians from fifty-three countries on the freedom of theology. It made a number of points which were likewise reiterated by Küng in several of his communications to the Vatican, and later also to the German Bishops, such as: (1) the representativeness of the Doctrinal Congregation (or Episcopal Commission) according to theological schools and approaches, (2) access by the accused to all the documentation, (3) communication in writing to the accused of the complained-about opinions, and (4) if necessary, ultimately a publicly *argued* refutation by the Congregation of the opinions in question. The declaration is as follows:

(7)
Declaration of 1,360 Catholic Theologians
on the Freedom of Theology (1968)

In complete loyalty and clear fidelity to the Catholic Church, the undersigned theologians see themselves compelled and obliged to point out publicly and in all seriousness that the freedom of the theologian and of theology in the service of the Church, which was won anew in the Second Vatican Council, must not today once again be endangered. This freedom is a fruit and a demand of the liberating message of Jesus himself and remains an essential aspect of the freedom of the children of God in the Church proclaimed and defended by St. Paul. Therefore it is incumbent on all the teachers in the Church to proclaim the Word *opportune importune,* in season and out of season.

For us theologians, this freedom goes hand in hand with the heavy responsibility not to jeopardize the genuine unity and the true peace of the Church and all its members. We are well aware that we theologians can commit errors in our theology. However, we are convinced that erroneous theological opinions cannot be disposed of through coercive measures. In our world they can be effectively corrected only by unrestricted, objective, and scholarly discussion in which the truth will win the day by its own resources. We affirm with conviction a teaching office of the Pope and the Bishops which stands under the word of God and in the service of the Church and its proclamation. But we also know that this pastoral ministry of proclamation ought not to constrain or impede the teaching of the theologian. Any kind of Inquisition, be it ever so subtle, damages not only the development of a healthy theology. It at the same time inflicts incalculable damage on the credibility of the entire Church in the world of today. Therefore, we expect the pastoral office of proclamation of the Pope and the Bishops to exhibit an understanding trust in our ecclesial attitude and to support without prejudice our theological work for the welfare of men and women in the Church and in the world. We wish to carry out our obligation to search out and speak the truth without being hampered by administrative measures and sanctions. We expect that our freedom will be respected whenever, to the best of our ability, we voice or publish our reasoned theological conviction.

Because now again an endangering of free theological work appears to be growing, we find ourselves compelled to make a series of constructive suggestions. We hold their realization to be indispensable so that the Pope and Bishops can worthily and appropriately carry out their tasks also in relationship to the function of theologians in the Church.

1. The offices of the Roman Curia, especially the Congregation for the Doctrine of the Faith, will, even after a certain internationalization by Pope Paul VI, see itself exposed to the appearance of partisanship in favor of a specific theological orientation as long as in the composition of its personnel the multiplicity of contemporary theological schools and mentalities are not clearly taken into account.

2. This is true in the first instance for the decisive organ of the Congregation for the Doctrine of the Faith, the Plenary of the Cardinals (Plenaria). Here the age limit of 75 years should be introduced.

3. As Consultors only outstanding and generally recognized professional people should be called. Their term of office should be specifically limited and in no case should extend beyond the age limit of 75.

4. The International Theological Commission desired by the Bishops' Synod, which likewise should encompass the various theological directions and mentalities in the Church in a proper proportionality, ought to be immediately established. The Doctrinal Congregation should collaborate with it in the closest possible manner. Likewise the competencies of the Congregation and of the episcopal commissions

for doctrinal questions within the bishops' conferences should be fairly and clearly delineated.

5. If the Congregation for the Doctrine of the Faith believes itself to be impelled in extraordinary and weighty individual cases to object to a theologian or a group of theologians because of their teaching, this must in every case (religious order people not excluded) take place in an ordered proceedings. For this proceedings, following the indications of the Pope for the reform of the Holy Office, *Integrae servandae,* December 7, 1965, a clear and binding order of procedure is to be worked out and ultimately in legal fashion to be publicized. The competence of the Congregation for the Doctrine of the Faith should thereby be clearly limited to substantive theological questions. Concerning purely personal matters only the proper legal path may be followed.

6. In the order of procedure, the following, which also should find their expression in the revised ecclesiastical law book, would have to be guaranteed:

a) The investigation of doctrinal questions by the Congregation must take place on the basis of authentic publications of the author himself in the original language, not, however, on the basis of unauthorized reports or translations. From the very beginning an official defender of the theologian concerned (relator pro auctore) commissioned by the Congregation should be involved. After the resulting evaluation, all of the objected-to teachings will be communicated in writing to the theologian concerned, along with all of the evaluations, decrees, relationes, and important documents. The theologian concerned will make a written statement on this material.

b) If this statement is not satisfactory two or more professional evaluations of theologians who are acknowledged experts on the disputed questions are to be obtained, of whom at least one-half can be nominated by the theologian concerned himself.

c) If afterwards a personal discussion is viewed as necessary, the names of the discussion partners, the subject of the discussion, and the complete text of all existing evaluations, decrees, relationes, and otherwise important minutes and documents are to be communicated in sufficient time beforehand to the theologian concerned. The theologian can conduct the discussion in any language wished by him and can bring with him an expert for his support. An obligation to keep secrecy does not exist. Minutes of this discussion signed by all of the participants go to the Congregation.

d) If according to the judgment of the Congregation even after this Colloquium it is clearly shown that the objected-to teachings clearly contradict the really obligatory confession of the Church and that wide circles of people are endangered in their faith, the Congregation should publicly refute these teachings in a reasoned statement.

e) Without prejudice to the binding quality of the ecclesiastical teaching authority, in the present-day social situation further measures of an administrative and economic sort against authors or publishers are as a rule to be avoided as useless or indeed damaging.

7. Since all faith without love is nothing, all efforts concerning the truth in the Church must be conducted according to the fundamental principles of Christian charity.

In May 1970 there occurred the first public dispute between Küng and the German Bishops. It was over an article Küng wrote on the new Vatican rules for mixed marriages, which included the obligation of the Catholic spouse to promise to bring up the children Catholic—which Küng, Rahner, and many, many other Catholics felt treated the non-Catholic's conscience with disrespect. Küng's article perceived the problem to be one in which every effort should be made to help the couple act according to *their* consciences. Thus he urged pastors to "use whatever latitude the law allows for, as extensively as possible. If this is not enough in a particular case, make concessions to the spouses as much as possible, even contrary to juridical stipulations." Küng

felt that he was not recommending irresponsible action or an attitude that was out of line with that of the German Bishops' Conference, which less than two years before had, like so many other
national episcopal conferences in reaction to *Humanae vitae,* advocated that in the face of the papal ban on artificial birth control
the persons concerned act according to their consciences. He
wrote: "What are we then to do? The same as the bishops recommended with regard to birth control: act according to conscience,
and all the more so, since this very law attributes such great importance to the responsibility of conscience!" Küng's article in the
Frankfurter Allgemeine Zeitung was published on May 9, 1970.
On May 19 the German Bishops' Conference issued a public
declaration repudiating Küng's position, to which Küng replied
publicly on May 27, 1970. And that technically was the end of
the matter. But it provided a rather sour background to the dramatic confrontation which began with the publication of *Infallible? An Inquiry* in July 1970, the centenary of the proclamation
of the dogma of papal infallibility at Vatican I.

The "Infallible" Book

The re-raising of the question of papal infallibility did not drop out of the sky in 1970. Küng, like so many Catholics, was deeply disturbed by what he perceived to be a lack of sincerity and truthfulness in dealing with changes in doctrines and truth claims. It was felt by many to be less than truthful to describe the shift from Gregory XVI's solemn condemnation of freedom of conscience as "false, absurd madness (*deliramentum*)" in *Mirari vos* (1832) to Vatican II's Declaration on Religious Freedom: "The human person has a right to religious freedom. . . . It follows that man is not to be forced to act in a manner contrary to his conscience . . . especially in religious matters," as a *development!* Consequently, Küng devoted a whole book to the problem, *Truthfulness: The Future of the Church* (1968), in which he dealt with the question of infallibility relatively briefly. But other Catholics also took up the matter about the same time, even a bishop—a Dutchman, Francis Simons, the Bishop of Indore, India (*Infallibility and the Evidence,* Springfield, Ill. Templegate, 1968). The thrust of Bishop Simons' argument was that "if there is an infallible teaching authority in the Church, it must be demonstrated by evidence from these books [Bible]. It is not infallibility which can give certainty to these books, it is they that must give us certainty about infallibility." But, Bishop Simons argued, the New Testament did not prove or even strongly suggest the Church's infallibility; divine assistance was promised in a number of places, but it was not at all evident that this assistance would be the charism of infallibility. The book was published by an obscure publisher in America and did not get much distribution nor was it translated. Nevertheless, Bishop Simons was visited by a delegation from the Doctrinal Congregation (including Jérôme Hamer) with the suggestion that he resign because of ill health. His response was that he never felt better in his life. After that he kept public silence on the matter, and so did the Vatican.

I, too, have dealt with the problem of infallibility in a chapter entitled "Doctrinal Authority and Freedom in the Church" in my book *Freedom in the Church* (Dayton, Ohio, Pflaum, 1969). I wrote on pages 103–4:

(8)

Perhaps the most serious objection that could be raised against the opponents of the infallibility of the Church (it might be better to speak of the indefectibility of the Church and let infallibility be purged in the communal dark night of the soul) would be that if the Church could err in essential matters, that would be evidence that it had been deserted by the Holy Spirit (might it not also be evidence that the Church deserted the Holy Spirit?), that it could have no assurance of continuity with Christ, and that it would then be set loose on a sea of complete relativism. But does the guidance of the Church by the Spirit have to be described in terms of the Church's being prevented from ever embracing error? Could the Church perhaps be described as being guided in such a way that, if it did err, it would be capable of righting itself, or renewing itself—just as God's chosen people of Israel did under the Spirit's guidance? This constantly being recalled to the path of righteousness and truth by the promptings of the Spirit through prophecy and the "signs of the times" would provide the essential element of continuity and the Scriptures and Tradition would provide the breaks against the open sea of complete relativism. To be sure, this line of thought also contains difficulties and uncertainties, but does it not seem to match better the historical realities of man's life, which is full of difficulties and uncertainties?

Whatever Church authorities and other Catholics think of the arguments of Bishop Simons and others on this most crucial subject, it is to be hoped they will at least be taken seriously—and most certainly not suppressed. The world, and the Catholic Church, has had more than all the suppression it needs. What the world, and the Catholic Church, needs are not more shorn sheep but more responsible persons. But one cannot have responsible persons without having free ones.

Once Küng's *Infallible? An Inquiry* was published, a series of exchanges between him and the German Bishops' Conference, including a discussion with them and theologian members of their Doctrinal Commission, took place—but with little satisfaction on the Bishops' side. Küng's book, though cast in the form of an inquiry, finds that all the arguments in favor of *a priori* propositional infallibility are wanting and that the arguments in favor of indefectibility, whereby the Church is maintained in the truth despite individual errors, have possession of the field. The inquiry consists in asking whether this analysis and line of argumentation is not correct, and therefore to be adopted—or can someone come up with more persuasive counterarguments? Küng at that point obviously had not yet been persuaded by any counterarguments —nor has he been subsequently. The immediate result was that the German Bishops' Conference issued a Declaration on February 8, 1971 (though dated February 4), concerning Küng's book. It stated:

(9)

In Hans Küng's book, *Infallible? An Inquiry* (Einsiedeln: Benziger Verlag, 1970), basic questions are raised about the possibility of there being a normative statement of faith in

the Church. These touch in part on fundamental tenets of the
Catholic understanding of the faith and of the Church. The
German Bishops' Conference believes that some of these
tenets are not safeguarded in the above-mentioned book.
These concerns have not been removed even after further
declarations by the author and after a discussion with him
directed by the Bishops' Conference. It is not the task of
bishops to take a position on the controversial questions,
technical and theological in nature, which again are at issue
on account of this book. However, the German Bishops'
Conference feels obliged to mention some nonnegotiable
givens which a theology cannot deny if it is to remain Catholic.

1. The faith in the word of God, attested to in the Bible
and confessed by the Church in the Creed, presupposes that
even there, in spite of the ambiguity and historical changea-
bleness of human language, there should in principle exist
the possibility of statements:

a. which are true and can be recognized as true, and

b. whose meaning remains the same, and whose validity
remains unrescindable, even though thought patterns and
speech experience historical change.

2. The normativeness proper to God's word of revelation
is given concrete expression in the Creed of the Church. In it
the Church responds to God's word attested to in the Bible
and makes this word its own. To be sure, the faith of the
Church always needs to be reflected upon anew. To this extent, it remains open-ended until the end of history. Nevertheless, it includes an unchangeable Yes and an unchangeable No. The Yes and the No are not interchangeable, one for
the other. Otherwise the Church could not remain in the
truth of Jesus Christ.

3. Concerning questions raised anew in given historical
situations, it is the right and the duty of the Church on the
one hand to make room for a thorough reflection on the
faith, and on the other to express whenever necessary its
unchangeable Yes and No. "Dogmas" is the name we give to

formulations which help to clarify the Creed, thereby providing in fact an interpretation of the witness intended by the Scriptures. These are put forth by the Church with truly ultimate normativeness.

4. A dogma does not draw its own proper normativeness from the result of the theological debate, nor from the assent of a majority in the Church, but from the charism given to the Church to maintain the word once it has been proclaimed in the force of its own truth, and to interpret it unerringly. The task of ensuring that the Church should remain in the truth of the Gospel through binding statements of faith is entrusted in a special way of its own to the teaching office. The reception in the Church of such dogmatic statements may be important as a sign of the Church's agreement with the normative source, but it is not the basis of either the truth or the authority of the statements.

5. According to the common and clear teaching of the Roman Catholic Church and the Eastern Churches, the power to issue such ultimately binding statements is found first and foremost in the Ecumenical Councils, as representing the whole episcopacy. Together with Vatican I and II and with the tradition which these two Councils concretely expressed, the Catholic Church also believes that the exercise of this power pertains also to the Bishop of Rome, as successor of Peter and head of the college of bishops. The conditions for such authoritative utterances are derived from the tradition of the Church, and are laid out in both Vatican Councils.

The next day, February 9, Küng issued a brief, conciliatory response:

(10)

In its declaration on my book *Infallible? An Inquiry* the German Bishops' Conference happily refrains from any condemnation. The five points which the Bishops make permit different interpretations. To a large extent they support my concern. However, the question raised in the book concerning the possibility of propositions which are not only true but also guaranteed as infallible is avoided. Significantly, the word "infallible" does not occur once in the whole declaration. This means that the Bishops allow space for further constructive discussion of this issue, which is of basic importance for today's Church.

Shortly thereafter, on March 4, the Bishops' Conference felt compelled to issue a response to Küng's response. They wrote:

(11)

The Bishops' Conference did also deal with the statement of Professor Küng in its Declaration on his book *Infallible?* Among other things, this declaration likewise states that in his book some fundamental tenets of the Christian understanding of the faith appear not to be safeguarded. The Conference is pleased to note that in his reply to the President of the Conference Professor Küng does not contradict this declaration. The Conference must, however, reject his view that the infallibility question is not dealt with in this Declaration. The text makes it clear that the teaching office of the Church has the specific power to interpret the faith of the Church normatively. With this, the proper content of the doctrine of infallibility, which in Professor Küng is at least obscured, is expressed. He speaks of "propositions whose infallibility is guaranteed *a priori*," a formulation which is foreign to the tradition of the Church. The declaration of the Bishops avoided the term "infallible" and used other formulations, the term "unerringly," for example, so as not to be identified with the distorted interpretation of Küng. Therefore, a contradiction exists between the statements of the Bishops' Conference and what one must derive from the book and from subsequent utterances of Professor Küng.

Bad Honnef, March 4, 1971

In the meanwhile a letter came to Küng from Cardinal Šeper, who no longer maintained his earlier friendly tone. In fact, he obviously was very angry. He wrote his rebuke on solely formal grounds, the primary one of which was under the circumstances quite odd. He complained that the Italian edition of *Infallible?* had no *Imprimatur,* when it was long since the custom of the vast majority of significant—and not so significant—Catholic theologians no longer to seek an *Imprimatur.* What was even more revealing was that he suggested that perhaps Catholic theologians should not even raise the questions of truth, change in doctrine, infallibility, and the like. He wrote on February 12:

(12)

399/57/i   February 12, 1971
Dear Professor Küng:

Your book *Infallible? An Inquiry,* published by Benziger and also translated into Italian under the title *Infallibile? Una domanda* (Brescia: Quiriniana), has no *Imprimatur.* According to canon 1385, paragraph 1 and 2, the *Imprimatur* is required. Furthermore, you state in the body of the book itself that you have deliberately dispensed with the Church's permission to publish because you yourself believe that your book is still Catholic.

Prescinding from the question whether or not a Catholic may at all raise the questions you raise in your book, the following must be stated: unambiguously, and not for the first time, you have set aside a valid prescription of the Church which, in spite of many discussions, is by no means abrogated. You use your reputation publicly to urge people to disobey legitimate authorities, as for example in the matter of mixed marriages. Permit me to invite you to ponder the position which you hold in the Church and the impact and consequences of your actions.

In the hope that you will then conclude that one cannot truly love and serve the Church in this way, I remain,

Devotedly yours,
Franjo Cardinal Šeper

On February 26, Küng wrote back to Šeper—again in a conciliatory tone—emphasizing once again his willingness to participate
in a discussion—with the proper safeguards:

(13)

Dear Cardinal:
    I have taken note of your friendly letter of February 12,
1971. I will happily ponder your exhortations. Concerning
the question of the *Imprimatur,* Dr. O. Bettschart, director of
the publishing house of Benziger, has already submitted a detailed statement in a letter to you dated February 10, 1971.
You invite me, in addition, to ponder my position in the
Church. May I then take the liberty of sending you a manuscript which originated independently of your letter, but yet
summarizes my thoughts on this matter? It should be clear
from this manuscript that in all things, even when I must be
uncomfortable, I am concerned to be of service to the
Church.
    I have no intention of imposing my personal views on the
Church or of issuing a call to rebellion. Instead, what I want
is to make a contribution to the renewal of the Church in
obedience to the critical norm of the Gospel of Jesus Christ,
and this if you will, in season and out of season. I am available for any discussion in which arguments are brought forth,
not just verdicts. Evidence of this will be found in a little
volume of discussion on the book *The Church,* which col-
lects the most important reactions and reviews, gives an account of the debate, and expresses the author's position. I
hope I can send you this volume soon for your information.
    I send you friendly greetings.

                                        Very devotedly yours,
                                        Hans Küng

    The summer semester 1971 (April 15–July 15) was to be an
extremely dramatic and hectic one for Küng. The university semesters in Germany are always demanding for conscientious pro-

fessors, and especially popular ones who are in great demand by students, colleagues, and outside groups. Küng of course was always very conscientious about his lectures and his many doctoral students and the running of his Institute for Ecumenical Research. Just reading and answering his daily flood of mail was a grinding, time-consuming chore. Like all German professors, Küng senses a profound responsibility to engage in constant research and publication; hence in slightly over twenty years he has published some 28 books and over 250 articles—that's more than a book and ten articles per year! In this particular semester he had added to all this two letters from the Doctrinal Congregation with theses to be responded to and final preparations for a round-the-world lecture and study tour to start immediately after the semester ended.

Thus, almost three years after they were promised, the problem areas found in *The Church* were sent to Küng by the Doctrinal Congregation in a letter dated May 6, 1971. Unlike the other communications to Küng, this was a combination of German (the cover letter) and Latin (the two "theses" and the order of procedure). All other communications from the Congregation were in German. When one looks at the two theses the impression of a certain incongruity is given. The two points raised are not unimportant, but they are clearly the sort of thing that makes up the very stuff of ongoing theological and scholarly debate in scholarly journals and at scholarly conferences. Point two, about who can celebrate the Eucharist, even specifically notes that the point made by Küng has also been made by other theologians. Furthermore, Küng merely says that, for the reasons given (*The Church*, p. 403), whether in an emergency situation laypeople might not celebrate the Eucharist "is debatable." Such a tentative statement hardly seems worthy of the formal action of the Doctrinal Congregation. Worse still, the Congregation continued to gnaw on the matter, for in its February 15, 1975, statement it again referred to the question—in a less than fair manner (see pp. 160–64). That years of effort on the part of the most important agency of the Vatican should only result in its involvement at the level of every-

day scholarly debate seems at least odd. The cover letter and two
theses were as follows:

(14)

399/57/i   May 6, 1971
Dear Professor Küng:

As you already have been informed, the Congregation for
the Doctrine of the Faith is examining your book *The
Church*. In accordance with the new procedural norms of the
Congregation, "Ratio agendi in doctrinarum examine," a
copy of which I enclose, we send you in the enclosed the
theses in your book which the Congregation for the Doctrine
of the Faith regards as erroneous or dangerous.

I request that you reply to these theses in writing within a
month (cf. the Norms of Procedure, No. 13).

> Respectfully,
> Franjo Cardinal Šeper

Concerning Professor Hans Küng's Book The Church

The Congregation for the Doctrine of the Faith has some
difficulties concerning the book of Professor Hans Küng,
Die Kirche (Herder, 1967). Although it regrets that the
book often speaks exceedingly negatively about the Church,
it nevertheless acknowledges that the book has no small
merit and highly praises the author's great erudition, the syn-
thetic power of his presentation, and his ecumenical spirit.

The difficulties concern primarily two points, of which the
first is the unity of the Church; the second is the necessity of
the sacrament of orders for a valid celebration of the Eucharist.

I. The Unity of the Church (Die Kirche, *pp. 313–52*)

Does the author rightly understand the doctrine of Vatican
II on the Church of Christ which "subsists" ["subsistit"] in
the Catholic Church, governed by the successor of Peter and
the Bishops united with him (*Lumen Gentium,* 8)? He

translates "subsistit in" by "exists in" ["existiert in"], and seems to identify "church elements which are present else-where" with the other "churches and ecclesial communities" (p. 337). This could easily favor the conclusion that the Church of Christ exists, according to its primary element, in the Catholic Church, and, according to its other elements, in the other Churches or ecclesial communities. The Council reads: "This Church [of Christ] . . . subsists in the Catholic Church . . . although many elements of sanctification and truth can be found outside of its company. These elements, however, as proper gifts of the Church of Christ, possess an inner dynamism toward Catholic unity" (*ibid.*). These "elements" are not the Churches or ecclesial communities, but some sacraments, perhaps, or some revealed truths.

It seems as if the author's mind is inspired by the notion that the Church of Christ, whose unity is torn asunder, consists of all the Churches and ecclesial communities. Cf. "Eine Kirche," pp. 312–52. We have noticed that, unless we are mistaken, the author does not acknowledge the following: "Only through the Catholic Church of Christ . . . the fullness of the means of salvation can be obtained. It was to the apostolic college alone, of which Peter is the head, that we believe our Lord entrusted all the blessings of the New Covenant" (*Unitatis redintegratio,* 3). "For although the Catholic Church has been endowed with all divinely revealed truth and all means of grace . . ." (*Unitatis redintegratio,* 4).

II. The Necessity of the Sacrament of Orders for the Valid Celebration of the Eucharist
(Die Kirche, pp. 519–22)

Chiefly on the basis of an argument from silence, the author believes that at the time when First Corinthians was written the faithful in the Corinthian church celebrated the Eucharist without the bringing in of those made ministers by the imposition of hands. From this belief, from the doctrine of sacraments received by desire, and from the doctrine of

the priesthood of the faithful (with the addition of remarks
of minor importance), the author conjectures that, in abnormal cases, the Eucharist may be consecrated by baptized persons without sacerdotal ordination. Therefore the traditional
judgment that the celebration of the Eucharist in many Protestant communities is invalid due to the lack of an ordained
priesthood can perhaps be corrected. Vatican II speaks
differently. Cf. *Unitatis redintegratio,* 22.

We know that other theologians (most of them, however,
later than the author) have expressed such views as these, at
least conjecturally. However, the arguments of the author do
not appear valid to us. We feel that, in this matter, he should
take into consideration what the Magisterium teaches, especially Fourth Lateran, Trent, and also Vatican II.

Although the Doctrinal Congregation has consistently refused
Küng access to the documents in his Vatican dossier, one document from it did accidentally become available and was published
in a German translation in Hermann Häring and Josef Nolte
(eds.), *Diskussion um Hans Küng "Die Kirche"* (Freiburg:
Herder, 1971), pp. 32–43. It is an official evaluation of *The
Church* done for the Doctrinal Congregation by a papal curial
theologian, the Magister Sacri Palatii Father Luigi Ciappi, O.P.
When one reads this document it is immediately apparent that it
served as the basis for a number of actions and statements by the
Doctrinal Congregation—the initial complaint to the Bishop of
Rottenburg about his having given his *Imprimatur* to *The Church*
and the attempt to have translations of it prevented, the statements in the two theses about questions of the unity of the
Church and "subsistit," as well as who can consecrate the Eucharist.

It is also immediately apparent why the Doctrinal Congregation
would not want to make such a document available to the accused author: parts of it are quite sarcastic, especially toward the
end; it misquotes and sometimes badly distorts Küng, as is
pointed out partly by Häring and Nolte in their footnotes; it is
very derogatory toward Protestants; it falls into the traditional
error of Catholic historians, that of trying to defend everything

Catholic officials ever did or said, such as Ciappi's defense of the medieval Popes and Pius XII and the German Bishops; the "ecumenical" statement about the Catholic Church having "everything," even freedom (!), was stunning in its triumphalism. Except for the later historical references, Ciappi's document could have been written in 1667 rather than 1967 after Vatican II. Presumably if it was known ahead of time that all documents that led to the initiation of a proceedings against an author would become available to that author, and perhaps ultimately the general public, the Congregation would bear that in mind when it picked its evaluators (for example, in the Catholic theological scholary world Ciappi had no weight at all, nor indeed Lemeer, whom he quotes several times), and most certainly the evaluator would also bear that in mind as he wrote his evaluation. Most difficulties would doubtless be thereby eliminated ahead of time by this simple device. But it has not yet come to that. The document was as follows:

(15)

I. General Observations
Strengths and Defects of the Work

1. Strengths:

a) *The intention was good* to attempt to present an ecclesiology which is less apologetic and more inspired by the example of the Second Vatican Council, that is, based on a historical-positive method with a broad use of scriptural texts and documents.

b) The *honesty* and *frankness* in admitting the moral defects of the Catholic Church and a certain overstress of the juridical-human element to the injury of the charismatic element are praiseworthy; also praiseworthy is the *demand* for a reform, for a renewal which makes the Church more capable of its mission of service of humanity, of witness to the truth and Christian life.

c) Worthy of praise is the *understanding* and *respect* for the non-Catholic communities, that is, for the doctrinal, charis-

matic, sacramental, and apostolic values which still exist in
them.

2. Defects:

a) *A certain devaluing of the divine origin of the Church,*
that is, of the intention on the part of Jesus Christ to found a
social, hierarchical organism which is designated for all peo-
ples and will remain standing over a long period of time until
the end of time.

b) *A certain devaluing of the nature of the Church* as a divine institution which is furnished with true and authentic
powers of teaching, sanctifying, and ruling which are appropriate exclusively to several members, namely, the holy hierarchy, and as such in no way can be shared with the faithful.

c) An arbitrary setting in opposition of the institutional and
charismatic elements of the Church whereby an excessive
significance is attributed to the latter to the injury of the former.

d) *Unfounded exegetical and theologically insufficient,*
partly heterodox, *explanations* of the marks of the Church:
unity, holiness, catholicity, apostolicity.

e) *An arbitrary setting in opposition* of the First Vatican
Council and Vatican II regarding the power of the bishops.

f) *Tendentious questions,* taken over from Protestants, regarding the nature of the primacy (of Peter) and its trans-
ferability, which then are not resolved.

g) *Tendentious questions,* taken over from Protestants, regarding the existence and nature of the Roman Pontiff, which
then are not resolved.

h) *Excessive ecumenism* which raises a doubt not only concerning the correct (objective) faith, but also concerning the
good faith of the author.

II. *Specific Observations*

1. The historical reality of the Church
Küng: The Church did not in the fixing of the canon of Holy
Scripture wish to reduce it to the true "Gospel." On the con-
trary, today many Catholic theologians would like to expand

it by the reference to the Apocrypha and "tradition." The
Holy Scripture is the "norma normans Traditionis ecclesi-
asticae."

Response: It is not understood in what manner the Catholic
theologians are supposed to be responsible for an attachment
of that sort. The divine Tradition, declared by the teaching
office of the Church, is the norm, not of the Holy Scripture,
but of the faith of the Christian and his understanding of the
holy text.

2. The Church, Christ, and the Reign of God

Küng: The question is raised: Is the Church grounded in the
Gospel? Christ proclaimed the Reign of God, which is
eschatological, imminent, and dependent on the sovereign
will of God; it is not an earthly-national or political-religious
theocracy, but rather a purely religious reign. Historical
research does not allow the positive claim that Christ had
foreseen a series of generations and centuries before him. In
the Gospels the announcement of the Reign of God by Christ
opens the way to the Church, but seen as a whole, it appears
to be illusory to base the juridical constitution of the Church
on such an announcement. That, however, does not exclude
the fact that in the proclamation of Christ there were elements which the young Church in its totality recognized as
constitutive elements of the greatest significance.

Response: The claims of Küng are unfounded. He
overstresses the opposition between the theological explanation of the Church as it is given in Catholic schools and the
Protestant explanation which he gives.

Moreover, Küng distinguishes excessively between the
Reign of God and the Church, while in the Gospels the
claim is better grounded that the Reign of God has two
levels: the earthly, relatively eschatological level, namely, the
pilgrim Church, and the heavenly, completely eschatological
level, which is the definitive Reign of God. The first is ordered to the second. Contrary to the opinion of Küng, the
definitions of the Church have an eternal value since they
are objectively the word of God. It even has the right to

threaten and to judge for the sake of salvation. And it is not true that the Church gives its laws out as the laws of God, or higher; rather, they are only their application.

3. Fundamental structure of the Church

Küng: It cannot be historically proven that Christ issued a mission command regarding the pagans. The Church very early passed over the Jews; likewise, it has sinned through their persecution; Nazism would not have been possible without the many centuries of Christian anti-Semitism. To such anti-Semitism there were reactions by individual Christians, but many personalities, and even the highest representatives of the Church, preferred to clothe themselves in silence, or out of opportunism and political reasons they did not speak out with energy.

Response: The reply follows from the observation that there are numerous Gospel witnesses from which one can derive a mission command by Christ, even if it then was stepwise better formulated by the community.

Küng appears to criticize Pius XII and the German Bishops.

According to Küng's claims, the charismatic structure of the Church was for a long time neglected because of clericalism and juridicism, while St. Paul (in his specific letters) shows a universal charismatic structure which the office structure encompasses and goes beyond: to these claims of Küng, Lemeer responds by establishing that even in the specific Pauline letters (cf. Corinthians) the charisms are subordinate to the hierarchical structure.

Further, Lemeer argues against Küng's position that historically one can doubt the baptismal command of Christ; or that the expressions "The Church is a human-divine reality," "the Mystical Body of Christ," are not legitimate, even if they could provide an occasion for false interpretations (which were rejected by Pius XII in the encyclical *Mystici corporis*).

4. Dimensions of the Church: Unity

Küng: Concerning the union of the Churches, he maintains—

after the enumeration of various erroneous attempts to justify the division of the Churches—that it is likewise mistaken to declare oneself in favor of the only Church of Christ, for thereby one does not acknowledge the others as Churches. One cannot in fact deny the baptism in them, by which one is made a member of Christ, nor can one deny that even the Catholic Church has many "vestigia Ecclesiae" which are really actualized in the other churches. Vatican II purposely undertook many corrections, especially with the identity formula: *"non est, sed subsistit."*

Response: Response with the observation that the Catholic Church rightly identifies itself with the Church of Christ, even if it calls the other confessions Churches; also, it is not true that Vatican II wanted to undertake the referred-to change. Thus it is not conceivable what are the "vestigia Ecclesiae" which in the Catholic Church have not yet been realized. Küng has the tendency to place the Catholic Church on the same level as the other Churches and to believe that for the sake of reunion it must give up some of its prerogatives.

Concerning the marks of the Church: holy, catholic, apostolic

Küng: He prefers to say "the sinful Church," rather than "the Church of sinners" (Journet). On *catholicity:* He holds that the Catholic Church cannot realize the necessary unity and catholicity without reconciliation with the others. He interprets the axiom "extra Ecclesiam nulla salus" only in the positive sense, that is, "intra Ecclesiam salus," whereby he does not exclude the possibility of salvation for those who are outside. On *apostolicity:* He prefers to speak of "apostolicity in the following" rather than of "apostolic succession" because the theological problem should not be obscured by secondary juridical and sociological considerations.

Response: The axiom must be understood in the moral sense, namely, for those who with guilt are outside the Church. The Church can also be understood in a wider sense, even if this

is not strictly according to the Scriptures. The explicit desire
for the Church of Christ includes the implicit desire for the
Catholic Church, even when in good faith someone is opposed to it.

On *holiness:* The Church is objectively holy since it was
made holy by Christ; actively holy because it sanctifies; subjectively holy because many of its members are holy. That
which Christ has set up is in no need of reform. The forgiveness of sins is available as a fullness of power to the
Church through the mediation of the hierarchy alone insofar
as the latter represents Christ, not the whole Church.

On *apostolicity:* One cannot abstract the formal element
from the "apostolic succession." Certainly Christ maintains
the Church in the apostolic faith, but he does so *by means of*
the infallible apostolic teaching office, after he had thus set
up his Church.

5. Offices in the Church

Küng: Not only priests may be called the leaders of the community, in order to form a special class between God and
men, which hinders the immediate relationship between God
and humanity.

The terms authorities, government, hierarchy, etc., do not
stem from the New Testament; likewise the others, right,
power, knowledge, worth, are not constitutive for the following of Christ. Only service (diaconia) in love is evangelical.

In the Pauline communities there was no episcopate, also
no presbyterate and no ordination with the laying on of
hands.

This therefore has the following consequences for the contemporary Church: a frightening distance between present-
day structures and the original ones. Vatican II introduced
several corrections in relation to the Council of Trent; the
decisions of Trent and the other Councils cannot be viewed
as the definition of problems which have arisen only today.

Not only the general charismatic service, but also the special, underlies the judgment of the whole, for *all* have re-

ceived the Holy Spirit and the special gift of the discernment of spirits.

One may not forget (which has happened often in the past) that there is a charismatic succession in the Church besides the apostolic succession, and it is of the highest significance. Although the shepherds alone have a *special responsibility,* and from that a special authority, the *whole* Church, the individual members included, stand in apostolic succession; besides this there is the succession of prophets and teachers.

Regarding the Petrine *power* and the Petrine *service:* One may deal with them only at the end of the tractate on the Church since the Petrine service stands *within* the Church and therefore is to be understood in relationship to it, and not the other way around. Roman theology, on the contrary, is gone about in reverse fashion; this has led to a rigorously unified, juridically organized Church with the monarchical universal episcopate and with centralization, even to the definition of the primacy and the infallibility of the Pope at the First Vatican Council. Eastern theology prefers to proceed from the community of the faithful, from the local Churches and their bishops: a collegially ordered confederation of Churches.

The immense service of the primacy in history is not to be overlooked; however, it must likewise be granted that centralism and absolutism of unity has led to division.

The *definition of primacy,* established by Vatican I (with certain limitations) was renewed by Vatican II, which added the new modifications so as to eliminate false interpretations. Among these are the following: The Bishop receives his *entire* power not through the election by the Pope, but rather by the force of the episcopal consecration. The Pope stands in the service of the Church; he may not separate himself from the Church, lest he become schismatic; The Council of Constance had maintained that it had received full power immediately from Christ, on the basis of which even the Pope owed it obedience.

Concerning the *continuation of the primacy of Peter* it must be noted that Vatican I (Denz. 1824 ff.) defined it without biblical arguments. Historically it is disputed whether the Petrine witnesses testify to the non-repeatable *laying* of the foundation, or also the *continuing* foundation function; whether the terms "bearer of the keys" and "representative shepherd" are to be interpreted as a primordial image for later shepherds or as the first bearer of the ongoing fullness of leadership.

On the *continuing of the Petrine primacy in the Roman Pontiff* Küng affirms: Vatican I defined it because it based itself on the witness of Irenaeus and others of the fifth century. Viewed *historically,* even renowned Catholic scholars have been skeptical about a constant tradition. The witness of Irenaeus (cited by Vatican I) is not concerned with a legal obligation; it is surprising that in the first centuries the witness of Matthew 16:18 was not adduced for primacy.

Despite such difficulties Catholic exegesis and theology claim the Petrine primacy and its continuation in the Roman Pontiff. Orthodox and Protestant theology must at least grant that it is not *contrary* to the Scriptures. Many probably would be prepared to admit that it is *according to* the Scriptures if it would be carried out in conformity with it. If a legitimate successor does not act in the service of the Church, of what use is his "apostolic succession"? If, on the contrary, an illegitimate successor exercises his office in the service of the Church, could he not even view the question of his legitimacy as secondary? What is decisive is not the "right" and "apostolic succession," but rather their "exercise." Without a relinquishing of "power," the reunion of the divided Churches and the radical renewal of the Church is impossible.

Response: The *forgiveness of sins* and the *eucharistic consecration* are within the exclusive competence of the priests, the representatives of Christ. Therefore, they alone are the heads of the community in a special sense; they form their own class; they do not hinder the immediate approach to God, but on the contrary they make it easier and more complete.

Küng incorrectly views the structure of the Church only in the light of the Pauline epistles which are accepted by all, even the Protestants, whereby he excludes the Pastoral epistles and the Acts of the Apostles; on the contrary, the Catholic Church also acknowledges these writings as having Pauline origin or as reports of his office. Küng neglects the "sensus Ecclesiae" in order to rely solely on exegesis in the interpretation of the Holy Scriptures. He does not keep in view that the epistles are occasional writings (cf. *La Sainte Bible de Jérusalem*).

If *centralism* and *absolutism* historically *could* have called forth division, it is not certain that confederation and collegiality could not have done the same.

The Dogmatic Constitution *Lumen Gentium* (No. 21) does not claim that the Bishop receives the "fullness" of power at his consecration, but rather "munera," and it explains in the Nota explicativa, c. 2: "In consecratione datur *ontologica* participatio sacrorum munerum."

The case of a *Pope being separated from the community* of the whole has never happened and never will happen. If it were to happen, one would have to see on which side the truth was.

Küng raises doubts regarding the Gospel witnesses which Vatican I cited for the *primacy* (John 1:42; 21:15–17; Matthew 16:18 ff.), as if they were not sufficient to ground a true primacy of jurisdiction, and he does not resolve them. The teaching office of the Church, on the contrary, bases its teaching on such texts because it declares that "according to the witnesses of the Gospel the primacy of jurisdiction over the entire Church of God was promised and handed over immediately and directly to the Apostle Peter" (Vatican I, Denz. 1822).

In like fashion Küng raises a doubt concerning the *historical* proofs for the *continuation of the primacy of Peter* and he does not answer them. Now it is, however, certain that his interpretations, which tend toward a denial of those proofs, are taken from O. Cullmann (cf. *Saint Pierre*).

Likewise the questions of the *continuation of the primacy in the Roman Pontiff* he does not answer after he has brought them into doubt. He does not, as other Catholic theologians in general do, attend to the fact that the dogma of the primacy of the Roman Pontiff was not known and practiced explicitly and in complete fashion in antiquity, as is the case in our day.

Regarding the use of Matthew 16:18, it is true that this text was used in early times as an argument for other questions which were discussed. That lies close to the thought that the primacy was undiscussed in this time.

Küng unwarrantedly assumes that one can have "office" ("munus") only from the charisma. If one cannot have it, the illegitimate superior cannot effectively practice it, because he has been suspended therefrom. That shows that legitimate succession is not a secondary question.

Küng unwarrantedly condemns the authoritative and authoritarian interventions of Popes St. Stephen, St. Innocent, St. Gregory VII as a misuse of power to the injury and not to the *use of the Church.*

The titles "Servus servorum" and the primacy of jurisdiction "supremi et universalis pastoris" are not irreconcilable; the second is at the service of the servant of God. Further, it is not evident that the spirit of service would have hindered the Eastern schism.

Concerning *ecumenism:* It is true that all the Churches have their own proper specialties and riches; however, the Catholic Church has them all: the papacy, tradition, Bible, freedom, and agreement among them. That is the truth criterion of the Church.

Conclusion

It is a wonder that a work such as this, which in many fundamental ecclesiological questions reveals a more Protestant than Catholic mentality, received the ecclesiastical *Imprimatur*.

Are we in the age of "dialogue"? Is it accordingly permitted to doubt and place in discussion doctrinal points which are already defined or solemnly declared or undisputed among all Catholic theologians?

It is easy to foresee that this work of Küng—decked out with the approbation of the Vicar General of Rottenburg—will soon, as were his other works, be translated into various languages. No wonder. Küng in fact is also a member of the executive committee of the journal *Concilium* and director of the Ecumenism section. Now one knows, however, that this journal likewise has published rather sharp, sometimes partly heterodox, articles with the approbation of all the episcopal chanceries where it is published.

While the bishops are silent and approve such publications, do the theologians have the right to practice their "charism" ad libitum?

Is all that in agreement with the declarations of Vatican I and Vatican II? It appears not. "A better judgment not being observed"—"Salvo miglior parere."

The second enclosure in the May 6 letter was the order of procedure of the Doctrinal Congregation, issued some five years after it was ordered by the Pope. In a number of important ways it falls short of the recommendations by the 1,360 theologians, which Küng noted in his response. Three matters that he did not call attention to nevertheless merit consideration. One is relatively small: the question of timing. Although the Congregation allows itself unlimited amounts of time for its actions—and indeed took months and even years in its dealings with Küng, for example—it imposes a thirty-day deadline on the accused. Secondly—and Küng does allude to this one briefly—the provision for an "extraordinary procedure" in Article 1 of the "Norms" is, to say the least, extraordinary; it allows the order of procedure to be aborted at any time without challenge, even at the very beginning. Thirdly—and this issue was raised by Küng and many other

Catholics elsewhere and earlier—there is the perennial question:
Quis custodiet ipsos custodes? (Juvenal, *Satires,* vi, 347). Who
will guard the guards? How does one become a Consultor? What
are the qualifications? How representative are they? Why is it that
the Catholic world's most respected theologians never become
Consultors—e.g., Rahner, Congar, de Lubac, Danielou, J. C.
Murray, Schillebeeckx, Metz? The order of procedure is as follows:

(16)

1. Books, other publications or conferences, the contents of
which fall within the competence of the Sacred Congregation
for the Doctrine of the Faith, are sent to the staff meeting
[*congressum*], which is made up of the superiors and officials
[of the Congregation] and which meets every Saturday. If
the opinion under examination is clearly and certainly erroneous and if, at the same time, it is expected that its
diffusion could lead, or is already leading, to real harm of
the faithful, the staff meeting can decide that the extraordinary procedure be adopted. That is, that the case be
brought at once to the attention of the Ordinary or Ordinaries concerned and the author be asked through his own
Ordinary to correct the error. Once the answer of the Ordinary or Ordinaries has been received, the Ordinary Congregation [the regular meeting of the cardinals, officials, etc., of
the Congregation] will adopt suitable measures in accordance with the following articles 16, 17, and 18.

2. Likewise, the staff meeting decides whether certain publications or conferences should be more closely examined according to the ordinary procedure. If it decides to do so, the
staff meeting will elect two experts to prepare studies and a
Relator "pro auctore." The staff meeting will also establish if
it is necessary to advise immediately the Ordinary or Ordinaries concerned, or if this is to be done only after the examination has been completed.

3. Those in charge of the preparation of the study are to

examine the authentic text of the author to determine if it is in conformity with the Divine revelation and with the teaching office of the Church. They also are to express a judgment on the doctrine contained therein, suggesting possible actions.

4. The Cardinal Prefect, the Secretary, and in their absence, the Undersecretary, can entrust the study in case of urgency to some of the Consultors [of the Congregation], but at the same time the staff meeting always designates an expert from outside the Congregation [*ex commissione speciale*].

5. The study or studies are to be printed, together with an office report, in which all useful details are to be given for judging the proposed case and indicating precedents. Lastly, the documents which are suitable for providing a thorough examination, particularly in the theological context of the matter treated, are printed.

6. The report, together with the study mentioned above, will be given to the Relator "pro auctore," who has the right to examine all the documents concerning the case in the possession of the Congregation. The task of the Relator "pro auctore" is to show in a spirit of truth the positive aspects of the author's doctrine and his merits, to cooperate in the genuine interpretation of the thought of the author in the overall theological context, and to express a judgment regarding the influence of the author's opinions.

7. The report itself, together with the study and other documents, is distributed to the Consultors at least a week before it is discussed by the Consulta [the weekly meeting of the Congregation's Consultors].

8. The discussion in the Consulta begins with the exposition of the Relator "pro auctore." After him each Consultor expresses either orally or in writing his own opinion of the content of the text under study. The Relator "pro auctore" can then speak in answer to observations or ask for possible clarifications. When the Consultors formulate their opinions,

the Relator leaves the room. Finally, at the end of the discussion, the opinions are read out and approved by the Consultors themselves.

9. The entire report, together with the opinions of the Consultors and the "pro auctore" report and the summary of the discussion, is then distributed to the Ordinary Congregation of the Cardinals at least a week before it is to be discussed by the Cardinal members of this same Congregation. The seven Bishop members who live outside Rome can take part with full rights in the Congregation.

10. The Cardinal Prefect presides over the Ordinary Congregation, presents the matter, and expresses his opinion; the others follow in order [of seniority]. Opinions are then collected in writing by the Undersecretary to be read and approved at the end of the discussion.

11. The Cardinal Prefect or the Secretary, at the weekly audience which one of them will have with the Holy Father, will submit these decisions for his approval.

12. If during the examination no erroneous or dangerous opinions are noted in relation to Article 2, the Ordinary is notified, if he has previously been informed of the examination. If, on the contrary, false opinions are noted, the author's Ordinary or the Ordinaries concerned are notified.

13. The author is informed of the opinions regarded as erroneous or dangerous so that he may submit his answer in writing within a full month. After this, if a discussion is considered necessary, the author will be asked to attend a personal meeting with representatives of the Sacred Congregation for the Doctrine of the Faith.

14. The representatives must draw up and sign a report in writing, which must be at least a summary of the discussion. The author will sign it also.

15. Both the written answer of the author as well as the summary of the discussion, if any, will be presented to the Ordinary Congregation for a decision. If, however, either from the written answer of the author or from the discussion, new doctrinal elements should arise which demand further

study, this written answer or the summary of the discussion is to first be submitted once again to the Consulta.

16. Should the author not send his answer and not appear at the discussion after he has been invited to do so, the Ordinary Congregation will make the suitable decisions.

17. The Ordinary Congregation also decides if and how the result of the examination is to be published.

18. The decisions of the Ordinary Congregation are to be submitted for the approval of the Supreme Pontiff and are to be communicated later to the author's Ordinary.

On June 21, 1971, Küng replied to the Congregation's letter about his book *The Church,* registering a somewhat detailed critique of the order of procedure—which was to remain a bone of contention till the present—and responding to the points raised about his book. Though his critique of the order of procedure was firm, the overall tone of the letter was cordial. He wrote as follows:

(17)

Dear Cardinal:

Various responsibilities during an arduous semester have hindered me from replying earlier to your letter of May 6, 1971. I beg for your understanding.

The reply to your letter would have been easier for me if the new norms of procedure had cleared away the objections which I raised against the procedure of your Congregation in my letter of May 30, 1968, and have since reiterated in various letters. Unfortunately this in no way has happened. I applaud the publication of the norms. I have studied these carefully. As the Congregation for the Doctrine of the Faith no doubt knows, these norms have aroused sharp criticism in the Catholic and non-Catholic public, and in my opinion rightly so. There are improvements in details, which I gladly acknowledge. However, the norms are not at all free of the spirit of the Inquisition, and they surely fall short of the very moderate demands which the 1,360 theology professors the world over have set forth in a declaration for the freedom of theology.

In your letter of January 24, 1970, you informed me that "the Congregation will proceed with loyalty, equity, and without arbitrariness." But I cannot regard a proceedings as loyal, equitable, and free from arbitrariness in which I am still being denied access to official documents, since I am kept entirely in the dark as to the course of the still secret proceedings, in which I cannot choose my own "defender" (Relator "pro auctore"), who is, in fact, entirely unknown to me. Besides, within these "ordinary proceedings," "extraordinary" ones are possible any time outside the parameters of legality. One merely needs to compare the new procedural norms with the norms which are routine in constitutional states to see immediately that the norms of the Congregation for the Doctrine of the Faith must, unfortunately, still be characterized as inquisitional and discriminatory. I consider it my obligation to uphold in every respect my objections against such norms and to confirm these objections. In my letter of June 1, 1970, I have already made it abundantly clear that I do this impelled by an ecclesial fundamental attitude, so that here I need only to refer to what was said there.

Meanwhile, I would not want to fail to acknowledge with gratitude that, for the first time, the Congregation for the Doctrine of the Faith has recognized that "the merits of the book are not slight." Regarding the two difficulties of the Congregation I would respond as follows:

1. Concerning the Unity of the Church

My interpretation of the expression "subsistit in" (*Lumen Gentium,* 8) as meaning "exists in" is based on the interpretation which I personally discussed in the Council with Monsignor Gérard Philips (Louvain), the second secretary of the Theological Commission of Vatican II. I refer further to the Commentary of Professor A. Grillmeier, S.J., another expert on the Commission, in the Supplement to the *Lexikon für Theologie und Kirche,* Part I. On p. 175, he writes: "No absolute, exclusive judgment of identity is stated, such as, for instance, that the Church of Christ 'is' the Catholic Church. . . . Hence the one true Church of Christ does exist. It is recognizable, and visible in its own way. . . . But 'ecclesiality' does not simply coincide with the Catholic Church, because ecclesial elements of sanctification and truth can also be found outside it. This brings up the question of the 'ecclesiality' of the Churches and communities apart from the Catholic, which involves on the one hand their character as mediators of salvation, and on the other hand, the necessity of the Catholic Church for salvation. These problems are not fully discussed here." The pertinent section in my book *The Church* was meant to carry forward the clarification of these problems.

2. *The necessity of ordination for the valid consecration of the Eucharist*

It is not the argument of the lack, but the argument of the presence of an ordained presbyter in the community of Corinth that seems to be an argument from silence. I raised the question because it emerges from the texts, because it was ignored in pre-conciliar Catholic literature and it could not be answered by competent Council theologians whom I questioned during the Council. If one could name me one serious theologian who can offer a serious argument for the presence of an ordained presbyter in Corinth, I would be grateful. Unfortunately, not even *Unitatis redintegratio* (22) answers this question. At the end of the pertinent passage, it says explicitly: "For these reasons, dialogue should be undertaken concerning the true meaning of the Lord's Supper, the other sacraments, and the Church's worship and ministry." In the aforementioned Commentary (Part II, pp. 118 f.), Professor Joseph Feiner, Consultant of the Secretariat for the Unity of Christians, writes: "Neither the Reformation Churches nor the Catholic Church may regard the present state of their understanding in the field of the sacraments as something final and complete. Consequently the last sentence of the article stresses the necessity of dialogue between the churches on this subject in the hope that it will lead to a more profound understanding of faith and to the drawing together of the churches." This is precisely what I have tried to do. In fact, the dialogue on this question has made considerable progress in the meantime, as it appears from the volume edited by Hermann Häring and Josef Nolte, *Diskussion um Hans Küng "Die Kirche"* (1971), where other exegetes and theologians and I discuss thoroughly and constructively the exegetical and dogmatic questions raised. I may, therefore, draw your attention to this volume, which I sent to you my dear Cardinal right after its publication. If it has not arrived, please let me know, and I will gladly send you a second copy.

My dear Cardinal, I hope that these remarks will have satisfactorily responded to the difficulties of the Congregation.

With the expression of my singular esteem, I remain,

Devotedly yours,

Hans Küng

It was not thirty days but rather over two years before Küng received any kind of a response to his June 1971 letter about *The Church,* and then it would be a general public Declaration (*Mysterium ecclesiae,* June 24, 1973) to the Church at large, with no specific mention of Küng or his book *The Church.* The matter obviously would not have developed in that fashion if the much more serious problem caused by Küng's book *Infallible? An Inquiry* had not cropped up in the meanwhile. As it was, with no reference to his response concerning *The Church,* a second letter was sent by Cardinal Šeper to Küng about his book on infallibility. This second letter was dated July 12, 1971, again in German, with the "theses" of complaint about the book *Infallible? An Inquiry* in Latin.

It was in the cover letter that Cardinal Šeper referred to a decree of the Congregation—as had Archbishop Philippe before him—to which Küng this time took sharp exception. Also, this time the theses were more extensive and serious. One of the examples offered by the Congregation, supposedly to prove their viewpoint in their fourth thesis, was most strange, for it seemed to disprove their position most eminently, and that, out of their own mouths. The Congregation quoted *Quicumque* as a presumably infallibly true Church definition; the statement held that whoever did not hold the Catholic faith was most certainly condemned forever. But as recently as 1948, the Holy Office issued a response to Cardinal Cushing of Boston against Father Leonard Feeney stating that a Catholic could not hold that all outside the Catholic faith were condemned. Was the 1971 Doctrinal Congregation somehow unaware of this glaring self-contradiction? The communication was as follows:

(18)

399/57/i   July 12, 1971
Dear Professor Küng:

The Congregation for the Doctrine of the Faith has initiated doctrinal proceedings against your book *Infallible? An Inquiry.*

By a decree of June 23, 1971, approved by the Holy Father on June 25, 1971, the plenary assembly of this Congregation decided that you should be informed in writing of the theses in this book which, on the basis of the examination of this Congregation, seem to be incompatible with Catholic doctrine.

In the enclosure, I am sending you the list of these theses which cause difficulties for the Congregation as far as a Catholic interpretation is concerned. I ask you to explain to the Congregation in writing within thirty days whether and in what way you believe that these theses and opinions can be reconciled with Catholic doctrine.

With the expression of my esteem, I remain.

Devotedly yours,
Franjo Cardinal Šeper

Questions on the book: H. Küng,
Infallible? An Inquiry (Zurich, 1970)

In the carrying out of its office the Sacred Congregation
for the Doctrine of the Faith requests Professor Hans Küng
to explain certain statements in his book *Infallible?* and to
answer some questions relative to these. It has noticed that
on the one hand Professor H. Küng proposes his opinions as
if they were open to discussion, and on the other he indeed
thinks that opinions, even when proposed by a Catholic theologian in this manner, must remain within the limits of Catholic doctrine.

I. On the Authentic Magesterium in the Church

The author writes: "Certainly some popes in recent times
. . . have continually attempted absolutely and exclusively to
reserve to themselves (and, when it suited them, also to the
bishops) the 'authentic' explanation of the 'deposit of faith'
. . . From all that has been said in this book, from beginning
to end, it is clear that the Holy Spirit is not given only to
pope and bishops in authentic fashion for the salvation of the
Church . . . [and] that the 'authentic' proclamation and exposition of the Christian message is not 'reserved' to anyone"
(p. 234).

This Sacred Congregation notes:

(1) "Authentic Magisterium" is a technical expression
which refers to the Magisterium of those who "endowed with
the authority of Christ preach to the people committed to
them the faith they must believe and put into practice. By the
light of the Holy Spirit, they make that faith clear" (*Lumen
Gentium,* 25). It is to the Magisterium, precisely because it is
made up of those who teach with the authority granted by
Christ in various ways and degrees—depending on how it is
exercised—that the Christian faithful "are . . . to adhere to
with a religious assent of soul" (*ibid.,* 48).

(2) According to the Constitution *Dei Verbum,* "the task
of authentically interpreting the word of God, whether writ-

ten or handed down, has been entrusted exclusively to the living teaching office of the Church, whose authority is exercised in the name of Christ" (10).

(3) The Constitution *Lumen Gentium* credits the authentic Magisterium to no one except the Bishops and the Supreme Pontiff (25). However, it clearly acknowledges that the Holy Spirit through the "sense of the faith" arouses and sustains the whole people of God (12).

(4) All this is traditional in the Church. The theologian is not being prevented by this from devoting himself to scholarly teaching, which is not to be confused with "authentic" teaching. Nor does it suppress the office in which the Magisterium has prudently to look into the investigations of theologians and the spiritual lights of "charismatics."

(5) The author denies that the authentic Magisterium is reserved to "some," that is, "to the Bishops and the Supreme Pontiff."

How can a Catholic theologian do this?

II. On the Infallibility of the College of Bishops and of the Roman Pontiff

The author writes:

(1) "The statements about an infallibility of the college of bishops, based on the traditional, unhistorical theory of a direct and exclusive apostolic succession of bishops, have feet of clay, exegetically, historically, theologically. That is to say, unless the substantiation were to be supplied by the basic source to which Vatican II, in Article 25 on the infallibility of pope and bishops, constantly refers" (p. 86).

(2) "If the foundations of neo-scholastic doctrine on infallibility are so fragile and its expression, both in connection with the pope (Vatican I) and in connection with the episcopate (Vatican II), creates so many unsolved and perhaps insoluble problems, would not the simplest and best solution be to abandon altogether the whole doctrine of ecclesiastical infallibility?" (p. 125).

It seems to this Sacred Congregation that, at least by expressing doubt, such assertions conflict with the doctrine of Vatican II, which is in accord with the doctrine (as to things defined about the Supreme Pontiff) and with the constant practice of the Church, starting with the first Ecumenical Councils. The author seems to be denying the infallibility of Ecumenical Councils as well.

If this interpretation of the text of the author is correct, how can he justify his opinion?

III. Indefectibility Instead of Infallibility

The author would prefer to admit the "indefectibility" rather than the "infallibility" of the Church. He describes indefectibility as follows: "A fundamental remaining of the Church in truth, which is not annulled by individual errors" (p. 181).

It seems to this Sacred Congregation that this ought to be said: Either the "individual errors" which, according to the author, "indefectibility" would allow for do not refer to what the supreme Magisterium of the Church proclaims as the doctrine of faith or morals, or on the contrary, they do. If the author intends the first, he preserves Catholic doctrine, but his manner of speaking obscures it. If the author intends the second (the context inclines in this direction), he departs from the doctrine of Vatican I (DS, 3011) and of Vatican II (*Lumen Gentium,* 25). How can a Catholic theologian think that he is permitted to do this?

IV. On Infallible Propositions (*Sätze*)

The author admits that the faith of the Church needs propositions which are to be believed, since one section of his book bears the caption "The faith of the Church is dependent on propositions of faith" (p. 144). However, he adds that it cannot be proved that faith needs infallible propositions. He writes: "It has not been proved that faith is dependent upon infallible propositions" (p. 150). But for centuries the Church has been requiring that symbols and professions of faith be assented to with the firmness of a most certain assent. Does this not show that in these symbols and professions of faith infallible propositions, that is, definitions, are set forth by the Church? The author explains that the faithful can "throughout all perhaps ambiguous or perhaps in particular even false propositions, commit themselves in their whole existence to the message, to the person proclaimed: they can believe in Jesus Christ. It is this faith alone," he adds, "that can give certainty: the peace that surpasses all reason" (p. 192).

However, this Sacred Congregation notes that in many professions of faith the Church demands a very firm statement of faith, even to specific propositions, especially concerning the person of Christ. (All these contribute to an extent to exhibiting the mystery of God which saves us through the Christ.) For example, the Symbol *Quicumque,* which begins thus: "Anyone who wants to be saved must first of all hold the Catholic faith. Unless this faith be preserved in its integrity and inviolability, one will most certainly incur eternal damnation" (DS, 75). Likewise the heading "firmly" of Council Lateran IV: "We firmly believe and unambiguously profess that . . ." (DS, 800). Likewise, the Tridentine formula of faith says: "I, N., believe with a firm faith and profess each and every doctrine contained in the (Constantinopolitan) Symbol of faith" (DS, 1862).

We request of the author that, even with regard to this question, he submit an explanation.

As it happened, it was not possible for Küng to comply or to do anything at all about the letter since it arrived literally just hours before he was to depart on his round-the-world trip—I know, I happened to be in Tübingen doing research at the time and was helping Küng with some suggestions of topics he might address in his lectures in America later that fall when the letter arrived. On July 19, 1971, he sent a brief note of explanation from his first stop—the Kremlin:

(19)

399/57   Moscow, July 19, 1971
Dear Cardinal,

Your express letter reached me a few hours before my flight starting a journey around the world. I am writing, therefore, from my first stop, where I am engaging in conversations with the Russian Orthodox Church. Unfortunately, for the time being, it is totally impossible for me to answer your letter in a manner commensurate to the seriousness of the business at hand. This will be possible only after I return home and look at the records. I, therefore, beg you to be patient until that time.

With sincere regard, I remain,

Devotedly yours,
Hans Küng

Having become somewhat anxious about time slipping away, Cardinal Šeper sent Küng a reminder dated December 17, 1971, which, given the Italian mails, would arrive just about Christmas time—again:

(20)

399/57/i   December 17, 1971
Dear Professor Küng:

On July 12, 1971, I sent you various questions, with the request to answer them for the Congregation for the Doctrine of the Faith. These questions concerned your book *Infallible? An Inquiry*.

In a letter from Moscow on July 19, 1971, you answered that you were traveling, and you asked for patience until after your return.

I hereby again request that you answer the questions put to you within thirty days after receiving this letter.

With the expression of my esteem, I remain,

Devotedly yours,
Franjo Cardinal Šeper

Küng clearly was irked at the reminder, both because it intruded again on the Christmas season, a time of Christian peace and reconciliation, and because he assumed, doubtless rightly, that the Vatican would have known full well that he had returned only on December 6, and from that time the thirty-day deadline was still over two weeks off on December 17. Nevertheless, he sent a substantive reply. It focused first of all on a critique of the *modus operandi* of the Congregation, requesting in brief: (1) access to his official records, (2) the right to name his own "defense attorney," (3) a delineation of competencies and a right of appeal, (4) mutual deadlines. However, his critique was much more extensive and severe than previously, referring aggrievedly to the "secret decree," the like of which had been passed over in silence in 1968. Küng also dealt at length with the substantive issues of infallibility that had been raised by the Congregation. Küng's response of January 24, 1972—within thirty days of having received Cardinal Šeper's December 17 letter—was as follows:

(21)

Dear Cardinal,

In a registered special-delivery letter dated July 12, 1971, you informed me that the Congregation for the Doctrine of the Faith had inaugurated a doctrinal proceedings against my book *Infallible? An Inquiry;* with the decree of June 23, 1971, which was approved by the Holy Father on June 25, 1971, the plenary meeting of the Congregation resolved to inform me in writing that on the bases of the investigations by the Congregation the theses contained therein seem to be incompatible with Catholic doctrine, so that within thirty days I should explain in writing whether and in what way I believe I am able to reconcile these theses and assertions with Catholic doctrine.

In a letter from Moscow on July 15, 1971, I informed you that your letter reached me only a few hours before my departure on a lecture and study trip around the world, and that during the trip it would be impossible for me to respond to your letter in a manner fitting the gravity of the situation. Therefore I had to request that you be patient until I returned home and could examine the documents.

After I, having returned to Tübingen on December 6, had already outlined the present response, I received your December 17, 1971, letter of warning, which, like the prohibition of the further distribution and translation of my book *The Church* communicated to me four years ago by your predecessor Cardinal Ottaviani, arrived precisely at Christmas. I have not taken the answering of your inquiry lightly, and I wish to respond from two perspectives.

I. Objection in Principle to the Proceedings of the Congregation

Already on May 6 of the same year (1971) you had sent to me a similar-sounding letter with questions in reference to my book *The Church,* which had already appeared in 1967; on June 21, I responded and indicated again my misgivings in principle to the Congregation's manner of procedure. Since you have not responded to these misgivings but instead only declare the inauguration of a second doctrinal proceedings, against my book *Infallible? An Inquiry,* I cannot but express anew, with even greater clarity, if possible, my misgivings on this manner of "doctrinal proceedings."

Here I refer to my letter of May 30, 1968, to the Secretary of your Congregation, Archbishop Paul Philippe, O.P., in which my misgivings were articulated and explained. Several of these misgivings in the meantime have been cleared up in an exchange of letters with the Congregation. Others, however, remain. Even the new order of procedure of the Congregation of January 15, 1971, the publication of which I desired and have welcomed, unfortunately does not resolve the matter. This is not merely my personal interpretation. As is certainly known in the Congregation, this order of procedure has met with sharp criticism from the Catholic and non-Catholic public.

I must therefore repeat: Despite improvements in detail, which I gladly acknowledge, this order of procedure is not free of the spirit of the Inquisition. It remains in any case far behind the very moderate demands which some time ago 1,360 professors of theology from the entire world drew up for the freedom of theology.

Thus I ask myself how this proceedings is consistent with your communication of January 24, 1970, "that the Congregation will proceed loyally, equitably, and without arbitrariness." Permit me to add parenthetically that according to this "ordinary" procedure there is still possible at any time an "extraordinary" proceedings in which the Congregation is not at all bound to the ordinary norms of procedure established by itself; thus the door to inquisitorial arbitrariness remains open. Also in reference to the "ordinary" procedure in question here I must make clear: It is impossible for me to recognize as "loyal, equitable, and without arbitrariness" a proceedings which

1. Permits me no access to the documents,
2. Prescribes a Relator "pro auctore" whom I have not chosen myself,
3. Permits the absence of clear definitions of competence and the possibility of appeal,
4. Is bound only to unilaterally decided time limitations.

Measured by modern legal consciousness this order of procedure of the Congregation for the Doctrine of the Faith must regrettably be described as still inquisitorial and discriminatory. As already in my response of June 21, 1971, in reference to the proceedings against my book *The Church,* so now also in reference to the new proceedings against *Infallible? An Inquiry,* I must *proclaim, or confirm, my objection in principle to such a procedure.* That this occurs not from an unecclesial, but rather from a basically ecclesial attitude, I have presented in detail in my letter of June 1, 1970, so that I can refer here to what was said there.

In reference to the book *The Church* I responded to the questions of the Congregation with the supposition that my fundamental misgivings on the proceedings in the Congregation would be taken seriously. From the inauguration of a further proceedings against *Infallible? An Inquiry,* I perceive that I have deceived myself in this hope. Under these circumstances it should certainly be understandable that I thus can look upon the entire proceedings of your Congregation as meaningful only if, in line with my requests, the following stipulations are fulfilled:

1. You refer in all your writings again and again to your dossier 399/57/i, which obviously refers to my person. Only with *full knowedge and free use of my documents* can I recognize the proceedings as loyal, equitable, and without arbitrariness. In this regard several things are unclear to me: In your letter of July 12, you speak of a new decree of the assembly of Cardinals of your office and explicitly mention that this decree was shortly thereafter approved by the Pope. But up until now I have received neither a copy of the decree nor the record of its approval.

I must confess that it is incomprehensible to me how still in this century secret decrees can be issued without the slightest attempt being discernible to present this decree at least to those concerned. The secrecy regulations of your Congregation may have their reasons. Nevertheless the impression arises that this mysteriousness does not serve the matter or those concerned, but rather your office and its officials.

In the previous century the old Congregation of the Index still had enough self-confidence to hand over to an indexed author those secret documents which later were nevertheless used as the basis of the Congregation's "secret decrees," so that he could learn the line of argumentation and reasoning and thereby orient himself; see the *Diaries* of the German church historian Franz Xaver Kraus (edited by H. Schiel, Köln, 1957, p. 484). Why may one today not see the critiques if this was already possible in the past century? Does not the impression necessarily arise that your office wishes to conceal something which it is afraid to present openly? As in my letter of May 30, 1968, and often since then, I therefore ask you for the written confirmation that I may see the decrees, critiques, and documents relating to me.

2. The Relator "pro auctore" foreseen in the new order of proceedings was provided with quotation marks in a remarkable fashion by the Congregation itself. In fact the expression is ambivalent. If the Relator "pro auctore" is named by the *Congregation* and acts in the name of the Congregation, which for its part has introduced a proceedings "against" (cf. the letter of July 12) the book of the author, then the Relator himself is in an ambivalent position, because he must act pro auctore and contra auctore at the same time. However the Congregation views this juridical problem, I myself as the author cannot recognize such a Relator "pro auctore," whose name for all intents and purposes is still concealed from me, as speaking for me. If the Relator "pro auctore" really should speak for the author, then the author himself must appoint him and work together with him. I therefore ask that the Congregation modify the order of proceedings resolved upon by itself in such a way that the author himself can choose the Relator "pro auctore."

3. The inauguration of a Roman doctrinal proceedings raises the question of the *definition of competence* and the instigation of *appeal:*

a. Several episcopal conferences have already inaugurated such proceedings in reference to the book *Infallible? An Inquiry,* and concluded them with various results. Now in addition comes the proceedings of the Roman Congregation for the Doctrine of the Faith. My question is: How many doctrinal proceedings shall still be carried out against my book? Must I look upon the proceedings taking place in Rome as a revision or as an appeal of the proceedings of the Commission on the Faith of the German Bishops' Conference? Are thus the judgments of the various episcopal conferences or their organs (the commissions on the faith) repealed according to the old axiom "ne bis in idem"? How will the introduction of a proper Roman proceedings be founded at all? When in the declaration of 1,360 theologians mentioned earlier a definition of the competence of the episcopal and the Vatican doctrinal courts was demanded, among other things, I could not imagine that so soon a concrete case would come forth in which such overlapping of competencies would arise: the papally approved secret decree of June 23, 1971, and simultaneously a majority of the declarations of the corresponding organs of the episcopal conferences.

b. But not only your office and the organs of individual episcopal conferences seem to overlap in competencies. On the basis of various facts I had to conclude (cf., e.g., *Diskussion um Hans Küng "Die Kirche,"* ed. by H. Häring and J. Nolte; Freiburg, Basel, and Vienna, 1971, pp. 31 ff.) that obviously various curial courts believe themselves competent to take measures, intervene, and bring pressures against publishing houses, etc. The question arises: How many Holy Offices are there actually at the moment and which is the highest court?

c. Of special importance for those concerned: Is it guaranteed that I in the end can lodge an appeal against the various proceedings—also against that conducted by your office? Can this occur at the Apostolic Signature, which since the new curial ruling is called the highest Roman court of appeal? I would have found it fair and loyal if not only the inauguration of the secret proceedings and the existence of secret decrees had been communicated to me, but at the same time an instruction on legal redress had been given me. Or is the Congregation for the Doctrine of the Faith perhaps not at all qualified for this, and should I then turn to the Apostolic Signature?

4. A further aspect of the proceedings of your office concerns the *duration* and *limitation of time* of the proceedings. I speak out of a ten-year experience with the Holy Office and the present Congregation for the Doctrine of the Faith, experiences with colloquies, decrees, prohibitions, interventions, and letters of this office. I may then in all clarity state that I consider the length of the proceedings unacceptable. The sole time limitation which the new order of procedure of the Con-

gregation mentions concerns the thirty-day period within which the author must present certain answers to the Congregation.

But what are the time limitations to which the Congregation itself is bound? May it extend a proceedings for an indefinite length of time? In the order of procedure I find no such time limitation given. Traditional canon law too recognizes, among other things, a time limitation and the demand for an acceptable duration of a proceedings.

Year-long insecurity over the outcome of a proceedings can be a form of injustice; and it may well be on this basis that Paul VI directed the Roman Rota in the past year to shorten the proceedings there considerably. In the interest of justice and loyalty a corresponding change in the procedures of the Roman Congregation for the Doctrine of the Faith would be urgent.

Permit me to recall the following experience: In the year 1967 the Congregation for the Doctrine of the Faith issued a secret decree on my book *The Church*. In the year 1971, thus four years later, after the book has appeared in numerous editions in the most varied languages, the Congregation forwards to me the questions which are then, of course, to be answered within thirty days. But even today, more than six months after my response of June 24, I still do not know whether the proceedings was suspended, whether a new proceedings against my book was inaugurated, whether everything was adjourned or what was concluded. Instead of leaving the writer in uncertainty for years, a state which the above-mentioned pressures and interventions of various snipers make possible, the Congregation should first set itself appointed times within which a proceedings must be inaugurated and concluded, or else it is to be considered suspended, or must be begun anew. This also belongs to the demands which I must submit for a proceedings to be just, loyal, and acceptable to the author, and which I see guaranteed neither through the practice nor through the wording of the Roman order of procedure.

On other important questions which are connected with the practice and the norms of procedure of the Congregation —for example, a possible bias of a consultant or of a member of the deciding committee—I do not wish to go further in this regard. It may be permitted me, however, to note that according to contemporary legal understanding concerning the incontestability of a proceedings, the impartiality of those judging—even if they are not judges in the strict sense —must be established. Indeed what has been detailed may suffice to make clear that certain curial prescriptions and practices in no way correspond to modern legal consciousness.

This is the reason why wide circles consider the present proceedings against my books harmful to the image of the Catholic Church; this is expressed in, among other places, a "Declaration of Solidarity" addressed to your office, which originated without my assistance and during my absence from Europe in the summer of 1971, and in a short time had more than 300 signatures. [See below, p. 82.]

A painful impression was also left on the public when the *Osservatore Romano* published recently several lengthy articles against the writer without even once reporting in an objective manner on the content of the book *Infallible? An Inquiry.* Is it from such practice that the Vatican newspaper even in good Catholic circles is again and again compared with the Moscow *Pravda?* Only at the end of this exposition on the kind and manner of Roman procedure do I wish to note how much the various questionable actions of the most various Roman organs have harmed my theological image in certain Catholic circles. The question occurs not only to the author: what actually do those in Rome intend to do in order to make reparation in suitable form for this damage, most especially the immaterial?

II. Preliminary Observations of the Questions of the Congregation

In reference to the questions placed by the Congregation to my book *Infallible? An Inquiry* I would like to observe:

1. I consider my questions admitted in principle. However, an affirmation of the contrary without argumentation is of little help. In fact my book is concerned to know precisely *how* certain utterances of the teaching office and especially the corresponding excerpts from Vatican I and II should be justified and proved theologically. My "Inquiry" in reference to the possibility of infallible statements was especially clearly formulated. If any official department of the Catholic Church ought to know a well-founded answer to this question, then that would indeed be the Roman Congregation for the Doctrine of the Faith. But here again to appeal only to those documents of the Magisterium which are the object of my questions is a vicious circle in which what must be demonstrated is presumed.

At any time I am willing to be convinced by arguments. Therefore I ask the Congregation to give me in at least brief form a reasonable argument for the possibility of infallible statements, one which does not ignore the difficulties in reference to certain texts of the Magisterium which have been pointed out by me, but rather takes them into consideration.

2. With this it is already clear that I do not in any way hesitate to enter into dialogue. Indeed, the *discussion* is in full progress. Besides the countless individual reviews in the short time since the appearance of the book, several volumes of discussion have already been published. I mention the collection edited by Karl Rahner, *Zum Problem der Unfehlbarkeit: Antworten auf die Anfrage von Hans Küng* (Freiburg, Basel, and Vienna, 1971), with numerous essays especially from the German-speaking world; then the essays by G. Baum, G. Lindbeck, R. McBrien, and H. McSorley published in the volume *The Infallibility Debate* (New York and Toronto, 1971); and especially the comprehensive Fall 1971 issue of the *Journal of Ecumenical Studies,* devoted to a study of the infallibility debate, as well as the important contributions of H. Stirnimann and A. Antweiler in the *Freiburger Zeitschrift für Philosophie und Theologie* (No. 3, 1971) and by W. Kasper in *Stimmen der Zeit* of December 1971. For me it would be of greatest value to know how the

Congregation judges the entire discussion. According to my observations up until the present, the following picture emerges:

a. There is scarcely any serious Catholic contribution to the subject which does not affirm the validity of my question.

b. There is scarcely any serious Catholic contribution to the subject which does not, even if it does not agree or agree completely with my solution, subject the traditional Roman understanding in some way to very sharp criticism.

c. My critics contradict one another very often, and this is true as much in reference to the interpretation of the Roman teaching on infallibility as in reference to the answer to my "Inquiry."

d. Up until now not a single author—and this is decisive in my opinion for the outcome of the debate—has offered a convincing argument for the possibility of infallible statements. The debate with Karl Rahner shows this especially; even this great theologian apparently is unable to adduce any proof for infallible statements. I therefore permit myself to send to you in the same mail my response to Rahner in Italian for your information. Together with my responses to M. Löhrer and K. Lehmann, it presents indirectly another contribution toward answering the questions of the Congregation.

3. For my part I will submit all responses to my book, including those in the future, to an attentive *study*. Besides apologetic articles in the traditional sense, like those in the collection edited by Karl Rahner already mentioned, other continuing contributions to the discussion of great importance have appeared, as, for example, the historical investigation by Brian Tierney on the source of papal infallibility, along with other contributions, in the above-mentioned issue of the *Journal of Ecumenical Studies,* which fills a gap in my argumentation; according to it, the first advocate of papal infallibility seems to have been Peter Olivi, who however was immediately condemned by the Pope of that day.

Likewise in the next summer semester I wish to give an advanced seminar on the infallibility discussion, in which the most important German opponents of my book will be treated in detail. In order to guarantee that the opinions of my opponents are expressed just as clearly as those of the author, I am inviting each individually to come personally to the pertinent meeting of the seminar; the Institute for Ecumenical Research of the University of Tübingen assumes the travel and hotel expenses. Should the Congregation for the Doctrine of the Faith show an interest in sending one of its experts to this advanced seminar, we will of course gladly give him an opportunity to present his views and arguments in detail.

4. All this shows clearly that I am aware what is at stake for the Church and Christianity in this question of infallibility. Inversely, it is certainly also known in your Congregation that any unilateral Roman position taking will not determine this affair, but at best will heat up the discussion. And the history of the decisions of the Congregation for the Doctrine of the Faith (or the Holy Office) and other Roman offices from the Galileo affair and the clash over rites up to the condemnation of historical-critical exegesis and various living theologians, who were then named as *periti* in Vatican II, shows that a problem can, or could earlier, be suppressed in the Church for a certain time, but that it then returns in heightened form.

To me personally nothing matters but the *objective clarification* of this question, so decisive for the theory and practice of our Church; my own theological position matters little to me. I occupy myself in the meantime in detail with very many other central questions of the Christian message. But after my inquiry on infallibility in the books *Structures of the Church* (1962), *Theologian and Church* (1964), *The Church* (1967), and *Truthfulness* (1968) remained without answer in Catholic theology, I saw it as my—not especially pleasant—duty to expound an inquiry in all moderation and fairness, yet also with the necessary decisiveness and unmistakable rigor: "non in destructionem, sed in aedificationem Ecclesiae." In this sense I would also apply to my little book the words of Acts 5:38 f.

Dear Cardinal, I do not know how you judge the present situation in the Catholic Church. I refer to that mistrust by the clergy and laity of the organs of leadership of the Church, including and especially of Rome, which in its negative consequences is immeasurably widespread. This mistrust does not arise from bad will but from disappointment. I have had opportunity to substantiate this in thousands of conversations all over the world, in letters and statements which come to me daily from Catholic laity, theology students, and priests from the most various sections of the Church. Rome's loss of credibility since Vatican II is dramatic and must to a great extent be seen as a result of the situation in Rome. Today in our own Church I must not seldom put up with the reproachful question why I in general still waste so much time and strength with Rome and the institutional Church, why I write a book expressly on papal infallibility and take the trouble to carry on correspondence with Roman offices. To this I have always answered that I myself have not written Rome off and am not working for the decline of the Catholic Church. I am not of the conviction that almost everything must be demolished before we can begin to build anew.

In a declaration which has been much noticed and very positively accepted I have publicly explained why I, with all my criticism of certain institutions and transactions, remain in this my Church and further intend, despite all assaults on my Catholic views, to work unwearied within it as I have done until now.

In a time when tens of thousands of priests and nuns have left the service of the Church or communal life, I have in countless letters, conversations, and lectures everywhere encouraged students, priests, religious, and laity to persevere and to make a renewed contribution in the Church, in ecclesiastical office, and in religious communities. Also on my most recent trip of many months around the world I have sought everywhere to battle energetically against the unbounded frustration and resignation, by showing from the Christian message itself how much meaning involvement in the Church has despite all difficulties. I have experienced moving oral and written witnesses from men and women who gratefully reaffirmed their existence in the Church with new strength and hope.

Dear Cardinal, with basic renewal and convincing reforms according to the gospel of Jesus Christ himself, Rome could also again instill into Christians new courage and new confidence. I do not consider myself infallible. I am not self-righteous and let myself at any time be corrected by such as know more than I. I do not wish to "demolish Rome," as certain circles reproach me, and I obviously do not imagine that I would be able to do so; only Rome itself is capable of that through imprudence, obduracy, and backwardness.

In my theology I occupy myself also with "Rome," although other Catholics no longer want to hear the word, because I am convinced of the necessity and the usefulness of a Petrine service not only for our Church but also for all of Christendom. What I strive for is a Church which acts in the spirit of the gospel of Jesus Christ even more than before for the people of today, their sorrows, and needs. For the sake of this gospel and the salvation of men and women I take upon myself much extra work and many tasks to which I am in no way obligated by my position. On the same grounds I also exercise my criticism of the Roman offices, of various traditional ecclesiastical forms and theological ideas. If in this letter comparatively much must be said about several formal questions, about certain demands for justice and fairness in the Church and in the Roman Curia, then this is all completely secondary to my theological work, but it must in this connection be said to you as the representative of a Roman office. The management of a Church which speaks so much of "Justice in the World" must likewise let humanity and justice also fundamentally rule first of all within its own walls if it is to be credible in the world.

I close my detailed response to your letter, dear Cardinal, with the repeated request that the Congregation send to me a positive response on the four formal questions raised as well as particularly on the material question at issue.

With singular esteem, I remain,

Devotedly yours,
Hans Küng

cc: Cardinal Dr. Julius Döpfner, President of the German Bishops' Conference

Dr. Carl Joseph Leiprecht, Bishop of Rottenburg

Professor Dr. Johannes Neumann, Rector of the University of Tübingen

Professor Dr. Walter Kasper, Dean of the Catholic Theology Faculty of the University of Tübingen

The "Declaration of Solidarity" that Küng referred to in his response did have over 300 signatures, both Catholic and Protestant, and was sent to Cardinal Šeper on September 30, 1971. It read as follows:

(22)

Declaration of Solidarity

We the undersigned members of different Churches and denominations are deeply disturbed over the manner and form in which the Holy Congregation for the Doctrine of the Faith is conducting its investigation of the two books by Professor Dr. Hans Küng of Tübingen, *The Church* and *Infallible? An Inquiry.*

The method of this investigation radically contradicts the spirit of Christ; it dishonors a man who has always understood himself as a loyal son of his Church, and who afterwards as before holds himself to be obligated to the message of Jesus Christ.

If this investigation, which injures not only the international reputation of Küng as a scholar and teacher of theology but also the reputation of the Catholic Church in general, must indeed be continued, we request and expect a procedure that will at least be conducted in a manner commensurate with human dignity and in a spirit of Christian brotherly concern.

We declare our solidarity with Professor Küng in his demand that an unconditional and unrestricted access to the pertinent dossier of the Sacred Congregation for the Doctrine of the Faith be granted him so that he may respond in every appropriate manner out of a full knowledge of the objections brought against his books.

Again, rather than a response from the Doctrinal Congregation within thirty days, there was a silence of almost a year and a half, and again the Congregation abandoned its order of procedure: it did not answer his formal requests concerning the proceedings, nor comment on his substantive theological responses, nor, according to Article 13 of the order of procedure, invite Küng to a discussion. Rather, the Congregation "decided, with the approval of the Holy Father, to prepare a declaration which sets forth for the benefit of the whole ecclesial community Catholic doctrine over against today's erroneous opinions in the area of ecclesiology. With regard to the doctrinal proceedings relative to the examination of your two books mentioned above, two options are open to you: First, the order of procedure provides for the possibility of a discussion with the representatives of the Congregation for the Doctrine of the Faith on the doctrinal points contained in the two letters of the Congregation. Second, you can accept immediately the doctrine contained in the Declaration. In this case, the doctrinal proceedings now in progress concerning your two books would be terminated" (July 4, 1973, letter of Cardinal Šeper to Küng).

But even then the possibility of a discussion was not an automatic assumption. The Walter Jens documentation noted: "Originally Küng was to have been presented by the public Roman action with an ultimatum to immediately subscribe to this declaration. Through last-minute negotiations with the Secretary of the Doctrinal Congregation, Archbishop Jérôme Hamer, who brought the declaration to Germany, Cardinal Döpfner, Cardinal Volk, and Bishop Leiprecht of Rottenburg succeeded in pushing through the possibility of a discussion with the Congregation as an alternative" (Walter Jens, ed., *Um Nichts als die Wahrheit,* Munich: Piper Verlag, 1978, p. 24).

The declaration, dated June 24, 1973, and entitled *Mysterium ecclesiae,* was enclosed with Šeper's letter to Küng. Two of the sections, 1 and 6, focused on the two points of contention in *The Church.* Point 1, about the unity of the Church, would seem to cause no major difficulty. Point 6, about the celebration of the Eucharist by someone other than an ordained priest, would appear to aim past the problem: there was no discussion of the Church at Corinth, the basis of Küng's argument, nor was there any discussion of abnormal situations, which was Küng's whole point. Points 2 to 5 all dealt with the claim of infallibility in the Church. However, "it was not the intention of this declaration . . . to prove . . . that divine revelation was entrusted to the Church so that she might thereafter preserve it unaltered in the world. But this dogma, from which the Catholic faith takes its beginning, has been recalled. . . ." The Congregation may have considered this simple affirmation sufficient for its purposes, but it did not respond to Küng's request for argumentation on how the affirmation was to be grounded.

The declaration, along with accompanying letters, was delivered to Küng on July 4, 1973, and was made public on July 5. On that day Küng also issued a press statement complaining about the manner of the proceedings and the simple affirmative nature of the declaration. He wrote as follows:

(23)

The Roman Doctrinal Congregation has juridically and theologically disqualified itself by its procedure. In the year 1967 it initiated a secret proceedings against my book *The*

Church and in 1971 a second against *Infallible? An Inquiry.*
Likewise in 1971 Pope Paul VI issued procedural regulations
for the Doctrinal Congregation so that the notorious misuses
of this old Inquisition office should be eliminated. Nevertheless the Doctrinal Congregation apparently did not see itself in the position to carry out and finish in these long years
the two proceedings in a manner corresponding to the papal
procedural regulations. Instead of this they intervene now in
the ongoing proceedings by a general public declaration on
the questions raised in these two books.

This procedure and the declaration with simple assertions
without substantive foundations make clear that the Doctrinal Congregation is incapable of making a contribution that
leads us further in the questions concerning Church, office,
and infallibility which today are discussed throughout the
world in Catholic theology and in the Oikoumene. Thereby
this selfsame Roman authority again appears as both the
prosecutor and the judge and gives proof through the entire
procedure—now even before the entire public—of its prejudice in the difficult proceedings.

On the next day, July 6, Küng published a lengthy article giving his arguments on the proceedings and the infallibility question
in a number of newspapers in Germany, Switzerland, England,
Holland, Italy, France, Spain, and Finland. It was as follows:

(24)
Incapable of learning? Roma locuta, causa aperta

In the post-conciliar period Rome has published a series of
worthy documents which have not solved all of the standing
questions, but rather have really just opened them up and
sharpened them: the celibacy encyclical (1967), the encyclical *Humanae vitae* (1968), decrees about Nuncios
(1969), marriage annulment procedures (1971), norms for
the nomination of bishops (1972), declarations on the sacrament of Penance (1972) as well as on the Sonship of God

and the Trinity (1972). It is to be feared that the latest
Roman declaration on the Church will have a comparable
counterproductive effect.

Rome passed up an extraordinary possibility. For clearly
in the ten years since John XXIII at the opening of Vatican
II had spoken—as the first Pope to do so—about the changing garment of the formulations of the faith, a large number
of questions about the Church and dogma have burst forth
which call for a response. Many would be thankful for constructive, orienting help somewhat in the style of the encyclicals of John XXIII on peace and social problems.

The latest Roman declaration, however, regrettably has another character. It stems from the Inquisition office founded
in the Counter-Reformation ("Sanctum Officium") which
became famous through the condemnation of Giordano
Bruno and Galileo and which together with the later-ab-
sorbed Congregation of the Index placed more than 4,000
books under reader prohibition with the penalty of excommunication. The most significant Catholic theologians of our
century—from Karl Adam to Chenu, Congar, de Lubac,
Teilhard de Chardin, Karrer, Rahner, Schoonenberg, and
Schillebeeckx—all had serious difficulties with this office.
Even under Pius XII they could bring the legalized purge
waves into action with removals, bannings, teachings and
publication prohibitions. John XXIII rehabilitated several of
these theologians and named them Council advisers. Paul VI
eliminated the Index, set up an International Theological
Commission, and introduced a reform of the Sanctum
Officium. However, despite its new name (Congregation for
the Doctrine of the Faith) and new procedural regulations,
the Roman Doctrinal office attempts again to take up various
of its old Inquisition practices. It likes to remain in the background itself (Holland, the Pfürtner affair) and, insofar as
they cooperate, sends the generals of religious orders and
bishops. The diplomatic service of the Vatican stands ready
to provide help in information and execution. But enough:
What all these practices in the Palazzo del S. Uffizio, which

have done the credibility of the Catholic Church and its theology incalculable damage, have to do with the gospel of Christ is asked about today no longer only by the readers of Dostoevski's *Karamazov* but also by many bishops and even not a few Roman curialists.

In 1967 a secret proceedings against my book *The Church* was introduced by the Roman Doctrinal office (at that time with the prohibition against distribution and translation) and in 1971 a second one against *Infallible? An Inquiry.* As early as 1965 Paul VI ordered that the Congregation should establish new, more just regulations of procedures and also publicize them. Only six years later did the Congregation publish such regulations, which, however, because of their inquisitorial character (no separation of powers, no access to documents for the accused, no appropriate defense possibilities, no right of appeal, absolute secret dealings), met with strong public criticism.

Nevertheless, even with the assistance of these procedural regulations prepared by themselves, the Congregation did not consider themselves in the position to carry out these two proceedings according to the correct form and to close them in these long years. Instead, they now, against right and justice, intervene by a generally public Declaration on the questions raised in the two books concerning the Church, office, and infallibility in the ongoing proceedings. Again the one and the same Roman office steps forward as the accuser and judge and shows through the whole undertaking its prejudice in the strenuous procedure now also before the whole public. In this matter its own Theological Commission was not consulted. Likewise the international Catholic and ecumenical discussion was not taken seriously, nor the two comprehensive discussion volumes on *The Church* and *Infallible?*, nor finally the "operative agreement" with Karl Rahner, the weightiest of the opponents in the infallibility debate.

Much more than an individual case is involved here. Through this statement on the unity of the Church, apostolic succession, universal priesthood, ecclesiastical offices, eu-

charistic celebrations, and infallibility, many are affected:
Unnumbered involved laity and pastors "on the front," Catholic exegetes, dogmaticians and ecumenists in the whole
world, who have similar interpretations and probably will
also continue to hold them. Significant ecumenical attempts
at understanding in recent years, as in the United States on
the Eucharist and office between official commissions of the
Lutherans and the Catholic Bishops' Conference (1970),
further, the document of the study commission of the Lutheran World Federation and the Roman Secretariat for Unity
(Malta Report, 1971), the French document for the reconciliation of offices between Catholics and Protestants
(Gruppe de Dombes, 1972), the Memorandum of the task
force of German University Ecumenical Institutes on the
reform and mutual recognition of ecclesiastical offices
(1973), as well as finally the *Ecumenical Catechism* edited
by J. Feiner and L. Vischer (1973)—all these are affected.
In all of the above-mentioned questions in which an understanding on the basis of the situation of Christendom is coming forth, the Roman document unfortunately shows itself to
be anti-ecumenical. Instead of interpreting Vatican II objectively and according to the Scriptures in the sense of theological, inner-churchly and ecumenical development, it is read
in a pre-conciliar spirit. This Council, which opened so many
doors and wished not to close others, is misused to block the
further progress of theology, the renewal of the Church, and
ecumenical understanding.

Of course it would be extreme to maintain that the Doctrinal Congregation had learned nothing. Under the pressure of
the "inquiry" the "historical conditionedness" of doctrinal
formulations, viewed as timeless, not only is touched upon
for the first time in a Roman document and not rejected, but
even is positively reflected on: the incompleteness and the
possibility of improvement of dogmatic statements are emphatically underlined. The meanings of the dogmatic statements are at least partly dependent upon the use of language
in a specific time and situation and must be newly elicited by

the theologians. Even the statements of the teaching office often bear the marks of a time-bound thinking in themselves. Not all dogmatic formulas are equally and for all times fit for the transmission of the truths of revelation. Sometimes new explanations and statements will have to be added; sometimes even old formulas will have to replaced by new ones. All this which is to be read in a Declaration by the Doctrinal Congregation deserves to be highlighted.

Should one not have been able to expect, on the basis of this relatively intensified consciousness of the problem, that the "Inquiry" pertaining to infallibility would be honestly and seriously addressed: Whether these so manifoldly historically conditioned, dependent upon the situation, incomplete, capable of being improved, expandable, replaceable doctrinal formulations could not also perhaps once be *false?* Does not the granting of the "historical conditionedness" also demand with it the implication of the "possibility of error" also, which indeed the history of theology and dogmas appears to substantiate? For, why should the Holy Spirit, who the office bearers so gladly see very busy, absolutely have to prevent errors in individual cases?

In this central point one is painfully disappointed. The "Inquiry" into an infallibility of specific statements or agencies guaranteed by the Holy Spirit was *not responded to, but rather gone around:* Where one expects reasons, one hears affirmations, where explanations, admonishments, and finally the admission: The infallibility dogma should not be "demonstrated by an investigation of the foundations of our faith," but rather only "be recalled to memory" through the Roman doctrine.

Whether this Roman doctrine today still can be found responsible was precisely what was asked. How much in dogmatics, exegesis, morals, church discipline, and politics was "recalled to memory" for the believers by the same Roman doctrinal office since the time of the Reformers, and which ultimately nevertheless even in Rome *de facto* had to be given up! And yet: *Despite* all errors the Church simply has

not fallen away from the truth of the Gospel; it was time and
again maintained and renewed in it. What will one say in a
reasoned fashion against such an interpretation? The arguments brought forth in *Infallible?* and later manifoldly
strengthened were in any case not refuted.

Thus the "Inquiry" remains standing: *causa aperta.* And
since even the Doctrinal Congregation knows of no reasoned
response, the prospect that the Roman infallibility doctrine
in the sense of the nineteenth century can be sustained fades
ever more. The recent Roman document will accelerate this
development, for:

1. The summary résumé of the Roman infallibility doctrine makes the weak points especially visible—obviously
also those in the doctrine of apostolic succession;

2. The word "infallible" is strikingly often replaced by
other words such as "unchangeable," "irreformable," "in-
defectible";

3. The question disputed even in Rome concerning the infallibility which stands behind the doctrine of *Humanae vitae*
is neither affirmed nor denied;

4. One no longer dares as earlier to speak unambiguously
of "infallible sentences or propositions."

To this extent the success of the "Inquiry" is apparent.
Moreover, the Roman document exposes itself to the suspicion that it is not speaking in infallible fashion about the infallibility of the ecclesiastical teaching office, but is rather
(even according to Roman interpretation) speaking in a fundamentally fallible manner. But conversely would it have
been more convincing if it had spoken about infallibility with
the claim of infallibility? One so easily presumes what is to
be proven!

In conclusion, one should nevertheless not be silent about
something pleasant: In the document not only were no
names mentioned, but likewise no formulas of excommunication and condemnation were used. It appears also that
one has learned this in Rome from the previous development: Questions like the present ones cannot be answered by

condemnations; a concern such as this cannot be regulated with disciplinary measures: the creation of martyrs does not pay. Catholic theologians—and the author has always unhesitatingly described himself as a Catholic theologian—will centainly pay attention to Rome. And they will do it even gladly whenever constructive, helpful, and reasoned answers are given to the needs and hopes of these times. Rome has in the course of centuries shown that it is capable of learning. And thus the hope is not unfounded that the Roman Doctrinal office will learn and that out of the organ of a doctrinal inquisition nevertheless one day an organ of doctrinal proclamation will come, as Paul VI in the decree on the reform and change of name of the Holy Office of December 7, 1965, described it as the task of the Congregation: The protection of the faith is better served today not through the exclusive persecution of errors but through the positive fostering of Christian doctrine.

On July 10 Küng felt compelled to issue another press statement against press reports coming from Rome that he had often refused to participate in a discussion. The pertinent part was as follows:

(25)
Vatican circles attempt to falsify the statement of Cardinal Döpfner

In contrast to Döpfner, who is concerned about a "satisfactory clarification" of the controversy with the Roman doctrinal authorities concerning the Church and infallibility, news agency announcements, which have their source in Vatican circles, maintain that I was invited ten times to Rome—in vain. I reject these assertions as untrue. I was always prepared for a dialogue with the Roman Doctrinal Congregation, as my letter of May 30, 1968, documents, and I likewise continue to be so. Until now, however, neither a time could be agreed upon nor has my written statement concerning just and fair conditions for such a colloquium been answered. Until today I have not been granted access to the documents, proper defense possibilities, the name of the defender appointed for me by the Congregation, specified time limitations for both sides.

I support Cardinal Döpfner's efforts for an "objective discussion" and would be extremely grateful to the German Bishops' Conference if it would take action in Rome for such a discussion under just and fair conditions so as to fend off greater damage to the credibility of the Catholic Church. In Germany there is agreement that the freedom of theological research should not be suppressed, that the progress of ecumenical efforts not be stopped, that the beginnings of the Second Vatican Council must not be rolled back.

On July 10 Cardinal Volk of Mainz also wrote a letter to Küng urging him to enter into discussion with Rome so as to settle the matter amicably. Küng answered with a lengthy letter on July 27, in which he stated that he was still committed to discussion with the Vatican, as he had been all along, but that under these new and extraordinary circumstances he needed time to reflect. His letter is as follows:

(26)

Dear Cardinal,
The concerted action against me has within the space of a week produced:
A declaration of the Doctrinal Congregation (delivered to me twice—through a courier from the Nunciature and by registered letter),
Two Vatican press conferences,
Two articles in the *Osservatore Romano,*
Two declarations of the German Bishops' Conference,
A bishop's visitation at its instigation,
And finally your special-delivery letter—to say nothing of the numberless telephone calls, letters, conversations, press

reports, radio and television broadcasts. All this is a bit much for a single man who stands over against a gigantic and powerful apparatus.

You will, in view of this, certainly understand if, against this entire background, I received your letter on the morning of July 12, around 7 A.M., brought to the house by special delivery, with somewhat mixed feelings. It would really have been a simple matter to have long since taken up contact with me at complete leisure. Since the proceedings of the Roman Doctrinal Congregation, of which until very recently you have been a member, had been running for three (*Infallible? An Inquiry*) or indeed for six (*The Church*) years, since my last letter to the Congregation of January 24, 1972, was not answered and instead on April 26, 1972, a now published document was in secret decided upon, I cannot now exactly understand why five days after the publication of the document I would have to be thought of with a special-delivery letter. At the risk that I will once again be charged with bad "style" if I express my wonder at such methods, I must nevertheless assert that I feel myself placed under the most massive pressure, which precisely in my case is not the appropriate method to attain something.

I am convinced that you personally are well intentioned toward me and have an honest interest in an amicable ruling on this matter which has been handled in such a way by the Doctrinal Congregation. I was extremely pleased at the friendly tone of your letter precisely because it distinguishes itself from another public statement to which I only indirectly replied (cf. the enclosed press statement of July 10, 1973, and the likewise enclosed offprint of a dialogue for the next number of the *Herder-Korrespondenz*) in order not to intensify still further the situation which has already been sufficiently dramatized by the Roman actions.

It was less understandable to me why you so urgently have pressed me to make positive theological contributions. It should not be at all necessary to list my bibliography, from *Justification* and *Council Reform and Reunion* to *The*

Church and *God's Becoming Human* [*Menschwerdung Gottes*]. I would only like to emphasize that critical writings such as *Truthfulness, Infallible?*, and *Fallible?* [*Fehlbar?*] likewise have an eminently positive goal and are thus understood by numberless people. The deepening of the faith and faithfulness, which is rightly demanded by you, appears to me and others in the present-day situation meaningful only when it is bound together with a frank critique of the ecclesiastical situations, good and bad, a critique which the bishops should not leave to only the theologians and laity. I have permitted myself to send you on the occasion of your being raised to the cardinalate my lecture—which everywhere was taken positively—"What Must Remain in the Church," where in all brevity is expressed how in my theology the critical and constructive elements necessarily hang together; the one without the other has no sense. I intend to continue on this path *opportune importune*. I would have already finished an introduction to *Christianity* if I had not been forced to produce my own volume of essays by the volume of essays on the infallibility debate in which I was not allowed to participate, and which volume goes back precisely to the instigation of the German Doctrinal Commission.

The urgency of your wish for a dialogue with Rome I can understand completely. If I am correctly oriented by German colleagues, I have above all you to thank that this possibility again was taken up in the written statement of the Doctrinal Congregation. I am extremely grateful to you for this since in this matter a frontal encounter with this authority, with all its unavoidable effects, could for the time being be avoided. Therefore I can immediately respond to your wish expressed in such a friendly fashion: I was always prepared for a dialogue with Rome and, regardless of all events, likewise continue to be so. At the public request of Cardinal Döpfner I have likewise declared myself in public prepared to contribute to a satisfactory clarification with an objective collaboration.

An objective collaboration is of course demanded of both sides. I was astonished in this connection that neither the letter of the Doctrinal Congregation of July 4, 1973, nor your own letter dealt with the central question of just and fair conditions for such a dialogue, as I had already developed in my letter of May 30, 1968, to the Doctrinal Congregation and had repeated in my last letter of January 24, 1972 (published in *Fallible?*). Time and again in various manners I made it clear that I am prepared for every genuine dialogue, but reject ahead of time every sort of inquisition. Twice in Germany I have participated with you in discussions, which should bear witness to my sincere readiness. With Rome, however, until now neither a time nor a catalogue of themes could be agreed upon. The questions in my last letter concerning just and fair conditions were not answered with a single word by the Congregation. Access to the documents, an appropriate possibility of defense, the name of my defender appointed by the Congregation, as well as time limitations for both sides have still always been denied me. Instead now the Congregation in a sensational manner intervenes in the proceedings which is in process by a general public declaration concerning the questions dealt with in the two books, and functions thereby simultaneously as the prosecutor, lawgiver, and judge. Despite this unusual way of proceeding I wish to stand by my readiness for dialogue. However, after my letter waited for a year and a half in Rome for an answer and now the result of the conversation in ununderstandable fashion has been prejudiced by a public declaration, I will certainly be granted the necessary time to reflect on the consequences of this new, juridically as well as theologically complex, situation for such a colloquium. I therefore ask for your understanding that at present I cannot yet speak to the matter more precisely. I am well aware that the entire matter must be handled with the greatest of caution if still greater damage to the credibility of the Catholic Church in Germany and in the world is to be avoided.

You will already have realized that the Roman declaration

has everywhere, and even in Italy, received the worst possible press and neither by the clergy nor by the people is really "accepted." The effects for the *oikoumene* would be devastating if the declaration would be "received" by the Church, which of course is unlikely. All the more so has it caused general wonder that the German Bishops have uncritically placed themselves in support of the Roman action and against one of their own theologians. For the welfare of our Church it would have been hoped from the heart that the Bishops, who again were not consulted concerning the text of the document, would force themselves to an unprejudiced view of the matter. In Rome, in this as in other cases, it is hoped that the bishops will pull the chestnuts out of the fire for the Curia. In Germany, however, as I understand the declarations of the Bishops' Conference, the Bishops and theologians are agreed that freedom for theological research should not be suppressed, progress of ecumenical efforts should not be stopped, the beginnings of the Second Vatican Council should not be reversed.

Concerning my own position in the whole matter it is also important for Rome to know what I here in briefest possible manner affirm: that I intend with all legitimate means to defend myself in this case, which truly is not only mine. I may neither act against my conscience, which I in all fallibility attempt to orient on the Gospel, nor disappoint the numberless men and women who throughout the world place their hope for the future on this path and expect from me personally— as in these days has been expressed in numberless letters and conversations—a remaining in the Church and an unpretentious standing firm. And after I have now for about ten years dealt with the Roman inquisition authorities, I will perhaps be believed that, if then I must, *Deo bene volente* I will likewise endure still another ten years. In any case—and this is said very clearly—any disciplinary measure would not be the end, but rather the beginning of the real debate, whose end would not be foreseeable. The effects in the intra-church-pastoral as well as in the state-political-university and finally also in the ecumenical areas I would not wish to paint for you and me. Certainly you likewise have experienced in the past weeks how numberless men and women in and outside of our Church, especially many priests and theology students, have been most deeply disturbed by the actions which have been prepared in general fashion against me. I have utilized only in limited fashion the possibility of enlightening the public and have at the same time turned away a further escalation, in that until now I have not only not called for public statements of specific groups and actions of solidarity, but rather I have hindered them. At the same time I would on the other hand be extremely thankful to the Bishops if on their side, out of their pastoral responsibility, they would work energetically against a Roman escalation, whose consequences we jointly would have to bear. Even in Rome one is clear on this matter: Rome can push through no measures in Germany against the will of the bishops.

May I in conclusion, my dear Cardinal, address you in a somewhat more personal form: it makes me very sad, and I have already expressed this in an earlier meeting, that a more constructive collaboration between you and me has not been realized. Therefore, I would like precisely in this dispute, which for both sides is more than unwanted, to lift up the profound commonness in fundamentals and in goals. You have for so many years known me well enough to realize that in all my theological efforts I have striven according to my best knowledge and conscience to do what is truly Christian in the Church and in the world, whose erosion I have at all times resisted not only on the right but also on the left. From that alone it should be understood—although this naturally can be easily described as pride, arrogance, and "infallibility"—that I, thoroughly aware of my own fallibility, must in certain matters speak so clearly and unmisunderstandably, which I have likewise done in this letter where the seriousness of the hour allows no making light of the matter. I promise you, nevertheless, that without concern for protocol or personal prestige I will gladly contribute in a Christian spirit to any honorable, honest, and just solution. At the same time I request that you along with your fellow bishops would work so that likewise in Rome an honorable, honest, and just solution would be striven for. I expect in principle no more and no less than that I can do research and teach in peace, which is proper to my task as teacher of theology in the Catholic Church. I will always stand by it in full loyalty and clear fidelity.

In upright allegiance I send you heartfelt greetings.

Yours sincerely,
Hans Küng

enclosures: Press declaration of July 10, 1973
            Interview with *Herder-Korrespondenz,*
            August 1973

cc: Cardinal Dr. Julius Döpfner
    Bishop Dr. Carl Joseph Leiprecht

The Catholic Theology Faculty of the University of Tübingen —Küng's colleagues—sent a rather lengthy letter on the same day, July 27, to all the bishops of Germany, urging them to do everything possible to see to it that the proceedings against Küng be, and appear to be, correct and just. It is a document strongly supportive of Küng, which curiously is not reproduced in the German Bishops' December 18, 1979 *Documentation* against Küng (nor in its English translation: *The Küng Dialogue,* Washington, D.C.: U. S. Catholic Conference, 1980—not on p. 68 or anywhere else). The letter stated:

(27)

Honored Cardinals!
Honored Archbishops and Bishops!

The undersigned professors of Catholic theology of the University of Tübingen turn in serious concern to the German Bishops on the occasion of the proceedings of the Congregation for the Doctrine of the Faith against our colleague Hans Küng.

At the beginning we wish to expressly affirm that we are conscious of the responsibility of the theologian for the genuine unity and true peace of the Church and its members. We affirm the teaching office of the Pope and the bishops and understand our task as a participation in their responsibility. Teaching office and theology live from the struggle within the faith for a living understanding of the truth. This struggle must, however, take place in a manner that will serve the essence of the search for truth and the credibility of the Church.

1. Our colleague Küng has with his objected-to books *The Church* and *Infallible? An Inquiry* set in motion a worldwide intensive theological discussion which in no way has yet led to a scholarly consensus. In view of the extremely difficult questions which are under discussion we hold that a proceedings, as the Doctrinal Congregation on this occasion is carrying it out, is objectively inappropriate. According to our conviction, disputed questions within the realm of scholarly theology as a rule cannot be settled through disciplinary measures without calling forth serious negative consequences. The anti-Modernist measures and the decisions of the Biblical Commission give testimony of that in manifold fashion. The proceedings against Hans Küng means unfortunately nothing other than the taking up again of a practice which has damaged the reputation of theology as a science and the Church as a whole.

We especially regret this, therefore, because at present much more serious dangers threaten the Church. One has the impression that the ecclesiastical teaching office overlooks the fact that today the fundamental spiritual debate is carried out in a completely different direction and on other fronts.

2. The undersigned hold that it is necessary that whenever the Congregation for the Doctrine of the Faith or the bishops believe it necessary to object to a specific teaching opinion, this must happen not only in an orderly and correct proceedings but also in one that is objectively appropriate and built on a clear theological foundation. The German Bishops' Conference has attempted to reckon with this fundamental

principle by the setting of norms for a doctrinal complaint proceedings. On the contrary, the proceedings regulations of the Doctrinal Congregation of 1971 for the investigation of doctrinal opinions leaves out of consideration the essential assurances of the rights of the one concerned—recognized by everyone today. Today in the civil rights administrative practice of civilized states governed by law it is accepted by all that the one charged has the right of access to his file and an appropriate defense—and this not only in penal proceedings.

In this regard we refer to the pertinent fundamental principles which were subscribed to by more than 1,300 theologians and on December 17, 1968, sent to the papal Secretariat. We stand behind this declaration and request that the bishops act so that these procedural fundamental principles will be observed in the spirit of *aequitas canonica* by the Doctrinal Congregation, as well in the interest of the truth as in the interest of the reputation of the Church and the personal worthiness of the one charged. We permit ourselves to enclose these fundamental principles.

3. In this connection we further request the German Bishops to reflect also on the pastoral consequences which a proceedings that many do not feel corresponds to contemporary basic principles of justice and the essence of theological scholarship will draw in its train. Doubtless for not a few —whether correctly or incorrectly—its judgment about the Church and the progress of the renewal stimulated by the Council depends essentially on how the teaching of the Church conducts itself with a man whose ecclesial mentality and whose efforts for the credibility of the Church are not disputed even by those who theologically in individual matters represent other viewpoints.

On this point the question is raised whether the Church wishes before the public of our land to give up a broad effectiveness, a trust in its justice, and a high evaluation of the purity of this message and the corresponding attitudes. The German Bishops will also have to test whether the counsel of those who, under the call of the word of a "small flock," demand severe restrictions corresponds to the universal task of proclamation of the Church and its tradition.

4. Finally we ask that the German Bishops reflect that in recent years the question about the continuance of ecclesiastical theology in state universities is again being discussed as much as the question of the constitutionality of the Church tax. Because of this several universities have already set up their own study programs of religious studies or are planning to. One must likewise note that in the present situation the withdrawal of the *Missio canonica,* and especially a doctrinal complaint proceedings which is not conducted according to fundamental principles which are clear and unobjectionable in their procedural regulations and according to clear theological criteria, will certainly encourage these and still further efforts. A proceedings which does not correspond to all the contemporary usual demands of justice will in any case give a political stimulus to the forces which are submitting the special legal status of the Church on the basis of the Concordat to a growing criticism. If the Holy See and the German Bishops do not deal with the ongoing theological discussions with the necessary intelligence and care, a historically developed position of the Church in the Federal Republic of Germany will suffer damage.

For this reason we request the German Bishops urgently to use their influence to see to it that the proceedings concerning the works of Professor Küng can likewise stand before the eyes of the critical public as correct and according to justice.

Finally we wish to not omit thanking the bishops who until now have already made efforts to hold open the possibility for an objective clarification of theologically disputed questions.

> Yours very sincerely,
> A. Auer, G. Greshake,
> H. Haag, W. Kasper, W. Korff,
> J. Neumann, R. Reinhardt,
> M. Seckler, H. J. Vogt

The Doctrinal Congregation sent Küng a reminder dated August 16, 1973, that it expected a reply from him on the declaration—with the usual deadline given. On September 22, 1973, one month after he received the Vatican letter, Küng replied. He also wrote a letter to Pope Paul VI the same day (also not reprinted in the Bishops' *Documentation*) in which he outlined his objections to the procedure of the Doctrinal Congregation and in the end asked him in effect to declare a cessation of hostilities. The letter stated:

(28)

Your Holiness,

The good will which you have shown me in various ways encourages me likewise this time to turn to you personally as the highest shepherd of our Church. Indeed I have felt myself obliged to speak openly my critique on this our Church according to my best knowledge and conscience. However, in my last books it was as always a critique out of love. Moreover, you have known me for many years and realize how very concerned I am with a complete loyalty and clear fidelity to our Catholic Church, from which I in no case will allow myself to be driven.

For several years now there have been running in the Doctrinal Congregation proceedings concerning *The Church* and *Infallible? An Inquiry*. They have until now produced no results. Full of trust, I would like to permit myself to state to you concerning this proceedings in brief and—for which I ask understanding—not in *stile curiale* the following:

1. I had to time and again raise fundamental objection concerning the justice of the proceedings and at the same time pose weighty questions concerning the theological problematic. However, concerning both matters I have till now received no answer from the Congregation.

2. The recent escalation of this matter set in motion by the Doctrinal Congregation in connection with the declaration *Mysterium ecclesiae* is being followed by many bishops,

priests, students of theology, men and women, and above all by the entire world press, with the greatest concern. Should I find myself forced to a further escalation, I will have to undertake it. However, the effects would be unforeseeable; it would intesify the polarizations, unleash unnecessary public and private protests, further shake the public credibility of the Catholic Church and Rome, and loose a dispute without end. Not only within the Catholic Church but even in the *oikoumene* have these stepped-up attacks against me encountered incomprehension.

3. For myself I am concerned that a *causa maior* of the post-conciliar Church history not be made of this matter. Along with every intervention for the freedom of theology I am gladly prepared to contribute to any honest, honorable, and just solution in a Christian spirit. I expect in principle no more and no less than that I will be able to do research and teach without suspicion, as corresponds to my task as teacher of theology in the Catholic Church.

4. Through its "declaration" the Congregation has said what it believed it had to say completely before the public. If it is the truth, it will of itself prevail. On my side I have taken a position in the discussion concerning *The Church* and *Infallible?* in detailed publications and will likewise continue, being conscious of my fallibility, to be open to and thankful for founded criticism of my interpretations. For the rest, I am not fixated on this theme. Already I have proceeded to concern myself with other, more central theological themes—in particular, an introduction to the Christian faith.

5. My question to the Congregation is the following: Would it not be the time, after both sides have said what is necessary, to allow Catholic theologians to discuss to the end, unhindered by disciplinary measures, these complex questions on the basis of the statements already made? Would it not be better to let this question between the Congregation and myself rest and leave the judgment about the answer to history? I am little concerned about being judged

right. The truth should see the light of the day, no more and
no less.

6. For all of these reasons I have made a concrete suggestion to the Congregation: Let the proceedings which have already been continuing in ecclesiastical agencies so long and
from which neither for one side nor for the other anything
good can come, finally and without further consequences be
closed.

I know that a word from you, Your Holiness, would be
sufficient to set this matter on the right path. Not only is my
person concerned in it, but also our Church, which should be
the steward of Jesus Christ. I therefore very earnestly request
from you your helpful mediation, and I greet you,

Most sincerely,
Hans Küng

Küng's September 22 letter to Cardinal Šeper was much longer,
objecting to the pressures he had been placed under and the proceedings against him and commenting on the theological position
of the declaration. In the end he again suggested that a mutual
agreement be reached to leave the matter rest. He wrote:

(29)

Dear Cardinal:
Your letter from Rome, dated July 4, 1973, reached me in
Tübingen on the morning of July 5. I will forgo a detailed account of the extraordinary circumstances that surrounded
this letter, which also have been well noted by the public.
—The letter was first brought to my house in Tübingen by a
courier from the Nunciature in Bonn;
—half an hour later, it was conveyed to me by the postal
service, registered mail from the Nuncio;
—one hour later, it was made known to the public, together
with the declaration *Mysterium ecclesiae,* and its contents
were commented upon by spokesmen of the Congregation for

the Doctrine of the Faith in a Vatican press conference summoned especially for the occasion;

–it was flanked by articles in the *Osservatore Romano*, and further by a Vatican press statement;

–it was supported in Germany by two declarations of the German Bishops' Conference and through the personal interventions of many bishops—also instigated by Rome.

One can only surmise what your Congregation and the other Vatican and episcopal bodies which were asked to join in wanted to achieve through this coordinated initiative. Be that as it may, I am entitled to ask for understanding if my answer is late. For me, an individual theologian who does not have at his disposal the powerful machinery of the Vatican and who has been exposed to a massive pressure of this kind, it would have been irresponsible, in such a situation, to comply immediately with your request to reply "soon." However, I did confirm at once receipt of your letter in a letter to the Nuncio in Bonn, Archbishop Bafile. May I, in self-defense, remind you of how much time the Congregation itself has taken to answer my own letters:

–My answer to your letter relative to the proceedings against my book *Infallible? An Inquiry* is dated January 24, 1972. The Congregation required one year and a half to acknowledge receipt of this letter.

–My answer to your letter relative to the proceedings against my book *The Church* is dated June 21, 1971. The Congregation has needed two years to confirm receipt of this letter.

–In a letter of August 31, 1968, the Congregation assured me that the "topics" for a discussion on my book *The Church* would "soon" be given to me. To date, that is, five years later, the Congregation has not sent me anything of the sort nor has it given me any reasons or explanation for not keeping its promise.

This being the case, I was certainly entitled to assume that you would give me more time to answer, especially during the summer vacations. But, after all the extraordinary demands made on me, your letter of August 16 came in the middle of my vacation, and demanded that, by September 20, I should answer your letter of July 4. Once more, your Congregation sets deadlines unilaterally, similar to the earlier thirty-day time limit, and within that deadline demands an answer in a manner that resembles an ultimatum.

Without relinquishing my objection against your unilateral deadlines, I would like to answer your letter today, September 22, since your admonition arrived at my summer address in Switzerland precisely one month ago.

By way of introduction, may I take the liberty to make the following point, which concerns the infallibility issue only indirectly: In your letter of July 4, an error has slipped in. You maintain that on May 6, 1971, I answered the Congregation concerning my book *The Church*. A letter written by me on that date to your Congregation does not exist. I surmise that the letter in question is the one dated June 21, 1971.

With regard to your letter of July 4, I would like to declare my position under two headings:

I. Fundamental Protest Against the Proceedings of Your Congregation

Your letter informs me that the "Ratio agendi" [the procedural norms] of your Congregation makes provisions for the possibility of a discussion on the doctrinal points contained in two letters of your Congregation, in case I should not want to subscribe "immediately" to the doctrine contained in the Declaration. This is exactly what was announced to the public in the press conference in the Vatican and commented upon in the *Osservatore Romano*. This raises several questions:

1. To my distress both spokesmen of the Congregation for the Doctrine of the Faith in the press conference failed to inform the public as to what is actually the case with the discussions with the Congregation. May I recall the following: The Congregation invited me to Rome five years ago to par-

ticipate in a discussion on my book *The Church*. I declared, and later confirmed time and again, that I was willing in principle to do so (cf. especially my letter of May 30, 1968). A discussion ensued as to the just and fair conditions for such a discussion. Some questions could be settled to the satisfaction of both parties. Among other things, the Congregation promised to inform me soon about the list of topics to be discussed. The Congregation never invited me to take part in a discussion on my book *Infallible?* until its declaration was published. In this declaration it was announced that a discussion was "possible." If the Congregation was of the opinion that the whole affair was worth a press conference, truth and veracity would have demanded that the true state of affairs should not be withheld from the public. Hence my question: Is the Congregation, which has imparted to the public the dissimulating and, in fact, deceitful information mentioned above, prepared to inform the public with the same degree of emphasis how things actually stand?

2. To my even greater distress the latest letter of your Congregation, on July 4, does not say a single word on the question which has now been at issue for five years, namely, the question about the just and fair conditions. In contrast to earlier statements of the Congregation, this letter makes it all look as if these conditions have never been discussed. My last two letters to the Congregation, to which your letter explicitly refers, raised and underscored my fundamental reservations against the legality of the proceedings of your Congregation. On January 24, 1970, you were so kind as to assure me unrestrictedly "that the Congregation will proceed loyally, equitably, and without arbitrariness." In my last letter of January 24, 1972 (but see also my letter of May 30, 1968), I took the trouble to substantiate in many pages of writing what I do not need to repeat here in detail: I absolutely cannot regard as "loyal, equitable, and free from arbitrariness" proceedings which:

—allow me no access to official records;

—prescribe a Relator "pro auctore" not of my choice and whose name I do not even know;

—neglect to clearly delimit competence and to provide for the possibility of appeal;

—are bound only by deadlines unilaterally set.

In my earlier letters (July 1, 1970, and January 24, 1972), I already explained in detail that my fundamental protest against both proceedings, which I must reiterate and underscore here once again, is not to be traced to animosity against the Church, but rather to a deeply ecclesial fundamental attitude. Here I need only refer to what was said there.

Therefore my question: Is the Congregation prepared to accede to these wishes which, by the standards of our modern sense of legality, go without saying? If it has come to such proceedings, that is what the Congregation ought to do in order to proceed "loyally, equitably, and without arbitrariness."

3. Since my last letter of January 1972, the situation has worsened because of the way the Congregation has acted publicly at various levels. I did not intend this to happen. Instead of responding to the objections I had expressed, the Congregation decided, as far back as April 26, 1972, to go to the public by way of a declaration. Your letter makes it clear that this "Declaration in Defense of the Catholic Doctrine on the Church Against Certain Errors of the Present Day" was prepared in connection with the two proceedings pending against me, and so comes through, in fact, as a "Lex Küng." It is clear, then, that, instead of standing by its own procedural rules, and contrary to right and equity, the Congregation is intervening in the proceedings still pending and undecided by a general and public declaration on the questions raised in both books. In so doing, the Congregation plays the role of lawgiver, accuser, and judge, all at the same time, as it were.

In view of these events, highly extraordinary as they are in terms of modern legal sensitivity, and so difficult for the public within and without the Church to understand, it is not easy for me to stand by my own willingness to participate in a discussion. I have declared even in public how badly shaken is my confidence in the legitimacy of the way the Congregation is proceeding. It is only in order to preclude still greater harm to the credibility of the Catholic Church, and of Rome in particular, and to show good will on my part, that, at the public urging of Cardinal Döpfner, I have already declared that I will stand by my willingness to participate in a discussion, no matter what happens, and so to contribute through substantive cooperation to a satisfactory resolution.

This substantive cooperation, urged by Cardinal Döpfner for the sake of a satisfactory clarification, I am certainly entitled to expect also from the Congregation. But since the action of the Congregation itself has shown that its present rules of procedure are obviously inadequate, a revision of the whole order of procedure seems to be needed. As early as April 1969, 1,360 Catholic theologians from fifty-three countries—among them some of the best-known names in Catholic theology—submitted to the competent Roman authorities a "Declaration on the Freedom of Theology." All these theologians call on the teaching office of the Church to proceed differently with regard to the theologian. Unfortunately, the proposals of the theologians have been implemented only to a small extent in the "Ratio agendi" adopted by the Congregation in January 1971. I would like, therefore, to renew my support for this declaration which is written "in complete loyalty and clear fidelity to the Catholic Church." I would also like to request that the Congregation should do the same.

Therefore my question: Is the Congregation for the Doctrine of the Faith prepared to accede to the wishes of the 1,360 theologians "so that the Pope and Bishops can worthily and appropriately carry out their tasks also in relationship to the function of theologians in the Church"? I take the liberty of sending you the aforementioned declaration in German, Italian, French, English, and Spanish.

4. Finally, the conduct of the Congregation also raises the

question whether the proposed discussion makes sense at all. You have not as yet made a proposal about which topics should be addressed in this discussion. The question, then, is whether the published declaration of the Congregation does not, in fact, so prejudice the outcome of the discussion that it turns into a "farce," as the press has surmised. Actually, you are proposing an alternative to the discussion, namely, that I should accept "immediately" the doctrine contained in the declaration. In this case, the proceedings pending against my two books would be "concluded." Many find that this alternative is cynical, since any proceedings are "concluded" if the accused "immediately" subscribes to his condemnation even before the sentence is passed. I do not want to quarrel about this point. What I want to know is whether, under the present conditions, a genuine and fair discussion is at all possible. Until now I have taken part in every discussion on infallibility that held out a promise of success. I have done this not only in Frankfurt, Paris, and Bern with theologians of a different persuasion, but also with bishops and theologians of the German Doctrinal Commission in Stuttgart. In all these cases, a genuine dialogue was involved, a genuine speaking with one another, in which both sides could learn something. In Rome, too, I would like to engage in a genuine dialogue of that sort. On the contrary, a discussion in which one side demands the surrender of the other or which is only the veiled beginning of disciplinary measures is of no help either to the common cause or to me personally. It rather blocks a genuine solution of the question still pending and is prejudicial to the credibility of the Catholic Church.

Therefore my questions:

a. Can the Congregation guarantee me a genuine discussion, or am I to expect a dictatorial act in which what is not being "immediately" subscribed to is then supposed to be endorsed? In other words, is the purpose of the discussion to ascertain the truth, or is it submission and the initiation of disciplinary measures? Is the Congregation prepared to implement the theologians' "Declaration on the Freedom of Theology"?

b. How does the Congregation explain the contradiction between its two letters? In its earlier letter of July 12, 1971, it speaks of theses in my book which *"seem* to be incompatible with Catholic doctrine" and "which cause *difficulties* for the Congregation as far as a Catholic interpretation is concerned." You ask me to explain "whether and in what way I believe that these theses and opinions can be reconciled with Catholic doctrine." And yet in your letter of July 4, 1973, the same Congregation speaks of "points which do not conform with the doctrine of the Church," as well as of "theses which this Congregation has found incompatible with Catholic doctrine." It seems as if, here too, the verdict is already being anticipated.

c. If the discussion is to be genuine, how are we to explain the statement of the spokesman of the Congregation in the press conference of July 5, 1973, that anyone who does not subscribe to this declaration of the Congregation is already "outside the Church"? How does this statement relate to the fact that the declaration itself happily refrains from formulae of excommunication?

d. Is there any truth to the report which has appeared in Catholic papers in Germany to the effect that the Congregation for the Doctrine of the Faith has opened a further proceedings against my book *Why Priests?* (1971)?

Permit me to add a final remark relative to this complex of questions. For five years now—to say nothing about earlier proceedings—I have made all the efforts I could think of to reply to the various letters of your Congregation extensively and to the point. Time and again for five years, I have raised the same questions as to the legality of your procedure. But your Congregation does not answer, not even the most fundamental questions about right and equity in the manner of procedure being forced upon me. The Congregation knows very well that we are dealing here with presuppositions in the absence of which a substantive discussion is out of the question. Under these circumstances, many would have stopped exchanging letters with your Congregation, which is what several people have advised me to do. But because of the concern I have for the common cause of the Catholic Church, a cause to which you and I are dedicated, I have always examined your letters, I have informed you of my readiness to participate in a discussion, and I have taken pains to achieve a scholarly resolution of outstanding problems from within a Catholic faith conviction. The Congregation on the contrary has steadily escalated its own initiative, and in a way totally incomprehensible to me has carried it forward to the point of publicly disqualifying me without delivering a judgment. I ask whether the Congregation is sufficiently aware that through its action it is putting a strain on the patience, loyalty, and sense of faith of a Catholic theologian. At any rate, out of this section of my letter this much emerges with unmistakable clarity: Without a clarification of the essential preconditions the discussion requested by the Congregation is senseless for both sides.

II. Questions on the Theological Problematic

Because of the way the Congregation proceeds I had to speak a great deal about questions of justice. I now come to the theological questions.

1. The declaration of the Congregation does not aim to "prove" the dogma at issue "through an inquiry into the foundations of our faith," but only "to call to mind" what is already known especially from Vatican I and II. With this the declaration bypasses the questions raised in my book without examining them in the least. The texts which the declaration quotes from Vatican I and II are, of course, known to me. Not only did I take part in Vatican II in my capacity as *peritus,* but for over ten years I have submitted the pertinent conciliar texts to thorough historical and theological analysis. As I wrote to you in my letter of January 24, 1972, in my book I am trying to ascertain precisely *how*

certain doctrinal statements, and especially the corresponding texts from Vatican I and II, are to be theologically grounded and responsibly supported. To merely refer to these documents of the teaching office to which my questions are addressed, is a vicious circle. What is to be proved to be so is, in fact, assumed to be so. I will any time be convinced by arguments. This is why then I have already begged the Congregation to produce, at least in abbreviated form, an argumentation that would prove the possibility of infallible propositions. In this argumentation, however, the difficulties I have raised concerning some texts of the teaching office should be addressed, not ignored.

After the publication of this declaration I have no choice but to reiterate with even greater insistence my request to the Congregation for an argumentation. As the reactions to my book and to the declaration of the Congregation show, these questions are not only my own. The declaration of the Congregation has been met with incomprehension in broad segments of the Catholic clergy and laity because it clarifies nothing. It only calls to mind what is in need of clarification. People expect arguments and what they get is assertions.

2. In connection with the latest declaration of the Congregation, I am struck by a contradiction. The letter of the Congregation on July 12, 1971, contains a whole section on "infallible propositions" (Section IV. On Infallible Propositions). But the declaration, in spite of everything it has to say about infallibility, nowhere speaks of "infallible propositions," which is indeed surprising. Should I take this silence to mean that there are no such "infallible propositions"? If so, my "inquiry" could be looked upon as substantially closed.

3. In the same connection, another question emerges. I am pleased to notice that the declaration speaks in detail of the "historical condition" of doctrinal statements. It maintains that the articulations of the faith are contingent on the situation, that they are imperfect, perfectible, open to additions, replaceable. If so, a question emerges for the teaching office

to answer: If these articulations are in many ways historically conditioned, if they are contingent on the situation, if they are imperfect, perfectible, open to additions, and replaceable, why could they not, under certain circumstances, also depart from the truth? Why wouldn't "historical condition" entail in particular cases even the possibility of error, as in many ways history seems to show? To what extent is the assertion that in determinate individual cases the Holy Spirit absolutely prevents errors a form of theological wishful thinking, rather than an utterance grounded on "the foundations of our faith"?

4. It is obvious that the declaration has not adequately taken cognizance of the most recent international *discussions* on infallibility. Unfortunately, the Congregation for the Doctrine of the Faith failed to respond to my invitation to send one of its representatives to our graduate seminar in Tübingen in the infallibility debate, a seminar which was attended by numerous experts from other universities; such as Professors H. Fries, K. Lehmann, K. Rahner, and J. Ratzinger. Thus, the Congregation missed a good opportunity for a genuine discussion. In this connection, I shall not fail to mention that the Institute for Ecumenical Research at the University of Tübingen has established archives on the infallibility debate. Documents of the most various kinds which have come to us and relate to the infallibility debate are collected there and subjected to disciplined investigation.

As a sign of how much I have endeavored to be amenable to serious theological discussion, how I am gathering and responding to all the arguments against my book, and how I am trying to make my own views ever more precise, may I send you a 524-page volume on the infallibility debate which I edited. It is entitled *Fehlbar? Eine Bilanz*. This volume is dedicated to the Congregation, "non in destructionem, sed in aedificationem Ecclesiae." This shows what sentiment is behind this book.

5. Parallel questions would have to be raised on the undifferentiated statements about the uniqueness of the Cath-

olic Church, the apostolic succession, the office of the
Church, the sacramental character and validity of the Eucharist. But in order not to prolong this already lengthy letter, I
would like to defer these questions.

III. A Personal Word

I am well aware, my dear Cardinal, that my various formal
and substantive requests strive for a larger measure of freedom which the teaching office of the Church ought to guarantee to the theologians as they minister to the Church. But
you yourself know that numberless true Catholics find that
Rome's measures against Catholic theologians detract considerably from the credibility of the Catholic Church in today's
society and put a strain on their own faith. On my side, I feel
that I am being supported not only by numberless positive letters and encouragements, but also by the aforementioned
declaration of 1,360 theologians made public five years ago.
In its introduction, this declaration voices what concerns me
most deeply in this whole affair:

> In complete loyalty and clear fidelity to the Catholic
> Church, the undersigned theologians see themselves compelled
> and obliged to point out publicly and in all seriousness that
> the freedom of the theologian and of theology in the service
> of the Church, which was won anew in the Second Vatican
> Council, must not today once again be endangered. This free-
> dom is a fruit and a demand of the liberating message of
> Jesus himself and remains an essential aspect of the freedom
> of the children of God in the Church proclaimed and de-
> fended by St. Paul. Therefore, it is incumbent on all the
> teachers in the Church to proclaim the Word . . . in season
> and out of season.
>
> For us theologians, this freedom goes hand in hand with
> the heavy responsibility not to jeopardize the genuine unity
> and the true peace of the Church and all its members. We
> are well aware that we theologians can commit errors in our
> theology. However, we are convinced that erroneous theo-
> logical opinions cannot be disposed of through coercive meas-
> ures. In our world they can be effectively corrected only

through unrestricted, objective, and scholarly discussion in which the truth will win the day by its own resources. We affirm with conviction a teaching office of the Pope and the Bishops which stands under the word of God and in the service of the Church and its proclamation. But we also know that this pastoral ministry of proclamation ought not to constrain or impede the scholarly teaching of the theologian. Any kind of Inquisition, be it ever so subtle, damages not only the development of a healthy theology. It at the same time inflicts incalculable damage on the credibility of the entire Church in the world of today. Therefore, we expect the pastoral office of proclamation of the Pope and the Bishops to exhibit an understanding trust in our ecclesial attitude and to support without prejudice our theological work for the welfare of men and women in the Church and in the world. We wish to carry out our obligation to search out and speak the truth without being hampered by administrative measures and sanctions. We expect that our freedom will be respected whenever, to the best of our ability, we voice or publish our reasoned theological convictions.

Although I stand up for the freedom of theology, I am anxious to assure you that, in a Christian spirit, I will contribute my share to any honorable, honest, and just solution of this difficulty. A further escalation of this affair, an escalation which is being watched with the greatest anxiety by many bishops, priests, theology students, men and women the world over, could have incalculable negative consequences for our Church. I, therefore, urgently beg of you to see to it that in Rome too efforts are made to achieve an honorable, honest, and just solution. Basically I ask nothing more and nothing less than to be permitted to inquire and teach without being suspected. As a theology teacher in the Catholic Church this is my vocation. I will always preserve my complete loyalty and unequivocal fidelity to this our Church.

In an effort at achieving a good solution, permit me to make the following proposal to your Congregation: Through its declaration the Congregation has publicly said about the matter at hand what it believed it ought to say. If what it has said is the truth, it will prevail by its own resources. On my side, I have taken a stand in detailed publications concerning the discussion on *The Church* and *Infallible?* Conscious of my fallibility, I will continue to be open to and grateful for criticisms directed at my views. I have already moved on to other and more central theological themes.

Under these circumstances, has not the time come to close this affair which is unpleasant on both sides and holds out no great promise for the future? Has not the time come to let Catholic theologians debate these difficult questions freely on the basis of the declarations issued to date?

Has not the time come to speak a final word of reconciliation, as I did in my exchange with Karl Rahner about the infallibility of the Church? What I wrote to Rahner I would also like to write to my dear Cardinal and to your Congregation:

> Has not the time come to drop the question between you and me and leave to history the task of deciding what the answer should be? I am not particularly anxious to be right. If it was given to human beings to produce such [infallible] propositions with the help of the Holy Spirit, why should that disturb me? If anything, I would ask that, for the sake of humanity, more use should be made of this possibility. For the time being, it does not look as if we are moving toward such rosy times. But so what? We are not concerned with our "subjective opinion." It is the *truth* that is to have its day, nothing more and nothing less. In a couple of years we should already be able to see more clearly. At any rate, I would like to make peace with you in this matter, if at all possible. This does not mean that you should espouse my way of thinking. But it does mean that you should agree that my way of thinking is Catholic.

In brief, the unpretentious proposal which I ask the Congregation to consider with benevolence is this: Without further discussion or other consequences, stop the proceedings which for years have been in progress against me and from which nothing good can come for either side. In this case, the questions raised in Part I and II of this letter will no longer require an answer, not as far as I am concerned.

In the hope that your Congregation will examine this proposal, I greet you with singular esteem.

Most devotedly yours,
Hans Küng

cc: Cardinal Julius Döpfner, President of the German
   Bishops' Conference
   Cardinal Dr. Hermann Volk, Bishop of Mainz
   Dr. Carl Joseph Leiprecht, Bishop of Rottenburg
   Professor Dr. H. J. Vogt, Dean of the Catholic Theology
   Faculty of the University of Tübingen

enclosures:
1. The "Declaration on the Freedom of Theology" in German, Italian, French, English, and Spanish
2. H. Küng and K. Rahner, "Versöhnliches Schlusswort
   unter einer Debatte," *Publik-Forum* (June 1, 1973)
3. *Fehlbar? Eine Bilanz* edited by Hans Küng (Zurich Einsiedeln, and Köln, 1973)—under separate cover

In a registered letter dated October 22, 1973, Cardinal Šeper
acknowledged—on the thirty-day deadline—Küng's letter, saying
that it raised many difficult questions, so that it would be some
time before it could be answered in detail. That turned out to be
something over five months. In the meantime, after a good deal of
effort, a mutually possible time was found for Cardinal Döpfner,
Cardinal Volk, and Küng to meet for a several-hour discussion of
the matter. The discussion took place on February 19, 1974. On
March 30, 1974, the promised detailed response came from the
Doctrinal Congregation. Basically they—it was signed by both
Cardinal Šeper and Archbishop Hamer—rejected all of Küng's
requests. It was as follows:

(30)

Dear Professor:
   The Congregation for the Doctrine of the Faith has received your letter of September 22, 1973. As was already
communicated to you in the confirming letter of October 22,

1973, the Congregation reserved for itself a detailed response, which here follows.

With the letter of July 4, 1973, to you the Congregation for the Doctrine of the Faith laid out its position before you in reference to the doctrinal points dealt with in the declaration *Mysterium ecclesiae*. In the event that you accept the teaching of this declaration, approved by the Pope, the Congregation will view the current proceedings against your doctrinal opinion as ended. It is not apparent why this position is "cynical" on the part of the Congregation, or why it is an "injury" or a "condemnation" of a Catholic theologian if he is required to accept the teaching of the Church. In the event that you do not accept the teaching of the declaration *Mysterium ecclesiae*, the Congregation offered you the possibility of a colloquium.

In your long letter you now deal with many questions under the following themes:

1. Objections against the order of procedure of the Congregation and against the concrete proceedings in your case, with the request for information about the meaning of the colloquium.

2. Several remarks concerning the theological problematic.

3. Your personal suggestion.

To the major content of your questions the Congregation answers as follows:

I. The Proceedings

Your letters to the Congregation are a constant attempt to shift the main weight of the dispute to procedural questions and to divert it from the problem of your doctrinal opinion. For the rest, we are of the conviction that our manner of proceeding is just and loyal, if also still capable of being improved.

1) THE RULES OF PROCEDURE

The fundamental error (and not only yours) apparently consists in viewing the proceedings of the Congregation as a penal proceedings in a criminal case. Rather, it is much more

concerned with investigating whether or not a theological
opinion "is in conformity with the Divine revelation and with
the teaching office of the Church" (Art. 3). It concerns not a
private opinion which is known only to the author, but rather
a doctrinal opinion which the author has openly spread in
the ecclesiastical community. This investigation and judgment takes place in two phases. In the first phase, internal to
the Congregation, the Congregation, after a testing of the investigated writings through its collegial organ, comes to the
judgment whether or not the doctrinal opinions in the writings under investigation contradict the rule of faith. This investigation takes place in a serious and collegial manner with
the special assistance of an expert; this expert has the task to
always draw attention to the positive arguments and intentions of the author (Relator "pro auctore," who of course
must not be confused with the defense attorney in a court
proceedings). All documents of this phase have only the
value of investigative documents of the individual experts.
This whole testing can lead to the result that the investigated
doctrinal opinion contradicts the binding doctrine of the
Church. In this case there begins the second phase of the
proceedings, which is no longer internal to the Congregation.

The first action of the Congregation as such, where its authority comes into play, is therefore not the submission of
other foregoing expert testimonies, but rather the formulation
of opinion through the vote of the Cardinals and its approval
by the Pope. The result of this official act will be communicated in writing to the local Bishop and to the author.
This letter contains those statements which, according to the
conviction of the Congregation, appear to be incompatible
with revelation and the teaching of the teaching office. At
this stage—after the Congregation has already specified its
objections—the author will be invited to explain himself.
The author, therefore, himself takes over the "defense"
(since the Relator "pro auctore" has already ended his function within the Congregation-internal phase of establishment). The author turns in his written explanation: if

necessary, a colloquium is likewise foreseen. After these explanations of the author have been examined, and depending on the result of the examination, the Congregation collegially decides what is to be done. This decision is communicated to the author and to the Ordinary.

The "Ratio agendi" does not specify further possible steps, nor does it speak of the possibility of an appeal since such matters are regulated by the general norms.

2) THE PROCEEDINGS AND THE EXAMINATION OF SEVERAL OF YOUR WRITINGS

a) The Congregation for the Doctrine of the Faith is constitutionally to hold to the specifications of *Integrae servandae* and the "Ratio agendi." The Congregation grants that the examination proceedings of your two books have drawn out too long; however, the Congregation was forced into this procrastination not least by your attitude. Upon the invitation to the colloquium concerning your book *The Church* you answered that "an unplanned journey to Rome is out of the question during the semester at the University of Tübingen"; in addition you requested that "the conditions . . . be agreed upon before my departure," and enumerated five "essential" conditions; as the Congregation responded to this request you came forward on July 27, 1968, with a new request, namely, that "the order of procedure of your Congregation as worked out on the basis of *Integrae servandae*" be sent to you. In order to respond to your wish we waited for the publication of these procedural regulations, which already before their publication were applied in practice. These procedural regulations foresaw as the first step, not the colloquium, but rather a written response of the author to the objections raised. Therefore a written explanation addressed to the individual objections was requested of you. Naturally these individual points are the same as the themes of an eventual colloquium. To the letter of the Congregation of July 12, 1971, you answered then on January 24, 1972, and to the referred-to writing of July 4, 1973, you responded on

September 22, 1973. Indeed, the Congregation had requested your answers within thirty days, according to the procedural regulations, which are valid for all similar cases; however, they awaited your answers even when the deadline was past without undertaking further steps.

I hope that these brief and incomplete remarks will cause you to moderate your complaints concerning the procrastinations and the one-sided deadlines.

b) The above statements concerning the nature of the procedural regulations already implicitly contain the response to your questions and "conditions."

The "full knowledge and free use of my documents" at the Congregation (your letters of May 30, 1968, and September 22, 1973) are not foreseen by the procedural regulations since the examination proceedings is not a juridical action or a penal process and because the documents of the respective dossiers do not have the value of the documents of a proceedings. The public writings of the author, and not the eventual complaint or the documents of the dossier, form the documents which are valid for the purpose of establishing the teaching opinion of the author. The position of the Congregation results only from the decision approved by the Pope after the closing of the examination, and this result has been communicated to you in two letters of May 6, 1971, and July 12, 1971. Therefore the letters and expert testimony of individual experts, Consultors, or members of the Congregation can only be viewed as temporary internal working instruments.

The Relator "pro auctore" (whom one must not confuse with an attorney in a trial) is seen by the procedural regulations as appointed by the Congregation itself; the Relator has the task during the Congregation-internal examination phase of being helpful to the Congregation itself in a dialectical fashion so that the Congregation can form the most objective judgments of the teaching opinions of the author as possible.

If after a while the examination concludes with the judgment that the examined doctrinal opinions are compatible with the doctrine that has been revealed and transmitted by the teaching office, or that they belong to the opinions which may be freely discussed among theologians—in this case the proceedings will be closed without the author having heard of it or having been unnecessarily disturbed.

The right of defense belongs to the author himself: he is required to explain himself in writing and if necessary is invited to a colloquium.

The right of appeal is guaranteed to the author by the general norms of valid rights in case the author believes that irregularities have been present.

3) THE COLLOQUIUM

You ask about the point of a colloquium between the Congregation and you; you ask this above all after the publication of the declaration Mysterium ecclesiae, which you call a "Lex Küng" and say prejudices the result of the colloquium.

In connection with what has been mentioned at the beginning it must be clearly stated here that the Congregation obviously will not change the teaching of the two Vatican Councils or, likewise, the declaration Mysterium ecclesiae in an eventual colloquium. How can a Catholic theologian call this teaching of the authentic teaching office a "dictate"?

A further clarification: This colloquium may not be understood as a free academic discussion among theologians or as an exchange of opinion in a manner of a congress. Rather, it will be much more a colloquium on a scholarly level which the author conducts with theologians named by the Congregation for the purpose of learning to know the teaching of the author as precisely as possible and to confront the statements of the teaching office. The Congregation does this by the power of the authority delegated by the teaching office of the Roman Pope. The colloquium therefore would have the purpose of giving you once again the possibility of clarifying your reasons why you hold your opinion to be a freely discussable one which would not thereby injure the doctrines which are obligatory and binding for a Catholic. At basis, therefore, the colloquium is a renewed possibility for the clarification of the opinion, and in this sense for the "defense," of the author.

Your charge that the Congregation proceeds against you in an unloyal fashion because it published the declaration concerning your teaching opinions before a colloquium was held cannot be accepted by the Congregation. First of all, it must be established that the declaration is concerned not with your personal views alone, but rather with the opinions of some other theologians as well.

Now, concerning your writings, it is to be noted that according to the procedural regulations a colloquium with the author is not obligatory, but, rather, optional. The Congregation is obliged only to request from the author a written explanation of the points in question; this has taken place. The publication of the declaration *Mysterium ecclesiae* was likewise therefore necessary because, despite the proceedings in process and contrary to the express invitation of the Congregation of December 1967, and with the disregard of the valid law concerning the *Imprimatur* (cf. the letter of the Congregation to you of February 12, 1971, and your answer of February 26, 1971), you proceeded to spread in various parts of the world opinions which, through your writings in many languages and in lectures, have disturbed most deeply the faith of the Church community. The responsible authority of the Church was not least therefore also obliged to take measures for the defense of the faith and to intervene in a clarifying manner, concerning which the faithful have a right.

You complain about the "intensification of the situation . . . through the public action of the Congregation." The Congregation is surprised that you raised such an objection since it was rather you who already long since have published the letters of this Congregation, issued press statements, given interviews concerning your "case," spread in various ways your doctrinal opinions during the examination proceedings, whereas on the other hand the Congregation remained silent, even when you described it very negatively in public.

II. The Theological Problematic

1. You request from the Congregation above all "an argumentation that would prove the possibility of infallible propositions . . . and how the corresponding texts from Vatican I and II are to be theologically grounded and responsibly supported." This is in fact the fundamental main question (in order not to say, the fundamental doubt) of your book *Infallible? An Inquiry*. It is certainly allowed to a Catholic theologian to pose a question which touches upon a truth of faith and then to search for an explanation. However, even if he did not immediately find an understandable justification for this truth, a Catholic theologian cannot bring the truth of the faith itself into doubt or indeed deny it. No Catholic theologian, as long as he is Catholic, holds the denial or doubting of a dogma of the faith as allowed in the name of theology. And insofar as it concerns the theological problems connected therewith, many competent authors have already answered your inquiry.

2. The distinction between infallibility and "infallible propositions" which you make is interesting and could be the subject of the colloquium in the following sense: how can one uphold infallibility as it is dogmatized in Vatican Council I and II if one denies the possibility of infallible propositions?

3. "Why wouldn't 'historical condition' entail in particular cases even the possibility of error, as in many ways history seems to show?"

As a theologian the prerequisites of infallibility are known to you and the answer to this question is likewise known to you: The Catholic Church believes (cf. Vatican Council I) that these prerequisites, because of the assistance of the Holy Spirit, exclude the possibility of an error in what has been defined as the content of a dogma (cf. *Mysterium ecclesiae*

No. 5). The questions which in this connection you raise in your letter show with sufficient clarity that this matter rests on the level of dogma and not on the level of a free theological discussion. Do you believe that your statements stand in agreement with the teaching of the two Vatican Councils?

You maintain that the declaration *Mysterium ecclesiae* does not take sufficient account of the international discussion concerning infallibility. You express your regret that the Congregation did not send its experts to the advanced seminar on infallibility in Tübingen. What is expressed in your books is "non in destructionem, sed in aedificationem Ecclesiae."

As is known to you, the competence of the Congregation extends to the teaching of the faith and not to freely discussable doctrinal opinions, even when through its international dimensions the Congregation is thoroughly aware of them; the Congregation, however, is not a theological faculty, but rather an organ in the service of the teaching office of the Pope.

Whether your teaching opinions are "in aedificationem Ecclesiae" or not is not a question of your intentions, but rather a question of the facts. It would not be "in aedificationem Ecclesiae" to represent doctrinal opinions which contradict the defined teaching of the Church.

III. A Personal Word

1. You call upon the freedom of the theologian. The Congregation, however, must remind you of the supreme principle of such a freedom: the theologian as well as the teaching office stands *in the service* of the revealed truth. Hence, for a believing Catholic there is not the freedom to deny a revealed truth in the name of theological freedom. Consequently, there is likewise a *responsibility* of the theologian to the ecclesiastical community and to the Church authority to whom Christ himself entrusted the task of teaching and protecting the revealed truth (*Lumen Gentium*, 25; *Dei Verbum*, 10).

For the good of the community of the faithful, who have a right to receive healthy teaching, the Congregation published the declaration *Mysterium ecclesiae,* not as some kind of theological contribution, but rather as commissioned by and with the approbation of the Pope. If you represent theses which stand in opposition to the declaration, you must pose yourself the question whether or not you still recognize the teaching authority in the Church.

This question in fact is not superfluous. For indeed in all your answers the dogmatic level appears as plainly nonexistent, just as if the doctrinal opinions put forth by you were all subjects of free theological discussion and as if they did not touch truths which are binding for a believing Catholic. Consequently the question is raised: What value do the dogmas and the statements of the ecclesiastical teaching office have for you? Do you accept the dogmatic character of Vatican Council I?

2. Finally you suggest as a solution that both you yourself and the Congregation should remain silent; history would show who was correct.

The Congregation regrets that it cannot accept your appeal to the judgment of history as the criterion of faith. In the Church there is another criterion than the judgment of history: this is the authority of the living teaching office which has been set up for service to the revealed truth. Concerning the infallibility of the Church and of the Pope the declaration *Mysterium ecclesiae* calls upon a defined dogma; it is not to be seen how such a defined teaching could be left to the "judgment" of the future.

If, therefore, your suggestion of silence should veil or cover over the definiteness or clarity of the teaching of the faith, the Congregation cannot accept your suggestion.

If, however, this silence could be understood and clearly interpreted as an act of your respect for the teaching office and as a time for reflection so that you might review your teaching opinions and could bring them into line with the teaching office, your suggestion would perhaps have meaning.

The Congregation, therefore, views your proposal of a colloquium as an expanded defense possibility for you as acceptable so that you can better explain yourself. As already mentioned, the subject of such a colloquium would be those questions which the Congregation posed to you in its writings of May 6, 1971, and July 12, 1971.

The Congregation is interested only that the Catholic teaching be proclaimed in purity and loyalty to Christ. The Congregation has no intention whatsoever of persecuting persons, but it wishes only to make certain that the Catholic community receives that spiritual nourishment to which it has a right. In view of the responsibility which the Congregation and which likewise you bear, each in his own manner, for the proclamation and the confession of the teaching of the Church, every question of human regard or prestige is of a second rank. In humble service to the word of God we, and indeed all of us in common, must maintain the "regula fidei," which is twofold: loyalty to that which has been handed on, and a dynamic orientation to the future. Only the service of the truth of Christ is concerned. We thus place great trust in your priestly spirit that you will deal with this truth in authentic loyalty.

Please let the Congregation know whether you intend to utilize this your defense possibility and when you can come to Rome. The date and the participants of the colloquium will be agreed upon immediately after your agreement since the Congregation wishes to resolve this question as soon as possible.

With friendly greetings,

Francis Cardinal Šeper, Prefect
Fr. Jérôme Hamer, O.P., Secretary

Cardinal Döpfner wrote Küng (addressing him as "Dear Fellow Brother"—*Lieber Mitbruder*—and with the familiar *"Du"*), saying that he had spoken to Hamer about a discussion with Küng. Küng responded on June 22 (also with "Dear Fellow Brother" and *"Du"*) that matters had been complicated and worsened by a long published interview by Hamer in which he defended the procedure of the Congregation, and that he would have to think things over in the light of this. Two other Catholic theologians, Johannes Neumann of Tübingen and Josef Blank of Saarbrücken, published critical responses to Archbishop Hamer's interview, and so then did Küng himself on July 25, 1974, in the *Frankfurter Allgemeine Zeitung* and other international newspapers. He wrote:

(31)
Concerning the Roman Belief Trial

There are things about which one would rather remain silent. However, the rumors and inquiries have so piled up that remaining silent can no longer be responsible.

The infallibility dispute appears to be extinguished. In numerous scholarly publications positions were taken concerning the complex theological problematic and in the course of the discussion a larger agreement in the matter showed itself than was at first expected. The major theological opponents arrived at an "operative agreement." It appears as though the question finally has gone into a calm phase of discussion. After the Roman Doctrinal Congregation on July 5, 1973, took a position concerning the problematic through a solemn declaration, *Mysterium ecclesiae,* and a press conference, one could have assumed that everything there was to say from the Roman viewpoint at that moment concerning the matter had been said for all Catholics to hear.

Instead of that, however, it became ever clearer that with the generally not very convincing document a better basis for the further procedure against the books *The Church* (1967) and *Infallible? An Inquiry* (1970) should be created since the Congregation obviously viewed its previous position as juridically and theologically too weakly grounded. At that time it was of course thanks only to the decisiveness of the German Bishops that literally at the last minute an ultimatum demand from the Roman side was dropped and a confrontation with unforeseeable effects could be prevented.

The author involved went to great lengths in a detailed response to the Congregation to convince the Roman authorities of the almost insurmountable juridical and theological
difficulties involved in a further proceedings: it would be best
to let the matter rest on both sides and allow the theologians
to discuss further in complete freedom. A private visit in
Rome in October of last year and private conversations with
the responsible persons appeared to bring a relaxation of the
tension and allowed to grow on all sides the hope for a quiet
laying aside of disputatiousness since the author had said on
his side everything that at the moment was to be said in a
theological summing up of the debate and a statement on
Mysterium ecclesiae."

In view of this situation it is all the more regrettable that
the Roman doctrinal authorities nevertheless finally did not
wish to be satisfied with the cessation offer of the author. The
repeated request for a fair proceedings, for access to documents and fair conditions for a theological colloquium, was
not granted. The simultaneous request to take into consideration the suggestions of 1,360 theology professors from
over fifty-three countries "on the freedom of theology" was
ignored. Instead, in a long memorandum the Congregation
pressed on the author a quick closing of the proceedings and
a colloquium in the Vatican, which, according to the present
guidelines, is very close to an interrogation, and then makes
possible the closing of the secret proceedings without the
presence of the one concerned. Despite this theologically
questionable and procedurally problematic manner of acting
by the Congregation, the author nevertheless wished to settle
the juridical and theological questions with the Congregation
in an objectively measured manner.

Unfortunately, however, in the meanwhile the second-
ranking man of the Congregation, Archbishop Hamer, went
to the German public with a several-page interview (*Herder-*

Korrespondenz, May 1974) and attempted to defend and justify the inquisitorial practices of the Doctrinal Congregation, the erstwhile Holy Office. With this surprising escalation the Congregation assumes the responsibility for a renewed and intensified discussion of the various Roman proceedings in the press and for an immense unrest in wide circles of the Catholic clergy and people.

It is understandable that it was precisely in the Swiss homeland of the author, where the Catholic people along with their episcopacy felt themselves overrun in the case of the moral theology professor Stephan Pfürtner, who was forced to resign by Rome, that the most tangible upheaval to date occurred. Alongside many individual voices now, the Synod in Bern, the largest of the Swiss bishoprics, likewise demanded the closing of the Roman proceedings. A few days later two additional Cantonal Synods (Basel and Lucerne) joined in. A petition of signatures initiated by Catholic laity was launched for the observation of human rights in the Church, in a manner for which one is to be no less grateful. All these actions are to be understood as a sign of the solidarity and the watchful consciousness of contradictions to the Gospel and to human rights in the Catholic Church. They have, beyond the individual case in question, likewise a significance not to be underestimated for other proceedings which are current. For the person afflicted, however, they are a support and encouragement in a difficult situation.

On all sides now, however, it is asked, what further should be done. The answer can only be: it is now up to the official organs, even of the Church in Germany, to help here and at the same time to make further spontaneous actions superfluous.

In February 1974, the Swiss Bishops accepted the following recommendation of the general Swiss Synod concerning the teaching office and theological research: "In every case the person concerned in a doctrinal proceedings has the right himself to name a defender and to have access to all documents." With reference to this general Swiss resolution, the diocesan Synod of Basel, on June 16, 1974, issued almost unanimously the following resolution:

> Already a proceedings which does not correspond to these conditions, and thereby human rights (United Nations Charter Articles 10 and 11), and all the more so an eventual possible condemnation, contribute to an intensified polarization in our Church, endanger the credibility of ecclesiastical authority, burden pastoral care and ecumenical collaboration.
>
> In the questions raised by Professor Küng there is concern for problems which were not created by him, but rather move a broad public, and were merely lifted up by him and placed in discussion. The problems which such questions call for can be solved only in an open dialogue and not through a simple statement of power.
>
> The Synod expects that the bishops will decide for themselves and will unhesitatingly intervene so that the presently conducted proceedings, which clearly contradict our recommendation, will be closed.

It is to be wished that the Synod of the Catholic bishoprics of Germany and the German episcopacy would make this balanced resolution their own. A decisive word precisely from the German Bishops would receive a hearing in Rome. The previous Bishop of Rottenburg contributed a great deal to the avoidance of an intensification of the conflict. The vacancy in the bishopric of Rottenburg should not be an occasion for immediate fear and further spontaneous actions of solidarity. The author himself wishes in this matter no further church political escalation, but rather an inner-churchly pacification and theological clarification. That the present important disputes despite everything are concerned with marginal Christian questions shall be shown in the near future in a book entitled *On Being a Christian*.

Hans Küng

Cardinal Döpfner was disturbed with his *Mitbruder* Küng's article and wrote him the next day, June 26, 1973, as follows:

(32)

Dear Fellow Brother,

In all brevity I wish immediately after the arrival of your letter of June 22, 1974, to make several remarks, without now entering into the substantive questions in detail. First I note that for several weeks it has been bruited about that you are referring to the letter of the Doctrinal Congregation of March 30, 1974. I myself hear nothing from you despite my request at the discussion of February 19, 1974, to join with me in making contact with the Congregation. Then I wrote you on May 30, 1974, and only now receive the response after you have published a statement on the memorandum of the Congregation, a statement in which again one is played out against the other. One cannot avoid the impression that finally you have no interest in working toward a good solution, but rather that you are playing the usual game of arousing the public. It cannot go on so.

With fraternal greetings,

Julius Cardinal Döpfner

The very next day, June 27, 1974, Küng wrote Döpfner a long explanation:

(33)

Personal

Dear Fellow Brother,

If I respond to your letter immediately it is not so as to respond to the charges with more charges. Likewise, I do not wish to write to the President of the Bishops' Conference, but rather to you personally. I can thus write more openly. For several misunderstandings appear to me to be explainable:

Naturally I have always answered truthfully the questions which are constantly put to me, that I have received another letter from Rome and that contrary to expectations Rome nevertheless continues to make further efforts. However, I have not "made known" the letter of March 30, 1974, although the plan of a new dossier on the progress of the infallibility dispute has been proposed to me. It appeared unnecessary to me to notify you about this letter since I assumed that a copy of the letter would be sent to you. Of course I was astonished to learn that even the Bishop of Rottenburg had not received a copy, and so I immediately had one sent to him. I still have not sent my response because new complications are always arising from the interview of Monsignor Hamer, which I am waiting to see the course of. A statement on the memorandum of the Congregation, as you write, I have only indirectly given insofar as I had to respond to Hamer's interview. Had this interview not appeared, I would have had no occasion to go to the public.

Perhaps, however, it would now also be helpful if I openly told you why at this point I view a further discussion in Munich as having little meaning. I thought that I had indicated this clearly enough in my letter. However, there were above all three facts which made me reflect:

1. The last letter of the Doctrinal Congregation was, with a very binding tone, so hard in its composition—and indeed juridically as well as theologically—that I could only conclude from it that the conversation with you and Cardinal Volk in Rome had no encouraging effect in my case. Again the juridically as well as theologically untenable procedure of the Congregation is defended; again the theological inquiry is not responded to; again the conditions for a just and fair colloquium are not spelled out. I had gone into all this with sufficient emphasis in Rome as well as in Munich so that it appeared to me simply without much sense or expectation to speak again of that once more. Can you not also understand that with the best of will I cannot deliver myself to such a colloquium—precisely in the interest of avoiding a confrontation—in which I can only against my conviction recant my understanding or then even be condemned? In Switzerland the uproar is so great precisely because Pfürtner had submit-

ted himself to all these things and precisely thus—after he had submitted to the colloquium—fell under the wheels. My entire effort was until then to avoid such a direct confrontation with unforeseeable effects.

2. I was very disturbed that you did not orient me concerning the action by Hamer, in which Monsignor Homeyer participated. I had to assume that you were in agreement with this procedure. If that is not the case I ask for an explanatory word. For me it was apparent that the matter was being worked simultaneously on two levels: with the letter direct to me and then with the interview to the public, which fulfilled a function of appeasement. To be sure, Hamer miscalculated this time again if he thought he could through such actions deceive the public concerning the true status of things in the Doctrinal Congregation. I am surprised that he did not take seriously my warning in this regard. For I had said to him clearly that he will not get by in public with a juridical and theological justification of the present practices of the Doctrinal Congregation, which, whether one likes it or not, still signified the Inquisition, and that I could no longer feel myself bound to my suggestion of silence if the Congregation pushed the matter against me still further. With *Mysterium ecclesiae* a frontal attack was attempted, and after it failed, now roundabout means. One heard the news early already from Freiburg [Germany]. But even the actions of Hamer in Fribourg/Switzerland got into the press—without my involvement—where this interview in a mendacious manner was said to be distributed to the Swiss Synods "upon the commission of the Bishops' Conference." From Paris one could hear that Hamer's interview was more or less forced on the *Documentation Catholique,* whereas now the publication of the response by Professor Neumann is strictly refused. I do not wish to go into further details. However, that all of this does not exactly foster my trust for my discussion partners you will certainly also be able to understand.

3. From North Germany I learned—and in this case from very reliable sources—that the Secretary of the Bishops'

Conference had stated in a private circle that my case would
be settled by August. When one sees the name of Homeyer
in the same Roman guest book, then one knows that such
remarks are to be taken seriously. As to the will of the Congregation in this regard there has until now been no lack.
What in this context, however, has disappointed most, and
together with all the other things has held me back from the
request for a new colloquium, was your answer in the
Munich discussion to my clear question of which side you
would stand on in case of a ("legally correct") Roman condemnation. You said that then even that would have to be
endured, although on the other side you granted that the
theological truth question in no way appeared clear. Can you
not understand that with the renewed pressure in the matter
from the side of Rome my skepticism would be strengthened
as to whether I might expect serious assistance from you if
the matter became critical?

After everything which I have said to you and after Rome
has written I find it painful when I am still always accused of
having no interest in a "good solution." It would have been a
simple matter for the Congregation to accept my suggestion
of a mutual silence (after the Congregation of course had already spoken extraordinarily clearly). This was not done and
the matter has even gone public. Why not address the accusations to those to whom it should be addressed? From your
side one hears until now in public not a single critical word
on the entire procedure of the Congregation, while I always
had to serve as a whipping boy of the Bishops' Conference
and not return the accusations of the Bishops' Conference.

For twelve years now I have constantly had to deal with
the Doctrinal Congregation, for seven years concerning the
book *The Church,* and for four years concerning *Infallible?.*
Letters are written and discussions are conducted eternally:
how long now shall this really go on? For our Church, however, the question is raised whether the Roman Inquisition,
which in the past four hundred years has damaged orthodoxy
so much, should also still be dragged into the third millen-

nium—to the injury then not least of theologians who are not able to defend themselves as well as I can. The articles by Neumann and Blank say it all more than clearly, and I am astounded only that at least in Germany this problematic which consists of a sensitivity to rights, especially from the perspective of the Gospel, is not seen through.

In view of this entire development then you too must grant that my last article in the *Frankfurter Allgemeine Zeitung* was extraordinarily moderate in tone and content. One could here have spoken and demanded things quite differently if one had "arousing the public" in mind. What has happened in Switzerland has not happened because of my doing, but rather occurred on the basis of the uproar which since the Pfürtner case has not yet died away. For myself these involvements come at a most unhelpful time because I need every hour to finish the manuscript for my next book. From that alone you could perceive that I have been forced to this escalation. And the fact that nevertheless night and day I attempt to work further on this book should perhaps also show you that for me this entire debate despite everything is peripheral in comparison to the true Christian concern, which we all in common have to represent.

There would now be sufficient time for a reasonable regulation of the matter before the sitting of the Synod in November. My answer to Rome, which because of the Roman "publicity work" (Hamer) was postponed, will contain once again my offer of silence. I am convinced that a clear word from you that out of all these things nothing good can come, and that one should at least temporarily put the matter on ice, would find a hearing in Rome. You speak of a "good solution" without indicating how you visualize that. With a colloquium without guarantees it certainly will not happen. I cannot imagine a "good solution" in this situation other than the *de facto* closing of the matter. Then public responses from me would of themselves be taken care of, as the situation in this matter was indeed very quiet in recent months— before Rome started it up again. In Switzerland at least it is very clearly seen that this demand for the cessation of the proceedings is not only my personal demand. You know yourself how many in Germany think the same thing. I would prefer it if the whole matter would be settled before November. However, if that cannot be attained in Rome I would also nevertheless personally ask you seriously to stand behind the declaration of the Basel Diocesan Synod, to which Bishop Hänggi has already promised to give consideration. If one should wish to block the handling of this not unimportant matter for the German Church at the Synod, things would not therefore become more calm. This whole matter concerns much more than my personal situation, as some will still better understand after the articles by Neumann and Blank than before.

My response to Rome is already conceived and can be sent off at any time. If you still have a suggestion to give me for this letter I would ask you to send it to me in writing or even by phone. I will gladly take up everything which can contribute to a good solution.

You see, my dear fellow brother, that I write very openly and unguardedly. I would be happy if you would receive the letter as it is intended by me. I am grateful to you always when you allow this same openness to prevail and I do not need to say to you that I will handle letters that are written to me personally as such.

With the repeated request for a little understanding I send you

Brotherly greetings,
Hans Küng

enclosures: Article of Prof. Neumann
                Article of Prof. Blank

The reaction to Hamer's interview was strong and negative, especially in Küng's homeland, Switzerland, where a small committee in Lucerne drew up a petition supporting Küng that quickly gathered 20,000 signatures and was submitted to the Swiss Bishops. The President and Vice-President of the Swiss Bishops'

Conference, Bishop Nestor Adam of Sitten and Bishop Anton Hänggi of Basel (Küng's home diocese) then hurried to Rome for conversations with the Doctrinal Congregation—but were apparently rather badly informed by it, to judge by their press statement, which Walter Jens (*Wahrheit*, p. 28) remarked "had been prepared for the two bishops by the Doctrinal Congregation." It was issued on July 8, 1974; the pertinent part was as follows:

(34)

The two bishops were informed of the contents of the last letter of the Doctrinal Congregation to Professor Hans Küng on March 30, 1974, in which he was invited to a discussion by the Doctrinal Congregation without his being forced to participate. This letter has until now been unanswered. The Doctrinal Congregation declared to the two bishops that Professor Küng could choose a defender for himself who would be allowed to accompany him to this discussion. All documents on which the Doctrinal Congregation has based itself are now already in the hands of Professor Küng. Moreover, the Secretary of the Doctrinal Congregation is prepared to come to Switzerland for a discussion with the Bishops' Conference to discuss and clarify further the still open questions. The petition of Synod 72, which was passed on by the Bishops' Conference, has arrived in Rome. The Doctrinal Congregation is preparing a written statement. These presuppositions permit hope for a just solution of these questions.

On the same day, July 8, Küng issued a press statement in response in which he of course denied that he had been supplied documents by the Congregation and noted that it was strange that only now was his own bishop informed by Rome of the proceedings against one of his own priests. His remark that the "defender" newly mentioned apparently would only be allowed to accompany him to the discussion, but not participate in it, might have seemed presumptuously cynical of him at the time. How-

ever, when Professor Schillebeeckx took Professor Bas van Iersel
with him to his "discussion" with the Doctrinal Congregation in
December 1979, van Iersel had to sit outside and could talk with
Schillebeeckx only during the coffee breaks. Küng's statement was
as follows:

(35)

To my great regret the Swiss Bishops have let themselves
be deceived by their Roman discussion partners. However,
now indeed even for the Bishops there can no longer be any
doubt that a Roman proceedings against the author of the
books *The Church* and *Infallible? An Inquiry* is being conducted and at any moment serious disciplinary consequences
can develop.

It is consequently a gross deception of the Swiss public
when the Prefect of the earlier Holy Office maintains that
"all documents on which the Doctrinal Congregation has
based itself are now already in the hands of Professor Küng."
Outside of the letters of the Congregation, which I am gladly
ready to publish, I have received nothing from the Doctrinal
Congregation. Rather, even in the last letter to me of March
30, 1974—which astonishingly the Swiss Bishops could be
made aware of only in Rome—I was again refused any access to my dossier. Even the letters and evaluations of the individual experts, Consultors, or members of the Congregation
are provisional internal working instruments and may not be
seen by the author.

If I reject the invitation to a discussion in the Vatican,
which under the existing rules is like a hearing, the proceedings nevertheless continues without the discussion. In any
case, this secret proceedings can at any moment be brought
to a close without the accused. Throughout the many-year-
long proceedings a defender has never been granted me. The
defender who now apparently has been described for the
Swiss Bishops would have no legal basis in the order of procedure of the Congregation; according to the formulation of

the communiqué he appears to be nothing more than a companion on the way to the discussion.

I very much welcome the fact that the Secretary of the Doctrinal Congregation, Archbishop Hamer, wants to come to Switzerland, hopefully also to inform himself about the actual attitude here in our country. I am quite prepared on this occasion to conduct a public discussion with Archbishop Hamer about the proceedings for the sake of an objective orientation of the public.

I feel a deep debt of gratitude to all those who in recent weeks have worked for the termination of the proceedings.

On September 24, 1974, Küng answered the Doctrinal Congregation, again spending a great deal of time on procedural matters, which really had become the heart of the whole debate. But he also addressed the substantive theological issues raised by the Congregation. Again he pressed for an "armistice." He wrote:

(36)

Dear Cardinal,

The response of your Congregation to my letter of September 22, 1973, with the date of March 30, 1974, reached my hands on April 6, 1974, through the mediation of the Apostolic Nuncio in Germany. May I courteously confirm to you hereby its reception. I also had to reflect for several months on the response. Moreover, the newest initiatives from the side of the Congregation and the ensuing complications forced me to postpone my response once again.

I appreciate the fact that the Congregation for the first time in the course of this now already more than seven-year-long negotiation concerning the books *The Church* and *Infallible? An Inquiry* has dealt with most of my questions in a detailed fashion and attempted to provide a rationale for its standpoint. I am especially thankful for the clarification of the legal situation insofar as this cannot be readily seen from the procedural regulations of the Congregation—which, if I am not in error, is taking place for the first time in my case. Likewise the spelling out of the theological problematic helps me to see the entire affair in a clearer light.

Of course my expectations expressed in my last letter concerning the ending of the proceedings unfortunately have not been carried out. On the contrary, to my great regret the Secretary of the Congregation, simultaneous with the response to me, turned to the public in an interview of many pages in the *Herder-Korrespondenz* in order to defend and to justify the self-understanding and the methods of the Congregation as they come into play against me in the proceedings. On the basis of this surprising escalation the Congregation shoulders the responsibility for a renewed and intensified discussion of the various Roman proceedings in the press and for an enormous unrest in wide circles of the Catholic clergy and people. It is understandable that precisely in my Swiss homeland, where because of the Pfürtner case a bitterness and outrage, not easy to eliminate, against the methods of the Congregation has remained, the reaction has broken out in the most tangible fashion until now. It expresses itself not only in many individual voices, signature collections, and press statements, but also in the Synod of my own home diocese of Basel, with which several cantonal Synods and many other church groups have already associated themselves. They all raise serious doubts against the manner of procedure of the Congregation and demand a cessation of the proceedings against me.

Likewise the most important theological reactions to the interview of the Secretary place the self-understanding in the methods of the Congregation along with the juridical as well as theological arguments in most profound question and urge upon the Congregation a general revision of its procedures. I allow myself to enclose the especially balanced and well-documented statements of Professor Dr. Johannes Neumann, "Es ginge anders besser" (*Herder-Korrespondenz,* June 1974), and of Professor Dr. Josef Blank, "Macht und/oder Wahrheit? Zur Problematik der römischen Glaubenskongregation als einer Wahrheitsverordnungsbehörde" (*Publik-Forum*, 13, 1974). There can be no doubt that there are clear conclusions even for the proceedings against me from these competent contributions of renowned experts.

Against the background of these very serious fundamental questions to the Congregation, now likewise raised by others, it appears to me at the moment not very opportune for me once again to go into every individual point in order to confirm my objections against the entire proceedings and especially the "concerted action" against me this past July and to defend myself against the accusations of the Congregation, as for example concerning the many-year-long prolongation of the proceedings and other matters. If one reads the letter of the Congregation, and especially the simultaneous justification by the Secretary of its methods appearing in the *Herder-Korrespondenz,* then the action of the Congregation at first glance appears correct. However, perhaps in Rome it will be understood that for me as the one accused—as for several in the past decades who through such proceedings, which according to your letter are not supposed to be penal proceedings, were made to conform, or indeed were punished with removal from their teaching chair—these methods appear less correct. It is understandable that your Congregation would gladly be rid of the rumor of Inquisition. But in the eyes of the public an apologetic can attain the desired impression only if one decisively revises the still inquisitorial characteristics of the procedural regulations of the Congregation as demanded. In the long writing of the Congregation and in the still longer press interview of its Secretary there was not a single word mentioned why the Congregation does not accept the suggestions of the 1,360 theology professors from all over the world ("Declaration on the Freedom of Theology," 1968), for whose realization I have in my letter again most emphatically pleaded. Had the Congregation taken up these suggestions, whose justice, fairness, and practicability no one doubts and which could only serve the reputation of the Congregation and the Roman Church, all such apologetics would be unnecessary. At the same time the Congregation could turn itself to its positive commission of the "promotion of the faith" given already in 1965 by Pope Paul VI. I would like therefore again to entreat the Congregation to accept the desiderata of the 1,360 theologians, which I enclosed in my last letter to you in several languages.

Now at the very beginning of your response to me is the accusation that my letters to the Congregation are "a constant attempt to shift the main weight of the dispute to procedural questions and to divert it from the problem of your (my) doctrinal opinion." However, after the Congregation has simultaneously launched two "proceedings" (with possible disciplinary consequences) against me, I must perforce turn to the "procedural questions" and ever again request the Congregation at least to take a position concerning these "procedural questions." At least this repeated request was now finally responded to. I have, however, thereby never wished to divert attention away from my doctrinal opinion, but rather have always time and again made the Congregation aware of my "Inquiry." Only now have I succeeded in bringing the Congregation to express itself on the "theological problematic," whereby it of course does not answer my "Inquiry" concerning infallible statements, but rather, if I have understood correctly, takes the position that it has already been answered. However, I cannot understand that as a reasoned response to my inquiry which I would be prepared to accept with complete respect.

Concerning precisely the legal situation of the proceedings I would now still have numerous important individual questions. For example:

Concerning the until now unknown to me two-phase theory and especially the "Congregation-internal" secret phase;

Concerning the non-penal character of the proceedings, which nevertheless can have penal consequences;

Concerning the Relator "pro auctore," who is to be "helpful in a dialectical fashion" to the Congregation and whom the author himself may not know;

Concerning the "examination documents" drawn up by the Congregation ("letters and expert testimony of individual experts, Consultors, or members of the Congregation"), which the accused may not see, for reasons which escape me;

Concerning the thereby renewed general denial to me of access to the documents, and its incomprehensible background;

Concerning my exclusion from the decisive first phase, the "accusation" of the proceedings, and likewise from the final phase, which is decisive for the judgment or condemnation;

Concerning the "further possible steps," which are not dealt with in the procedural regulations but which are mentioned in your letter;

Concerning the still unclear appeal possibility for me on the basis of the Apostolic Constitution *Regimini ecclesiae;*

Concerning the colloquium, which is conducted "on a scholarly level" and nevertheless is not to be "a free academic discussion" and in which apparently it is not foreseen that even once the Congregation could theologically be mistaken;

Concerning the prejudging of the entire proceedings through the declaration *Mysterium ecclesiae,* which in various respects goes beyond Vatican I and II, etc.

However, all these questions only show how justified the demand for a general revision of the proceedings of the Congregation is. Before I now turn my attention to the theological problematic, I would like at least briefly to take up an accusation which I in this connection cannot allow to pass uncontradicted: The Congregation accuses me of having in various ways turned myself to the public, "whereas the Congregation remained silent." Apparently one does not remember in the Vatican any longer that it was the clearly intended indiscretion of Vatican circles which on June 12, 1968, spread abroad in the Italian and later also in the rest

of the world press that in the first session of the "Ministerial
Council" of the Curia Cardinals, newly set up by the Pope, it
is supposed to have been decided that measures against the
author, because of "insult to the Pope," were to be taken.
Since there was no denial forthcoming from the Vatican and
your Congregation persistently remained silent before all rumors and never took my Catholic reputation under protection, I saw myself forced to give an account to the press and
likewise later to orient the public to the state of affairs. One
could not expect that I should allow the interested public to
remain uninformed when in a secret proceedings without my
hearing of it your Congregation decreed (as happened in the
"express invitation of the Congregation of December 1967,"
cited in your letter) that further distribution and all translations of my book *The Church* were forbidden. Since then
from Germany to Korea and New Zealand a well-aimed
"publicity campaign" of Vatican organs against me was to be
observed. Against this background the "silence" of the Congregation might appear in another light, as well as my public
reactions.

In the meanwhile the Congregation intervened in the proceedings in process with a "declaration" which goes beyond
Vatican I. Since in this connection the desire was made clear
from both sides in the fall of 1973, I proposed to the Congregation in writing and orally that I would no longer express myself in public on the infallibility question if the Congregation itself does not force me to. In this manner the not
very fruitful public debate about difficult theological problems would be brought to an end. I have held myself strictly
to this voluntarily given assurance. Again, however, it was
likewise now the Congregation which drew the attention of
the press to this matter and thereby likewise challenged me
to my defense against a manner of proceeding which now as
before appears to me as neither just nor appropriate.

In the area of misleading information to the public there
also belongs the communiqué concerning the announcement
from the Swiss Bishops' Conference by your Congregation.

Although access to my dossier No. 399/57/i and especially to the documents of the proceedings against the books *The Church* and *Infallible? An Inquiry* has been denied me for years by the Congregation as well as the assistance of an attorney, the Swiss Bishops were informed that both are accorded to me. This—at least misunderstood—public statement I likewise unfortunately had to publicly contradict.

The latest involvements which have arisen from the action of the Congregation, which others can only too easily follow, show once again that it would have been better immediately to adopt my suggestion and temporarily to leave the matter to theological discussion: namely, to find out—and it is about this that my "teaching opinion" is concerned—what, in the point raised by my inquiry, the "revealed truth" is, in whose "service," also according to your interpretation, not only the theologians but also the ecclesiastical "teaching office" must stand.

Of the "responsibility of the theologian to the ecclesiastical community and to the Church authority" and above all to the Lord of the Church and his Gospel, I truly do not have a low opinion. In fact, there is for no one in the Church the "freedom to deny a revealed truth." Insofar as the ecclesiastical teaching office "stands in the service of the revealed truth," I have likewise always acknowledged a "teaching authority in the Church." Indeed, I have at various times wished that the "teaching office" might—in the decisive statements of the Christian message—represent the "healthy teaching" in a more emphatic, concentrated, and convincing manner.

Thus the aim of my entire inquiry is precisely to know what on the "dogmatic level" are the "truths which are binding for a believing Catholic." That this is not so simple is shown by many problematic matters today even in Rome, in the Roman doctrinal decisions from the Galileo case through the Syllabus of Errors to the encyclicals *Humani generis* and *Humanae vitae*. That is shown also, however, by the various interpretations of the definitions of the First Vatican Council, about which in my theological publications I would have not concerned myself so intensively if I had not acknowledged in them a "dogmatic character."

That my inquiry concerning infallibility has struck an unclear point in the teaching of the Church is generally granted. And that in the Catholic Church and theology there exists no unity on the answers given to the inquiry is known certainly even in Rome and was demonstrated for all to see in the volume edited by me entitled *Fehlbar? Eine Bilanz* (1973). In a manner for which one is to be grateful, even the Congregation indeed grants that it "is concerned not with your (my) personal views alone, but rather with the opinions of some other theologians as well." Precisely this admission of the Congregation hardens the fundamental doubts concerning the appropriateness of such a proceedings. I am not able to see why the Congregation carries through such a proceedings precisely against me alone. I am likewise unable to see why of all the theologians in the world only I had the declaration *Mysterium ecclesiae* officially sent to me at my house and why only I should formally "accept" it. For this reason the presumption is not groundless that this *declaratio* of the Congregation is nevertheless ultimately only a "Lex Küng."

Finally I would like to put an important theological misunderstanding of the Congregation to right: For me the "judgment of history" is not the "criterion of faith," as the Congregation falsely attributes to me. The "criterion of faith" is for me as for the Congregation the "revealed truth." But obviously even for the ecclesiastical teaching office sometimes only in the course of history has it become clear what in a specific point the revealed truth is, to which "the authority of the living teaching office which has been set up for service to the revealed truth" likewise must adhere, as also do the theologians. For the Congregation grants even in its declaration *Mysterium ecclesiae* in a happily clear manner that the formulations of the faith of the teaching office are situation-bound, incomplete, capable of being improved, expandable, replaceable. From that it seems to follow that in the question of the "revealed truth" no one ahead of time may number himself among the "beati possidentes."

My suggestion to let the matter rest after the public statements given from both sides and to grant time for the clarifying discussion of the theologians had therefore precisely not the goal "to veil or to cover over the definiteness or clarity of the teaching of the faith," but rather on the contrary to bring it into full light. I have from my side at the present hardly anything to add to what has been said and renew therefore my personal suggestion made in my last letter. On the other hand, is it not also recognizable that from the side of the Congregation something decisive could be said beyond what is in your "declaration." And if this "declaration" in fact has the revealed truth in precision and clarity behind it, it will certainly come through in the Church even without disciplinary forced measures.

Concerning my "respect for the teaching office," wherever this teaching office bears witness to the revealed truth, there will be no lack. And likewise for me it will not be excluded that in the course of time I will recognize the revealed truth better, more clearly, and more precisely. On the contrary, it is for this that I strive every day, always prepared for every kind of correction which with reason is required of me. And insofar I also gladly draw upon the "time for reflection" granted to me by the Congregation, in a manner to be thankful for, in order to "review my teaching opinions," as this is the duty and task of every serious scholar and especially a serious theologian. Thus I will certainly not exclude the possibility that in the course of time my teaching opinion could conform to that of the teaching office, as certainly likewise the Congregation will keep itself open to new developments and insights. As at the beginning was laid out with reference to weighty voices, a fundamental reflection on the self-understanding and the methods of the Congregation is especially to be recommended. I myself likewise would like to reflect on the whole matter in a broader theological and ecclesiastical

context: in order to make clear for me and others what the
"revealed truth" in general, and thereby and also the "teaching of the Church," and thus finally the content of our faith,
is.

With the assurance that it is always my concern to serve
the community of the Church and its faith, I greet you

With sincere respect,

Yours truly,

Hans Küng

cc: Cardinal Dr. Julius Döpfner, President of the German
Bishops' Conference

Cardinal Dr. Hermann Volk, Bishop of Mainz

Bishop Nestor Adam, President of the Swiss Bishops'
Conference

Bishop Dr. Anton Hänggi, Bishop of Basel

Chapter Vicar, Auxiliary Bishop Anton Herre, Rottenburg

Professor Dr. Wilhelm Korff, Dean of the Catholic
Theology Faculty of the University of Tübingen

enclosures: The referred-to statements of Professor Josef
Blank and Professor Johannes Neumann

The years 1971–74 saw a great deal of scholarly activity on the
infallibility question, and not just by Küng. Besides the flood of
books and articles there were Küng's Tübingen seminar (1972),
to which a number of the best Catholic theologians of Germany
came, another colloquium sponsored by the Jesuits in St. Georgen
in 1971, and another sponsored by French Catholic theologians
in Paris in 1972, as well as one by the Catholic–Old Catholic
Commission in Bern the same year. The Lutheran-Catholic Consultation in the United States conducted an eight-year-long study
of infallibility (1973–80) before issuing its statement, *Teaching
Authority and Infallibility in the Church* (Minneapolis: Augs-
burg, 1980). The Canadian Protestant-Catholic Consultation,
also after long study, issued its statement on infallibility in 1980
(see *Journal of Ecumenical Studies,* XVIII, 3, 1981). In 1971

there also appeared a volume of collected essays on Küng's *Infallible? An Inquiry* (*Zum Probleme Unfehlbarkeit, Antworten auf die Anfrage von Hans Küng,* Freiburg: Herder), edited by Karl Rahner (Küng was quite displeased with it because he was not allowed to respond to his critics in the volume itself, and because he felt many of them were unwarrantedly negative). Küng responded with a volume of essays by various theologians in 1973 entitled *Fehlbar? Eine Bilanz* (Zurich: Benziger). On January 9, 1971, Küng appeared at a hearing of the Doctrinal Commission of the German Bishops' Conference composed of Bishop Volk, Bishop Wetter of Speyer, and Professors Joseph Ratzinger and Heinrich Schlier. On February 8, 1971, the German Bishops' Conference issued a Declaration against *Infallible?* and the Italian Doctrinal Commission did the same on February 21, 1971.

During these years, the early 1970s, Küng was also hard at work on a book that turned out to be almost 700 pages long, *On Being a Christian.* Actually the phrase "hard at work" is a gross understatement, for each chapter would go through anywhere from four to six drafts before Küng would be satisfied with it conceptually and stylistically. Küng thought of it as a positive contribution to making Christianity understandable and meaningful to contemporary critical men and women. Although the book was widely acclaimed as just that, Küng was deeply disappointed at the largely negative reaction from a number of Church authorities and some German dogmatic theologians—never really for what the book said, but rather for what it supposedly did not say. In any case, Küng launched its publication in Frankfurt with the following description of his purpose on October 10, 1974:

(37)

Time and again from the left and from the right it is asked whether a Catholic theologian with my interpretations can remain in the Catholic Church. Allow me upon this occasion a personal remark: Today on October 12, 1974, exactly at this hour Cardinal Döpfner is ordaining in the Roman

Church of St. Ignazio eleven students of the Papal Collegium
Germanicum as priests of the Catholic Church. One could
call this an accident, for I did not myself choose the day and
the hour of this press conference: precisely twenty years ago
today, on October 10, 1954, at the same hour in the same
Roman Church of Ignatius of Loyola, I myself as a student
of the same Papal Collegium Germanicum was ordained a
priest of the Catholic Church. And after I for twenty years,
throughout all the unavoidable constant criticism, have maintained loyalty and allegiance to this Church, have worked,
studied, and struggled for it, you will perhaps understand:
said frankly, I have had my fill of always having to prove
anew that and why I intend to remain in this Catholic
Church as a logical consequence of the Gospel. In my new
book I have once again spelled it out. In any case, after
twenty years I feel myself not less Catholic than on the day
of my ordination, which in our ecumenical age of course
does not exclude but rather includes the realization of the
justified evangelical demands.

A second matter should immediately be added: One could
likewise call it an accident that I today after twenty years am
not in parish duty, to which I at that time felt myself drawn,
but rather in an academic teaching office, into which I had
not pushed myself. The pastoral intentions have remained
the same as those of the then chaplain of the Collegium Germanicum, of the later curate in Lucerne, of the spiritual director in Münster/Westphalia, as well as now after fifteen
years of work as an academic teacher and researcher in
Tübingen. The work therefore of a theologian is the sober
and extremely effort-full task of "theo-logy," the "speaking of
God": how one can speak of God and the divine in the
world today so that men and women do not repeat prayers in
ununderstanding, but really with understanding. And not just
any kind of a theology, but rather a "Christian" theology:
how one can speak of this Christ Jesus so that men and
women do not merely repeat the traditional Christian formulas, but rather can convincingly live and act out of the

Christian message in the society of today. Theology therefore understood as a "service" to men and women who, as in contemporary industrial society one is ever more aware, have other needs than just material ones.

Twenty years of theology have gone into this book. Despite the first press report, the book is not a look back in anger, but rather a realistic look forward. It is not a reckoning with the twenty years; I do not have any theological past to overcome. It is a working out of twenty years in which it slowly became clearer to me what it can mean to be human and to be a Christian: From the evangelical source for the man and woman in the present. This book, which in many directions is doubtless very critical, is not written against Rome, but it is written even for Rome—and for the World Council of Churches. It is written as a defense and justification, a clarification and challenge of the Christian faith and life in a time in which the churches unfortunately have lost rather than won in credibility. It would like to bring to light for today the original Christian message and especially the form of Jesus of Nazareth. It would like of course not only theologically to proclaim, declaim, or declare. It would like to give reasons: That, why, and how even a critical man or woman can be responsible today before his reason and his environment to be a Christian. Perhaps this book will now nevertheless finally disavow the cheap Küng-clichés of the destructive Church critic, enemy of the Pope, and destroyer of dogmas. This book would wish to be nothing more and nothing less than an encouragement to be Christian.

Of course this book leaves nothing critically unquestioned, but it drives through all negative criticism always to positive answers. And because it everywhere sorts out things as comprehensively as possible and in the decisive points attempts to differentiate and interpret precisely, it cannot be brief. It deals with a body of material which in other places is brought together in several volumes.

Do not expect, therefore, cheap sensations from this book. The real sensation is what here and today this Jesus of

Nazareth himself has to say for the individual and for society about God and humanity through his word, deed, and fate. Therefore, simply another Jesus book? In no way. What, however, then is the originality of this book? In any case, not everything which is said here about miracles, authentic and inauthentic words of Jesus, virgin birth and empty grave, ascension and descent into hell, founding of the Church and the many-formed New Testament Church constitution, which one long since could have read in leading Protestant and Catholic exegetes—if one wished to.

The originality lies elsewhere. In this book the attempt is:

Not to go into only individual questions and individual areas of theology, but rather to lay out the entirety of the Christian message before the horizon of contemporary ideologies and religions: in a comprehensive synthesis which in itself is correct and is systematically unifiedly structured even in the details and even as it must be attempted in the specialization of the discipline of theology;

To speak the truth without church-political regard and without concern for theological forming of fronts and modish trends of inerrancy: upon the latest scholarly position of research and in intellectually honest argumentation and un-narrowed theological critique bound up with an unshakable trust in the Christian cause;

To move logically not from the theological posing of questions in the past, but rather from the wide-ranging and many-leveled questions of contemporary men and women and from there, by way of the fullness of information, to drive through time and again in concentration to the center of the Christian faith: so that the human, the generally religious, the extra-Church-based matters can be taken seriously, and nevertheless at the same time the differentiatingly Christian element can be crystallized out, and the essential distinguished from the inessential;

To speak in the language of contemporary men and women without biblical archaisms and scholastic dogmatisms, but also without modish theological jargon: the greatest possible linguistic efforts to formulate matters simply and understandably for our contemporaries who are not theologically trained, and yet at the same time precise, differentiating, and captivating;

To integrate on the basis of personal research into the doctrines of justification to Christology and ecclesiology likewise the confessional differences, and thus to set out the common elements of the Christian confessions as a renewed call for finally also a practical-organizational understanding: no new theories alongside of others, but rather today's possible fundamental consensus not only between the Christian churches, but rather also between the most important theological directions;

To bring to expression the often hardly perceivable unity of theology—on the foundation of exegetical and historical research from fundamental theology through dogmatics and ethics to practical theology—in such a way that from the God question to the Church question the steadfast connection between incredible theory and a livable practice, of the individual and the social, of critique of the times and critique of the Church, of personal piety and reform of the institutions, can no longer be overlooked.

In conclusion I wish to fend off a possible misunderstanding: as the author of this aid on how to be Christian for modern men and women, I in no way hold myself to be an exemplary Christian. Therefore let a single sentence be quoted from the book: "The author has not written the book because he holds himself to be a good Christian, but rather because he holds being a Christian to be a good thing."

Hans Küng

On December 4, 1974, Cardinal Döpfner wrote to Küng with a generally encouraging reaction to a quick perusal of *On Being a Christian* but also with some misgivings; he also reported on his continuing attempts to attain a resolution in Rome. He wrote:

(38)

Dear Fellow Brother!

Unfortunately only now do I come to thanking you for sending me your new book, *On Being a Christian.* I received the book during the Bishops' Synod in Rome. The constant burdens during the Synod and the manifold responsibilities which awaited me after my return have unfortunately not yet made it possible for me so to read your book, outside of the perusal of several selected sections, that I could form a final judgment for myself. You have poured out a great deal of energy and work, and the pastoral care which motivates the book is tangible. I hope therefore also that your book will contribute to a real renewal of the faith and of our Church. You will not be surprised that in this book I also have found a series of expressions of which I am convinced that they will not be useful for this goal, and even make it difficult. They will not precisely foster a reasonable closing of the doctrinal proceedings in Rome.

The stay in Rome offered the opportunity to discuss several times the question of the doctrinal proceedings. I have the hope that in the end despite all difficulties a reasonable solution will result. It is of course clear to me also that without your collaboration such a closing will not be attainable. I cannot at the moment say more about it because I await precise news and confirmations from Rome itself. This presumably will take a little while longer. You can in any case be certain that I will inform you in good time as soon as a clear line makes itself known.

In this sense, brotherly greetings, and precisely in this Advent time, all good wishes for your work and your personal path.

Yours,
Julius Cardinal Döpfner

Küng responded on December 11, 1974, indicating among other things that he still felt an agreement to silence on both sides would be the best solution. His letter said:

(39)

Dear Fellow Brother,

I thank you very much for your friendly letter. I was happy above all that with all the critique of individual points you nevertheless evaluate my new book positively. Naturally this book, especially, presumes that one has read from beginning to end in order to make a real evaluation. One notes then also how clearly a critique to the right *and* to the left is carried out.

The news from Rome has naturally interested me, especially since I note with concern that my letter of September 4 to the Doctrinal Congregation has still received no answer. If I understand your letter correctly, then the news spread about by the Rome correspondent of the *F.A.Z.* [*Frankfurter Allgemeine Zeitung*] sometime past in connection with his private audience with Pope Paul VI was nevertheless not correct. Of course a reasonable solution is something also desired by me. This still appears to me to lie in silence on both sides. Every kind of public act from the Roman side would call forth a proportional response concerning the procedure and result; after all that has gone on before, even if I wished to, I could not avoid such. Therefore, I still always hope that my proposal of silence will be accepted in Rome. This possibility looms still even in the last letter of the Doctrinal Congregation to me.

I would not wish to neglect to expressly thank you for your efforts in "my" matter in Rome; I know very well how unpleasant such duties are. I am likewise happy that you will inform me in plenty of time as soon as a clear line becomes discernible. It would mean much to me to avoid further public controversy after my new book has found this kind of positive reception in the Catholic as well as the non-Catholic public, which permits even my earlier publications to be better understood. I was able to gratefully confirm that last Sunday at the conference in the Munich Academy.

I likewise wish you a not all too busy Advent time, a happy Christmas feast, and God's blessing for the coming year 1975.

Yours,
Hans Küng

A copy of *On Being a Christian* was also sent by Küng to Cardinal Höffner of Cologne, who on the surface of things did not yet play a great role in the relations with Küng, but would very soon. Hence, it is worth quoting Cardinal Höffner's December 23, 1974, letter to Küng. The letter is somewhat odd, not attacking Küng directly, but rather ridiculing theologians in general— odd also because there really was no apparent reason for writing the letter: Höffner had long since received Küng's book, and it wasn't simply a thank-you note; and he still hadn't read the book, so he couldn't comment on it. The letter was as follows:

(40)

Dear Professor:
After my return from the Synod of Bishops in Rome, I found your friendly letter of October 17, 1974, and your new book, *On Being a Christian*. I thank you kindly for both.

In my interview with the newspaper of the Diocese of Cologne on October 11, 1974, I was not concerned ultimately either with the discipline of theology as we learned it at the Gregorian or with the position of the Roman Congregation for the Doctrine of the Faith, but with the faith of the Church as proclaimed by Vatican I and confirmed by Vatican II. It is with this faith of the Church that I cannot reconcile your view of the infallibility of the Pope and of the Councils.

Do the latest developments in theology and society have the authority required to change the faith of the Church? Besides, today there is no such thing as *the* teaching of theology. Some profess with the faith of the Church that the Pope is infallible when he speaks *ex cathedra* and issues definitive decisions about the faith. Others say that neither the Pope nor the Councils nor the Apostles could proclaim faith propositions which would be infallible.

Some profess that God has created not only the visible world but also the angels. Others say that there are no angels and that, when Holy Scripture mentions angels, it refers only to God's loving care for us.

Some profess the existence of evil spirits, that is, of evil beings who had been created by God good in their nature but fell away from God through their own fault. Others take leave of the devil and explain that the belief in the devil is a dubious heritage of time-conditioned biblical conceptions.

Some profess that the Virgin Mary gave birth "to the Son of God on earth without having known a man, overshadowed by the Holy Spirit." Others say that Mary conceived her Son through intercourse with a man.

Some profess that Jesus Christ arose from the dead and appeared to his own. Others say that after Jesus died his memory was so powerful in the disciples that they dared to say in metaphorical language that he was dead no longer, but had been raised from the dead.

Some profess that the eucharistic sacrifice can be validly offered only by an ordained priest. Others say that all the faithful are empowered to consecrate the Eucharist.

Some profess that a sacramental marriage which has been consummated is indissoluble because God wills it to be so. Others say that the indissolubility of marriage is only a commandment one ought to strive to observe, so that remarriage is to be allowed during the lifetime of the other spouse if the earlier marriage is hopelessly wrecked, that is, "dead."

Some profess that Jesus gave the mandate to make disciples of all nations and to baptize them in his name. Others say that missionary work should be concerned that a Hindu become a better Hindu.

Obviously, there is no such thing as *the* doctrine of the theology professors. Not a few of them not only say it differently; they say different things. Who decides who is right? The stronger arguments? Both sides claim to have the stronger arguments.

The question I am asking is this: By what authority do you profess your opinions?

Your new book, *On Being a Christian,* has been sitting on my desk for quite a while. I haven't yet found the time to read it. Your dedication "In the Service of the Common Christian Cause" has pleased me.

Sincere good wishes for Christmas and the New Year.

Yours,
Joseph Card. Höffner

Küng responded rather quickly in straightforward fashion on January 10, 1975:

(41)

Dear Fellow Brother,

I have read your letter attentively. Of course totally contradictory statements cannot be true at the same time. The question is then who is correct about the particular points. It is, however, too simple a solution to appeal to the "doctrine of the Church," since even the "teaching office" is being asked how it understands that doctrine. Even according to Vatican II the teaching office does not stand above the Word of God; it must serve that Word. Whether it does this in all the points is at least a question. You asked me: By what authority do you profess your opinions? My reply would have to be: By the authority of the Word of God, which I as a theologian must serve.

Whether I do this correctly is of course an open question.

However, the representatives of the teaching office should in turn argue on the basis of the Word of God, instead of merely decreeing again what has been handed down. I have given reasons for all the questions I raised and the views I set forth. With regard to the question you have raised, I have expressed myself in great detail in the volume of essays entitled *Fehlbar?*, which sums up the infallibility debate. To date, no one has refuted me.

In my opinion, a discussion in which both sides always appeal formally to an authority is not likely to take us far. One ought to speak about the thing itself. I would, therefore, be very pleased if you, as bishop, would find the time to read this book which so many are reading at this time.

I sincerely wish you God's blessings for the year already begun and send you cordial greetings.

> Yours,
> Hans Küng

February 15, 1975, was an important day for Hans Küng. On that day a letter was sent from Cardinal Šeper which "closed" (*einzustellen*) the proceedings against Küng's two books *The Church* and *Infallible? An Inquiry*. In the letter there was no modifying phrase, "for now" (*für jetzt*), as there was twice in the accompanying Declaration. The Declaration stated that the proceedings would be "ended for now" (*für jetzt beendet wird*), which phrase would be used in December 1979 as the legal basis to move unannounced against Küng. What the phrase might be argued to have allowed would be the reopening of the proceedings against Küng, but surely not unannounced judgment and sentencing. Moreover, the phrase "for now" was also used earlier in the Declaration when it stated that "this Congregation . . . for now imparts to Professor Küng the admonition not to advocate these doctrines any longer" (on infallibility, which the Congregation disagreed with). Obviously Küng was not being admonished against his opinions on infallibility indefinitely. That sentence, however, was not attended to in December 1979. The letter and Declaration were as follows:

(42)

Very Honored Professor!

In order to meet the mutual wish to end the proceedings concerning your books *The Church* and *Infallible?* the Congregation for the Doctrine of the Faith has decided to close both proceedings with the enclosed Declaration.

We are of the conviction that this Declaration will be received in that positive spirit in which it was composed. With friendly greetings,

> Yours sincerely,
> Francis Cardinal Šeper, Prefect
> Fr. J. Hamer, O.P., Secretary

(43)
Declaration of the Congregation for the Doctrine of the Faith

In carrying out its task of promoting and defending doctrine concerning faith and morals in the whole Church, the Congregation for the Doctrine of the Faith has examined two books of Professor Hans Küng, *The Church* and *Infallible? An Inquiry,* which have been published in many languages. In two different letters, dated May 6, 1971, and July 12, 1971, the Congregation informed Professor Küng about the difficulties it had found in his views and requested him to explain in writing how these views were to be reconciled with Catholic doctrine. In a letter of July 4, 1973, the Congregation offered Professor Küng the further opportunity to explain his opinion by taking part in a discussion. In his letter of September 4, 1974, Professor Küng left this opportunity unused. In his answers he failed to establish that some of his views on the Church do not contradict Catholic doctrine. He rather persisted in them, even after the publication of the declaration *Mysterium ecclesiae.*

So that no doubt about the doctrine which the Catholic

Church holds should exist and so that the faith of Christians should in no way be obscured, the Congregation recalls the doctrine of the teaching office as set forth in the declaration *Mysterium ecclesiae* and declares:

In the two above-cited books of Professor Küng, there are views which, in various measures, contrast with the doctrine of the Catholic Church which is held by all the faithful. Because of their particular importance we mention only the points to follow, while abstaining from passing judgment on other views which Professor Küng advocates.

The view which at least doubts the dogma of the infallibility of the Church or reduces it to the Church's fundamental indefectibility in the truth, with the possibility of error in propositions which the teaching office of the Church teaches definitively as propositions to be held, contradicts the doctrine defined by Vatican I and confirmed by Vatican II.

Another error which heavily burdens the teaching of Professor Küng relates to his view of the teaching office of the Church. He does not apply the genuine notion of authentic teaching office, according to which the bishops are "authentic teachers, that is, teachers endowed with the authority of Christ, who preach to the people committed to them the message of the faith which they must believe and put into practice" (Vatican II; Dogmatic Constitution *Lumen Gentium,* 25), for "the task of authentically interpreting the Word of God, whether written or handed down, has been entrusted exclusively to the living teaching office of the Church" (Vatican II; Dogmatic Constitution *Dei Verbum,* 10).

Further, the view already suggested by Professor Küng in his book *The Church,* namely, that, at least in the case of necessity, the Eucharist can be validly consecrated by a non-ordained baptized person, is not compatible with the doctrine of the Fourth Lateran Council and with Vatican II.

Because in his letter of September 4, 1974, Professor Küng does not at all exclude the possibility that, given adequate time for thorough study, he could bring his views in line with the authentic doctrine of the teaching office of the Church, in spite of the importance of these doctrines, the Congregation, so directed by Pope Paul VI, for now imparts to Professor Küng the admonition not to advocate these doctrines any longer and recalls that the ecclesiastical authority has authorized him to teach theology in the spirit of Christian doctrine, but not to advocate views which distort that doctrine or call it into doubt.

The bishops in Germany and in other places where the situation requires it, especially where the aforementioned doctrines are advocated in theological faculties, seminaries, and other institutions dedicated to Catholic or priestly education, are to see to it that the faithful are appropriately instructed about the doctrine of the Church, about the declaration *Mysterium ecclesiae,* as well as this declaration.

Priests who, by virtue of their office, are proclaimers of the Gospel, teachers of the Catholic faith, and catechists are obliged faithfully to profess and set forth the doctrine of the Church concerning the questions at issue here.

Finally, theologians are again requested to investigate the mystery of the Church and the other mysteries of the faith in the obedience of faith and to the true edification of the Church.

With this declaration, the proceedings of the Congregation for the Doctrine of the Faith in this matter are ended for now. In the audience granted to the Prefect of this Congregation on February 14, 1975, Paul VI has approved this declaration and ordered its publication.

Given in Rome, at the Congregation for the Doctrine of the Faith, February 15, 1975.

Franc. Cardinal Šeper, Prefect
Fr. Hamer, O.P., Secretary

The Attack on Küng's
Being a Christian

However, for Küng it was out of the fire into another frying pan, for the German Bishops' Conference also issued, on February 17, 1975, a Declaration in which it not only greeted the termination of the proceedings against Küng's two books, but also delivered to him a set of instructions on how to proceed theologically and initiated their first statement against his new book, *On Being a Christian*. The Conference espoused the curious position that the teaching office, or Magisterium, is to adopt dogmatic positions without any argumentation or proof for them and that then the theologians were supposed to come up with the proofs—and they accused Küng of reversing the order of things in this matter. The Declaration stated:

(44)
Declaration of the German Bishops' Conference
on the Closing of the Doctrinal Proceedings
of the Congregation for the Doctrine
of the Faith on The Church and Infallible?

I

On the occasion of the closing of the doctrinal proceedings on the books *The Church* and *Infallible? An Inquiry* by Pro-

fessor Dr. Hans Küng the German Bishops' Conference
thanks the Doctrinal Congregation in Rome for the decision
taken. The renunciation of the application of severe disciplinary measures should not veil the unambiguous, clear
statements on the question of truth. The "Declaration" of the
Congregation of February 15, 1975, affirms this with complete clarity and in detail. After the declaration *Mysterium
ecclesiae* (July 5, 1973) and the present decision the German Bishops' Conference need no longer make a statement
concerning the book *Infallible?* by Professor Küng. For the
rest it maintains unchanged its statements concerning these
on February 4, 1971, and March 4, 1971, and confirms these
again.

The decision issued by the Congregation for the Doctrine
of the Faith and approved by Pope Paul VI renounces other
measures and counts thereby on the solidarity of Professor
Küng. The German Bishops' Conference therefore joins in
the admonition of the Congregation for the Doctrine of the
Faith and expects that Professor Küng will not further represent the position that he has manifoldly been directed away
from by the ecclesiastical teaching office. This is valid at the
same time for all those who by the commission of the
Church proclaim and teach, insofar as they have made these
theses their own and have declared them compatible with the
self-understanding of the Catholic Church.

II

In this connection the German Bishops' Conference recalls
several principles which belong to the fundamental understanding of Catholic theology and which in individual theological works of Professor Küng (especially *The Church, Infallible?, Fallible?, Why Priests?,* and *On Being a Christian*)
are not sufficiently perceived. All rest upon the fundamental
stance of the theologian and of every Christian toward the
tradition of the faith and thereby ultimately upon the understanding of the Church itself.

1. NORMATIVE SIGNIFICANCE OF THE CHURCH'S TRADITION OF THE FAITH

With justification today the necessity of a constant orientation of Church life and theological work by the witness of the Scriptures is demanded. That the proclamation of the faith and theology ever again lets itself be asked whether it corresponds to the spirit and content of the Scriptures and is unrelentingly prepared to learn from them also belongs thereto. The historical-critical exegesis is thereby a valuable, and today indispensable, help. Nevertheless, the legitimate dealing with the Scripture within the framework of the Church is in no way exhausted by it. The Catholic faith lives from the entirety of the Scripture and does not allow in its explanation and in its theological use any one-sided or indeed exclusive priority of several, mostly "earlier," levels, with the simultaneous denigration of the later levels of development. The substantive connection of the various statements and the development of the teaching within the New Testament is acknowledged by the acceptance of the Scripture into the Canon.

The post-biblical interpretation of the revelation through the Church reflects in its manner and with the respective historical means on the truth of revelation testified to in the Scripture. This unfolding of the apostolic Gospel is not only a piece of theological history, but rather forms above all in its authoritative decisions, under the assistance of the Holy Spirit, a true and inalienable history of the faith of the Church. Therefore this binding tradition of faith in its function of interpreting the origin has still even today a normative significance.

This normative significance of the ecclesiastical development of the faith plays too small a role in the writings of Professor Küng investigated by the Congregation for the Doctrine of the Faith, but also in the above-mentioned writings of Professor Küng. Instead of that, Professor Küng in his theological thinking often makes a leap from the New

Testament to our present without bringing in or sufficiently valuing the rich history of the faith of the Church with its manifold experiences and insights. This unhistorical confrontation of the Scripture and the present is in its implementation not infrequently therefore problematic because the changed spiritual and especially theological situation is not observed and therefore questionable parallelizations are the result. Only with the help of the entire Scriptures and the entire tradition of the faith, and thereby in acknowledgment of the historical development of doctrine, is it possible to proclaim the Gospel of God materially correct and appropriate to the situation so that no conforming to momentary and short-lived tendencies follows, to which even scholarly theology remains subject.

2. CONCERNING THE RELATIONSHIP OF THE TEACHING OFFICE AND THEOLOGY

Every claim of faith is in need of—precisely in light of the Catholic description of the relationship between revelation and reason—an accounting, and today especially of a scholarly analysis and reflection. Theology is, nevertheless, from the very beginning and inalienably referred to the witness of the Scriptures and the binding explanation of the word of God by the teaching of the Church; it shows whether and how a truth of faith or a theological statement is grounded in the Scriptures and in the tradition of the Church. Thereby theology also has a thoroughly critical function: it tests the agreement with the primary witness of the Bible and with the normative Church tradition; it deepens understanding; it opens up hidden presuppositions or as yet undiscovered connections, then discusses and clarifies them. There is nevertheless—likewise in the application of all scholarly methods— no position outside of the Scriptures and the living tradition of the faith of the Church from where the role of the umpire on the basis of a principle of objective neutrality could be taken vis-à-vis the entire tradition, *and* at the same time a valid theology be offered for the entire framework of the

Church. Just as the Scriptures did not arise outside of the primitive Church, so also there is no Catholic theology outside of its concrete faith community. Catholic theology, therefore, in all of its scholarly illumination of the faith, places itself fundamentally on the ground of the ecclesiastical conviction of the faith and seeks with its means its rationale and explanation. Thereby, for example, the arising of new questions can lead at first to tensions. However, in principle the Catholic theologian trusts the ecclesiastical tradition of faith on the basis of the promises of Jesus Christ and attempts convincingly to present its spiritual power even for the present.

Professor Küng has many times, especially in his book *Infallible? An Inquiry*, left this structure of Catholic theology and appears to argue from a standpoint outside of the community of the faith when he lays upon the ecclesiastical teaching office alone the "burden of proof" for dogmatic decisions, and until the furnishing of this evidence of a binding truth of the faith he refuses a clear agreement. Professor Küng demands from the ecclesiastical teaching office "proof" which precisely the *theologian*—and indeed not only in the manner of historical-critical research of the Scriptures—should bring forth. Here a reversal in principle of the relationship of a Catholic theologian to the tradition of the faith of his Church is threatened.

This tradition of the faith must indeed be theologically grounded in its claim; still more in need of grounding, however, is the contradiction of the faith of the Church. For no scholarly method may grant such a certitude about the Holy Scripture and its explanation, about the reality of the faith in general, so that we could ground our life and death in the Christian hope thereon if the Church in the power of the Spirit that has been sent did not say to us what the Holy Scripture is, what the legitimate explanation of the Scripture is, and what the legitimate development of doctrine is.

Concerning this the theologian can never alone finally make a judgment about the ecclesiastical tradition, if the unity of the faith is not to be lost in favor of subjectively measured decisions. This is true first of all when one recalls that theological research with a certain necessity is subject to a constant shift, and in addition today suffers not infrequently from a contradictory pluralism.

Therefore the staying within the teaching office of the Church belongs inalienably to the method of theology. To be sure, the theologian cannot immediately put forward the ready answer to new questions. For this there must be attempts at clarification within the framework of the Church; only these may not be given out as the assured truth or indeed as the Church teaching. That this is possible is shown by the history of the development of the faith in the Church which unfolds the faith without taking its identity away.

3. CONCRETE BINDING CHARACTER IN FAITH

Whoever grounds himself and his entire life in faith in the revelation of God in Jesus Christ must have the certitude that he builds on the truth. In the service of this certitude the Catholic Church has always insisted upon the trustworthy and understandable statements of the content of the Christian faith and its unfolding. Likewise the Christian faith itself demands from its side this certitude because the Christian message possesses a decisive and irreversible character from the eschatological event of Jesus Christ: Because God really came to men and women of concrete history he on his side also makes a decisive claim on us. This happens through the Church which is sent and made capable of this in the Holy Spirit. The speaking in full power and the sacramental acting of the Church belong to the concrete form of the decisive existence of God for men and women in their history. Thus in all of the historicity of the linguistic formulations and the time-conditioned posing of problems in the dogmas of the Church there lives a final and insurpassable truth, which precisely therefore binds in all seriousness and concretely, and which, beyond the actual situation of how it arose and its first formulation, places an obligation. The Church, and more precisely the Pope and the Bishops as the successors of Peter and the rest of the apostles, has been given the task by the Lord of the Church and has been promised the grace with careful listening to the revelation to lay out in full power and, therefore with obligation, the word of God. The "infallibility" of a universal Church, of the college of Bishops, and of the Pope serves no other goal. It is not grounded other than in the promise of Jesus Christ and in the working of his Spirit.

Professor Küng does not deny the possibility of binding propositions. Nevertheless, he appears to limit their necessity and the historical range of their validity to emergency situations without giving the material criteria for them. The specified and continuing binding quality of ecclesiastical doctrinal decisions is not preserved in his theology.

III

The German Bishops' Conference is aware of the fact that without destroying all the unity in the faith today there are different outlines and forms in the methods of carrying out theology (for example, a more biblical, or a more speculative orientation, etc.). The fundamental propositions laid out above, which in no way are exhaustive, remain, nevertheless, binding and unrenounceable for every Catholic theologian in general.

If Professor Küng does not observe the norms of ecclesiastical faith expressed in these principles as the foundation of his theological work, conflicts with the ecclesiastical teaching office cannot be avoided. Therefore even "declarations" on individual positions of Professor Küng, as necessary as these might be, are insufficient. Thus even the new book of Professor Küng, *On Being a Christian* (Munich, 1974), whose theological effort and pastoral goals are acknowledged, contains a series of statements about which it cannot be seen how they can be brought into conformity with the just-mentioned fundamental propositions (cf. especially the Christology, the doctrine of the Trinity, the theology of the Church and the sacraments, the salvation historical position of Mary).

With this fundamental attitude there likewise is closely associated the renewed requests put forth to change by his own power the order of the Church in contradiction to the responsible declarations of the competent organs of the ecclesiastical office through so-called "reform demands" (cf., for example, now again in *On Being a Christian,* pp. 491 ff., 525–27: a recognition of offices, intercommunion, etc.).

The German Bishops' Conference therefore issues to Professor Küng the urgent appeal to review his methodological procedure and the complained-about substantive statements of his theological thought in light of the fundamental propositions here laid out.

On February 20, 1975, Cardinal Döpfner held a lengthy press conference at Bad Honnef in which he outlined the long history of the affair, most of which would be repetitious here. However, it is important to quote one paragraph where Döpfner spoke about what Church authorities had never done in regard to Küng and also stressed that they had had a number of discussions with Küng. The pertinent part is as follows:

(45)

One would certainly have to say that this proceedings is fair and presents a new style. . . . It is therefore not justified to speak of a publication prohibition. . . . At the closing of this point I wish to make clear and to emphasize that the high level of commitment and the pastoral goals of Professor Küng were never brought into doubt. He writes in a simple and understandable language. At no time was the condemnation of the entire theology of Professor Küng in question, but rather the setting aright of several—of course very essential—questions. This critique has nothing to do with the integrity of Küng as a priest and as a Christian. I can with an honest heart say that the German Bishops' Conference has never taken part in such statements. There have of course likewise in the meanwhile been frequent conversations with Küng. I have the hope that in the future the things in common will be emphasized more than the things that divide, even if it is also to be reckoned that the public presumably will be less interested in this.

On the same day, February 20, 1975, Küng also issued a press statement, which was a combination of criticism, gratitude, and cordiality:

(46)

I am not here to insist that I am right as over against Rome and the Bishops in the much disputed questions of infallibility and church order. Not who is right, but rather what is right is the question. The truth, with whomever it lies, will come through. As a theologian and a pastor I am concerned only to provide a convincing Christian answer to the pressing questions of men and women of today, and numberless reactions confirm me in this.

Now Rome and the Bishops have answered from their side. Even these "declarations" have not refuted anything which I have said in a theologically grounded way. The Declaration of the Roman doctrinal authorities is much more the public admission that the secret proceedings against me have shown themselves to be incapable of being carried out and are now being closed. Such Inquisition proceedings contradict indeed the Gospel, human rights, and likewise the spirit of the "holy year of reconciliation."

Since 1968 I have time and again requested access to the documents, time and again for permission to have a legal counselor—in vain. Of course the latest Declaration of the doctrinal authorities is silent about this, and they, as likewise in other cases, would like to transfer to the accused the burden of proof for his innocence. I have never rejected a colloquium in Rome. But I have insisted upon just and human conditions. An Inquisition proceedings I could never submit myself to. The doctrinal authorities unfortunately have never responded to my repeated suggestion of mutual silence. Indeed the Roman ex-Holy Office, under pressure from the German Bishops, have turned away from disciplinary measures against me—for which one is to be thankful. However, I see myself required to respond, even publicly, to the renewed attack on my Catholic correct belief, which substantively offers nothing new beyond what was in the declaration *Mysterium ecclesiae* (1973).

In the prevailing circumstances I greet the fact that the German statement now addresses the disputed points in a more differentiated fashion than before and fundamentally acknowledges "that there must be attempts at clarification within the framework of the Church." One can now compare the positions and form a judgment for oneself. I have never, as the Declaration of the German Bishops' Conference submits, done theology "from a standpoint outside of the community of the faith." Consequently I will likewise not allow myself to be held back from continuing to fulfill my service to men and women in critical solidarity with the Catholic Church and in an ecumenical spirit and to teach that which shows itself to be from the New Testament and the great Christian tradition as Catholic doctrine. Naturally in this I will time and again reflect in theological responsibility on the methods and content of my theology, as hopefully the Roman Curia likewise will adopt the theological fundamental principles of the German Bishops' Conference for themselves, even if that would have no small consequences for the method and content of Roman theology.

A short time later, on February 26, 1975, Küng wrote another letter to Cardinal Döpfner. This time again as *"Lieber Mitbruder."* It was a letter totally given over to gratitude—not a word of reference to the public criticism of *On Being a Christian:*

(47)

Dear Fellow Brother,

It is now eight days since I received the two Declarations and I can already look back with some distance on the very rapidly developed past events. I would at this time like to write you a personal letter since, assuming that I do not hear otherwise from you, the two Declarations do not necessarily demand an official response from me. In this manner I do not here need to come back to the painful defects in the proceedings nor to the theological questions which remain unanswered in the two documents.

Even at this distance I am still of the opinion that it would have been better for all concerned if the proceedings had been quietly closed or if my questions had been posed in a more positive manner. However, I can on the other side likewise understand that nothing more was to be attained in Rome and that the situation was very difficult for the authorities there.

Thus I can in this letter limit myself to expressing to you an honest, heartfelt word of thanks after all of the not easy exchanges which unfortunately there had to be even between us. I am well aware how much effort in Rome and probably even in Germany it has cost you to attain such a solution in which the two sides could save face. That you have had the patience and perseverance to do all this stirs up in me no small amount of gratitude; the threatening general confrontation could have brought with itself not only for our Church but also for me personally unforeseeable developments. That I have been spared this I know more than all concerned how to appreciate.

I was likewise well aware that my own public statement at the moment could not have been pleasant for you; for me, however, it was the minimum that seemed necessary to say in view of the defective proceedings and the unanswered theological questions. All the more so I was astounded that in the press conference, which I could follow live in the Tübingen radio studio, you spelled out the standpoint of the Bishops' Conference from beginning to end in a fair and friendly manner without injuring me in any way.

Your honorable declaration in complete openness had in general decisively influenced the really very mild reaction: In interviews in the press, radio, and television I could precisely therefore maintain a moderate attitude, as is rather generally acknowledged, and renounce counterattacks especially concerning the here discussed doctrinal points. It was likewise because of your attitude at the press conference that I have damped down all the already prepared solidarity actions in my favor. And finally, I have also given up the writing of a large article for the *F.A.Z.*, planned a week ago, which would present my own theological position—other than as in the Bishops' Declaration—and very clearly posed counterquestions. I will not exclude thereby, naturally, the possibility, as you indeed also intimated, of taking a theological position on the "declarations," but for the time I have nothing planned and would like in any case not to heat up the discussion unnecessarily. If after these "declarations" not all too much results, probably no statement of my own from my side would be necessary.

With this now, as you have made clear in public, an unpleasant period for all concerned has been closed. If I very often had to take a "hard" standpoint and could not deviate from specific juridical demands and theological positions, this happened then—and I beg you to believe me in this—never because of stubbornness and self-will, but because of an obligation of conscience based on Christian faith which makes me answerable *opportune importune* for these demands. The resolution, which seen as a whole is surely happy, and which has earned Rome partly even the reputation of "wisdom" and has gained you personally a great deal of sympathy even in otherwise critical circles, now gives the distinct hope that the Congregation will revise its procedural regulations from the ground up and will not allow matters to develop so far in other proceedings. Let me, however, once again repeat my very personal thanks: It would give me great joy if in the future we could together stand up for what is doubtless the more important thing for both of us: a common Christian concern.

With every good wish for your pastoral task, so full of responsibilities, I am with hearty greetings

Yours,
Hans Küng

Küng was approached by a Representative in the Federal Parliament about raising his case on the floor of the Parliament. Küng responded: thanks, but no, thanks. This and other matters were reported by Küng to Döpfner in another letter, and all was responded to by Döpfner in a letter of May 6, 1975. As was often the case between the two men, the exchange was open but critical —with good will and the lines of communication despite all remaining intact. Döpfner wrote to Küng on May 6, 1975, as follows:

(48)

Dear Fellow Brother!

Many thanks for your letter of February 26 and for the communication of March 20, 1975. First I thank you that you have done your part in the announcement of the ending of the doctrinal proceedings—which in any case was the substance of your statement—to bring about a rational closing of the matter in public. The public reaction has indeed in general indicated that there is a rather thorough appreciation of the direction taken in the solution. Of course I do not need to repeat my public declaration of February 20 on the decision of the Doctrinal Congregation and concerning your own person. Naturally I stand on that. Your proclaimed understanding and expressed gratitude for the efforts of the German Bishops I have with satisfaction taken note of.

Of course I would like for the sake of honesty not to keep silent about my disappointment that not only not a single word of thanks, but rather only hard accusations and objectively unjust attacks ("public admission," "secret proceedings," "Inquisition proceedings," "doctrinal authorities," "ex-Holy Office," etc.) is all that you could find for the Doctrinal Congregation. Without a high level of readiness on the part of responsible circles in the Doctrinal Congregation for the decision taken, the solution that was found would certainly not have been possible. Perhaps you have observed that several commentators of liberal papers, otherwise well intentioned toward you—and even if only in subordinate clauses —have indicated at this time even the limits of your response. In distinction to this "Declaration" I was—several passages apart—rather relieved by your balanced response in the TV discussion on the evening of February 20, 1975.

The publication of the unsigned article "How Often Yet— Herr Küng?" in the German edition of the *Osservatore Romano* of February 28, 1975, happened without my knowledge and without any discussion. It would have been better if some things in this form had not been written. Within the German Bishops' Conference we do not allow ourselves to be influenced by articles of this type. But you should not be entirely surprised at the tone and style of this response: If you read through again your "Declaration" of February 20, 1975, then it will not be difficult for you to recognize that the article in some regards indeed was not very masterful but perhaps was an unavoidable echo to your attack.

I heard of the statement of the Archbishop of Freiburg on *On Being a Christian,* but I do not know the exact text. Such individual statements of bishops about which I myself know nothing ahead of time naturally depend on the judgment and good thinking of the individual fellow brother. You of course understand that I cannot in the least "direct" such contributions, and also indeed fundamentally do not wish to.

Many thanks for the transmittal of the correspondence with the Parliament member, Peter Conradi from Stuttgart.

You have certainly decided correctly in not allowing yourself to become involved in particular interests. Although I am happy when as in this case and on other occasions unnecessary and unfruitful "disturbing fires" can be avoided, I nevertheless judge the questions posed by Mr. Conradi as inadequate, "politically" too transparent, and therefore his plan extremely painful.

What concerns me the most is the background of your more theologically oriented references, and indeed in the press declaration of February 20, 1975, as well as in your letter of February 26, 1975. First of all I find unacceptable the way you reduce the referred-to faith questions in the proceedings to a large extent to the level of Church politics (in the broadest sense) and of pragmatic tactics. This begins with the term "proposal of mutual silence" (*Stillhalteangebot*) and continues likewise through the tenor of your letter (for example, ". . . that nothing more was to be attained in Rome and that the situation was very difficult for the authorities there"). I will not deny such aspects in general and their relative significance. But the problem is therewith in no way resolved. At a specific point the concern nevertheless is very intensely with the unavoidable question of the truth of our faith and about the maintenance or the loss of the identity *in principle* of our Church. I hold the reducing of the whole problematic to the "church reform" and likewise to tactical maneuvers consequently as absolutely impossible.

In the same connection I have a further doubt: You speak in your Declaration of February 20 and in your letter of February 26, 1975, of the Declarations of the Doctrinal Congregation and of the German Bishops' Conference as having refuted nothing which you had said was theological grounding. I find it difficult not to see an extreme stubbornness in such statements which could have very easily placed the outcome of the entire proceedings in question. For one, you cannot—even after *Fallible?*—overlook the weighty objections from a large number of theologians to the central thesis of *Infallible?*. For another, you confuse, even after the

Declaration of the German Bishops, time and again the various levels of the ecclesiastical teaching office and of theology. Otherwise a number of sentences and statements in your utterances could not come out in the form they have. However, as long as here the distinction of the legitimation, the function, and therefore the kind of argumentation of the respective language is blurred, and you allow to the "teaching office" only an extremely limited "pastoral" service, I fear for an unavoidable flaming up again of the conflict as soon as you take a stand on questions concerning the teaching of the Church. I will not deny in this connection that the ecclesiastical teaching office could be thought through more deeply concerning its function and that it could be still more precise in its utterances. But here we are concerned with the fundamental principles.

These reflections well up in me with the rethinking and frequent rereading of your letter and your Declaration. I ask you therefore once again for a fundamental and serious reflection precisely on these matters. If we would again have to have disputes concerning these difficulties and if no rapprochement were possible, I would hardly know how to help any further.

In hope for a fruitful collaboration in the common task of our Lord I wish God's blessing for you and your work and am with hearty greetings

Yours,
Julius Cardinal Döpfner

Essentially all was quiet for well over a year after the February 15, 1975, Vatican Declaration. Then, on April 6, 1976, Küng was in Rome for the publication of the Italian translation of his book *On Being a Christian* and took the occasion to have lengthy discussions with both Cardinal Šeper and Archbishop Hamer of the Doctrinal Congregation—much as Küng had earlier suggested to Cardinal Šeper when he asked that they have discussions after the proceedings against *The Church* had been terminated. (This, of course, was the second time in the 1970s that Küng had lengthy theological conversations at the Doctrinal Congregation, the earlier one being in 1972—see above, pp. 129–32.) According to a detailed report from Küng to Cardinal Döpfner on April 27, 1976, the discussions went very well. Küng registered his displeasure with Döpfner about the actions of Father Jean Galot, S.J., a professor of dogmatic theology at the Gregorian University. It was the same Galot who also impugned the orthodoxy of Edward Schillebeeckx on the Vatican radio on December 4, 1979, just eleven days before Galot turned up as one of the three interlocutors for the Doctrinal Congregation in a "discussion" with Schillebeeckx at the Palazzo del S. Uffizio in Rome. In his book *Cristo contestato: Le cristologie non calcedoniane e la fede cristologica* (Florence: Librerìa Editrice Fiorentina, 1979) Galot attacked a whole range of contemporary Catholic theologians besides Küng and Schillebeeckx, including the Americans David Tracy and Monika Hellwig. In Schillebeeckx's 1974 book, *Jesus,* he mentioned that most theologians say privately that Galot's 1971 book, *Vers une nouvelle théologie,* is based "on a completely mistaken interpretation of the authors dealt with, and so does not make the grade as a piece of scholarship." An American publisher who was approached about translating the Galot book was advised by readers that the scholarship was too inferior to warrant translation. He is a Consultor for the Doctrinal Congregation. It should perhaps also be noted that a year later, December 1980, Schillebeeckx received a letter from the Doctrinal Congregation which cleared his orthodoxy and dropped the proceedings. Did the massive worldwide reactions to the Schillebeeckx and Küng affairs have any influence on that decision?

In the letter to Döpfner, Küng also spoke about the volume of essays critical of his book *On Being a Christian* (*Diskussion um Hans Küngs "Christ sein,"* Mainz: Matthias-Grünewald, 1976) edited by his friend and former "patron" Hans Urs von Balthasar. As with the Rahner-edited volume against *Infallible?* Küng was not permitted to respond to his critics within the volume itself. He was told by Šeper and Hamer that that was a quarrel among theologians—it pleased Küng that Rome was allowing such theological matters to be worked out on the scholarly dialogue level, which was what he wished the German Bishops would do too (unfortunately not to happen)—and that they had no difficulty with his replying publicly to his critics. It is also clear from the April 27, 1976, letter to Döpfner that Küng thought himself "corrigible" in theological matters, and spelled it out in some detail. This probably was partly in response to Döpfner's criticism in his May 6, 1975, letter above.

Walter Jens in *Wahrheit,* p. 173, notes: "Through the unjustified publication of this letter in the Bishops' *Documentation* (November 17, 1977) the confidentiality assured by the Roman agencies was violated."

(49)

Dear Cardinal,

A visit in Rome and a private conversation with Cardinal Šeper and Archbishop Hamer as well as two more lengthy conversations with the Bishop of Rottenburg, Dr. Georg Moser, provide me with the occasion to send you a report, which presumably might also be of interest to the members of the Bishops' Conference.

The occasion of the visit to Rome was the appearance of the Italian edition of *On Being a Christian:* a press conference there with a prepared statement concerning the Catholicity of the book (see the enclosed) appeared to me to be the best method to avoid precisely at the beginning of the discussion tendentious and indeed false reports (as at the earlier time with the German edition in *Der Spiegel*) in Italy. As the press echo indicates, this has likewise largely succeeded. There were no unpleasant sensations concerning individual doctrinal points after I gave a clear expression of my loyalty to the Catholic Church and its teaching. The single shrill tone came in the Italian press and then also in the international press through a statement by Pater Galot, S.J., on the Vatican radio on the same day which personally discredited me and was brimming with misinterpretations and insinuations. Nevertheless I have not allowed myself to be turned aside by this Vatican provocation with a corresponding reaction. Likewise I succeeded in taking up the penetrating questions of the journalists concerning the Vatican sexuality document, divorce, abortion, Italian internal politics, etc.

In any case I hope that despite Galot's and similar falsification of my book in individual ecclesiastical organs, the great majority of Catholics and Italians will receive and understand the book as has happened in Germany: as an aid for men and women within and without the Catholic Church for their Christian belief and life. Afterwards Rome and the Bishops doubtless will also receive complaints and denunciations, but I would like at this opportunity only to indicate that no other of my books has received such a wide approval even and precisely by Catholic pastors, teachers of religion, ministers, and men and women engaged in church work as has *On Being a Christian*. I have often reflected therefore whether or not it would be useful to publish representative expressions of this "sensus fidelium."

Private conversations first with *Cardinal Šeper* and then with *Archbishop Hamer* lasted around five hours and were conducted in the usual openness and friendliness and touched upon just about all of the important questions of the day. It was acknowledged that I had remained loyal to the "admonitiones" of the Doctrinal Congregation of February 15, 1975. It was further clear that no new Roman proceedings are now planned against *On Being a Christian*. On the other hand, however, they were not prepared to give any kind of assurances that nevertheless in the near future a proceedings would not be initiated. Of course, in both conversations I indicated emphatically that the Declaration of the Doctrinal Congregation and the supplemental Declaration of the German Bishops' Conference, which indeed also already made a statement concerning *On Being a Christian,* will be so understood by the international public and also by me that therewith all matters up till now had then been taken care of and that in general in similar disputes concerning doctrinal questions a "new style" would be practiced in the future. In Germany, in Switzerland, and far beyond it would not be understood if again—and precisely against a book that has been so helpful to so many, *On Being a Christian*—a new proceedings would be initiated. In any case, a new proceedings with its own mechanism would likewise nevertheless again lead to the same dead-end situation as all of the previous ones. That can only damage the credibility of the Catholic Church and its theology. In any case both discussion partners appeared to be clear that a new conflict contained within itself completely incalculable risks for all sides.

I brought the discussion around to the volume of essays *Diskussion um Hans Küngs "Christ sein,"* by von Balthasar and others, which against my will provoked a public confrontation. I was told that this was a "lis theologorum" which did not involve Rome. I acknowledge that it doubtless was a step forward if theologically disputed questions would be discussed in a scholarly manner among theologians rather than be disciplined by the teaching office. Of course, I could not understand why then—aside from the very one-sided composition of the authors—the author under discussion was not allowed to participate as a discussion partner in the same discussion volume, as is customary in such discussion volumes; only so, indeed, could the reader form an objective judgment concerning truth and untruth. I was told that I could indeed answer this collection of essays in an article.

Given the weight of the authors and the broad effects of a book, I felt that I had to respond not only in a scholarly journal but rather in a widely distributed serious newspaper. This article will shortly appear. I hope that even in the German episcopacy it will be understood that a newspaper article which is to serve as a defense of my Catholic integrity concerning highly complex questions—if it is accepted at all —must be written in a manner other than as in a theological scientific article. I have taken the greatest effort not only to study the collection of essays carefully in detail, but also to discuss it with expert colleagues and finally in a special several-day colloquium. Nevertheless this article shall not be the last word on this matter. I hope in the foreseeable future to find time to devote myself anew in a scholarly manner to the exegetical, history of dogma, systematic and hermeneutical questions that have been brought up in the collection of essays and elsewhere. Of course, a renewed theological concern with the material includes clarifications and corrections, expansions and deepenings of my own standpoint as well. I am convinced that, as has already been expressed in various ways in the book itself, in connection with various doctrinal points—and likewise precisely concerning those complained about by the German Bishops' Conference—a positive going further is thoroughly possible and indeed desirable.

Of course, I have the impression that critics skipped over important statements of *On Being a Christian* or have not taken them sufficiently seriously. Thus, for example, my clear affirmation of the fundamental intentions of the Council of Nicaea against Arius: "In Jesus the one true God is present, not a second God or demi-God. Our whole redemption depends on the fact that in Jesus we are concerned with the God who is really God" (p. 448). Or the interpretation of the Chalcedonian "vere Deus": "The whole point of what happened in and with Jesus depends on the fact, that for believers, *God himself* as the friend of men and women was present, at work, speaking, acting, and definitively revealing himself *in this Jesus* who came among men and women as God's advocate and deputy, representative and delegate, and was confirmed by God as the Crucified raised to life" (pp. 449 f.). Or concerning the Incarnation: "It was in Jesus' *whole* life, in his *whole* proclamation, behavior and fate, that God's word and will took a human form. In his whole speech, action and suffering, in his whole person, Jesus *proclaimed, manifested, revealed* God's word and will. Indeed it can be said that he in whom word and deed, teaching and life, being and action, completely coincide is the embodiment of God's word and will . . . he might almost be called the *visage* or *face of God* or—as in the New Testament itself—the *image* or *likeness of God*. The same thing is expressed also in other terms: when Jesus is called the *Word of God* or even the *Son of God"* (pp. 443 f.). After all that it is apparent that I have never intended to doubt the Sonship of God of Jesus (or the Trinity)!

Whether or not interpretations represented not only by me are sufficient, one can of course likewise with me—as well as with other contemporary Catholic theologians—discuss. The difficulties of christological interpretation—from the perspective of New Testament exegesis, from the history of dogma, and from modern consciousness—are for every Catholic theologian today, but also for every preacher and proclaimer of the Christian message, significant. Of course I am aware that my book—or more often rather tendentious press announcements or reviews!—can under circumstances at first make traditional Catholics uncertain, especially if they have not been correspondingly further educated through religious instruction and proclamation and have read my book only in part, if at all. In any case, I would like to underline this: my presentations do not in any case wish to abbreviate, veil, disturb, upset, but rather help the uncertain, create clarity for the confused, overcome polarizations, and strengthen the Christian faith, for which unnumbered persons are thankful to me.

I have been pleased by and have likewise publicly called attention to the fact that you, my dear Cardinal, as President of the German Bishops' Conference, in February 1975, in your press conference, expressly acknowledged my "high level of commitment" and my "pastoral goals," as well as my "integrity as a priest and as a Christian." Several—not all—authors of the collection of essays and a few other theologians (in part even members of the German Doctrinal Commission) have once again sunk below that level which was attained in the exchange. I would therefore like to ask you and the German Bishops expressly to intervene even further

for this my "integrity" and to call upon your theological advisers to act other than in the collection of essays and, as you
did in that press conference, hope that "in the future the
things in common will be emphasized more than the things
that divide."

The usefulness of a pastoral doctrinal or proclamation office
of the Pope and Bishops in our Church has constantly been
affirmed by me myself in the most difficult phases of the infallibility debate. Nevertheless I have also now again in
Rome attempted most emphatically to make understandable
that this teaching and proclamation office in contemporary
times can attain its goal only if it is not one-sided, but rather
is really catholic and does not attempt ahead of time to exclude representative tendencies of contemporary Catholic
theology. Likewise the declaration of the episcopacy on the
Council of Nicaea would have found a greater and more positive echo if the Catholic theologians who (perhaps quite
without the knowledge of some bishops) were cited verbatim
had been invited to the discussion and to collaboration. Only
thus can the much-complained-about polarization and negative pastoral effects be avoided; only for this reason have I
likewise renounced making a public statement on this document. Rather I used the opportunity to express once again
my readiness for every possible kind of constructive collaboration with the episcopacy "in aedificationem Ecclesiae."

In sum may I say: In the matter of On Being a Christian,
after the official declaration of the German episcopate on On
Being a Christian, the declaration on Nicaea, and above all
the referred-to collection of essays, in my opinion a calm can
now descend. Official and officious critique has been issued
and my reply, as far as it has been necessary at the present
time for my self-defense, has also.

I would be thankful to you, my dear Cardinal, and to the
German Bishops if I could be left in peace and calm to do
my theological work. I hope that with my restraint and also
with this letter to have said some things contributing to a sub-

stantive clarification of the present situation and send to you
along with my best wishes my friendly greetings.

Yours sincerely,

Hans Küng

cc: The Bishop of Rottenburg, Dr. Georg Moser

enclosure: Statement for the press conference in Rome

On May 22, 1976, Küng responded to his critics, as he reported he would, in a detailed article in the *Frankfurter Allgemeine Zeitung* (*F.A.Z.*). It speaks for itself:

(50)
Response to my critics. Theology for men and women?

Hans Küng, the Swiss Catholic theologian, since 1960 Professor Ordinarius for dogmatics at the University of Tübingen, is as significant as he is a battling theologian. For almost twenty years, since the first book, *Justification: The
Teaching of Karl Barth and a Catholic Reflection,* he has
made many fellow believers uneasy. His books always
arouse attention. Küng, the Küng Affair, became known beyond the borders of the Catholic Church when in 1970 his
book *Infallible? An Inquiry* led to a conflict with the
Roman Curia. His last book, an almost 700-page-long book
on the teaching of the faith, which appeared under the title
of *On Being a Christian* in 1974, published by Piper, had
difficulty in finding indifferent readers. At the publication of
the Italian edition a few weeks ago in Rome, Küng felt himself compelled to say: "I am no destroyer of dogmas, no
enemy of the Pope. . . . I hope that those who read the
book in the Vatican do not simply go hunting for heresies."
Likewise in Germany opponents of the position of Küng have
published a collection of eleven essays with the title *Discussion of Hans Küng's "On Being a Christian."* Küng's wish to
participate in this discussion, his request for the acceptance of
at least a brief response by the person concerned, was re-

jected. The programmatic character of this controversy about the course of Catholic theology induces us to print here the unabridged response of Küng to his critics.

F.A.Z.

The doves are cooing now even on the roofs of the Roman palazzi: the dispute—apparently set aside less than a year ago—goes on: unfortunately. One bit of progress is that the Pope and Bishops apparently are convinced of the inadvisability of authoritarian disciplinary measures. Now, however, it is the theology professors who continue the dispute.

In the infallibility debate they were still fifteen. This time —after rejections—they come forward in the strength of a football team: eleven, again against one. Very vigorously supported, of course, on the tribunes by a handsome number of theologically zealous pennant wavers and the trumpets of archconservative Catholic postilions. Are some of the individuals not standing on already lost positions?

Is This Discussion?

*Discussion of Hans Küng's "On Being a Christian":** discussion on what? Theological discussion rather than ecclesiastical inquisition would be welcome. But is this really discussion? In no way: the real partner always stands ready for discussion, but he is missing. Reason: the one attacked on 143 pages was denied a defense on the spot. Indeed the editor (who does not profess himself as such), Hans Urs von Balthasar, at the same time strikes a completely different tone in a private circular letter to the Swiss clergy and recommends against taking *On Being a Christian* as a "signpost in a foggy countryside." But he who in his official contribution writes specifically about the "disadvantage of resentment in theology"—as well as the Catholic publishing house —decided against accepting even only a brief response of the

* With contributions by H. U. von Balthasar, A. Deissler, A. Grillmeier, W. Kasper, J. Kremer, K. Lehmann, K. Rahner, J. Ratzinger, H. Riedlinger, Th. Schneider, B. Stoeckle; Matthias-Grünewald-Verlag, Mainz, 1976. 15.80 DM.

author of *On Being a Christian* into the volume whose name
in the book title is used to attract the public. Therefore, it is
in truth not a discussion volume, but rather a partisan volume of carefully sought out professors who in the majority
are members of the likewise one-sided papal or episcopal
Doctrinal Commissions—all very honorable theologians.

What is an individual to do when he is besieged before his
goal? How can he catch all of the balls when each one
brought his own with him? One would have to have at least
eleven arms and at the same time be able to defend oneself
against feints, charges, and fouls. What should be done?

Keep silence? Perhaps. One would certainly be spared a
great deal of irritation. Nevertheless, to keep silence would in
this unstable church-political situation be fatal for the one attacked. It would be too easy for a dictum (non probatum!)
to be used for a theological and ecclesiastical discrediting or
indeed for a new "doctrinal proceedings." And the cases of
professors Stephan Pfürtner, Franz Schupp, and even almost professor Uta Ranke-Heinemann, the cases of numerous quietly disciplined pastors, chaplains, religion
teachers, lay theologians, make one be "sober and watchful."
Thus, a first response must be given. However, it is nevertheless painful to be forced to counter those with whom one
has so often collaborated—painful to have to defend oneself
in one's being Catholic—Churchly—Christian against those
with whom one so gladly would make common cause—in
theology, Church, Christianity. What should one do? Should
one perhaps take up the numberless misrepresentations, insinuations, condemnations of the dogmatician Joseph Ratzinger: this Being a Christian is an "option for a label which
in reality is an empty formula"; the Christian would be withdrawn "out of his life-and-death seriousness into the questionable interest of the literary"; the Christian faith would be
"handed over to corruption at its very foundation"; the community of the Church would disappear "literally into the saying of nothing"; such a teaching would be "an undisguised
arrogance"; a theology that is "rootless and ultimately un-

binding," "as it were in a going it alone, alone with oneself and modern reasonableness," in "unseriousness"; a "school certitude, party certitude, not a certitude for which one can live and die, a certitude for comfortable times in which the ultimate is not demanded"; such a theology "lands ultimately in the abstruse," "leads nowhere" . . . ? No, the discussion here shall not be on such a level.

But what of the numberless orthodox suspicions and verdicts of the other opponents: Should one protest against all of the sentences torn out of context, against the false undertones, the false concealing of what was also said by me? Can a false statement simply be balanced by a counterstatement, an incorrect assertion simply by a denial, an ungrounded denial by an assertion? Unfortunately not. For a response one would need space, very much space. What then is to be done? Can a newspaper page balance out a volume of many pages? Naturally not. But perhaps nevertheless the critical transitional situation of Catholic theology, as it is reflected in that volume of collected essays, can be briefly sketched on a newspaper page for the unprejudiced reader so that he will understand what the game here is about—a game in all seriousness. For it concerns—note well!—indeed not only "my" book. That would not be worth the effort. It concerns the questions, problems, and needs which burden very many men and women inside of and outside of the Church which are dealt with in this book.

One thing appears immediately to those who know the situation: the team that from the outside appears so homogeneous is by no means so united within. If one looks more closely, the colleagues are not only playing against the one, but also against themselves: goals against themselves are thus unavoidable, and the game then is somewhat more even than appeared at first. Who is really playing against whom here? Who belongs to which party?

Extraordinary: one of the strongest parties yet has not even gone onto the playing field: the Roman Curia (there is at the papal universities a Roman non-curial party). Is it

being held in reserve? Is it perhaps running on the edge of
the playing field keeping warm, planned by the trainer and
manager for the second half? In earnestness: it is not a par-
ticipant because none of the players on the field will have
anything to do with this Roman curial theology. Not even the
veterans Rahner and Balthasar (with Grillmeier), who—do
they still remember?—themselves earlier had to absorb
rough blocks and indeed low fouls which even today leaves
them groggy, because they were not completely orthodox.

No Curial Theology

What is it that characterizes this neo-scholastic theology
which, despite the Second Vatican Council, still dominates
the Roman Curia? It takes all ecclesiastical propositions of
faith literally—just as positivist jurists interpret and apply a
law without asking where it came from, how it has changed,
whether it has still another meaning, how could one formulate it better: a dogma positivism which corresponds formally to legal positivism. Unbiblical, unhistorical, unecumen-
ical, this theology reached its brilliant high point with the
infallibility definition of 1870, but was decisively weakened
one hundred years later through the Second Vatican Council and has shown itself no longer representative of the Catholic Church. As a serious scholarly theology it has played itself out today. However persistent it still is in the matter of
error, it has nevertheless until today not admitted openly any
of the numerous serious errors of the ecclesiastical office in
matters of faith and morals. Still in the most recent, much
criticized Roman "Declaration on Several Questions of Sexual Ethics" there is the unbroken self-conscious calling upon
the "assistance of the Holy Spirit" under which "the Church
protects in unbroken fashion the truths of the moral order
and transmits them without error."

But wait: the authors of our collection of essays are no
curial theologians, even when they come out of neo-scholas-
ticism. Who in Germany wishes still to be a curial theologian? Even the theological seniors, Rahner, Balthasar, and

Grillmeier, are presumably not prepared to identify themselves fully with the "traditional teaching" in the sense of the Roman Curia. Would they today give their honest agreement: to the condemnation of Galileo and the numerous corresponding measures against the new natural-scientific theories as they were still during the time of Pius XII; to the condemnation of specific Asiatic worship forms in the rites dispute; to the theological affirmation of the Papal States as a hundred years ago; to the numerous condemnations of the results of the new historical-critical exegesis in this century (pertaining to the authorship of the biblical books, source research, historicity, literary genres); to the massive condemnations and forced measures in connection with "Modernism" (theory of development, development of dogmas); to the purging measures of Pius XII in connection with the encyclical *Humani generis* and the worker priests, or the excommunication (still valid today) by the same Pope of all Communists in Italy and elsewhere? Presumably not.

No, our German theologians are truly not curial theologians! On the contrary: those who in contrast to the author of *On Being a Christian* throw themselves on the bosom of a self-conscious Catholic orthodoxy also, when looked at more closely, do not take such a Catholic orthodoxy quite so precisely. If they speak about their own concern or about something that is not meant for the public, one can thus hear precisely from them astonishingly liberal criticism of the Roman teaching office. Indeed even in the volume of collected essays which is pious vis-à-vis the teaching office but sharply polemical against *On Being a Christian*, fundamentally critical tones occasionally poke through which from their writings easily could be composed into a handsome symphony:

Even here Rahner criticizes the traditional ecclesiastical teaching (test case: the founding of the Church), the Second Vatican Council (papacy), and the Doctrinal Commission of the German Bishops' Conference (the question of office).

Even here Balthasar demands that "we have to critically illuminate tradition from the origins and perhaps newly formulate it," which—one hears and is astounded—"today no one disputes."

Even here Grillmeier demands almost modernistically "a new description of what is Christian that is understandable, easily perceivable, doable," as an "urgent necessity."

But, thus the perplexed reader asks himself, how did these Catholic theologians, who from the Roman curial point of view in no way are orthodox, nevertheless come to their orthodoxy? They who neither can defend nor wish to defend so many of the things which the Roman teaching office theology defended and defends in its literal meaning? Well, each has his own way—one loudly and the other quietly—to make an arrangement with the official teaching in the critical points as far as they are urged by Rome. One simply does not love Roman theology, but does one nevertheless marry it!? Several typical possibilities of an arrangement—one should observe, we are not concerned here with a comprehensive evaluation of these theologies!—show up also in our controversy:

Forms of Arrangements

Arrangement I: Here a reinterpretation of the doctrine on the Church. Example: Karl Rahner on the question: "Did the historical Jesus found a Church?"

The traditional Church interpretation is clearer here: the historical Jesus did found a Church. Rahner, however, knows that this traditional interpretation turns up historical and exegetical difficulties. Therefore, he reinterprets it. He must indeed admit that the expectation of the early end of the world by Jesus forms a "difficulty and question" for an authentic foundation of the Church by Jesus "which was not seen or was supressed in Catholic ecclesiology until the most recent times";

That the connection between Peter and the later popes, between the Twelve and the later college of bishops, was "simplistically" described even by Vatican II yet;

That no founding of the Church could be derived from a "couple of founding words of a juridical sort."

In clear language then: that—as was detailed by me in agreement with the leading New Testament scholars of both confessions—there can be no talk of a founding of the Church in an authentic sense by the historical Jesus, but rather that the Church—as a post-Easter community of faith —was founded on the death and awakening of Jesus.

But one is astonished: Rahner, after the indication of all these exegetical difficulties against a founding of the Church by Jesus, states with the pathos of a confessor: "We Catholic Christians will also in the future say with the ancient faith: Jesus has founded the Church. . . ." He would like only to understand this proposition in a "more differentiated" manner than before the Second Vatican.

How will theologizing to be understood, which at bottom in an apparent dialectic can only say both things: Jesus did not found the Church and he did found it! How does one understand this ambiguous manner of speaking which continues then in Rahner's "modest remarks" on the historical development of the leadership offices and their recognition in the other Churches on the understanding of grace and the spirit: May "we Catholic Christians" then never know how it really is?

The most important thing for Rahner's theology, which in programmatically "systems-immanent" fashion is based on the ecclesiastical dogmas (not measured against the statements of the Scripture), is always that the dogmatic formula, because infallible, must absolutely be preserved. Even if it perhaps must be "differentiated" into a completely other meaning: unhistorically reinterpreted, and perhaps even interpreted into the contrary. No question. With the help of such "differentiating" verbal dialectics one can indeed arrange matters and thereby at once be orthodox and modern. The formulas—for the Roman curial "orthodoxy" very important —remain; the content, however—decisive for modern men

and women—is really re-formed (to "found" a Church then
means precisely something other than to "found" in general
human use of the language). A theology truly helpful for
present-day men and women?

Arrangement II: By a flight into aesthetics and mysticism!
Example: Hans Urs von Balthasar on theological method.
The theologian from Basel, who earlier wrote against
Rahner, accuses me first of all of not having completely covered the "attempts at understanding Paul" in reference to his
theology of the cross, which no reader will understand who
knows the long sections in *On Being a Christian* on the subject (justification, grace, redemption, representation). But
with *On Being a Christian* Balthasar is irritated above all by
the logical beginning with the questions of men and women
of that time or of today ("from below") and the critique of
the institutional Church. Silently suppressing my critique toward the "left" of the revolutionary alternative in tendentious, often false fashion, he follows in my sketch of the
proclamation, behavior, and fate of Jesus only those strokes
which run contrary to him and attempts to reduce this interpretation—although there is constant talk about God—to
the "sociological-ethical level."

Balthasar expressly affirms "demythologization." But an
authentic understanding of a consistent historical-critical exegesis and dogmatics is something Balthasar has as little of
as Rahner: for him all that is not a struggling for the truth,
but rather merely a "making understanding easier" for modern men and women and thereby "a loss of weight"! Allergic
to all "modern knowing better," he searches in the Scripture
and tradition for the "secret freight." And on such a mystical
height the dark clouds of critical exegesis, history of dogmas,
and the Church change their color into a rosy red. Even very
real alternatives before which Jesus himself stood appear in
that kind of spiritualized church—where is it?—harmoniously reconciled: the political-religious establishment, the
monkish emigration, the moral compromise, and apparently
also the social-political revolution can be made harmless

and be reinterpreted into "special missions" for the whole of the Church. Thus everything, "even the institutional hierarchy," appears here in a "beautiful" light.

Who however does not find such beautiful exegesis and theology so beautiful, will be admonished to interpret the New Testament Scriptures (and naturally also the witnesses of the tradition), instead of in their rich, tension-filled, often contradictory history, so as to cultivate the little trees in the forest, "fir, beech, spruce," organically and harmoniously. Whereby the theological "forester" Balthasar apparently is opposed to this strenuous forest work, all cultivating, uprooting of stumps, clearing, indeed even chopping of wood and collecting of dry branches. It is no wonder if with such a luxuriant theological aesthetics "energies, signs and symbols overflow their banks" and men and women need only gratefully and traditionally "float along in the stream from the origin of God into the future of God."

A theology for the men and women of today? In any case theology can in such a manner dispense with demanding Church reform. Which according to Balthasar means: "To run against institutions as Don Quixote against the windmills." *De facto* all the unnumbered persons suffering under the institution (birth control, divorce, celibacy, official arrogancies of the most various kinds, etc.) will in a "serious case" hardly find support from this subtle spiritualized theology: such a theology, although it constantly has the word "love" in its mouth, floats past the real suffering of men and women, precisely that of many men and women in the Roman Catholic Church. Thus one relatively easily makes an arrangement with all of the problematic elements in Church history and the present: through an aesthetic excessive elevation and a mystical transfiguration.

The dilemma of such a theology is shown by the contribution of the Freiburg dogmatic theologian Helmut Riedlinger on Mariology in a moving form; his inner conflict between faith and knowledge finds respect. Concerning Mary he has to admit: "the cleft between historical-critical knowledge and the faith of the Church is deep." However, he does not enter into debate with a single argument of historical-critical exegesis and history of dogmas; he grounds not a single one of his mariological affirmations. Stat pro ratione voluntas: all exegetical, historical, systematic, practical difficulties must be ignored in order to justify all of the developments of Catholic Mariology up to Pius XII and to hold off the self-prophesied "collapse" of the Roman Catholic faith.

The Heretic Hat of Arius

Arrangement III: Through the harmonizing of dogma history! For example: Alois Grillmeier on the Sonship of God.

With much historical erudition the Frankfurt Jesuit demonstrates at first, in many pages, undisputed items (Hellenistic elements in heretics, juridical elements in the Greeks). However, he precisely did not refute that which was maintained by me: that already the first Ecumenical Council of Nicaea in A.D. 325 expressed the original message of Christ through the dogma of the "Son of God, one substance with the Father" in a very time-conditioned Hellenistic language, conceptuality, and thought form. The heretics (and the hereticizing) had at that time "Hellenized"; the Councils (naturally only the orthodox), however, "de-Hellenized": thus sounds the touchingly simple information of the historian who is directed by dogmatic interests concerning this Council which nevertheless (despite "de-Hellenizing") unmistakably remains within the Hellenistic horizon and its imagery ("essence," "substance," "hypostasis," "homousious"!). For the genuine concerns of many Christians and the founded difficulties of Jews and Muslims with the belief in one God, as well as for the doubts of many, even Catholic, exegetes and historians of dogma (not only the Harnacks and Bultmans) concerning the Hellenization (already prepared for in the later New Testament writings) of the Christian original message by Greek theology and Church, our historian has nothing but apologetics and polemics (the lantern of historical-critical reason!).

Already Grillmeier's jubilee article for the 1,500-year celebration of the Council of Chalcedon (1951) on the development of the Christ dogma was a parade example in the Catholic area of an ever more knowledgeable but yet apologetic-harmonizing writing of the history of dogma: which certainly made possible an apparently modern arrangement with dogmas which today are difficult to reconstruct, but which in reality nevertheless do not help contemporary men and women any further. Grillmeier's present article makes no decisive progress. Indeed, even he now demands a "new description of what is Christian which is understandable, perceivable, and implementable." But his own contribution peaks in a pleading for a stereotypical repetition of Hellenistic formulas and energies of the Trinity and Incarnation formed 1,500 years ago—as if precisely the two major doctrines were thus simply biblical, had not already divided the ancient Church, and for the non-historian today were still "understandable, perceivable, and implementable"! Against such traditionalism I hold fast to the thesis which was worked out by Rahner and myself jointly and was accepted by the International Congress for Theology in Brussels in 1970: "The great christological confessions and definitions of the past have their abiding significance also for the Church of the present. However, they cannot be interpreted outside of their historical context or indeed only stereotypically repeated. In order to speak to men and women of different times and cultures, the Christian message must ever again be stated anew."

Five years later I attempted to make good this thesis of that time in a "new description of the Christian," without expecting gratitude for it precisely from Grillmeier. I certainly do not contemplate putting on the heretic's hat of Arius which is proffered by him. And I also do not allow it to be put on the pre-Nicaean Fathers: Grillmeier, who tendentiously gathers together my sentences which are suspicious of heresy to him, also holds the great theologians of the first 300 years before Nicaea to be *de facto* (material) heretics

because they subordinated Jesus as Son to the Father ("sub-
ordinationists"). I must, however, mention one scandal (and
one understands now also why it was not wished that I be
granted even one page for my response in the volume of
collected essays!), that Grillmeier smoothly suppresses my
central statement on the problematic: the express information not only of the great intentions of the Council of Nicaea
(*On Being a Christian*, p. 448), but also of the Sonship of
God of Jesus (the "vere Deus" of the Council of Chalcedon,
A.D. 451, interpreted according to the Scripture and the
times): "The whole point of what happened in and with
Jesus depends on the fact that, for believers, *God himself* as
the friend of men and women was present, at work, speaking,
acting, and definitively revealing himself *in this Jesus* who
came among men and women as God's advocate and deputy,
representative and delegate, and was confirmed by God as
the Crucified raised to life" (*On Being a Christian*, p. 449).

With this summary formula an acceptable (even for theologians more dependent upon the letter), broadly common
christological consensus might be formulated with which a
contemporary woman or man can in any case live as a Christian and which could possibly be theologically broadened: of
course not through the repetition of old saws, schoolmaster's
instructions, and sniffing out of heresies, but through understanding, fair discussion in the consciousness of the difficult
problematic for both sides. Catholic theology is, as precisely
this volume bears witness, a theology in transition.

No: Whither?—There Is Only: Halt!

Not everything in this volume of essays is gray against gray
and black against a black background. At least subliminal
differences, indeed contradictions, are discernible, which
should be listed.

The exegetes are interested above all in whether the join-
ing of systematic theology to biblical theology which has for
a long time been desired has finally been obtained and suggest discussable improvements of detail. Orthodoxy is not

their problem, suspicion of heresy not their concern. The Freiburg Old Testament scholar Alfons Deissler: "Here the essential element of the Old Testament message of God is set in relief as it seldom is in the non-exegetical literature." Also the Viennese New Testament scholar Jacob Kremer: The book offers a "by no means uncritical," but extremely "outstanding evaluation of the fullness of exegetical investigations which can hardly be covered by the professional exegetes themselves": this may—in contrast to Balthasar's judgment—"be numbered among the best writings which in recent times have come out about Jesus of Nazareth."

One sees: between the exegetes and the dogmaticians characteristic contradictions show themselves in this transition phase! Balthasar: "The Protestant thesis that the prophets were against the institution (temple, priesthood, hierarchy) is historically absolutely false." In contrast Deissler, not a Protestant: "known cult-critical (and temple-critical!) texts of the prophets can in this connection not be simply ignored." Or Rahner as we heard on the founding of the Church: "We Catholic Christians will . . ." In contrast Kremer, also a Catholic Christian: "the rather assured results of the recent exegeses: that, namely, Jesus on the one hand maintained an imminent expectation of the eschaton and did not immediately intend any founding of the Church." Kremer's explanation that "a naïve, uncritical reading of the Bible," which there "has been for centuries," "is for the reader of the twentieth century no longer the ideal and proper approach to the Holy Scriptures," could be written directly against Balthasar, Grillmeier (and Riedlinger's Mariology). Catholic theology in transition! With the passage of time will dogmatics nevertheless work constructively with the results of exegesis?

In view of this "discussion volume" itself, that hope is not to be given up. For example: in contrast to Grillmeier, the Mainz theologian Theodor Schneider works very progressively. Listen: This dogmatician grants the notorious difficulties of the classical triunity doctrine, affirms the critique from the perspective of the New Testament, acknowledges the efforts for a continuity with the great tradition: "Küng consciously stands on the ground of the Church's doctrine of the Trinity and repeats this in all brevity correctly and even in its content. From that it would be wrong to accuse him of 'heretical' thoughts or to wish to insinuate such an impression!" However, if Schneider now looks at Grillmeier, Balthasar, and Rahner, he can certainly understand even better the necessity of constantly critical "disengagements" from the traditional doctrine. Concerning the inner-Divine triunity many more today are inclining toward a "theologia negativa" because they are not convinced not only by the unbiblical "very abstractedly constructed speculation" of the "School tractates," but also by those mentioned here by Rahner, Ratzinger, and Kasper. Schneider himself unfortunately offers no further suggestions. Precisely that is symptomatic for this entire volume: It raises only a halt, never a whither!

Ecumenical perspectives in this otherwise so little ecumenical volume open the inquiry of the Freiburg dogmatician Karl Lehmann. With the exegetes and other younger dogmaticians he affirms fundamentally a new theology which "could entice many men and women out of their reserve toward the Christianity handed down and perhaps after many years of alienation for the first time be brought closer to the spirit of Christianity." Lehmann's inquiries, although, as with his teacher Rahner's, they are made all too securely from the rock of Roman Catholic truth, must be seriously discussed. *On Being a Christian* assumes *de facto* an understanding in the Church-dividing controversial questions, which, having been theologically prepared by many, is possible today, and long since has been carried out by numberless individuals. Only through such a finally, yet-to-be-implemented ecumenical union can the "Church homelessness," complained of by Lehmann, of so many Christians between the Churches be overcome.

How problematic, however, the here-noted progress of a theology in transition is, is shown by the dogmatician Walter

Kasper, who newly asks about the ecclesial quality of my being a Christian. Even he has long since passed the point of no return. Even he finds the Scripture to be the "authoritative original witness," and wishes to attend to the "signs of the time." Even he appears to "implement theologically the modern turn toward humanity"; historical-critical research can "help" "faith to be responsible before itself and before others." Thus he "candidly" demands "a breaking out of the prison of traditional School theology." "No going back!" Even he!

Where Is the Consistency?

And yet concerning the relationship between Scripture, tradition, and the teaching office—since Luther's days the cross of Roman Catholic theology—he would like to turn back the time about twenty years. He critically investigates my "development" and wishes that I might nevertheless be as I was at the time of my doctoral dissertation, as though development were something bad—more precisely: as if a system-conforming development were the best for a churchly-thinking theologian. As if it were not much more important that a development—according to the standard of the Christian message itself—should be correct, consistent, and well grounded.

Kasper sees in me the danger of subjectivism, immanentism, functionalism—incorrectly, I believe. What, however, provides for him an unshakably objective certitude? Kasper, with the late Johann Adam Möhler (1835): "Nothing but the Church, Church, Church!" The Church, however, understood as the teaching office church, and this then the "presupposition of all presuppositions," in a churchly doctrinal system which circles within itself. Numerous compromises and harmonizations between traditional doctrine and the results of contemporary exegesis and history of dogmas —from apostolic succession to Christology—are the consequences. As with others in this group, this theology, at least up until today, lacks consistency. The book *The Church*

(1967), against which only in the past year the Roman Inquisition proceedings was closed, Kasper names today my
"most beautiful book." Too much honor. However, who
knows what the future will yet bring . . .

A Missed Chance

This volume—with its subliminal anxieties, glaring contradictions, fundamental hermeneutical-methodological unclarities, and covert denunciatory tendencies—is for Catholic
theology a missed opportunity—viewed in general, a theology in an ivory tower without a positive result: Those who
know better know nothing better! A volume by theologians:
not for contemporary men and women and their real problems, but rather for theologians and their inner-theological
needs. A professor's theology for theology professors!
Throughout, an allergy against criticism of the institutional
Church—without counterarguments! Throughout, an anxiety
about what has been officially defined—without their own solution! Throughout, an anxiety about reason, reasonableness,
plausibility—without alternatives! All this a signal of the
fundamental crisis of a theology in transition whose foundation is not truly critically questioned.

I do not intend *a priori* to deny dogmatically defined elements. I do not intend to maintain that my interpretations
are infallible. However, in distinction to my counterplayers,
whose action in the first line is about dogmas, tradition, and
the teaching office, I am above all concerned about the Scriptures explained for today, about the living Christ, about the
practical being a Christian. And for this—in the midst of the
Church community!—I also wish to continue to work. I am
little concerned about a dispute concerning dogmas, as important as they are. What is more important to me than a
Christ theory is a theological and churchly Christ belief and
Christ following.

One could have done something really great and helpful
for theology and for all men and women who wish to believe
with an authentic discussion volume. Nevertheless, there hap-

pily are even in the German language area respected Catholic theologians like J. Blank, H. Fries, M. Löhrer, G. Lohfink, O. H. Pesch, F. Schierse, who likewise take a critical-positive attitude toward the interpretations put forth in *On Being a Christian,* as well as many Protestants (E. Schweizer, L. Raiser, H. Zahrnt), but also very many practical pastors, religion teachers, theology students, and unnumbered representatives of a non-Catholic public; but their views are not allowed to come to expression in this volume. Only the German (Catholic) dogmaticians are (to some extent) proportionately represented: not the exegetes, not the historians, not the fundamental theologians, not the ethicists, not the pastoral theologians, not the religious educationalists—not to speak at all of Protestant or of non-German theology! Also from this perspective a missed opportunity.

The only consolation: of the eleven gathered together here —in order to come back to the initial image, which with its humor allows one to bear the too great seriousness—each plays much more convincingly on his own playing field. Would it not have been better in general to have formed a common team instead of attempting to outmaneuver a player in this or that manner? Would not collaborative effort be a proper reaction to a book like *On Being a Christian?* Would it not be better finally to have done with suspicions? Would it not be more sensible, instead of getting stuck in negative defense and protection, to put forth a common effort toward better theological answers for the men and women of today? —and all that without over-anxiety about the truth, according to the great intentions of John XXIII or the Second Vatican Council: "The 'vital' point of this Council is not, therefore, a discussion of one article or another of the fundamental doctrine of the Church, which has repeatedly been taught by the Fathers and by ancient and modern theologians, and which is presumed to be well known and familiar to all." But rather, "a step forward toward a penetration of doctrine and a formation of conscience in faithful and perfect conformity with the authentic doctrine, which, however, should be studied and expounded through the methods of research and the literary formulations of modern thought. The substance of the ancient doctrine of the deposit of faith is one thing, and the way in which it is presented is another. And it is the latter that must be taken into consideration with patience if necessary, everything being measured in the forms and proportions of a teaching office which is predominantly pastoral in character."

Then on June 24, 1976, Cardinal Döpfner responded to Küng, acknowledging the discussion Küng had had at Rome and spending a large measure of his letter commenting on Küng's response to his critics and implications he saw therein. Tendentiously the German Bishops' Conference's December 1979 *Documentation* (and the English translation, *The Küng Dialogue*) published this letter of Cardinal Döpfner's but not the precipitating article by Küng or his long response in which he vigorously defended his position. Moreover, it should be noted that this exchange of letters was consciously on a more formal basis, with Cardinal Döpfner fulfilling the role of the President of the German Bishops' Conference. Hence matters were probaby put more sharply than they would have been had they been "personal" letters characterized by "Dear Fellow Brother" and *"Du."* Cardinal Döpfner wrote:

(51)

Very honored Professor Küng,
    Unfortunately only today after my three-week journey in Africa can I confirm the reception of your letter of April 27 of this year and to thank you for it.
    I have taken note with interest of the report on your conversations with Cardinal Šeper and with Archbishop Hamer as well as the presentation of your view of the critique published until now of your book *On Being a Christian.*
    Since I also am of the opinion that this letter is of interest to the members of the Bishops' Conference I have first of all

handed over your letter to the chairman of the Doctrinal Commission and requested that the Doctrinal Commission discuss the substantive questions which have once again been brought up through the conversations.

Of course I must state that your "response to my critics" in the *F.A.Z.* of May 22 has disappointed me not a little. After your letter in which you report of your comprehensive dealing with the essays in the volume of collected essays, *Discussion of Hans Küng's "On Being a Christian,"* I had expected a response which was more related to the substance of things.

Indeed in your letter you spoke of the desire to take up the questions and doubts of your critics in a scholarly fashion and you emphasized expressly that clarifications and corrections, expansions and deepenings of your standpoint were quite possible. But, my dear Professor Küng, I have long waited for these clarifications. Time and again in various connections during recent years you have made such promises.

Your response to the "critics" would have been an extremely apt opportunity to prove this in fact.

Therefore I must recall to you the urgent appeal which the German Bishops' Conference made to you at the conclusion of their Declaration of February 17, 1975, namely, "to review his methodological procedure and the complained-about substantive statements of his theological thought in light of the fundamental propositions here laid out."

If you, however, value your "critics" so little as your answer in the *F.A.Z.* makes apparent, it is hardly believable that this review after well over a year has even begun.

Such a serious review I have always understood as an essential constitutive part of the "new style" of clarification of doctrinal opinions which can be described as mistaken or as false. I could quite rightly also expect this from you.

Repeatedly in public and in your letters to me you have declared yourself ready to review the complained-about utterances from your side. Unfortunately to this hour this has *de facto* not happened. On the contrary, the statements in your *F.A.Z.* article give the impression that such a review of your standpoint is ultimately out of the question for you. In your letter of April 27, you merely again express the hope of finding time in the foreseeable future to take up again in a scholarly fashion the questions raised.

With all of this you create for the Bishops a new situation. That I regret this very much needs of course no emphasis.

Therefore I once again urgently ask of you seriously to reflect on the complained-about methodological procedure and the substantive statements that have been questioned in the Declaration of the German Bishops' Conference of February 17, 1975, and to review them.

With friendly greetings,

Yours,

Julius Cardinal Döpfner

Küng responded almost immediately to Döpfner on June 28, 1976, outlining a detailed defense of his actions. It was his last letter to Cardinal Döpfner. On July 24, 1976, Döpfner was suddenly stricken with a heart attack and died. For all the hardheaded communications, both in writing and in speech, the two men had with each other, there was a fundamental mutual respect and sympathy and a willingness on the part of Cardinal Döpfner to exert himself strenuously in all directions to keep dialogue going between Küng and Church authorities until acceptable solutions could be arrived at. Given such an attitude and record, as the Archbishop of Munich, the most populous and powerful see in Germany, and as the President of the German Bishops' Conference, Cardinal Döpfner was in a position to translate his attitude into effective action and thereby allow Küng to do his theology fully within the authority structures of the Catholic Church. After his death he was replaced by Joseph Ratzinger as Cardinal Archbishop of Munich and Cardinal Joseph Höffner of Cologne as President of the German Bishops' Conference. Both men's attitudes and actions leaned in quite other directions than did

Döpfner's as far as Küng and progressive theology were concerned. That dramatic change in Germany and the coming of the new Pope, John Paul II—with a very conservative theological and disciplinary bent—presented a "new situation" far beyond whatever Cardinal Döpfner had in mind when he used the phrase in his last letter. Küng's June 28, 1976, letter to Cardinal Döpfner was as follows:

(52)

Very honored Cardinal,

I thank you for your letter of June 24, 1976. Therein you present the view that the Doctrinal Commission will discuss the substantive questions raised again by the conversations and you presume several times that I am not prepared to subject my interpretations to a serious review. I am not a little astonished by this. Allow me the following comments:

1. In what concerns the infallibility and Church questions —the sole subjects of the last Roman Declaration—I have reviewed the entire literature that has appeared, carefully examined the reasoned criticism, and attempted to work up in the form of a balanced report the many positive aspects of the ecclesiastical teaching integrated with theological tradition. After this volume of collected essays no further theological responses came forth.

2. In the discussion of *On Being a Christian* I have since the appearance of the book devoted myself to the clarification, review, and deepening of those disputed dogmatic questions which I myself likewise in the book declared to be in need of further theological examination. I spelled all this out in my last letter to you. To show that we are dealing here not with simple lip "promises," I would like to refer to the following facts:

A three-day colloquium with doctoral students on a comparison of Walter Kasper's *Jesus the Christ* and *On Being a Christian;*

A further three-day colloquium with doctoral students on the volume of collected essays *Discussion of Hans Küng's "On Being a Christian"*;

Several colloquia lasting many hours with well-known exegetes on the substantive questions which are under debate, especially in Christology;

A seminar during the summer semester which has just ended on the referred-to "discussion volume," which ended with a disputation between Walter Kasper and myself;

With a large number of the authors of the volume of collected essays I have carried on discussions about the problems concerned or have exchanged letters, etc.

All this shows, my dear Cardinal, that I in no way "value my critics so little" but that I attempt to give a conscientious reckoning of the points which have been complained about to me. Of course, for a long time I also awaited truly helpful constructive contributions from my colleagues which took seriously the present exegetical, history of dogma, and systematic state of research. The volume of collected essays which was co-edited by various advisers of the Doctrinal Commission was in this aspect not just for me an extremely large disappointment.

3. Concerning the discussion that was provoked by the referred-to "discussion volume," may I in addition to what I said in my last letter make the following supplementary remarks:

a. A completely different reaction from my side would have been possible if the contributions from Balthasar, Grillmeier, Rahner, and Ratzinger had also shown the same constructive willingness to engage in discussion as did the contributions of Deissler, Kasper, Kremer, Lehmann, and Schneider; if one had not, to my great regret, called forth a decisive defense of my Catholic orthodoxy with general putdowns and *de facto* hereticizations; and if my response to the questions of the colleagues could have followed in the same volume of collected essays.

b. Since the "discussion volume" had experienced an enormous and above all also an indirect publicity (through a defamation campaign in specific papers and elsewhere), I was forced to an answer in a larger forum. Since unfortunately there is no longer a Catholic weekly newspaper which could have given such an article the necessary space, I had to turn to the serious daily press. Concerning my *F.A.Z.* article may I make the following remarks:

My response moves on the purely theological level and refrains from all dispute with the doctrinal office. My article gives a response that is completely appropriate to the material and indeed precisely also to the "methodological procedure" that you say needs to be clarified.

In reference to the "substantive statements" I limited my newspaper article to a clear confession of the Sonship of God of Jesus; to say more about substantive questions like preexistence, Incarnation, Trinity, Church, etc., in a daily newspaper was impossible. Perhaps the title, "Response to my Critics," which was chosen by the editors of the *F.A.Z.* itself, did not sufficiently bring out the notion that this was only my first response to my critics, in which I expressly spoke out in favor of a "common effort toward better theological answers for the men and women of today."

Further publications on remaining substantive questions are in preparation. First I must now, as already announced in *On Being a Christian,* deal with the many substantive questions lying at the basis of the God question. In order not to escalate the matter further I have until now not responded to the letter to the editor by Balthasar and other theologians in the *F.A.Z.*

In conclusion may I, my dear Cardinal, say: This "discussion," which likewise is not very pleasant for me, was not set in motion in this form by me. From my side I have, as before so also now, no interest in a further escalation and would be thankful if I could be spared it. The discussion contributions of the authors of the volume of collected essays have made only too clear how difficult it is to answer these questions even by those very theologians who criticize me. Construc-

tive further work will be the most important thing for all
sides. A "new situation," in view of the above, does not
appear to me to be at hand.

I hope, my dear Cardinal, with this supplementary information to have provided a help for the evaluation of the situation, and send you my friendly greetings.

Yours sincerely,

Hans Küng

cc: Cardinal Dr. Hermann Volk, Mainz, President of the
Doctrinal Commission
Bishop Dr. Georg Moser, Rottenburg

The Stuttgart
Colloquium, 1977

As the President pro tem of the German Bishops' Conference, Cardinal Höffner forwarded to Küng a letter Cardinal Döpfner had drafted to him but which could not be typed before his death. It was a proposal of a discussion or colloquium. The August 31, 1976, letter of Cardinal Höffner was as follows:

(53)

Dear Professor Küng:

On the day before his unexpected death Cardinal Döpfner had drafted the letter below. The letter was to be typed the next day, July 24, and mailed, but that never took place.

The following was the text of the letter:

Dear Professor Küng:

Many thanks for your letter of June 28, 1976, which you also sent to Cardinal Volk and Bishop Moser of Rottenburg.

In the meanwhile the Doctrinal Commission of the German Bishops' Conference, at my request, has discussed the newly arisen situation. On the basis of the responses I have received, I suggest a discussion to clarify some key questions concerning *On Being a Christian*. I hope that this discussion will lead to a clear agreement in our common faith and eliminate some confusing matters which have arisen in connection with your book.

If you wish, I would happily agree to inviting one of your colleagues to participate in this discussion. On my side I would like to bring Cardinal Volk, Bishop Moser, as well as Professors Lehmann and Ratzinger as participants in the discussion.

Today I would like to ask for your agreement in principle to this discussion. The discussion could take place at the Catholic Academy of the Diocese of Rottenburg in Stuttgart-Hohenheim.

After I receive your answer I will ask Prelate Dr. Homeyer, who returns from vacation on August 8, 1976, to arrange with you the exact date of the discussion. I am thinking of the second half of September or October of this year.

With friendly greetings,

Yours,
(Julius Card. Döpfner)

After speaking with Cardinal Volk, I suggest that the discussion be held as proposed by Cardinal Döpfner. Therefore, I have asked Dr. Homeyer to get in touch with you about the precise date.

Probably the discussion could not take place before October. By that time the new President of the German Bishops' Conference will have been elected. If need be, he will be able to participate in the discussion.

With friendly greetings,

Yours,
Joseph Card. Höffner
President pro tem of the
German Bishops' Conference

Küng immediately (on September 4, 1976) answered Höffner, saying: "It touches me deeply that the President of the German Bishops' Conference, who was always greatly appreciated by me, even immediately before his death—which has also personally hit me hard—had drafted a letter inviting me to a discussion, which now his successor will conduct for him. I am happy to declare myself in principle prepared for a discussion which will clarify several central theological questions in reference to *On Being a Christian.*"

In an October 19, 1976, letter to Cardinal Höffner, who had just been elected the successor to Cardinal Döpfner, Küng noted: "That means that the minutes of such an openly conducted discussion will in no way be used against me. I request that you, my dear Cardinal, expressly assure me of this." In his December 9, 1976, letter to Küng, the Secretary of the German Bishops' Conference, Monsignor Josef Homeyer, wrote: "Cardinal Höffner is prepared to arrange at the beginning of the discussion that the tape recording and the minutes will be utilized by neither side. Cardinal Höffner expressly confirms that this discussion is not a discussion in the sense of section 5 of the Doctrinal Complaint Proceedings of the German Bishops' Conference." Among those who had been suggested from the Bishops' side as participants in the Colloquium was then Professor Joseph Ratzinger of the University of Regensberg, formerly a colleague of Küng's at Tübingen and later the Cardinal Archbishop of Munich. Walter Jens in *Wahrheit,* p. 213, noted that "the objections of Professor Küng against Monsignor Professor Ratzinger stem from his unobjective contributions to the discussions in the volumes of collected essays against *Infallible?* and *On Being a Christian.*" Hence, he did not take part in the Colloquium.

Jens also explained why (p. 214) Küng allowed the transcript of the four-hour Colloquium to be published in the book of documentation edited by Jens (*Wahrheit*) as a corrective to what was considered the improper and tendentious *Documentation* of the German Bishops. Jens wrote (p. 214): "Despite this assurance [of confidentiality by Cardinal Höffner], however, the Colloquium was later used against Küng in connection with the second as well as the third public Declaration of the German Bishops' Conference on *On Being a Christian* and was used as an argument for the doctrinal complaint action. Since the German

Bishops' Conference, through the use of the Colloquium minutes against Küng as well as the inclusion of his personal letters to the President in a 'documentation' that was made public, broke the expected confidentiality, they forced Küng to a public defense: only with the full knowledge of this Colloquium and the previous and following correspondence is it possible objectively to evaluate the later public objections of the Bishops' Conference as well as the dispute in general."

The Colloquium took place at the Catholic Academy (a conference center) of Stuttgart-Hohenheim from 10 A.M. to 2 P.M. on January 22, 1977. The transcription of the minutes from the tape recording was done at the office of the Secretariat of the German Bishops' Conference and sent to all the participants on April 12, 1977. The transcription is as follows:

(54)
April 12, 1977

Participants: Cardinal Joseph Höffner, Archbishop of Cologne; Cardinal Hermann Volk, Bishop of Mainz; Dr. Georg Moser, Bishop of Rottenburg; Professor Hans Küng, Tübingen; Professor Johannes Neumann, Tübingen; Professor Karl Lehmann, Freiburg; Professor Otto Semmelroth, Frankfurt

Concerning: Colloquium on January 22, 1977, in Stuttgart-Hohenheim

Transcript of the Colloquium

Reverend gentlemen!

In response to the commission given in the Colloquium on January 22, 1977, the ladies here in the Secretariat have taken pains to provide a transcription from the tape recording of the Colloquium at that time.

The recording was technically extremely defective, so that the transcription was almost impossible for the poor secretaries.

I am therefore all the more grateful that I am now able to forward to you the transcription.

At the same time may I recall the agreement to treat this transcription in confidence.

With friendly greetings,

Yours,
Homeyer
(Dr. Homeyer)

Enclosure: *Confidential*

Prefatory Remark

The following transcription is the stylistically worked-over version of the tape recording. Only in a *few* places *within* individual statements—which are indicated by parenthetical markings (. . .)—what was spoken could not be accurately reconstructed because of phonetic-acoustical defects. Since in no case did this concern central statements it appeared better to leave out these statements. Citations, above all from *On Being a Christian,* were verified. The Colloquium lasted from 10 A.M. to 2 P.M.

Cardinal Höffner:

Gentlemen, I greet you all very warmly and I am grateful to the two of you (= Professors Küng and Neumann) that even at the last minute the appointment could be moved up to 10 A.M. Further, I understand that it is agreeable to all that we have planned to continue the Colloquium to about 1 P.M., until lunch. Much more than three hours is likewise hardly to be considered (*Cardinal Volk:* at most).

Now a couple of prefatory remarks, first of all concerning the character of the Colloquium:

It is not a Colloquium in the sense of section 5 of the Doctrinal Complaint Proceedings. Such a Colloquium would indeed also have to be conducted with the competent local bishop, with you (= Bishop Moser), but rather this should be a Colloquium with the representatives of the episcopal office. And you, Professor Küng, have indeed also in your last letter formulated the matter thus expressly With the representatives of the episcopal office, and indeed we are here

upon the commission of the Bishops' Conference, therefore
not as the Doctrinal Commission of the Bishops' Conference,
but rather as representatives of the Bishops' Conference insofar as we likewise represent the episcopal office.

Now, what should be the goal of the Colloquium? According to my reflections, we should think back to the Declaration of the German Bishops' Conference of February 17–20,
1975. In this Declaration it was stated that your book, Professor, *On Being a Christian,* contained a series of statements
which did not show themselves to be compatible with the
three fundamental principles which we at that time, in February 1975, at the Bishops' Conference had put forth: namely,
(1) how certain statements of your book would be compatible with the normative meaning of the ecclesiastical tradition
of faith, and (2) how they fit into the correct relationship
between the teaching office and theological scholarship, and
(3) how they could correspond to the concrete binding quality of the faith. We also indicated at that time which points
in your book had occasioned us to make this statement. We
indicated statements concerning Christology, the doctrine of
the Trinity, the theology of the Church and sacraments, and
the position of Mary in salvation history. When I look at this
Declaration of February 1975, then I believe that the role of
the Colloquium today should be to clarify these difficult
doubts and—if possible—to erase them. Your letter likewise
gives me special hope in this matter, that is, the letter which
you wrote in April of the previous year to the late Cardinal
Döpfner. It probably would be well for the thematic of our
Colloquium—we indeed do not have unlimited time at our
disposal—if we were to discipline ourselves somewhat to
concentrate on the following themes, and indeed I would
think if we would then also remain with your book, that is,
the text of your book.

(1) There would be a first question area, the question
concerning the binding quality of the christological decisions
of the Councils of Nicaea and Chalcedon. (2) One could then
here immediately specify the first point somewhat, namely,

the binding quality especially in connection with the Sonship of God and the eternal pre-existence of Jesus Christ. (3) A third question area would be taken from soteriology, as it, for example, comes out in your statements concerning the significance of the death of Jesus and the representing of Jesus. And finally (4) a fourth question area: the status of the doctrinal decisions of the Councils in relation to Christology. What status do these ancient Councils have? From all this it emerges that in the four points which I have mentioned there stands behind them really an ecclesiological question, namely, your understanding of the Church.

Concerning the method of the Colloquium I would suggest the following: that (1) our fellow brother Cardinal Volk, as a former dogmatics professor, be made the moderator. Then (2) that we—and this has already been agreed upon in our letters—record the Colloquium on tape, and (3) if so, then the third would be that a résumé would be drawn up in writing and the tape recording would also be transcribed so that then the transcription would be given to all participants. That would perhaps be sufficient for now concerning method. However, I would still like to add something further concerning the confidentiality of this Colloquium. According to my conviction, it would be correct if we proceeded on the assumption that we will keep this confidential, that it, for example, not be given to the mass media, but that it must be kept confidential. We have to indeed agree upon this *here* and now. Would there be something to say relative to this question of confidentiality? Or perhaps would something result only from the Colloquium itself? However, for the moment I would in the beginning see the matter as I have just now described it.

These are the few prefatory remarks that I wish to state beforehand. Would there be any further remarks concerning this?

Professor Küng:

Might I perhaps at the very beginning make a few fundamental remarks which I believe could help in part to provide an answer for the questions which come up here. I would not like to neglect to thank you, first of all, the Bishops, for extending the invitation to this Colloquium, for I believe that it is not in vain that I come to this Colloquium. It appears to me that this is precisely the right way to speak of these matters, and I know that you (= the Bishops) in the midst of your various burdens must nevertheless ascribe an enormous weight to such a matter if you take out this time. I applaud that sincerely. I cannot really imagine that matters will appear worse afterwards than before this attempt to formulate something in general.

I had perhaps eight points which already move somewhat in the direction of a response. I would naturally like to make them as brief as possible.

1. The first is: one will indeed understand this book (*On Being a Christian*) only if one understands the pastoral intention which stands behind it. If it concerned pure scholarship then perhaps the matter would have been attacked with less verve, certainly with less passion. I am concerned to take up the questions of men and women of today and—as well as I possibly can—to answer them. I have not, I insist, invented a single question which is in there, but rather, they are questions which are widely discussed among men and women of today—this is likewise the opinion of my colleagues in theology; in this sense therefore I attempted to give a pastoral response. And I have likewise appreciated it that in the "Declaration" (February 1975) that was seen and emphasized really for the first time, that in any case in my own manner I attempt to serve the Church. I believe—and I may say this honestly—that otherwise one could probably not explain the persistence with which I—both opportunely and inopportunely—pursue certain matters. That is really the first thing which I wish to say.

2. A second is connected somewhat with the selection of the questions. I have nothing to object to them insofar as here there are special difficulties. However, I would nevertheless from my side emphasize that the entire book of

course is a great deal more! While I look at the questions here then they are in essence concerned with fifty pages, and even there again entire large sections provide probably no difficulties, for example, concerning God and suffering, etc. . . . . If one would look precisely at where the problems lie, they cover a relatively small space. I am naturally concerned—I have, I believe, made an unusual effort—to bring Jesus himself as the crucified and awakened one nearer to the men and women of today. And, I believe, the sharpest opponents have granted that here also something not unimportant has taken place. I have just now read the review of Helmut Riedlinger, the second contribution to the discussion by Helmut Reidlinger (cf. "Radikale Rationalität," in *Theologie und Philosophie,* 51, 1976, pp. 185–95), who brings this out really more clearly than anywhere else. I would nevertheless like to request that whatever is discussed here always be seen within the context of the whole. It would be indeed possible that, especially under the circumstances, the dogmatic questions, whose importance I do not wish to dispute, could now be somewhat overdrawn in their significance on account of the pastoral concern, if one views them in all too isolated a manner. In any case, I believe, many have understood those things which I have wanted to say very positively.

3. The third point concerns somewhat the question of method, which here indeed certainly plays a very great role, as in all questions, which you (= Cardinal Höffner) have just now alluded to. The material questions, one would have to note, are indeed addressed clearly enough in the book. It is the so-called method "from below" that is followed, certainly not in the sense as if here in some way God and his reality and everything which at the same time comes "from above" should be excluded; on the contrary, I have—I believe—in these matters taken a very clear position, even in the question of the Awakening. However, it should be on the one hand gone at from the questions of men and women and on the other hand likewise from what the disciples of Jesus had seen at that time, as reported in the New Testament.

From there I slowly come to the higher questions which now
lie especially here before us in discussion. I grant that coming as I do "from below" I naturally have greater difficulties
in embracing the dogmatic statements of the tradition. I
would like only to raise the point that conversely the traditional dogmatics, as it is widely conducted, has extremely
great difficulties very often in taking the historical Jesus himself seriously and integrating such things as, for example, the
Sermon on the Mount, etc.; it concerns therefore the connection, which is very important to me—and this already indicates progress—between dogmatics and ethics and how to
express it. They are, therefore, things which I can again
make easier, but I acknowledge the difficulties. I would only
like to raise the point that I know the starting point "from
above" and you can assume here in the entire conversation
that on the basis of my seven Roman years the current explanation of the dogmas is very well known to me. I have, I believe, properly passed my exams and I have studied the matter very well and I know whereof I speak. Likewise, I began
with Karl Barth with the starting point "from above" and
have likewise written the book *Menschwerdung Gottes* completely from the perspective of "from above." I have, however, there likewise shown why this starting point does not
appear satisfactory to me. Therefore, one would have to, I
believe, see what the method "from below" means.

4. A fourth point is probably also important and has been
expressed by me in various letters. I have always clearly expressed my readiness to learn and also my readiness to make
corrections. If one says to me that is only verbal, then I cannot view that as correct. My books and the entire path which
I have followed show that I have undertaken a not merely
usual measure of constant new learning. It is also not correct
if one says I would not take seriously the objections of my
colleagues in theology. I know no one who has so thoroughly
engaged in an exchange with the objections. I do not see
that, for example, with Karl Rahner, who from one side was
attacked at least as much and to this very day has hardly en-

gaged in an exchange on certain matters. I say that only for comparison: I have in the infallibility debate published a volume of over 500 pages in order to spell that out. I have likewise now again taken the latest volume of collected essays (namely, *Discussion of Hans Küng's "On Being a Christian"*) very seriously. I have conducted a three-day colloquium with my doctoral students on the comparison of Walter Kasper's Christ book with my book. I have conducted another three-day colloquium with doctoral students on the volume of collected essays concerning *On Being a Christian*. I have conducted several colloquia of many hours' duration in order to clarify those matters with well-known exegetes (Catholic as well as Protestant), for example, Jeremias (therefore also traditional exegetes) and exegetes such as Ernst Käsemann, Gerhardt Lohfink, and others. Finally, I have conducted an entire seminar on this discussion volume. This shows that I take this matter completely seriously and that certainly likewise in the future I can probably clarify still other things. I cannot do everything at once, but perhaps I can still provide some information. This, therefore, concerning my readiness to make corrections—it is meant seriously.

5. The fifth point: concerning the discussion. I am certain —and that was likewise expressed by Cardinal Döpfner at that time in his letter—that my article in the *Frankfurter Allgemeine Zeitung* (May 22, 1976) in any case was not so understood as I would have liked to have it understood. One must see that my disappointment with the reaction precisely also from the advisers from the Bishops' Conference in this matter (they are indeed in great part represented in the volume of collected essays) was extremely great. I could understand that the disturbance in connection with *Infallible?* was great. I was conscious that I had taken up a tabooed question and that naturally something was stirred up—how very much I was at that time concerned to avoid these matters, as, for example, in the discussion with Karl Rahner, which then finally did come out. I could speak on this for a long time.

But good. I could understand that. What I could not understand at all, and what explains the vigor of my reaction, is that no one helped at all to work through this great exchange between Christianity and modern society in view of all those who today in the Federal Republic of Germany, and far beyond it, do not wish to know anything at all of things Christian: that no one had supported me at all in that!

I had expected that one naturally would raise difficulties, that one naturally would not be in agreement with everything, but from the entire volume of essays, except for acknowledgments in several contributions, I saw little that helped me. I viewed it as an outright shot in the back, that I, standing in front of the Church—for I thus understood myself—now was being shot at by my colleagues, so that therefore again the question was raised by unbelievers, disbelievers, or even believers: well, for whom does he really speak? That pained me very deeply. I say this openly and that explains to a large extent my reaction. I would definitely say that if all of the responses had been on the level of those by Karl Lehmann, of Theodor Schneider, of Walter Kasper, and of the two exegetes Kremer and Deissler, then certainly my reaction would have been completely different. What hit me especially were the responses of Balthasar, Ratzinger, Karl Rahner, and Grillmeier. And indeed because—and that is the second thing I wish to say relative to this—because I was in a way attacked in my Catholic orthodoxy, which simply had to challenge me. If I had been indifferent to that, if I had been the liberal, rationalist, radical rationalist—as it is lately said—theologian to whom therefore human reason was more important than the Church of God, then the matter would have been one of indifference to me. Then I could have smilingly walked off and said: Write on, that doesn't touch me. But it did touch me when I was attacked in my own Church as if I were no longer Catholic, especially when this partly took place with a kind of marshaling of evidence and argumentation which indeed was devoid of all careful theological method, which in part contained simply only attacks and indeed no evidence, only misunderstandings, etc.

And the third concrete matter concerning the volume of collected essays: that I was not allowed to respond. This I did not understand. My whole response would have been different—that is, of course, completely understandable—if I had been allowed to respond. I asked Balthasar; I asked the publishers: it was not allowed me. One could really think that I was already excommunicated. That was already the case by the time of the volume of collected essays on infallibility and I had thought that one would have learned from it that nothing good could arise therefrom. I do not wish thereby to defend everything I have written in the *F.A.Z.* I can only say that I thought the matter over thoroughly. It was read over by many, but I did consciously compose it in that sharp manner. I was, honestly said, fed up with my older colleagues, when the three or four I have named constantly preached from above in such a manner as to smear my Catholic orthodoxy—that was simply unacceptable. I consciously said once that if that were ever to happen, then I would make it clear. Whether in the end that was right or not, or whether that was helpful or damaging to me, I do not here wish to judge. I do not wish to defend everything, I would like only to have it said to you how I experienced it.

6. A sixth point I can now make more briefly. This shows, therefore, the reality of the attacks. The reaction to this book was indeed extremely varied, even among theologians themselves. It varied according to discipline. We received in essence the criticism of the dogmaticians. We had hardly any criticism from exegetes. Up to now, except for the two exegetes in the volume of collected essays, no one has stated that the essential matters were not presented or criticized faithfully according to the New Testament. Even the two exegetes in the volume of collected essays presented the matter in a completely different fashion; I can at any time accept, for example, the critique of Deissler concerning the rela-

tionship of Jesus and the Old Testament. There is certainly much more to be said about the matter. Kremer stated what in essence I had already brought forth in the book *The Church*. There too I have nothing to object to. Likewise, I have received no critique, except for Mr. Stoeckle, from the side of the ethicians, but rather they are essentially in agreement. And precisely because Mr. Stoeckle has recently been brought onto the Doctrinal Commission, it is natural for persons like me to raise the question about how far this Commission then is representative. Several colleagues and moral theologians have likewise thus sensed the matter. From the practical theologians I have received very great acknowledgment, above all orally. They say: With this we can work.

It varies according to the discipline; it varies also according to the nation. Only in Germany was there this disturbance and only here did it come to this intense interchange which I personally did not wish and which I personally did not provoke. I should say that despite my image among the public (it is well known to me: as a "quarrelsome person" and all such lovely things), one can check the literature to see that I never personally attacked anyone. As far as I was concerned I have always only defended myself. That is true of my book *Justification,* my book *The Church,* also *Infallible?,* although I should have criticized Karl Rahner severely: there is not a single word said against individuals. Subsequently I simply defended myself, although there was a challenge to do so only in Germany. In Italy, where I held a press conference and made people aware of what I was concerned about, namely, the constructive side of things—I also reported at that time to Cardinal Döpfner, when I had the occasion, that I likewise spoke with Cardinal Šeper and Archbishop Hamer in order to make that point clear—until now there has been absolutely no disturbance there. That is also the case for the United States, which I visited in November. In New York I made it very clear what I was trying to do. The same is now true for Ireland, whence I have just returned, truly a good Catholic country, and also for England: there until now everything has been received extremely positively. When I compare the criticisms which appear to me to be very serious and which give me much to think about, as, for example, from Avery Dulles, indeed a well-known man here, a serious theologian; when I compare that with what was otherwise said, for example, by individual vigorous opponents in the volume of collected essays, then one can easily see the difference even in the tone and manner in which it was made! Or when I see the review of a man who works on the Roman commissions and enjoys the highest reputation, namely, Raymond Brown—which review was reprinted in the *Tablet!* These two were really the outstanding Catholic reactions till now. For they are imbued with a completely different spirit, and I have written to the journal *America* of the American Jesuits, where these two reviews first appeared, thanking them that they even published such reviews in that the two colleagues expressed their doubts so openly, but in such a form that a hereticization did not come into question. Had that or something similar happened in Germany things would have developed completely differently here also.

7. The seventh—and this continues only what was already said—concerns the reaction of the public. Here too there was an extraordinary contrast between the large public reaction and that which now and again was expressed on specific matters by theologians, especially by dogmaticians. In public one saw the book as an enormous help. I reflected on whether or not I should send you several letters, namely, positive ones, after you (= the Bishops) certainly received many negative letters concerning my affair. I did not do this, which indeed you yourselves can understand. I can communicate to you, just to give one example, the following: This book was read with approval all the way from convicts in the Stuttgart-Stammheim, over there where the Baader-Meinhof people are, up to the Federal Finance Minister, who read through the entire book during the Christmas vacation (1975–76), from the first to the last page—and indeed with approval. I

do not say these things in public, but one needs to see precisely these things—the contrast and the impression which it now makes when we in Catholic theology come to such battles. Mr. Neumann can likewise confirm that in the past weeks a guest lecture took place in Tübingen, by one of the leading persons of the Jewish-Christian dialogue, Pinchas Lapide, a rabbinic theologian, who clearly expressed the idea that the starting point "from below" opened an entirely new possibility to Jewish theologians to conduct the dialogue. And indeed not only as till now was forever and always the case, namely, on the question of anti-Semitism or always only the question of human rights, but also concerning the central question which divides Christians and Jews, namely, Jesus of Nazareth. And he stated that as a Jew he can now go a very large part of the way with us, and we have—I believe—held an extremely positive discussion before the two theology departments, completely in public, which shows what new possibilities were opened up in the Jewish-Christian dialogue. That the entire ecumenical relationship could be relieved of tension in this manner, I need not say.

8. A final point—it is likewise very important because it certainly was very often spoken of—is the comparison that was always made—most recently again in the German daily press—between Küng and Lefebvre. The Bishops will have said something on this matter themselves. One says: On the right one is hard, and on the left one does nothing. I have on various occasions always emphasized the same point, that in no case can I agree if these two persons and also the two aspects of the problem and their inner structure are placed on the same level. I mention here once again four points which I have constantly repeated, even now in Ireland, where I spoke before the Irish Theological Society without meeting any serious resistance; and that did not surprise me. I have always spoken about these things there; but I raised there—as already earlier—four points:

1. I was always different from Lefebvre in that I have never disputed the Catholic orthodoxy of the Pope and the

Roman authorities. And I would never dream of doing such. And I can say that I have time and again drawn attention to the pastoral intentions of the Pope, with all of my critical statements, to which I adhere, and I have time and again defended these intentions. The same is also true for his moral integrity and so many things which people from the "right" and "left" have cast in doubt.

2. I have likewise never, as has Lefebvre, fundamentally placed myself in opposition to the Second Vatican Council; I have not placed myself against any Council of the Church.

3. I have likewise never formed my own organization. I have resisted all temptations which were brought to me by various groups to become the leader, if one will, of the "opposition." I did not then go, as I was asked to by many, to the Bishops' Synod (1971) in order, along with those people who at that time stood with the groups of priests outside, to give the matter a little more visibility and also perhaps more power. All those things I did not do. I will not spell that out now in detail. I only wish to say that in contrast to Lefebvre I have never attempted to form an organized opposition here.

4. I have likewise never striven to shape the education and training of priests according to my own opinions. We in Tübingen are all different persons and we have likewise, I believe intensively, discussed all of these questions. We in the Theological Faculty are made up of many individual minds, but it is also where theological questions are discussed. It was not so completely unusual that, for example, Walter Kasper and I expressed these various positions in writing, and that we then conducted jointly in my seminar— it was my initiative—discussions on the matter with practically scholastic precision, with exact times, etc.—and it was carried out wonderfully. Thus for my part I renounced entirely having my own concluding session with my people because I said that everyone can judge for himself. I mean that we in the Theological Faculty now could maintain peace despite all the tensions that have existed for a long time because of the volume of collected essays.

You see, I am happy that I could present all this calmly here in context. I would only like to say in conclusion: I have never made it a secret that I am a Catholic theologian, that I can give the reasons why, and that I intend to remain one. The entire passion, which certainly is present in my scholarly commitment, which, I believe, does not make me blind to any direction, is to be understood from this starting point. And from there I likewise think that the Colloquium should and can be conducted, and from there, I likewise believe, I can now respond to all the concrete questions which you (= Bishops) have.

Cardinal Volk:

Thank you very much for this explanation. We look upon the Colloquium as an opportunity for all the participants. This is true first of all in view of our information from you (= Professor Küng). But we also see the Colloquium as an opportunity for you. The situation is thus: the Doctrinal Commission of the Bishops is asked, should we do this or do that, or what can one do in the situation? Therefore representatives of the Doctrinal Commission are also here. But the matter is concerned much more primarily with understanding. Our goal is to provide the possibility here to understand what is meant. We have often emphasized that you have always been able and prepared to expand your position and to develop it further. Cardinal Döpfner was obviously of the opinion that until now this had not taken place in the measure that was expected by him.

I suggest therefore that we turn to several limited questions, for there are indeed dozens and dozens of questions which are raised in the book. These cannot be discussed in a colloquium and the point is that, as Cardinal Höffner remarked, we therefore are essentially concerned with Christology and the salvific reality of Christ here. Concerning Christ's salvation for us, wherein does this exist and why can he mediate it? I proceed from the opinion which I have always had that a certain wholeness is proper to theological truth. A half-truth can theologically be a whole error. I have always emphasized that. I do not know whether you picked that up in Münster [where Cardinal Volk earlier was a theology professor and Küng was his assistant for a short time], but that is my conviction. There is hardly any sort of matter in Church history where there is not some kind of truth present. . . .

The small catechism must likewise contain the theological truth without its being identical with a book of dogmatics. And here in Christology it fundamentally concerns who Christ is in order to do that which he does. It concerns naturally the action of Christ. He is of course sent to work, to act, and to complete the saving deed through teaching, living example. Thus he is in fact this absolute turning point through the revelation.

Now the question is, who is this Christ that he can do that? You have an abundance of statements about the Christ titles which you designated as no longer effectively usable today. It concerns likewise the two-nature doctrine. I refer for example to page 131 in your book. It is concerned with these Councils as with the theology which stands behind them, an advanced work of translation. "The entire so-called two-nature doctrine is an interpretation in a Hellenistic language and conceptuality of what this Jesus Christ really means! The importance of this doctrine should not be diminished. It has made history. It expresses a genuine continuity of the Christian faith and hands on significant guidelines for the entire discussion and likewise for every future interpretation. However, on the other hand the impression cannot be given either that the message of Christ can or may be expressed today only with the help of these categories of the then unavoidable but insufficient Greek categories, with the help of the Chalcedonian two-nature doctrine, with the help of the so-called classical Christology." The question is raised: There were indeed still further christological statements that were necessary from Nicaea to Chalcedon in order to preserve everything that was said earlier from new misunderstandings.

But you do without the two-nature doctrine in your interpretation. Which Christ is really the true one? The posing of
the question comes up once again, for example, on page 449,
where in summary fashion you speak about Christology. You
say: "Truly God: the whole point of what happened in and
with Jesus depends on the fact that, for believers, *God himself* as the friend of men and women was present, at work,
speaking, acting, and definitively revealing himself *in this
Jesus* who came among men and women as God's advocate
and deputy, representative and delegate, and was confirmed
by God as the Crucified raised to life. All statements about
divine sonship, pre-existence, creation mediatorship and incarnation—often clothed in the mythological or half-
mythological forms of the time—are meant in the last resort
to do no more than substantiate the uniqueness, underivability
and unsurpassability of the call, offer and claim made known
in and with Jesus, ultimately not of human but of divine origin and therefore absolutely reliable, requiring men and
women's unconditional involvement."

That therefore is the great statement about Christ. However, there is a question whether or not the Church teaching
is thereby given expression and indeed not only in the sense
of whether or not the classical formulations of the dogma are
present here. It is not a question whether or not the two-nature doctrine must absolutely be stated, but rather a question
whether or not in Christ the Father proclaims himself most
fully, which naturally in the letter to the Hebrews (cf.
1:1 ff.) is without a doubt the case. Therefore there is no
further revelation—it is unsurpassable in Christ. But for us
there is the question whether this description of what Christ
is can describe what he does. For there must indeed exist a
connection here. It concerns the action of Christ. And to this
there belongs certainly the humanity, otherwise one could
not speak at all of the significance of the God-man. It would
likewise not be thinkable that a sacrament of the Eucharist
existed: "Who does not eat my flesh and does not drink my
blood cannot have life in me." Is the humanity forgotten

there? The question is now: Is your Christology sufficient to ground the action of Christ and the effectiveness, fruitfulness of the actions of Christ as is proper to the Christian faith? The question is therefore not about this or that formulation, but about the total statement itself. With this it becomes apparent—and you yourself speak of it—that the Johannine Gospel is largely missing, although in several places you make detailed remarks about and also cite John. In general, nevertheless, the question is raised whether a Christology "from below" obtains everything which becomes visible through a complementing by a Christology "from above"; one must likewise see that the totality of the Christian doctrinal statement must make it possible to speak not only about what Christ is but also about what Christ does. Is therefore a Catholic Christology possible as a pure Christology "from below"? That is, as it appears to me, at least one of the central questions. And it appears to me that we should speak about this, for everything which you say concerning "true God" on pages 449 ff. does not yet express the totality of the Church doctrine: *Vere homo et vere Deus.*

That is not covered by what is said here. Should we call this an aspect of the question? Must there be a Christology "from below"? . . .

But the question is whether or not that is sufficient, whether a Christology "from above" must not also be included so that a Christology "from below" is correct. Likewise the other way around, the starting points of a Christology "from above" can be insufficient in itself if a Christology "from above" is not complemented by a Christology "from below." That is the question, whether the Christology "from below," as you consciously practice it, is sufficiently complemented by a Christology "from above."

Professor Küng:

Yes, may I then attempt to give an answer? To be sure I also am concerned with the totality and I indeed know from Münster your concern, and it is also mine. I have likewise

stated sufficiently often in the infallibility debate what a half-
truth is—that is true also of course for the official formulations: that under some circumstances naturally there also an
error can very easily creep in when in these formulas likewise
only perhaps half of the matter is expressed in the interpretation. But I was only concerned that totality not simply
lead to, in its Latin form, integrity [integralism was an archconservative movement at the beginning of the twentieth
century]. You certainly do not understand it thus either,
but it is naturally a horizon which—to describe my own
position—in every case is always demanded from the "right."
It must represent "integrally," that is, "totally," the object of
faith—so have I in any case understood it. Right?

Cardinal Volk:
   I am far from that. I did not use the word "integral." It is
not a question of words, but rather of matter.

Professor Küng:
   Right, therefore I see a fundamental agreement. That was
indeed likewise the *first* point of my answer. One must simply see that for all questions: it is simply not the case that I
should stand here—if you wish—on the spectrum of theology perhaps simply "to the left," although certainly this is
dominant in the impression of the Bishops; but I have no
hesitations about that. "Left" is for me where—and this also
the case even in Catholic theology today—the revelation of
God is *de facto* emptied in Christology, where in essence the
prophet Jesus of Nazareth is a replacement, and where likewise the concept of God is so completely emptied out or interpreted into being with humanity that it in fact is no longer
there. To that extent I would therefore definitely not confess
myself to this doctrine. I would not of course—and that is
what I wanted to indicate—even be able to confess myself to
a pure repetition of *this* formula! It must indeed be interpreted! Therefore I see a consensus, in any case, in reference
to the fundamental attitude toward these matters. That would
be the first point.

The *second* point you have already happily clearly highlighted, and there are very many substantive statements in this sense that were made; that is now only the concretization of the position: there is no question for me but that a Christology where God himself is not expressed as revelation, where the revelation of God himself is not expressed, makes no sense. I see nothing at all therein which could be *unconditional:* I see therein no claim which could force me to follow it! One must see everything, that is completely clear to me; and I have, I believe, said so clearly to the "left" as well as to the "right."

A *third* point: You speak of action. That is correct, of course. I will, if you so wish, state, from the perspective of the action of Jesus, what he is, but I wish indeed to say that simultaneously. So very often one finds here the misunderstanding of setting the "functional" in contrast to "really" —I find it time and again. I set "functional" in contrast to "ontological." Functional certainly does not mean unreal. I do not mean that Jesus is not what he does. These are simply general statements. How that is specified more precisely is another question. However, all statements about action and about the action of Jesus are also naturally statements about his being. That is true in the sense of "agere sequitur esse." That is completely clear. For me there is no question about that.

The *fourth* point: What you now have said about the two-nature doctrine is for me in any case affirmed in this light, which I clearly express: I would not only like to uphold completely, but would also like to bring to a new effectiveness, the great intentions of the two-nature doctrine, especially insofar as they were defined at the Council of Chalcedon.

Therefore, the *fifth* point: What you say of the formulation "vere Deus" is to be understood and also to be so presented that a new interpretation should once again bring the men and women of today closer to it. You understand—I do not need to tell you certainly as trained theologians—how

much effort must go into this kind of undertaking before one
can bring it into such a formulation. I have thought so long
over a few sentences of the book and have attempted so
strenuously to bring it to expression as positively as possible
—as precisely here. It appears in this sense to be the decisive
point, that in Jesus there is the revelation of God himself and
that in Jesus God himself is near, is at work; in Jesus he has
himself spoken, acted, definitively revealed himself (cf. p.
449)! That is what I wished to say here with this theistic
power and that appears to me to be the decisive matter.

A *sixth* point: You say correctly that it is not a matter of
the words but rather of the substance. That makes things
easier, certainly. When therefore one asks, does what is
there indeed contain the matter or not?—that is a justified
question; that goes without saying. However, I would not in
any case, from the fact that I view these terms ("hypostasis"
especially and likewise the entire presentation) as inapt for
today, state ahead of time that I would not maintain the substance. That is a question which must be investigated in individual cases. And thus I have likewise understood your question. We must therefore see whether in individual cases the
substance was brought to expression or not. The questions
then of course diverge as to how far one can go and what the
substance is. For me the substance, which must be expressed,
is very clear, and it is thus seen certainly by the great majority of the New Testament scholars: That Jesus is the revelation of God the Father himself. That in any case is a response to the question which in this connection of the
Christology "from below" I use as a supposition to this text:
"Jesus is the true revelation of the true God." That appears
to me to be the decisive point. I do not wish to say that one
could not now unfold that, but it seems to me that that is the
real point.

A *further point* which you (= Cardinal Volk) toward the
end have alluded to: the Johannine Gospel is no way missing with me! It is true that compared to Paul it is utilized
much more briefly. But one cannot do everything. I grant

that it is a weakness of the book—one could have developed it completely differently. But you yourself said that I have cited the Johannine Gospel. And I have not cited it simply from anywhere, but I believe—I do not need to read it out here now—I have cited the absolutely decisive quotations, and indeed precisely there where it comes to your point, namely, in relationship to the unity of the Son and the Father: "The Father and I are one." I have not "demythologized" this classic statement of, if you will, high Christology. I did not simply, for example, leave it out. On the contrary: I have related the statement very positively. And it fundamentally expresses very well what I myself wish to say, namely, that indeed who sees him sees the Father in him, that indeed here there is a unity. But Karl Lehmann can confirm that we in Lucerne in the Society of Catholic Dogmatic and Fundamental Theologians had also discussed this question of Christology and had received precisely from Mussner, who indeed is not over-progressive in these questions, clearly as the result of his exegesis of the Gospel of John, the information that the unity between Father and Son can be spoken of as only (one may not really say "only," for there really is not an "only"), must be specified, as a unity of revelation and a unity of action. That is likewise my interpretation. Mussner himself raised the question whether that is what Nicaea meant. Whether that is what "the same essence" meant he could not as an exegete decide. The dogmaticians had to decide that. The opinion among the dogmaticians was various. . . .

This interpretation I by no means hold alone, but rather it is likewise how New Testament scholars commonly think today; I can say that without hesitation. I naturally have systematically and compactly composed the matter. Whether, therefore, there is a bridge between the christological dogmas and what in general is presented as the interpretation by New Testament scholars today is of course the central question. That is disputed in part by the volume of collected essays referred to. Colleagues like Grillmeier interpret this in the sense of a history of dogmas which for me is a harmonizing sort. However, there are also others. There was just now an article—I know of it only by accident—in the *Christlichen Sonntag* (actually: *Christ in der Gegenwart*) by a colleague whom I no longer recall who handled precisely this question: Is there a bridge? He affirms the question. There certainly is a whole row of people who affirm it. I would like to do something that is still better. I would like to do something which would more positively be a help to the colleagues as well in presenting the matter in a positive manner. I have put forth an enormous effort in order to make it positive.

A *final* item: The Christology "from above" and "from below." It has probably already become clear that it was a misunderstanding from the beginning to place the Christology "from below" in opposition to a Christology "from above," as if God were not involved in the former. I have also never disputed that one can start out "from above." I myself have said that I learned it so, and not only on the basis of my education: I myself dealt with matters thus throughout the entire book *Justification.* The entire book *Menschwerdung Gottes* already says what it is in the title: I myself have done this and likewise admit it to everyone. And I would say to your question, whether in this sense it works methodologically "from below," I would say: Yes, to me it appears to work, methodologically seen. . . .

I stand at the foot of the mountain and come now, if you will, up the Mountain of Transfiguration and attempt then to grasp what therefore this Jesus is, and come then to the insight that he is not simply one of the prophets: I come, that is, "from below." It is impossible, if I wish to argue methodologically correctly, for me at the same time to stand already on the top of the mountain and then always converse with myself there below. I have attempted to be logical about it. And personally I would affirm the question which you pose. I mean, that one can arrive there "above." Incidentally, I have at an earlier time when one could still speak with Mr. Ratzinger, when he was still here (= Tübingen), discussed the question with him at length. At that time, when I had hardly worked on the matter yet, he said that it must never-theless be possible to present everything "from below" with-out the essential elements being simply dissolved. He meant at that time that it must really be possible.

Whether it succeeded, my dear Cardinal, in individual points one can always discuss. There are always still a large number of points. I do not wish to gloss over that ahead of time. I would only like to say a final thing, namely, to the two-nature doctrine . . . this would be, if you will, I believe a counterquestion, whether you also would grant what I have spelled out as a foundation. These things are not only my foundations, but there are also relatively traditional Protes-tant theologians, such as Pannenberg: they say indeed ex-actly the same about their Christology! Whether, therefore—and this is now my question—the two-nature doctrine is re-ally still understandable today, whether in the practical proc-lamation it is not much more misunderstood. Whether the two-nature doctrine at that time really, according to the wit-ness of the history of dogmas, solved the difficulties, whether still further contradictions did not follow therefrom in the subsequent centuries. And then the question of exegetes which likewise was not positively answered ahead of time: whether therefore this kind of terminology, this kind of rep-resentation really corresponds to the original witness; and whether it does not precisely in a very decisive point go be-yond the Johannine Gospel, beyond the peak statements of the Johannine Gospel. I would like from my side to raise this question. And these are my questions. If and when someone can answer them better, then that is fine with me. But they are still naturally there and they are not only my own ques-tions.

Cardinal Volk:
Two wish to speak, Cardinal Höffner and Bishop Moser.

Cardinal Höffner:
I will attempt to make somewhat concrete on the basis of the text what you (= Cardinal Volk) have just said. When we read on page 449: Christ is the Son of God, that means

the uniqueness of the call of God to humanity, or on page
443: In life, in behavior, in fate Jesus manifests the word
and will of God itself, manifests likewise the call itself, or on
page 444: Father and Son are one; this means: In the work
and in the person of Jesus one meets God, God manifests
himself. Or on page 456: What is said in the Johannine Gospel concerning Father, Son, and Spirit is not to be understood ontologically. That would be "static." Rather they are
likewise statements about the manner of the revelation of
God. Or on page 390: Jesus lives "from an ultimately
unexplainable experience of God." Everywhere there are
functions. I at one time excerpted the book and have here
about eighteen pages, but nowhere do I find a single place
where I would say that I find myself confirmed here in the
"deum de deo, deum verum de deo vero." Rather, there is always something functional that is said. And then I asked myself, cannot these statements likewise be made about St.
Francis of Assisi, who was also an advocate of God among
us? In him the experience of God had revealed itself in a
wonderful manner. Or Paul, indeed, likewise says, I live, not
I, but Christ lives in me. Or, we have 10,000 Muslims in Cologne. If one speaks with the Iman [sic—should be: Imam;
Iman means something like "faith"] and others then one can
also say that Mohammed is the representative of Allah—not
Allah for God's sake; but in a wonderful manner Allah reveals himself in this human being. Therefore I have the question, where do I find this statement in your book: "genitum
non factum," that is, the eternal pre-existence of God? And
how should I interpret the statement that "ontological"
means static when I say that God is? God is being: that is
the most fantastic dynamic. Those would be several questions
which came to me as I looked through the book in amplifi-
cation of what Cardinal Volk has already said.

Cardinal Volk:

May I perhaps ask Bishop Moser, or do you wish to respond immediately?

Bishop Moser:

My question goes practically in the same direction. I would like to be allowed once again to come back to the first complex of questions. I am concerned with the pastoral intention already mentioned in your introduction to *On Being a Christian*. Of course this does not exclude your taking a stand *expressis verbis* within the book perhaps to normative statements from Councils, e.g., in this connection, the Council of Nicaea. Where is a binding statement and the statement about the binding quality of this statement in the book? One can now say from the discussion which we are conducting: there is always discernible a certain ambivalence. You have clearly or indirectly placed question marks. Would it not be necessary to clarify that in an expansion of the book *On Being a Christian?* That was spoken of at the very beginning of your remarks under your point four. It is necessary to go into the matter there. The Bishops' Conference on February 17, 1975, said: "The normative significance of the ecclesiastical development of the faith plays too small a role in the writings of Professor Küng which were examined by the Congregation for the Doctrine of the Faith and just mentioned." And I believe that that is likewise true for the question of the Johannine Gospel. I agree completely that that is not sufficient. I have indeed already said that beforehand and one will acknowledge that here also. But on the other side there is the question: Does it have the weight or the context, or could a way be found to clarify this context in another accent so that the totality of the Bible is expressed? "Functional" was just now spoken of. Then one must naturally speak of the Sonship of God. And at one of these most important places in the entire dispute the questions must be raised whether there are still other titles, and what is the truth concerning the Son of God. . . . How does that now stand pastorally, where does it lead? . . . If all these titles are only seen as functional, then indeed Jesus Christ is a business manager of God according to contemporary relations, but he is not God himself. Where is that now said *expressis verbis?* Is that expressed sufficiently and appropriately? Here I would suggest that these matters, these ambivalences, and these over-accentuations should be discussed and opened up. One must also make it understood that these things are spoken of in the sense of making a statement about them. If these statements about them—and we have already discussed this elsewhere—were forthcoming, then I believe your intentions and this normative mention of the formulation of the faith finally could be brought together. For otherwise these questions remain standing. And otherwise a deficit remains in these intentions. And the deficit could lead then to an image of Jesus which in reality no longer presented the entire Bible. It would fundamentally be another . . .

Cardinal Volk:
Please.

Professor Küng:
May I respond to the two together. Therefore, a first remark. Cardinal Höffner, I am happy that you have seen the matter so precisely. One would probably have to look at individual instances, where the individual matters stand. When you, for example, cite the sentence concerning an ultimately "unexplainable experience of God" (page 390), that is said of the *historical* Jesus. And this is an expressed approach to the mystery, if you will; it is not simply the only approach, it is stated in the context with very many others. And in addition to that the transition must be found to that which the community afterwards said of him as the *one raised up,* which was very much more than this. Thus this would in a sense be only a presupposition. Thus, only in this sense, a making more precise.

"Statically": There I can grant that you are completely correct. Naturally everything that is seen in connection with God I would view as highly "dynamic." . . . You are correct, and I have already granted ahead of time that I am speaking functionally. But it nevertheless also cannot be overlooked that it concerns precisely this unity between Jesus and the Father and that in this sense it concerns not only functions. Therefore I would not, for example, view myself correctly understood if one did not very decisively see what is first said here in relationship to the underivability, etc., regarding the Sonship of God as the explanation of the sentence which precedes it: namely, that in Jesus, God himself was near, was active, and had ultimately revealed himself. Whether this unity is sufficiently emphasized, whether we can go as far as very often now is done in dogmatics (above all in following these two Councils) from the perspective of New Testament exegesis, is certainly a question.

I would clearly reject the manner, the comparison, the question (which you clearly would negatively answer) which you have posed about whether perhaps the same thing could be true in Francis of Assisi. With all admiration for Francis of Assisi, I naturally could never make all these statements about him which I here make about Jesus. I would never say that in Francis of Assisi the God who is friendly to men and women had himself spoken as in Christ. I would never say that he had acted in him. I would not make this definitive statement: for me something once and for all has taken place here. And I have, I believe, made clear throughout the entire book that everything else *afterwards* can only be handed on in faith in *him*. Not simply that we could have "more" in Christ. One would likewise have to speak about Paul. Especially enlightening, it appears to me, nevertheless, is the comparison with Mohammed. That is indeed probably the decisive distinction between Islam and Christianity, that precisely the Muslim naturally would not make these statements about Jesus. The decisive thing for Islam is indeed precisely not Mohammed, but rather naturally the Koran! Where with us Christology stands, where with us the living person of Jesus Christ stands for God and indeed in this unity with God which is likewise a norm—there in Islam stands the Book! That is the true revelation of God. That is what even Mohammed must orient himself toward. He *brings* the Book indeed, only in reality the angel brings it to him. That is perhaps the real difference between Muslims and Christians. Therefore, I would in no case see Jesus on the level of Mohammed.

Concerning pre-existence one would perhaps have to discuss the matter for itself. It will indeed have to be addressed once more. I would like to put it for a time in parentheses because otherwise I might stray a bit too far, and then attempt to clarify it somewhat in the response to Bishop Moser: The *pastoral intentions* are given expression in precisely these matters. The question of who succeeds more is, I believe, still an open one. Whenever I say "I," I never mean myself alone; I say this expressly. I believe that a significant part of the preaching today of the younger generation who in fact have studied is done very much more in *this* manner than in that which simply proceeds from the two-nature doctrine. Pastorally I would think precisely that it would be better to proceed in this manner; in any case that was my purpose. Whether it has succeeded will probably only be shown by history—ultimately, therefore, that which can remain. That the Johannine Gospel in fact could be set into relief more clearly I have already said. One could do that certainly if one had, for example, more space! The architectonic structure also naturally demands certain things; I believe that everyone who writes a book knows how difficult it is simply to bring everything in. It was indeed, I believe, an acknowledged difficult undertaking and I simply had to stop somewhere. That could of course have been done in a further section.

I do not believe that it was very necessary to go into the *binding quality* in reference to the Councils, and indeed because in my book *Infallible?* I had already spoken with extremely great clarity concerning the binding quality. I have also very much regretted that the positive aspects were taken up all too little by the opponents, who in time of course noticed that the yes is affirmed. I have not drawn the binding quality into doubt, but rather the question of the infallibility of this definition. That is naturally always still an open question. And then I can say I likewise regret that from the side of the teaching office until now really very little more was done than to repeat documents, which of course were already known to me. And essentially likewise my colleagues, since the extended response which I gave in the summing-up volume *Fallible?*, have not gone any further into the question. Not a single one has made a statement on that volume. One should doubtless have been able to see that I was not aiming at making the activity of the teaching office impossible today. My critique in large measure was that it is perceived really too little in a constructive sense. I would say that of Rome as well as the Bishops' Conference: that one really would expect a much more positive and helpful proclamation, and in this sense the carrying out of the teaching office. I not only have nothing against this; rather, I wish it. Whereby I likewise clearly stated that I have nothing against the idea that *in extremis,* that is, when it is really necessary, one would naturally draw limitations. I have clearly distinguished *two categories* concerning binding quality: I have affirmed that the *symbols of the faith* are to be taken seriously! I have now devoted the major course of the whole semester to the Apostles' Creed—I am now at the Ascension. And I have affirmed that even *definitions of the faith*—not only, therefore, summaries, but also limitations—are not only possible, but rather under circumstances even to be desired. I have indeed gone even further into the matter than Karl Rahner, who believes that that is no longer possible today because things have become too complex. I am of the opinion that they have not become too complex, above all when it really concerns in some question an "Articulus stantis et cadentis ecclesiae." And of course it can be done. I would only think that then one would have to base it on trust, namely, on the believing trust in what now really the Spirit of God says . . . but those indeed are then really different questions. Therefore, I affirm the binding quality.

Indeed the difficulties begin fundamentally there where it

must be interpreted. Everyone today must indeed interpret—
Cardinal Höffner, you mention that also. I believe that you
also interpret the *social doctrine* of the popes. And if I were
to ask you what you think about certain social documents,
about certain expressions, for example, in this area by popes
of the first half of the nineteenth century, you would probably also give extremely differentiated answers. We have, I
would say, fewer difficulties with Leo XIII as compared to
everything that went before. We likewise have in the *dogmatic* area naturally things which are easier for us and still
others which are less easy for us. And I will attempt to make
the best of it. Were I simply an attacker of dogmas then I
would probably go at things in a completely different way.
Then I would make the matters laughable or I don't know
what. I do not do that. I think that I state my criticisms very
seriously but I do not bring them forth in a derisive manner.
I set the problem in relief and attempt to give positive solutions. How far in individual cases it succeeds, I as someone
with a vested interest cannot judge. I would take the inquiry
which Bishop Moser has directed to me completely positively. I intend of course to work further in this area. I
would, however, nevertheless request my colleagues—and
precisely those who are not present now—to collaborate . . .

Cardinal Höffner:
I would say again . . .

Professor Küng:
May I just finish my sentence?

Cardinal Höffner:
For me it was, however, indeed almost horrifying precisely
on this point. When I now look through the whole book and
ask myself where is the "genitum non factum" stated, and
when I then almost with horror should have to say that I do
not find it, but rather only the functions, but the functions
are still not the same as the other . . .
We can very well say of Mohammed that is one commis-

sioned, a plenipotentiary speaker, ambassador, trusted one and friend of Allah. I can likewise say the love of God has been revealed in Francis of Assisi. That has indeed horrified me. I must as bishop nevertheless find this in this confession. The other thing, that one of course can also still interpret ecclesiastical decrees and statements in the social area even after 1850 and sometimes 1870 is certainly clear?

Cardinal Volk:

Lehmann wishes to speak.

Professor Küng:

May I perhaps only briefly likewise give a response? I naturally presented the "genitum non factum" where I speak of the Sonship of God. This formula intends to express nothing other than the Sonship of God. How the Sonship of God again must be understood is of course a question, right? The whole problem is: How is the Sonship of God to be understood? One already sees even in the New Testament itself a development. There I attempted to interpret this more from the perspective of the Old Testament, as it certainly originally was understood in the community. I would give this as an answer. The "genitum non factum" is precisely the question of the Sonship of God. Whether my answer is sufficient is a question, but I certainly would not say that the matter itself is not there.

Cardinal Volk:

Lehmann.

Bishop Moser:

I would for a moment like to intervene, excuse me. Page 449 once again. There indeed the uniqueness, underivability, unsurpassability is spoken of. One can also, I believe, say that in connection with St. Francis. But on the other page it now goes further, it concerns the "calling" and "claim," "which ultimately . . . is of divine origin and therefore unconditionally concerns humanity in an absolutely trustworthy manner." That is in the uppermost section. If I may once

again raise a question: Why then is not simply some sentence
or reason stated—in a subordinate sentence even—with the
statement: For he is God himself in person? Then what we
are discussing here would be said. That is our dilemma that
only the claim and the vocation is spoken of as of divine origin. I wished only to clarify in one place where the question
comes from.

Cardinal Volk:
   Professor Lehmann.

Professor Lehmann:
   Yes, I would like to dig a little further at this point. We
are certainly at one that the so-called "functional" view of
Christology is completely legitimate and that it likewise
brings forth from a pastoral view very many positive possibilities. One can, I would even say, express better precisely
the salvific work of Jesus and many other things from that
perspective. That truly the confession of Christ has been
preached so little certainly is connected precisely with the
difficulty of the "practical" Christology, precisely the crisis in
which we are. I have, however, a little hesitancy about using
the word "functional" here, and that for several reasons:
first, at the time of the New Testament and also long afterwards naturally there was no refined meaning of "functional"
in distinction to "ontological." We are bringing a category
into the New Testament which one may bring only very cautiously. I can of course apply the term "functional" as the
first characteristic; if I, for example, express the working of
Jesus in its significance and if I would like to distance myself
more from—let us not say "ontological"—but rather from
purely "static" concepts. However, I would not view it as
good if one now instead of "static" (in itself manifold in
meaning!) one now substituted "ontological." For likewise
Mr. Küng had indeed said before with clarity, for which we
are to be thankful: "agere sequitur esse!" That, however,
then can naturally have enormous consequences! That means
that even behind the function statements, which are is-state-

ments, an ontology stands. And at this point one must, I believe, now likewise observe the ancient ecclesiastical Christology somewhat more precisely.

I find very many formulations in Küng's book excellent, in a certain fashion fascinating, but I ask myself why the christological statements then simply suddenly break off. For example, the famous sentence on page 390: "Without any title or office he appears in all his action and speech as advocate in the completely existential sense: as the personal messenger, trustee, indeed as confidant and friend of God. He lived, suffered and struggled out of an ultimately unexplainable experience of God, presence of God, certainty of God, indeed out of a singular unity with God, which allowed him to address God as his Father. The fact that he was first of all called 'Son' in the community may simply be the reflection which fell upon his countenance from the proclaimed Father-God." And then I ask myself now can and may I really remain, in the interpretation of the *concrete form of this unity,* exclusively in the categories of self-manifestation, self-revelation, making visible, representing? Naturally I do not say that these statements are false. They are indeed helpful. But the question is whether the matter can really end with that. Here in my opinion the classical Christology provides an unmistakable indication that there is still a further dimension to be taught. Naturally I would likewise say with Mr. Küng that the classical statement was to be interpreted. We are certainly aware that the classical Christology was thought of and spoken of more in a dependence on physical, material things. The model was the "being at hand" of things rather than more personal categories. Hence the category "physical" here without a further explanation is extremely problematic. However, something—and this is the point—is expressed here which we also always must hold fast to in other patterns of thinking. And that is precisely the answer to the question of how to explain more precisely this *form of unity.* Very briefly: (1) There is here an *unchangeable* unity, beyond "only" of consciousness. (2) Therefore even the question of the unsurpassability of the claim is in essence not sufficient, but rather it concerns the question: Is there indeed also a uniqueness, underivability, unsurpassability *of the person,* and indeed in principle, not only in the perspective of a *de facto* comparative history of religion, as important and indispensable as this is? Is there a ground for this *in principle underivability, uniqueness of person?* One could read that out of the formulation of Mr. Küng, "ultimately . . . of divine origin" (page 449), but why is the clarification of what the "hypostatic union" means in this matter missing here? The answer to this is not provided with the tag "static." It concerns a unity which is no longer dissolvable, which also— and that is not a complaint about Mr. Küng—cannot be interpreted only in terms of action, or which one can even allow to disappear again ultimately unexplained.

It is concerned here not "only" with Nicaea and Chalcedon, but also and precisely with the Scripture. It is impressive that at the beginning of the Johannine Gospel it states: "In the beginning was the word and the word was with God and *the word was God."* This statement "was God," that is, is God, with which one must certainly be very cautious, is missing, for example, in the entire book *On Being a Christian.* Further: That Johannine Gospel, which Rudolph Schnackenburg has drawn attention to, did not probably completely by accident have still another such indication at the end of the twentieth chapter (apparently the original conclusion): "My Lord and *my God."* The Gospel, apparently with compositional intent, as far as one can determine such things, concluded so that the whole thing was in a theological bracket. And I can therefore only regret that Küng's book did not deal with this central structure and with these texts. And here is the point where for me neither the biblical nor the classical Christology was sufficiently worked through in several points in the book.

I grant gladly that here in theology, therefore likewise outside of the book of Hans Küng, what is necesssary for the clarification of the interpretation has not yet been done. That is therefore the task of all of us. But sometimes I ask myself: Must one not here or there where one—perhaps now—still has not mastered something, perhaps at first "powerlessly" simply repeat one or another document? Must one not simply recall to oneself and others that here is something that has not been invalidated—and I think also that the practice of the teaching office gains a certain meaning here—in order to come back to the matter of the beginning—to recall through the citation of completely well-known documents something which now is *before us* as a task. At this point—I do not wish to prolong this—I believe that from the concepts "functional," "ontological," etc., down to the precise specification of the goal of the christological unity (what is that for an is-statement?) there remains in the book, I feel, a palpable uncertainty. For me therefore a genuine conversation is necessary because I believe that it is a positive uncertainty. It probably will allow itself to be expanded. I would not say simply: That is already a closed system which is no longer expandable. However, then it must likewise be expanded. And then simply for my theological interest there would be the question: Do you see here, Mr. Küng, a possibility of clarifying the matter so that—as seen by you—"misunderstandings" soon and for good can be eliminated? These are my questions.

Professor Neumann:

Yes, I would perhaps like to point only to one thing. One may not, I believe, simply separate the various levels in Küng's book from one another and for example place citations from one level on an equal basis next to others. When above all matters are cited which Mr. Küng stated concerning the historical Jesus, then one must likewise bring in other things—excuse me if I as a complete non-exegete intervene in the discussion here—but it is above all things, indeed even the normative statement, which were addressed by Bishop Moser. And I feel myself somewhat co-responsible for norms. I believe that Mr. Küng, for example, under "clarifications," where he draws up the theological résumé (page 441), says, for example, that at the high point of this progressing revelation and education of the generation of humanity . . . there occurred: "God himself in his Son and Word stepped into the world and took on a human nature." I mean, here he says then: "Definitively" is "humanity liberated from darkness, error and death," "in order in this manner to attain to God." I believe therefore that in the theological explanation there are some things which he had left out in the introductory analysis of the historical things. And I believe that even this book wants, as do the Holy Scriptures, to say more, and it might be that perhaps in the book too little —as Mr. Lehmann has said—attention has been paid to the Johannine Gospel and to the embracing bracket between John 1 and the conclusion of the Johannine Gospel. The statements are in themselves, I believe, nevertheless at hand.

Professor Küng:

Yes, may I (*Cardinal Volk:* Please.) immediately respond to this? I believe that between what Mr. Lehmann says and what I say there is a very large agreement. For example, I share the doubts concerning the term "functional." One uses what is available, right? I have said in various places time and again that I am *not* concerned with the terms. For example, a colleague in Ireland asked me recently whether one ought not better say "relational," whether I could not also say that; then I said: Yes, of course, I could also say that. But in German we see rather little, all too little in that, and one would again have to explain things very much at length. I did not invent the word "functional" either. I have taken it over. I perceive it as I have already said, not really in contrast to "real," but rather to "ontological." Precisely here, I believe, are many misunderstandings—as if that then were not existential [*Seinshaft*]. I of course also understood that as a reality. I can therefore perhaps only explain the matter thus, that there is a very large difference whether I make a Christology with a Greek essential concept—we see that indeed in the two-nature doctrine—*or* whether I speak more in the terms of happenings. I would naturally, precisely in the sense of the previously emphasized dynamism, truly not think that this was then less real. This can indeed on the contrary be still more real. However, it appears to me to be very important that one does not interpret the word "functional" weakly. It is precisely stated so as to present a distinction— one could even say: the distinction between an essential and a happening Christology. But I would again further likewise underline the reality. When, for example, precisely page 390 is cited—that is essentially the place which Cardinal Höffner already referred to—then one must unconditionally, if one does not really wish to misunderstand fundamentally, add to it page 391. Page 391 is indeed only an attempt, on the basis of what has been made available in exegesis, to make clear how one really can use this title of Jesus, e.g., the Son of God. That is a difficult problem—everyone grants that—and I have made an attempt here. But if I ask whether one could not go further here, then I would say: Yes, of course, one can do that and one must also go further. Do I not say in paragraph two on page 391: Only after the Awakening was he recognized as the Son of man and the Son of God, the Son of man also in the sense of a title of highness and not only a title of lowliness, as it is in the Scriptures? "Only now was he recognized as the Son of man and the Son of God, as the redeemer and reconciler, as the only mediator and high priest of the new covenant between God and humanity, indeed as the way, the truth, and the life of God for humankind" (page 391). Of course I say that likewise. And I say this now, not, for example, as "an interpretation" or as an opinion of another, but rather that is my own statement. Mr. Neumann also correctly said that I then attempt to say additional things about this . . .

Cardinal Höffner:

Perhaps I can—I have read that somewhat differently— cite the text which you now also mention here. On page 441 it says indeed: "God himself in his Son and Word stepped into the world." However, this sentence is to be interpreted in connection with the entire section. There Professor Küng explains what is said in Greek theology. But he does not identify himself with it very much, for in the next section he then says: that is indeed wonderful and at the same time this theory is "a Hellenization of the Christian message of salvation and liberation which included a large number of negative elements." Therefore one cannot simply cite that as the opinion of Professor Küng—you (= Professor Neumann) do not so simply present it. Otherwise I would have been overjoyed! Then I could have said: There is *one* place in the 680 pages! You must understand me: I have as bishop read the book and have searched from page to page to find where it is. And then I came to this place; there I likewise was not satisfied; I of course read that, but I read it in the entire context. It is again not *your* (= Professor Küng's) opinion.

Professor Küng:

Well, this I can and wish to say openly. I declare my reservations concerning the formulation. That is certain. I can likewise immediately make that still clearer if I were to respond still further to the question of Mr. Lehmann. Now concerning the categories of the representative, etc.—there I indeed for the rest also said still more: I include indeed likewise the Sonship of God clearly in that. I am very happy that you, Mr. Lehmann, have said still more clearly and directly that one must likewise speak of the underivability of the person (meant: not only of the claim). I would without hesitation subscribe to this. Hence, I have already said: This sentence is indeed only a subsequent sentence to what was already previously stated. Of course I mean that. For what is the claim supposed to be if it is not incorporated in the person? (*Cardinal Höffner:* Yes, one would have to say that! Yes, if that . . .)

Cardinal Höffner:

Again, the Muslims say that of Mohammed and the claim which he proclaimed. The claim which is in the Koran is underivable. There is no human being before, no human being after who was sent by God as he was.

Professor Küng:

No, but Mohammed—in order to make that once again clear, and I have actually discussed this with Muslims—is indeed for the Muslim fundamentally nothing at all as a person. Right? Mohammed is not put forward in this sense as a model. With all desirable clarity I have likewise shown: Death indeed is only the point of what indicates that the person fundamentally means nothing. (Here the words on the tape recording are garbled.) It will from there . . .

Cardinal Volk:

I suggest that we not speak anymore about Mohammed. We are interested in the Catholic faith and not Mohammed.

Professor Küng:

Yes, I am likewise completely of the same opinion. But look, I could have perhaps written into this sentence here (cf. page 449) this statement about the underivability *of the person.* I have now remarked that where it was thus stated one perhaps could really interpret it minimalistically. However, I do not do so. I understand it from the perspective of the previous sentence (cf. page 449 above); I thought *this* was so clear that it was apparent. I stated it thus because precisely these terms and this presentation were used in connection with the *origin.* Hence I have here stated the underivability of the origin, right? However, I have absolutely no hesitation to state this likewise about the underivability of the person. This separation of action and being I could from the very beginning and fundamentally not accept at all.

A further matter where I likewise can agree without hesitation: namely, that it is here concerned with an indissoluble unity. This naturally is not to be understood as a merely accidental or current unity; it is an indissoluble unity. And everything which is implied with the "ephapax" (once and for all), which was underlined variously by me, is likewise intended. Right? And here I would say: Good, whoever can

say it better, let him say it! The difficulties really begin—and
I say this completely openly and admit it totally (Cardinal
Höffner and Bishop Moser have spoken to the same point)—
when now it is simply said: Jesus is God. I would not indeed
deny this, it is nowhere denied. But I would nevertheless
base myself on the fact that—if I look at the entire Scripture
and think of the synoptic Jesus—Jesus himself is called precisely the *Son* of God and that outside of the Johannine Gospel only in several relatively late, Hellenistically influenced
exceptional cases is Jesus directly described as God. The hesitations, indeed, come from the fact that—as is emphasized
likewise by other theologians—a good part of the practical
piety (in this I also see the pastoral concerns in the background) is fundamentally "monophysite." Karl Rahner was
probably the first to state this thus clearly. Those are the hesitations. And this likewise has already been stated against
me, that I do (not) say: There on the cross hangs God.
Well, of course this is not so simple: On the cross there hung
the *Son* of God. Otherwise we get into things against which I
have already made statements, as for example concerning
Moltmann, who in general fundamentally sees only the
"crucified God" and in my opinion gets into difficulties there,
for who then awakened? . . . [God himself as in Hegel's
dialectic?]

If he wishes to make things so that God himself dialec-
tically deals with himself, then we are into "necessity"; but
that is likewise also not dogmatically tenable. Hence, the
problems simply follow.

I have always spoken in this sense of the *"Son"* of God because it is important to me, as likewise to the classical doctrine of the Trinity, that this *"distinction"* be made clear.
And I see a whole host of misunderstandings by believers
and naturally also by unbelievers who simply think that is a
mythologem which is demanded of us. I call attention to this
—and here I have been essentially influenced by Josef
Andreas Jungmann—that in the aftermath of the anti-Arian
resistance the liturgy, fortunately not in its totality, but fun-

damentally the German liturgy, the Frankish liturgy, was diverted thereto, as he expressly says: The entire conversion took place really from the God Wotan to the God Jesus, or similar. And he saw—and this is really a shame—that one did not hold fast to the classical form of the Latin oration: Prayers to the Father, *per dominum nostrum Jesum Christum in spiritu sancto.* In this same sense he also clarifies the *gloria patri et filio et spiritu sancto;* this all likewise comes in. My intention in these matters is to make clear again the original relations and to set forth in this sense precisely the Father *through* the Son *in* the Spirit. That would be something in regard to the doctrine of the Trinity which is always involved here and which it would not occur to me at all to deny. I am precisely concerned that all this be made clear from the scriptural origins. And it appears to me in this sense that precisely the authentic statements are more understandable than what often becomes of them afterwards.

I would indeed only like to say this much, that that [is not] the complete answer: the work of expansion which Karl Lehmann demanded right at the conclusion I affirm wholeheartedly. I intend and presume to be able to say more if I once again could "dive into" these matters, which I sooner or later certainly would do. This is simply a question of time and, I believe, also of joint research by theologians. If more can be said here, I am the last one who would close it off. And there are, which was just now justifiably emphasized by Lehmann, no closed systems. This is true for all questions. I have always rejected this. It is no problem, it changes nothing essential for my understanding—it can on the contrary only enlighten it—if one, for example, continues the development of christological peak statements about pre-existence, the Sonship of God, or other matters. I believe that I can—from my perspective—only affirm this. It would be completely different if I had closed doors here and had said that this does not come into the question whatsoever, if I had taken a fundamentally [contrary] position. There are indeed in this connection sufficient theologians, Protestant in

any case (and the Catholics do not always say it!), in regard
to specific statements, e.g., in regard to the "vere Deus." Had
I said that this does not come at all into the question, then
one would have had to say: Well, he is firmly fixed. I am not
firmly fixed in these questions. And I have indicated
sufficiently that with every book I have learned so much
more that I likewise hope in the future not to stand still.

Cardinal Höffner:

Now it would indeed be important to know what that concretely signifies. You would indeed likewise lift a care from
us.

Professor Küng:

Yes, concretely that means for me (*Cardinal Höffner:*
How that could happen.), what I now can say very precisely:
One of the contributions which in the discussion has
impressed me most is the one from Helmut Riedlinger (who
made relatively sharp statements, but I have had absolutely
nothing against that) which appeared in the journal *Theologie und Philosophie* (51, 1976, pp. 185–95). He examined
the method of "radical rationality," as he designated it. He
showed, I believe, an unusually large measure of acknowledgment of what was accomplished in this book. This lack of
jealousy—this I must say—is rare in German theology—not,
however, in American and in French. Because of this there is
simply another basis present. I must say this so that it can be
correctly understood. Even Karl Lehmann likewise, I believe,
found words of acknowledgment, which naturally also did
dry hearts such as mine good. However, Riedlinger presented
very clearly what *de facto* was there accomplished in order,
naturally, from that point on to present his inquiries with all
sharpness. I would truly not close myself off to these questions. I would not think it completely correct to designate the
method ahead of time simply as radical rationality. I have
used the expression in a very specific connection, namely, in
connection with the God question and in the debate with
critical rationalism and similar tendencies. I did not use this

concept—as far as I can remember—in the same proportion
in Christology. Well, good, the questions are there. I mean
that he (= Riedlinger) is right when he here *and* there
alludes to the complexity of the questions and the totality
in the now long-standing question about the relationship between *reason and faith*. For one notes that, whether concerning the Sonship of God, or the pre-existence and all that is
involved in it: there is always the question of how faith and
reason are related to each other! And that is simply a question, in my opinion, which has been present since the Middle
Ages, after above all Thomas Aquinas arrived at this solution, which was done in an authoritative manner for that
time. This synthesis is then indeed, after the coming of the
modern period, especially with Descartes and the consequences of his thought, placed in question. No one would
dispute that today. And to me personally the most urgent
thing appears to be—and I also believe it will help to forward that debate itself most of all—that I take up this question which I have been involved in since my Roman study
days and which I elsewhere developed further and which I
likewise dealt with in my first Tübingen lecture on faith and
knowledge (at that time as a fundamental theologian). My
plan—and it is not only a plan, but rather it is already
carried out quite far—is to handle this question of reason
and faith *ex professo* and thereby to present the God question anew and to offer from there a background against
which presumably Christology likewise again could be better
seen. I cannot here—in order not to give a false impression
—shield ecclesiastical position, traditional theological position from all criticism. But the center of gravity of the whole
work will doubtless be on the debate with the critique of
religion so that precisely from there presumably a number of
these hopefully can be accepted gladly even from the side of
the teaching office. For I do not believe that up till now there
has been such a debate with Feuerbach, Marx, Freud, and
Nietzsche and a presentation of the problematic since Descartes as I in any case not only intend but so far have al-

ready completed five of the seven chapters. I hope to be
finished this year, assuming that my health holds out and that
other demands do not become too great. I would likewise—
and perhaps I may also say so here—like to use the opportunity of the great academic festival lecture on the occasion of
the 500th-year celebration of the University of Tübingen not
for church-political purposes or other such things, but rather
I would really like to deal with the question of what the reality of God means for science today and for the science of the
contemporary university. To this extent I can only say: this
in any case is what I can accomplish. I hope to be finished
with these matters by the time of the university Jubilee. I
must of course put forth very great effort and hope to be able
to present at least a clarification in the christological question
insofar as at the conclusion of the book, after the question of
the God of the philosophers has been dealt with, the God of
Jesus Christ will also be dealt with once more. How far I can
get I do not know. Those for now are the goals. I cannot—
and I say this to you completely openly—from a purely
physical point of view endlessly continue at this intensity. I
must likewise at some time bring this to an end, but I would
in any case then have come so far that I could connect up
with *On Being a Christian*. To this extent I am hard at work
on these questions. I could well think that some things which
concern me will be somewhat better understood after this
book and likewise several hesitations which are still present
will fall away precisely in reference to the fundamental presentation.

Cardinal Volk:
Bishop Moser.

Bishop Moser:
I did not know of the article by Riedlinger which you have
just referred to. But when I page through it now, I see there
precisely the questions which we have just discussed. You
will also recall the sentence which, basically understood,
was the central question also of our conversation. It says

there: "Unfortunately I cannot doubt that Küng's demythologization concretely means the taking away of the belief in the becoming human of the eternal Son of God" (page 193). That must now once again be seen pastorally. And here is the real point at which we have difficulties and where from the parishes there are time and again inquiries of why you say nothing concerning it. It would certainly be the most helpful thing, Professor Küng, if on this point you could provide a clear explanation or expansion, however one would want to formulate it. You would thereby certainly make an essential contribution to the relaxation of the situation, for this inquiry is not simply a theological inquiry, but rather an inquiry of faith of our people who naturally are made uncertain by weakening and one-sided elements of the book. These people want to know, what now? Do the bishops say nothing, do they let everything go? Can we accept that here the God-man will be spoken of no longer in a completely clear manner? I believe that we would make relatively quick progress on this point—if I may take up what Cardinal Höffner has said—if it were to come to a concrete agreement in the sense that you would say that I will also clarify myself on this point. We, indeed, may not undervalue a pastoral matter in the face of the entire situation. You have yourself in your point number eight spoken of such a situation. You know this now also from your own experience. Each of us could present x number of letters where it is said: there one makes a world movement in the sense that resistance is mounted against Lefebvre, and here one allows everything to pass, here nothing contrary happens and also nothing clarifying. I wanted to say this in the sense of the concretization of the Colloquium.

Cardinal Volk:

Pater Semmelroth, can you respond?

Pater Semmelroth:

My remarks go quite in the same direction. I wanted only to point out something precisely from the perspective of your pastoral concerns, which can very clearly be seen in the book and which are in any case extremely welcome to me. There is attributed to Jesus Christ, and this is, as we indeed have already very often seen, stated precisely in functional—to remain one more time with the word—fashion, which I maintain is extraordinarily important. Now naturally there arises in the reader, in the reader who is not educated as an expert theologian, the question of wherein this uniqueness of the relational position of Christ is grounded. From the tradition and from the Councils that would indeed be ontologically responded to. And there I have had the uncomfortable feeling, and I still have it, that the statements of the ancient Councils nevertheless are placed too much—in the sense of questionableness or even of being in need of denial—in the light of speculation, naturally of Greek and Hellenistic speculation. In my opinion there is not a sufficient attempt to make clear to the reader and to present what it is these Councils really meant with their ontological statements (for example, the consubstantiality statements) and whether and how far that is still valid for Christology even today.

This question remains rather unanswered and it seems to me that it would be an important one. Otherwise, people, when they read all these things thus, very easily get the impression: Good, that is Greek speculation and therefore is no longer valid for contemporary men and women and hardly needs to be taken seriously anymore. In this direction perhaps a certain expansion would be possible, if not indeed necessary. One cannot simply say to these people that the statement of the ancient Councils, because they are Greek-formed, thereby no longer have any significance for us.

Professor Küng:
    May I perhaps ask something here?

Cardinal Volk:
    Yes, I ask only—you have the floor—please, Bishop Moser, just read the sentence (of Professor Riedlinger) out

loud. I would then gladly have a response afterwards from you (to Professor Küng).

Bishop Moser:

"Unfortunately I cannot doubt that Küng's demythologization concretely means the taking away of the belief in the becoming human of the eternal Son of God" (page 193).

Cardinal Volk:

You (= Professor Küng) have the floor.

Professor Küng:

I immediately put a question mark there in my text. I am not prepared to subscribe to that. I believe that he (= Riedlinger) does not wish to say precisely this. I would simply reject it as a correct interpretation. I do not in any case wish to take back the belief in the Incarnation. I am concerned to interpret the belief in the Incarnation; and indeed to interpret it from the perspective of the cross and the Awakening, as it indeed likewise occurs in the Scripture. I am critical of the placing of the Incarnation belief in the center whereby—and that is also my critique, but truly not only mine!—with this Greek conception the cross is placed in the shadows: it is only a misfortune. The decisive thing took place fundamentally at Christmas. Hence, critique [by me] exists, but indeed in no case in the sense that the Incarnation should be denied or simply taken back. That is certainly not correct and also does not correspond to what I have said about the Incarnation. One could say that it is too little or whatever, but one cannot say that I simply take it back. That would be one thing. Then to Pater Semmelroth: On this point I have entered into a very intensive exchange with the tradition so that I have worked through up to the medieval theories concerning the becoming human of God. To this also belong those matters which I have been dealing with now for almost a lifetime. Naturally I have long attempted to work my way through here and my first attempts in this direction, as far as they were personal attempts of theology, dealt indeed also only with these matters. Then these things are incidentally to be found in the book which probably is the most difficult to read of my books and has been probably the least reviewed: *Menschwerdung Gottes* [which is the presupposition for *On Being a Christian*].

Pater Semmelroth:

From the point of view of your pastoral concerns these matters must nevertheless be so presented that one who reads this and only this book can nevertheless perceive that these Council statements are not simply no longer valid because they were attained through speculation. I believe—you perhaps do not wish to say that or probably do not wish to say that—but here an attempt which would point out positively what is significant in the Council statements, what is meant and what today is still applicable, should be worked out more positively.

Cardinal Höffner:

The book indeed was also read by believers, not merely by those who stand at a distance or who have become indifferent, but also by believers of the central communities.

Professor Küng:

Right.

Cardinal Höffner:

It is from these that we receive the letters.

Professor Küng:

Indeed, but one will of course also be able to say that many have likewise been made nervous by theologians. When one sees how—and I should also be allowed to say this—a member of the Doctrinal Commission, as for example my colleague Scheffczyk, can distribute an essay, which I can only describe as calumniating, throughout all Germany without reproof (cf. *Concerning "On Being a Christian,"* Schaffhausen: Christiania-Verlag, 1976), without him on his side being reproached, I cannot understand. These people are mounting a campaign against me. And such writings are then distributed by members of the Bishops' Conference yet; I may be allowed to add this.

At the beginning there was no such discussion as this. That came only later. On the contrary, in the beginning there was extremely wide agreement. One said: Here is something that for once helps us move forward! But naturally when one reads these matters as above, then I can understand the reaction. When someone constantly reads the German daily press, then I can understand all this. It is because of this that the people were later made uncertain of themselves. The pastor from Tübingen sent the article by Scheffczyk to all of the members of the parish council. Indeed, what should one do? Against this certainly I cannot react. I cannot counteract it sufficiently. I would have to constantly be at work everywhere and write refuting essays. The whole thing is spread by means which can only be compared to an intrigue. Thus in the *Schweizerischen Kirchenzeitung* a prospectus for this writing (of Scheffczyk) was enclosed, stuffed inside, and indeed against the will of the editor-in-chief. The prospectus alone had such a defamatory character that everyone who saw this prospectus of Scheffczyk's book would have to say: Well, if Küng says that then I don't need to read the book at all. And I believe . . .

Professor Lehmann:

Of the prospectus, yes: According to my information, Professor Scheffczyk disassociates himself from the blurb on the dust jacket.

Professor Küng:

Indeed?

Professor Lehmann:

In any case he declared that a blurb on the dust jacket for his book has been used by the publishing house which he had not seen and that it is painful to him that such a text has been spread about.

Cardinal Höffner:

We note today that you are fighting especially with Mr. Scheffczyk or Mr. Ratzinger, with these two? Would not then a colloquium also be necessary there? I cannot easily imagine that these two wish to malign or put someone down. I presume that they likewise had real doubts as a result of their reading.

Professor Küng:

I am still not completely finished with my response. I am prepared for every colloquium. I have not wished the absence of Mr. Ratzinger here because I do not wish to speak to him, but rather because I had at least imagined (which has been confirmed here) that there might enter into this Colloquium a fundamental sharpness and emotionality which would not be wished by me and which in any case I would not beforehand expect from the two colleagues here present. For me it is a quite extraordinary feeling when I, for example, go to the Society of the German-speaking Dogmatic and Fundamental Theologians, where Mr. Scheffczyk presided as the chairperson, where everything was full of friendliness, and where not a single word was said to me—and afterwards such an attack was forthcoming! The same was also the case with Karl Rahner, who was with me for days in Brussels in 1970 and said not a word of objection against *Infallible?*, likewise did not follow my wish to present the matter [in *Publik*], and afterwards suddenly the matter appears not on the table of the house but rather in public!

These defamations have gone throughout the entire world. In Ireland I was on a Saturday-evening television program which literally the entire nation was watching (because it is a large national program) and again was asked how I respond to the accusation of Karl Rahner that I am a "liberal Protestant." So it goes. Therefore I defend myself against this. And this also pertains a little bit to my response to Bishop Moser concerning my own making things more precise: would that the colleagues also contributed something *positive* thereto! They all have granted that these are authentic questions. Ratzinger admits that. He knows why. He is too smart and knowledgeable not to know that all these matters are very difficult issues. Indeed, then they should all do something jointly for once and also individually.

And I would like to say something further since I have the opportunity: It is not only my impression that precisely the official organs and especially the Doctrinal Commission—I do not indeed wish to say anything here against the gentlemen who are "on it"—appear to people to be extremely one-sided in their composition. That also has to do with an earlier reaction to the "Memorandum on Offices." I have until now refrained from raising the question of the representation of Catholic theology in Germany. The criteria according to which they are sought are in any case personally unclear to me. I do not see the competence in discipline and in subject matter which really must be the criterion for advisers of the Bishops' Conference. There must be some sort of secret canon of orthodoxy which I do not know which determines things. In order not to be misunderstood: I do not like commission sessions and have absolutely no desire to be called! However, there is no question but that a number of documents would have come out somewhat differently if other colleagues had been involved and other specific persons (as the complaints increased) were not simply dismissed, such as, for example, my colleague Haag, who in friendly fashion was pushed out of the Bible Subcommission. I mention that only because to me there . . .

Cardinal Volk:
The entire Subcommission has been dissolved.

Professor Küng:
The entire Subcommission has been dissolved? Well then! One has the impression that here—I say this not as an accusation—perhaps many things would have gone better if people who were in the opposition had participated, if the representation had been broader. I have heard bitter com-

plaints from moral theologians that the only moral theologian (you know of this of course from the colloquium with them, Cardinal Höffner) who represents certain positions in ethics, that is, especially conservative positions, that precisely he is the one who was put on the Doctrinal Commission. Other colleagues whose reputation in the discipline is completely otherwise do not get placed on it!

I would not wish to criticize this now in specifics. I am not concerned now with detail but with an accusation, and it is not concerned with the presentation of particular interests. I mean only that confrontations as they now sometimes have taken place were certainly grounded in the fact that on the side of the teaching office a relatively one-sided composition predominated. I gladly acknowledge that individual persons on the Doctrinal Commission have likewise put forth great efforts—I mean colleagues—to see to it that it does not become one-sided. To this extent I would therefore not wish in any way to pass judgment on individual persons. But the outer spectrum appears not to be large enough.

Bishop Moser:

I believe that we are drifting somewhat away from the subject now. However, I would like first to say something about the referred-to prospectus. I do not wish at all to speak of the content; that would be a subject in itself. However, in any case, the prospectus of Mr. Scheffczyk's book has produced bad blood and even agitation has developed out of it. I believe that no one will defend that nor can defend that. I would welcome it very much if Professor Scheffczyk would say out loud that he has not participated in such a prospectus. That would certainly be a service to an understanding.

You (= Professor Küng) have not made a secret of your thoughts and I likewise will not make a secret of mine. At the beginning under point four you underlined very clearly your readiness for correction. We have taken seriously the objections which have come forth till now and you tell us, as you have emphasized in the course of the Colloquium, that you say yes to the work of expansion. Cardinal Döpfner admonished you further; three days before his death we had a discussion. There he said that also, and I would like to be able to say it here in all openness and without any kind of aggression—you know that—: This would also at some time have to find a published expression. If that which you say is to go out: good here, here I make corrections, here and here I expand things, then certainly some things from the one-sided attacks—if there in fact are such—would no longer be possible. And thus I would simply think that from the Colloquium—without its becoming a gigantic undertaking—something somewhere should be felt and read. You will be helping with an essential step further, Professor Küng—of this I am absolutely convinced—you yourself, your book, your pastoral concerns, and also the Bishops. Without this, it appears to me, we cannot come to a permanent solution. We had already spoken of this, spoke of it in complete calmness, and I wish likewise to say this in complete calmness: there must also at some time be something expressed aloud on your part which at least blunts the point of such possible misunderstandings. I would be very thankful if we could go further together in this direction.

Cardinal Höffner:

What comes to us is an accusation. It is said: You already declared eight years ago that Professor Küng may no longer spread about the things concerning infallibility and against infallibility. We are likewise saying this again. Every new affirmation of this book is nevertheless a new affirmation, every new edition of *On Being a Christian* where the same thing as before is found in it . . . you simply repeat it. What should we do? This is simply not a proclamation of the clear doctrine. You change nothing. Then you say that for at least one or two years now you have noticed how easily injured the unity of the Church is. Everyone no longer allows everything to collapse in the Church; others react in another manner. We sense that it is beginning to break apart! Here the Bishops cannot keep silence. Thus the question now is—we are coming gradually indeed to the conclusion—: What do we do now? How can we help the Church here? That would be my question: How does it go further?

Cardinal Volk:

May I say something to this? For me the concern is that I myself be convinced that the book presents the Catholic faith. I would like to dismiss all objections if I myself were of the conviction that here the Catholic truth is adequately stated. This demands a certain level of statement. For one can indeed say many true things which, however, are not sufficient to express the Catholic truth. I am decisively concerned that the indispensable statements of the Catholic faith in fact be presented. That is my concern. Therefore, once again what I said at the beginning: I consider the Colloquium a chance for me, but also for you, to understand better what I have until now understood from the book. That an interpretation of the book is necessary in order to be convinced about the presentation of the Catholic faith appears to be clear. And therefore the question of Bishop Moser: Would not something be necessary in the sense that something complementary be stated which then can be affirmed by us as the interpretation itself—thus have I thought of the matter, thus have I understood it. For I must indeed be convinced that this states the Catholic truth. I must indeed have the conviction: that is to be represented—and not in the next book or the one after will it be set aright! Therefore every word which you say is of the greatest importance to me; I wish to understand you optimally. But that demands an interpretation because there are so many sentences here. One can say all these things. However, is the indispensable thereby stated? That has indeed become clear here in several statements. I would like once again to underline the question of Bishop Moser. Is not something possible, something in hand from you, so that we ourselves are covered when we are time and again asked?

Dr. Homeyer:

That is really the same thing I would wish to say. Would it then not perhaps be a help if the questions which have become clear here, from the validity of the Councils to the detailed questions as they were developed by Professor Lehmann, if these questions were very precisely formulated from the side of the Bishops' Conference? And if you, Professor Küng, were requested to also make a written statement on them? And when one then reflected, afterwards this also then would be published? Would that then not be a form, as one such, which could here issue as the recognized necessary expansion?

Professor Küng:

Only very briefly to a matter which was remarked on. It is indeed not correct when one says that I would simply repeat. One recognizes even in Rome very expressly that in the infallibility debate I have very loyally held to the—if you will—compromise. I cannot, however, when I am asked, simply say: I do not speak. In our Church this also would make a bad impression. However, I have neither propagated my opinions on the infallibility issue since the Roman Declaration was issued, nor have I for example [done this] in *On Being a Christian,* where it would have been very easy to make an appeal once more very powerfully on two pages. I mentioned the question once more, referred to the literature, and nothing more.

Cardinal Volk:

May I say a word in between? You have somewhere made the remark that there was a difference between the Roman Declaration of that time and that of the German Bishops' Conference.

Professor Küng:

Yes, that can—I do not know for certain . . .

Cardinal Volk:

Yes, you have done so, Professor Küng. But I cannot imagine that two declarations would appear here without their having been compared down to the last crossed *t!*

Professor Küng:

I can imagine that the coordination does not work so badly . . .

Cardinal Volk:

We do not know everything either, Professor Küng. But that you write such a thing really amazed me. Is Küng really so naïve? I thought.

Professor Küng:

No, no, I certainly am not so naïve.

Cardinal Volk:

To the very last dot and crossed *t* the statement which we wrote and the Roman Declaration were compared with one another . . .

I wished only to say that parenthetically. I ask that we continue.

Professor Küng:

Yes, I was saying something concerning the infallibility issue. I have the unity of the Church very much at heart. And I have always shown this when it came to the point— Bishop Hänggi can tell you this more clearly—for example, to the high point of the crisis immediately after *Humanae vitae* when in an extraordinary manner I had the opportunity to give the "word on Sunday" in Switzerland. It was indeed a difficult time when everyone expected that I now would energetically come forth in opposition. However, at that time I urged understanding and unity. Likewise in the Lefebvre issue—I do not know whether anyone here has seen it—I very clearly attempted not to play the matter up but rather to help unity.

Cardinal Volk:

For this we wish to thank you expressly. It is known that you did not play the matter up here. For this we wish to thank you!

Professor Küng:

I am happy that one has seen this. It also truly expresses my inner attitude. Now, pertaining to all of the corrections, I wish to raise the following concerns: One should not play up a book in such a manner as though there were no others. Indeed, at that time three came onto the market which were completely new. Walter Kasper's book says certain things also. Why must in one of them now everything be so perfect that there is nothing whatsoever to admonish? I have no worry but that it will be balanced out. What Walter Kern says, namely, that one should take Küng and Kasper together (cf. the review in *Stimmen der Zeit,* 1976)—this is not exactly my interpretation—is probably done by many. And these people say: Yes, Küng is perhaps more difficult in dogmatic matters. The other is better there, for these things let us therefore take the book of Kasper.

Cardinal Volk:

May I say a word to this? Why do we turn to you? That comes from the fact that your book has had an enormous circulation—not only here in Germany but now it is translated into almost every civilized language. . . .

For us the question is whether a reduction of the faith has taken place here. That is our concern. And for this we have to bear a responsibility. . . .

You know my old thesis: Theology has the essential task of hindering the system. One cannot therefore proceed from one sentence and from it develop the whole theology. . . .

Professor Küng:

I am completely in agreement.

Cardinal Volk:

This complementarity indeed has an advantage, that is true. It is a somewhat complicated thing, but it is true. And when you put the question to me why precisely you are asked about it, then I say to you because the book has had such a circulation and is circulated ever further. . . .

I have likewise read it. And it is an agony, I must grant you, it is an agony. . . .

[At this point in the minutes there are two omissions important in this connection; the recollection is that they concerned the comparison of the above-named books of Kasper and Küng.]

The question is so acute that we cannot simply pass it up. Therefore the question . . .

Pater Semmelroth:

Could we not perhaps ask Mr. Küng whether the suggestion of Monsignor Homeyer would not be realizable. I mean there would then be the possibility that you (= Professor Küng) would make a statement from your side concerning what the Bishops miss in this book. Whether afterwards that would be published—that is indeed the suggestion of Monsignor Homeyer—is a second question which then could be jointly clarified.

Cardinal Volk:

Professor Neumann has asked for the floor.

Professor Neumann:

I would perhaps like to make a mediating suggestion. I mean, the reasons which you (= Cardinal Volk) have given for the questions asked of colleague Küng are indeed enlightening. I would like, however, to raise a doubt about the suggestion of Monsignor Homeyer: The list which the Bishops' Conference presents, or could present, could be so detailed and comprehensive that it then really would be—if Mr. Küng were to respond—what he wished it would not be, namely, a "Summa" or a "Summula."

Therefore, it appears to me that another way—rather than questions to colleague Küng—would be worth considering. According to his own assertions, a number of very substantive responses have already appeared, e.g., by H. Riedlinger and also several others. Here in this Colloquium today several points have been mentioned which particularly concern the Bishops. Would it not be possible to limit oneself to those problems which were addressed here in this room and these perhaps could be looked into in a number of serious scholarly exchanges? Would not then perhaps a not very long but nevertheless clarifying explanation, in the sense of how Küng has attempted here today to explain himself, be given by him? This could happen in a twofold manner, perhaps in a form like the little booklet *Twenty Theses to "On Being a Christian,"* which has appeared separately. One could, however, also consider whether such statements—I would not under any circumstances wish to describe them as corrections but rather as clarifications, expansions, deepenings, explanations—could be brought in as an addition in a new edition. Then probably your concern—that one unchanged edition appears after the other—would be taken care of.

Of course, this would be a question of how it fits in with the work program of Professor Küng. On the other side it appears to me that this matter perhaps need not indeed be so comprehensive. If we receive the transcript of this Colloquium I could imagine that perhaps it would be a matter that could be accomplished within the space of three or four weeks. It would then be an expansion which would not be comprehensive, would not address all problems. What concerns the Bishops likewise is this, that it should be visibly shown. Küng says—reflect also on what you have quoted from Cardinal Döpfner—that he wishes to learn, but that will be expressed perhaps only in his next book after the forthcoming one. It would be fitting if this false impression could somehow be cleared up. I would like to ask both sides whether this might be an acceptable way.

Cardinal Volk:

I would like to mention still another subject which should not remain unmentioned. That is the following: Is—we have indeed also communicated this to you—is the fruit of salvation of the saving deeds of Christ satisfactorily presented? Here I personally have enormous doubts. The impression should not be given that only "ontological" questions are concerned. Is it the uncreated, eternal pre-existent Son of God? That is of concern, of course. That is an indispensable statement. But the saving fruit is also of concern. Namely, whether the saving fruit has the character of mystery, and indeed mystery not in just any sense. There is nothing which we understand entirely, I have already said that a hundred times. There is nothing concerning which we know everything. That is a mystery, a mystery in the theoloical sense, namely, that here there is a connection in the sense of grace, which we would not at all be able to say if we did not have to say it. We have in the meanwhile heard more. But it pains me inwardly when on page 442 it is said: "However, does *today* a reasonable human being wish to become God?"; the sentence ultimately, as you doubtless know, comes from Professor Topitsch. May I ask, have you ever met Topitsch?

Professor Küng:

No.

Cardinal Volk:

I will tell you, I met him in a . . .

Professor Küng:

I have taken it [that sentence] from somewhere else, if I remember correctly.

Cardinal Volk:

Met him in a two-week course . . .

Afterwards, during the discussion, I was asked: Why did you not bash him in the head and why did you not speak more sharply against him? Fundamentally the question behind that was: Is the saving fruit only the answer to the question which we ourselves have? Naturally it is also that. But when Paul said God gives us more than we ask for, indeed than we can think of, then the question is also raised whether that is an answer to our question. What men and women ask *we* respond to—or do we have a message in which more is said as an answer to our question than we demand? . . . The question is thereby raised that for me your ethical section appears downright weak. This question of the suprahuman dimension of the reality of salvation is indispensable. The Scripture is no longer acceptable at all if I wish to respond only to the questions of men and women. No human being can expect something so that it will serve his salvation and will set up here a connection in a way which we do not ask for, but in a way which is conceded to us. Ultimately it proceeds from the question—here one can be expectant about your book concerning God—of how far here it *de facto* is a mystery, how far creation signifies a connection with God which transcends our understanding, and how far the saving act of Jesus Christ signifies a connection with God which transcends our understanding. *For me your book is too plausible* [emphasis added]. It definitely does not concern the character of mystery of the saving deed of God. You do not need to respond to this now. You can do so, but I would rather address the subject . . .

Whether men and women ask about this or not is not decisive. What is decisive is whether we must speak on the basis of what is found in the Scripture. I wished only to have that said so that there are no misunderstandings here. It was stated therefore only so that it would not remain outside the table of this Colloquium. Please!

Professor Küng:

I likewise do not wish to respond to that, but I also do not wish that misunderstandings remain here and I would like only very briefly to say to that: The sentence that man becomes God I consider, from a purely dogmatic standpoint, unusually questionable.

Cardinal Volk:
Absolutely not!

Professor Küng:
Yes, good.

Cardinal Volk:
Absolutely questionable, one cannot say that. For indeed man becoming God is not the point.

Professor Küng:
Yes, then . . .

Cardinal Volk:
It is indeed not . . .

Professor Küng:
I mean . . .

Cardinal Volk:
But that a connection arises which transcends our understanding.

Professor Küng:
I hold the sentence "Man becomes God" to be an un-Christian sentence. Well, can someone explain to me how that is the most fatal sentence in the book, as Rahner partly maintained? I have not understood that at all. For one thing, the sentence as such is for a traditional dogmatics not acceptable in this sense. What the Fathers meant by "exchange" is somewhat implied. Naturally. Of course I also meant to have said that. There is also the second point: When it concerns presenting the "connection" then it indeed always concerns only—even according to the most outspoken statements of the New Testament (2 Peter 1:4)—a "participation" in God. And that is in no way disputed by me; that was also very beautifully explained by Blank. There is also the third point: with me this all comes fundamentally under the term "eternal life," concerning which I hold a great deal. In view of it, according to general conviction, as in relationship to

the Awakening, I believe I have said things more clearly than most other books have, and indeed without hesitation. . . .

There is also a sentence which you, Cardinal Volk, especially like: God is all in all. For me that is also a fundamental sentence of hope. And I have, I believe, said that in all clarity. The "connection" is likewise there. That this is not "plausible" in an everyday sense I have constantly said. With all his doubts H. Riedlinger clearly highlights that. I constantly speak of trust. I hold everything not as purely rational in the usual sense. I say that from beginning to end. May I . . .

Cardinal Volk:

Does the formulation "according to the Scriptures *and* reasonable" turn up?

Professor Küng:

Yes, of course, I likewise hold to it very strongly. (*Cardinal Volk:* Not I.) You would nevertheless not . . . (*Cardinal Volk:* Not I.) You . . . (*Cardinal Volk:* Not I.) . . .

Cardinal Volk:

Because I say there are things in the Scriptures which I must accept.

Professor Küng:

Yes, well, Thomas Aquinas would not say that. Thomas Aquinas would have nothing against "proportional to reason," on the contrary! But this is not important now. I would also like in this connection to explain when Mr. Ratzinger says that everything is placed under "plausibility" and then this is seen as a disqualification: that would be justified if I here appeared as a pure rationalist. I have always said, and that goes for the whole book from beginning to end: as soon as the reality of God itself is in question, whether that is creation, the Awakening, or the completion, reason reaches its limits. Here I even go very far: here only a relationship of trust is possible, whereby, however, I likewise at the same time emphasize knowledge! Therefore only in this sense do I wish to effect plausibility. One indeed cannot say that we have had very many books which today make Christianity plausible. Karl Adam, one of my predecessors, was also bitterly criticized because of his book *The Spirit of Catholicism.* Cardinal Bea himself said that he had intervened for it. . . .

It was also thought then that that was unacceptable, and today that all appears very orthodox. Therefore I think that would now be part of an answer to the questions which were raised earlier.

Cardinal Höffner:
What is to be done?

Professor Küng:
What is to be done? Well, now for once let's be fundamental.

Cardinal Höffner:
Two suggestions have been presented.

Professor Küng:
May I say something fundamental now? If, therefore—now said very clearly—what is put forth in this book is only from a human being and further is the poor work of a theologian, then indeed even from the side of the Bishops one could wait a little bit without nervousness! It is just not so that a book, however widely distributed it is—and I notice and also do my very best, I gladly grant that—can shake up the Church. It is just not so. If it does not come up with something worthwhile in the fundamental points about which, I grant you, it is concerned, then it will just disappear of itself. When you bring up the *teachers of religion,* then these people have indeed also an opposite question for the Bishops: Are not specific things said here in a powerful way such that they can be presented even to contemporary youth and even in this extraordinarily difficult situation faced by our religion teachers who perhaps for the first time are confronted with a generation which did not receive the faith at

home. That is a completely new situation. They (the religion teachers) and naturally also many pastors, even relatively conservative monsignors, say then (I heard this for the first time from a diocesan chancery office in North Germany): "One must in any case grant that from Küng's book one can preach a hundred sermons." That is perhaps the opposite question which ought to concern you in the irrelevancy of the pastoral ecclesiastical situation: That a great part of our clergy—in any case, the younger generation—is of the opinion that it would help them in this very much. In any case, very many say that and also write it. Then there is naturally the question: Good, is then everything now complete? I affirm the question in its justification. And one will indeed also be able to see here what can be done in the future. I mean, however, only that from the side of the Bishops' Conference and also from the side of Rome the matter could be observed with a bit more Christian trust. How that develops —I am not yet finished, that is not yet the end of my answer —will be seen. I grant already that all that should be clarified.

I would also like to say something about "Summa" or "Summula" because the sentence indeed is constantly cited and constantly falsely cited [it is from the foreword of *On Being a Christian:* "What then is the aim of this book, which now in fact nevertheless has become something like a little 'Summa' of the Christian faith?"]. If one looks carefully at the quoted sentence of the foreword, then one sees that this statement (1) is in a subordinate clause, (2) is limited, (3) is in quotation marks, and (4) was described as "in fact." First there is an interrogative clause: "What then is the aim of this book?" And now comes the relative clause, that now in fact, that is, against my will, against my original intention, nevertheless something like, and then still further: *little* "Summa," and Summa in quotation marks, of the Christian faith. I say only this, and this will perhaps show you something of what stands behind it all in regard to the

mental motivation: Had I consciously undertaken to write
this book, I would view myself as presumptuous; I say this to
you very clearly. What I wished to write, and I have just now
heard it from my London publisher, who in a press conference said: "The last time he was here he promised to write a
small book of 200 pages!" And that was my purpose. And
thus I likewise at that time began on a small island somewhere in the wide world and wrote it without any scholarly
apparatus. What one would have perhaps seen was that completely without fear I had drawn the borders toward the left.
As I came back I saw that I could not do it so. (May I explain that further because it appears important to me. If I
made it so short it would not work.) Thus I began to spell
out section C. Afterwards I had to, whether I wanted to or
not, continue further in this style, that is, three levels deeper.
Consequently in the end I also had to write section A and B
once again. I say this only because it always comes in connection with the "claim" of the book. I do not mean that I
would have simply written the Summa: My purpose here is
not to offer the all-comprehensive explanation!

What can I then do? Indeed, and I wish to say this once
again and in all seriousness: The questions are so complex in
these matters which are addressed that one cannot (1) rele-
gate them to an individual, and (2) Monsignor Homeyer, I
appreciate your completely well-intentioned suggestion, but
this is too complex to be able to answer with brief statements. It is too difficult and I would indeed presume that
that is already known by everyone.

Cardinal Volk:

Professor, you yourself, however, have edited *Twenty
Theses*. Have you not yourself considered something like this
possible? Otherwise you would indeed not have done that.

Professor Küng:

Indeed, precisely these twenty theses are evidence for what
I mean, namely, not that I started with twenty theses, but
after I had written 680 pages I abstracted these theses out.

Cardinal Volk:

But you have edited them also as an independent item. (*Professor Küng:* Yes.) That is some indication that one nevertheless can proceed in this manner, that one does not pose only individual questions.

Professor Küng:

But only if one has done the research.

Cardinal Volk:

There are three suggestions now: there is (1) the suggestion of Monsignor Homeyer: questions by the Bishops' Conference and the usable responses from your side; (2) the suggestion of Professor Neumann: write an afterword or a separate small volume; and (3) your own suggestion: why does one not trust me more? If it is nothing then it will of itself disappear. That means for the Bishops: let God's water pass over God's land.

Professor Küng:

The latter I do not mean at all. I will say it once again: you have indeed completely different means at your disposal to contribute to the clarification of the situation. How then can you expect a single individual to perform the entire work? I have already—and I say this in complete modesty—accomplished an enormous work in order to make Christianity again more understandable to contemporary men and women. If in your interpretation that has not succeeded with these statements which concern the traditional dogmatics and the Councils, then I understand that. However, I cannot as a single individual now again immediately shake everything out with a flick of the wrist. What is demanded in my opinion is (1) that the colleagues likewise and in all disciplines, above all dogmatics, New Testament, and also ethics, constructively collaborate here; and (2) it is necessary that I myself again do research. If I now really am supposed to do something constructively new, then I need more time. I cannot now simply so quickly write something in addition. That all requires an enormous amount of work.

Cardinal Volk:

Do I understand correctly that you reject the former suggestion as well as the latter suggestion?

Professor Küng:

No, I do not reject out of hand the suggestion of Mr. Neumann, which, incidentally, was made without my knowledge. I only say in this connection: I cannot (1) do that alone and (2) simply with the flick of a wrist. That would be irresponsible and would be of little help to us in the present situation. But I can—and this would be my own suggestion in the sense I have already indicated—I can now attempt to clarify this question of method, which is the fundamental question: What is the relationship between reason and faith? I can also attempt to clarify at the same time the God question, to which one time and again returns and which you likewise have addressed with the connection between God and humanity. And then I can do yet a third thing (and that would take up somewhat the item from Mr. Neumann. I would not wish to say now ahead of time what will come of it because I myself honestly do not know): I can attempt in the last chapter, where I must make a statement anew about the Christian God—and this is what is of concern—to say several things, some of which I also stated here, perhaps to clear up several difficulties. That I can do. But you should not expect too much from me, not even there. I do not wish somehow to give an impression which then might not be realized. I cannot possibly in this context go into the question of pre-existence. Certainly I can make several things clearer. I do not yet know myself how this Chapter 7 (God of the Philosphers and the God of Jesus Christ, the Old Testament and New Testament God) will look. I also do not know how far, from a purely physical standpoint, I am in a position to do that. But this much I can say, that I now and in this manner can attempt to do at least something which could be of help to you. I can add still one last thing: Afterwards I will then need a break! I have a free semester ahead of me. With

On Being a Christian I was at the end of my powers, even physically; my collaborators can report on it. Many people likewise say I should rest. That would also do my theology good. Well, good. But naturally I do not exclude the expansions. On the contrary, I see them as desirable.

I simply would not want to make a promise now; rather I would immediately again have to think about what I would have to do; I would then have to go into individual questions —even under the circumstances as intended by Mr. Neumann—*expressis verbis,* that is, *ex professo.* Then I could see what would have to be worked through; I would hope of course that other people would also have something constructive to say about these problems. And I hope also that perhaps the Doctrinal Commission will at times constructively attempt to clarify several things—as I had expected to happen in this discussion. Then it would be made considerably easier for me. As I have now indicated, I believe I can also go into and clarify such things even in response to the substantive suggestions of Lehmann (concerning functional, relational, ontological, etc.). The question of pre-existence would have to first be clarified by exegetes. In any case, that is what I now honestly believe I could say.

Cardinal Volk:

Well, but the procedure of the Doctrinal Commission is somewhat different. Think of the contributions of Kasper, Ratzinger, Lehmann, etc. Individual theology has indeed already been done there. But Professor Neumann has asked for the floor.

Professor Neumann:

Yes, I wanted only to say (1), it's true my suggestion was not discussed with Mr. Küng. But (2), you (= Cardinal Volk) have also frightened me again with what you demand of Mr. Küng with such a declaration, when you, for example, come to speak of the fruit of redemption, for this would virtually mean a commentary of Küng writing on Küng. If the Bishops' Conference presents here a theses catalogue, then I

fear that here indeed a single individual will be burdened
with a task which a single individual neither can accomplish
nor should accomplish. Above all, Küng's book—would in
fact take on the character of a quasicatechism—if he
answered the theses of the Bishops' Conference so to say to
their satisfaction. I believe that is neither desired by you nor
would that be Küng's intention. It is likewise not reasonable,
and I would if I were in his place also reject it, to go into all
possible objections and problems now. I believe that my
suggestion was very clearly limited to the themes which were
stated at the beginning, especially by Cardinal Höffner, by
you (= Cardinal Volk), and by Bishop Moser, but also
by the two colleagues and above all in reference to the
inquiries by Mr. Riedlinger. I mean that now, in any case,
Küng would have to be free to take up again *the* questions
in which he felt himself really to be misunderstood and
misinterpreted. And it must indeed, as already said, likewise be doable in a certain manner. I believe Küng has already indicated that in many things an individual is asked to
do too much. You put it rightly: You have written this book
alone, now likewise give the answer to these questions alone.
However, I believe everyone, even in theological work, en-
counters a sound barrier of not being able to do more.
Therefore I would like to have my question so understood
that Mr. Küng now really has the freedom (1) to say which
questions he wishes to answer. Then it would still be the
business of the Bishops' Conference to say afterward: Yes,
that is not sufficient, we now have further concrete questions.
(2) He must also have freedom in the question of the form
of publication. It is one thing if I make an extract of twenty
theses out of a book of 680 pages, and another if I have to
be precise once again about *very specific* questions. It appears to me that the last, colleague Küng, would be almost
simpler, namely, to be precise about a couple of misunderstood questions. I would not say here: Bore deeper, go
still further down, etc., but rather simply say: I did not mean
that which was attributed to me, or as I have been misin-

terpreted. This appears to me to be doable, whether it be in the newly expected book on God or, as said, in any other form. I believe one should not expand the list of all possible questions and inquiries too far.

Cardinal Volk:

Absolutely not.

Professor Neumann:

Then there would come . . .

Cardinal Höffner:

Then over against this naturally there is the conscience of faith of the Bishops. Can we simply let these serious doubts which we have expressed, can we simply let them stand and say: Let us allow the future to decide, for in the history of the Church the development indeed sometimes has led to completely different results when one allowed something to run. Then that would indeed also be for us the question: Can we in the questions which now really press upon our conscience of faith, can we simply wait there?

Professor Küng:

But that indeed is not my interpretation, Cardinal. My understanding was: By no means should one simply let things run. I only say: One, there should not have to be only *one* person who clarifies things, but rather everyone should help; they all indeed grant—one can even read that in the volume of collected essays—that they are not only Küng's problems; Mr. Ratzinger says that in all clarity. I must also indeed still live, I simply cannot do everything. This year alone, because of various things which come up and which I cannot easily turn down—e.g., when a publisher wishes that I be there [for the publishing of a foreign edition of *On Being a Christian*]—is heavily overcommitted. I believe that I have likewise done a great deal so that everywhere *On Being a Christian* will be correctly understood. I have said everywhere that these questions which are disputed do not stand in the foreground. That has certainly, as is granted even in

Rome, contributed to the relaxation of tension. In Italy as well as in England and in Ireland, I have been able to prevent the sensational things, which in the beginning were played up in *Der Spiegel,* from being made into the main things. However, I must for the same reason go to Spain. I mean, to be able to likewise do something there—exactly as in Ireland—for the Church. You can indeed also inquire there as to whether now everything is so negative. If one can say something in Spain in the present unstable situation concerning the things which should remain in the Church, then that is indeed also a pastoral service. In any case I must do all these things. I must in February again go to Washington to the Kennedy Institute for various matters. I must then go once again to America. Unfortunately that must happen three times within a half year, which I normally would not do; and I have not been there for a long time. I can almost count the days of this year wherein I can work further. I must really gather together all the hours and I attempt to do so just to realize even just these possibilities. For the same reason, Cardinal Volk, as earlier because of the theses, I must personally ask for understanding. I cannot speak before the entire university, the President of the Federal Republic, and many guests in the Tübingen Stiftskirche on the difficult question of whether "God" has something to do with the sciences (or however I will formulate it—I still do not know) if I have not studied the matter thoroughly for myself. I have a seminar with my colleague Oeing-Hanhoff in view, perhaps on the questions of the theory of knowledge and all of the questions wherein the other disciplines cause our theology difficulties.

These are the kind of complex questions which often really horrify me in the face of all these things. I must do this now; I cannot in any way avoid these things. Then please let me do them and you will indeed likewise see more results. It is indeed not so simple. That is only my answer to your question about nothing happening. Something from the side of the theologians and from my side should happen.

Cardinal Höffner:

But now there comes precisely the problematic of the two things, the pre-existence of Jesus Christ and what you (= Cardinal Volk) have said about soteriology. Indeed, can we as Bishops, who have the responsibility of the teaching office, can we simply allow that to stand—and other things as well? That is indeed the question for us.

Cardinal Volk:

Professor Lehmann.

Professor Lehmann:

Yes, I would like to return once again to the suggestion of Mr. Neumann. Naturally the form in which that takes place more precisely is a matter which remains first of all for Küng. For example, whether he writes an essay, edits a small volume, or wishes to make an addition. Something or other of this sort. That is first of all . . .

Cardinal Höffner:

Or in the text itself.

Professor Lehmann:

Naturally. And I also can understand the time question. Only I ask Mr. Küng, this time as an advisory member of the Doctrinal Commission, also for a little understanding for the fact that the dispute has now lasted seven, eight, soon nine years. I myself have invested a great deal of time. And I could have easily written a good book or a couple of them if I had used this time for myself. I may also say that here.

The question has come down to one specific point. I hope that this point will not become a conflict which is difficult to resolve. We are in agreement about the expandability of several statements. That is a great deal. There remains the question, however, of with what urgency this expandability is seen. I can somewhat understand that the Bishops hold several expansions to be, simply from the point of view of the subject matter, unrelinquishable.

If we could discuss further we would naturally have to

clarify yet whether, for example, the uniqueness of the person of Jesus which came into existence includes certain dimensions even of the pre-existence statements and the statements about the mediation of creation, whether one can bring this matter to a settlement at all without these dimensions. We have, for example, still not spoken in sufficient detail about the Sonship of God; we have almost not spoken about pre-existence, and hardly about soteriology. It appears to me that, without using a formal pressure or anything like it, because of the subject matter itself simply more precise statements are necessary.

Can one now wait "indefinitely" until a clarification of these questions follows? That is a genuine problem for me. When I think of the exchanges, the disputes, the misunderstandings, the polemics and everything, then I ask myself whether nevertheless it would not be worth the sweat of Mr. Küng, and certainly also of others who can collaborate with him, to at least take up in an essay the questions which here today have been addressed and thus to answer them so that one can say: Several things are now in any case clarified. That need not indeed be an exhaustive answer, a last word.

In the questions which we have dealt with here today there is likewise a pastoral side concerning the effect of the book in other countries. It can be—as Mr. Küng believes—that there have been no difficulties in the reception. However we indeed know, without mentioning anyone, our earlier fellow students, and we understand what they have often taken home with them in theology and Christology. How helpless they often are. I'm not certain whether for these people it is not also necessary to do something more to help them maintain to some extent their own identity. When one comes to Italy, Spain, etc., then one indeed has the impression, amid this enormous change which is taking place, of an inner need, and there is likewise naturally still the question (without this leading to a harmonization of the response!): how does everything which the people once learned—perhaps only externally—how does that really now fit with what is at present going in upon them? That is of course not primarily a question for us here in Germany (although it plagues us sufficiently!). And when this book pours into these lands with a certainly great success, it brings with it the entire burden of the questions and problems which have naturally also turned up here today. Is it then not really possible in the course of the year to respond somewhat to the questions in two or three articles? That would even be a sign. I believe that this really basically would relieve the tension.

I make—so to speak, wearing two hats: as an advisory member of the Doctrinal Commission and also as a colleague —the heartfelt request to you to reflect whether or not such assistance is necessary. The rest of us must indeed likewise speak of these same questions in lectures and engage in discussion with them. I do not have so much time that I can thoroughly enough work through all this in order to publish; that can perhaps even yet happen. It will thus perhaps be the same with some others. However, if one makes these things public with the total use of all powers, even *literary,* as does Hans Küng, then one would likewise have a corresponding responsibility. And here now are the difficult points. It should nevertheless be possible to make a further step here, a further authentic step. The Colloquium today really gives me hope that in two or three of these points that should be possible. It is unfortunate that we could not speak here about pre-existence and the Sonship of God. I believe that, even from the exegetical perspective, it would still be possible to accomplish several things. I would likewise say, in this perspective, that progress has been made there. It certainly looks somewhat different from the way I first learned it. Of that I am convinced. However, that is not the decisive question. Rather, it is: When one makes a global statement about these matters may one leave out elementary essential parts over the long term? That is my question to Mr. Küng. There should nevertheless also be awakened in Mr. Küng a greater sensitivity for the fact that the Bishops are in what for them is really a pressing situation. I wish to call that to mind once again.

Cardinal Volk:
  Bishop Moser.

Cardinal Höffner:
  It is 1:30.

Bishop Moser:
  I will be brief. I am also of the opinion that we should now not set up a maximal catalogue or a maximal demand, but rather we should hold to the rule of proceeding by steps. It must nevertheless be possible to move forward in stepwise fashion. This would likewise mean that there be a proportionate concern for the situation in which Professor Küng finds himself. Nevertheless, something from all of the expectations can be realized.

  If I may systematically repeat it. A couple of points have been mentioned which would not demand a large employment of time. An article was mentioned, for example, an essay relative to questions of Professor Riedlinger. The article could, so to speak, serve as a vehicle in order to bring several points into this response which have played a role in our Colloquium. If one wished still less, one could see the first step in this, namely, that on the basis of the pastoral urgency of the matter—and on this we are certainly at one—a couple of letters with questions and answers could be exchanged. What Monsignor Homeyer said could make the matter easier. One could draw into all of this even what will be available in writing from the recording of the Colloquium. Then the suggestion of Professor Neumann would stand out: a possible appendix to *On Being a Christian,* or what was mentioned by Professor Küng, namely, a chapter within the book on God. This would then of course also contain an inclusive answer whereby indeed the accents which you especially emphasize would depend completely on you. The whole matter can now be brought together, I believe, in the sense of a suggestion and with an agreed-upon time schedule. It would, however, have to be clear—and here I would very much like to ask your understanding, Professor Küng—that something in fact "would be going on," that something in fact would happen. Immediately it would become clear that the matter in general was discussed here, that critical questions back and forth were raised, and were raised here, that they were openly answered here also, that here nothing was veiled —all this would be a help for the necessary relaxation of tensions. Also, from the perspective of the pastoral urgency, a service would be done. Indeed at present it is that which burdens us the most, that from everywhere it is said: Indeed, he (Hans Küng) is allowed everything—and how the formulations are stated! I believe that such general judgments and such mistrust could in fact be turned aside through such a first step. I would like to say this once again: This would not be a tactical move or a beating of a straw man, rather this would certainly be a service to us all and thereby a service to unity. I would be extremely happy if we could at least move further in this direction. I would also like to ask Cardinal Höffner again that all this be publicized. Perhaps at lunch we can also clarify what is meant by "confidentiality of the Colloquium." Whether or not we should speak at all, namely, to communicate that such and such themes were handled and that something concerning them is to expected. I believe that all this would be a help.

Cardinal Höffner:

The public should indeed learn of the manner in which we seek . . .

Bishop Moser:

. . . That that at least has been addressed. I would be concerned here if one declared everything to be confidential and shoved it aside! Concerning this I would like to conclude, Professor Küng, with one more sentence. I understand that on the basis of your work program you say: The others should do something! However, here your word naturally has a decisive weight. Your word, if it goes in the direction and outlines the perspectives as you stated at the beginning: Good, here clarifications will come, here likewise further differentiations will come, here (which Cardinal Volk said) the complementary element will not be suppressed but is even desired. Then much will be won.

Cardinal Volk:
Professor Neumann.

Professor Neumann:
In your sense, Bishop Moser, I would perhaps next like to address the question of making the Colloquium known to the public. I do not hold with the practice widely followed in the Church of confidentiality. Something nevertheless will come out. I would therefore be completely in favor of, for example, Monsignor Homeyer and Mr. Küng or—if he does not wish to do it—Monsignor Homeyer and I or Mr. Lehmann or someone giving notice that such a Colloquium with the Bishops took place, that specific questions which appeared pressing to the Bishops were discussed, and that the expandability, the possibility of the expansion was affirmed on all sides.

Cardinal Höffner:
Indeed, with that we naturally again call up the question of the public: What now?

Professor Neumann:
Indeed, we can also say that there has been agreement, for example, on some things which Mr. Küng can develop in the next weeks. Now you have also said further, Bishop Moser, that Küng's word carries great weight. There comes a very heartfelt request to the Bishops and to the episcopal teaching office, namely, to ask themselves how that really should come about. You see, Mr. Küng has referred to a festival lecture which he is supposed to give. I am on the Jubilee Commission and I suggested all possible names—you can believe

me—but not that of Mr. Küng, indeed simply because I come from his faculty and because it would have looked odd for me to vote for him. I mentioned the name of another colleague from our faculty and one other from the Protestant faculty because in this gathering of the Jubilee Committee the God question was first. And they said, we do not wish on the occasion of the Jubilee to hear something about some questions of the theory of knowledge or indeed something on the history of the university, but rather about the central question of our human existence, about God. Then it was said that the only one that we can have confidence in that he will speak in a language which we non-theologians will understand is not this one or that one, but rather is Hans Küng. Some of these were highly renowned members of our teaching faculty. And if I may say to you that in this room in which we met, the guest house of the university, among many profane works there was also Hans Küng's *On Being a Christian*, then you can see that even here Küng in fact moved into a vacuum of even the episcopal proclamation, that simply therefore his book is snapped up. Therefore it appears to me also conceivable that the burning questions could be answered in some kind of a response, be it in his lecture on the God question, be it in an extension of the introduction to a new edition of *On Being a Christian*, be it in his concluding chapter of the book on the God question. What is then not clarified could indeed still be addressed in clarifying fashion by the Bishops' Conference. I believe therefore that there are still more possibilities than merely the three mentioned. That is what I would still like to say concerning the possibilities.

Cardinal Höffner:

We would like to come to an agreement.

Cardinal Volk:

Yes, I would say that the possibility of the expansion is naturally conceivable. Where in the world is there something which is not expandable? The possibility of the expansion

exists with any book, as theology, the history of theologians
in general in the course of history shows. Therefore the possibility of expansion is a completely harmless statement.
Please, Professor Küng!

Professor Küng:

Yes, I would like to now request the Bishops not to be
over-demanding on me: I am not one of those who say something here but do something else. I promise nothing which I
do not hold to. And I would likewise request that you not
pressure me: not only because it is not possible to force me,
but rather because I would like also very much that that be
done which also makes sense. I have a simple doubt about
all of the "brief things" in this matter because they help little! I mean, you have indeed now an example outside of our
discussion, namely, the *Dutch Catechism*. There it was attempted with such means to do something. Nothing at all has
come of it. There is this fasicle and long negotiations about
what is acceptable and what is not acceptable. The fasicle,
however, has not been taken notice of. And it would indeed
also not be taken notice of if in my case such a catalogue
would be published as something added on. If it is to be,
then one would have to enter into the matter with great
power of persuasion for specific things.

However, a second doubt is added thereto. My experiences
till now have not been so positive—I mean with my colleagues, especially from dogmatics—that I would so quickly
place myself on icy footing. I knew very well why I
addressed only the question of method in the *Frankfurter
Allgemeine Zeitung:* namely, because I know what I can do
in this area and what I cannot. I know very well that if I
were now to write an article that the gentlemen who until
now have not through personal discussion and likewise not
through contributions with understanding, but rather through
heavy polemics and other things have come forward, that
they naturally would take this article to task. Consequently,
when I do something I wish to do something solidly, some-

THE STUTTGART COLLOQUIUM, 1977

thing which likewise is assuredly within the realm of the possible.

Thus therefore I would like from my side now to make two constructive suggestions which in any case—this does not indeed have to be immediately answered—would help still more in the long run. *The first:* Whether or not what at that time was done in Frankfurt [1970, after the appearance of the book *Infallible?*]—Cardinal Volk was likewise present: a workshop could be undertaken among the most competent people (and indeed balanced out). That was on the initiative of [the Jesuits] of St. Georgen. I greeted that warmly in the infallibility debate. There for once things were simply discussed, and were discussed very seriously. I have indeed been the only one until now who has constantly organized the discussion further. I even personally paid the colleagues so that they could come to Tübingen and participate at that time in the infallibility seminar, namely, Lehmann, Ratzinger, and Rahner; Mr. Scheffczyk incidentally at that time turned down the invitation to come. I could imagine that a discussion among the experts could clarify many things. *The second:* It would be really more important to me if now the Bishops' Conference or the Doctrinal Congregation, which probably is even more competent, were to instigate studies on the points concerned. One must take the competent people, whether they are more from this direction or from another direction, for example to do a study precisely on pre-existence or on the Sonship of God. That would be something. I could also imagine that the question of Cardinal Volk concerning the "fruit of redemption" (or however one would want to designate it), that that also could be such a theme. Or likewise the formal question relating to the binding quality of the Councils. There one would indeed have to include not only dogmaticians but also exegetes and likewise historians of dogma, historians, etc., in order to obtain something. That could happen without my participation. I am of course gladly prepared to collaborate and likewise prepared to take a position; then I myself would gain something. I cannot, however, only repeat myself or "correct" myself through a purely external measure. . . .

I could imagine that something would come of it. Those would be two constructive countersuggestions which either with or without my participation, as one would wish, could be realized. I would gladly be prepared then also to respond to all of these questions. You can likewise be certain that this would happen in the appropriate form. I would not have brought these polemics into the "collection of essays"; it would not have occurred to me at all. I was always objective. I also conducted myself thus vis-à-vis Walter Kasper.

What I could say as yet a *third* thing from me is the following: Simply on the basis of my physical capabilities I can at the present time not possibly promise more for this year than that in the last chapter of my new book I will reflect carefully from this perspective and likewise state that which I can at the moment contribute to a clarification. That in any case from my perspective would be something immediate. But I can only promise you that I will take this seriously and —I said already—I promise nothing that I cannot do. I take it seriously and I would attempt to say and do by way of clarification at least that which at the time is possible. However, I promise myself very much more if such studies would be initiated! In the next years I would likewise be again free to think over such things much more. I am convinced that very many things would be clarified and that this would likewise help the proclamation. What I have written is nowhere simply by me. That is quite clear: originality in the usual sense was in no way my goal; I have gathered together what is there; for almost every sentence I can bring forth some reference. As a consequence, at some time others of these matters would also have to be spoken of and discussed. We would simply have to ask the individual expert persons. Then I also could take a position. And I believe that the present day has shown that the matter is not without prospects and that several things nevertheless will become still clearer.

Cardinal Höffner:

This concerns not simply us, but rather it concerns the collegium of the bishops in the whole world. It is indeed not a matter that we would have to virtually halt the proclamation of the faith—until such a study group could come to a conclusion—concerning the pre-existence of Jesus Christ, the fruit of salvation, and the binding quality of the Councils.

Professor Küng:

No, indeed, I do not mean that. You in fact are fortunately not stopping! Here one must really not overestimate the significance of my book. The Archbishop of Cologne would nevertheless always say what the truth is. And you are fortunately now truly not the only one who now also constantly emphasizes the other side. It is indeed in no way the case that that will not be said! With all of the unfortunate accompanying appearances of the debate one will in any case say: It is impossible today that a pastor or a chaplain or a religion teacher has not heard about what is debated. Therefore: It is not so that my opinions are unopposed. It is known, it has been said by the Bishops' Conference, the "volume of collected essays" has now been read by the theologians, and likewise many pastors and chaplains have naturally at least looked into it. It is not so that one would have to suspend the proclamation—how could one do that?

Cardinal Höffner:
It's now 1:45!

Cardinal Volk:

That means that the book will continue to appear unchanged.

Professor Küng:

Indeed, what should that mean now? There are 160,000 copies in print. At present no new edition is foreseen. What sort of sense would it make if I were to add something now?

Cardinal Höffner:

You said indeed you wished to use the seventh chapter of your book in order to . . .

Professor Küng:

In the next book, yes!

Bishop Moser:

I cannot refrain from saying that now as before I have the impression—for all of the positive reasons which have been mentioned: we will in some way have to make a statement. I extend the heartfelt request to you to think over how such a statement—for example, in connection with a news release about the Colloquium—can appear. The moment that you, for example, agree to the possibility of expansion . . . that you declare that you certainly will think further about the emphases and will come back to the questions in further publications, at that moment—and this is now most important to me—a moderating element will be introduced. I believe that we should not take leave of each other after this Colloquium full of understanding but without having such a minimal consensus clearly expressed. It may not be that it simply state: Yes, we have indeed spoken with each other and afterwards we again took leave of each other: there was nothing in principle that was made clear. But something indeed has been made clear! A number of clarifications have been confirmed, which of course likewise would not have been simply excluded ahead of time. I believe that we are also obligated to the public for such a statement, and not only to the Bishops' Conference in connection with the points which Cardinal Höffner mentioned in the beginning. Therefore once again my very urgent request that this be set down in an appropriate composition.

Cardinal Höffner:

That would be taking the suggestion of Professor Neumann: You said it would indeed come out.

Professor Küng:

I believe that it is not possible in a sensible declaration to deal with theological questions. And I did not understand it thus. What is possible—of course, this should not in any way have a disqualifying character—is the expansions. In this sense I wish once again cautiously to say that I could conceive of something like that. I mean that even if it were made known that here matters were very thoroughly discussed: that would show that everything wasn't simply "let go." My readiness to state in this sense publicly that I of course am reflecting on this matter or that matter shall not be lacking. I would not now want to tie myself down to specifics. One would have to reflect on that seriously. But I would not find it good if we did so immediately because, I believe, that takes some time. . . . I have, I believe, also in earlier cases, likewise concerning the Doctrinal Commission, held myself to matters very loyally. It is not my custom to trumpet this in public. I do not know, but perhaps—in order to make a concrete suggestion—Mr. Lehmann could sketch out such a matter and that perhaps it could then be discussed. Perhaps Mr. Neumann and Mr. Homeyer could also help; in principle it does not matter. I believe only that formulations must be found which will make this clear to the public and which also are acceptable to me. I believe that that is possible.

Cardinal Volk:

Homeyer.

Dr. Homeyer:

If I may say something further in conclusion, Mr. Küng. You of course appreciate a candid word. I am not very pleased with the result of the Colloquium, as good as its course perhaps was. I simply fear that the Bishops feel themselves obliged to say something in addition to it or to make a statement. And it would really be my very well-intentioned urging that you do this yourself, for this certainly would be much more sensible and a much greater service to the matter at hand and the Church. That you flatly reject this for this

year—if I may speak so openly—does not really make me
very happy. And I say this in connection with the request
that perhaps you would nevertheless still think it over.

Professor Küng:
It is physically impossible for me! I tell you this very
honestly. I do not even know whether I can do all the other
things; they all depend on each other; I cannot sleep less
than five hours! This is very clear: one cannot simply do that
so quickly! Even fourteen days is an enormous amount of
time. Moreover, I consider it impossible that one could do
anything serious in these fourteen days. I must then go over
the literature. If I wish to take seriously merely an article, as
the one from Mr. Scheffczyk, against which I have many objections, I would nevertheless have to reckon with it thoroughly. I tell you, I do not even make it through reading all
of the reviews—I have stacks of them—although they of
course interest me a great deal. I simply cannot get through
all of them (I believe there is also no one else who would get
through the reading of all these reviews). I read only the most
important ones; now a number of them are coming from all
over the world. Always more are being collected by me
which I simply have not yet read. I will of course read them
sometime; I hope that perhaps sometime it can be done in a
seminar or in some other manner. But now I simply physically cannot do it! I really cannot do it!

Cardinal Höffner:
The minimal suggestion was that the two professors and
Monsignor Homeyer somehow (*Bishop Moser:* Professor
Neumann)—yes, I mean Professor Neumann and Lehman as
well as Monsignor Homeyer—somehow would attempt to
draw up a brief text about the Colloquium today. You (=
Professor Küng) yourself just now said that it should be
declared that the Colloquium had taken place, that several
questions—one could also name them—were discussed, and
that you are prepared to consider these. You said that.
We indeed are not competent, we can indeed only report

to the seventy fellow confreres of the Bishops' Conference. We are indeed not competent to say what they will do; we do not know what they will then say.

Cardinal Volk:

I personally do not find such a statement which we have discussed very helpful.

Cardinal Höffner:

No. From us . . .

Cardinal Volk:

One will say: What has he (= Professor Küng) said then and what really are the positions? And that leads indeed to a sackful of questions!

Cardinal Höffner:

However, we would likewise believe that it could remain confidential on our part.

Cardinal Volk:

I could imagine that with collaboration between Bishop Moser and you (= Professor Küng), the immediate contracting parties, a statement with this or that content could be made, which of course would bring with it a sackful of questions. The priority should be that it says: We are in dialogue. That would indeed be the positive meaning: We are in dialogue.

Bishop Moser:

Those emphases can certainly be included which proceed from the fact that we were here not bickering but dialoguing. Naturally it must also come out that—if I have heard correctly this was also mentioned—several major points were clarified in this discussion. And perhaps from what was said on both sides in the beginning, a couple of sentences could be included which would be formulated somewhat otherwise now that we have spoken with one another. I do not hesitate to say that perhaps when a sketch is there before us we could discuss it again expressly. That cannot be done in five lines.

Cardinal Höffner:

A short press release saying that this and that point was discussed can of course be confusing to many—we will naturally then receive letters. Then one will see: you Bishops are no longer even certain on this point, etc. Indeed, the letters will come as soon as the day after tomorrow.

Professor Küng:

That of course is not the intention of such a notice.

Cardinal Höffner:

Those are his (= Cardinal Volk's) doubts about a short notice.

My suggestion is that a mini-notice be given out now and shortly afterwards a detailed notice about the Colloquium. For if a mini-notice is given out and afterwards only a short release, that would be rather thin fare.

Cardinal Höffner:

Then indeed perhaps it would be better not to publicize anything. For I am convinced that the Colloquium will not remain confidential.

Professor Küng:

I believe that the fact that there was a discussion cannot be kept secret. One will of course have to be able to say to one's colleagues that the Colloquium took place. I have always thus understood things in these matters: whether one issues a one-page press release or in some other manner brings the issue before the public. I believe that it would be quite extraordinary if it were done in this fashion (a mini-notice). I indeed did not make the suggestion; I only responded to the question. I am gladly prepared to collaborate. In fact, the matter has two sides. I likewise do not know what will be a greater help to the situation of the Church—it is indeed this that is at stake in this case; this surely is the criterion. I could imagine—I'm just saying this now thusly—that a text could be so formulated that the stand of the *Bishops* and their positions would not be damaged, but rather could be expressed in some way to show that the matter is not simply being let go. And on the other side it must also be so spoken that it will not in any manner be interpreted as a dressing down of me or the like. And thus I can from my side say something helpful on this occasion. However, I believe that this depends on you. I can only express my readiness.

Cardinal Volk:
Professor Lehmann.

Professor Lehmann:
If one does not take up questions of content—in such short declarations one can do that all the less—then its function would be primarily that of a press release. More than that probably cannot be done at all now. If the matter went on for more than a page or so, this would then also mean definitions (which are not possible now). It seems to me that such a press notice could be comprised of ten or fifteen lines. It will indeed not be difficult to say that in connection with the discussion of *On Being a Christian* representatives of the German Bishops' Conference met with Hans Küng, etc., in order to review disputed questions. Why should one not say that christological questions were discussed, but also it was found by Professor Küng that here expansions are completely possible, that the expectation was expressed by the Bishops that these expansions will be carried out in the near future. Or something similar. More will not be possible in such a notice. One could also say—if one wished to—that the Colloquium should be continued, perhaps in other forms. Of course there would have to be discussion of this. I could imagine something like this.

Cardinal Höffner:
That would not be more than the content of the earlier letters.

Professor Lehmann:
If one wishes to prevent uncontrolled rumors about today's Colloquium one must issue a press release. Or do we think

that the people are all walking blind through the house?
There is a conference here this afternoon. It's absolutely impossible in fact to prevent this from being spoken of. And
then when individuals are asked, what should they say in the
absence of such a declaration? It is also not good of course if
then different persons respond and speak in their fashion:
The one says a bit more and the other says a bit less! To this
extent I would therefore welcome a short press notice, which
of course then may not appear later than Monday (meaning:
January 24). Therefore it would have to be done here. It
would make no sense to brood about it once again for a long
time at home. Then it in fact would be too difficult and too
late. A decisive question appears to me now to be: Does one
wish such a press release with a limited function, or does one
believe that a communication can be dispensed with altogether? Another kind of "declaration," a substantive-
theological sort, does not appear possible to me now. Then it
is likewise not good to speak formally of a "declaration," but
rather of a press release.

Cardinal Höffner:
    In Cologne forty to sixty bishops are already waiting [for a
celebration of the seventieth birthday of Cardinal Höffner].
There is still a four-hour trip.

Bishop Moser:
    But you will still eat something?

Cardinal Volk:
    Can we then agree on the suggestion of Bishop Moser and
Professor Lehmann? I also opt for: (a) there was a discus-
sion, (b) it cannot be said that everything would be "let go."
There is indeed no reason to be quiet about this . . .

Professor Küng:
    Then probably the best suggestion is that we should sit to-
gether here immediately, that is, those who can do so now. It

should be done immediately. Any hesitation, I believe, would be of no use.

Bishop Moser:

Who could sit together a little longer after lunch? (Küng, Lehmann, Moser, Neumann indicate their readiness.)

Dr. Homeyer:

I also am a bit on pins and needles. (*Cardinal Höffner:* What? *Homeyer:* A bit on pins and needles.) Cardinal Tarancón is waiting.

Professor Lehmann (to Monsignor Homeyer):

But you surely could have a brief limited time? It would indeed be very good if you could be present.

Cardinal Höffner:

But we will still all eat together. We can speak of the matter at the table.

The Colloquium was ended around 2 P.M.

As agreed, a joint press communiqué was issued which noted the fact that the Colloquium took place, who was involved, what was discussed, and that "agreement was reached that several christological presentations are in need of expansion. . . . Professor Küng has declared himself prepared to contribute to the clarification of the discussed questions in an appropriate manner." Then on February 21, 1977, Küng sent a long detailed letter to Cardinal Höffner in time for the next meeting of the German Bishops' Conference that month. In it he surveyed the ground of the dispute, responded to specific theological questions, but pointed to his soon to be published book *Does God Exist?* as a place where the needed elaborations referred to would be found, and ended the letter with a series of suggestions on how theological research might be carried forward and fostered by the Bishops' Conference in conjunction with theologians. The letter was as follows:

(55)

Dear Cardinal:

On January 22, 1977, in the Catholic Academy in Stutt-gart-Hohenheim, the discussion of *On Being a Christian* took place with you, Cardinal Volk, and Bishop Moser. You had invited Professors Lehmann, Semmelroth, and Prelate Homeyer to join, and I had invited Professor Neumann. I am grateful to the Bishops that this time a personal discussion with me was preferred to a new public declaration and that the discussion was conducted in an open and friendly atmosphere. All participants no doubt realized that in this way many important points could be clarified. As suggested to me, I would like to commit to writing some of these points for the attention of the German Bishops.

1. My book *On Being a Christian,* as well as my earlier books, can only be understood if one perceives that the objective they pursue is pastoral. Although I do substantiate my views in scholarly fashion, I am never interested in a purely academic, ivory-tower scholarship, but in positive answers to the questions people ask today, in the light of the Christian message. Among all the questions discussed in connection with *On Being a Christian,* there isn't a single one which I have myself fabricated. Everywhere I have addressed questions that beset people within and without our Church. Anyone who has read this book can recognize that I have gone to great lengths to provide constructive answers to these questions.

2. One does justice to the book only if one sees it as a whole, and refrains from taking into consideration in a 675-page book only the 50-page chapter entitled "Interpretations," which deals mainly with the history of dogma. The extraordinary success of the book among pastors and religious educators, a success the Bishops often mentioned, can only be traced to the fact that there the Christian message of the earthly, crucified, and risen Jesus has been elabo-

rated in a manner that is convincing to them and helpful in their pastoral activity. No other book of mine has yet met with such wide acclaim among Catholic pastors, religion teachers, sisters, and men and women engaged in Church work. I often wonder whether it might not be useful to publish some impressive expressions of the "sense of the faithful." Above and beyond, this book has appealed to circles outside the Church which are hardly ever reached by theological literature or by the Christian proclamation. Thus it has already proved to be a new basis for the difficult dialogue with Jews about Jesus Christ. This is connected with the points to follow.

3. One does not do justice to the book unless one perceives that, from beginning to end, something like the perspective of the first disciples of Jesus is being consistently adopted, which is the perspective of the questioning person of today, the historical difference, of course, being taken into account. This is the way in which to construct on solid historical foundations a Christology "from below," as suggested by the whole historical research of the last two hundred years. The Christology "from above" is known to me from my seven years of study in Rome, as well as from the new Catholic and Protestant interpretations of our time. From *Justification* (1957) to *Menschwerdung Gottes* (1970), I myself have tried to elucidate this Christology through research in the history of dogmas, philosophically, theologically, and systematically. I still regard it as a legitimate Christology. Yet I have already explained in *Menschwerdung Gottes* why today it seems to me to be objectively right and pastorally appropriate to approach Christology "from below."

Every Christology is dependent, to be sure, on the witness of the New Testament, the witness of the Church of the Apostles, but this is not what is meant by the expression "from below." In every Christology "an element of a theology from above" does play a role insofar as *God,* the Kingdom of God, the will and action of God are already involved in the proclamation, the conduct, the claims of the Jesus of history, and not only in his resurrection. But even if this figure of speech be regarded as unimportant, it makes a decisive difference all the same, methodologically, whether, in dealing with the interpretation of the New Testament witness, as well as with the traditional Christology from the Fathers to Karl Barth, a doctrine of the Trinity and of the Incarnation is the premise from which we start, and then move deductively from God ("from above") to the man Jesus of Nazareth; or whether I, as well as various other Catholic and Protestant theologians, begin by taking stock of modern exegetical discussions, and, placing ourselves time and again in the perspective of the first disciples of Jesus, as it were ("from below"), we systematically think our way to God, inductively and interpretatively. When one attempts an exact definition of the concepts, one cannot think with methodological consistency "from above" and "from below" at the same time. From a methodological point of view, we have here a genuine either/or! An illustration: If you want to climb a mountain step by step from below, you cannot at the same time keep on calling down from the top. Obviously, we are dealing here with two different interpretative models (paradigms) of the Christian message. Both have their advantages and disadvantages. By competing with each other in an honorable theological contest, they both can prove what service they can render to the Gospel and to the people of today.

4. I have no doubts that, when we engage in our critical inquiry into exegesis and the history of dogma, we must adhere if not to the letter, then certainly to the broad objectives and substance of the Ecumenical Councils and especially of the Councils of Nicaea and Chalcedon, which are of fundamental importance in classic Christology. Even in the book *Infallible? An Inquiry,* I have shown something to which too little attention is being paid: the Church is dependent both on short recapitulative propositions of the faith (professions and symbols of faith) and, in extreme cases, on propositions

of the faith which are defensive and defining (definitions and dogmas of faith; cf. pp. 143–50). Thus, practically for the past twenty years I have tried over and over again to achieve a positive understanding of the great and even of the little-known conciliar tradition, from the christological Councils of Nicaea and Chalcedon to the late Byzantine councils (cf. *Menschwerdung Gottes*), from the medieval papal synods, the Councils of Constance and Basel (cf. *Structures of the Church*) and Trent (cf. *Justification; Why Priests?*) to Vatican I and II (cf. *Structures of the Church; The Church; Infallible? An Inquiry; Fehlbar? Eine Bilanz*). With regard to the elaboration of the christological tradition, the explicit "prolegomena" to *On Being a Christian* are constituted by *Menschwerdung Gottes,* a fact which has also been too little noted. From the beginning and always since, it seemed indispensable to me that the ecclesial and also the conciliar tradition should be measured against the Christian message as originally witnessed to in Holy Scripture, in fact against Jesus himself, as the primary criterion of every theology.

5. Although time and again, I am being publicly compared with the "Lefebvre case," I must for the reasons already indicated absolutely refuse to let my position be equated with that of Archbishop Lefebvre.

a. It has never occurred to me to pose as infallible in my own right or to contest the orthodoxy of the Roman authorities, as Monsignor Lefebvre has repeatedly done. In my confrontation with Rome I have criticized, asked questions, made proposals, urged discussion and reform, but all the while I have acknowledged that there was also another Catholic opinion and that I am fallible.

b. In all the criticisms I directed at the halfheartedness of many conciliar documents, I certainly had no cause to discredit Vatican II globally as a neo-modernistic, neo-Protestant, and heretical council. I have rather shown clearly how much the "novelties" of Vatican II—relative, say, to the reform of the liturgy and the adoption of the vernacular— have on their side not only the New Testament but also the old Catholic tradition, a tradition of which Monsignor Lefebvre seems to be ignorant.

c. I have founded no ("progressive") group of my own. I have deliberately recoiled from all sectarian endeavors. I have never intended to be more Catholic than the Catholic Church. To the best of my ability, I have spoken and worked everywhere for the unity of our Church, last but not least in connection with the Lefebvre case.

d. Nor have I ever tried, in exclusive and doctrinaire fashion, to impose my views particularly on priests in training or even in a seminary of my own. In a regular church-affiliated or state-run school—and also among us here in Tübingen—the students are exposed from the first to the most diverse influences (more conservative or more progressive), and this I have always welcomed.

In short, I have never made a secret of the fact that, in spite of all the difficulties which have been created for me in this my Church almost since I received my doctorate in theology, I remain loyal to this my Church and I stand up passionately on her behalf. I am happy to say that numberless Catholics, clerics as well as lay, at home and abroad, have time and again given me strength along this path.

6. With regard to the christological dogmas which presuppose the doctrine of the two natures, I have taken considerable trouble to safeguard the great objectives and the substance which have the authority of the New Testament and to show their relevance. In keeping with the well-known word of John XXIII, the conceptual and representational framework need not be adopted as if it were normative. The "substance" of the faith must be safeguarded; the formulation, which is the "garb," can change. This applies also to the dogmatic assertions concerning pre-existence, incarnation, redemption, and Mary, all questions on which I have much to say in *Menschwerdung Gottes* and *On Being a Christian*.

I do have the impression that critics overlook or fail to take seriously enough important assertions of *On Being a Christian,* as for example my clear agreement with what represents the basic aims of the Council of Nicaea against Arius: "In Jesus the one true God is present, not a second God, or demi-God. Our whole redemption depends on the fact that in Jesus we are concerned with the God who is really God" (*On Being a Christian*, p. 448). Or the interpretation of the formula "truly God" in the Council of Chalcedon: "The whole point of what happened in and with Jesus depends on that fact that, for believers, *God himself* as man's friend was present, at work, speaking, acting and definitively revealing himself *in* this *Jesus* who came among men as advocate and deputy, representative and delegate, and was confirmed by God as the Crucified raised to life" (p. 449). Or about the Incarnation: "As became clear through all the previous chapters, it was in Jesus' *whole* life, in his *whole* proclamation, behavior and fate, that God's word and will took a human form. In his whole speech, action and suffering, in his whole person, Jesus *proclaimed, manifested, revealed* God's word and will. Indeed, it can be said that he in whom word and deed, teaching and life, being and action, completely coincide *is* the embodiment of God's word and will . . . he might almost be called the *visage* or *face of God* or . . . even the *Son of God*" (p. 443 f.). According to all this, it is obvious that I have never thought of denying the divine Sonship of Jesus (or the Trinity)!

7. Whether or not these interpretations, which I do not alone advocate, suffice is open to debate also in my case— just as in the case of other Catholic theologians of our time. Today the difficulties entailed in christological interpretation, deriving from the exegesis of the New Testament, the history of dogmas, and modern consciousness, are considerable for every Catholic theologian, but also for every preacher and proclaimer of the Christian message. I am certainly aware that my book, or more often biased press reports or reviews of my book, can at first disquiet traditional Catholics, especially when they have not been appropriately instructed through religious education and preaching and when they read only parts of my book or none of it. In any case, I

would like to stress this: my expositions are not at all meant
to curtail, conceal, disquiet, trouble, but to help the dis-
quieted, to afford clarity to those who are at a loss, to overcome polarizations, to strengthen the Christian faith. For this
help numberless people are grateful to me.

In this connection I was glad, and have said so publicly,
that the late Cardinal Julius Döpfner, as President of the Conference of German Bishops, in his press conference in February 1975, explicitly acknowledged my "high level of commitment" and my "pastoral goals," as well as my "integrity as a
priest and as a Christian." A few theologians (some of them
members of the German Doctrinal Commission) have de-
scended again below the level to which the discussion has
risen. I would like, therefore, explicitly to beg you and the
German Bishops to keep on upholding this my "integrity."
They should urge on their theological advisers "the hope that
in the future the things in common will be emphasized more
than the things that divide."

8. As far as the discussion of *On Being a Christian* is concerned, I have tried since the publication of the book to clarify, re-examine, and deepen those controverted dogmatic
questions which are in need of further theological investigation, as I myself had already declared in the book. This is
not just an empty "promise," as the following facts prove:

—A three-day discussion among doctoral students on the
comparison between *Jesus the Christ* by Walter Kasper and
On Being a Christian;

—A further three-day discussion among doctoral students
on the volume of essays entitled *Discussion of Hans Küng's
"On Being a Christian";*

—Discussions of many hours' duration with well-known
experts on the questions at issue, especially christological
questions;

—A seminar on the aforementioned volume by Walter
Kasper which ended with a discussion between the author
and myself;

—I have conducted discussions or exchanged letters on problems still pending with most of the authors who contributed to the aforementioned volume of essays.

9. While trying conscientiously to come to grips with the points at issue, I have also been waiting for a long time for constructive contributions from my colleagues, contributions, namely, that would be truly helpful and take seriously the present state of exegetical, historical, and systematic research. In this respect, the volume co-edited by various advisers of the Doctrinal Commission of the Conference of German Bishops was a major disappointment for me. Hence, some remarks on my reply in the *Frankfurter Allgemeine Zeitung* of May 22, 1976, a reply which the Bishops have found objectionable.

Last spring in my conversations with Cardinal Šeper and Archbishop Hamer I acknowledged that, without a doubt, progress has been made when controversial questions in theology are discussed by theologians in scholarly fashion, instead of being settled magisterially through disciplinary measures. Of course, I could not understand then, and still cannot understand, why—considering the one-sided choice of contributors—the author being discussed was not allowed to have his say in the same volume as a partner in the discussion. This is customary in a volume of discussions and is the only way in which the reader can form an objective judgment about truth and error. I was told in Rome that I could certainly reply to this volume in an article. Given the importance of the authors and the ripple effect of a book and of the attacks on my Catholic orthodoxy, I thought that my reply should appear, not in a scholarly journal, but in a serious newspaper of wider circulation. I hope that the German Bishops, too, will understand that, if a newspaper article on highly complex questions in defense of my Catholic integrity was to be understood at all, it had to be written differently than a technical article. A totally different reaction would have been possible on my side:

a. if the articles by Balthasar, Grillmeier, Rahner, and Ratzinger had shown the same constructive willingness to dialogue as the articles by Deissler, Kasper, Kremer, Lehmann, and Schneider;

b. if a firm defense of my Catholic orthodoxy had not, to my chagrin, been called for because of general allegations and accusations of heresy;

c. if in the same volume I should have been permitted to answer the questions of my colleagues.

This "discussion," as unpleasant as it is even for me, has not been provoked in this form by me, since on my side I have never started a personal polemic. I am still not interested in a further escalation and would be grateful if I could be spared such escalation. The articles of the authors who contributed to the volume have made it all too clear how difficult it is, even for the theologians who criticize me, to answer these questions. The most important thing now is constructive cooperation on all sides. At any rate, one thing is clear: I alone cannot be saddled with the burden of clarifying questions shared by all.

I may also remark that, as has been the case earlier in the infallibility debate, this "theological rage," replete with hateful personal attacks by fellow theologians, has only been the case in German-speaking countries. These polemics—spread about in all kinds of leaflets and pamphlets—have contributed to the unsettling of the Christian people more than my book has. Before my critics began to engage in polemics the book had been received by the public in an entirely positive way. Upon my return from Ireland and England, I was able to report in the discussion in Stuttgart how positively my book had been received there. The same is true of the United States, which I visited in November, and in Italy, where the book was published last year and caused none of that excitement, and later also in Brazil. In all these countries—soon this will no doubt be the case also in Spain and France—people seem to have understood the book for what it intends to be. It aims to help people in their Christian life and faith within and without the Catholic Church.

10. It goes without saying that the article I wrote for the *Frankfurter Allgemeine Zeitung* is not my last word in the matter. As I have already mentioned in a letter to Cardinal Döpfner, I hope to find time in the near future to address anew in scholarly fashion the exegetical, historical, systematic, and hermeneutical questions raised in the volume and elsewhere. It goes without saying that a theological reconsideration of the subject matter includes clarifications and corrections, completions and deepenings of my own position too. As already stated in the book itself, I am convinced that a positive updating is quite possible, and indeed desirable with regard to the various doctrinal points—also and especially with regard to those which the German Bishops' Conference finds objectionable.

In our discussion in Stuttgart we came to agree that some christological expositions need to be complemented. In keeping with the basic attitude I have already often explained, I have declared that I am prepared to contribute in an appropriate way to the clarification of the debated questions. For the time being, this will be done especially in my book *Does God Exist?* to be published next year, which is a complement to *On Being a Christian*. In this volume I will extensively address the basic problematic many critics have addressed, namely, the relationship between reason and faith, as well as the understanding of God which is at the root of all the questions. I will also touch upon the question of Jesus' relation to God the Father. In connection with this question one could, for example, clarify some things that came to expression in our discussion, namely:

—that "functional" christological assertions should not be regarded as "unreal" assertions, so to speak (Jesus *is* really the Son of God);

—that in Jesus Christ acting and being cannot be separated;

—that uniqueness and underivability apply not only to the origins of Jesus Christ but also to his person;

—that the Johannine Christology, which had to be dealt with with relative brevity in *On Being a Christian* (although very emphatically, and in considerably more places than many critics have noted in their superficial reading of the book), can be brought out more extensively, etc. . . .

11. Even during the most difficult phases of the infallibility debate, I have consistently affirmed that it is beneficial to have in our Church a pastoral office of teaching or proclamation of which the Pope and the Bishops are in charge. Yet, even in Rome I have recently tried with all possible emphasis to make the point that this office can serve its purpose in our time only if it is not one-sided but truly Catholic, and does not attempt to exclude out of hand distinctive representative directions in today's Catholic theology. This is the only way to avoid much-lamented polarizations and unfavorable pastoral consequences.

12. I, therefore, take the liberty of reiterating here the proposals I made in the discussion in Stuttgart for the purpose of attaining to a common clarification of the issues pending for all theologians:

a. Study projects relative to important individual issues (for example, the pre-existence of Jesus Christ, divine Sonship, soteriology) should be promoted and funded with the participation of the most qualified experts from pertinent disciplines;

b. Symposia should be promoted and funded in which important individual issues would likewise be discussed by specialists with openness and collegiality;

c. For the sake of its own credibility, the German Doctrinal Commission should be so composed as to represent all important currents of today's Catholic theology, in order to preclude the impression that some theologians pass judgment on other theologians who are just as competent as they are. In the selection of advisers competence should be the criterion, not good conduct.

d. The Doctrinal Commission, whose statements to the public have been hitherto almost exclusively negative, in the manner of the Roman Congregation for the Doctrine of the Faith, should address more positive tasks in the service of proclamation.

In conclusion, may I repeat what I have written in the past to Cardinal Döpfner: as far as *On Being a Christian* is concerned, after the official Declaration of the German Bishops on *On Being a Christian,* after the Declaration on Nicaea, and especially after the aforementioned volume of essays, I am of the opinion that the time has come to let peace enter. Official and semi-official criticisms have been heard and I have responded to the extent to which it was necessary to do so in my own defense at this particular time.

I would be grateful to you, my dear Cardinal, and to the German Bishops if I should be permitted to do my theological work in peace and quiet. I hope that, by means of this letter too, I may have said something that will contribute to a proper resolution of the present situation.

I would like to ask you to send this letter to all the members of the Conference before the next meeting of the Bishops' Conference.

With best wishes and cordial greetings, I am,

Devotedly yours,
Hans Küng

cc. Dr. Georg Moser, Bishop of Rottenburg

Judging from the optimistic tone of the letters Küng sent on the same day to Monsignor Homeyer and Bishop Moser, he felt that his lengthy letter to Cardinal Höffner would satisfy the German Bishops at least until his book *Does God Exist?* came out several months later, where his christological views would be elaborated with the Bishops' concerns taken into consideration. On March 3, 1977, the German Bishops' Conference issued a Declaration about the Colloquium, the results of which they found unsatisfactory. Given the obviously aggressive personality of Cardinal Höffner as President of the Conference without an effective coun-

terweight in Cardinal Döpfner, one wonders how much the negative judgment of the Declaration reflects Cardinal Höffner's hard-
driving attitude. Still, on the basis of the Declaration alone, one
would have thought that the Bishops would nevertheless be content to wait and see what Küng would do in the promised elaborations in the soon to appear *Does God Exist?* However, in an accompanying letter to Küng, Höffner said that the Conference
directed him to "impart to you the questions which emerge about
On Being a Christian, and out of the Declaration of February 17,
1975." Those questions were promised later. The March 3, 1977,
Declaration was as follows:

(56)
Declaration of the German Bishops' Conference to the Press Concerning the Discussion with Professor Küng

The German Bishops' Conference has examined the results
of the discussion with Professor Küng arranged by the
Bishops' Conference and held in Stuttgart on January 22,
1977, Cardinal Höffner presiding. As it appears from the
communiqué released to the press by the Secretariat of the
German Bishops' Conference, the main theme of the discussion was constituted by the assertions of Professor Küng concerning the person and saving action of Jesus Christ in his
book *On Being a Christian.* In this discussion Professor
Küng recognized that some christological explanations in his
book need to be complemented. The Bishops felt that the
amendments were urgently needed, since they concern assertions which are central to the Catholic faith. Professor Küng
declared that he was ready to contribute "in an appropriate
way" to the clarification of the questions at issue. What he
has presented thus far is not sufficient.

In spite of initial moves toward agreement, the German
Bishops' Conference regards the inadequate and ambiguous
assertions of Professor Küng as so momentous that it must
again request Professor Küng to provide the necessary precisions and emendations.

The German Bishops once more reinforce what they said in their Declaration on the Creed of Nicaea on September 24, 1975: Jesus is not only an exemplary human being, not only God's spokesperson and administrator [*sic;* the Bishops wrote *Sachverwalter,* "administrator," instead of *Sachwalter,* "advocate"]; he is rather the eternal Son of God. "God from God, light from light, true God from true God, begotten, not made, of one substance with the Father," as the Church teaches in its profession of faith. Only if Jesus Christ is presented unequivocally and witnessed to in accordance with this profession of faith as true God and true human can the Christian message of redemption and salvation remain uncurtailed and unadulterated. Because the book *On Being a Christian* fails to do justice to this central truth of faith, the German Bishops' Conference insists on a prompt correction or supplementing of the pertinent assertions of Professor Küng in keeping with normative Church doctrine, so that readers may not be misled and confused. On February 17, 1975, the German Bishops' Conference drew attention not only to the Christology but also to the doctrine of the Trinity, the theology of the Church, and of the sacraments, and to the place of Mary in the history of salvation.

This declaration of the German Bishops' Conference has been imparted to Professor Küng. The assembly would welcome it if Professor Küng should do what is required for a clarification.
Essen-Heidhausen
March 3, 1977

A little more than six weeks later Cardinal Höffner sent Küng the "questions" in a letter dated April 22, 1977. Of this letter Jens wrote: "As was stated by a very reliable source, this letter was written for Cardinal Höffner by a known dogma professor and member of the Doctrinal Commission." In this letter Küng is obviously being pushed to state again in traditional fashion the christological formulas of the Council of Chalcedon (A.D. 451). However, it is precisely doing only that which Küng thinks would

be a betrayal of the obligation of the late-twentieth-century Western theologian. The Chalcedonian formula was developed in a period and culture when mythological language was *au courant,*
when Greek ontological categories were *the* thought patterns,
when "divine human beings" were familiar and meaningful. All
of those cultural givens have for some time been fast disappearing
in Western Christendom. Now the historical-critical, scientific
world views tend to prevail, and consequently theologians must
work with those givens in order to "evangelize" their contemporary world, just as the "good news" of Jesus was translated
from the Jewish world view into the Greek world view in the
early centuries of Christianity. Hence, simply to repeat the ancient ontological, mythic language of the early Greek Councils, as
Cardinal Höffner wanted, was seen by Küng, along with perhaps
the majority of substantial contemporary Western Christian theologians, as worse than worthless. In this letter—regardless of who
wrote it—we find a classic example of the impasse so frequent in
contemporary Christianity between the ontological, static world
view and the historical, dynamic world view. Höffner was asking
ontological, static questions; Küng was giving historical, dynamic
answers. The trouble was that Küng's answers were *not* all Greek
to Höffner—he wished they were in Greek ontological categories.
The letter was as follows:

(57)

Object: Your book *On Being a Christian*
           Here: Answers to specific questions
Reference: Discussion between representatives of the German
           Bishops' Conference and you, January 22, 1977,
           in Stuttgart-Hohenheim; your letter of February
           21, 1977; my answer of March 4, 1977

Dear Professor Küng:
    On March 4, 1977, I informed you that the German
Bishops' Conference was not satisfied with the outcome of
the discussion of January 22, 1977, and with the contents of

your letter of February 21, 1977, and that I had been directed to impart to you some questions relative to *On Being a Christian.*

Today I would like to attend to this task. I deliberately limit myself to a few questions, although the compass of the controversial themes is not thereby exhausted.

1. In your letter of February 21, 1977 (no. 6), you declare that it had never been your intention to doubt the divine Sonship of Jesus or the Trinity. We acknowledge this helpful statement and a few others. And yet your statements in this matter, both in your book and in your letter of February 21, 1977, remain ambiguous. The long quotation from *On Being a Christian* (p. 443) at the bottom of page 4 of your letter, goes only so far as to assert that *"in his whole person, Jesus proclaimed, manifested, revealed God's word and will,"* and that he *"is the embodiment of God's word and will."* You do not go beyond the formula: "in Jesus we are concerned with the God who is really God" (p. 448). You thereby admit a functional unity of manifestation and action between the Son and the Father, but obviously you do not want to go on to raise and answer the question that necessarily must be asked next, namely, about the relation that exists between the Father and the Son *at the level of being,* as the faith of the Church teaches. In this way, however, you do not do justice to the whole of Scripture. One cannot decide on the basis of your statements whether Jesus is Son of God because he is God's indispensable agent, or whether he is this agent because he is the Son of God. As a result, the divine Sonship, too, emerges as *one* of many possible *constructions* which is, at bottom, replaceable (cf. also pp. 442 f.; p. 445). You avoid, deliberately it seems, clarifying statements such as Holy Scripture and the statements of the Councils of Nicaea and Chalcedon demand as constitutive elements of the Catholic profession of faith.

You may of course refer to the fact that in your letter of February 21, 1977 (no. 10), you declare: "Jesus *is* really the Son of God." Unfortunately, this is an incidental state-

ment which strains against almost all the others in your book
or even stands in contradiction to them. The difficulty of a
discussion consists in the fact that, time and again, you use
statements with more than one meaning, and soteriological
expressions to which you can refer when questions are
asked. In so doing, however, you dodge, in key christological
statements, a categorical profession cast in a language that
allows for no equivocation.

In conclusion, then, I would ask you the following first
question: *Is Jesus Christ the Son of God, eternal, not made,
one in being with the Father?*

2. On pages 444 ff. of *On Being a Christian,* you deal with
the God-human formula, "true God and true human." There
is no way of finding in your book a firm profession in this
connection. For you, "true God" means obviously "nothing
more" than *the UNIQUENESS, UNDERIVABILITY AND
UNSURPASSABILITY of the CALL, OFFER, and CLAIM
made known in and with Jesus ultimately not of human but
divine origin and therefore absolutely reliable, requiring men
and women's unconditional involvement"* (p. 449). This unequivocally bespeaks a curtailment and undercutting of the
dogma of Nicaea and Chalcedon. You declared in your letter
of February 21, 1977, that you adhere to the faith of
christological dogmas, and that you would like to show their
relevance (cf. nos. 4 and 6).

In this context a key soteriological element is also contained which I cannot unfold in this letter, but the consequences of which I would like to mention. If it were not *God
himself* who offered himself up for humanity, the core of
Christian revelation collapses. The same applies to the emphasis on the humanness or the humanity of Jesus. All assertions about Jesus' humanity have any relevance at all for the
faith only if they are intrinsically connected with the "true
God." This fundamental ambiguity accounts for the defi-
ciency that has been repeatedly noted in the trinitarian doctrine of *On Being a Christian.*

In conclusion, then, here is my *second question:* Taking for granted that explanations and deepenings are, ultimately, always necessary, *do you concur without reservations with the profession of the Church that Jesus Christ is truly human and truly God?* Since you always appeal to the Scriptures, and rightly so, precisely in this context I may remind you of the Johannine Christology (cf., for example, John 1:1 and 20:28–31).

3. For the moment, I will overlook further christological themes. I will, however, mention a key methodological problem closely connected with the questions above. You often say that you would like to sketch a Christology from "the perspective of the first disciples of Jesus" (no. 3). To the extent to which you refer to the normativeness of the original witness of the Apostles, what you are saying is essential. However, you delcare at the same time that "the ecclesial and also the conciliar tradition should be measured against the Christian message as originally witnessed to in Holy Scripture, in fact against Jesus himself, as the primary criterion of every theology" (no. 4). You seem, then, to be of the opinion that, by the means available to historical reason, the theologian can transpose himself directly into the perspective of the first disciples (and of Jesus himself), and *thus* reconstruct the mystery of the person of Jesus Christ and his work, and from this position, the position of a detached observer, assess the Church's profession of the Christ, and eventually raise questions about "discrepancies" within that profession.

I may, therefore, ask you the *third question,* which I would like to unfold in two parts (while bracketing out the hermeneutical-historical problems):

a. *Does not the return to the "perspective of the first disciples" require*—at least in a theological sense—*a mediation on the part of the living faith-consciousness of the Church?*

b. *Is not the Church's confession* (for example, of the divine Sonship of Jesus) *the pre-given which a theologian must explicate with the help of all his methodological tools? Or do you maintain that a hypothetical historical reconstruction is per se sufficient to give us access to the theological under- standing of Jesus Christ?*

This question has already been put to you with all possible clarity in the Declaration of the German Bishops' Conference on February 17, 1975 (cf. II, no. 1). You were asked to con- sider it. To this day, you have not adequately responded.

I will not discuss here many important problems, for ex- ample the Christology "from above" and "from below," even though I cannot at all subscribe to the positions you take in your letter of February 21, 1977 (no. 3). I would, however, comment on at least two sets of problems from your letter (no. 12).

1. Study Projects and Workshops

The German Bishops' Conference is not disinclined to ex- amine more closely your proposals, which, incidentally, are not at all new. Workshops of a similar kind are conducted regularly within the full assemblies of the German Bishops' Conference. All the same, your proposal does raise some fundamental questions. Such study projects should not ob- scure the fact that certain faith assertions are entirely clear as to their basic meaning. Therefore, they are already normative at the outset of any such project (which is, of course, con- cerned with the quest for a deeper understanding). In no case should any such symposium, which is always conceiv- able as a project within theological circles, obscure the difference between the function of theology and that of the teaching office, and make a discussion among theologians the only criterion for decisions about doctrine.

2. Composition of the Doctrinal Commission

In the name of the German Bishops' Conference I most decisively disavow your contention that advisers to the Doc- trinal Commission are chosen on the basis of "good conduct" and not the technical expertise of the gentlemen in question (cf. no. 12). I regard it as a particularly regrettable blunder on your part that you should have used your letter to me to denigrate your colleagues who are of high repute, even internationally. As I can personally testify, it is precisely your case that for many years has been taken under advisement by the Doctrinal Commission with the utmost objectivity, circumspection, and patience.

Dear Professor Küng, I beg you for an answer especially to the three substantive theological questions mentioned above. As you answer, please abstain from a great many references to your books, since in our opinion these do not answer these questions with an adequate measure of clarity.

Nor can the Bishops go along with you when you believe that you can respond to these questions by making declarations of intention as to projects you intend to undertake. Your answers can be very brief and pointed since, in the first and second questions, we are dealing above all with formulations taken from the Creed. This is also the reason why the Bishops cannot let the fundamental answer to these questions be contingent on study projects and workshops.

In the discussion of January 22, 1977, you had the opportunity of convincing the representatives of the German Bishops' Conference that in fundamental christological questions you agree with the faith of the Church. In spite of some important contributions to the discussion on your part, the overall outcome is not sufficient. Unfortunately, you did not take advantage of your letter of February 21, 1977, to clarify anew the questions and answers addressed in Stuttgart-Hohenheim, even though the Bishop of Rottenburg in a letter of January 28, 1977, had especially drawn your attention to this opportunity and to the importance of the matter. You will, therefore, realize that in the name of the German Bishops' Conference I must again insist on a clarification of the questions at issue.

I urge you, then, in spite of the many and sundry tasks of a semester in progress, to answer these questions in writing by June 15, 1977. Understand that your answer is of utmost importance for the German Bishops' Conference.

In the hope of receiving a satisfactory answer from you,
and with cordial greetings, I remain

Yours,

Joseph Cardinal Höffner

There was then an exchange of letters in June and July between
Höffner and Küng, the former wanting the latter to set other matters aside and answer the questions asked, and the latter saying
that he was overwhelmed with work with the academic semester,
the finishing of his 900-page book on God, and preparing the lecture for the 500th anniversary of the University of Tübingen, and
that he thought he had already done a great deal of answering.
On September 12, 1977, Küng summed up these thoughts again
and asked Cardinal Höffner to have a little patience until his
"God book" came out in a very few months. He wrote:

(58)

Dear Cardinal:

I would have been glad to answer your letter of July 8,
1977, in the way you wanted it answered, but, as I tried to
explain in my letter of June 13, 1977, I am extraordinarily
burdened at this time. The completion of my book on the
God question and the speech at the celebration of the fifth
centenary of the University of Tübingen must be given absolute priority. Many personalities in public life, including the
Federal President, will take part in this celebration.

I have nevertheless tried to add precision and concreteness
to the terms of the very complex questions you have raised,
and especially to those which relate to Christology. In my
opinion, these are questions that cannot be given a catechism
answer. After having already exhaustively answered your
questions for hours in Stuttgart, after addressing a long explanatory letter to the German Bishops' Conference, after
many thorough discussions with the Bishop of Rottenburg, I
have once again reflected radically about the whole problematic in connection with the God question, and the fundamental

question of faith and knowledge, and have consigned my reflections to writing in a 900-page book. I am of the opinion that by locating your questions in a broader theological context one makes a more helpful contribution to the clarification of the situation. I will take the liberty of sending to you a copy of this book as soon as it is published, which will be soon. I hope that the German Bishops' Conference will know how to appreciate not only the pastoral intentions which motivate this book, but also the importance of the substantive theological statements which are broadly set forth in this my "Answer to the God Question of Our Time."

With cordial greetings,

Devotedly yours,
Hans Küng

Cardinal Höffner was obviously coolly furious when he responded on September 21. The most revealing sentence was "These questions could have been answered merely with the unrelinquishable profession of this faith." He wrote:

(59)

Dear Professor Küng:

I acknowledge receipt of your letter of September 12, 1977. In this letter you again refuse to answer questions with regard to your book *On Being a Christian*. You have been asked questions about the fundamental truths of the Christian faith. These questions could have been answered merely with the unrelinquishable profession of this faith. I very much regret that you failed to do this. You have thereby made it obvious that from within the theology advocated in your book an unequivocal yes to fundamental assertions of the Catholic faith is not possible.

Cordial greetings.

Yours,
Joseph Cardinal Höffner

Now it was Küng's turn to profess amazement and cool anger
in his November 7, 1977, response to Höffner:

(60)

Dear Cardinal:

With amazement I have taken note of your letter of September 21, 1977. I regret having to state that this letter
shows hardly any appreciation for the difficult theological
problematic or for my own personal burdens at this time,
which I have repeatedly mentioned. Under these circumstances I would like to say here briefly what I regard as
decisively important.

I emphatically reject your allegation that I have again refused to answer questions in connection with my book *On
Being a Christian*. On the contrary, on January 22, 1977, in
Stuttgart, I participated in a four-hour discussion with you
and other bishops and theologians in which you had the opportunity to ask all the questions that beset you. Above and
beyond that, on February 21, 1977, I addressed to the German Bishops' Conference a long explanatory letter which,
among other things, also contains a clear profession of the
divine Sonship of Jesus. Finally, in two further letters, June
13 and September 12, 1977, I explained that I would answer
your questions in the context of my next book, *Does God
Exist?*, which will appear in February 1978. In view of all
this, how can you maintain that I am refusing to answer
questions relative to *On Being a Christian?*

You further maintain that the questions you have raised
could have been answered merely by making a profession of
Catholic faith. I am outraged that a profession of faith
should be demanded of me, a full professor of Catholic theology, as if I had denied that faith. In this connection, I
emphatically reject the allegation, already made against me
in the Declaration of the Bishops' Conference on March 3,
that I regard Jesus Christ only as a "spokesperson and administrator" (*sic!* [the Bishops wrote *Sachverwalter,* "adminis-

trator," instead of *Sachwalter,* "advocate"]) of God and that
I deny assertions of the Council of Nicaea. To these allegations, which defame my Catholic orthodoxy at home and
abroad, I will come back in terms of a public retraction on
your part. Here I will say only one thing: It has never occurred to me to deny the essential tenets of our faith, nor do
I see any basic contradiction between the statements of my
book *On Being a Christian* and the statements of the first Ecumenical Councils. Naturally, I regard it as indispensable
that an interpretation be provided for the people of our time.
I would like emphatically to request of you that in the future
you should always start by taking for granted that you and I
stand on the ground of a common Catholic faith.

Finally, you maintain that an unequivocal yes to the basic
assertions of the Catholic faith is not possible from within
the theology advocated in *On Being a Christian.* As it appears from the foregoing, this too is an indefensible allegation. Of course, I do not let anybody force upon me the way
in which I should answer these questions. As it appears also
from other christological publications of recent years, we are
dealing here with extremely subtle and complex problems,
which face all theologians, and which, also in the opinion of
other Catholic theologians, cannot be coped with by means
of catechism answers. In my book I hope to contribute to the
clarification of the situation, which is what can be equitably
expected of me.

I would be grateful to you if you would at least take cognizance of the fact which, to no avail, I have tried to explain to
you in two letters. At present my work load is excessive. This
year I have not been able yet to take one day off, and I am
once again fully immersed in academic work. I had mentioned to you that I would give the address at the celebration
of the fifth centenary of the University of Tübingen. I have
given this address on "Science and the God Question." The
reaction tells me that the address has been looked upon far
and wide as a great service to the cause of the Christian
faith. It will appear in print in the next few days together

with the address of the Federal President, Walter Scheel. I
take the liberty of enclosing a copy of the manuscript. As I
also promised you, I will also send you a copy of the new
book as soon as it is published. I still hope that the German
Bishops' Conference will appreciate not only the pastoral intentions that motivate these books, but also the importance
of the substantive theological assertions they contain.

  With cordial greetings,

Devotedly yours,
Hans Küng

enclosure: Address given at the celebration of the fifth centenary of the University of Tübingen on "Science and the
  God Question"

  cc: Dr. Georg Moser, Bishop of Rottenburg
      Dr. Anton Hänggi, Bishop of Basel

Ten days later, on November 17, 1977, the German Bishops'
Conference issued a Declaration on *On Being a Christian* (its
third). It contained some strange inaccuracies, such as in the second paragraph. There the Declaration stated that Cardinal
Höffner put several questions to Küng, which he "failed to answer." What is meant, of course, is that Küng did not answer to
Cardinal Höffner and others' satisfaction, which is not the same
thing as not having answered. On September 12, 1977, Küng had
remarked to Cardinal Höffner: "In my opinion, these are questions
that cannot be given a catechism answer. After having already exhaustively answered your questions for hours in Stuttgart, after
addressing a long explanatory letter to the German Bishops' Conference, after many thorough discussions with the Bishop of Rottenburg . . ." Then too, despite Küng's oral and written dis-
claimer about the accuracy of the description of *On Being a
Christian* as a "little Summa," the Declaration nevertheless bases
most of its objections to *On Being a Christian* on the presumption that it claims to be a "little Summa," and therefore criticizes
it not for what is says but for what it does not say. But it is clear
to any reader that there was no claim to comprehensiveness in the

remark about a "little Summa" in *On Being a Christian*. In Küng's German the sentence is extremely relativized. (*Was also will dieses Buch, das nun faktisch doch so etwas wie eine kleine "Summa" des christlichen Glaubens geworden ist?*) To begin with, the word Summa is put in quotation marks, obviously indicating that the term is used only in an extended, specialized sense. Then the analogical use of the term is re-emphasized with the modifying words *so etwas wie*, "something like." The three words before pile up the stress on the notion that it was not at all the intention to produce anything like even a quasi-Summa: ". . . this book which *nun* (now) *faktisch* (in fact) *doch* (nevertheless) has become something like a little 'Summa' . . . ?" In the process of spelling out the minimum he thought necessary, Küng touched on a great number of points in Christian doctrine; but that *fact* does not constitute the further *claim* to comprehensiveness.

There is also a puzzling inadequacy in a central point of the Declaration. In section 1 a long portion of John's Gospel is cited, followed by: "Words such as these would be totally unintelligible if Jesus . . . were not himself God." But there is absolutely nothing in the citation that at all necessitates Jesus' being God himself. In fact, especially with the phrases about Jesus being sent by the Father and having life from the Father, these words written in a late-first-century Semitic context would be much more "intelligible" if it were *not* presumed that Jesus were God himself. The citation allows such an interpretation, but does not necessitate it, nor indeed in a Semitic context is it at all probable. But the Bishops seemed unaware of this, which only emphasizes the differences in starting points between Küng, along with many, many other theologians, and the Bishops; the latter start with the Church statements—here as found in the early Councils—and the former with the historical data as found in the New Testament.

A final example apparently has in the background Cardinal Volk's complaint that *On Being a Christian* was "too plausible." Such could not be the complaint about the portion of the Declaration here being considered. It cites, "with regret," Küng as saying: "But does a reasonable man today want to become God?"

Apparently the Bishops think man does become God, for in the next sentence they say: "Does anyone think . . . man ceases being a man because he has become God?" But two sentences later in referring to man the Bishops contradict that statement with the following: "He has not become God . . . This too is a mystery." But if man does not become God, why is it regrettable to say that a reasonable man today does not want to become God? Was not such a desire precisely the temptation offered to humanity in the Garden of Eden: "you will be like God" (Genesis 3:5)?

In addition, the Bishops also published a large *Documentation* on the dispute—without Küng's permission. The Declaration was as follows:

(61)
Message of the German Bishops
to Those Proclaiming the Faith Declaration on the Book
On Being a Christian by Professor Hans Küng

In the Declaration of the German Bishops' Conference of February 17, 1975, at the termination of the doctrinal proceedings of the Congregation for the Doctrine of the Faith relative to Professor Küng's books *The Church* and *Infallible? An Inquiry,* the German Bishops' Conference defined its position also with regard to the book *On Being a Christian,* published a short time earlier (*Nachkonziliare Dokumentation,* Vol. 43; Trier, 1975, p. 206; cf. also all the other entries until 1975). With reference to the normative significance of the Christian tradition, the Declaration states: "When Professor Küng fails to observe, as basis for his theological work, the norms of the Christian faith that come to expression in these principles, conflicts with the teaching office of the Church are bound to emerge. Hence, even Professor Küng's 'declarations,' necessary as they may be, are not sufficient. Thus, even in the new book of Professor Küng, *On Being a Christian* (Munich, 1974), whose theological concern and pastoral purpose we recognize, there is a series of assertions which do not exhibit conformity with the principles mentioned above (cf. especially its Christology, the doctrine of the Trinity, the theology of the Church and of the sacraments, the place of Mary in the history of salvation)."

A theological discussion among experts ensued (cf. many individual articles, and the volume *Diskussion über Hans Küngs "Christ sein,"* Mainz, 1976). Until the last hours before his untimely death, Cardinal Julius Döpfner, then President of the German Bishops' Conference, pressed for a clarification of these misgivings, especially with regard to the person and work of Jesus Christ. In a discussion with representatives of the German Bishops' Conference, Professor Küng was urgently requested to make necessary emendations and additions to the aforementioned book. He has never complied with this request; he merely promised possible clarifications in a forthcoming book.

In a very extensive letter to Professor Küng dated April 22, 1977, the President of the German Bishops' Conference raised specific questions regarding various assertions in *On Being a Christian*. Even after repeated urgent exhortations in subsequent letters, Professor Küng has failed to answer these questions.

The book *On Being a Christian* is being disseminated without emendations and translated into other languages. Since this book presents itself as a kind of "little 'Summa'" (p. 20) of the Christian faith, and is also being understood and used by many as a text in teaching Catholic faith, the German Bishops' Conference feels impelled to define again its position with regard to this book. It would not do this if it did not feel that it is its duty to do so for the sake of the faith of believers. As we are often told, Küng's *On Being a Christian* has contributed considerably to a distressing undermining of the faith.

In this Declaration we do not intend to make a judgment as to what Professor Küng personally believes or does not believe. Nor are we dealing here with what Professor Küng has written in earlier books, or will write in books to come.

Here we are concerned rather with the book *On Being a Christian*, although this book is premised on a way of thinking and doing theology set forth in earlier books. With regard to this theological method, the German Bishops have already defined their position in the aforementioned Declaration. Although *On Being a Christian* thinks of itself as of a "little 'Summa,'" it does not deal with everything that pertains constitutively to the Catholic faith, as, for example, the seven sacraments and their significance for Christian life. We must ask, however, whether what is treated in the book is treated in accord with the Christian faith. Here we do not propose to mention in detail everything that is inadequately set forth, as, for example, the doctrine of the Trinity, the doctrine of the Church, of the sacraments, and of Mary. Consistently applied, the theological method used by Professor Küng, the shortcomings of which have already been mentioned in the Declaration of February 17, 1975, brings about by way of consequence a rupture with traditional faith and doctrine in matters of importance. The dissociation of theological method from the previous tradition of the Church and a prejudiced and selective use of scriptural texts lead to an abbreviation of the faith. We do not thereby question the positive concern of Professor Küng. Yet, he fails to present to the reader the whole Christ and his saving action in all its fullness. It is not enough to proclaim in a general way one's fidelity to the constitutive articles of the faith. These must be unequivocally affirmed and their contents unfolded.

1. Jesus Christ, True God and True Human

Prescinding from the theological method and the truths of faith just mentioned, we need to advert here to the abbreviations inherent in a one-sided and inadequate Christology. The doctrine of the Christ is the foundation of the Christian faith. It needs to be especially stressed. (With regard to the doctrine of the Church, cf. the Declaration of the Congregation for the Doctrine of the Faith, *Mysterium ecclesiae,* of

July 24, 1973, and the Declaration of the German Bishops' Conference of February 25, 1975.) In the book the divinity of Jesus is slighted. Jesus of Nazareth is true human and true God. These two assertions may not be abridged; the one is not to be collapsed into the other. For Jesus Christ cannot do what he does if he is not what he is. In the Incarnation, the eternal, uncreated Son of God, divine as the Father is divine, one in being with the Father, is bound in personal unity with the human Jesus. This is indeed a great mystery, but it must be held and also affirmed; otherwise the doctrine of salvation, as the fruit of the redemptive deed of Jesus of Nazareth, will be seriously impaired, and the Gospel, the good news of our salvation in Jesus Christ, in whom God himself has ultimately bound himself to our humanity, can no longer be asserted as to its constitutive contents, or proclaimed. The casual statement that Jesus was the Son of God does not suffice as a description of the Christ, since even the gracious act of redemption, for instance, affords us the status of children and sons, as it is said in Gal. 3:26: "Each one of you is a son of God because of your faith in Jesus Christ." According to the word of the Lord, we too can and should call God our Father.

Our Creeds clearly and unequivocally assert who Jesus is. In the Great Creed it is said: "[We believe] . . . in one Lord, Jesus Christ, the only Son of God, eternally begotten of the Father, God from God, Light from Light, true God from true God, begotten, not made. For us humans and for our salvation he came down from heaven: by the power of the Holy Spirit he was born of the Virgin Mary and became human." In the Apostles' Creed we confess: "[We believe] . . . in Jesus Christ, his only begotten Son, our Lord." This too is an unequivocal profession of the divinity of Jesus Christ, for the words "only begotten" profess the oneness in being, as asserted in the doctrine of the Most Blessed Trinity. Besides, Jesus as the Christ could not be our Lord, as he is, if the human Jesus were not so much one with the divine Son

that in him God himself and his saving Lordship are present
and operative.

In *On Being a Christian* we find a whole string of titles of
office and designations which are to apply to Jesus the Christ
in a unique way. Thus, Jesus is often called advocate. But
even if this title should apply to Jesus Christ in a unique
way, it is not enough as an adequate description of what
Jesus Christ really is. There have been many agents of God:
before Christ, Moses and the Prophets; after Christ, the
Apostles and the envoys of the Church. But all these agents
point above and beyond themselves to the Messiah to come,
or to the Messiah who has come. Jesus, on the contrary,
points directly to his own self. Thus Paul can write: "It is
not ourselves we preach but Christ Jesus as Lord, and ourselves as your servants for Jesus' sake" (2 Cor. 4:5). In the
Gospel of John, Jesus says about himself: "I am the way,
and the truth, and the life; no one comes to the Father but
through me" (Jn. 14:6). In the discourse about the bread of
life, which refers to the Eucharist, we read:

> I am the living bread which has come down from heaven.
> Anyone who eats this bread will live for ever; and the bread
> that I shall give is my flesh, for the life of the world. . . .
> Anyone who does eat my flesh and drink my blood has eter-
> nal life, and I shall raise him up on the last day. . . . As I,
> who am sent by the living Father, myself draw life from the
> Father, so whoever eats me will draw life from me.
> (Jn. 6:51,54,57)

Words such as these would be totally unintelligible if
Jesus, unlike all the other agents of God, were not himself
God, the eternal, uncreated Son of God. Because of this
unique claim on the part of Jesus, it is said, in connection
with the passage quoted above: "From this time on, many of
his disciples broke away and would not remain in his company any longer" (Jn. 6:66). Jesus is not the Son insofar as,
and because, he is God's advocate; rather he is God's advocate because he is God's Son. We do not understand in what

sense Jesus is and how he claims to be the advocate of God unless he be also the eternal, uncreated Son of God.

2. God's Self-Surrender for Us in Jesus of Nazareth

It is a mistake to consider all this a quarrel about words. What is at stake here is rather that Jesus is not only our teacher and model, but also the redeemer and life eternal, if we unite ourselves to him with a total faith. Numberless are the witnesses who by their lives and deaths have borne witness to their faith in God. The Letter to the Hebrews speaks of a "cloud of witnesses" and says that "the world was not worthy of them" (Heb. 12:1; 11:38). But these witnesses could not redeem us, not even through their lives and deaths. Jesus, however, did redeem us through his life and death because he was not only true human, but also God's divine Son, sent by the heavenly Father to effect our redemption. In the First Epistle of Peter it is said: "Realize that you were delivered from the futile way of life your fathers handed on to you, not by a diminishable sum of silver or gold, but by Christ's blood, beyond all price: the blood of a spotless, unblemished lamb" (1 Pet. 1:18 f.). Hence, we are right to pray: "We adore you, we bless you, because through the holy cross you have redeemed the world." For we have not been redeemed by just any sufferings; only the passion and death of the Son of God become human, who once and for all becomes one with all human beings, embody the power to redeem.

When the divinity of Jesus of Nazareth—true human and true God—is not asserted and held with unmistakable clarity, a distorting abbreviation of the Gospel follows as the inevitable consequence. For the core of the Gospel as the message of salvation is this: God himself loves us, he loves every human being, even the sinner, even us as sinners.

We were still helpless when at his appointed moment Christ died for sinful humans. . . . But what proves that God loves us is that Christ died for us while we were still sinners. Having died to make us righteous, is it likely that he would now

> fail to save us from God's anger? When we were reconciled
> to God by the death of his Son, we were still enemies; now
> that we have been reconciled, surely we may count on being
> saved by the life of his Son?
> (Rom. 5:6,8–10)

God's love for us is not just sentiment. God's love is not
an inactive, but an active love. In his love God not only
does something for us; he goes all out for us in that he sends
his one and eternal Son to us and for us in order that in him
we may have access to life eternal, which we had lost and
missed.

> Yes, God loved the world so much that he gave his only Son,
> so that everyone who believes in him may not be lost but
> may have eternal life. For God sent his Son into the world
> not to condemn the world, but so that through him the world
> might be saved.
> (Jn. 3:16 f.)

Abraham, who was prepared to sacrifice his only son
Isaac, is only a weak prefiguration of what the heavenly Father has done. The angel from heaven said: "Do not raise
your hand against the boy . . . Do not harm him" (Gen.
22:12). The heavenly Father on the contrary does not hold
back. He gives up the only Son, his beloved, and thereby he
gives himself for us. It is not for us to ask whether God
could have saved humankind in some other way. The Father
did go out of his way for us without consideration for himself, which is the reason why God's own self, as well as our
own self, is involved in what is Christian and no substitute is
possible. For what is actually involved is that in the Incarnation of the divine Son, God's covenant was sealed with our
own selves once and for all. Hence, the covenant in Jesus
Christ is the new, the final, the eternal covenant. This also
means that through Christ humanity not only achieves
fulfillment in and for its own self. As it now relates to itself
in the all-encompassing depth of its heart, it achieves fulfillment through and in Christ and, in Christ, also through the
Father.

This self-surrender which the Father effects in the sending of the Son becomes embodied without curtailment or reservation in Jesus, the Son become human. Jesus prolongs that surrender. When, in the Garden of Gethsemane, Jesus in mortal dread begged to be spared, the cup of suffering did not pass away from him. Jesus accepts suffering and death. Thus, in his surrender to the will of the heavenly Father, Jesus makes his own God's love for us without curtailment. "No one can have a greater love than to lay down one's life for one's friends" (Jn. 15:13).

Note here that the unconditional surrender of Jesus Christ on the cross does not mean that he had failed or that he missed the purpose of his life. On the contrary, through his unconditional surrender to the design of the heavenly Father for sinners, he achieves fulfillment for his own self. His words on the cross, "Now it is finished" (Jn. 19:30), mean not only that his life has come to an end, but also that he has carried out his mandate, that he has fulfilled it. In the Letter to the Hebrews we read: "Although he was Son, he learned to obey through suffering; but having been made perfect, he became for all who obey him the source of eternal salvation and was acclaimed by God with the title of high priest of the order of Melchizedek" (5:8–10). The resurrection, then, is the incontrovertible sign that his self-surrender did not imply his own undoing. Rather, it paved the way to his glorification in eternity.

> But God raised him high and gave him the name which is above all other names so that all beings in the heavens, on earth and in the underworld, should bend the knee at the name of Jesus and that every tongue should acclaim Jesus Christ as Lord, to the glory of God the Father.
> (Phil. 2:9–11)

All this is of the greatest importance for our faith and for our understanding of our own Christian life and destiny. It makes it clear to us that Christian life hinges on love and that in love our own selves are at stake, our own disposition of ourselves, the surrender of our own selves to Jesus Christ and to the Father. Since God has loved us first and loves us unconditionally in Christ to the point of self-surrender, therefore love for God and neighbor is the chief commandment. "On these two commandments hang the whole Law, and the Prophets also" (Mt. 22:40). Hence "faith makes its power felt through love" (Gal. 5:6). The self-surrender of Christ in death is the sacrifice of the New Covenant, which becomes present in the holy Mass, so that inner participation in the holy Mass entails unconditioned self-surrender to God, in fulfillment of the chief commandment. As was the case for Jesus Christ, the Christian too achieves his own self and attains to fulfillment before God and in God through such surrender of his own self to Christ and, in Christ, to the Father.

Our love for God and for neighbor must come to fruition in our conduct.

> Anybody who receives my commandments and keeps them will be one who loves me; and anybody who loves me will be loved by my Father, and I shall love him and show myself to him.
> (Jn. 14:21)

Love then is not a substitute for deeds. Nor are deeds a substitute for love. Rather, love finds expression in deeds. Love does not cease when the deed is done; it outlasts the deed. "Love does not come to an end" (1 Cor. 13:8). We cannot then want to do good in order to escape the obligation to love. In this case we would take shelter behind our deeds. We would do a deed in order not to make ourselves available to others in love, not to surrender our own selves. A deed of this kind would be compliance with law; it would not be love, nor a response to God's love, for God not only does something for us, but surrenders his own self for us in the Incarnation of his Son.

All this fails to come to the fore in the book *On Being a Christian*. True, Jesus of Nazareth is God's advocate among us and for us, but it is not clear that, in the sending of the Son, God manifests himself as love. The Scripture says:

"God is love. God's love for us was revealed when God sent into the world his only Son so that we could have life through him" (1 Jn. 4:8 f.). In the last section of the book, some 100 pages long, entitled "Practice," the commandment of love is mentioned but not treated thematically. Like Peter, we are being asked: "Do you love me?" (Jn. 21:15). This fact does not receive its due in a "little Summa" on being a Christian, such as we have in *On Being a Christian*. We cannot then regard this presentation as adequate. God's saving action in Jesus Christ is abbreviated there in a fashion which we once again disavow.

3. Abbreviation of the Reality of Redemption

Since the saving action of God in Jesus Christ is slighted in its presentation, it is inevitable that the fruits of the redemptive deed of Jesus Christ should also be described in an abbreviated manner. The fruits of redemption are a mystery. This does not mean that we do not know anything with any precision about the matter. Mystery means rather that the gracious deed of redemption joins us with Christ more closely than anyone ever could—so closely that our capacity and our notions are transcended. This union is affirmed in the simile of the vine and the branches, in the designation of Jesus Christ as the head and of the Church as his body, and of the individual as a member of his body. This is stated in over one hundred passages of the New Testament, which declare that we are in Christ and Christ in us. Only because of such an assimilation with Jesus Christ, which does not come about unless we become his members, do we call God Father. In the gracious deed of redemption, Jesus has made us his own brothers and sisters. "But when the appointed time came, God sent his Son, born of a woman, born a subject of the Law, to redeem the subjects of the Law and to enable us to be adopted as sons. The proof that you are sons is that God has sent the Spirit of his Son into our hearts: the Spirit that cries 'Abba,' 'Father,' and it is this that makes you a son, you are not a slave any more; and if God has made you a son, then he has made you heir" (Gal. 4:4–7). In the Second Epistle of Peter, we read: "In making these gifts, he has given us the guarantee of something very great and wonderful to come: through them you will be able to share the divine nature and to escape corruption in a world that is sunk in vice" (1:4).

Because of this union with Christ which God effects, we share his destiny, his death, which is indeed the consequence of sin, but can be transformed by us into a surrender of our life and, thereby, of our own selves. But we share with him also the destiny of his resurrection. "As this earthly man was, so are we on earth; and as the heavenly man is, so are we in heaven. . . . our present perishable nature must put on imperishability and this mortal nature must put on immortality" (1 Cor. 15:49,53). Thus this graced union with Christ becomes the ground of our hope. For nothing that may happen to us can curtail or dissolve this union with Jesus Christ. Only we ourselves can destroy it through mortal sin. The fact that nothing of a temporal nature can separate us from Christ (see Rom. 8:38 f.), this fact is the supreme ground of our hope.

In the Mass, as we mix water with wine, we pray: "By the mystery of this water and wine may we come to share in the divinity of Christ who humbled himself to share in our humanity." Professor Küng, on the contrary, adopts this quote "But does a reasonable man today want to become God?" (p. 442). One can read this only with regret. Does anyone think, or is it being taught anywhere, that in the redemption man ceases being a man because he has become God? In the Incarnation, the divine Son does not cease being God; in the redemption, man does not cease being man. He has not become God, but partakes of the eternal life given him, and thereby of the blessedness of God. The sign and content of that life is the resurrection from the dead, as assured participation in the eternal and blessed life of God. This too is a mystery; it surpasses our understanding. And yet, in the ab-

sence of a description of that mystery the Christian faith is
diminished. In the book *On Being a Christian* the description
of the reality of salvation, of the fruit of God's redeeming action in Jesus Christ, is abbreviated, and this distorts the reality described.

The Bishops must, therefore, stress that, in regard to the
points indicated here by way of example, *On Being a Christian* cannot be regarded as an adequate presentation of the
Catholic faith. The Bishops issue this Declaration because it
is their duty to bear witness to the true faith and to defend
that faith.

The required emendations and additions also call for the
use of another theological method. The assertions of Sacred
Scripture in their totality and the normative doctrine of the
Church must be incorporated without abbreviation. One is
not entitled to look upon this demand as if it were a way to
make the faith in Christ unnecessarily complicated. Jesus
Christ is truly human and truly God. This is the content of
our faith in Christ. This double affirmation permits no alternative, that is, neither the choice of a Christology one-sidedly
or even exclusively "from below" (centered, that is, on the
humanity of Christ) nor that of a Christology only "from
above" (centered, that is, on the divinity of Christ). Both
affirmations can and must be made together; both must be
given their due. In a presentation of the Christ and of what it
is to be a Christian this is indispensable, and the Bishops insist that it is so.

This double affirmation, that Jesus of Nazareth is truly
God and truly human, is the essential affirmation of the first
Ecumenical Council of Nicaea in the year 325, which condemned as erroneous the doctrine of Arius, who maintained
that the Son of God is the highest creature (cf. the Declaration of the German Bishops of September 24, 1975, on the
occasion of the 1,650th anniversary of the Council). To
identify with the faith as established at Nicaea does not detract from an ecumenical concern. The witness of the first

Ecumenical Councils is shared by Catholic, Orthodox, and Protestant Christians. This is precisely the basis for efforts to achieve unity among all Christians. If this basis is questioned or merely permitted to grow dim, the striving for unity is deprived of its foundation. If by chance a unity should emerge, it could not be regarded as standing in continuity with the origins of Christianity.

The Bishops would not want anyone to think that they do not esteem the theologian's proper task or that they are not grateful to theologians for their genuine assistance in the deepening of the Christian faith in our time. All of us labor for a renewal of the Church stemming from its source, Jesus Christ. This is precisely the reason why we cannot dispense with the task of bearing witness to the mystery of his person and setting forth that mystery without abbreviation.

With appreciation for the legitimate concern of Professor Küng, the Bishops insist that faith in Christ must be witnessed to in its entirety and that this witness must extend to all the articles connected with that faith. They are convinced that an unabbreviated faith in Christ is more credible than an abbreviated one, even though an unabbreviated faith includes mysteries and the affirmation of the same. "The mysteries of God are more credible than human solutions."

Küng's initial reaction was brief, it being reported by the German Press Service that he "regretted that the Bishops had not had enough patience and insight to wait for the clarification of the theological questions concerning in particular the divine Sonship of Jesus, which he has never denied, in his forthcoming book. The Bishops knew that this book would be published in three months. The theologian also strongly objected to the fact that his personal letters to the President of the Conference of German Bishops had been published in a biased context, without his consent and without giving him the opportunity to define his own position. 'When will the Bishops let me work in peace?' asked Küng in the end, with reference to the fact that this is the third time the

Bishops have made a statement about his book *On Being a Christian.*"

Küng also reacted in two more substantial ways. One was to allow one of his colleagues at the University of Tübingen, Professor Walter Jens, to edit the full documentation of the disputes between Küng and Rome and the German Bishops; entitled *Um Nichts als die Wahrheit,* it was just short of 400 pages and in February 1978 an edition of 50,000 copies appeared. The second was an "Appeal for Understanding," which Küng wrote in January 1978 and was published both in the Jens documentation and in the later documentation edited by two other colleagues of Küng, Norbert Greinacher and Herbert Haag, *Der Fall Küng* (Munich: Piper Verlag, 1980). (This important document was not published in the Bishops' *Documentation.*) It was a passionate defense of his actions and a plea for fraternal collaboration rather than contentious dispute:

(62)
An Appeal for Understanding

Often the following question is raised: Is it necessary to take issue at all with the most recent Declaration and *Documentation* of the German Bishops' Conference against the book *On Being a Christian?* Do we not know from experience that such actions are dead letters in themselves, ununderstood and ignored by many of those for whom it is specifically intended? Doubtless this is a reason why until now Catholic theologians, to whom this Declaration nevertheless is pertinent, have hardly issued any remarks. Likewise, a larger public, both within and without the Church, have "had enough" now that after Rome the German Bishops' Conference once again attempts to cast an individual theologian as a whipping boy so that many will subscribe to traditional formulas which do not answer the questions which so many pastors, chaplains, teachers of religion, people in religious life, and engaged laity have today. As though

there were no more pressing problems in the Catholic
Church of Germany . . .

A New Style?

The Declaration and *Documentation* of the German Bishops' Conference have surprised not only me. After the concluding Declarations of the Roman Congregation for the
Doctrine of the Faith and the German Bishops' Conference
concerning the proceedings against the books *The Church*
and *Infallible? An Inquiry,* I limited myself to a terse
counter-declaration and left many unrectified matters stand
—although my "inquiry" concerning infallibility was in no
way substantively responded to! I proceeded on the assumption that the German Bishops' Conference with its simultaneous statements against *On Being a Christian* had said what
they felt they had to say on the grounds of orthodoxy and
that I now could conduct research and teach undisturbed in
the service of the "common Christian concern," as I had expressed the matter in a personal letter to Cardinal Döpfner.
This letter, as with so many other items, is missing in the
Documentation of the Bishops. One spoke at that time in
general praise of a "new style." Good! But what has become
of this "new style"—especially now after the death of Cardinal Döpfner, who had worked so hard for an understanding? To be sure, a proceedings had not been initiated
and the Damocles sword of the withdrawal of the *Missio
canonica* or indeed of excommunication was withheld, although the pressures continued further. After that first "Declaration" against *On Being a Christian* there were constant
letters, telephone calls, conversations. Then there came a
second public "Declaration" against the same book, and
finally a third together with documentation, and even this
Declaration was said to be again only a "temporary closing
of the matter." Is the matter, therefore, now to continue in
this style, even possibly again against my next book and the
one after that?

This time also the matter proceeds as an action well
prepared ahead of time and well coordinated by a long arm.

Only immediately before the publication of this "documentation" was I informed by telephone that my personal letters to the President of the Bishops' Conference would be handed over to the press in this "documentation," knowing full well that I could do nothing more against it. I protested energetically against such an abusive utilization of my letters. Not because they had something to hide from the light of day or because a disclosure would be somewhat "painful" to me. Rather, it was because a bureau had here arrogated to itself the right to use my personal letters without my agreement and to publicize them in a tendentious selection and with a tendentious commentary. Nevertheless, the new President of the German Bishops' Conference, Cardinal Höffner, ignored my protest and had published a "documentation," which of course did not document precisely the important matters. Is that the manner in which bureaus should deal with citizens, and bishops with their theologians? Because, however, the ecclesiastical authorities have themselves broken trust in so brazen a fashion and have turned the express agreement of the Stuttgart Colloquium against me, they forced me to a defense, not for my person but for the sake of the cause. For the matter concerns nothing but the truth! But here it does not suffice simply to report or to summarize what has been held back from the public. Leaving items out would only arouse the suspicion that one likewise wished to channel information and direct the discussion. Here the public cannot be satisfied any longer with a selection of documents for a particular purpose, but rather demands to be fully informed so that it can form its own judgment itself. I am grateful to Walter Jens that he has done this with his documentation. Precisely the Stuttgart Colloquium will show how vigorous an effort I myself made to end the conflict: it is a singular appeal for understanding to the German Bishops.

A Declaration Which Clarifies Nothing

When we now turn to the "Declaration" itself, we do not wish to bore the reader with a detailed refutation of all the half-truths, distortions, misconceptions, misunderstandings, indeed untruths, which this paper contains. In comparison with some clear, polished Roman documents, this somewhat confused, choppy, and diffused "Declaration" is of obviously lesser quality. Even some pastors ask themselves: Is this the theological level of the entire German Bishops' Conference? The "Declaration," as is heard, was not even seriously studied and discussed by the Bishops, but rather (on the authority of a commissioned eminent author and only after a few improvements) was simply "issued." In our analysis we wish to limit ourselves to a few significant points.

Even the point upon which the entire document hangs is a falsification: It is "declared" to us that *On Being a Christian* is put forward as a "little Summa" of the Christian faith and will be used as such and therefore demands a response from the Bishops' Conference. Contrary to better knowledge—for even in the Stuttgart Colloquium the Bishops were expressly made aware of the matter—that phrase is taken in isolation from a subordinate sentence of the foreword and the limiting context is done away with. Namely, the book "in fact (!) nevertheless (!) has become something like (!) a little (!) 'Summa' (in quotation marks!) of the Christian faith." Can one be more cautious in a formulation? And so as to set aside any final doubt one can read on the same page: "There is not offered here a miniature dogmatics which would give knowing answers to all the old and new controversial questions."

One asks oneself at the very beginning of the "Declaration": Did the author really read this book, read it entirely? From the *a priori* misleading perspective of a "Summa" the "Declaration" accuses the book *On Being a Christian,* for example, of not dealing with "the seven sacraments and their significance for Christian life." Even this charge itself is false: two compact sections are devoted to the Eucharist; likewise Baptism, Confirmation, and priestly Ordination are referred to briefly with reference to the specialized publications of the author. Moreover, already in the book *The Church* Baptism, Eucharist, Penance, and Ordination were handled, to which should be added *What Is Confirmation?*

and *Why Priests?;* beyond that, a longer and comprehensive book by the same author on the sacraments has been already publicly announced! The "Declaration" then also misses (in the fourth part of *On Being a Christian*) a thematic handling of "the chief commandment of love." However, whoever has eyes to read can read about this theme whole sections in the third part. No, we are not imagining things: the author of the "Declaration" did not really read this book.

Nevertheless he engaged in debate with the book! Did he really do so? In an almost casual manner. The "Declaration" cites Bible texts and creeds, which are neither unknown to the author of *On Being a Christian* or denied by him. Further, the main tensions of the book are nowhere taken into account. Nowhere are the emphases correspondingly analyzed. Nowhere are the lines of thought of *On Being a Christian* seriously gone into, nowhere really argued with. Walter Wolf of the Swiss Evangelical Press Service was correct when he said: "As incredible as it may sound, the Declaration of the Bishops which is supposed to distance itself from Küng deals only marginally with the embattled theologian. For pages a Catholic—and only a Catholic—Christology (doctrine about Christ) is developed, without a single word in reference to Küng. The divinity of Jesus is presented, without, however, reference to Küng's *On Being a Christian*. Thus upon reading, the question involuntarily arises: Does what the Bishops say about the divinity of Jesus stand in any way in contradiction to the teaching of Küng? Could not that theologian transfer into his thought categories that which the Bishops postulate as the substance of faith which cannot be given up? Are not *artificial divisions here thrown up* where in reality there are none?" No, it must also be clearly stated that the author of the "Declaration" has not in reality debated with the book *On Being a Christian*.

Nevertheless he sought for possible "abbreviations" in several pages of the book! But did he even really find such after he time and again belabored the "abbreviations," up to four times on a single page? He at least claims that he found them, and does so with the certain awareness of the happy possessor of truth—as though there could be no "abbreviations" in episcopal statements and pastoral letters, as though no "abbreviations" could be sought for in the cathechisms and prayer books approved by the German Bishops' Conference, as though there were not precisely here a promising subject of investigation for a self-critical "Doctrinal Commission" of the German Bishops' Conference!

Whoever has read this paper will not be able to avoid the impression that here an anonymous "declarer," undisturbed by modern historical-critical method, is going about his business. Otherwise how could he so misunderstand the contemporary hermeneutical posing of the question in Christology? He has nevertheless confused the substantive theological question of whether the man Jesus of Nazareth is the "Son of God" (which is affirmed by me) with the methodological question of whether one must start out in Christology "from above," from the perspective of God (which is denied by me in favor of a logical beginning point "from below," from the point of view of the disciples at that time and of humanity today). And how could he otherwise show such little understanding of serious exegesis? Where the New Testament—for example, in connection with the new covenant—speaks of the cross, he speaks of the incarnation. Where the New Testament speaks of the self-giving of the Son, he speaks of the self-giving of God, of the Father, indeed ascribes to him— who unlike his "prefiguration" Abraham did not "hold back" from the sacrifice of the son—the unwilling murder of his son!

After all this it is no longer a surprise that our "Declaration" shows itself to be incapable of making the message of Jesus Christ even just to some extent understandable to contemporary humanity—and all the more the, high christological statements of the "eternal, uncreated Son of God" and "true God." The calling upon the "mystery" to be found here serves, as so often, a convenient alibi. Where the author does not quote the Bible or the Creed, he expresses himself in a dogmatics and in a theological and metaphorical language ("fruit of the redemptive deed") which was already passé before the Council and today has an almost painful effect. . . . The "Declaration" bristles with theological platitudes ("God's love is not an inactive, but an active love"), abstruse sayings ("we cannot then want to do good in order to escape the obligation to love"), contradictions (redeemed humanity has "become God" and nevertheless "not become God"). Should these and similar things perhaps be persuasive "for those who have the responsibility of proclamation"? Should we allow such "unabbreviated" truth in preaching and religious instruction to be thus proclaimed?

The Catholic exegete Professor Josef Blank is right when he says: "It is to the point to say that the book of Küng, in the first instance, bases itself on the secure foundation of the research results of modern exegesis as they already long since have been represented by many noteworthy Catholic exegetes. This exegesis along with its methods has already long since had the blessing of Rome. If the Bishops were to be consistent, they would really have to forbid the entire modern exegetical enterprise as well as the historical-critical thinking that is connected with it. From this starting point there are so many dogmatic statements whose truth content appears problematic today and must be interpreted in another way. If one is going to work with the argument of 'unabbreviated Catholic truth,' then one would first of all have to explain what that should mean. One could just as well turn the spear around and say that the dogmas are abbreviated biblical statements and that in the proclamation of the official Church the Gospel of Jesus is often enough abbreviated; it is not certain which has damaged the Church more."

No, it does not truly help the Church when in matters concerning nothing but the truth, it is decreed instead of argued, and instead of being convinced one is convicted. It especially damages the Church when in the well-known integralist manner it is time and again demanded that the faith must be brought to expression in an integral—in modern language: "unabbreviated"—fashion and one does not thereby notice to what a grandiose abbreviation one has oneself fallen victim to. How often here is the Jesus of history permanently put into deep freeze in favor of the "Divine Son of God": there is a single quotation from the three synoptic Gospels while all the rest are Johannine and Pauline texts—and even these are misunderstood! In fact it is precisely to this abbreviation, which of course is widespread in the neo-scholastic school dogmatics as well as in the traditional proclamation of the faith, that the Catholic exegete Karl Hermann Schelkle referred when in 1973 he wrote: "An abbreviation of Christology can arise when it is developed from the pre-existence, which perhaps the general consciousness of the faith and also the school dogmatics widely attempt to do. Then Christology concentrates itself on the Incarnation in the wonderful birth of Christ. The resurrection discloses the significance of the birth event. The eschatological awaiting of the coming again and the fulfillment become inessential." Thus, a perhaps classic case of abbreviation—our "Declaration"!

But it is precisely the neo-scholastic school dogmatics which so often both overpowered and ignored the Scriptures, which in fact has made the tradition the norm of the Scriptures and the teaching office the norm of the tradition, which from the stream of the great Catholic tradition occasionally lets through only rivulets—precisely it in fact is once again recommended by this "Declaration" to those who are "responsible for the proclamation," as though there had never been a Council! In *On Being a Christian* the supreme norm of course, as is freely admitted, is the Gospel of Jesus Christ himself. Vis-à-vis the Gospel as the norm which determines all other things (*norma normans*), of course the solemn conciliar doctrinal documents and confessions of faith are indeed important, but, however, dependent, that is, determined norms (*norma normata*). That is the ancient Catholic understanding, and the new President of the German Bishops' Conference himself has affirmed in his letter to me that the normativity of the apostolic primordial witness is "something inalienable." Our "declarer," however, maintains that the method employed in *On Being a Christian,* which in dogmatics constantly builds on the results of New Testament research, would produce—if it is consistently applied—"by way of consequence a rupture with traditional faith and doctrine in matters of importance"! A rupture? By no means. But doubtless a difference! The urgently needed difference in "the lively consciousness of faith in the Church"—which is very important to me, but which also stands under this norm—between the authentic Catholic and the pseudo-Catholic, so that thereby throughout all discontinuity the authentic Christian continuity will become visible! For the German Bishops' Conference itself will indeed not wish to maintain that everything is Catholic which is given out as Catholic *both* in practice *and* in doctrine. Or would the German episcopacy, not to speak of other things, perhaps wish today to be reminded of its condemnation of the Darwinian theory of evolution because it allegedly was incompatible with the Catholic faith as it proclaimed at the provincial Council of Cologne in 1860—even at that time more Roman than Rome?

Even the non-theologian can thereby recognize that this "Declaration" of the German Bishops' Conference is a declaration which for my book does not substantively clarify anything, but rather itself needs clarification. It is not even capable of keeping the Councils of Nicaea (A.D. 325) and Chalcedon (A.D. 451) carefully distinct from one another and attributes to the first that double statement ("true God and true human") which for the first time appeared in the second!

Perhaps against the background of this "Declaration" one will better understand why I had to and still have to raise a protest in every form:

That already the first episcopal "Declaration" on *On Being a Christian* issued a general condemnation totally without foundation;

That the second episcopal "Declaration" attributed to me

the notion that Jesus Christ is "only an exemplary human being" and "only the spokesperson and administrator (*sic!* [*Sachverwalter*]) of God" and that I deny the christological statements of the Nicene Creed;

That the third episcopal "Declaration" in connection with ecclesiology, the doctrine of the Trinity, the doctrine of sacraments and Mariology again comes forward with unfounded and unspecific charges;

That finally precisely this exegetically as well as dogmatically weak "Declaration" in an unserious manner charges me with "departing from the prescribed tradition of the faith" and with a "prejudiced and selective use of scriptural texts," and thereby de-emphasizes my confession of the Sonship of God, which reaches its high point in an explanation of the "truly God" in a manner which is appropriate to the Scriptures and to the times, as simply a "casual statement."

Must one accept all this as a loyal, if also critical, Catholic theologian? Must one allow oneself to be taught by such a teaching office which is incapable of learning, without being allowed to inquire after authentic reasons? What sense is there in the amply documented preparedness to discuss, all the endlessly clarifying conversations, correspondences, and publications, if in the end such a "Declaration" as this comes out? No, it cannot be thus in our Church! All this is not the method which serves the truth.

An Opportunity

The German Bishops' Conference had at the time of the Council the reputation of being moderately progressive. And indeed in fact it had—Cardinal Döpfner especially—no small merit in the positive results of Vatican II. At that time the German Bishops and theologians of the most varied directions worked together constructively. Since the Council that has changed—and still more so since the all too early death of Cardinal Döpfner. In many questions of faith and morals the German episcopacy appears not only distant from every open theology, but also distant from all the wishes and hopes of the greater part of our people and even of its own clergy. Should one not for the sake of credibility both within and without return to conciliar cooperation? Would there not lie here a new opportunity?

Many people within and without the Catholic Church have found themselves encouraged in their Christian faith and life by the book *On Being a Christian*. Indeed, many have themselves even felt challenged anew to be Christian. Hundreds of letters from all over the world give testimony of this to me, which indeed even the Bishops confirm when they in their "theological efforts and pastoral setting of goals" say that the book is constantly being widely distributed, even published in other languages, and "is being understood and used by many as a text in teaching Catholic faith." The questions arise: Are all those people then on a dead-end street, those numberless persons who have understood the book in a different way, much more positively than have the German Bishops' Conference and their court theologians? Would not many of them be "disturbed" and "made uncertain" only in the moment that the official and officious attacks on *On Being a Christian* begin? Are not many of these of the opinion that in this book "the entire Christ" and the authentic "reality of redemption" are thoroughly again presented to the people of today and in a fresh manner in their eyes? And is not the discussion in other lands, from the United States to Spain and from Ireland to Brazil, conducted in a completely different, constructive fashion than in Germany, where in the discussion of theologians so many non-theological factors are also at play?

If I may state the matter so directly and unmistakably: I am not alone in holding my book to be thoroughly Catholic —indeed I also have always conducted my theology completely in the midst of the Catholic believing community. But even if *On Being a Christian* "abbreviated" individual points of the Catholic truth more than other theological books or official ecclesiastical documents, would it not nevertheless be better, as ultimately is the case with other Catholic theolo-

gians (and even official teaching documents themselves),
that the incompleteness would be supplemented for the sake
of being helpful, and be done in good will and in mutual fraternal critique? Would it not be better, instead of always only
allowing oneself to be disturbed by the "disturbance" of several traditionalist Catholics, that one be encouraged more by
the affirmation of many critical people within and without
the Catholic Church who have found a helpful answer in *On
Being a Christian?*

And may not one expect from the Bishops, instead of only
constantly repeated dogmatic declarations, also for once a
self-critical, constructive statement on the demands for reform which until now have always only been fended off: a
revision of *Humanae vitae,* recognition of the validity of
Protestant ministerial offices and celebrations of the Eucharist, intercommunion, joint building of Churches, ecumenical
and religious instruction, dearth of priests and celibacy
and . . . ?

The unsolved problem of all episcopal declarations and actions is the relationship between theology and the ecclesiastical teaching office. Theologians certainly should not wish
to play bishops and insert themselves into the Church leadership where they are not competent. However, on the other
hand bishops ought also not wish to play theologians, even
when they were at one time theologians, but today no longer
are. They should not think they can solve with simplifying
questions and simple confessions complex theological questions which for centuries exegesis and dogmatics have been
struggling with and in the course of time have approached in
extremely different manners. Thus it is also with unrenounceable confessions of faith in different situations: that cannot
mean that theologians would have to provide proportionately
simple answers to all too simple catechism questions if they
are posed to them as theologians. Of answers, constructive answers, there is truly no lack in my book, and if I do not respond as a model student so promptly to every question put
to me by the teaching office, that is because this inquisitorial

method appears to me to be unworthy of a professor of theology—and indeed not only for him! Professor Josef Blank believes that it is a "bad situation as far as service to Christian truth (the truth of Jesus Christ) is concerned if one equates such a service always primarily with the affirmation and defense of dogmatic formulas and demands from the theologian that he/she confess to such a 'catalogue of formulas.' This is an unfitting simplification of intellectual work as well as a disregarding of the theological truth conscience. It is precisely the theologian who has the public reputation of the Church at heart who can no longer give the appearance today, for the sake of representing the claim of truth, that his theological statements are made upon the command of the official Church rather than from a free, believing, scholarly conviction. He must be able to freely and honestly formulate not only his consent but also his dissent, his critique."

In the interest of mutual understanding it should be here again clearly affirmed what was expressed already in *On Being a Christian* and again in *Does God Exist?*, namely, that I confess to the divine Sonship of Jesus and also to the "truly God and truly human" statement of the Council of Chalcedon, that, however, at the same time everything depends upon one's understanding this correctly. Are not there also exegetical, dogmatic-historical, philosophical, and theological difficulties in this question which are to be confessed within the German Bishops' Conference—difficulties which I indeed never invented myself? For example:

1. That according to the consensus of contemporary scholarly exegesis Jesus himself did not proclaim himself as the "eternal, uncreated, divine Son of God";

2. That even the first Jewish believers did not thus speak of Jesus as the Son of God and were no less Christian than were the Fathers of the later Councils;

3. That the statements of the Councils of Nicaea and Chalcedon were time-bound in their Hellenistic terminology and manner of presentation and that even such official doc-

trinal statements, even according to the most recent declaration of the Roman Congregation for the Doctrine of the
Faith, *Mysterium ecclesiae,* are dependent upon the situation,
incomplete, capable of being improved, capable of being expanded, and capable of being replaced by another;

4. That the numberless thinking persons of good will
today—and I turn to them—have genuine difficulties of faith
in connection with the "eternal, uncreated, divine Son of
God," and would be extremely thankful for every helpful
clarification.

Within the broader horizon of *Does God Exist?,* broader
than in *On Being a Christian,* one will find expressed the interpretation of many Protestant and Catholic theologians:

1. The christological problems can only be clarified within
the framework of a comprehensive rethinking on the basis of
the original belief of Christianity within the total modern horizon, whereby a new interpretation of the relationship between reason and faith and a modern understanding of God
must be presupposed.

2. Likewise, the presentation of Jesus as Son of God is according to a broad consensus of contemporary research not
something which fell directly from heaven, but rather a—
justified—post-Easter description of the Risen One, which
within the New Testament communities themselves had already gone through a significant, substantive development.

3. The primordial community which consisted of Jews had
understood the Sonship of God from the perspective of the
Old Testament as the justice and power position of the one
awakened to life and raised to God ("Today have I begotten
you"); under Hellenistic influence, however, an eternal be-
getting according to nature from the bosom of the Father was
drawn into the foreground.

4. The unity of the Father and of the Son was understood
from the beginning as a revelation unity ("Who sees the Son,
sees the Father") and not, as it was increasingly later, as an
a priori given nature-metaphysical unity.

5. The eternal pre-existence of the Son of God does not,

according to the interpretation of other Catholic theologians, need to be understood in a literal sense (this question is at present being investigated in the Institute for Ecumenical Research).

6. The center of the Scriptures, according to the general conviction of contemporary Catholic as well as Protestant exegesis, is not pre-existence, incarnation, and supernatural birth, but rather the cross and raising up of Jesus Christ.

7. On the basis of the New Testament evidence, the Sonship of God ("vere Deus") can today be very cautiously stated thus: the truly human Jesus of Nazareth truly is for the believer the actual revelation, Word, Son of the one true God.

After all that it should be clear that I am prepared at all times to confess to the faith of the ancient Church. Likewise I can say: *Credo in filium Dei unigenitum!* But I am not prepared through a comfortable, purely formal repetition of traditional formulas to contribute to the obscuring rather than the clarifying of the substantive problems which were not invented by me but which stem from the New Testament, to the situation that once again the central problems of faith of contemporary humanity simply are not being taken account of by the hierarchy, and that once again instead of a mature Christian faith being proclaimed an immature ABC faith is required. Present-day men and women, with all of their doubts and hopes, expect from theologians *and* from bishops not the simplistic repetition of the confessions of faith, but rather their interpretation for today, responsibly tested by the original Christian witness of the New Testament. These men and women feel a debt toward the book *On Being a Christian* and I cannot free myself from the suspicion that the doctrine of the "eternal, uncreated, divine Son of God" remains just as ununderstandable to these men and women after as before the episcopal Declaration.

Therefore, why should we not enter here into a fair theological competition: not who can best repeat the old formulas, but who can best make the ancient Christian truth un-

derstandable? Or has the German Bishops' Conference
completely forgotten what John XXIII said concerning the
substance of the faith, which remains, and the clothing of the
formulation, which can change, concerning the uselessness of
the simple repetition of the traditional statements of faith,
which are well known to us, concerning the necessity of the
teaching office today to speak in a pastoral perspective concerned with the care of the souls, in a language and concep-
tualization which men and women really understand?

To be sure, we are not speaking of a superficial adaptation
to the modern, indeed modish, consciousness, a falsely understood plausibility. The questions are serious and should
likewise be seriously investigated. For my part I have attempted to make my answers precise, clear, and in depth in
the book *Does God Exist? An Answer to the Modern Question of God,* whose appearance the Bishops' Conference, for
reasons which escape me, did not wish to wait for. However,
even these answers should not be understood as finished answers. Rather, I await the constructive contributions precisely from my theological critics. However, may I expect
from the German Bishops' Conference that this book, which
wishes to bring contemporary men and women closer again
to the reality of God, will be received with more understanding and sympathy than my previous books, and that
they will not confuse and make uncertain with renewed "declarations," and thus foster polarization, those men and women
whom this book wishes to help? My further suggestions are
well known to the German Bishops' Conference. They
should not be fended off with disarming moralism or with
pretexts such as claims that specific statements of faith are *a
priori* clear:

1. Study projects on important controversial questions in
which all the various orientations within German Catholic
theology (and if possible also with representatives of Protestant theology) should participate;

2. Study conferences with the best-trained experts (more
exegetes and practical theologians!) of whatever tendency;

3. An impartial composition of the German Doctrinal Commission so that specific orientations are no longer excluded.

Conflicts even in the Church certainly are unavoidable. They are witness to vitality and in any case are to be preferred to the graveyard peace of totalitarian systems. Conflicts must be endured. No, they must be fruitfully worked through. No group may simply overrun the others. In the community of the faith the leadership service of the bishops and pastors as well as the scholarship service of the theologians each have their own tasks, function, competence, calling. For the good of the entire community of the faith and each individual the forcing through by one group at the expense of the others is no help. Neither a hierarchy church nor a professor's church will help. Rather, only the tension-laden working together in service for the common Christian cause will help. Or do we perhaps not come from the Gospel of Christ, whose proclamation each of us in our special way must serve, whether it is through leadership (to which superior preaching and administration of the sacraments belong) or through research and teaching? And are we not there for the same men and women who today once again are beginning to be aware of the significance of the ethical-religious dimension in the life of the individual as well as of society and who precisely now expect from us not opposition to each other but collaboration with each other?

Therefore my honest appeal to the Bishops: Let us finally cease the superfluous quarreling about orthodoxy and "abbreviation" of Christian truths. Let us cease secret negotiations, endless correspondence, inquisitorial interrogations, hearings by authorities, public hasty judgments. Let us dismantle mistrust, overcome polarizations, and settle disagreements fairly. Let us again work together on the true front on which we stand jointly in order to meet the challenges of the time and to be a genuine help to men and women in their individual and social problems: in order to bring the still divided churches toward unity and again "give an account of

the hope that is within us" to the men and women in our
land. Let us finally in common address the very concrete
tasks in Church and society whose accomplishment the men
and women of today expect from us. Let us end the quarrels!
We have more important things to do!

On February 10, 1978, Küng sent a copy of *Um Nichts als die
Wahrheit* to Cardinal Höffner with the following important letter
—which was also not published in the Bishops' *Documentation:*

(63)

Dear Cardinal,
   On Monday, February 13, there appeared a documentation
edited by Walter Jens, initiated by the Piper publishing house,
on the quarrel between the German Bishops' Conference and
myself: *Concerning Nothing but the Truth: The German Bishops' Conference contra Hans Küng* [*Um Nichts als die
Wahrheit: Deutsche Bischofskonferenz contra Hans Küng*].
   With this letter I wish to make this fact known to you. At
the same time it is my intention to give you an explanation
concerning it.
   I very much regret that such a reaction became necessary
through the one-sided publication of an episcopal *Documentation.* Immediately before its publication the Secretary of
the Bishops' Conference, Dr. Homeyer, notified me by telephone that my personal letters to the President of the
Bishops' Conference would be made public in this *Documentation.* I immediately protested energetically against such an
abusive use of my letters, not because they had any reason to
avoid the light of the day, but rather because they were being
used without my agreement in a tendentious selection and
publicized with tendentious commentary. Dr. Homeyer
promised me to make you, as the President of the German
Bishops' Conference, aware of my objection. Nevertheless
you allowed the publication to proceed. I have felt this a severe breach of trust which has forced me on my side to agree

to a comprehensive informing of the public and to make the necessary materials available.

For me it was self-understood that even the official ecclesiastical statements should have been published in their complete text for the sake of informing the reader. A comprehensive informing, however, includes likewise the Stuttgart Colloquium, for which under these circumstances I no longer claim the confidentiality which you publicly assured me of even in the *Documentation*. As you know, I entered into this Colloquium with the understanding that it was not a Colloquium involving a doctrinal complaint process and "the minutes of such an openly conducted discussion would in no way be used against me" (letter of October 19, 1976), on which matter you, my dear Cardinal, in your letter of December 9, 1976, agreed. Despite these assurances, however, the Colloquium was later—in connection with the second as well as the third public Declaration of the German Bishops' Conference on *On Being a Christian*—used against me and utilized as argument for an official doctrinal complaint.

After the German Bishops' Conference thus through the utilization of the minutes of the Coloquium against me as well as through the publication of my personal letters has broken the expected confidence, my public defense has become unavoidable. For it is only with a complete knowledge of this Colloquium and of the foregoing as well as the following exchange of correspondence that the public can at all objectively evaluate the later complaints of the German Bishops' Conference and the entire development of the dispute.

I wish to make expressly clear, my dear Cardinal, that I have not from my side generated any escalation in this affair, nor do I wish to generate any in the future, and I hope also that it will not be forced upon me. I am much more concerned that bishops and theologians in all mutually necessary objective critique engage no further in public personal feuds, but rather in the interest of contemporary men and women fulfill their service to the proclamation of the Gospel. In this spirit I wrote my conclusion to the documentation as an "Appeal for Understanding." I would be grateful if it were taken as seriously on the side of the Bishops as it was intended by me.

Furthermore, the book *Does God Exist? An Answer to the God Question in Modern Times,* which will appear in about a month, will show clearly how positively concerned I am in matters of theology and the Church. I understand this book, which you unfortunately did not wait for, as likewise already *On Being a Christian,* as a not insignificant service to the Christian cause which we commonly represent. At the same time my closest collaborators, Dr. Hermann Häring and Dr. Karl-Josef Kuschel, have edited a small book with the title *Hans Küng / His Work and His Way,* which likewise has a constructive function: it should provide an overview of my theological and ecclesiastical activity to date, dismantle prejudices, and solicit trust in my work. Concerning the disputed dogmatic questions, and especially those which deal with the Sonship of God, after these publications one will no longer be able to accuse me of not taking the objections of the Bishops seriously: I have done everything within the realm of present possibilities to deepen and clarify these questions in the "documentation" as well as in *Does God Exist?,* as well as in *Work and Way,* as well as, finally, in a radio lecture. One cannot reasonably expect more from a theologian.

In conclusion may I also direct my public appeal for understanding to you personally. I ask you, my dear Cardinal, to do everything possible so that the Catholic Church in Germany will be spared such disputes in the future and that a collaboration in mutual critical loyalty will become possible. Closing with friendly greetings,

Yours sincerely,
Hans Küng

Copies to the participants in the Stuttgart Colloquium

On March 19, 1978, Küng sent a copy of his newly appeared book, *Does God Exist?,* to Cardinal Höffner and Bishop Moser.

In it he elaborated his christological explanations, as he had promised. The demand has been made often by Cardinal Höffner that Küng state plainly that Jesus *is* the Son of God. Küng does so a number of times on pages 683–88, making, for example, the following statements: "Jesus Christ is not merely God's Son but God's Son from all eternity." "He . . . *is* in person, *is* in human form, God's Word, will, Son." "He not only functions for me as God's Word and Son, he *is* this and he is so not only for me but also in himself." "For me, Jesus of Nazareth is the *Son of God* . . . he as the only one, 'only-begotten,' *unigenitus!*" On the one hand one might have thought these elaborations would satisfy Cardinal Höffner and the other bishops. However, the two different methodologies are still present. The above phrases Küng uses of Jesus are all scriptural, and according to Küng, and most other theologians, naturally are to be understood and interpreted within their historical contexts; all subsequent Christian statements are to be understood and determined from them, not the other way around. That of course also includes the statements of Councils, etc. Hence, the statements of the Councils of Nicaea and Chalcedon on Christology and Trinity—*deum de deo, vere homo et vere deus,* etc.—are to be understood and determined by the contextually understood Scriptures. However, for Cardinal Höffner and other "scholastic," "non-historical" Christian thinkers, it is the other way around: the Council statements determine what the Scriptures really meant—regardless of the historical context of the Scriptures. There's the rub. And it is still rubbing.

New Pope, New Problems

On August 6, 1978, Pope Paul VI died and on August 11 Küng published the following statement about him in the *Die Zeit:* "Personally I am grateful to Pope Paul that through all the years he held his protective hand over me. I came to know him personally when he was a cardinal and also spoke with him later. No one could have prevented him from intervening in the intense infallibility debate with a severe punishment. Indeed, he could have gone as far as excommunication. It was known to me that it was his guideline, even in my case, to proceed *con carità,* that is, not with juridical, disciplinary measures, but rather nevertheless to attempt to find a solution—in any case, to avoid an open break. There were and are persons in the Church who have not understood this stance and wished for a stronger action, and probably still wish for it. I am well aware that it needed only a sign from the Pope to bring these forces into action."

Cardinal Luciani, an Italian, was elected as Paul's successor and took the name of John Paul. While he was still cardinal Küng had sent him a copy of the German edition of his *On Being a Christian,* and received a cautiously encouraging letter from him after a partial reading.

Pope John Paul reigned only for about a month before his sudden death and was succeeded by the Polish Cardinal Wojtyla, who took the name of John Paul II. For Christmas 1978, Küng sent Pope John Paul II a copy of his book *Does God Exist?* with the hope that he would "bring the men and women of today again closer to God." That the Pope received the book was confirmed by a letter from his secretary, though as to its reading nothing is known.

Early in 1979 it became known that the Pope was planning to issue a lengthy document on Holy Thursday concerning the reconfirmation of the priestly celibacy law in the Western Church. On March 30, Küng sent the Pope a personal letter urging him rather to set up a representative commission to study the entire problematic. At the same time he asked for a similar action on the infallibility question and enclosed a copy of a newly appeared little meditation booklet entitled *The Church—Maintained in the Truth?*, which dealt with the infallibility question in a quite positive manner and concluded with the request for the establishment of such a commission. This action at this time is important to note because that meditation was one of the two items specifically mentioned in the December 15, 1979 Vatican Declaration against Küng as the reason for the condemnatory move. Was the Pope angered by the letter and did he hand the booklet over to the Doctrinal Congregation for action? There was no response to Küng's letter or the booklet. . . . Küng's March 30, 1979 letter was as follows:

(64)

Holy Father,

The press report of an imminent exhortation to the Catholic clergy is the reason for my writing this letter. It is written with a trust in you as a human being, a Christian, and the highest shepherd of our Church who certainly will not take it amiss if a priest and theologian out of honest concern for our Church turns directly to you.

I have been impressed with the sympathetic humanity, the decisive power to act, and the pastoral engagement with which you have taken up your boundlessly important service

in the Church and in the present-day world. I am grateful
that from the beginning and also now in your first encyclical
you have placed Christ Jesus in the center in order precisely
from this center of Christianity to demand a new turning toward humanity, its hopes and its needs. I find joy in the fact
that you have spoken out clearly for the progress of ecumenical understanding among the churches, and above all that
you have so powerfully intervened for human rights in the
West and East, North and South. A new Christian humanism
indeed!

But you are in no need of my praise and my acknowledgment. They will be richly expressed to you from many
sides. Many men and women in our Church, clerical and lay,
are burdened, however, with the concern whether, if we wish
to stand with credibility before the world as Christians and
as Church, we must not do very much more. For:

Of what value is all the preaching to the world for conversion if the Church itself does not practically lead in such
conversion?

Of what value is it to speak to men and women today of
conscience if at the same time within the Church and its very
leadership a self-critical examination of conscience with corresponding results does not take place?

Of what value is all the talking of a fundamental renewal
of human society if the reform of the Church in head and
members does not also proceed decisively?

Of what value is the intervention of the Church for human
rights in the world if human rights are not fully guaranteed
in the Church itself?

Holy Father, you perhaps will say that all this, however,
goes without saying in the Church. However, individual in-
timations in Mexico and in your encyclical cause many to be
concerned that the connection between the Church's mission
outwardly and Church reform within, between human rights
in society and human rights in the Church, might not be
sufficiently taken account of. Many ask themselves:

Can we credibly hold up before the contemporary society

of the capitalistic West and the socialistic East their failures
if at the same time we do not honestly and concretely admit
the clearly indisputable failures of the Church and correct
them in practice?

Can we in Latin America and the Third World credibly
stand up against poverty, illiteracy, unemployment, under-
nourishment and sickness, all of which of course are closely
related to the high birth rate, if we at the same time do not
stand up decisively for a humanly reasonable family planning
which includes a conscientiously responsible birth control by
the marriage partners?

Can we credibly stand up in contemporary society for the
rights of women if we still always treat women in the Church
as subjects with lesser rights and withhold ordination with
theologically unconvincing arguments?

Can we credibly stand up for an active ecumenism if we
still after almost a half millennium after the Reformation dispute the validity of Anglican and Protestant offices and
eucharistic celebrations?

Can we with credibility call for a better Christian proclamation and practical pastoral activity if on the basis of our
own human laws we still constantly rob communities in the
whole world of their pastors of souls and—what is no less
weighty—the regular celebration of the Eucharist?

This last point in a clearly incomplete list is what in view
of the expected exhortation to the Catholic clergy fills me
with a special concern. You know, Holy Father, that the celibacy encyclical of your predecessor Paul VI, which in its first
portion spoke in an astoundingly open fashion of the difficulties of the celibacy law, did not end the discussion about celibacy, but rather intensified it. I am convinced that future admonishments to obedience and loyalty will likewise not solve
this difficult problem. I cannot in this letter enter into the entire problematic. Nevertheless, I can express some of the
concerns and objective problems that are abroad among the
clergy and the people:

1. The Gospel of Jesus Christ knows a personal vocation of an individual to celibacy in service to humanity, as it was lived by Jesus himself and by Paul, certainly in an exemplary fashion for our time as well. However, Jesus as well as Paul expressly guaranteed to every individual a complete freedom: "whoever can take it, let him take it" (Mt. 19:12). "Everyone has his own charisma from God, the one thus, the other so" (1 Cor. 7:7). This expressly guaranteed freedom —celibacy as a free charisma—militates against a general law of celibacy for the clergy.

2. The ancient tradition confirms the Scripture: Peter, upon whom you in your office call in a special manner, and the Apostles were and remained—Paul himself witnesses to it—married, even in the complete following of Jesus. And this remained the model for bishops and priests throughout the first millennium. "The bishop shall be without fault, a man with only one wife" (1 Tim. 3:2). From the call to fullness, readiness to sacrifice, and the following of the cross at that time—entirely on the basis of the Scripture—a mandatory celibacy was never derived.

3. The charismatic celibacy, which above all had its original place in the monastic communities, was misunderstood in later centuries as an express prohibition of marriage and was extended to the entire clergy and in part was forced upon them with gruesome means.

4. In the Eastern churches—with the approval of Rome even in the churches united with Rome—the biblical tradition of priestly marriage was adhered to, as indeed also all of the churches of the Reformation gave up the medieval marriage prohibition for their pastors. This marriage prohibition therefore concerns a special law of the Latin portion of the Roman Catholic Church, which even according to Roman interpretation is not a divine, but rather a purely ecclesiastical law: *ius humanum,* which at any moment can again be suspended.

At the Second Vatican Council discussion about the law of

celibacy—as likewise that concerning birth regulation!—
which was desired by many bishops and theologians, was forbidden by the Pope himself, who then in the encyclicals concerning celibacy and birth regulation many times called upon
that very same Council for his own interpretation. Apparently it was feared in the Curia that these two questions
would lead to a complete turnabout—exactly as did the open
questions in the Council concerning freedom of religion and
conscience and the Jewish question.

In the post-conciliar period, despite all papal measures, the
conviction increasingly grew among the clergy and laity that
this uncommonly cutting legal intervention in the personal
rights of men and women was not only contrary to the Gospel and the originally free order of the Church but also contrary to the contemporary understanding of the freedom of
the individual—contrary even to the papally affirmed human
right to marriage. Likewise, various bishops' conferences
have consequently requested a fundamental change in the
celibacy law from Rome, as indeed the Roman Bishops'
Synod had also clearly in its majority affirmed, if this were
not contrary to the will of Pope Paul VI.

Holy Father, the sacrifices are massive which our Church
has paid for the disregard of freedom of the Gospel and of
the human right to marriage, and which it must still pay
every day:

Tens of thousands of priests in recent years all over the
world had to give up their priestly office against their will
above all because of the celibacy law.

Tens of thousands of thoroughly qualified young people
throughout the world have therefore not entered into priestly
service.

Tens of thousands of pastoral positions are already now
unfilled, and every day more are abandoned. In your Polish
homeland the situation because of special historical and political conditions is indeed different. But you know how
numerous are the problems in this area even there. In our
lands, in any case, the catastrophic situation will soon no

longer be such that it can be covered over with organizational measures (a single pastor for an increasing number of congregations; laity as substitutes for pastors; the celebration of communion as a substitute for the Eucharist). The unrest among the clergy and among the faithful increases. What Cardinal Joseph Höffner, President of the German Bishops' Conference, said in connection with the lack of priests in Germany is unfortunately true for most regions of the Catholic Church: "the situation is one that causes anxiety."

At the same time today there are very many young people in the West as well as in the East who are prepared to work for humanity in Church offices. The number of theology students particularly in the German-speaking area has increased greatly. However, except for a small minority, they are not prepared to submit to the celibacy law.

Reflecting on all these things, I am, along with many in our Church, of the following opinion: renewed admonishments with an insistence on the celibacy law, and indeed a further restriction on the practice of dispensation, which will only pile up the problems and provide a stimulus for new dishonesties, will accomplish nothing. There can be no calm concerning this question until celibacy is again returned to what it was at the time of Jesus and the Apostles, namely, the subject of a free decision of the individual, and the Church law which brought it about under the most dubious of circumstances is, as already is the case everywhere outside of the Roman Catholic Latin rite, removed.

I would like, therefore, Holy Father, to express to you the wish of many Catholics, clerical and lay, men and women, in all openness:

Call back into priestly service those priests who had to give it up only because of the celibacy law; everywhere we miss them.

Spare our theology students throughout the world the choice that is forced upon them between priestly service and God-willed marriage; everywhere we urgently need young priests. Give back to the Church of the Latin rite the ancient Christian freedom in this matter; the Gospel itself demands this.

Eliminate this barrier to the reunion of the Christian churches; the Reformation would have taken another course if Rome had immediately approved the justified demands for the vernacular in the liturgy, the chalice for the laity, and priestly marriage. Four hundred and fifty years passed before this error was perceived and the vernacular and the chalice for the laity were granted. How many priests must we still lose until the justification of priestly marriage, with which other churches have had a good experience, will be perceived and acknowledged?

Holy Father, you will now say that the fulfillment of such demands would be at least premature. However, then certainly a binding expression on your part in this matter would likewise be premature. Therefore I urgently request of you concerning that one matter and appeal to you thereby as a pastor: Let the celibacy question and similar disputed questions be open in your exhortation to the Catholic clergy! Much more, let the entire problematic be fairly and objectively clarified by a commission representative of the entire Catholic Church and composed of the best experts in the world.

This letter gives me the opportunity to inform you that I have also publicly expressed the same wish for an objective and fair clarification of the disputed question of infallibility. The stimulus for this was the publication of an important book on the infallibility debate in Vatican I. In the booklet *The Church—Maintained in the Truth?*, which I am at the same time sending you under separate cover, I have myself attempted to make a contribution to the positive clarification of the infallibility question. You yourself know how closely connected this matter is with several of the above-discussed problems.

Please forgive, Holy Father, my open speech which, however, is prompted by the love of the Christian concern and of our Church. I am ready at any moment even personally to lay before you these concerns of many people, if perchance you should wish so and should have sufficient time at your disposal for a conversation about these complex problems.

May God bless you in your primacy of service to the Catholic Church and to the whole of Christendom. Greetings to you in sincere respect.

Hans Küng

Somewhat earlier, on February 19, 1979, Küng had written to his local bishop, Georg Moser of Rottenburg, telling him of his two new brief publications dealing with infallibility. He explained why he felt he should write the introduction to his friend August Hasler's book, and why as a balance he wrote the theological meditation. A reading of the two article-length essays does show that they are indeed complementary. The introduction essentially described the *status questionis* of infallibility as it was in 1975 when the Vatican proceedings against his book *Infallible?* were concluded and what developments there had been since— basically reportorial. He stated that the question had not yet been resolved and that that lack of resolution was causing increasing, deep-seated difficulties. Hence, he concluded with the request that an international commission of experts be set up to deal with the problem—this request was made directly to the new Pope. The meditation, on the other hand, did not describe the negative side of the infallibility problem. Rather, it was basically an attempt to persuade wavering Catholics and non-Catholics that there was indeed reason to trust in and be committed to the Catholic Church. This essay, too, he ended in almost identical language, with a plea to the new Pope that he set up an international commission—an ecumenical one—on infallibility: "Under the new pontificate the infallibility issue should be researched again exegetically, historically, theologically, with objectivity, scholarly honesty, fairness, and justice. As was done earlier for the birth control issue, an *ecumenical commission* should be established for the infallibility issue, a commission composed of internationally recognized experts in the various disciplines (exegesis, history of dogmas,

systematic theology, practical theology, and pertinent non-
theological disciplines)." For Americans the idea of an ecumenical commission on infallibility should not be at all strange, since
the Lutheran-Catholic Consultation in the United States had concentrated for over eight years precisely on the infallibility question and had just brought out their joint statement in 1979. It
should also be noted that Küng stated explicitly that with these
two writings he had no intention of provoking a new infallibility
debate. He repeated as much in his February 19, 1979, letter to
Bishop Moser, which was as follows:

(65)

Dear Bishop,

In the forthcoming weeks the Piper publishing company,
which has also published several of my own works, will publish a book of a countryman of mine, Dr. August B. Hasler:
*How the Pope Became Infallible: The Power and Power-
lessness of a Dogma.* Already in 1977 Hasler published a
two-volume historical monograph on this theme: *Pius IX
(1845–1878), Papal Infallibility and the First Vatican Council: Dogmatization and Implementation of an Ideology.* The
Frankfurter Allgemeine Zeitung had at that time asked me
for a review of his work. In the meanwhile, because of the
episcopal *Documentation* on the dispute about *On Being a
Christian,* a confrontation resulted which I did not wish
to intensify. Hence, I withdrew my tentatively granted agreement.

Now, however, Dr. Hasler asked me for an introduction to
his new book. The request of a countryman of mine, whom I
have known since his student years, was something which in
these circumstances I could not deny. I attempted to compose this introduction as objectively and unpolemically as
possible. In the first section I summarize the results of the
earlier debate. In this I have not gone any further than what
I had already expounded in detail in *Fallible? A Balance*

(1973). The second part reports briefly the results of the Hasler book. Finally, in the third part I attempt once again to respond to the question of the churchliness and catholicity of such a theological position. The introduction ends with a petition to the Roman authorities to set up an ecumenical commission composed of internationally acknowledged experts in various disciplines for the clarification of this question which through the Hasler book again has become a burning one.

Because within the framework of an introduction it was impossible to respond in a convincing manner to the fundamental question posed to me by Hasler concerning the Church's remaining in the truth despite all errors, and because the positive, edifying aspect of my theory is of more concern to me than its critical, delimiting aspect, I had at the time I wrote the introduction also written a *Theological Meditation* with the title *The Church—Maintained in the Truth?* This meditation, likewise, merely illustrates what I already had spelled out in the referred-to evaluation ("Bilanz," the last chapter of *Fallible?*).

It is important to me, my dear Bishop, to emphasize that with my introduction and the accompanying *Theological Meditation* no new infallibility dispute should be provoked. Rather, I am concerned now as before that the infallibility question be investigated exegetically, historically, and systematic-theologically, in total objectivity and scholarly sincerity. For the sake of this positive concern I have likewise rejected requests for a separate (or indeed prior) publication of my introduction. (Naturally I cannot exclude the reprinting of individual passages.)

For the sake of completeness in this information I will send you as soon as possible prepublication copies of the Hasler book as well as of my *Theological Meditation*.

With friendly greetings I am,

Sincerely,
Hans Küng

The middle months of 1979 were quite calm on the surface. When I was with Küng in early June we planned what eventually became a special issue of the *Journal of Ecumenical Studies* (of which I am the co-founding editor and Küng a charter associate editor), which also was produced as a book *Consensus in Theology? A Dialogue with Hans Küng and Edward Schillebeeckx* (Philadelphia: Westminster Press, 1980). There was concern expressed then about the ideologically conservative bent of the Pope, but nothing more. However, the mills of Rome were grinding away. In September 1979, Pope John Paul II visited Ireland and the United States and made a number of very conservative theological statements. Shortly thereafter Küng published an assessment of the first year of the Pope's pontificate in a number of major world newspapers; his evaluation was not completely uncritical. It was subsequently strongly rumored that the Pope was quite displeased personally and that this was not without its effect on the subsequent withdrawal of Küng's *Missio canonica,* his Church commission to teach theology in the name of the Catholic Church. There of course is no proof of this. However, in the book of documentation they edited, *Der Fall Küng* (Munich: Piper Verlag, 1980), Norbert Greinacher and Herbert Haag noted that on October 16, 1979, the now Cardinal Joseph Ratzinger of Munich gave a radio interview on the Pope's first year during which he was critical of Küng's criticism of the Pope.

Then from November 5 to 9 there was a meeting of all the cardinals in Rome, during which the German cardinals (Ratzinger, Höffner, Volk) were received by the Pope in a private audience. "Immediately after his return Cardinal Ratzinger expressed himself about Küng in a completely different manner, whereby in extraordinary fashion for the first time the phrase *Missio canonica* turned up." They then quoted the news service of the Catholic News Agency: "This the Cardinal declared . . . the reality is that Küng 'very simply no longer represents the faith of the Catholic Church. It is a question of honesty and uprightness to say that he does not present the faith of the Catholic Church and therefore cannot speak in its name'" (p. 77). The term *Missio* occurs a little later. After comparing this extraordinary statement with the

Vatican decree of about a month later, which withdrew Küng's *Missio,* using almost the identical language that Ratzinger had, it is transparent that Ratzinger knew rather precisely about the forthcoming Declaration. Of course, the fact that on the same day the Roman Declaration appeared (December 18, 1979) the German Bishops' Conference issued their own Declaration supporting Rome, along with a printing of a book-length *Documentation,* eliminates any doubt about the German cardinals' collaboration with Rome long ahead of time in the move against Küng. It clearly was all extremely well coordinated and kept absolutely secret.

Although Küng was completely unaware of all this, he engaged in a correspondence with his former colleague Cardinal Ratzinger, objecting to the challenge to his orthodoxy. Ratzinger's last letter to Küng, on November 16, was very friendly. It was the calm before the storm.

The Challenge
to Küng's "Catholicity"

Greinacher and Haag provide the following immediate background to the Vatican Declaration (*Fall Küng,* pp. 87 f.): "On the basis of the conciliatory letter from Cardinal Ratzinger . . . the impression was given that the clouds around Küng had dissipated. However, the calm was deceptive. Already on Friday, December 14, 1979, a stringently secret meeting of Roman and German authorities took place in Brussels. Participants: Archbishop Hamer, Secretary of the Roman Doctrinal Congregation; Archbishop Mestri, Apostolic Nuncio in Bonn; Cardinal Höffner, President of the German Bishops' Conference; Monsignor Homeyer, Secretary of the German Bishops' Conference; and Bishop Moser of Rottenburg-Stuttgart. Main purpose: coordination of actions in the imminent withdrawal of the *Missio* from Hans Küng. Bishop Moser, the competent local bishop, according to the Concordat, was placed under a special obligation of silence, the *Sigillum* of the Doctrinal Congregation. He expressed serious doubts about the entire procedure of the Congregation and communicated this both by telephone and in writing to Cardinal Šeper, the Prefect of the Doctrinal Congregation, who was absent because of illness. After Cardinal Šeper as well as the other participants insisted on the measures decided upon in Rome, Bishop Moser allowed his doubts to be overcome, agreed to the procedure and to carry out the penal measures, for which according to the Concordat he alone is competent.

"The Secretariat of the German Bishops' Conference called a press conference for Tuesday, December 18, 1979, at 11:30 A.M. in Cologne, without announcing the subject. Toward 10 A.M. a courier from the Nunciature in Bonn delivered the Latin text of the Declaration along with an accompanying letter of Cardinal Šeper's to Hans Küng's house. Küng, however, was traveling in Austria. He was informed by telephone of the Roman measures, which struck him completely unexpectedly. He commissioned a colleague urgently to request Bishop Moser not to deliver any legally binding declaration on this matter before Moser spoke with him. In the meanwhile, however, Cardinal Höffner in Cologne delivered the Roman Decree together with an extensive Declaration of the German Bishops' Conference to the press, and Bishop Moser woud not speak on the phone. He had himself already laid out in a declaration of his own intention to communicate to the Minister for Science and Art in Stuttgart the withdrawal of the *Missio*." The Declaration of the Doctrinal Congregation was dated December 15, 1979, and was made public on December 18, 1979:

(66)
Declaration of the Sacred Congregation
for the Doctrine of the Faith
on Some Major Points in the Theological Doctrine
of Professor Hans Küng
December 15, 1979

The Church of Christ has received from God the mandate to keep and to safeguard the deposit of faith so that all the faithful, under the guidance of the sacred teaching office through which Christ himself exercises his role as teacher in the Church, may cling without fail to the faith once delivered to the saints, may penetrate it more deeply by accurate insights, and may apply it more thoroughly to life.[1]

---

[1] Cf. Conc. Vatic. I, Const. Dogm. *Dei Filius,* cap. IV "De fide et ratione": DS 3018, Conc. Vatic. II, Const. Dogm. *Lumen Gentium,* n. 12.

In order to fulfill the important task entrusted to itself alone[2] the teaching office of the Church avails itself of the work of theologians, especially those who in the Church have received from the authorities the task of teaching and who, therefore, have been designated in a certain way as teachers of the truth. In their research the theologians, like scholars in other fields, enjoy a legitimate scientific liberty, though within the limits of the method of sacred theology. Thus, while working in their own way they seek to attain the same specific end as the teaching office itself, namely, "to preserve, to penetrate ever more deeply, to explain, to teach, to defend the sacred deposit of revelation; and in this way to illumine the life of the Church and of the human race with the light of divine truth."[3]

It is necessary, therefore, that theological research and teaching should always be illumined with fidelity to the teaching office since no one may rightly act as a theologian except in close union with the mission of teaching truth which is incumbent on the Church itself.[4] When such fidelity is absent, harm is done to all the faithful, who, since they are bound to profess the faith which they have received from God through the Church, have a sacred right to receive the word of God uncontaminated, and so they expect that vigilant care should be exercised to keep the threat of error far from them.[5]

If it should happen, therefore, that a teacher of sacred doctrine chooses and disseminates as the norm of truth his own judgment and not the thought of the Church, and if he continues in his conviction, despite the use of all charitable means in his regard, then honesty itself demands that the Church should publicly call attention to his conduct and

[2] Cf. Conc. Vatic. II, Const. Dogm. *Dei Verbum*, n. 10.

[3] Paulus VI, Allocut. ad Congress. Internat. de Theologia Conc. Vatic. II, 1 Oct. 1966; A.A.S. 58 (1966), p. 891.

[4] Cf. Ioannes Paulus II, Const. Apost. *Sapientia Christiana*, Art. 70; Encycl. *Redemptor hominis*, n. 19.; A.A.S. 71 (1979), pp. 493, 308.

[5] Cf. Conc. Vatic. II, Const. Dogm. *Lumen Gentium*, n. 11 and 25; Paulus VI Exhort. Apost. *Quinque iam anni*; A.A.S. 63 (1971), pp. 99 f.

should state that he can no longer teach with the authority of the mission which he received from it.[6]

This canonical mission is, in fact, a testimony to a reciprocal trust: first, trust on the part of the competent authority that the theologian will conduct himself as a Catholic theologian in the work of his research and teaching; second, trust on the part of the theologian himself in the Church and in its integral teaching, since it is by its mandate that he carries out his task.

Since some of the writings, spread throughout many countries, and the teaching of Professor Hans Küng, a priest, are a cause of disturbance in the minds of the faithful, the Bishops of Germany and this Congregation for the Doctrine of the Faith, acting in common accord, have several times counseled and warned him that he must carry on his theological work in full communion with the authentic teaching office of the Church.

In this spirit and in order to fulfill its role of promoting and safeguarding the doctrine of faith and morals in the universal Church,[7] the Sacred Congregation for the Doctrine of the Faith issued a public document on February 15, 1975, declaring that some opinions of Professor Hans Küng were opposed in different degrees to the doctrine of the Church which must be held by all the faithful. Among those opinions, it noted especially those which pertain to the dogma of faith about infallibility in the Church, to the task of authentically interpreting the unique sacred deposit of the word of God which has been entrusted only to the living teaching office of the Church, and finally to the valid consecration of the Eucharist.

At the same time, this Sacred Congregation warned Professor Küng that he should not continue to teach such opinions, for it expected, in the meantime, that he would bring his

[6] Cf. *Sapientia Christiana*, Tit. III, art. 27, par. 1; A.A.S. 71 (1979), p. 483.

[7] Cf. Motu proprio *Integrae servandae*, n. 1, 3, and 4; A.A.S. 57 (1965), p. 954.

opinions into harmony with the doctrine of the authentic teaching office.[8]

However, up to the present time he has in no way changed his opinion in the matters called to his attention.

This fact is particularly evident in the matter of the opinion which at least puts in doubt the dogma of infallibility in the Church or reduces it to a certain fundamental indefectibility of the Church in truth, with the possibility of error in doctrinal statements which the teaching office of the Church teaches must be held definitively. On this point Hans Küng has in no way sought to conform to the doctrine of the teaching office. Instead he has recently proposed his view again more explicitly (namely, in his writings *The Church—Maintained in the Truth?*—German edition, Benziger Verlag, 1979—and an introduction to the work of A. B. Hasler entitled *How the Pope Became Infallible*—German edition, Piper Verlag, 1979), even though this Sacred Congregation had affirmed that such an opinion contradicts the doctrine defined by Vatican Council I and confirmed by Vatican Council II.

Moreover, the consequences of this opinion, especially a contempt for the teaching office of the Church, may be found in other works published by him, undoubtedly with serious harm to some essential articles of the Catholic faith (e.g., those teachings which pertain to the consubstantiality of Christ with his Father and to the Blessed Virgin Mary), since the meaning ascribed to these doctrines is different from that which the Church has understood and now understands.

The Sacred Congregation for the Doctrine of the Faith in the aforesaid document of 1975 refrained at the time from further action regarding the above-mentioned opinions of Professor Küng, presuming that he himself would abandon them. But since this presumption no longer exists, this Sacred Congregation by reason of its duty is constrained to declare that Professor Hans Küng, in his writings, has departed from

[8] Cf. A.A.S. 67 (1975), pp. 203–4.

the integral truth of Catholic faith, and therefore he can no longer be considered a Catholic theologian or function as such in a teaching role.

At an audience granted to the undersigned Cardinal Prefect, the supreme pontiff Pope John Paul II approved this declaration, decided upon at an ordinary meeting of this Sacred Congregation, and ordered its publication.

In Rome, at the Sacred Congregation for the Doctrine of the Faith, on December 15, 1979.

> Franjo Cardinal Šeper
> Prefect
> Jérôme Hamer, O.P.
> Titular Archbishop of Lorium
> Secretary

The accompanying letter from Cardinal Šeper to Küng spoke of the two small writings on infallibility early in 1979 as violating conditions of the February 15, 1975, Declaration from the Congregation, and that they were "therefore compelled to . . . issue a new public Declaration." It is obvious, of course, that they were not "compelled" to bring out a new Declaration. If the Congregation was compelled to do anything, by their own procedural rules it would have been *not* to have issued a new Declaration or anything else until after they had reinstituted a new proceedings against Küng, with all the written and oral procedures which that entailed. A further extraordinary element is the fact that in the December 15, 1979 Declaration the Doctrinal Congregation publicly condemned him on questions of his Christology and Mariology, neither of which questions had ever been raised by the Vatican; here they condemned without any proceedings at any time whatsoever. Moreover, although there had been much discussion about at least one of these areas, Christology, with the German Bishops, there was never instituted a proceedings against Küng on this, or any other, matter even by the German Bishops on the national level. However, Cardinal Šeper seemed unaware of, or at least unbothered by, all these points. His December 15, 1979 accompanying letter—which interestingly does not appear in the

German Bishops' Conference *Documentation* (nor, therefore, in *The Küng Dialogue*)—was as follows:

(67)

Rome, December 15, 1979

Very Honorable Professor,

The Congregation for the Doctrine of the Faith had to, with great displeasure, take notice of the publication of your two new writings on the infallibility question, namely, *The Church—Maintained in the Truth?*, Benziger Verlag, 1979, and "Zum Geleit," foreword to the book by A. B. Hasler, *How the Pope Became Infallible,* Piper Verlag, 1979. Therein you put forth in a new and even more express manner your earlier expressed opinions on the theme of infallibility in the Church. This Congregation had already earlier, in following its specific task (cf. the motu proprio *Integrae servandae*, C. 3, 4), taken a position thereto in a Declaration of February 15, 1975, whereby the following condition was expressly set forth: ". . . haec S. Congregatio, de mandato Summi Pontificis Pauli VI, pro nunc Professorem Ioannem Küng monet, ne tales opiniones docere pergat . . ." (A.A.S., 1975, p. 204).

This Congregation, however, must view the condition placed in the cited *monitum* as not fulfilled by the publication of your two above-named writings. It sees itself therefore compelled to reckon with the situation which has been changed by you, and issue a new public Declaration, of which we enclose a copy for you.

In the hope that after this our new step you will wish to ponder your present position in the Church, I remain yours bound in Christ,

Franc. Card. Šeper, Prefect

The statement issued on December 18 by Cardinal Höffner fully supported the action of Rome, but strangely went far beyond it, for it spent a large portion of its space condemning

Küng's Christology in great detail—which was not at all what the Vatican Declaration was about; the latter concentrated on the infallibility question. The legal problem about there not having been any formal proceedings against Küng's Christology also did not seem to bother Cardinal Höffner. He specifically stressed again that he did not find any statements by Küng that Jesus *"really is* the Son of God." Recalling the above citations from *Does God Exist?* in which Küng several times over stated very explicitly that Jesus *"really is* the Son of God," one wonders whether Höffner's remark to Küng in his letter of April 24, 1978, thanking him for the copy of *Does God Exist?,* that "I hope I find the time to read the book," went unfulfilled. His December 18, 1979, statement simply dismisses the efforts of *Does God Exist?* as unsatisfactory. One also notes the attack on Küng for his reform efforts, which are unspecified and globally condemned. Archbishop Lefebvre turns up again. Cardinal Höffner's presidential statement sounds very much like a checklist of the complaints he registered at the Stuttgart Colloquium, with no particular regard to whether they were answered by Küng or not. The most pertinent portions of this statement—which also is not printed in the German Bishops' *Documentation*—were as follows:

(68)

. . . The German Bishops' Conference regrets that it had to come to this painful decision. It places itself unreservedly behind the position of the Congregation for the Doctrine of the Faith and for the resulting step by Bishop Moser. On the basis of the total development there was no other way out.

The Doctrinal Congregation sees the main reason for this decision in Professor Küng's teaching about infallibility in the Church. . . .

The theological method practiced by Professor Küng, whose dangerous narrowing was addressed many times, has resulted in many cases in a breaking with the Catholic tradition of belief and doctrine. This is above all apparent in Professor Küng's statements concerning the person of Jesus Christ. In the central christological question—whether Jesus Christ *really is* the Son of God, that is, that he has, undiminished, the rank and the level of being of God—despite all attempts at clarification, he has avoided a decisive confession formulated in binding words. Since ancient times Christians confess that "we believe . . . in one Lord Jesus Christ, the only born Son of God, born of the Father before all ages: God from God, light from light, *true God from true God,* begotten not made, one substance with the Father" (thus in the great confession of faith of Nicaea of A.D. 325). This has consequences for our salvation: if *God himself* had not given himself for men and women in Jesus Christ, then the central piece of the Christian revelation falls. All statements even about the humanity and being human of Jesus are really significant for Christian faith only if they are inwardly bound up with the true being God of Jesus Christ. Professor Küng indeed solemnly asserts in general form that he preserves the content of the christological dogmas and wishes to give them meaning; however, *de facto* he darkens and diminishes their clear statements. Fundamental unclarities about the mystery about the person who is Jesus Christ threaten the center not only of the Catholic but also of the Christian faith in general. It is therefore no accident that Professor Küng presents unsatisfactorily also the doctrine about the Trinity of God, the Church, the sacraments, and Mary.

This defect has contributed to a pressing disturbance of security in the faith. The faithful, however, today have a right to a full and clear presentation of the indispensable truths of the faith. The teaching and shepherd's office in the Church must bear the concern for this. . . .

As many efforts for an expansion on the part of Professor Küng collapsed (cf. also the several-hour-long Stuttgart Colloquium on January 22, 1977), the German Bishops' Conference published a "Declaration" on the book *On Being a Christian* on November 17, 1977. At the same time the pertinent correspondence was published. Professor Küng's further promise to clarify the objected-to themes—in his latest work, *Does God Exist?* (Munich, 1978)—has again not been fulfilled. . . .

In the same connection there belongs his almost unbridled attacks against the discipline and order of the Church. . . . The ecclesiastical office has often been charged in recent years with tolerating deviant doctrinal opinions of this sort within the Church. . . .

Neither the President of Tübingen University nor the Catholic Theology Faculty were informed of the ecclesiastical measures against their colleague, which of course affected them directly. Understandably, they were incensed. Having heard the news on the radio, the faculty—eleven professors without Küng—met and issued the following signed declaration:

(69)
Declaration of the Professors
of the Catholic Theology Faculty
of Tübingen
(December 18, 1979)

From the radio we have learned that our colleague Professor Dr. Hans Küng, according to simultaneous declarations of the Nunciature and the German Bishops' Conference, on the basis of a decision of the papal Doctrinal Congregation of December 15, 1979, will have his ecclesiastical teaching commission withdrawn by the Bishop of Rottenburg. We are most deeply disturbed by this intervening step taken by the Doctrinal Congregation and the way and manner of proceeding in concerted action. We draw back in horror in face of the incalculable consequences. We see deep dangers for the credibility of the Church in contemporary society and for the freedom of theology and research and teaching.

Dean, Professor Dr. Wolfgang Bartholomäus
Pro-Dean, Professor Dr. Gerhard Lohfink
Professor Dr. Alfons Auer
Professor Dr. Norbert Greinacher
Professor Dr. Bernhard Lang
Professor Dr. Rudolf Reinhardt
Professor Dr. Max Seckler
Professor Dr. Hermann Josef Vogt
Professor Dr. Ludger Oeing-Hanhoff
Professor Dr. Walter Kasper
Professor Dr. Herbert Haag

Küng, hurrying back from Austria, arrived in Tübingen in the late afternoon, and on that evening, December 18, 1979, issued the following emotion-laden statement:

(70)

I am ashamed of my Church which still in the twentieth century can carry out secret inquisitional proceedings. It is for many men and women a scandal that in a Church which calls upon Jesus Christ and which lately attempts to defend human rights defames and discredits its own theologians with such methods.

In the objected-to new little writing on the infallibility problematic I only repeated the old and still not yet answered questions and at the same time requested the Pope to set up a commission of internationally recognized experts for their clarification. The objections, however, against the book *On Being a Christian* were not the object of a Roman proceedings. Finally, I have made in my last book, *Does God Exist?*, further precisions concerning Christology, which until now have not been complained about by any Church office. However, all these obviously are only excuses in order to si-

lence an extremely uncomfortable critic. And while the
Dutch cardinal Willebrands has defended his theologian Edward Schillebeeckx by a personal intervention with the Pope,
very specific German cardinals and bishops have collaborated with the Roman Inquisition in order to destroy the
credibility of one of their own theologians in his own Church
in a pre-Christmas night and fog operation. Even after the
Pope, 350 years later, finally admitted that the Roman Doctrinal Congregation had committed a fundamental error
against Galileo, this same Roman Inquisition Bureau has
carried out its false tactics against not only me but also
against many other theologians.

Nevertheless, I expect even in the future to present, as a
Catholic theologian in the Catholic Church, the Catholic
concerns of numberless Catholics, and I know myself to be
in agreement in this with unnumbered theologians, pastors,
religion teachers, and laity in our Church. At the same time I
will struggle so that in our Church this disciplinary measure
will be repealed in all forms as John XXIII in his time
repealed the condemnations of prominent French theologians
like Teilhard de Chardin, Congar, de Lubac, and others. I
hope in this to have support both within and without the
Catholic Church. I am certain that the struggle of so many
men and women for a more Christian Church cannot in the
long run remain without success.

Cardinal Höffner was obviously stung; the next day, December 19, 1979, he issued another declaration—strangely this
was included in the Bishops' *Documentation,* although Küng's
December 18 statement to which it responds was not. This is really quite an extraordinary statement and deserves careful reading. Höffner said that the Doctrinal Congregation tried for ten
years to get Küng in a discussion but that Küng refused. Of
course, as the documentation shows, that simply is not accurate.
Cardinal Šeper himself wrote to Küng that it was not at all
Küng's fault that the discussion had not taken place (January
24, 1970), and then followed long negotiations about the condi-

tions for a fair discussion. Finally the matter was satisfactorily closed on February 15, 1975, without a discussion. However, *Küng then did in fact have a five-hour discussion with Seper and Hamer in Rome* (as he also had conversations with the Doctrinal Congregation in Rome in 1973), which Küng reported to the German Bishops. Höffner then went on to make the surprising statement that Rome had no other choice but to act in his absence—apparently also unaware somehow, that according to the Congregation's own rules the only appropriate action Rome could have taken was to initiate a proceedings against Küng, not to skip it and move directly to sentencing. All the more extraordinary is the fact that later in his statement Höffner said that "the Doctrinal Congregation had to reopen the proceedings." But they didn't, at least not according to their own procedural rules. Then in his paragraph 3 Höffner seemed again to be unaware of the procedural rules which the German Bishops' Conference had set up for a formal proceedings on doctrinal matters and that they in fact were never initiated against Küng, which is what Küng said in his statement. Unfortunately the readers of the Bishops' *Documentation* (*The Küng Dialogue*, p. 168) will never know that, since his statement was not included. The questions Höffner referred to in paragraph 3 were not within the context of a formal proceedings and consequently do not refute Küng's statement. Cardinal Höffner's declaration of December 19, 1979, was as follows:

(71)

1. Professor Küng speaks of an Inquisition proceedings in which the German Bishops collaborated. In this connection, he refers to Professor Schillebeeckx, who contrariwise was defended by Cardinal Willebrands.

It must be said in this regard that the Congregation for the Doctrine of the Faith has tried for ten years to engage in a discussion with Professor Küng. Time and again, under a variety of pretexts, Professor Küng has refused to take part in this discussion. The Congregation for the Doctrine of the Faith had no other choice except to come to a decision in his absence. The extensive exchange of letters shows plainly that there have been no inquisitional proceedings. Professor Küng knew very well what the problems were. He has disappointed the German Bishops, and especially the late President of the German Bishops' Conference, Cardinal Döpfner, and his own local ordinary, Dr. Georg Moser, as they tried to settle the conflict through dialogue. He must, therefore, take full responsibility for the present situation. The reference to his colleague Professor Schillebeeckx has a strange ring. Professor Schillebeeckx was willing to take part in a discussion with the Doctrinal Congregation. In contrast to Professor Küng he summoned up the measure of humility and willingness required to engage in a dialogue. It is, therefore, inappropriate of Professor Küng to refer to his colleague Schillebeeckx.

2. Professor Küng speaks of a night and fog operation which took him by surprise. There was no such operation. To begin with, it must be assumed that before the end of the semester Professor Küng had not yet gone on vacation; in other words that, on December 18, it was still possible to reach him in Tübingen to deliver to him the decision of the Doctrinal Congregation. Besides, Professor Küng knows that by writing the introduction to A. B. Hasler's book *How the Pope Became Infallible,* he has violated the 1974 agreement to proceed no further on this question. Because of this violation the Doctrinal Congregation had to reopen the proceedings. On April 5, 1979, in a letter to Professor Küng, Bishop Moser had written in part: "I therefore take it for granted that an unpleasant aftermath is inevitable and that great difficulties will ensue." Bishop Moser added that even after the objectionable statements has been repeated a dialogue was still possible. Professor Küng was fully aware that he had violated the agreement.

3. Professor Küng maintains that he was not fully informed about the objectionable statements. This is not so. For example, on April 22, 1977, in a letter to Professor Küng, I put to him three questions. These questions showed what objections were involved.

4. Professor Küng declares that he intends to exhaust all the possibilities to have the decision of the Doctrinal Congregation revoked. If Professor Küng is prepared to conform his statements in all areas with the doctrine of the Church, there is nothing to prevent the rescinding of the present action.

5. There can be no valid reason why anyone who fails to advocate the whole doctrine of the Church should teach priests who are entrusted with the task of handing down the doctrine of the Church. The Bishops are responsible before the faithful that this should be done.

On December 18, the Chancery Office of the Diocese of Rottenburg issued a statement as to what the Vatican decree meant and what it did not mean; the latter especially is helpful to bear in mind. The pertinent part is as follows:

(72)

The decision of the Congregation does *not* mean:

That Professor Küng is no longer to be viewed as a member of the Catholic Church. He remains after as before within the community of the Catholic Church.

That Professor Küng either is hindered in the exercise of the priestly office or has been removed from its functionings. He remains a priest with all the rights and obligations which are connected with this office.

That Professor Küng as a scholar may no longer teach and do research. The freedom of scholarship as an objective principle of our constitution and an individual right of the university professor gives him the further possibility of working in a scholarly manner. His status as a civil servant, including his salary, remains untouched.

The decision of the Congregation does mean:

Professor Küng can no longer make the claim to teach *with the commission of the Church*.

He can no longer function as the holder of a *Church-related state office*.

There were frantic efforts by Küng's colleagues to arrange some
solution with Bishop Moser—all this amidst meetings of 2,000
student supporters of Küng and a parade demonstration of 1,000,
the founding of the Committee for the Defense of Christian Rights
in the Church, etc., etc. Moser finally agreed to go to Rome to
try to arrange a resolution with the Pope, and Küng was tó write
a statement for the Pope. It was as follows:

(73)
Statement for the Hands of the Pope

I have always considered myself a Catholic theologian and
will continue to do so. Now as before, I regard myself as a
priest of the *Ecclesia Catholica*. As a Catholic theologian,
what was and is particularly important to me is the "Catholic" Church, that is, the entire, universal, all-encompassing,
and whole Church. Hence, my task has always been and is to
teach Catholic truth with Catholic breadth and depth. Thus,
all my life I have promoted the continuity of faith and of the
faith-community, a continuity which endures in spite of all
breaches. This is Catholicity in time. Likewise, I have promoted Catholicity in space, that is, the universality of the
faith and of the faith-community, which encompasses all
groups. It is in this spirit that I would like to continue to advocate Catholic doctrine as a Catholic theologian. I know
that in this I am of one mind with numberless theologians,
pastors, religious educators, and lay persons.

With regard to the latest Declaration of the Doctrinal Congregation, I would like to state the following. I begin with a
few *general observations*.

In the latest publications on the infallibility issue my purpose was not to aggravate the issue, but to resolve it constructively and without any stubbornness (*pertinacia*). In my
introduction to Hasler's book, after reporting on his findings,
I have merely summaried thoughts from my "balance sheet"
["Bilanz"] on the infallibility debate published in 1973. Likewise, the little *Theological Meditation* entitled *The Church—*

Maintained in the Truth?, written at the same time, states: ". . . the point here is not to provoke a new infallibility debate." My task was and is not to accuse but to inquire. I am prepared to submit my ideas to a new investigation. To this end, in the introduction as well as in the *Meditation,* I have made reference to the French theologian Yves Congar and submitted to Rome the proposal to establish an ecumenical commission of internationally recognized experts in the various disciplines. My theological work to date has not been characterized by "a contempt for the teaching office of the Church," a reproach I strongly reject, but by an effort at enhancing anew the credibility of the Church's teaching office within the Church and in the world. Nor have I in any way given preference to my own judgment as a "norm of truth," even in opposition to the Church's own "sense of faith." On the contrary, I have based my whole theological work on the Gospel of Jesus Christ and Catholic tradition with scholarly honesty and loyalty to the Church.

I cannot conceal the fact that I still entertain strong reservations with regard to the order and mode of procedure of the Congregation. In particular, I cannot understand the fact that, before the latest gravest step, the Congregation has not even granted me the opportunity of defining and defending my position. In addition, the order of procedure is being violated when in its Declaration the Congregation makes severe accusations against my concept of "some essential articles of the Catholic faith" (Christology, Mariology), although these points have never been the object of Roman proceedings against me.

After these general considerations, some remarks on the key issue at hand. In the Declaration of the Doctrinal Congregation, my concept of the *teaching office* and *infallibility* is being perceived one-sidedly and negatively. Here, for purposes of clarification and with reference to statements of the German Bishops' Conference on February 4, 1971, may I state the following. In my earlier publications on the infallibility issue, I have never called in question the proposition that there are Church utterances which are true and can be recognized as such. Their meaning remains the same, as patterns of thinking change in history; it remains in force beyond challenge and demands an unequivocal Yes or No response.

I likewise profess that the Church has the duty and the task of proclaiming the Christian message witnessed to in Scripture and of bringing out clearly and bindingly the significance of that message. In this connection, of course, the statements of the declaration *Mysterium ecclesiae* (1973) relative to the historically conditioned character of all formulae of faith should be taken seriously.

In addition, I have always maintained that officeholders are in a special way entrusted with the task of making sure that the Church remains in the truth. They must express Christian truth bindingly and in certain situations they must define the extent of that truth (definitions of faith or dogmas) over against what is un-Christian. In this respect, a special authority belongs to the Ecumenical Councils, as representing the whole Church, to the college of bishops, and to the bishop of Rome, as the head of that college. In view of this special significance of the Ecumenical Councils, I also stand fundamentally on the ground of the Councils of the ancient Church, and especially so in christological matters. I have made a special effort to make these Councils understandable to people in our time.

As far as Vatican I is concerned, I have never intended to deny the definition of faith which it issued, to question the authority of the Petrine office, to make of my own opinion the yardstick in theology, nor to trouble Catholics in their faith. On the contrary, in view of the well-known theological problems, I have merely inquired how one can substantiate, on the basis of Scripture and tradition, the possibility of propositions being infallibly true in the sense of Vatican I. For me, this is not a fictitious, but a genuine issue. The infallibility debate conducted internationally on this issue has had at least this result: A great many people, including Catholic theologians whose Catholicity is unquestionable, have admitted that the issue must be raised and that it is legitimate to raise it.

I, therefore, in all seriousness ask to be believed when I say that, fully conscious of the risk involved for me personally, I intended in this to be of service to our Church. In the spirit of Christian accountability, I intended to bring about a resolution of this issue which burdens so many people within and without the Church. The issue is of particular importance for the reconciliation with the Eastern Churches, a reconciliation to which Pope John Paul II has given a new and hopeful impetus by establishing a special commission. A fresh discussion of the issue is also required from an ecumenical point of view.

In making this statement, I am sustained by the confidence that the present confrontation, which is grave and fraught with unforeseeable consequences, can be positively resolved in the spirit of genuine Catholicity.

> Dr. Hans Küng
> Professor of Dogmatic and Ecumenical
> Theology at the Catholic Theology
> Faculty, and Director of the
> Institute for Ecumenical Research
> of the University of Tübingen

December 20, 1979

On Thursday morning, December 20, 1979, a representation of the Catholic Theology Faculty of Tübingen (Dean Bartholomäus, Pro-Dean Lohfink, and spokesman for the professors Haag) met with Bishop Moser and read him their letter of December 18. Moser then wrote them a letter the same day, which according to Haag basically repeated their conversation. However, Haag added (*Fall Küng,* p. 125): "Orally the bishop of course added that it was perhaps an error on his part from the beginning to allow himself to be placed under the obligation of the *Sigillum,* the strict rule of silence of the Doctrinal Congregation (Secretum Sancti Officii). According to the *Codex Iuris Canonici,* Canon

1623, § 1, the violation of this rule of silence *ipso facto* incurs an excommunication '*specialissimo modo reservata,*' the lifting of which is reserved to the Pope personally (Canon 2245, § 3), 'for outside of the danger of death and extreme cases no one—not even the Grand Penitentiary—has the power to absolve from this censure' (Heribert Jone, *Gesetzbuch der Lateinischen Kirche,* vol. III, p. 510)." Küng's later objection to being condemned without a hearing—and especially at Christmas time *again*—was also Moser's initial objection. However, his resistance to being made at the last minute the cat's-paw for the authorities in Rome and the President of the German Bishops' Conference (According to German law only Moser as the local bishop could withdraw Küng's *Missio canonica*) was unavailing. Moser's December 20, 1979, letter—which of course is *not* in the Bishops' *Documentation*—to the Catholic Theology Faculty of the University of Tübingen was as follows:

(74)

Very Honorable Dean!
Very Honorable Gentlemen!

To the letter of December 20, 1979, which through the Dean and the Pro-Dean and your spokesperson you have handed to me today, may I summarize what I already have declared orally in the following answer:

I deeply regret that the Faculty was not informed about the decision of the Doctrinal Congregation in proper time. Until the beginning of the press conference by Cardinal Höffner on December 18, 1979, I was obliged to discretion. In conformity with this, therefore, I also informed my Cathedral Chapter only on the morning of December 18, 1979. In consultation on the question of which places had to be informed immediately, I placed great value on making the informing of the Dean of the Catholic Theology Faculty in Tübingen a first-rank matter. A courier was sent to him with the appropriate documents. The sending of a courier seemed to me to be the more appropriate and serious form of communication. Therefore I preferred this manner of communication to one by telephone. Simultaneously with the leaving of the courier Auxiliary Bishop Franz Josef Kuhnle proceeded to inform by means of the same documents the responsible leaders of the Wilhelmsstift and the theology students there. Thus I had to assume that at the moment that Cardinal Höffner gave his press conference the necessary information was likewise available to the faculty as well as the living quarters of the theology students.

I was extremely surprised that the Dean was apparently informed only much later. My investigations turned up the following: The courier was given the information at the University that Dean Bartholomäus was not available. He thereupon gave the documents to the porter of the University with the request for an early delivery. The *de facto* late delivery was for some time unknown to me. To the extent that I bear guilt for it, I hereby express a wish to apologize—as I have already done to the representatives of the faculty.

Concerning the criticism of the faculty of the manner and timing of the procedure against Prof. Küng, I can tell you that I have complete sympathy with it. I would like you to know that on December 14, 1979, I was requested on very short notice to come to a consultation in Brussels. As the decision of the Doctrinal Congregation was officially handed on to me there, I sent a letter to Cardinal Šeper. In this letter I told him that in the planned procedure against Prof. Küng it was necessary that every appearance of an unjust or unreasonable harshness be avoided. Moreover, I urgently requested that Prof. Küng again be heard personally before the publication of the measures planned against him, or that he be given the opportunity of making a written statement. Finally, I indicated that I held the publication of the declaration immediately before Christmas to be unthinkably unfavorable and unacceptable. In opposition to the attempt to reject this intervention I defended myself and was able to speak to Cardinal Šeper on the telephone and lay out and explain my arguments even during the negotiations. Cardinal

Šeper took these into consideration. However, he insisted on
the carrying out of the decided-upon measures and indeed at
the planned time.

To the urgent request of the faculty that the *Missio* of
Prof. Küng not be withdrawn, I must state the following: I
cannot respond to this request under the present circumstances either in a positive or in a negative sense. For my
part I made an effort to enter into a conversation with Prof.
Küng on December 19, 1979. On the basis of the results attained there I will approach the Holy See and attempt to obtain for Prof. Küng the possibility of another hearing, or a
conversation, or of a statement. Throughout this difficult and
delicate undertaking I will need room for negotiation on all
sides. I have personally taken the risk of temporarily post-
poning the measures which were expected of me. I must
therefore ask the Faculty for understanding if I do not take
on myself a still further commitment.

Finally, I would like to request the members of the Faculty
to remain steady in an effort to build a basis of trust, as I
also attempt to do. Only thus can the conflicts that have now
arisen be directed into a course which will lead to a solution.

With friendly greetings,

Yours sincerely,
Georg Moser, Bishop

In agreement with the Catholic Theology Faculty, the Presidium
of the University of Tübingen issued a declaration on December
21, 1979, concerning the legal situation of Küng. It provided the
context within which the subsequent maneuvering was to take
place:

(75)

In recent days there have been many speculations concerning the effects of the Declaration of the Roman Congregation
for the Doctrine of the Faith of December 15, 1979, which
stated: "Professor Hans Küng, in his writings, has departed

from the integral truth of the Catholic faith, and therefore he can no longer be considered a Catholic theologian or function as such in a teaching role."

The University of Tübingen affirms that Professor Hans Küng, after as before, is Ordinary Professor of dogmatic and ecumenical theology in the Catholic Theology Faculty of the University and in this capacity possesses an unhindered commission to teach.

According to the stipulations of the National Concordat, only the competent diocesan bishop could declare to the Baden-Württemberg state government that the prerequisites for the *Nihil obstat* are no longer present and the *Missio canonica* granted fourteen years ago to Professor Küng at his call to the University of Tübingen would be withdrawn. Until this action all statements of the Roman Curia and the German Bishops' Conference are a part of the inner-ecclesiastical formation of objectives and establishment of decisions. They do not touch, however, the legal corporation rights and especially not at all the civil servant status of Professor Küng.

In the event that the diocesan bishop of Rottenburg-Stuttgart should inform the Minister for Science and Art as the competent minister that a serious charge against the teaching of Professor Küng in the sense of the National Concordat is present and that this entailed the request to look for a corresponding replacement to fill the teaching needs of the Tübingen Catholic Theology Faculty, the following would be drawn into consideration:

The Catholic theology faculties are integral component parts of the state university and according to the formulation of Article 19 of the National Concordat likewise stand under state law. Only in their relationship to the ecclesiastical offices do the specifications of the Concordat, and the thereto-connected concluding protocol, with the observation of the relevant ecclesiastical prescriptions, apply in supplementary fashion.

According to Article 5 of the Fundamental Law, the Ger-

man universities are free in research and teaching. This freedom is in addition protected as an institutional right in Article 20, 85 of the State Constitution of Baden-Württemberg.
According to the legal decision of the Federal Constitutional
Court, Article 5 of the Fundamental Law likewise contains an
individual as well as an institutional protection. Vis-à-vis it,
however, there is the religious freedom of Article 4, 140 of
the Fundamental Law, from which, alongside individual
rights, a claim by the Church as an autonomous structure
concerning matters of its own corresponding to its own inner
self-understanding is to be derived.

According to the decision of the Federal Constitutional
Court in Volume 6, pages 309 ff., the National Concordat of
July 20, 1933, continues to be valid as a state law, and has
the rank of a simple right in law and can make no claim of
precedence vis-à-vis the freedom of research and teaching
which is protected by the Fundamental Law and to which the
organization freedom of the university in this area also belongs. Article 5 of the Fundamental Law, however, is
modified concerning the Catholic theology faculties by the
religious freedom (Article 4, 140 of the Fundamental Law)
which must be observed and protected by the State.

The university is not mistaken in seeing a genuine tension
of relationship between the specifications of the National
Concordat in connection with Article 4, 140 of the Fundamental Law and the fundamental right of freedom of research and teaching. It follows first of all, nevertheless, that
the right of the diocesan bishop to withdraw the ecclesiastical
teaching commission does not touch the legal corporation
status of a professor, so that Professor Hans Küng can continue to teach and do research at the university even if his
courses would no longer be acknowledged as requirements
for the reception of the priestly office or of an ecclesiastical
teaching office.

The Presidium regrets therefore that the establishment of a
replacement teaching chair or indeed the exclusion of Professor Küng from the Catholic Theology Faculty has been

precipitously spoken of in public. This is the case because the State and the University could respond to a possible demand by the diocesan bishop to look for a replacement in various ways.

The Church-state legal problems which arise with a recall of the *Missio canonica* are complex in the extreme and are subject to multiple juridical interpretations. Consequently, fundamental reflections are needed before individual steps on the basis of a possible decision by the diocesan bishop can be undertaken, above all a change in corporation rights, as for example would be demanded in a change of faculty.

The University observes with great concern the increasing conflict between members of the Catholic Theology Faculty and the ecclesiastical agencies. Simply on the basis of its claim for the security of its status as an autonomous corporate body, the University places itself in an unlimited protective stance before its University teacher Hans Küng, without wishing to express thereby vis-à-vis the Church or vis-à-vis the public the wish to influence or complain about the ecclesiastical procedure as such.

The University will also decisively represent this standpoint before the state government of Baden-Württemberg. Bound up with that is the hope that in the foreseeable future there will be a discussion that will clarify in what forms and according to which regulations future cases of conflict of this sort are to be dealt with.

The University hopes for itself that after a phase of joint reflection and cautious dealing with the public the possibility will exist to mediate between the Roman Catholic Church and Professor Küng.

Bishop Moser was told by telephone that he could have an audience with the Pope and hence flew to Rome on December 21, having Küng's December 20, 1979, "Statement for the Hands of the Pope" with him. However, when he got there he was not allowed to see the Pope but had to content himself with a meeting with Cardinal Šeper and Cardinal Casaroli, the Secretary of State

of the Vatican. Küng's statement was given to the Pope, and
Moser was told that he would receive a delegation from the German Bishops sometime before New Year's. Moser returned home
on December 22, informed Küng by phone of the results, and arranged for a conversation the next day. "In this discussion of almost three hours the focus, besides the report on the Rome visit,
was on the further mediation efforts. After Küng explained to the
Bishop that it would be improper and irresponsible, under pressure and in such a brief time, to make still further declarations to
the Declaration, Moser asked for a collection of theological material from Küng's writings on the disputed questions, for they
could assist him in his arguments during the upcoming negotiations. After Küng prepared these materials he left for his vacation
place to pass the Christmas tide in peace and thus to contribute to
the calming of the public—this all was discussed with Moser"
(*Fall Küng*, p. 131).

However, "although in the discussion between Bishop Moser
and Hans Küng on December 23, 1979, it had been agreed that
Küng would not issue any further theological declarations, and although Moser knew of Küng's departure, late on Christmas Eve
he sent the following letter to Küng's Tübingen address, which in
content and tone differed significantly from the discussions between Küng and Moser up until now. Possibly Moser felt himself
forced from other ecclesiastical quarters to obtain still more concessions" (ibid., p. 132). Bishop Moser's following Christmas
Eve letter does have the hardness and ring of Cardinal Höffner's
style and language. Moser did not wish Küng a "Merry Christmas!":

(76)

Dear Professor Küng:
    Over and over I have read your December 20, 1979,
"Statement Relative to the Declaration of the Congregation
for the Doctrine of the Faith on Some Major Points in the
Theological Doctrine of Professor Küng dated December 15,
1979" ["Statement for the Hands of the Pope"]. In our con-

versation on Sunday, December 23, 1979, I declared that I am grateful for this statement on your part, but that I can see in it no more than a first and minimal step which, given the situation of the hour, is not sufficient. Because I am full of worry and anxiety and because I intend to do all I can for the sake of mediation, I take the liberty of summarizing once more the questions and requests and giving my reasons in writing.

1. Your statement deals mainly with infallibility in the Church. I notice that you consistently avoid the word "infallibility." You also overlook the declarations of the Doctrinal Congregation concerning the other two points mentioned there; namely, "the task of authentically interpreting the unique sacred deposit of the word of God which has been entrusted only to the living teaching office of the Church," and "the valid consecration of the Eucharist." How is it that you are not disclosing your views on these points?

You quote from the Declaration of the German Bishops' Conference on *Infallible?* dated February 4, 1971. Unfortunately, you did not include in your quotation the important statement in which the Declaration speaks of formulations "which help to clarify the Creed," thus providing in fact an interpretation of the witness intended by the Scriptures, and which are set forth by the Church with truly ultimate normativeness. This is precisely what is at stake.

I find it regrettable that you do not speak about the Ecumenical Councils in the way the Bishops do, namely, "as representing the whole episcopate." Your version is: "as representing the whole Church." Thus you embark on an interpretation of the Councils which has often been challenged on historical and dogmatic grounds.

2. With regard to the christological questions, you only manage to go as far as to say that you stand "fundamentally" on the ground of the Councils of the ancient Church. Specifically, what does this mean? Your statement to the effect that the task of caring for the truth is entrusted "in a special way" to the teaching office, to which there belongs a

"special authority," needs to be more precisely and clearly formulated. What do you mean by "special authority"? Any teacher, for example, enjoys an authority which is special.

3. One cannot discern from your statement whether a normative teaching office of the Church exists *for you yourself,* a teaching office whose judgment you acknowledge. True, you disclaim the intention of making your "opinion the yardstick in theology." You take no position as to the form which an official assessment of your doctrines would take. Likewise the "new investigation" to which you want to subject your views, as you declare, remains very vague. What kind of investigation would it be? Who would conduct it? And to what purpose? In your statement, you make a host of declarations as to what you did and did not intend, and yet, apparently, you do not intend to accept any judgment passed by the authority of the Church on your theological doctrines and their effects. No one has contested that, subjectively, your intentions are positive.

4. Closely examined, even your remarks on "infallibility" turn out to be disappointing. It is not clear how you stand with regard to some of your earlier statements.

a. You write in your statement that you do not intend to deny the definitions issued by Vatican I. How can this declaration be reconciled with the following: "I only deny that this indefectibility of the Church in the truth is bound up with certain propositions and authorities" (see *Hans Küng: His Work and His Way*)?

b. You maintain that your "inquiry" is "not a fictitious, but a genuine issue." This might well have been true earlier. Later, you have indeed declared the opposite. Already in *On Being a Christian* one reads: "The 'inquiry' may largely be regarded as settled" (p. 677). In *The Church—Maintained in Truth?* you speak of the negative results of the infallibility debate. The old infallibility debate should be terminated "as soon as possible." A few lines above, you speak of "the questioning of the traditional doctrine of infallibility" and you pick up the fatal word "revision of the stipulations of Vatican I." In the introduction to A. B. Hasler's book *How the Pope Became Infallible,* you say explicitly that "there are no solid foundations for the acceptance of such infallibly true propositions or authorities," and that the Pope "can fulfill his service *better* without infallible doctrinal definitions."

As long as you insist on such statements as these, your declaration that the question is "genuine" is not credible. Please, do define your position with regard to these statements, for they cannot be objectively reconciled with your statement of December 20, 1979. I beg of you explicitly: as you do this, do not be easy on yourself.

Dear Professor Küng, I have cited these statements of yours only by way of example. I could cite more. Please make your contribution to an unequivocal clarification and write not primarily for the eyes and ears of the public but for the authority in the Church. In the present situation, as I explained to you orally, first and minimal steps are just not enough.

In the light of Christmas, I beg of you again from the bottom of my heart, do at least contribute to the resolution of the conflict the share which has long been expected of you; otherwise, to quote Cardinal Döpfner's words on May 6, 1975, "I would hardly know how to help any further."

In the discussion scheduled to take place in Rome on December 28, 1979, I can help effectively only if I am in possession of a written response from you by Thursday, December 27, 1979, at 8 P.M.

In spite of the Christmas holidays, I have no choice but to ask you for this response.

With cordial greetings,

Yours,
Georg Moser

As Bishop Moser knew, Küng was not at his address in Tübingen, but with his family for Christmas. Therefore Moser telephoned Dr. Hermann Häring, Küng's first assistant, and asked him to open and read his letter over the phone to Küng.

Greinacher and Haag reported that Moser would have been "completely satisfied if Häring were to answer his letter in Küng's name" (*Fall Küng,* p. 135). The text of the letter was worked out by long distance between Häring and Küng, starting 8 A.M. Christmas Day, and then was brought to Moser by Greinacher, who repeated Küng's earlier oral request that he be heard by the Pope before a decision was reached—which request has never been granted—though John Paul II has found time, for example, for a two-hour private conversation with the Protestant evangelical Billy Graham. The December 26, 1979, Häring-Küng letter was as follows:

(77)

Dear Bishop:

On Christmas Eve I received the letter you addressed to Professor Küng and opened it as previously arranged. After several unsuccessful attempts on the evening of that day I managed to reach Professor Küng on Christmas morning around eight o'clock. On the evening of December 25, I had another lengthy conversation with him.

The outcome of this conversation was as follows: Professor Küng appreciates how difficult the situation is in which you as mediator in such a grave matter find yourself; yet for reasons of time and substance he feels that he is not in a position to send you a personal letter within the deadline you have set. He has authorized me to impart to you what follows as an answer to your letter. I am using notes taken during our conversation.

1. Since in the days before Christmas Professor Küng had conversations with you lasting many hours, he feels that he has already given sufficient evidence that he is not unamenable to take part in a discussion. In these conversations he made all imaginable efforts to answer the substantive questions, while making it clear to you that, for reasons of time and substance, it was impossible for him to add still further written explanations to the written Statement he has already

submitted. As he has already declared, he is prepared to engage in discussion with the Church authorities. This readiness he has never denied. In his opinion, this readiness is indispensable. He regards it as essential and sees in it almost a master commandment for Catholic theology to observe. Yet he still insists that such discussions must be held under just and fair conditions. For years he has been asking himself why such conditions are not being guaranteed to him by Rome.

2. Professor Küng stated that, even in the last conversation with you on December 23, he tried to give substantive answers to substantive questions. In addition, he has sent you documentation concerning those of his views which have been questioned. He was all the more dismayed that suddenly he should be compelled to add further explanations to the statement already submitted, and this on Christmas Eve and on Christmas morning. He cannot understand why in Rome (where, as a rule, people think in terms of centuries) an attempt should be made to extract something from him by force in the space of a few days—and this between Christmas and New Year's—and precisely in relation to questions which are theologically highly complex and fraught with political implications. For reasons of time and substance, he regards this demand as irresponsible. At any rate, after the physical and psychological aggravations to which this unexpected Roman initiative has subjected him, shortly before Christmas, he feels that, to his chagrin, he is absolutely in no position to submit a new declaration now.

3. As to the detailed questions relative to his orthodoxy, which Professor Küng surmises were articulated by the hand of an expert, Professor Küng regards them as downright inquisitional. He regards them as partly inadequate, the citations having been taken out of context. There is no understanding of his position, nor any willingness really to identify with his intention. On the other hand, as he explained orally, he is certainly entitled to expect that an answer should be given to his well-known questions. In this connection he

made reference to the account he gave of the infallibility
debate in the book *Fehlbar? Eine Bilanz* (1973) and reiterated elsewhere. As other theologians also attest, the infallibility issue is still beset with basic ambiguities in Catholic
theology. For this reason, Professor Küng has urged that an
ecumenical commission of suitable experts be established to
remove these ambiguities. Until the unresolved problematic
is further clarified, by this or any other means, it would
hardly be possible for him to answer questions which, to
begin with, are the ones he himself has raised. If either you
or the Roman authorities are not merely interested in an act
of humble submission on his part, but in a genuine resolution
of the problem itself, then he is entitled to expect that his
proposal be in some form or other acted upon.

   4. Professor Küng is very much aware, as you yourself
are, that the situation is serious, not only for himself but for
the whole Church at large. In this situation, people in authority within the Church should indeed be asked how they
can take it upon themselves, just before Christmas, to trigger
in large segments of the Church and of the clergy so much
indignation, dismay, and deep sorrow at the fact that such an
action is possible in a Church which pledges allegiance to
Jesus Christ. Professor Küng has drawn your attention to the
fact that, should the measures decided by the Doctrinal Congregation be enforced with finality, the problem itself would
not be settled in the Church. On the contrary, a step would
have been taken toward a very difficult and critical future.
He could not and would not accept responsibility for these
consequences.

   All the same, Professor Küng reaffirms his willingness to
engage in discussion. Even in this hour he emphatically
wants to abide by this willingness. He stressed that even now
he is willing, although he must still require that the discussion be held under just and fair conditions, as he has said
and specified repeatedly in earlier statements and letters.
Moreover, in a personal letter to Pope John Paul II in the
spring of 1979, he offered to come to Rome any time to

speak with him about all the unresolved problems, should the Pope so wish and have the time.

In addition, Professor Küng would like to ask you urgently for a favor. As you go to Rome, would you take along his request that the Pope, who is entitled to take in his own hands many extraordinary matters, should find the time in this critical moment to speak with a theologian of our Church who for decades has tried as best he knows how to work for the cause of the Christian faith both within and without.

I very much regret that in this grave moment I cannot impart to you any other answer. I too would like to hope that the conflict might be so resolved that the credibility of our Church, and ultimately of the very cause of Jesus Christ, should not be harmed but enhanced.

With respect for the task before you in the next few days, I convey to you my greetings, and I wish you God's blessings.

Yours,
Dr. Hermann Häring

The German delegation consisted of Bishop Moser and his metropolitan, Archbishop Saier of Freiburg, and the three cardinals, Volk, Ratzinger, and Höffner. They were joined in Rome by Šeper from the Doctrinal Congregation and Casaroli, Vatican Secretary of State, and of course, John Paul II—of whom it was said on Swiss television (December 23, 1979) by Father Mieczyslaw Malinski, author of the book *Pope John Paul: The Life of My Friend Karol Wojtyla* (1979): "He could affirm 'with certainty' that John Paul had never read a book by Küng so long as he was in Cracow. 'He was in no way a theologian,' he added" (Peter Hebbelthwaite, *The New Inquisition? The Case of Edward Schillebeeckx and Hans Küng,* New York: Harper & Row, 1980, p. 110). Greinacher and Haag commented: "After Ratzinger had already earlier expressed himself negatively about Küng's orthodoxy, Cardinal Höffner now also showed his prejudiced position in a drastic manner in an interview before his departure. In view of such a composition of the delegation, there could hardly exist

any doubt about the outcome of the 'mediation'" (*Fall Küng,* p.
138). There then followed a six-page interview by Höffner which
to a significant extent was made up of earlier letters and statements of his scissored and pasted together; there was no moderation of Höffner's earlier exhibited hostility toward Küng.

The papal consultation took place at Castel Gandolfo outside
of Rome, without Küng. The result was negative. Greinacher and
Haag commented: "Indeed, concerning the decision which came
Friday evening [Küng] was left in ignorance until Sunday forenoon. Bishop Moser, who had returned from Rome by Saturday
midday, refused to be in touch with Küng in any way. Küng was
informed of the decision of the Holy See through the Nunciature.
The Nunciature announced on Saturday forenoon that the decision would be published only on Sunday forenoon. Küng himself
was first informed at this time of the negative Roman decision by a
Nunciature secretary. Later the letter of Bishop Moser was
brought by messenger. The press statement of the Holy See, December 30, 1979, was as follows:

(78)

1. The Declaration of the Doctrinal Congregation on December 15, 1979, concerning certain tenets in the theological
doctrine of Professor Küng had become unavoidable for the
sake of the conscientious protection of the right of the faithful that the doctrine taught by the Church be fully imparted
to them. Previous efforts on the part of the Holy See, the
German Bishops' Conference, and the local Ordinary to in-
duce Professor Küng to correct his erroneous views had all
failed.

2. Since in a conversation with Bishop Moser, Professor
Küng had declared himself prepared to clarify his doctrines
further, the local Ordinary, with great patience and personal
openness, once more sought to assist Professor Küng in solv-
ing his problem. Having been informed about a "statement"
submitted by Professor Küng after his meeting with Bishop
Moser, the Holy Father decided to invite to a special confer-

ence the German cardinals, Bishop Moser, and the Metropolitan Bishop of Freiburg im Breisgau, Bishop Saier. The Cardinal Secretary of State and the Secretary of the Congregation for the Doctrine of the Faith were also to participate.

After a thorough examination of the latest statements of Professor Küng, all participants in the conference came to the conclusion that these statements did not constitute a sufficient ground for changing the decision taken in the Declaration of December 15.

3. In view of this, Professor Küng cannot, of course, continue to exercise the commission to teach theology which has been entrusted to him by the Church. The competent local Ordinary has no choice but to draw the canonical consequences in keeping with the provisions of the Concordat.

4. For years, the Doctrinal Congregation has taken pains to clarify with Professor Küng the ideas he has disseminated, without finding a comparable willingness on his part. The conference of December 28 is further evidence of the fact that both the Holy See and the German Bishops have handled Professor Küng's problem with the best of good will.

The decision which has been taken with great regret after so many previous efforts is exclusively determined by a deep sense of pastoral responsibility. As already emphasized in the Declaration of December 15, that decision does not at all imply that the legitimate freedom indispensable for theological inquiry is being curtailed.

The decision does not in any way alter the attitude of the Church with regard to its efforts at promoting Christian unity, in keeping with the principles set forth in the Declaration of Vatican II, *Unitatis redintegratio*.

5. Although Professor Küng's statement cannot constitute sufficient grounds for changing the decision contained in the Declaration of the Doctrinal Congregation of December 15, the Holy See and the German Bishops do not give up hope that Professor Küng, who has more than once declared his intention of remaining a Catholic theologian, will, after reflection in depth, adopt a position which will make it possi-

ble for the Church to reinstate his canonical commission to teach.

The Holy See and the German Bishops will continue to commend this matter to the Lord in prayer and ask all persons of good will to do the same.

Bishop Moser's notification to Küng that the mediation effort in Rome had failed came, as mentioned, in the form of a letter—the letter withdrawing his *Missio canonica:*

(79)

Very Honorable Professor!

In connection with the *Declaratio* of the Congregation for the Doctrine of the Faith of December 15, 1979, which was delivered to you on December 18 through the Apostolic Nunciature, I communicate to you the following:

The conversations conducted in the meanwhile have not led to a lifting of or changing of the *Declaratio.* Thereby a state of affairs exists according to which the prerequisites for a teaching activity with an ecclesiastical commission no longer exist. Accordingly I hereby withdraw the *Missio canonica* which was granted to you.

As the local bishop I will notify the Minister for Science and Art of the state of Baden-Württemberg that a serious complaint against your teaching exists and request him in cooperation with me to bring about the appropriate remedy and to search for an appropriate replacement in the teaching position of the Tübingen Catholic Theology Faculty.

I need not emphasize to you that I have attempted on all sides with all the powers that stood at my disposal to address this development. After as before I remain ready to have conversations with you.

With friendly greetings,

Yours,
Georg Moser, Bishop

Küng then issued the following declaration on December 30, 1979:

(80)
For a Truly Christian Church

With sadness and incomprehension I have learned of the results of the Roman negotiations. The Pope condemned a man whom he had not heard. The Roman motto *"audiatur et altera pars"* (the other side should also be heard) does not apply in papal Rome. Although several times I have written to the Pope and lastly to the Bishop of Rottenburg, urgently requesting a conversation with him, the Pope did not find it necessary personally to hear a Catholic theologian who has attempted throughout a quarter of a century to serve his Church according to his best knowledge and conscience. An uncomfortable critic should be silenced with all possible spiritual force. John XXIII and the Second Vatican Council are forgotten. Rome obviously will accept no *"correctio fraterna,"* no loyal criticism, no fraternal bearing with one another, no inquiries required by the spirit of solidarity. Human rights and Christian love will be preached outwardly, but, despite many beautiful words, disdained inwardly.

I was struck by the Roman action without any mediation and during the Christmas season, and, thanks to the Roman strategy of negotiations, was always only an object and never a partner in the procedure. Nevertheless, through conversations with Bishop Moser and through a declaration which was put into the hands of the Pope and through the constantly repeated preparedness to discuss all disputed questions, I have done everything that I could responsibly do in this extraordinarily difficult and burdensome situation.

It was in vain. I was not listened to. Unheeded also remained the interventions of Christians throughout the world. Unheeded the vigorous protests of numberless theologians, pastors, and laity of various confessions. Unheeded even the admonition of the World Council of Churches. The Roman authorities and German Church leaders have not understood that this dispute is not only about the case of Küng, but also about the Church and that the chances of its being built up again after the Second Vatican Council are thereby being forfeited.

It concerns not only the case of an individual theologian, but also all those who, known or unknown, in the past and in the future, who have been and will be dealt with in mechanical fashion by ecclesiastical authorities.

It concerns not only the case of an individual believer, but also the unity of the universal Church and the credibility of the Church leadership.

It concerns not only the infallibility of the Pope, but also his moral authority both within and without.

It concerns not only an inner-Catholic dispute, but also the success of ecumenical understanding.

I ask myself how many of our theologians, pastors, and laity dare not now call themselves Catholic if I should no longer be a Catholic theologian.

Despite all this I perceive the Roman verdict not as a defeat, but rather as a challenge to our Church for a long-over-due clarification of the fundamentals of Catholic theology and proclamation. A dishonest compromise would have perhaps retained the ecclesiastical teaching commission for me and created a temporary respite; it would, however, have been no service to the Church and would have robbed me of my very Christian identity and moral credibility.

In order to counteract the negative consequences of the Roman decision I request the theology faculties and other teachers of theology, the diocesan and priest councils, the parish councils and other church committees and groups in the coming weeks and months to discuss the contemporary critical development, to express openly your opinion, direct your appropriate demands to the competent ecclesiastical units, and work for the repeal of the manifold Roman disciplinary measures.

In unreserved fashion I stand behind the demands of the Committee for the Defense of Christian Rights in the Church. I request the Committee to continue its work beyond the present case and wherever possible to institutionalize its actions on an international level.

What is necessary for the future practice of doctrinal procedures is utimately the—in my case inexcusably neglected —demand to realize that "the spirit of dialogue is to be felt in those measures which the Doctrinal Congregation or another judicatory might undertake in regard to theologians. That means that they must have the opportunity to be heard and to clarify their viewpoint, as is expected in today's sense of justice. In every case the person concerned in the doctrinal procedure has the right himself to name a defender and to have access to all documents" (conclusion of the general Swiss Synod of February 16–17, 1974).

Despite these disciplinary measures, whose removal I will continue to work for, I remain not only a member and a priest in the Catholic Church, but also an Ordinary Professor of dogmatic and ecumenical theology. I will continue to pursue my central concern, namely, to make the message of Jesus Christ understandable to the men and women of today, as decisively as before: open to discussion and learning there where collegial and fraternal discussion takes place. In this I know that I am not alone. Against all resignation I will struggle together with the many who until now have supported me and to whom I express my gratitude with my whole heart. Let us continue to work together for a truly Christian Church.

On the same day, December 30, Tübingen University stepped forward with a declaration in which it tried to re-establish calm and offered itself as a mediator toward a resolution of the dispute;

it also made clear that the University was not going to be rushed
into any hasty actions by Church authorities.

(81)

The University regrets that it was not possible to arrive at
an agreement between Professor Küng and the Curia. It
thanks the diocesan Bishop, Dr. Georg Moser, for his intervention in favor of Professor Küng. It hopes that in the foreseeable future the dialogue can again be taken up. It allows
itself to be guided by the conviction that the decision of the
Curia is reversible with continuing efforts if the discussion
can be successfully held within objective parameters. The
fronts may not harden themselves still further by formulations which would not recognize a continuing readiness for
discussion.

The University offers once again to serve as a mediator. It
hopes that both sides will enter into further discussions with
a will to attaining an agreement. They must always be conscious of the tension-filled relationship between religious
freedom and the freedom of research and teaching. The
placing together of two such fundamental basic rights lays
upon all participants a special measure of responsibility. Beyond that, the law of the love of neighbor should oblige them
to exhaust all possibilities of reaching out to one another.

What is needed now is discretion. In the conversations
with the Church the collaboration of State, Church, and University is in need of a renewed clarification so that in the
Küng affair the fundamental question of the function of the
theological faculties and their research and teaching freedom
need not be brought into doubt. It should be undisputed that
the theological faculties can justly carry out their double responsibility as institutions of ecclesiastical teaching and as
scholarly establishments only if the freedom of research and
teaching is protected for them and their members in appropriate measure.

As the University already in its declaration of December 21, 1979, emphasized, the test of the legal consequences of the withdrawal of the ecclesiastical teaching commission demands a considerable amount of time. During that time, in any case, the legal corporation status of Professor Küng remains unchanged.

On December 31, 1979, Bishop Moser sent the letter to Minister for Science and Art Helmut Engler of the state of Baden-Württemberg asking for the removal of Küng from the Catholic Theology Faculty of the University of Tübingen. The pertinent parts are as follows:

(82)

Very Honored Minister!

As you can gather from the enclosed "Declaratio de quibusdam capitibus doctrinae theologicae professoris Ioannis Küng," the Congregation for the Doctrine of the Faith in Rome declared on December 15, 1979, that Professor Dr. Hans Küng . . . in several of his writings deviated from the full truth of the Catholic faith and therefore can neither be considered a Catholic theologian nor teach as such. As the major points for this decision the doctrinal opinions of Professor Küng concerning the following truths of faith are listed: the dogma of the infallibility of the Church, the authentic interpretation of the deposit of faith by the ecclesiastical teaching office, the plenary power over the valid celebration of the Eucharist.

This decision has proceeded after long efforts by the Congregation for the Doctrine of the Faith in Rome, the German Bishops' Conference, its organs, as well as myself since 1968 and 1971 respectively, in order to arrive at a satisfying clarification of the disputed interpretations. As you can see from the attached documentation, these comprehensive efforts failed.

Likewise still in the very last phase, namely, after December 15, 1979, Professor Küng had an opportunity to express himself within the framework of conversations and an exchange of correspondence especially initiated by me as the local bishop. His statement was thoroughly discussed and evaluated at a final meeting of a delegation of the German Bishops' Conference with Pope John Paul II on December 28, 1979. This statement was found to be insufficient. In the end, therefore, the conversations conducted in the meanwhile have not led to a lifting of or a changing of the *Declaratio* of December 15, 1979, as is clear from the press declaration of the Holy See of December 30, 1979. I request that you look to the attached documents for the details in justification.

I have made the decision of the Congregation for the Doctrine of the Faith, which has the approval of the Pope, my own. In the power of my episcopal responsibility, therefore, I bring forth a serious complaint against the teaching of Professor Hans Küng and withdraw the *Nihil obstat*.

At the same time I request that in line with Article 19 of the Federal Concordat—in connection with Article 3 of the Bavarian Concordat, Article 12 of the Prussian Concordat, and Article 10 of the Baden Concordat (each with the concluding regulations that belong to them)—the appropriate remedy be undertaken and a proper replacement be sought for the teaching position at the Tübingen Catholic Theology Faculty.

In view of the fact that the Catholic Theology Faculty at the University of Tübingen possesses at once a state and an ecclesiastical status, I must affirm that Professor Dr. Hans Küng consequently is obliged to give up his Church-related state office within this faculty. Should he not of himself resign from the legal position which he as a member of the Catholic Theology Faculty holds, then I must request that his exclusion from this faculty be initiated.

On December 30, 1979, I communicated to Professor Küng that on the basis of the given state of affairs I withdrew the ecclesiastical teaching commission which had been given to him. . . . [There now follows a list of the attached documents.]

Of course I will be glad to be available for conversation concerning the situation that has arisen and its legal consequences.

With friendly greetings,

Yours,

Georg Moser

Copy of this letter with enclosures to the Minister President of the state of Baden-Württemberg, Herr Lothar Späth, Stuttgart

In the meanwhile thousands upon thousands of letters of protest against the Vatican and the German Bishops and other thousands supporting Küng poured in from all over the world. According to Greinacher and Haag, the German Bishops' Conference alone received thousands of such negative protests (Küng received over 5,000 letters of support). "In order to respond to this critique the German Bishops' Conference felt impelled to issue an apologia in the form of a 'pulpit statement' to be read in all the churches [after its date of issuance, January 7, 1980] and a further 'Declaration' (3,500,000 copies) [an-eight-page pamphlet]. Many priests of course refused to read the 'pulpit statement' in their worship service, so that for example Cardinal Ratzinger felt himself compelled to admonish his clergy in a circular letter at Easter time that his pastoral letter in any case would have to be read if a priest did not wish to commit 'a clear violation of the promise of obedience which belongs to the essence of the priestly ordination'" (*Fall Küng,* p. 158). An interesting aspect of the "Declaration" portion of the pamphlet is that there are many references to numbered documents, giving the appearance of weighty scholarliness. In fact, the bishops did print hundreds of thousands of copies of their *Documentation,* which ran to something over 200 pages in book form in the English edition (*The Küng Dialogue*)—the German was on double-columned tabloid newsprint. The "pulpit statement" and the "Declaration" were as follows:

(83)
Joint Pulpit Statement of the German Bishops
(January 7, 1980)

The Pope and Bishops have arrived at an important decision in the dispute with Professor Hans Küng. The commission to teach theology in the name of the Church had to be
withdrawn from him. Many seeking and questioning persons
have had approaches to fundamental religious questions
opened to them by Professor Küng; many faithful have, however, also been brought into confusion by the interpretations
presented by him.

We German Bishops see ourselves, in complete unity with
the Pope, despite many years of attempts at clarification and
conversation, unfortunately forced to state: Professor Küng
represents in important points of the faith teaching opinions
which stand in opposition to the binding teaching of the
Church. As long as this is the case he cannot be a theological
teacher in the name of the Church. We do not judge what
Professor Küng personally believes, but rather what he writes
and what he says in lectures.

Many and different people have in recent weeks expressed
themselves in the Küng case. Has the procedure against him
been conducted justly? Are not the disputed points really
marginal problems? Is the Church retreating behind the Second Vatican Council? How is it with freedom in the Church?
We Bishops are obliged to give a clarifying, helping word to
the faithful and to the public. This brief pulpit statement can
of course touch only a few points. We have explained the details in an extensive declaration.

1. In the foreground of the dispute there stands the word
"infallible." That no one in the Church, not even the Pope,
remains protected in all of his speech and acts from error
and mistakes is self-evident. The teaching of the infallibility
in the Church does not concern that. Rather it says: when
the Pope as the highest teacher of the Church or a general

Council or the Bishops in full accord with the Pope affirm something as revealed by God and presented as to be believed, then they are protected by the assistance of the Holy Spirit from an error (cf. *Lumen Gentium,* 25). This, however, Professor Küng calls into doubt. He is himself very clear about how the question of the infallibility in the Church very much concerns the foundation of the faith, Church, and theology.

2. Professor Küng repeatedly stresses that he does not wish to dispute the binding teaching of the Church, but rather openly "inquires" to it. There is, however, a tremendous difference between whether one questions what a statement means and how it is to be grounded, and whether one places this statement itself in question and thereby doubts it. Professor Küng, however, clearly draws binding Church doctrine into doubt.

3. Is infallibility in the Church not a marginal question? For the faith and for theology it is decisive that everyone knows wherein he or she can and must give the obedience of faith required by God. Consequently it is not a side issue whether God has promised to the teaching office of the Pope and the Bishops that assistance which in final questions of the faith excludes error and thereby gives us that certainty in faith upon which we found our life and our hope. Of course all human statements, likewise those of revelation and of the Church, are limited. But limitation and error are different things.

4. If we cannot depend upon the binding statements of the Church with an ultimate certainty, then even who Jesus Christ is can be drawn into doubt. Did God really give himself for us in that his eternal Son, like unto him in essence, took on our human existence and died for us? This is the faith which bears our life and our death. The great Councils of Christian antiquity proclaimed it in a final manner; in it they laid out the central message of the New Testament in a binding fashion. This confession is and remains the foundation for our entire faith and life as Christians. We make this

confession our own in the Credo of the Holy Mass: "God from God, light from light, true God of true God, begotten not made, of one substance with the Father." Professor Küng's statements remain—despite all attempts of the ecclesiastical office to arrive at clarity and unambiguity in discussion with him—behind what the Holy Scriptures, confession of faith, Councils, and liturgy bear witness to of Jesus Christ.

5. Time and again the question is raised whether the procedure against Professor Küng was just. We gladly grant that ecclesiastical rules for procedure can be improved. Nevertheless, we must unambiguously answer: the procedure was just. And it is not justifiable to shove the substance about which the dispute with Professor Küng is concerned behind the question of procedure.

A broad theological discussion was carried on in public concerning the opinions of Professor Küng on the doctrine of Jesus Christ and on infallibility in the Church. A large number of peer experts had taken a critical position toward the interpretations of Professor Küng.

A large number of letters, conversations, invitations to conversations from the side of the Apostolic See and the Bishops could not bring it about that Professor Küng made the necessary contribution to the clarification of the disputed points. Because Professor Küng let it be known that he would be prepared to review his statements, the Roman Doctrinal Congregation on February 15, 1975, refrained from requiring a recantation, and instead admonished him not to repeat his opinions which are not in agreement with the ecclesiastical teaching office. Professor Küng has not held to this. In a publication of 1979 he interpreted the non-withdrawal of the ecclesiastical teaching commission as a sign that the ecclesiastical teaching office itself was not certain about the matter in question concerning infallibility. With this the Pope and Bishops saw themselves impelled to act. They had to affirm: as long as Professor Küng contradicts the binding teaching of the Church he cannot teach theology with the commission of the Church.

To speak here of a violation of human rights or of Inquisition methods is not objective. Whoever considers the documentation of the German Bishops' Conference concerning the Küng case, and especially also the efforts of recent weeks, will be able to be convinced of the honest openness to discussion on the part of the ecclesiastical office. It is all the more regrettable that the withdrawal of the ecclesiastical teaching commission must remain in regard to Professor Küng. However, all of us, together with the Holy Father, do not give up the hope that Professor Küng will revise his attitude and opinion.

In conclusion we would wish expressly to state that the Church needs theological scholarship and theologians. The foundation of theology is the binding faith of the Church. However, this faith must be theologically penetrated, developed, and founded. This task of theology is important for the very life of the Church. Thus the dialogue between the ecclesiastical office and theology is something that cannot be given up. We will not be going astray by continuing to pursue it.

We German Bishops confirm our complete unity with the Holy Father and with each other. The worship of the Son of God become human, the confession to him according to the Credo of the Church, the yes to the gift of the Spirit, who protects the Church from error in faith, unites us and all the faithful. Let us guard this unity, let us pray for this unity. Würzburg, January 7, 1980

[Then come the names and sees of all the Ordinaries of Germany in the alphabetical order of the sees.]

(84)
Declaration of the German Bishops
(January 7, 1980)

The decision of the Church to withdraw the ecclesiastical teaching commission from Professor Dr. Hans Küng has drawn great public attention both within and without the

Church. We have received many disturbed but also many confirming written statements. Immediately after the Christmas time we came together in a session called by ourselves in order to issue to all of you a joint word of clarification and orientation which we have unanimously agreed upon.

1. An Almost Ten-Year Prehistory

Despite widespread news coverage by the media, the development of the conflict is not everywhere known in equal measure. Therefore the most important points along the way of a painful dispute will be mentioned. The German Bishops' Conference has made available to the public a comprehensive documentation of all the important previous events so that it can itself form an unprejudiced picture of the manifold efforts.

In May 1968, Professor Küng was invited by the Roman Doctrinal Congregation to a conversation concerning his book *The Church* (cf. doc. 1). A meeting did not take place and Professor Küng did not produce the requested written statement on substantive matters. In July 1971, a doctrinal proceedings against the book *Infallible?* was opened. Immediately a list of objections and difficulties was sent with the request for a response (cf. doc. 19). Since after two years despite renewed invitations no substantive discussion took place, the Doctrinal Congregation published the doctrinal document *Mysterium ecclesiae,* which without the naming of names and without the threat of measures attempted positively to clarify the truths of the faith that were in question. Since the conversation offered (cf. doc. 23 and 24) to Professor Küng likewise even after the publication of this declaration could not take place in the following two years, the Doctrinal Congregation decided on February 15, 1975 (cf. doc. 35), with the permission of Pope Paul VI, to take an unusual step: it admonished the theologian "not to advocate these doctrines any longer," and desisted for the time being from a further action, that is, it suspended the proceedings "for now." Professor Küng opened the way for this when in

September 1974 he communicated to the Doctrinal Congregation (cf. doc. 32) that with "a time for thought" he did not exclude the possibility that his teaching opinions in the course of time might "conform" [angleichen] to that of the teaching office. This otherwise legally not foreseen solution was de facto broken by Professor Küng in the spring of 1979, in that he presented his previous theses concerning infallibility in the Church in a sharper form (cf. doc. 55). Independent of this proceedings of the Roman Doctrinal Congregation, the German Bishops' Conference had in vain from 1976 until 1977 sought a further clarification of the teaching of Professor Küng concerning Jesus Christ (cf. doc. 43 ff.). Since 1970 public calls by Küng for action against the valid ecclesiastical order issued forth (mixed-marriage regulations, recognition of offices, intercommunion, celibacy, ordination of women to the priesthood, etc.—cf., e.g., doc. 10).

Despite urgent requests no colloquium with Rome took place. The conversations with the German Bishops' Conference reached no satisfactory clarification. Even the long-lasting theological discussion could not move Professor Küng to the expanded treatment which he himself granted was necessary, or indeed to corrections. All the means at their disposal to reach a successful clarification in dialogue were exhausted by the Doctrinal Congregation and the German Bishops' Conference. The Holy Father in an unusual step required a still further review before the issuance of the "Declaration." Even on the day before the conversation between a delegation of the German Bishops and Pope John Paul II on December 28, 1979, Küng, via a colleague, responded with a simple rejection of the urgent request by the competent local Bishop of Rottenburg-Stuttgart for several specifications of content (cf. doc. 62/63). With this the decision became unavoidable.

2. Bases for the Church Decision

In the expressions of opinion since the December 18, 1979, publication of the decision, the event itself has stood

in the foreground and the substantive questions, on the other
hand, have threatened almost to disappear. What does it all
concern?

a. It concerns not only the infallibility of the Pope, but
rather of the whole Church, indeed even concerning the truth
of the Holy Scriptures. Professor Küng acknowledges that
the Church of Jesus Christ has been promised a fundamental
remaining in the truth of God. Almost all Christian Churches
and Christian communities affirm in their confessional statements this maintenance of the Church in the unswerving loyalty of God. In Jesus Christ he turned once and for all toward the world and entrusted the word of salvation to his
Church for loyal protection and correct interpretation
throughout the passage of the ages. The indestructibility of
the Church in the promised truth of God of course does not
exclude individual errors. Professor Küng also believes that
such a general remaining in the truth is sufficient. Indeed—
and this now is the kernel of his thesis—this is consistent with
de facto errors in decisions concerning the faith which the
ecclesiastical teaching office has issued as irrevocable. Thus
Professor Küng denies that the "indestructibility of the Church
and the truth is bound to specific statements or agencies." He
thereby draws not only the infallibility of the Pope into
doubt, but also the prior and much more fundamental gift of
the guaranteeing of the Church in the truth of God accomplished by the Spirit. A defense against errors through the
active protection of the deposit of the faith and even indeed a
definitive decision in questions of the faith would *de facto* no
longer be possible.

b. With this fundamental thesis Professor Küng obscures
two further dimensions of the Christian faith. To these belong the decisive confession of the faith and a certitude
which stands the test through life and death. Therefore from
the beginning is the biblical faith closely bound to the binding word expressed in the Credo. Only thus can the Christian
through the trustworthiness of the faith retain joy and
confidence even in difficult situations. Even non-Catholic
Christian Churches and ecclesiastical communities also hold

fast to this. Professor Küng does not dispute that the faith is expressed in confessional formulas. Nevertheless, he draws the persevering validity of ultimately binding statements into doubt. Of course the Church does not deny that such statements of faith are conceived in their earlier horizon of understanding, that they can and must be more deeply understood and pastorally explained anew.

A second difficulty is closely connected with these fundamental theses. With Professor Küng it is no longer clear that the Church in its official agencies (the College of Bishops, Council, Pope) is able unerringly to explain in the face of a specific historical situation the Christian confession of faith in a binding statement in a legitimate manner and under thoroughly described conditions (cf. Constitution of the Church of the Second Vatican Council, *Lumen Gentium,* Art. 25). The competent officeholders in such situations act not out of an arbitrary fullness of power, but rather they are official and public witnesses to the purity of the living deposit of the faith. They speak for the witness of the faith of the entire Church. Their public ecclesiastical function is therefore bound to the message of the faith. "The teaching office is not above the word of God, but rather serves it" (Dogmatic Constitution on Divine Revelation of the Second Vatican Council, Art. 10). The Church was always convinced that a special assistance of the Holy Spirit was given to the responsible office in this specific unfolding of the service of witness. There can be no talk of an arbitrary and self-pleasing exercise of domination by the ecclesiastical teaching office.

c. These elements of the understanding of the faith are gathered together in the concept of the infallibility in the Church. It is certainly not as central a matter of faith as is the God question and the resurrection of Jesus Christ. However, it is by far not therefore a "marginal dogma." It serves the finding of truth and confidence in official proclamation and thus has been helpful to the members of the Church more indirectly. The faithful have a right to a full and unambiguous presentation of inalienable truths of faith. And therefore the theological statement on the ultimately binding statements of faith provides a deep insight into the inner understanding of revelation and history, Spirit and Church, office and word. When something is not correct here, there appear dangerous, even if at first hardly perceivable, cracks in the foundation of a theology and even in the faith consciousness of the community. We German Bishops have already pointed out in a detailed declaration of February 17, 1975, such consequences in the theological method of Professor Küng (cf. doc. 36). This also was in vain.

d. These defects are above all apparent in the statements by Professor Küng concerning the person of Jesus Christ. He indeed would like to hold fast "to the great intentions and substance of the Ecumenical Councils," but his concrete statements concerning the divinity of Jesus Christ and the Trinity of God fall short of the content of this traditional faith. For example, it is not false, but it is insufficient to say that "in the history of Jesus Christ true God and humanity are involved." For the Christian faith the confession is decisive that Jesus Christ in an unlimited manner is the word of God from eternity. "We believe . . . in the one Lord Jesus Christ, only begotten Son of God, born of the Father before all ages: God from God, light from light, true God from true God, begotten not made, of one substance with the Father."

To be sure, one must attempt to open up these words of the great confession of faith to contemporary men and women. However, theology may never be unclear precisely in this decisive point of Christian confession. For it concerns here the truth of our salvation: if God himself has not turned to humanity in Jesus Christ, then Jesus likewise cannot redeem us from sin and death. Here all the Christian Churches are at one. All statements about the being human of Jesus and his exemplary humanity are full of significance for faith only if they are inwardly bound up with an unlimited confession of "the true God." The Roman Declaration does not formally put the christological question forward as the basis for the withdrawal of the teaching commission. This is so because of legal procedural reasons, for the almost ten-year-long doctrinal proceedings did not include these problems. The fact that this is an incidental reference does not indicate, however, that this and other defects (for example, the view of the Mother of God and of the sacraments) are to be taken any less seriously. The German Bishops' Conference in its statement to "those proclaiming the faith" concerning the book *On Being a Christian* on November 14, 1977, thoroughly dealt with their substantive significance. It is precisely within an ecumenical perspective that these connections are important (cf. *Die Deutschen Bischöfe,* 13).

3. Integration and Consequences

After the unsuccessful efforts to attain a clarification above all in the important substantive questions, a decision became unavoidable. All the participants in this decision were painfully aware of the pastoral consequences. Küng's theological work was not being rejected in total, but only in the specified points. The pastoral goal of his work was already thoroughly recognized by us. A general rejection of his theology is not involved. However, there gradually arose in the midst of the Church an unbearable contradiction in that an influential theologian taught in the name of the Church and trained future priests and lay theologians while over the years he acted contrary to the accepted commission. It concerns the handing on of the undamaged Catholic faith to other generations, not a Roman power claim or maintaining a system in existence.

We understand the concern of many. We ask, however, for trust when along with Pope John Paul II we declare: we wish unmistakably to cultivate the spirit of mutual understanding and dialogue in the relationship between the teaching office and theology. No one can or wishes to lag behind the letter and the spirit of the Second Vatican Council. We are not anxious and narrow in the face of the necessary questions and research in theology. On the contrary, until most recently, difficulties between theology and the Church office—often unnoticed by the public—were worked out in a reconciling fashion. Please look upon the situation of Professor Küng as a very concrete exceptional case for which we for almost ten years tried to find an amicable settlement. We will in no case relinquish this style. Likewise the Pope and his Congregations do not desire to. However, we also cannot be untrue to our task of preserving the faith, concerning whose carrying out we must give a reckoning at the judgment of the Lord. At the assumption of his office the theologian was entrusted with the teaching of the living faith of the Church. There remains therein a broad field for his own questions and new research. Nevertheless, he should not forget that he should work for the building up of the Church. Whether he succeeds in this cannot be decided by him alone. If he one-sidedly breaks this received trust, makes himself to be the standard, and thereby must have his teaching capacity withdrawn, it is a specious dishonesty to speak of the injury to human rights. The freedom of opinion of Professor Küng is not limited.

The ecumenical dimension of the conflict is often spoken of. Catholic special doctrines are not herein exclusively, nor indeed even principally, concerned. Much more is at stake with the question of the irrevocable truth of the Bible and of the confessions of the ancient Church Councils on the genuine Christian fundamental questions. We believe that we do a service to the entire *oikoumene* much more with our insistence on the unabbreviated confession of Christ.

We do not wish to fall short of that which has already been attained, but we also do not wish to take any irresponsible steps which in truth would not mean progress. We all come closer together when we become more like Jesus Christ. For this we must change ourselves. A self-appointed task which would embarrass one's partner would be no help in the search for unity. We thank the many Protestant sisters and brothers for their discreet concern when a family conflict breaks out in the neighboring house. They know only too well that our questions and needs—perhaps in a transformed sense—are also their problems. They likewise are occasionally obliged to engage in doctrinal disciplinary proceedings, to use their terms.

We thank the theologians for their painstaking and selfless work. We ask them for patience and circumspection in the public presentation of their hypotheses. Self-discipline and true freedom and a self-critical mutual supplementation is better than a doctrinal proceedings.

We ask all the members of our Church and all those interested in the matter for a sober judgment of the decision taken. One cannot call for love without at the same time being concerned with the truth. Tolerance does not mean giving up on the finding of the truth. Pluralism in theology is not possible without the necessary unity in the confession of faith. Distrust the slogans and agitations which continually can endanger the peace and the unity of the Church.

In association with Pope John Paul II and the Bishop of Rottenburg-Stuttgart and all the faithful of this diocese we are conscious of the special responsibility to the universal Church. Finally, we request your prayers that God will protect his Church from injury and discord.

Würzburg, January 7, 1980

[Then come the names of the bishops as in the previous document.]

Everyone expected that on Sunday, January 20, 1980, when Küng celebrated Mass at St. Paul's in Tübingen, he would speak about the "pulpit statement" read against him almost everywhere the week before. But in fact he preached on the prescribed text, 1 Corinthians 12, on the various charisms. He contented himself with the previous issuance, on January 11, of a brief statement in response to the Bishops' massive nationwide attack on him. His statement was as follows:

(85)
Press Declaration on the Pulpit Statement
(January 11, 1980)

That the dispute has now also been carried even to the
pulpit I can only regret. With Church tax funds running into
the hundreds of thousands and printings into the millions the
entire apparatus of the Church is mobilized against a single
individual: documentations, brochures, pastoral letters, individual bishops, a pulpit statement of the entire episcopate—
all replete with incomplete information and one-sided interpretations. Justice and Christian brotherliness would have
demanded that one so attacked should be given the possibility of presenting his own theological position before the
German Catholics. Against all contrary claims I affirm the
following to be true:

1. I was always prepared for conversation and for correction and have had numberless conversations with the local
bishop, representatives of the German Bishops' Conference,
and even personally with the heads of the Roman Doctrinal
Congregation, and have likewise desired a conversation with
the Pope.

2. I have rejected only an Inquisition procedure where the
investigator, prosecutor, and the judge are identical, where
access to the documents are denied me, where I cannot name
a defender, where negotiations are handled in my absence,
and there is no possibility of appeal. That runs contrary to
the Declaration of Human Rights of the European Council,
Article 6.

3. Concerning my publications which recently have come
under discussion there has been no proceedings conducted
either in Germany or in Rome. This pertains to the book *On
Being a Christian* as well as the new publications concerning
the question of infallibility. The *Documentation* of the German Bishops' Conference concerning these is incomplete.

The presentations by the Church office of my Christology I especially feel to be profoundly inaccurate.

I appeal once again to all the organizations of the Catholic Church, especially on the parish level, to discuss the most recent development in an unprejudiced manner and to form their own opinion on the basis of comprehensive information.

On January 10, 1980, the expanded Faculty Council, the decisive organ of the Catholic Theology Faculty at Tübingen, voted by secret ballot on a brief declaration—the vote was 14 yes, 1 no, and 1 abstention (Küng was not present). In the later maneuvering this is an important document to note:

(86)

The declarations of the Bishop of Rottenburg-Stuttgart, Dr. Georg Moser, and of Professor Dr. Hans Küng permit a revision of the ecclesiastical decisions to be expected. In this hope the Faculty asks Professor Küng to do everything in his power to moderate the conflict. It asks Bishop Moser to allow provisional solutions during this provisional period which will make a revision easier. The Faculty asks the Senate of the University to exhaust all the legal possibilities to see to it that Professor Küng continues to remain a member of the Catholic Theology Faculty. It urges a rapid clarification of the disputed legal questions. In the meanwhile the functioning capacity of the Faculty, especially the capacity to have all examinations recognized, must be preserved.

As the statements, declarations, articles, demonstrations, letters, etc., mounted into the scores, hundreds, and thousands, and the legal dispute between the rights of the Church authorities and academic freedom and the state mounted and intensified, the pressure on the Tübingen Catholic Theology Faculty members to abandon Küng's struggle to remain a member of the Faculty increased greatly—until the ancient Roman tactic of *divide et im-pera* had its effect. Seven of the twelve (besides Küng) Faculty members broke ranks on February 5, 1980, and issued a declaration which was somewhat murky in its intent—at least to judge from the disclaimers of some of the signers afterward—but clear enough to seriously undermine Küng's position, to say nothing of his health, which was beginning to break under the long terrific strain (chest pains and other ominous symptoms).

Greinacher and Haag had the following introductory remarks to that declaration: "Among all the reactions to the Küng case, the following declaration by seven (of the total twelve) professors of the Catholic Theology Faculty of the University of Tü-bingen caused the greatest astonishment, alienation, and incomprehension. On February 1, 1980, Professors Auer, Lohfink, and Reinhardt spoke with Küng and revealed to him the intention of several colleagues to go before the public with a declaration of their own. Küng pleaded with them urgently not to do so in view of the negotiations in process and his imminent letter to Bishop Moser [February 12—see below pp. 454–80]. Nevertheless, on the evening of February 4, in connection with the farewell address of Professor Haag [becoming emeritus] in the Festival Hall of the University, the news was bruited about that the declaration would be published the following day. It appeared on February 5, in the *Frankfurter Allgemeine Zeitung* and the *Schwäbische Tagblatt* [Tübingen]" (p. 235):

(87)
Declaration of Seven Professors of the Catholic Theology Faculty of the University of Tübingen
"Church Struggle with the Help of Theology?
Opposed to Total Confrontation within Catholicism"
(February 5, 1980)

The withdrawal of the ecclesiastical teaching commission (*Missio canonica*) from Professor Hans Küng appears to have led to a crisis within the Catholic Church of Germany. Hans Küng has done very much for the aggiornamento of the

Catholic faith. He has unceasingly and publicly expressed the yearning of many Christians for a renewal of the Church and he has found language for their concerns which have spread far beyond the area of theology and the Church. Obviously Hans Küng has addressed matters which for a long time have moved many. They do not wish to have this understandable language and hope for further reforms taken away again. Therefore the shock and reaction which is now going through the Church. Such a shock contains within itself opportunities, but also dangers. The opportunities will be squandered if the whole affair leads to a total confrontation between "progressive" and "conservative" forces and to a Church struggle on the backs of theology and to the injury of the theological faculties.

How Christians Deal with One Another

Indications of such a confrontation have long since appeared. Positions have hardened, fronts are thrown up. The "terrible simplifiers" are at work. On the one side is the threat to battle for supposed or real rights with litigation in the state courts as far as possible, and a propagandistic campaign which in the area of language seeks to disqualify the "opponent" ("manipulator," "hierarchs," "inquisition," "a night and fog operation," "an arrogant archbishop," and so forth). On the other side there is a manner of procedure which does not correspond to the contemporary sense of justice and the spirit of Christianity, and (the statement came from Cologne) a public disqualification of contemporary theology. If all this continues only shattered remains will be left. This corresponds neither to the demands of the issue nor to the example of Jesus.

The Question of Truth Alone Gives the Dispute Its Value and Its Seriousness

One should not dismiss the whole controversy as a mere theologians' squabble, as a dispute about dogmatic subtleties, or as the dark machinations of Roman agencies, or indeed maintain that it concerns merely the silencing of an uncomfortable critic—with our freedom of opinion and the press such in any case would not be possible. It concerns the truth of the faith and the structural problems of the Church. Hans Küng himself claims that it concerns "nothing but the truth." That is to be taken seriously on both sides. The catchword "infallible" is certainly burdened, and the concept "infallibility" is likewise theologically disputed. It is not concerned with the privileges of persons, but rather with the service of the truth which the Petrine office must perform for the faith, and ultimately for the protection which the Church brings to the truth of the faith and to the trustworthiness of its witness. That is no marginal question any more than is the question of the relationship of Jesus to God.

The direction of the debate is apparent, among other things, in that the confessions of faith from the early period of Christianity are binding on all Christian Churches in their continuing truth to this very day. Therefore, here it concerns the essential and continuing foundation of the ecumenical rapprochement, and to that extent it provides a service to all the Churches. An ecumenism which ignored the truth question would be on a false path. Likewise should a Church separate itself from theological doctrinal opinions in which it sees its faith endangered, it should not be accused of threatening "Christian rights" or "human rights" and wishing to "enforce a particular understanding of the truth." Such a confusion of language has a completely demagogic effect when in addition it is likewise maintained that this takes place "at the cost of the happiness of millions of men and women."

It Is Completely Concerned with the Freedom of Theology

Theology as the science of faith has a special position and function within the witness to the faith and within the living practice of the Church. It has taken over the faith of the believing community in which it works, not only as an object of its research and teaching, but also it stands continually and constitutively upon the foundation and under the norm of this faith. Its task is the scholarly service of its truth. It is not the functionary of any ecclesiastical agency. It must be able to bring forth its contribution to the whole independently, critically, and freely. Every inappropriate limitation, dismissal, or suspicion of its work is damaging, regardless of whether it would come from without or from within. However, the theologian has not received his scholarly office in order to serve *his own* credibility or *his own* ecclesiastical interest. He is indeed responsible only for his own conscience concerning the truth, but the decision as to whether his convictions and doctrinal opinions in reality express the faith of the believing community can ultimately not be left to his own judgment.

The scholarly work of the theologian, particularly today when the truth of the Christian faith must win a new, credible, and well-grounded presence in the struggle of humanity for its future, is of great significance for the Church. The Church needs a theology which is free, capable of accomplishment, and committed to its task. But a theology without its Church would be nothing. This with-one-another and for-one-another of theology and the Church does not exclude oppositions, tensions, and conflicts, but demands regulation of the collaboration and likewise clarity about with whom the final word lies. Unfortunately the hopeful beginnings of a productive collaboration between bishops and theologians— a collaboration to which likewise and above all a respect for the varying responsibilities and charismas belongs—which in connection with the Council flourished, have in the post-conciliar phase been heavily burdened from both sides by a faulty readiness to engage in dialogue, dismissive judgments, and characteristics of style marked by limited personalities. Just as theologians should not arrogate to themselves the functions of the episcopal teaching office, so also bishops should not interfere in inner-scholarly work. Here also a new style, indeed in part a new structure of Church practice, is urgently necessary. Since the truth "does not raise a claim other than the power of the truth itself" (Vatican II, Decree on Religious Liberty), the solution to disputed scholarly questions should not be sought by administrative or disciplinary measures. Nevertheless, not every intervention by the teaching office into the work of theology is an unwarranted intervention. This is the case, for example, when an individual theologian sets up "as the norm of the truth his own judgment and not the thought of the Church" (*Declaratio* of December 15, 1979), for in this case he would arrogate to himself the highest teaching office in the Church.

Moreover, the freedom of theology is not only threatened by authoritarian ecclesiastical measures or by totalitarian ideologies and systems. It is likewise endangered when it is delivered into the hands of the objectivity-limiting mass media and the notions of plausibility which reign there. False friends, whose number never fails when resentments against the Church break out, injure the freedom of theology under certain circumstances more than does an official doctrinal call to the subject matter which again forces one to substantive argument.

The Theological Faculties in Danger

The freedom of theology in the Church (not from the Church!) is additionally assured within the Federal Republic in that the theological faculties are integrated within the state university and the freedom of research and teaching is guaranteed by the constitution. The structural tensions between ecclesiastical obligation and state office, which were foreseen and ordered in the Concordats, expose the theological faculties to special hazards. However, this status of the faculties has in practice proved to be extremely fruitful for the Church as well as for society. Whoever wishes a free theology and a free Church and a free state must stand up for this status of the faculties. A theology frightened back into the ecclesiastical ghetto should not be wished upon either Christians or upon society.

The theological faculties are nevertheless today endangered in their existence not only from without but increasingly also from within. Whoever allows or wishes that a theologian without a *Missio canonica* should belong to a theological faculty for an extended period of time undermines its scholarly theoretical status as well as its constitutional and Concordat guarantee. This protects indeed not only theology in general but also Catholic and Protestant theology. Where the connection with the Church is undermined or is given up, necessarily very quickly the ecclesiastical interest in the faculties will likewise cease.

It is not to be overlooked that thereby an unholy alliance between the integralist-minded clerics, for whom the existence of state faculties has long been a thorn in the side, and an ideologically blind liberalism will have been given a push forward. Supposedly progressive voices which neglect the ecclesiastical status necessary for the continued existence of the theological faculties add fuel to this fire. Compromises and arrangements which carry the seeds of destruction in themselves might be offered as short-term solutions to the conflict. In the long term they must show themselves as a time bomb of incredibly explosive force within the entire state-Church legal structure.

In the events of the past weeks the question of the freedom of research and teaching for theology has been brought before the public. Unfortunately in this question the following have often been overlooked: (1) The freedom of research and teaching is not only an individual right of a professor but also an institutional right which includes the functioning capability of the faculties and universities. (2) It does not place in question the individual right of the individual professor: he can continue to do research and teach—only he cannot do so with the teaching commission of the Church. (3) A state which has a neutral world view observes and protects the freedom of the religious communities to regulate their own affairs themselves. Therefore it may not install in the theological faculties any mechanisms for changing the function of theology. Indeed, whoever would wish to demand of state organs that they see to the observing of rights within the Church would burden anew the state with the long since overcome sovereignty over the Church.

In conclusion it may be recalled that precisely the program of the "Catholic Tübingen school" and its faculty, which has existed for over one hundred and sixty years, has taken upon itself as an obligatory standard the service to the Church and society by way of theological work which is bound in faith, but precisely thereby and therein is free. Its efforts likewise strive further to realize constructively the tension-filled unity of science, churchliness, and openness to the times, and to ward off its destruction.

Alfons Auer, Walter Kasper, Gerhard Lohfink, Ludger Oeing-Hanhoff, Rudolf Reinhardt, Max Seckler, Hermann Josef Vogt

(88)

The Dean of the Catholic Theology Faculty of the University of Tübingen, Professor Dr. Wolfgang Bartholomäus, made the following statement concerning the declaration of the "seven":

1. There are at present twelve professors in the Faculty, of whom ten are Ordinarii. The group of seven, therefore, excludes two professors [Ordinarii, in addition to Küng] in order to give the impression of an overwhelming majority of professors.

2. The five professors who did not sign the declaration of the seven were not asked to. They had no opportunity to express themselves concerning the declaration.

3. On January 10, 1980, with one negative vote and one abstention the Faculty requested the Senate of the University,

in view of our hope for a revision, to exhaust all legal possibilities to the end that Professor Küng could remain a member of the Faculty. In the face of this unity there now arises various questions:

If the declaration of the seven operates within the resolution of the Faculty, why then was not an agreement among all the professors sought out? If, on the contrary, the declaration of the seven contradicts the Faculty resolution, why then did the great majority of the seven vote yes on January 10, 1980? Or why did the seven afterward neglect making an attempt to revise the Faculty resolution within the Faculty?

4. The declaration of the seven is an expression of opinion of colleagues which as such cannot repeal the Faculty resolution. As Dean, I must, after as well as before, proceed on the basis of the resolution of the Faculty. The declaration is an expression of opinion which of necessity will disturb the delicate mediation attempts of the University after conversations between the parties concerned had already begun. The declaration is an expression of opinion which in content and in form is inappropriate for contributing to the resolution of the conflict and it has disturbed me in the extreme by the manner in which it came into existence.

There was a flood of criticism, often very strong, against the "seven," some coming from the majority of the junior faculty (academic counselors and assistants) and the student body of the Catholic Theology Faculty. Let the following event serve as a single example.

The historian Professor Dr. Christoph Weber, from Düsseldorf, had been invited to a guest lecture during the summer semester 1980 at the Catholic Theology Faculty of the University of Tübingen upon the suggestion of the Ordinarius Professor for medieval and modern Church history, Professor Reinhardt. On February 6, 1980, Professor Weber sent the following telegram to the Dean of the Catholic Theology Faculty:

(89)

Of all the documents of German Church history of the nineteenth and twentieth centuries which I know, today's declaration by the seven Tübingen professors belongs among the
most shameful. The servility, toadyism, and fawning obfusca-
tion that are here exhibited have never before existed in this
form. The torturous walking on eggs with its officious concern
merely gives witness to one thing, namely, cowardice and
hypocrisy. Therefore I naturally cannot now hold a lecture.
The signature of Professor Reinhardt especially pains me. I
am happy, my dear Dean, that you yourself have not signed.
Please notify Professor Küng of this telegram.

Professor Dr. Christoph Weber

Some two weeks earlier, on January 21, 1980, Küng wrote a
letter to Professor Helmut Engler, the Minister for Science and
Art of the state of Baden-Württemberg, to apprise him of how he
saw his legal situation and to ask for a clarification—this was in
preparation for a debate on the matter in a forthcoming session of
the Parliament. Küng's arguments are clear, quite simple, and
forceful. He makes two main points: that the Church authorities
both in Rome and in Germany had grossly violated their own
published rules of procedures in their measures against him, and
that therefore their request to the state to remove Küng from the
Catholic Theology Faculty had no proper legal basis; that the
local bishop, who alone according to the Concordat had the right
to ask for the removal of Küng, appears not at all to be acting for
himself, but for another, which would seem to be in violation of
the Concordat. It is not difficult to see why the Bishops were
nervous about the possible outcome of the case and were consequently spending hundreds of thousands of marks in their campaign against Küng. It is interesting to note that this enthusiasm
spilled over to the United States, where it was arranged for the
American Bishops' publishing arm to translate and publish in
handsome book form the German Bishops' Conference *Documen-*

tation against Küng (*Dialogue with Küng*), the first 5,000 copies of which were underwritten by Cardinal John Krol of Philadelphia. Küng's letter was as follows:

(90)

Professor Dr. Helmut Engler
Minister for Science and Art

Very Honorable Minister:

With my whole heart I would like to thank you for the detailed, open, and objective discussion which I was able to have with you on January 17, 1980. Especially important for me was your assurance that you and the provincial government will investigate the entire matter thoroughly according to juridical criteria and that thereby the fundamental interests of theology as a science within the German university will be kept in view.

In our conversation, among other things, I drew attention to the defects in the ecclesiastical "proceedings" conducted against me. These defects, juridical and political, appear so significant to me that I allow myself to spell them out to you once again in writing as follows. In my judgment the serious defects in the proceedings are to be found in two areas:

I. Proceedings defects in the inner-ecclesiastical procedure

In the Roman Catholic Church there exists a "new proceedings order for the investigation of doctrinal questions" of January 15, 1971, published in the *Acta Apostolicae Sedis* 63 (1971), pp. 234–36.

1. Without going into the details of this proceedings order, it is to be ascertained here that the Doctrinal Congregation through its decree of February 15, 1975, had "closed" the proceedings against my books *The Church* and *Infallible? An Inquiry* in all forms. See the following citations in the attached documentation, *Um Nichts als die Wahrheit,* pp. 142–45; letter of the Doctrinal Congregation concerning the termination decision, p. 142.

In the Declaration closing the doctrinal proceedings the

Congregation likewise affirmed that with this very same Declaration "the proceedings of the Congregation in this matter are ended for now" (pp. 144). "Ended for now" means, in the context of all official ecclesiastical statements of that time, that thereby the proceedings would be definitively ended without any legal conditions. The admonition in this Declaration "not to advocate these doctrines any longer" is not modified with any demand for recantation or with any sanction. Cardinal Döpfner, in his statement to the press on February 20, 1975, expressly confirmed and emphasized that "this proceedings . . . presents a new style": at the same time he likewise pointed out that this Declaration did not put forth any "publication prohibition" (p. 156).

If the Congregation for the Doctrine of the Faith now in its decree of December 15, 1979, refers to that "for now," it thereby obviously ignores the facts that (a) the proceedings against *The Church* and *Infallible?* had been closed and (b) a new proceedings in the sense of the proceedings order had not been opened against me. Since that Declaration of February 15, 1975, I have heard nothing further from Rome.

2. In the Roman decree reference is made to questions of Christology and Mariology which were dealt with in my book *On Being a Christian* (1974): the book itself is not mentioned. In this connection it is to be noted that likewise concerning this book and the doctrinal opinions contained in it no doctrinal complaint proceedings have been conducted either before the Roman Doctrinal Congregation or before the German Bishops' Conference (since January 1, 1973, there has also existed an order for "doctrinal complaint proceedings in the German Bishops' Conference"). There were merely written statements exchanged with the Bishop of Rottenburg and the President of the German Bishops' Conference. In addition, on January 22, 1977, a colloquium with representatives of the German Bishops' Conference and myself took place. The Secretary of the Bishops' Conference, at the instruction of Cardinal Höffner, expressly confirmed to me in writing "that this discussion is not a discussion in the sense of section five of the Doctrinal Complaint Proceedings

in the German Bishops' Conference" (p. 223). Cardinal Höffner confirmed this assurance personally at the beginning of the colloquium (p. 227).

On the basis of this conversation the German Bishops' Conference issued a press statement on March 3, 1977 (pp. 329 f.), and finally a comprehensive declaration on my book *On Being a Christian* on November 17, 1977 (pp. 349 ff.). Likewise in this declaration there is no mention of a proceedings or of legally binding obligations to which I would have to hold so that specific sanctions would not come into play.

On the basis of this state of affairs I can only conclude that according to Canon Law *the Roman decree of December 15, 1979, was not preceded by a procedurally correct proceedings.*

3. In particular there was no formal opportunity provided me to express myself in *this* "proceedings" which led to the withdrawal of the *Missio*. The Bishop of Rottenburg likewise, as the decision of the Doctrinal Congregation was revealed to him on December 14, 1979, in Brussels, by long-distance telephone and by writing pressed the Prefect of the Doctrinal Congregation, Cardinal Šeper, "to grant Professor Küng once again a personal hearing before the announcement of the anticipated measures against him." From this it can be concluded that Bishop Moser had obviously perceived this severe procedural failure. This defect was, however, not eliminated. It is noteworthy that there is missing from the Bishops' *Documentation* precisely this letter, so important for the entire proceedings, from Bishop Moser to Cardinal Šeper, whose content, however, can be confirmed from stenographic minutes of the Faculty delegation meeting with Bishop Moser on December 20, 1979, and likewise in his letter to the Dean of the Catholic Theology Faculty of December 20, 1979.

II. Procedural defects in the claims of the Bishop to the provincial government

1. Without referring to the question of the legal grounds from the Concordat that the complaint is to be based on, it is clear that this right is granted only to the appropriate local

bishop and not to the Holy See. Doubtless it is no concern of the state to investigate the manner of the forming of the will of the bishop. However, it should ascertain that the bishop acts by the power of his own right and not only as the implementation assistant of the Holy See. In this connection the doubts presented to you by the former Kultusminister, Professor Dr. Ernst Gottfried Mahrenholz, provide a thorough analysis. Concerning the independent responsibility of the measures by Bishop Moser there arise large areas of unclarity which make it questionable whether the bishop acted in accordance with the Concordat in this case. May I call attention to the following:

a. Just a short time before the Roman intervention Bishop Moser had defended my orthodoxy against the accusations of Cardinal Ratzinger: "objective criticism and inquiry, even against the Pope, are possible; whoever inquires is not less Catholic than anyone else. One does not need to have any fear for freedom in the Church" (Catholic News Service, Bulletin-KNA-No. 46 of November 15, 1979). It is striking that only a little later the bishop made the opposite viewpoint his own.

b. As was mentioned above under *I,* 3, the bishop both orally and in writing, while in Brussels, urgently pleaded with Cardinal Šeper: "to avoid every appearance of an unjust or improper harshness" and "to grant Professor Küng once again a personal hearing before the announcement of the anticipated measures against him . . ." Although the doubts of the bishop were not reckoned with, he nevertheless, upon the instruction of Cardinal Šeper, who insisted on the carrying out of the decided measures, publicly proclaimed the withdrawal of the *Missio* on December 18, 1979.

c. On December 20, 1979, the bishop declared to the nominated delegation of the Catholic Theology Faculty (composed of the Dean, Pro-dean, and Senior) that he felt himself to be "held to his given word . . . to maintain the *Sigillum* [seal of secrecy]." The bishop then indicated that "it perhaps was a mistake from the beginning to submit himself to this *Sigillum.*" He added: "The letter of the Bishop to the

Minister bears no date because he, the Bishop, always still hoped to find a means of mediation" (stenographic documentary note of the delegation of the Faculty). From this it follows that Bishop Moser obviously was not convinced of the justice of the Roman measures and had ultimately carried them out only under higher instructions. This, however, constitutes an *abuse of the Concordat specifications*.

2. At this juncture it should also be pointed out that the Holy See likewise in other cases has, through the bishop, intervened directly into matters regulated legally by the Concordat. The following is a single example from the most recent history of the Catholic Theology Faculty of the University of Tübingen (which of course in a disputed proceedings could be expanded further): The chair for Canon Law has been unfilled for two years now because, after the first choice declined the invitation, the episcopal *Nihil obstat* for the second choice is still not forthcoming. Judging from the statement of the bishop, there exists no objection from his side against the suggested candidate; rather, until now the Holy See could not be won over to the approval of the nomination. Here it is clearly seen that the decision, which according to the specifications of the Concordat should lie solely with the local bishop, today in fact is made in Rome.

From all this the conclusion appears clear that the bishop in the case under consideration has acted only as the implementation organ of the Roman Curia. The right of the Concordat, however, proceeds under the assumption that the bishops act in the power of their own responsibility and their own right. There appears here in fact to have come about that which the German episcopacy, after the definition of papal infallibility at the First Vatican Council, in a response to a circular statement of Bismarck in 1875 had so decisively rejected: namely, that the bishops "would become papal officials without their own responsibility" and that, according to Catholic interpretation, "it is an immoral and despotic principle" that "the command of the superior unconditionally releases one from one's independent responsibility."

I ask you, honorable Minister, to investigate the questions

spoken of here which pertain to the legality of the proceedings on decisive points. It appears to me that it is necessary
to have it clarified beforehand whether the state ought at all
to take up the petition of the Bishop of Rottenburg-Stuttgart.
Concerning the further implications which were also the subject of our conversation, I do not wish to go into in this letter.

    With friendly greetings I am

Yours sincerely,
Hans Küng

cc: President of the University of Tübingen
    Dean of the Catholic Theology Faculty
    President of the CDU-Caucus of the Provincial
    Parliament

As he had indicated to his colleagues at the beginning of February, Küng prepared a lengthy letter to Bishop Moser. Dated
February 12, 1980, it was the first contact between Moser and
Küng since Moser's terse letter to Küng withdrawing his *Missio*
on December 30, 1979. Küng was at great pains again to explain
his theological position concerning methodology, Christology, and
infallibility—and for that reason it is an important document. At
the end he proposed submitting himself to an official proceedings
on those questions by the German Bishops' Conference, the conclusion of which would decide the question of whether he would
remain in the Catholic Theology Faculty or not. Küng hoped that
this might serve to resolve the impasse, but he was not optimistic
—at least not as he expressed himself to me over the phone in
February 1980. Still, he felt it was worth an attempt. His letter
was as follows:

(91)

Very Honored Bishop,
    Since your return from Rome on December 29, 1979, be-
cause of your decision to withdraw my *Missio canonica* and
to approach the state "for help," the situation has developed

in a threatening manner: A deep unrest concerning the development of our Catholic Church has come over faithful, pastors and theologians, whole congregations, Catholic groups, societies, and faculties; latent polarizations have broken out openly and on all sides a threatening crisis is spoken of. I take this development with its severe consequences very seriously and therefore I now turn to you.

For I am convinced that an unprejudiced and above all an objective theological conversation will clarify at least what has allegedly allowed my Catholicity to appear questionable in the eyes of Church authorities. With a view to such a clarification I would here like to set several things aright, concerning Christology and infallibility at first, then come to speak of my own theological intentions, and finally to say something concerning the corresponding formulas.

I. Concerning Christology

CORRECTIONS

The claim that I had not clearly affirmed the *Sonship of God* of Jesus as it was understood in Scripture and tradition, that I had falsified it or explained it in an unchurchly sense, is incorrect and cannot be documented from my writings.

The claim that I had disputed the christological statements of the Councils of Nicaea and Chalcedon in their continuing *binding quality* for the Catholic Church is incorrect and positively refutable from my writings.

Therefore likewise the claim that it is impossible to give a clear yes to the *confession of faith* of the Church on the basis of my theology is incorrect and, in view of my various christological studies, ununderstandable. As everyone knows who knows me or has carefully read my books or heard my lectures, I give a decisive yes to the confession of faith of the Church and will continue to do this, above all in the worship service as the authentic locus of the Credo. Likewise, I thus have, as is clearly shown in my writings and the detailed analyses of my book *Menschwerdung Gottes,* nothing against

the interpretation of the Sonship of God of Jesus as such as
it was carried through in the fourth and fifth centuries.

The *connection* between my inquiry *into the infallibility
problematic* and my christological statements made in the
Roman document, in the pastoral statement, and in the Declaration of the German Bishops likewise appears incorrect,
and in view of my total theological work appears to me base-
less. The "defect" of my understanding of infallibility—thus
in the Declaration of the Bishops of January 7, 1980—would
become apparent in my "statements concerning the person of
Jesus Christ." This claim is completely unfounded; it raises
the suspicion that in doing Christology I deal carelessly with
the binding statements of Scripture and tradition, indeed that
I would write my Christology precisely at their expense.

Therefore, the impression given by the German Bishops
that according to my theology it was *"not God himself* who
has turned toward humanity in Jesus Christ" is erroneous
and injurious to me in my decisive intentions. On the contrary, one of the central christological statements in my book
Does God Exist? is as follows: "In the work and in the person of Jesus God himself is met in a unique and definitive
manner" (p. 749). Consequently the sentence from the joint
pastoral statement of the German Bishops could absolutely
be my own: "If God himself has not turned to humanity in
Jesus Christ, then Jesus Christ likewise cannot redeem us
from sin and death."

In this connection I must emphatically point out that my
detailed confession of Christ in *Does God Exist?*, which contains the clarifications promised in the Stuttgart Colloquium
with you and Cardinals Höffner and Volk, was not taken account of by the German Bishops' Conference, as I must conclude from the letter of its President. In a proceedings according to the rules this book would absolutely have had to
be taken into consideration. Moreover, you, my dear Bishop,
certainly along with me are of the conviction that the various
committees and agencies of the Church leadership which
have given stimulus to such false interpretations of my theol-

ogy stand under the moral obligation also clearly to set aright such errors.

WHAT IS CONCERNED

You know, my dear Bishop, that within Catholic Christology there is a legitimate plurality of opinions, as all the discussions of the past years in Germany itself have sufficiently shown. You know concerning this that with the confession of the fundamental and generally binding belief statements of the Church the *theological difficulties* do not cease, but rather begin. And certainly you are also of the conviction that theologians have to deal with these difficulties, of which the theological literature is everywhere full, so that on the one hand the meaning of these faith statements remains, and on the other hand the understanding of them will be newly opened to the men and women of today.

In this it is undisputed among Catholic theologians that theology has the right and obligation to take into service all useful *methods* for the research and explanation of the faith. And it is likewise undisputed that theology thus must always find new ways of making statements. These were often at first disputed; the Church condemnation, for example, of Thomas Aquinas and in our century the condemnations of the historical-critical method by the Papal Biblical Commission are only particularly striking examples of this. Nevertheless, many new ways of stating things have prevailed because their truth content won out through itself. And some ancient ways of stating things have despite official encouragement not prevailed when they have shown themselves scientifically and pastorally as inapt ways.

The dispute, therefore, according to my conviction, is not about the Christian *cause* which we have in common, but rather about the *manner* in which we can state it today. And I proceed now as before from the assumption that our common belief in Jesus Christ must be so stated that it can be understood not only by theologians, not only by practicing Catholics or Protestant Christians, but rather also by the

458 KÜNG IN CONFLICT

numberless questioning people outside of the Church. In
these efforts, which of course may not proceed at the expense
of the Christian truth, the Bishops and theologians should
conduct themselves so that unnecessary polarizations and
conflicts within the Church are likewise avoided.

Thus it is then also clear: in the present dispute the concern cannot primarily be about individual statements, but
rather about the *total coherence* of a theological conception,
about its methodological beginning points and real goals.
Only against this background will it be possible to form a
well-founded judgment about individual statements. For this
reason I would like to provide you with several fundamental
indications concerning the methodological and hermeneutical
starting point of my christological expositions.

1. *I am concerned with a theology that is consistently related to the Scripture:* According to the Second Vatican
Council the Scripture again should become the *"soul of theology."* It is proper therefore that the Scripture as the decisive and always present beginning of the Church tradition is
to be taken seriously and is to be made fruitful in a completely legitimate "mediating immediacy," which was time
and again practiced in the history of the Church, for the present proclamation and theology. In this I place myself in the
tradition of the great Catholic theologians who have understood theology as *"scientia de divina pagina"* (Thomas
Aquinas). This new listening to the Scripture, of course,
allows the time and again surprising, inspiring, and disquiet-
ing power of this never fully comprehensible fundamental
witness of our faith to be experienced. The Scripture has
time and again exercised such a critical-productive function
vis-à-vis the faith of the Church and it will likewise do so in
the future.

This being presumed, I defend myself against the claim
that such a theology related to Scripture places the "meaning
of the faith of the Church" over against a "historical-critical
understanding of the Bible." The goal is nothing other than
the understanding of the Scripture with the best possible

methods available to us today. The Catholic exegete was obliged by the encyclical *Divino afflante Spiritu* (1943) and the Second Vatican Council precisely to the historical-critical method. I have taken it seriously in dogmatics, and no exegete of rank has in the discussion concerning my Christology claimed that I did not have the broad exegetical consensus behind me on central points. This confirmed me in my way and was hardly sufficiently reflected on in the discussion —which above all was carried on by dogmaticians. I would like to ask you, my dear Bishop, expressly to once again reflect on this state of affairs. Some on the other hand are inclined to accuse me of playing the Scripture against the tradition. In this I am concerned only to eliminate the very much greater danger that the tradition would be played against the Scripture or that its power of statement vis-à-vis the tradition breaks through in only a limited measure. A tradition which is not according to the Scripture is not Catholic.

2. *I am concerned with a theology that is consistently historically responsible:* Also in this program I do not stand alone. The *historical conditionedness* of faith statements and indeed the historical conditionedness of the earliest witnesses to the faith preserved in the Scripture is no longer denied by anyone. It is even appreciated in the Roman document *Mysterium ecclesiae* (1973). Whoever thinks historically discovers immediately that "Church," "tradition," "development of faith," "development of dogmas," and the necessity to ascertain always anew one's Christian identity in binding faith statements, are most profound human and human-acting phenomena.

Faith statements, therefore, *cannot simply be repeated,* least of all by theologians. We rightly trust thereby in the Spirit who leads us always anew into the truth, which is nothing other than the "ancient" truth of Jesus Christ himself. Whoever thinks historically must therefore pose to himself precisely the questions which have constantly been posed to him from the origins of Christian history and the Church. Every confession of the faith, every Council, and every later statement of the teaching office or qualified theology must *legitimate itself* by the original message. This becomes especially clear within the First Ecumenical Council of Nicaea, which—still without conciliar "mediating authorities" —depended decisively on the Scripture and based its authority thereon. The tension between the origin (the original normative biblical tradition) and "tradition" (the derived, "normed," post-biblical tradition) must remain standing. It must not be flattened out by any static explanation, organic development, or dialectical speculation model. The original Christian message remains beyond our disposal and will *never be captured* by us or put into concepts, because for us—in close connection with the always new forms of a Christian practice of life—it is and remains constantly the future.

Whoever thinks historically will therefore—without denying the binding quality of earlier faith statements—know: Despite a binding canon and despite binding doctrinal statements we can neither predict nor determine ahead of time with juridical measures the path of further reflection on the faith and the language history of the faith. The historical dialectic of continuity and discontinuity forbids precisely the dividing *a priori* of the continuing (essential) and the passing (unessential), the core and the shell. New formulations of the faith and indeed new theological overall descriptions will time and again—as in the past—develop. And time and again we will face the problem that new "paradigms" or "understanding models of understanding" of the faith will arise which at first are disputed.

Whoever thinks historically has therefore an understanding of the troublesome situation in which disputes about the right belief can develop. Here it is easy to speak "past one another" and it cannot be prevented that the position put in question will be taken up by many committed Christians, will be accepted as a completely new possibility, and will be perceived precisely as a liberation for a new Christian faith.

I am convinced that we are standing in such a period of

transition. I see my books—*The Church,* but above all *On Being a Christian* and *Does God Exist?*—the profound disturbances of the past weeks precisely among many pastors and religion teachers point to this—in the context of a new Christian experience of reality. This has already long been prepared. However, it only slowly makes its way without being able to legitimize itself everywhere—it comes from a new immediacy to the Christian message of the origin, to the proclamation, action, faith, person of Jesus.

Theology in such a transition, my dear Bishop, stands in need not only of a constant testing of its orthodoxy. It stands in need even more of trust, of encouragement and fraternal well-wishing. And it stands in need therefore also of the acknowledgment of its own self-understanding: When a Catholic theologian understands himself as such, even if he comes to unwonted but argued results, then he must at first be taken seriously as a Catholic theologian. For he also has the right to claim this Church as his home until the non-Catholicity is proven by arguments. For he has the right to call this Church his home as long as his own up until now unwonted arguments are not refuted by the Christian message in its origin. Since in our Church that was at first so often condemned which later was shown to be at home there, one should be doubly careful today.

3. *I am concerned with a theology which unhesitatingly takes up the questions of the present day:* Every theologian should live in fraternal solidarity with the men and women of his time. I am convinced that he stands before God under the obligation to become a Jew to the Jews, a Hellene to the Hellenes, a contemporary person with the questions, hopes, and anxieties of our present day *to the men and women of today*—even to those who question, to the sceptics, to the despairing, to those who are disillusioned by the Church.

All this is true in special measure for the questions of Christology, where the Christian faith is in wide stretches still trapped in a world view which has lost its self-evidence. Bernhard Welte is one of the few Catholic theologians who

draws consequences from this for a future Christology:
"Does the continuity of the Christian self-understanding
break off entirely with this and with it the continuity in the
understanding of Jesus, the continuity of Christology? One
must say: Yes, what concerns the *form* of the language, of
the questions, of the thought breaks off the continuity. But it
does not necessarily break off in the question of the *cause*
[*Sache*] about which it is concerned, therefore in our case
of the cause of Jesus and his Gospel, that is, of the words
which proclaim him. There will always still be the ancient
words which bring us the witness of Jesus, for example the
words of the Holy Scripture and also the words of the
Church and its confessional formulas. In them the ancient
and always new cause of Jesus will time and again speak out
anew. But of course the ancient words and thereby the ancient cause will be questioned and understood on the basis of
a new world and thereby in a new language and a new question horizon, and they will therein take on a new form for a
new epoch."

Therefore Welte suggests—and I have attempted to think
along this line along with many exegetes—that in theological
thinking about Jesus we should let "the category of event become dominant instead of the category *Ousia-Substantia*":
"Therefore one always remains with the fundamental intention of the Councils, namely, to explain the Bible, when one
thinks beyond their form: The human being Jesus happens,
he expresses the incomparable of his self and his spirit in
words and deeds and faithful acts, he touches thereby in
manifold ways those who hear him and he calls forth in
those thus touched an echo. All this one can call the *event* of
Jesus or the happening of the history of Jesus. In this event
or this history there comes to pass a unique and complete
human being, and there occurs in the one and same event the
total and unique *God:* He expressed himself in a new manner
to men and women, judging and redeeming, in this event or
in this history of Jesus. If one attempts to think according to
this conceptual sketch then one also again has the unity of

the divine and the human, but no longer thought of in the manner of a static essence, but much more in the manner of a moved happening. One thereby preserves the biblical fundamental intention of the ancient formula of confession, but changes the manner and form of its thinking."

When a theologian thus attempts to speak in categories of event, of happening, of revealing, it is inappropriate to want to evaluate and indeed condemn him with the categories of essence: The statement that in the person of Jesus God reveals himself in a definitive and unsurpassable manner is not less than the earlier statement that Jesus "is" God. Karl Rahner has precisely again recalled how manifold in meaning that little word "is" in this connection is. Already at the Würzburg Synod he "issued a certain protest" against the statements of Cardinal Höffner: "Cardinal Höffner said that Jesus of Nazareth *is* God. I responded: Of course that is a Christian, irreversible, definitively binding truth. But one can also misunderstand this sentence. While other 'is-sentences' express an identity of a simple sort between [the subject and] the content of the predicate, such an identity between the humanity of Jesus and the eternal Logos of God is precisely not present. Here there exists a *unity,* not an *identity.* I say that only to make clear that concerning the christological dogma inside the Church and inside its orthodoxy there are continuing questions and even varieties of opinions. I wish thereby to make clear that for me in connection with Christology the question [of Küng] of what is possible is not to be answered so simply as perhaps the Cologne ecclesiastical statement makes out." Indeed, Rahner, who as is known is not in agreement with me on the question of infallibility, confirms after a careful reading of the book *On Being a Christian* that he "could discover no absolute affront against a defined dogma in Christology."

On this point an unexpected and surprising convergence between a modern personal-historical starting point and the starting point of the New Testament Christologies shows up. Precisely the New Testament encourages us to express the person and cause of Jesus ever anew for the faith with new thought images, symbols, metaphors, names, concepts, which will be understood today and therefore can unfold a power to enlighten the understanding. Precisely thus does the proclamation of the faith in Jesus remain *creative* and does not petrify in the fear that one might give up something of the true faith because one expresses it in another way.

Perhaps, my dear Bishop, you will counter that with such a conception the door and gate to arbitrary speculations would be opened. Because I see very well this danger in a time of transition I have devoted myself intensely to precisely this question. This leads me to a final point:

4. *I am concerned about a theology which consistently spells out the Christian belief of Jesus Christ:* Jesus Christ himself is what is specific to the Christian faith—this is my central and certainly legitimate response. The task of the Christian theologians, therefore, is above all time and again to answer the question: Who is this Jesus Christ? More precisely: Who is this Jesus of Nazareth who for us believers is the Christ and the Son of God? In face of the difficulties which many men and women have with the traditional christological statements, I have taken the path of exegesis which lies close by: I reported in a scholarly fashion about the proclamation and the lifestyle of Jesus of Nazareth, of the history of effects [*Wirkungsgeschichte*] before and after the death of Jesus.

This *methodological beginning point,* with which I am not alone in beginning, and its systematic development have in past years led to broad discussions. Critics, of course, have time and again proceeded from presuppositions which do not pertain to my methodological self-understanding. There was above all the officially formulated suspicion that a "historical *reconstruction hypothesis*" presents "alone and in itself a sufficient approach to the theological understanding of Jesus Christ." Two things are to be remarked on this:

First: Such a distortion of the fundamental question by an imprecise use of the terminology of the theory of science hides the true question: Can we know something about Jesus of Nazareth who indeed is not a myth? For it concerns—despite all the considerable problems of the hermeneutics of history—first of all the *report* about the person and cause of Jesus, the *report* of the experiences as the first believers had them with this Jesus. Since forever and ever this report has been inalienably at home in the Catholic Church. Since forever and ever one could proceed from the notion that a historical making-present of this person of Jesus is possible and is necessary for the faith. That this questioning back has led to the growing historical-critical consciousness, to an increasingly refined posing of questions and explanation possibilities, does not speak against but rather for the success of such a report.

Second: It is clear to every historian that he cannot limit himself to the reproduction of positive facts. Every text is formulated and understood out of a *pre-understanding*. Every comprehensive explanation of historical dates, persons, or events always presumes the standpoint of the interpreter. The alternative: The historical Jesus, or the Church's faith in him, is therefore inapplicable. Why?

Certainly: The methodological explication of the person and the cause of Jesus proceeds from the historically significant sources, from the historically-critically illuminated history of Jesus, which does not end with the death of Jesus, but rather through the Easter experiences has received a new quality. But this history is written by a believing theologian who stands before the question: How and why can we trust in this Jesus of Nazareth at all, how and why can he stand before us and for us in God's name? A Christology that methodologically comes "from below"? Yes, but precisely this from the standpoint of someone who believes in Jesus Christ. This Christology "from below" could only therefore be consistent and convincing for many because it was written *by a believer*. This historical reason therefore precisely does not exclude the approach to the revelation of God, but rather makes it possible.

I cannot go into the *many individual questions* which are bound up with this attempt here. For example: Will not the *true challenge* of Christianity be hidden and diverted by the method of the historical approach? I think not and am of the conviction that the challenge and non-simultaneity of the Christian message can only again be brought to comprehensive expression in the binding together of historical distance and present-day relevance. Will not through the method of the report and historical analysis a believing, *confessing yes or no* become superfluous? I believe not: Only in historical evidence will the alternatives and the central questions for a Christian faith again become so concrete that they will newly issue a challenge for a decision. Does not this method create unnecessary *uncertainties?* I believe not and am convinced that only through it will many things again become clear in which one can trust oneself in faith. Jesus whom we confess as the Christ gives our faith its true identity. Therefore a Catholic theologian must be allowed to present him as the great challenge even for the men and women of today in the Church and in society.

FORMULAS OF FAITH OR FIGURE OF FAITH?

On the basis of all these things that have been said, I would like, my dear Bishop, to come back to the christological questions which were put to me by Cardinal Höffner on April 22, 1977. While observing the hermeneutical principles here laid out, *I confess myself to the central christological formulas of our confessions of faith,* as I already declared at the beginning.

However, when you place this whole extremely complex problematic before your eyes, you will, my dear Bishop, now perhaps better understand why I at that time (to say nothing of the problematic of the justification for such questions) did not wish to give any final answers to abbreviated questions in the style of a catechism in which the true theological hermeneutical problems would nevertheless again be suppressed.

In view of the epochal transition in which the entire category system has moved, in view of the extremely difficult explication of the traditional christological faith statements, as well as in view of the growing faith needs of many men and women confronted with the traditional Christology, I request that you and your episcopal fellow brothers take seriously my conviction, which is shared by many: in my explanations, which have been criticized from the side of the Bishops, *the belief* in Jesus Christ is not *softened* or reduced to the prologue of a temporary speaking about Christ. It is concerned much more with the same intentions, connections, with the same cause—of course within the framework of another structure of the faith. Everything depends on this other context!

It is not just for the sake of being right that I insist upon this, but rather out of a fear that all those who have learned again to believe in Jesus Christ within the framework of a historical Christology will be *left alone* and sooner or later will fall back into skeptical reservations. It is precisely religion teachers and pastors who had to painfully bear the consequences. I also am concerned with the churchliness of theology. But the concern is still more about the continuity of the cause that is fixed in binding faith statements. It is concerned, therefore, also with formulas of faith, to be sure, but only within the framework of a specific structure of faith. Both are related to each other. Whoever has understood this has—I believe—understood the dispute which has broken out at present in the Catholic Church (and not only because of my person).

II. Infallibility

I need not here speak in as detailed fashion about the infallibility problematic as concerning the questions of Christology, although they also are to be resolved only within the framework of a theological total conception. As you know, my dear Bishop, this question has received *relatively little at-*

tention in the German-speaking area. For the Roman Doctrinal Congregation, however, it forms the decisive core of the dispute: Of course, they are dealing here with their own cause. It would be good, therefore, if with common effort a moderation of the discussion and a containment of the problematic could be attained. Consequently we should begin here likewise with the setting of several things aright.

CORRECTIONS

Certainly it has not remained hidden even from you that in recent weeks my inquiry into the infallibility definition has been *constantly expanded* and made into a fundamental question about my relationship to the Christian truth in general. Also here, I believe, I have the right to be protected by ecclesiastical agencies against unjustified overinterpretations. Therefore I affirm the following:

The claim that I deny the *continuing binding quality* of faith statements which demand an unmistakable yes or no is incorrect and is positively refutable from my writings. The opinion of certain interpreters that I reject the "ultimately binding" statements with the affirmations of binding statements is ununderstandable and without any objective basis. "Binding," of course, correctly understood cannot be further intensified.

Further, the claim that I set myself apart from the infallibility definition of Vatican I is incorrect and is not to be documented from my writings. The talk about the *"revision"* of Vatican I in my latest two publications stands in a very differentiating context and is related to the problem brought up by Yves Congar and hardly discussed, namely, that of the reception and the "re-reception" of conciliar decisions as well as the results of the newest historical research. Concerning the sense and meaning of my "inquiry" I will comment further below.

The general claim that in the dispute over my inquiry the "truth of the Scripture" is placed in debate is incorrect and completely contrary to the fundamental intention of my theological work (Declaration of the German Bishops of January 7, 1980). However, I gladly leave the judgment concerning this claim to the world of exegetical experts.

I find the claim that I draw the "much more fundamental gift of the *guaranteeing of the Church in the truth* of God accomplished by the Spirit" into doubt ununderstandable and in diametrical contradiction to my explanations (*ibid.*). It is precisely upon it that I place an increased weight in connection with my inquiry. In this connection I regard it as a serious false orientation of the public that the Bishops' *Documentation* printed only one of the writings incriminated by Rome (the introduction to Hasler's book). It did not, however, print the theological meditation which was purposely simultaneously published by me and expressly characterized as a positive expansion, as was already completely and fully affirmed by me in the title, *The Church—Maintained in the Truth?;* there it was made concrete and thus in no way remained a "general" protestation.

Finally, the claim of the Roman Declaration of December 15, 1979, that I hold the teaching office in contempt and place my own opinion over against the meaning of the faith of the Church is false and not without a disparaging effect. I have always presented my inquiry with arguments and have placed myself under the objective necessity of finding theological truth—indeed I have challenged myself precisely to theological argument. Even by my critics I have received the admission that here are difficult problems which were not invented by me and which concern the whole of Catholic theology.

You, my dear Bishop, are certainly of the same opinion as I am that an objective conversation is possible only if these corrections will be respected on both sides and wherever possible they be brought to the attention of the disturbed faithful also by the Church authorities. For here we are concerned with very fundamental questions which can be fruitfully discussed only within a larger *total context*. I would therefore again like once more to point to the background against

which, according to my conviction, the disputed questions
should be judged.

WHAT IS CONCERNED

It should be once again recalled that there are *four dimensions* (methodologically and content-wise not without consequences) in which my theological thinking moves: Even in
the question of the infallibility of the Church it wishes to be
consistently related to the Scripture, be historically responsible in its statements to the Christian origin, unreservedly
pose the questions of the present to itself, and finally make
Jesus whom we confess as the Christ the decisive standard of
our faith in speaking and acting. Within the framework of
these dimensions my inquiry moves and the hypothesis which
I myself have suggested as a solution of the problems moves.
I do not wish to go into these here—after all, the arguments
have long since been available.

You will counter that I have up until now left out of consideration that decisive dimension which is viewed as so necessary in contemporary theology, namely, *churchliness*. To
this I would like to respond that churchliness is already
carried out in all of the named dimensions: it is indeed concerned with the apostolic Church (relationship to the Scripture), with the Catholicity of this Church in time (historical
responsibility), with Catholicity in space (challenge by the
present) and finally the conviction that we are the Church of
Jesus Christ (Jesus Christ as the decisive standard). In the
infallibility question of course above all the questions of the
visible Church which is to be identified by specific *faith statements and offices* are under debate. Concerning this several
remarks are allowed.

1. *I am concerned with the service to the unity of the
divided churches:* In the dispute with Roman agencies as well
as in the various German statements of the past weeks it is
apparent that this viewpoint is almost entirely *excluded*. The
suspicion is simply expressed that I conduct an ecumenism to
the neglect of the truth question.

This judgment, however, does not take the true *seriousness* of the ecumenical problematic seriously. All the non-Catholic Churches view the infallibility dogma as a new Roman Catholic special doctrine. And for all non-Catholic Churches this dogma poses a major hindrance to a possible reunion precisely when they would be prepared fundamentally to acknowledge the Petrine service of the Bishop of Rome.

It is therefore the obligation of a theologian dedicated to an ecumenical theology and a director of an Institute for Ecumenical Research to take up this difficult problematic and think it through self-critically in view of the inquiry posed from the outside. Only thus can the cause of the *oikoumene* be effectively helped forward in this decisive point.

The present manifoldly documented *bewilderment* of many non-Catholic colleagues throughout the world shows how much of the credibility of our Church depends on the decisive working through of this problem area. Even in the declaration signed by many professors from the Catholic theological faculties of Germany it is stated: "If Catholic theology no longer possesses the freedom to inquire from what is to what was, from the present to the origin in order to open up once again the lost possibilities of unity and union, the ground will be pulled out from underneath the ecumenical discussion of theologians from the side of Catholic theology. With this, however, the ecumenical efforts of the Church in general lose their credibility; the developments to the present time would have to come to a standstill" (see pp. 624–28). No one in our Church can want that.

2. *I am concerned with a contribution to the clarification of the relationship between the teaching office and theology:* As you also know, the definition of the infallibility dogma occurred (measured against the history of the Church and of the faith) very late. Over many centuries there was no talk of the infallibility of the Pope. For further centuries it did not turn up as a formal point of Catholic theological criteriology. At the same time the self-understanding and function of a

"teaching office" underwent an *intense change* after the Middle Ages. From this it is not to be feared that the entire Catholic understanding of the truth will become destabilized by a discussion of the infallibility question. A glance at Church history and the other Churches shows clearly: the Christian truth developed through the witness of the Scripture, through the confessions of the faith, through the tradition common to all the Churches, as well as through the lived faith of the Christians, a high level of meaning, certitude, and saving power.

The Petrine service truly is not thereby declared superfluous; I have attempted time and again to make it significant for the Catholic Church and for the *oikoumene* understandable even for non-Catholic Christians. Also the claim of this Petrine office of realizing its service to unity for the Catholic Church if necessary by binding statements and also in the defense against errors is not superfluous. But this claim has sense only if it is understood as a service to the witness of the faith of the entire Church. Here a dialectic must be maintained which can relieve us of a great deal of anxiety: On the one side we are of the common conviction that the Church is in need of the service of a unifying witness. On the other side we must remain in serious discussion about the question of what space with its own laws is to be granted to theology within the Church.

The extremes of precisely our century have shown that a free theology dedicated only to the truth can contribute a great service to the *credibility of the Church*. In the face of the fact, however, that many significant theologians have been bridled or taken to task, we must today succeed once again in breaking through the atmosphere of a latent mistrust and in articulating ever more clearly the tasks of the teaching office and theology, each of which are independent.

You know, Bishop, that in my inquiry into infallibility I have posed a *hypothesis,* indeed I had to pose one: a hypothesis which would relax the problematic and could make the legitimate goals which are in this dogma understandable even to wider circles. I do not maintain that I have thereby clarified the relationship between teaching office and theology. Precisely therefore I ask you all to do something so that this comprehensive question also can be discussed comprehensively, without emotions and threatened sanctions. I see myself confirmed in this by the above-named declaration of German theologians: "Likewise the possibility to put forth and test hypotheses, to carry out controversies with reasons and arguments, and to correct and overcome errors through scholarly disputation—all of which belongs to the unrelinquishable freedom of theology—must be able to be claimed by theology in an unhindered fashion. The more unhindered the scholarly disputation can be, the more it will fend off subjective arbitrariness by the force of its strict argumentation and thereby serve the truth."

The two foregoing citations wished to describe the *horizon* from which the infallibility debate receives its ineluctable urgency. One might say that they are very general and leave my statements concerning the definition of infallibility itself still open. Therefore a third point follows:

3. *I am concerned with the clarification of the meaning and grounding of the definition of infallibility:* Whoever does not take the definition of papal infallibility seriously will not speak of it and nevertheless do theology. I take it *very seriously* and have undertaken since the beginning of the sixties to analyze it carefully in all respects and to explain its intention in a manner that is understandable to contemporary men and women. In the intensive discussion of the past decade a double problematic has appeared to me as well as to other Catholic theologians:

a. Exegesis as well as the history of dogma poses enormous difficulties for a reasoned argumentation. On this much has been written and thoroughly discussed in several study conferences at which I was present. Within the framework of this letter this need not be gone into in further detail.

b. *The meaning of the infallibility definition* has become unclear as a result of the progress of hermeneutical and linguistic philosophical reflection. The definition of material faith content can always be newly translated, illuminated, made explicit in reference to new questions, and reworked in relationship to the latest status of hermeneutical reflection. The infallibility definition, that is, a definition of the formal binding quality of the content of faith, nevertheless itself sets up a binding hermeneutic and thereby because of the changed hermeneutical consciousness falls into an interpretation conflict—which can only be briefly alluded to here. For example, a juridical hermeneutic lies at the basis of the infallibility definition: How then, however, are new exegetical results to be brought in? The infallibility definition accentuates the question of individual statements of faith ("propositions," "judgments," "definitions," "sentences"): How will it deal with the problem of the comprehensive unity of statement? The infallibility definition proceeds from the model of *a priori* infallibly true statements: How is that to be reconciled with the genuine scientifically theological goal of an argued grounding of faith statements, especially when one reflects that the teaching office, independent of new arguments about interpretation, claims to make judgments and thereby sets itself up as the final agency of interpretation, even of its own competence of interpretation?

Problems which—I say this in all seriousness and in all modesty—from the outside make us non-credible as long as we are not prepared to clean them up or clarify them. Problems at the same time which can be cleaned up only within the framework of an anxiety-free and *free atmosphere* which is as open as possible. Is it improper for a theologian to openly state this question and to undertake this act of honesty both within and without?

These indications, my dear Bishop, should suffice to make clear to you once again how urgently necessary and objectively demanded that inquiry was which I initiated several years ago and which in a remarkable manner entertained such great publicity.

QUESTIONS, DOUBT, DENIAL

The German Bishops have declared that in the matter of infallibility I not only asked what the definition means and how it is to be grounded. Rather, I had "placed this statement itself in question and thereby doubted it." I believe that this distinction in this difficult matter is not correct. Having been struck by the questions of many people, I as a theologian expressly inquired into the grounding of the infallibility definition and thereby perhaps brought it about that corresponding to the status of present-day theological research it appeared to some as being ungrounded. This is a doubt which was not deliberately raised by me, as if I were erecting my own understanding of the faith against the sense of the faith of the Church. Rather, this is a doubt which independent of me has arisen from the logical necessity of argumentation and counterargumentation.

Thus I have posed a formal inquiry and not a denial—out of an ecclesial concern, I believe. For I have never thought to associate myself with those who claim that a generally defined statement is nothing. I have only gone about the business of theology, which perhaps is unpleasant because it is full of risk. I believe, my dear Bishop, that whoever trusts the power of faith certainly also has the power to withstand all the questions which human reason poses to the faith. But also conversely: precisely whoever is able and ready to pose to himself all questions without forfeiting them ahead of time gives thereby a testimony of his own unbroken power of faith.

From this fundamental attitude I place myself unreservedly behind the referred-to declaration of the German Catholic theologians: "In order to fulfill its task as a science, theology must be able to make unhindered use of the freedom to utilize all appropriate methods for the research and explanation of the faith. Of the freedom to follow the force of logic and data and to be able to follow the methods dictated by this force of logic and data there can never be too much. Its utilization can never be arbitrary. The task of the episcopal teaching office can, therefore, not be to prescribe or to recommend to theology specific methods, and to forbid others, but rather—if this should be necessary—by the power of office to indicate when an explanation resulting from this or that method cannot be viewed as a legitimate explanation of the authentic faith witnessed to in the belief of the Church and proclaimed by the Pope and Bishops.

"Along with the Declaration of 1979, signed by 1,360 theologians, on the 'Freedom of Theology,' we emphasize that 'for us theologians this freedom goes hand in hand with the heavy responsibility not to jeopardize the genuine unity and the true peace of the Church and all its members.' On the other hand, we must with the same Declaration confirm that we 'wish to carry out our obligation to search out and speak the truth without being hampered by administrative measures and sanctions. We expect that our freedom will be respected whenever, to the best of our ability, we voice or publish our reasoned theological conviction.' "

These theological clarifications of mine, my dear Bishop, have become long and nevertheless must leave many things open which will need future clarification. Nevertheless allow me at the conclusion of this theological portion of my letter to quote what my colleague Heinrich Fries, who is also very much appreciated by you, has written about the most recent dispute: "Alongside of the believers who, as you say, feel themselves made insecure, one may not overlook the extremely large number of those who have found a genuine help for their faith through the books of Küng, above all through *On Being a Christian* and *Does God Exist?*, who were strengthened in their faith and have gained a new and credible approach of understanding and inclination thereby. For many pastors, religion teachers, and preachers the two above-named books of Küng have become a true and precious treasure. That is above all true if one reads what was written and does not always look for what is missing."

III. A Suggestion for a Solution

As was indicated at the beginning we find ourselves in an inner-churchly, political and juridical situation that is not simple. The consequences growing out of it are difficult to estimate. As even the debate in the Parliament of Baden-Württemberg has shown juridically above all two problems stand in the foreground:

1. Because there is no provincial Concordat for Württemberg and because the National Concordat states nothing about the departure of a professor after the withdrawal of the *Missio* and supplementary agreements were necessary in other provinces, the legal basis on the grounds of the Concordat for a dismissal from the faculty against my will are at least not clear.

2. The necessary inner-Church proceedings were not carried out against either of my two new publications on the infallibility question nor against my book *On Being a Christian:* As is known, the Roman Doctrinal Congregation suspended the proceedings against my books *The Church* and *Infallible? An Inquiry* legally through the decree of February 15, 1975. Indeed at that time wishes concerning my behavior were presented to me, but no sanctions were placed in view. If Rome now should wish to carry out disciplinary sanctions on the basis of new statements from my side, then a new proceedings in the sense of the Roman "new procedural regulations for the testing of doctrinal questions" of January 15, 1971, would have to be opened. That has not taken place. Also in reference to several christological (and mariological) questions which I deal with in my book *On Being a Christian* and which likewise were mentioned as reasons for the Roman measures, the necessary proceedings of a complaint against doctrine has not been carried out by either the Roman Doctrinal Congregation or the German Bishops' Conference. Since January 1, 1973, there is an

"order for the proceedings of a complaint against a doctrine by the German Bishops' Conference." There has also been nothing conducted against me according to these proceedings regulations. That means that before neither Roman nor German ecclesiastical courts has it been established in a correct proceedings that the incriminating publications damage essential Catholic elements of the faith.

It would be difficult to imagine how the state could proceed with a legal administrative act when the Church has not held to its own orders of procedure in the establishment of the serious charges against my theological statements. To that it must be added that the legal foundation according to the Concordat—which most of the "expert evaluations" that are floating about persistently overlook—bears little weight in the case of the University of Tübingen.

Should now a legal dispute about all this be carried on which could last for many years and would have to bring the problematic of the Concordat into public discussion? That certainly would not be in the interest of the Church and of the state, also not in the interest of the University, the Catholic theological faculties, and certainly in my personal interest, which is that I only wish to remain what I always was—a Catholic teacher of theology. No, truly I have indeed written critical theological books but I have never pushed the discussion onto the state-juridical level. And I am decisively of the opinion that the discussion should again be brought back from this level and cleared up on the inner-Church level. But how is this possible after the Roman action? With good will on all sides it seems to me that the following path could be trod:

The Diocesan Council of the Diocese of Rottenburg-Stuttgart in an extraordinary session on January 26, 1980, for the withdrawal of the *Missio,* under your presidency, urgently requested me to do everything to clarify the questions which have cropped up and at the same time requested the German Bishops to support you with all their power in your efforts to bring about an understanding: "The Diocesan Council is, along with the German Bishops' Conference, of the opinion that the 'ecclesiastical procedural regulations can be improved,' and demands therefore that the German Bishops' Conference unhesitatingly press for an improvement of these proceedings and to take up the 'Küng Affair' in an improved proceedings." This suggestion of the Diocesan Council, among other things, has been taken up by the Association of Religious Teachers in the Diocese of Rottenburg. It corresponds to the numberless voices in the international Catholic public which likewise demand a new, more just proceedings.

In response to this suggestion of the Diocesan Council, my dear Bishop, I declare myself hereby prepared to collaborate in a proceedings of the German Bishops' Conference on an objective clarification of my theological position in reference to infallibility and Christology as it is foreseen in the "order for the proceedings of a complaint against a doctrine by the German Bishops' Conference" of January 1, 1973. Until the close of this proceedings the withdrawal of the *Missio* should remain as until now suspended in its legal consequences. In order to foster a clarification in the situation and to relax the tension in the University situation I would be prepared to request the Minister for Science and Art for a semester's research leave.

According to the press declaration of the Holy See on December 30, 1979, "the Holy See and the German Bishops do not give up hope that Professor Küng, who has more than once declared his intention of remaining a Catholic theologian, will, after reflection in depth, adopt a position which will make it possible for the Church to reinstate his canonical commission to teach." This letter should indicate to you, my dear Bishop, my will for this demanded deepened reflection. I do not doubt therefore that the Holy See will empower the German Bishops' Conference to undertake such a proceedings according to the "order for the proceedings of a complaint against a doctrine by the German Bishops' Conference." Only through such a proceedings can the serious defects in the proceedings which have been discussed in the public be healed. Finally, the proceedings order of the German Bishops' Conference indeed likewise understands itself as a possibility for the "necessary defense of rights" for an accused author (cf. Preamble). Since according to Concordat practice the local bishop is the competent agent for the granting and withdrawal of the *Missio canonica,* such a request submitted with vigor would hardly be rejected in Rome.

In the hope that the German Bishops' Conference likewise will positively take up these requests of the Diocesan Council and numerous Catholics and present it in Rome, I extend to you

Sincere greetings,
Hans Küng

Greinacher and Haag remarked that "at first Bishop Moser expressed himself positively on Küng's letter when speaking to University President Theis" (*Fall Küng,* p. 511). However, from February 24 to 28, 1980, the spring meeting of the German Bishops' Conference was held, during which the Küng affair was discussed. "Before Küng himself received an answer, Cardinal Höffner expressed himself on Küng's letter, after the conference had ended, before journalists in Cologne on February 29, and judged that even in this letter of Küng's 'the decisive matter' was not clarified. Thus, for example, to the point complained of by the Bishops that he denied the essential equality [*Wesensgleichheit*] of God the Father and Jesus Christ, he wrote that one cannot evaluate his opinion with categories of essences. The theologian should profess the faith of the Church clearly as it is proclaimed by the teaching office. Everything further now lies with Küng. In this connection Höffner defended the Roman proceedings as 'really not so bad.' He granted, however, that they could be improved. Thus, he would suggest to the Pope that in the future the accused author be granted a defender of his own choice. The doctrinal complaint proceedings by the German Bishops' Conference which Küng had requested could not be opened because the matter was being handled by Rome and thereby would be decided by the superior agency (*Frankfurter Rundschau,* February 29, 1980). The following letter from Bishop Moser corresponds widely in content with this statement of Cardinal Höffner" (*Fall Küng,* pp. 511 f.). Moser's letter to Küng was dated March 1, 1980:

(92)

Very Honored Prof. Küng!

Thank you for your detailed letter of February 12, 1980, which in the meanwhile I have carefully studied. I have never left in doubt the fact that I stand ready when you are prepared to clarify your theological position in such a way that the granting of the teaching commission in the name of the Church will once again become possible. Consequently, it is from this viewpoint that I have attempted to read and evaluate your present explanations. I would like to communicate to you in all openness the impressions that I have gained thereby.

1. First of all I perceive in the clarification of your intentions and in the presentation of the hermeneutical foundations of your theology a helpful step forward. Objectively I have discovered several statements—above all in the area of Christology—which until now I was not able to find in such clarity in your works. You confess not only to the Sonship of God of Jesus but also to the continuing binding quality of the conciliar decisions of Nicaea and Chalcedon (p. 2); you state a clear yes to the confession of faith of the Church (p. 2); you wish to design your Christology for those who are seekers, but not at the cost of the Christian truth (p. 4); you hold the alternatives of the historical Jesus or Church faith in him as inaccurate (p. 11); finally, you confess "to the central christological formulas of our confessions of faith" (p. 13); you do not wish to turn aside from belief in Jesus Christ (p. 13). Likewise concerning the question of infallibility you make several clarifications which are extremely helpful. You do not wish to deny the continuing binding quality of state-

ments of faith which demand an unmistakable yes or no (p. 14). You declare expressly: "Also the claim of this Petrine of realizing its service to unity for the Catholic Church if necessary by binding statements and also in the defense against errors is not superfluous" (p. 18). You explain your inquiry into infallibility as "a hypothesis" (p. 18). You affirm that you do not make the claim that "a generally defined statement is nothing" (p. 21).

I believe that these expressions lead us further. However, are not the interpretations rejected by you not argued for in individual statements of your publications? It is likewise unclear whether and how far you are prepared formally to change such statements in new editions of your previous works.

2. Several questions in Christology as well as in the teaching about infallibility appear to me in every case still open. Thus, for example, the central question of whether Jesus Christ is the Son of God *from eternity*. The answer to that doubtless has enormous consequences for the further understanding of the Sonship of God as well as the Trinity. You confess to the christological formula of the Credo, but at the same time declare it inappropriate if someone wishes to "evaluate and indeed condemn . . . with the categories of essence" your christological outline (p. 9). How is it then with the essential unity of the Son with the Father? Such unclarities make your assurance that you did not dispute the christological statements of the Councils of Nicaea and Chalcedon in their continuing binding quality unfortunately again extremely ambiguous.

And if you already acknowledge a continuing binding character of statements of faith which demand an unmistakable yes or no, I must thus ask: How does this relate to your statement in *Infallible?* where it states that "with these defensive-defining propositions, even if they have a definitive and obligatory—and, to that extent, dogmatic—character for a particular situation, it is a question in the last resort of a ruling, not on principle and for eternity, but of a practical ruling on terminology conditioned by the situation" (p. 128)? How can one in the face of this statement, which in the text itself is characterized as the result of a lengthy reflection, speak in earnest of a *"continuing binding quality"?* This question therefore is so important because in the Church something can be *binding in faith* only if it is *true.*

3. The following state of affairs appears still more serious to me: The Declaration of the Congregation for the Doctrine of the Faith of December 15, 1979, in connection with the earlier Declaration of February 15, 1975, names three doctrinal points in which you deviate from the full truth of the Catholic faith: the dogma of the infallibility in the Church— the authentic interpretation of revelation through the ecclesiastical teaching office—the valid carrying out of the Eucharist. The christological and mariological questions on the contrary are not given by the Doctrinal Congregation as reasons for the measures taken, but rather are introduced as a consequence of your position on the specified points. Therefore it is decisive whether your letter goes further in the three first-specified points and deals with the detailed questions which I laid out before you in my letter of December 24, 1979. I do not wish to repeat these questions here, but only state that a response to them essentially is still missing. The relationship between theology and the teaching office appears to me not at all clarified; concerning the question of the valid completion of the Eucharist, you do not enter into it at all. Concerning the defective clarification of the infallibility question, I have already indicated above. Only by going into these questions and indeed in a formal reckoning with your earlier statements can the necessary clarification in the matter be brought about. A clear further development of your doctrinal opinions up to this point is otherwise not visible.

Your statement of December 12, 1979, was in these points already unsatisfactory. My urgent request for a precise response to the questions which I specified in my letter of December 24, 1979, has not been responded to by you. After the decision of the Congregation for the Doctrine of the

Faith was upheld a new situation has arisen in which only new and clear statements from your side can lead the matter further. Your explanations of February 12, 1980, in any case are not sufficient for a repeal of the decision contained in the Declaration of the Doctrinal Congregation of December 15, 1979. On the basis of this total situation I see no possibility for me to ask Rome for a review of the specified decision. For this there would be needed a decisive expansion and clarification, or explicit correction of your theological position on the indicated points. In any case unchanged new editions of your publications will not set this demand aright; by such you give rather a contrary sign to the public.

4. Under these circumstances I have no occasion to suspend the legal effects of the withdrawal of the *Missio* in any fashion. Likewise I cannot accept a postponement of the well-founded and demanded measures of which I wrote to the Minister for Science and Art on December 31, 1979. After the situation has once been placed on the juridical level it can be drawn back from there only when there develop from your side essentially new factual conditions.

In addition, the Concordat legal situation is evaluated by authoritative church-state lawyers differently than by you. Likewise I cannot but view your doubts about the *legality* of the inner-church procedures as unsound.

5. It is not correct that the doctrinal proceedings was finally and in every respect closed with the document of February 15, 1975. In this Declaration the Congregation for the Doctrine of the Faith in reference to your two books *The Church* and *Infallible? An Inquiry* referred to three interpretations which were not conformable to the teaching of the Church. Then it stated there further: "Because in his letter of September 4, 1974, Professor Küng does not at all exclude the possibility that, given adequate time for thorough study, he could bring his views in line with the authentic doctrine of the teaching office of the Church, in spite of the importance of these doctrines, the Congregation, so directed by Pope Paul VI, *for now* imparts to Professor Küng the admonition

not to advocate these doctrines any longer and recalls that the ecclesiastical authority has authorized him to teach theology in the spirit of Christian doctrine, but not to advocate views which distort that doctrine or call it into doubt." At the conclusion of the Declaration it expressly states that against this background "the proceedings of the Congregation for the Doctrine of the Faith in this matter are terminated *for now.*" The German Bishops' Conference for its part issued a detailed statement on this Declaration of the Doctrinal Congregation on February 17, 1975, in which among other things it said: "The German Bishops' Conference joins in the admonition of the Congregation for the Doctrine of the Faith and expects that Professor Küng will not further represent the position that he has manifoldly been directed away from by the ecclesiastical teaching office."

All that leaves no doubt that what is involved here is a temporary cessation of the proceedings. In logical fashion the Declaration of December 15, 1979, in the decisive passages repeats the result of the proceedings which by the document of February 15, 1975, was ended "for now." This closing did not take place unconditionally, but with the assumption that you would not express further the criticized doctrinal opinions. It was not only wishes that were expressed to you, but rather a clear condition was laid down.

Your two new publications (the introduction to the Hasler book and *The Church—Maintained in the Truth?*) provide the Declaration with proof that you have not held to the condition. To that extent a new proceedings was indeed not necessary for these two writings.

6. Your suggestion to undertake in the German Bishops' Conference a doctrinal complaint proceedings cannot be taken up in the present situation. The German Bishops' Conference cannot open a proceedings in a matter which has been taken to itself by a higher authority. Paragraph 35 of the doctrinal complaint proceedings of the German Bishops' Conference is clear here: "If the Sacra Congregatio pro doctrina fidei has begun . . . a formal doctrinal complaint pro-

ceedings, a doctrinal complaint proceedings against the same author on the same question cannot be initiated according to the present rules." This blocking effect properly takes effect only if a pending proceedings has been closed by a decision. If the Doctrinal Congregation with the active cooperation of the Pope has already made a decision which I as the local bishop have made my own, the German Bishops' Conference is no longer the competent agency for a proceedings to take up again a matter which should review and possibly revise the Roman decision. Likewise the suggestion of our Diocesan Council is no additional help.

7. For the moment neither I nor the German Bishops' Conference have the power to ask the Doctrinal Congregation for a reopening of the proceedings ("petitio novae audientiae"); you yourself, however, do. Such a request, of course, can succeed only if you credibly indicate that after a deepened reflection on the complained-of doctrinal opinions you find yourself in union with the complete truth of the Catholic faith. The possibility of a reopening of the proceedings lies therefore exclusively with you.

Very honored Professor, I would have preferred to send you a more encouraging response to your letter. However, the prerequisites for such are lacking in the present situation. We can move further only if together we take all the circumstances into consideration. I consciously say "together" because now as before it is possible to build bridges. For the sake of the Church and the Catholic Theology Faculty in Tübingen such efforts should steadfastly go forward. In any case I am available to you when it concerns further steps to accomplish substantive understanding.

> With friendly greetings,
> Georg Moser, Bishop

cc: The Minister for Science and Art, Stuttgart
    The President of the University of Tübingen

Küng obviously found Moser's letter not a little frustrating, irritating, and disingenuous. He clearly felt that Moser was not his own man, and that because he kept changing the rules of the game the true agenda was not the one on the surface. He asked Moser nevertheless to pluck up his courage and work for the proceedings he had asked for in his previous letter. The reader can judge for himself or herself as to the validity of Küng's argumentation. For his part, Bishop Moser adopted a hurt tone in his March 24, 1980, response to Küng, picking out a few points to reject specifically and then standing pat on demanding further clarification (submission?) from Küng before any movement from the Bishops' or Rome's side would take place. On March 13, 1980, Küng wrote to Moser as follows:

(93)

Very honored Bishop,

On February 12 I had a detailed essay sent to you in order that from my side a step toward understanding should be taken in a very difficult situation for our Church. Many who encouraged me to do this attached to this well-thought-out and, thus I believe, theologically comprehensively argued writing, no small hopes. All the more disappointing was your letter in response of March 1.

1. In my letter of February 12, 1980, I rectified various claims which ecclesiastical agencies had made concerning my positions and questions on Christology (pp. 2 f.) and infallibility (pp. 14–16). You, very honored Bishop, discover therein statements which you had not been "able to find in such clarity" in me before. In a fair dealing with my letter you would of course have had at the same time to acknowledge that likewise have I nowhere denied these statements. Apparently, however, the official interpretations of my writings have already for a long time been characterized by mistrust and a one-sided looking for holes. From this can be explained the fact which has been perceived by many in our Church that in the statements of the Bishops the true intentions and central statements of my theology indeed are no longer visible.

2. In my letter I expressed myself in detail about the background and the foundation of my *christological sketch* (pp. 3–13). You raise objections neither against the explanations of my methods nor against my hermeneutical explanations—which indeed likewise are part and parcel of contemporary theological analyses. Why then, my dear Bishop, do you not draw the conclusions which my explanations lead to? Why do you not wish to see that it is on the level of hermeneutical reflections that there can be a theological mediation which easily could have been taken up as a substantive discussion which would lead us further? Why do you take the rest of my explanations of Christology only with a mistrustful attitude and interpret them in a minimalist fashion?

Already my declaration of December 20, 1979, made to the Pope, in which in the questions of Christology I stood "fundamentally" on the *ground of the Councils* of the ancient Church, is taken by you on December 24, 1979, precisely not as a comprehensive statement in principle, but is misinterpreted by you as a diluting expression to which I could barely force myself. On September 21, 1977, Cardinal Höffner attempted to force me to say that I could not give a clear yes "to the confession of this faith which cannot be given up." My express and repeated confession to the *Credo* in my last letter (pp. 2–13) therefore should have easily been sufficient for you to erase this suspicion so as at least to find the basis for a discussion on the question of Christology. On the contrary, you again issue individual questions before the context is clarified and focus the discussion on individual theological statements without thinking about their connection.

Once again you insinuate in a fashion which twists the meaning of my explanations diametrically about, as if I wished to not allow my theological explanation to be measured by the *Credo*. Thereby—and this method has been employed for years—you *personalize* the substantive problematic once again: as though it concerned only my ideas, as though many Catholic exegetes, systematicians, and practical theologians had not put forth similar ideas, as if the *substantive problem* which is raised by so many and which is so widely discussed can simply be suppressed by ecclesiastical agencies. However, thus not only will my case not be regulated, but likewise the questions of a number of believers (pastors, religious, laity) will be challenged, as the reaction to the unexampled episcopal public efforts against me bear witness.

Since the Bishops have the task to care for in a special way the rather non-credible Christian proclamation in the present, the disappointment within and without our Church concerning this whole matter is all the greater. Precisely because in my theology we are not concerned with some sort of unfounded private opinions, but rather with scholarly well-founded theological statements which are congruent with a broad exegetical consensus, the Bishops by their actions consequently raise the suspicion that they cannot disarm the argument of a critical theology and cannot respond to the questions raised. Not only for me but also for other theologians the question is raised: Do the Bishops at all wish to allow a theological discussion on christological questions which is responsible to the Scripture and to *allow new attempts* to make the faith in Jesus Christ once again understandable for the men and women of today?

3. In my letter I undertook further a renewed attempt to explain the reasons, purpose, and directions of my inquiry into the *problematic of infallibility* which is related to the question of the authentic teaching office. Even here you apparently had nothing objective to object to in my basic explanations. But also here, my dear Bishop, you immediately again concentrate on individual sentences, which in fact are supposed to merely initiate a discussion of the substantive questions, and search for possible defects in them. The fact that you curtly characterize my nine-page comprehensive statement as not sufficient to warrant beginning anew a conversation, arouses doubts about your will or your ability for an understanding.

The method of interpretation focused on gaps had been seen earlier. On December 20, I based my declaration (for the hands of the Pope), at your own suggestion, on the statement of the German Bishops' Conference of February 4, 1971, in which the term "infallibility" is avoided altogether. In your letter four days later you asked why I avoid the term.

At the same time I affirmed that the Church has the "duty and task" to carry out the Christian message "clearly and bindingly." You miss the formulation of the Bishops' Conference: ". . . really with an ultimate binding quality." Had I not confirmed the binding quality of faith statements which are true and which are recognizable as true, whose meaning remains the same within the change of historical ways of thinking and statements, which are irremovable and which demand an unmistakable yes or no?

Unfortunately this manner of raising questions continues in your most recent letter of March 1, 1980. You accept my concept of the "continuing binding quality" as helpful and then, nevertheless, again seek to make it untrustworthy from the perspective of my christological statements ("unfortunately again extremely ambiguous"). Furthermore, you immediately juxtaposed to this my affirmation of a "continuing binding quality" a citation from *Infallible?* which, however, in no way provides the counter-evidence that you intend it should; for all of the limitations indicated there (situation-conditioned, not specified for all eternity, pragmatic) do not remove the truth of a definition of faith which has come about, but rather they make it more precise and do so completely in the sense of the explanations of *Mysterium ecclesiae* (No. 5). And if you quote from *Infallible?,* then please also quote what I have detailed concerning this question in *Fallible?* (pp. 391–96): "How can a faith statement persist through history" and "how can a faith statement at once be situation-conditioned and binding?" That you should charge precisely me that only *what is true* can be binding in faith reverses the sides. For it is precisely I who had been the one to constantly attempt to critically uphold the truth question time and again even against the formalistic claims of authority.

No, dear Bishop, on this basis of suspicion and misinterpretation and in this spirit of constant mistrust no fruitful dialogue can come about. What I miss at the same time is: When will you recognize the ecumenical implications of this problem? You do not mention a single word about this in your letter. Therefore I would like again to urgently request you to take seriously the questions raised and to be sensitive to ecumenical sensibilities in precisely this place. The profession of the Bishops in favor of ecumenism will appear credible only when a constructive theological solution for this central question for the Eastern Churches and for the Reformed Churches is striven for. The catastrophic echo from the *oikoumene* concerning the measures taken against me should have given even you and all the German Bishops cause to think.

4. Perhaps I do you an injustice if I were to doubt your sincere *will to mediate*. Nevertheless the question remains open whether such mediation attempts are not condemned to fail ever again within the framework of the playing rules as they are practiced at present. Indeed, the priority of themes which are to be discussed (Christology, infallibility, authenticity of the teaching office, questions of the Eucharist, Trinity, Mariology, among others) is not clarified; likewise, the expectations which you have of me are not clarified; finally, the consequences which you think to draw are not clarified either.

Although Cardinal Höffner places an extraordinarily great weight on the questions of *Christology,* in your last letter you attempt to show that the questions of Christology are of a lesser importance for a revision of the proceedings; indeed, Rome puts them forth only as a consequence of my alleged "contempt for the teaching office." However, at the same time you attempt to use my positions in christological matters as proof that I hold the teaching office in contempt.

Thereby a circle is formed whose maintenance makes progress in the dialogue absolutely impossible.

Although the Roman authorities base their proceedings on my statements concerning *infallibility,* they repeatedly insist on questions concerning the *Eucharist,* which after the closing of the "proceedings" in 1975 have played no further role in the discussion. And beyond these questions time and again further questions concerning *Mariology* are alluded to in undifferentiated fashion although there still has never been an official discussion with me concerning them. And if all of these questions were resolved, then—I fear this on the basis of the correspondence carried on till now—those doubts would probably again be brought into play with further theological problems of which the Bishops hinted already on February 17, 1975: those "demands for reform," in which the order of the Church would be "arbitrarily" changed, that is, in the language of Cardinal Höffner, those "in part unrestricted attacks against the discipline of the Church" (December 18, 1979). According to the report of the Catholic Press Agency (KNA) of February 28, 1980, concerning the last day of the German Bishops' Conference, I am considered by many people a "leading fighter for specific proposals of reform, like the lifting of celibacy and the ordination of women; the withdrawal of the teaching commission is associated with the condemnation of such proposals for reform." What all, therefore, does one expect by way of corrections from me? How many question complexes, I ask myself, do the Bishops probably still have *in petto* which they can haul out at any stage of the dialogue? It would seem that this or that argument is brought forth depending on the circle of addressees and the given situation.

The like is true for your *argumentation:* At one point you declare my presentations helpful. Nevertheless, they are only a "first minimal step" (December 24, 1979) and insufficient for a resumption of the dialogue or even of the process (March 1, 1980). What ends, therefore, have my presentations served? Only that you constantly again should pressure me and wherever possible involve me in contradictions? At one time you expect from me (as brief as possible) fundamental explanations. At others in your answers you use against me quotation upon quotation with which I then again should engage in a new discussion. I declared to you that according to a general theological consensus the relationship between the teaching office and theology is urgently in need of clarification. Your answer to me: "The relationship between theology and the teaching office appears to me not at all clarified." What, therefore, are the expectations which are attached to my statements?

It is similar concerning the *consequences* which in the future I should expect. First of all, it seems to me that the matter concerns clarifications which should make a new dialogue possible. Then in unexpected fashion it apparently concerns in this foreground area already the clarification of my earlier statements (brought forth with several citations out of context). Finally there now suddenly turns up—apparently also brought forth within the area of preconditions—the question of the revision of my writings. With this I would naturally with every just reason have to have clarified ahead of time the question of the justice or injustice, the founded or unfounded character of such demands.

What at the moment is becoming visible on the side of the teaching office in the multiplying, constantly changing arguments and doctrinal points, in the ever new horizons of expectations, in the unexpected changing of the charges, shows that the ecclesiastical courts themselves hardly have the will to hold an ordered procedure or proceedings. With the repeated reading of your letter one must ask oneself: What is it really about now? About a fraternal dialogue concerning disputed questions which existentially strike so many men and women, or finally and ultimately really only about the recanting and total submission of an individual theologian? Are substantive questions to be clarified, or is an example simply to be made of someone?

5. In my letter of February 12, 1980, I have asserted that

neither the Roman nor the German ecclesiastical courts have established in a *correct proceedings* that the incriminating publications violated essential elements of the Catholic faith.

Concerning the *German courts* you have not contradicted my assertion. Thereby it appears to me to be undisputed that concerning questions of *Christology and Mariology absolutely no court has carried out a proceedings.* I perceived this as a fact which expresses disdain for any sense of justice and which obliges no civil court to accept the declarations of ecclesiastical offices concerning my christological or mariological statements as grounds for any sort of civil action.

The ecclesiastical authorities themselves therefore stand under an *official obligation* either to rehabilitate me concerning questions of Christology and Mariology or to have the charges established in a correct proceedings. In this matter, in my opinion, you as the competent bishop have the obligation to be active since you have made the judgment of the Roman authorities your own.

Concerning the *Roman courts* you have in my opinion not sufficiently evaluated the complex situation which has developed. Contrary to your assertion, I have not maintained that the proceedings was closed "finally and in every aspect" in 1975. For me the statement is sufficient that, as always, the matter was closed according to legal effect, especially since the rules of proceedings in no way recognize a temporary closure.

What the matter concerned according to the judgment of the Doctrinal Congregation itself is clearly seen from the letter in which the Prefect of the Doctrinal Congregation, Cardinal Šeper, officially informed me of the closing of the proceedings: "In order to meet the mutual wish *to end the proceedings* concerning your books *The Church* and *Infallible?,* the Congregation for the Doctrine of the Faith has decided *to close both proceedings* with the enclosed Declaration." It is also clear that the Bishops' Conference issued a declaration "upon the occasion *of the closing* of the doctrinal proceedings" (December 17, 1975). And finally, it is certain that Cardinal Döpfner, then the President of the German Bishops' Conference, had in his letter on the same day likewise adopted the language of the ending of the doctrinal proceedings. In all of the official documents there never was talk of a "temporary closing" of the proceedings, which in the procedural rules for the proceedings is not even anticipated.

Indeed "admonishments" not "conditions" were issued to me. Sanctions, however, were precisely not envisioned, to say nothing about being specified in detail. A publication prohibition was expressly excluded. Already in my declaration of February 20, 1975, I made it clear that I did not understand the close of the "proceedings," against which I time and again until the closing had raised serious formal legal doubts, as an act of one-sided submission, but rather as an obligation to deepened reflection on both sides (cf. *Concerning Nothing but the Truth,* documentation edited by Walter Jens, pp. 160 f.).

If, therefore, within the framework of the February 17, 1975, closed proceedings no sanctions had been decided upon, then for the grounding of such a serious measure as the withdrawal of the *Missio* of December 15, 1979, a new proceedings would be necessary. This has not taken place. According to the Roman order for doctrinal complaint proceedings a new proceedings would have to be carried out in order to establish whether through the two new publications I in fact had acted against the warning of the Congregation for the Doctrine of the Faith.

In order to submit these two writings as evidence, contact with the author would be in order. In this regard it is admitted that you yourself, my dear Bishop, in your letter of the days of December 14 or 15, 1975, to Cardinal Šeper, expressed serious doubts about the manner of proceeding of the doctrinal authorities and urgently requested a hearing for me. Unfortunately you have not kept the promise that you gave to me to publish this letter (at the same time with my declaration made for the "hands of the Pope") and despite all your doubts have accepted the Roman decision.

I am, therefore, now as before, of the conviction that in view of the legal situation the *Roman decision cannot be sufficient* for the administrative act which is demanded from the Minister for Science and Art. I am convinced that if it only wished to, it would be a simple matter for the Doctrinal Congregation to agree with my argumentation in this matter. In that regard the discussion on this point is not primarily about a legal situation which is clear, and therefore necessary, but rather about a church-political decision.

6. In my letter of February 12, 1980, upon the suggestion of your Diocesan Council and of many others I offered my cooperation in a *proceedings of the German Bishops' Conference* according to the corresponding "rules for a doctrinal complaint proceedings" (1973). In this I already myself pointed out that the German Bishops' Conference in this situation of course cannot introduce a proceedings without a discussion with the Holy See. However, through an appeal to the Pope they could have done what was within their power in order to open a proceedings which would take place according to the criteria of contemporary justice. Therefore I expressly ask you again to work for this solution which, if there exists on the side of the Bishops only a little good will for an understanding, would be yet attainable even today.

Despite the very deeply disillusioning and in part negative content of your letter, you emphasize at the very end once again that now as before it is possible *to build bridges*. I share this view. However, you will understand that this cannot include the disavowal of the commandment of Christian truthfulness and scholarly honesty, to which my theology is committed, nor a *sacrificium intellectus et conscientiae*. However, it can include the discussion anew and clarification of the foundations of our faith for the welfare of our Church. And it must also include the pondering by the courts of the Church on a proceedings of rightness and justice which, as you know, in the presently practiced form even among the inner-church public is now as before widely rejected. Only with a *common* effort, and not in a "here is everything" and "there is nothing," can good still come out of the present situation.

With friendly greetings,

Yours sincerely,
Hans Küng
Professor of Dogmatic and
Ecumenical Theology of the
Catholic Theology Faculty and
Director of the Institute for
Ecumenical Research at the
University of Tübingen

cc: Minister for Science and Art, Stuttgart
President of the University of Tübingen

Although by March 24, Küng still had not received a response from his March 13 letter to Moser, he had little ground for optimism, and consequently investigated alternative solutions with University President Adolf Theis. Greinacher and Haag commented on the situation at this point as follows: "From the beginning Dean Bartholomäus worked untiringly for Hans Küng's remaining in the Catholic Theology Faculty. He was decisively supported also in this last phase by a portion of the professors, by the academic counselors, assistants, and students on the Faculty Council. The seven colleagues, however (four of whom are Rottenburg diocesan priests)—the majority of the professors—remained, despite all the mediation attempts of the Dean and Norbert Greinacher, firm in their attachment to their public declaration of February 5, 1980. Because the basis for Küng's remaining in the Faculty (even without a *Missio canonica,* if need be) was thus destroyed, and since on the other hand because of the unrelenting attitude of specific German bishops, the reissuance of the *Missio* was not to be reckoned with in the foreseeable future, Küng felt himself forced to search for a solution within the University. Such a solution was worked out in several constructive discussions with University President Theis: The constitutionally legally guaranteed research and teaching freedom of Küng and the functioning of the Institute for Ecumenical

Research should be protected by the University. The teaching
chair and Institute, however, at the suggestion of Küng, should be
withdrawn from the Catholic Theology Faculty, until a possible
reissuance of the *Missio canonica,* and placed directly under the
Senate of the University. In order to assure thereby above all the
possibility of doctorates and habilitations [Ph.D. and Doctor of
Habilitation, the second doctorate that potential university professors in Germany normally must have] for his students and co-
workers, Küng sent the following letter, which contains a reflection on the developments within the Faculty, to President Theis
as a response to the suggestions of March 19, 1980" (*Fall Küng,*
p. 526). The possibility of a positive response from Bishop Moser
alluded to at the end of his letter was of course dashed later the
same day, March 24, 1980, when Küng received Moser's letter by
messenger. Küng's March 24, 1980, letter to University President
Adolf Theis was as follows:

(94)

Dear University President Adolf Theis,
     Thank you for your letter of March 19, 1980, along with
the four enclosures. In confirmation of our discussions may I
briefly summarize my own standpoint and relationship to the
negotiations of the Catholic Theology Faculty as follows:
     It is well known to you, to the University, and also to the
wider public, how decisively since the surprising Roman
measure against me of December 18, 1979, I have spoken
out time and again in favor of and have endeavored to accomplish my retention in the Catholic Theology Faculty. In
this in the beginning I was likewise supported by all of my
Faculty colleagues, who even on December 18 itself publicly
expressed their dismay concerning the "intervening step
taken by the Doctrinal Congregation" and concerning the
way and manner of the proceeding in concerted action. And
on December 19, all the colleagues declared in a letter to the
Bishop of Rottenburg that they are "outraged" at the "secret,
precisely synchronized proceeding—and this immediately be-

fore Christmas" without hearing again from the person affected; "in general the entire procedure is burdened with defects . . . which contradict the contemporary sense of justice and the Christian ethos"; they had "no doubt that he [Küng] wished and wishes to remain in the Catholic faith and in the Catholic Church"; in view of the expected consequences for the Church, for the relationship between Church and state, and especially for our Faculty, they requested the Bishop "urgently not to take the anticipated step despite its already public announcement."

However, after the Bishop, following a "mediation action" of the German Bishops in Rome, nevertheless on December 30 did take the step, there took place indeed not among our students or in the University or in the wider public, but rather among several colleagues of the Catholic Theology Faculty, an unexpected change of mind. Indeed, still on January 10, members of the expanded Faculty Council agreed, with a single contrary voice and one abstention, that the Senate of the University of Tübingen should exhaust the legal possibilities toward bringing about a revision of the ecclesiastical resolutions so that Professor Küng would continue to remain a member of the Catholic Theology Faculty. However, while from my side I responded to this Faculty resolution to defuse the conflict by withdrawing almost entirely from the public and, in cooperation with you, my dear President, I worked intensively for an understanding, on February 5, 1980, seven of the twelve Professors of the Catholic Theology Faculty had barged off in a completely different direction with a declaration of their own to the public. There was no longer any talk of the earlier expressed serious material and legal doubts; the Roman penal measures were interpreted as "an official doctrinal call to the subject matter," the charges of the Roman Doctrinal offices were accepted and thereby it was insinuated that I am a theologian who puts forth "as the norm of the truth his own judgment and not the thought of the Church" (cf. *Declaratio* of December 15, 1979) and thus "arrogates to himself the highest teaching office in the Church." This acceptance of the attitudes and statements about me in the Roman declaration I perceive as discrimination and completely untrue. At the same time, however, the seven decided for themselves what in the Faculty resolution of January 10 was consciously left open: "Whoever allows or wishes that a theologian without a *Missio canonica* should belong to a theological faculty for an extended period of time undermines its scholarly theoretical status as well as its constitutional and Concordat guarantee." Because of such a public declaration of the majority of the professors the basis for me to continue to remain in this Faculty is destroyed.

As you know, my dear President, in the past weeks I have, according to my best knowledge and conscience, done everything through conversations with you and the Minister for Science and Art and finally through a 26-page statement to the Bishop of Rottenburg-Stuttgart of February 12 (concerning whose preparation the seven Faculty colleagues ahead of time had also been informed by me) in order to make my contribution to a constructive resolution and a reissuance of the ecclesiastical teaching commission. However, even this detailed statement on the questions of Christology and infallibility—at the end of which I expressed my readiness to place myself at the disposal of a legal doctrinal complaint proceedings by the German Bishops' Conference—received —at first by a press declaration of the (not even competent for this case) Archbishop of Cologne and then through a written statement of the Bishop of Rottenburg-Stuttgart of March 1, which was marked with the same spirit—a rough rejection. This for me incomprehensible attitude of the Bishops indicates to me that any understanding is at present shattered on the stubbornness of specific German bishops; unfortunately the reissuance of the *Missio* is thereby in the foreseeable future not to be reckoned with.

The situation which has thus arisen forces me to consequences which I regret most deeply, but which however unfortunately are unavoidable. For I have even publicly never left any doubt that now as before I understand myself as a Catholic theologian and in this sense will work for the renewal of my Catholic Church. I have assured you, my dear President, that I am prepared to do my part to bring about an agreed-upon resolution within the framework of the University. The unrenounceable presupposition for such of course is that my constitutionally legally guaranteed academic research and teaching freedom as well as the functioning of the Institute for Ecumenical Research, which is connected with my teaching chair, will remain completely protected. Above all that includes that my right to collaborate in unhindered fashion in the doctorates and habilitations of my students and co-workers remains guaranteed. I greet therefore the change in the statutes of the Senate suggested by you which expressly legally guarantee the membership which has existed until now in the Doctorate and Habilitation Committee of the Catholic Theology Faculty. This membership is necessary in order to work in an equal fashion and with equal effect on doctorates and habilitations. At the same time in order to avoid difficulties in individual cases the Faculty should likewise expressly confirm that the seminar certificates earned in the Institute for Ecumenical Research will be recognized by the Faculty as they were before. From my side I wish to notify the Faculty that because of the situation which has arisen I do not intend to collaborate in all of the doctorate and habilitation proceedings. Only where my students and co-workers are concerned will I take part in the sessions of the committee.

At the conclusion of this letter I feel compelled to confirm: I hold my objections against the illegal inner-Church proceedings and also my doubts about state-Church legalities, as I expressed them in the letters to the Minister for Science and Art, the delegates of the Parliament of Baden-Württemberg, and the Bishop of Rottenburg-Stuttgart, in full force. I cannot agree with the conclusions of the advisory opinion of Professor Scheuner relating to my belonging to the Faculty; my own interpretation moves along the lines of the presentations by Professor Scholder and Kultusminister (retired) Mahrenholz. Because I consider myself now as before a Catholic theologian I also will continue to think about how to bring about a revision of this proceedings, unjust in every manner, and a reissuance of the *Missio*.

Before a final step by the University it appears to me necessary to ascertain in this matter whether eventually, on the basis of my written statement to Bishop Moser on March 13, a change of attitude on the part of the Bishop is to be expected which would make further deliberations by the University superfluous.

I thank you very much, my dear President, for your intensive efforts for a justifiable solution. I leave it completely to you whether and how far you wish to make use of this letter of mine in relationship to the Catholic Theology Faculty.

With friendly greetings, I remain,

Sincerely,
Hans Küng

On March 25, 1980, a meeting of the expanded Faculty Council of the Catholic Theology Faculty was called during the between-semesters period. The session was chaired by University President Theis, who asked for their judgment on the possibility, after Küng's possible withdrawal from the Faculty, of his retaining the right to put forward candidates for the Ph.D. and D. Habil. In what Greinacher and Haag called a "tough" five-hour-long negotiation, in which the "seven" still always operated as a group, the Faculty Council nevertheless in the end did unanimously agree that Küng could be on the Ph.D. and D. Habil. committees of his students—assuming agreement between the Bishop, Minister, and Küng were reached. "While the Minister gave his fundamental agreement two days later, the Bishop asked for time to think. For also in this case Bishop Moser could decide nothing without a discussion with the Nunciature. Only days later did

he send on to President Theis his agreement to the 'acceptable solution' with the condition that Küng could only be an 'advisory'
member of the Doctorate and Habilitation Committee when he
was not mandated to give an evaluation" (*Fall Küng*, p. 534).
Küng agreed and on April 8, 1980, sent the following letter to
Theis:

(95)

Dear University President Adolf Theis,

On March 25, the Catholic Theology Faculty agreed to a
modification of the Senate statutes which guarantees to me as
the Director of the Institute for Ecumenical Research a
membership in their Doctorate and Habilitation Committee
concerning dissertations which are directed by me. This resolution was composed with the presupposition of a harmonious resolution between the Minister for Science and Art, the
Bishop of Rottenburg, and myself. This has become—among
other things through your intensive efforts—possible.
Thereby the condition expressed in my written statement to
you of March 24—complete academic research and teaching
freedom as well as the functional capability of my teaching
chair and Institute—is fulfilled, so that now from my side I
can agree with the inner-University resolution. On the basis
of the situation, which I again in summary fashion presented
to you in my above-referred-to written statement, I see myself forced temporarily to leave the Catholic Theology Faculty until an eventual reissuance of the *Missio canonica*. I
rejected a transfer to another faculty on the grounds of my
scholarly self-understanding and of my conviction of faith as
a Catholic theologian from the beginning. I request, therefore, that my teaching chair—with the title "Teaching Chair
for Ecumenical Theology"—as well as the Institute for Ecumenical Research attached to it be temporarily taken out of
the Catholic Theology Faculty and be placed as a central institution directly under the Senate of the University. At the

same time I would request that the Senate establish an institutes order corresponding to the document which you sent
out before me in your written statement of March 19, 1980.

In this connection may I make the following fundamental
observations:

1. I do not give up my commission after a twenty-year
Faculty membership voluntarily. For now as before I understand myself as a Catholic theologian who as priest, pastor,
and scholar knows himself to be bound to his Church. In the
past three months I have from my side undertaken various
steps to attain an understanding with the ecclesiastical authorities and a re-granting of the *Missio canonica*. However,
the unrelenting stand of well-known German bishops on the
one hand and the development within the corps of professors
of the Catholic Theology Faculty on the other hand force me
to a step which I never would have wished.

2. I nevertheless take this step because I do not wish that
the University be drawn into a tedious dispute because of the
Roman decision, have its peace endangered and its reputation damaged. In addition I would not wish that the state of
Baden-Württemberg should be drawn into a state-Church
legal conflict that would be difficult to resolve because of the
ecclesiastical measures in my case; the efforts until now by
the Minister for Science and Art, for which I'm thankful, to
arrive at a harmonious provisional resolution strengthen me
in this attitude. However, above all it would be irresponsible
for me as a theologian under the given circumstances to enter
into the path of litigation and involve the University as well
as myself in possibly many-year-long trials whose consequences are unforeseeable. I am a theologian and I wish to
remain a theologian; the requested resolution gives me the
possibility, despite all the ecclesiastical and University legal
limitations, to devote as before my entire energy and time to
the purely theological scholarly tasks in research and teaching. If the Church authorities have attempted in my case to
force through the truth with the means of power, as a Christian I trust that with time the truth will of itself come

through. Not last, because of this reason, I view the present striven-for "resolution" as provisional.

3. My proposal does not mean that I do not maintain completely my serious legal doubts against the inner-Church procedure. All the professors of the Catholic Theology Faculty agree that "the entire procedure is burdened with defects . . . which contradict the contemporary sense of justice and the Christian ethos." It would, therefore, be the task particularly of the Catholic Theology Faculty to engage itself unanimously and clearly in the revision of this inquisitorial "proceedings" which in my understanding from beginning to end expresses disdain for all justice and Christian fraternity. Likewise I myself intend—above all through the working through of the theological problematic—to strive toward a revision.

4. My proposal likewise does not mean that I do not maintain completely my serious state-Church legal doubts as I have formulated them in letters to the Minister for Science and Art, the delegates of the Parliament of Baden-Württemberg, and the Bishop of Rottenburg-Stuttgart. The conclusions from the expert testimony sought by the Ministerium in relationship to my membership in the Faculty I cannot agree with. The Minister for Science and Art is in my conviction in no way released from the duty to investigate whether in my case the ecclesiastical charge can be viewed at all as a sufficient basis for the administrative action demanded of the state. Article 19 of the National Concordat says expressly that the relationship of the Catholic Theology Faculty "to the ecclesiastical authorities is to be governed by the fixed specifications in the pertinent Concordats *with the observation of the pertinent ecclesiastical prescriptions.*" As is known, neither of my last two small publications on the infallibility question nor the books *On Being a Christian* and *Does God Exist?* have ever been the object of a doctrinal complaint proceedings in Rome or in Germany. Furthermore, the statements and decisions of the ecclesiastical authorities concerning these took place without a proceedings

according to the rules. Thus the prescriptions of neither the Roman Doctrinal Congregation nor the German Bishops' Conference were held to. Thus, in the end what is involved in the measures against me is a papal power claim, not however, the result of an orderly proceedings. The responsible politicians and above all the Minister for Science and Art, but also the expert adviser, must ask themselves whether they wish to allow the inner-state rules of justice to be influenced from outside by measures which are not characterized by the standards of justice and law.

Likewise in my opinion there is needed a fundamental clarification of whether or not after the Roman intervention, which is not covered by the Concordat, the constitutionally guaranteed freedom of teaching and research in the Catholic theological faculties is at all still preserved. My case is no individual case. It has raised fundamentally exemplary questions about the present dominant interpretation of the Concordat of 1933: there exists the danger that every Catholic theological faculty of our state universities in fact will become in research and teaching a state-financed ecclesiastical institution and the "Church-bound" civil office of the professors a Church office salaried by the state. The question is posed whether or not the balance of the rights and obligations of the two Concordat partners is maintained in reference to the Catholic theological faculties if the state has to bear the burdens of such ecclesiastical measures.

I thank you anew, my dear President, that despite all resistance you have untiringly striven for an acceptable resolution and unto the very end in all decisiveness have intervened for the protection of my position at the University.

With friendly greetings,

Sincerely,
Hans Küng

cc: Minister for Science and Art Prof. Dr. Engler

President Theis acted immediately on the matter on April 9, 1980, and on April 10, Minister Engler issued a decree which made it legally binding. On the same day Küng and Theis held a press conference at which Küng issued the following statement:

(96)
The Questions Remain!
(April 10, 1980)

1. In the future, as professor of ecumenical theology and Director of the Institute for Ecumenical Research at the University of Tübingen, I likewise will hold lectures and seminars, do research, teach, and publish. As a Catholic theologian I will continue to struggle for a Christianity which is oriented more toward the message of Jesus, for ecumenical understanding, and for the renewal of my Catholic Church which I now as before understand myself to be bound to as a priest, pastor, and scholar.

2. I will continue to work for the revision of an inquisitorial "proceedings" which from beginning to end contradicted all justice and Christian fraternity; I thank all those many persons who have supported me and likewise those who in the future will support me.

3. Because of the unrelenting stand of some well-known German bishops and because of a defective support—for a variety of reasons—of a majority of Faculty colleagues, I saw myself consequently forced, after a twenty-year membership in the Catholic Theology Faculty, temporarily, until the eventual reissuance of the ecclesiastical teaching commission, to withdraw my teaching chair and the Institute for Ecumenical Research attached to it from this Faculty and to have it placed directly under the Senate of the University. I am grateful, however, to my University, its President, and the Minister for Science and Art that they have guaranteed my academic research and teaching freedom within a wider University framework.

4. Indeed I must thus—except for doctorates and habilitations of my present and future students—give up above all my right to lectures which are relevant to examinations, to

the hearing of exams, and participation in the calling of new professors. Nevertheless, through this resolution I am freed to devote myself anew with my entire power to my true theological scholarly tasks in collaboration with my co-workers at the Institute, who stood loyally at my side during this difficult time. For the sake of theology and also for the sake of the peace of the University it appeared to me as a theologian that under the given circumstances it would be irresponsible to follow the path of litigation and thus involve the University as well as myself in years-long trials whose consequences are unforeseeable. If the Church authorities have attempted in my case to force through their opinion with the means of power, I trust as a Christian that the truth will with time of itself come through.

5. I completely maintain my serious legal doubts concerning the inner-Church proceedings. The Minister of Science and Art in my opinion has now as before the duty to investigate whether in my case the ecclesiastical charges can at all be viewed as a satisfactory grounds for the administrative act demanded of the state. For obviously Rome and the Bishops were not concerned in my case for a just proceedings and a constructive resolution of the questions—which were not invented by me. Rather they demanded *de facto* the denial of specific critical inquiries and total submission to an ecclesiastical teaching system which in many ways is outdated. I could not reconcile these either with the freedom of conscience of a Christian or with the scholarly honesty which I also as a Catholic theologian understand myself always to be obliged to.

6. My case shows with pressing clarity that a fundamental clarification is needed to determine whether the constitutionally guaranteed freedom of research and teaching in Catholic theological faculties is, after the direct Roman interventions, which are not covered by the Concordat, at all still conserved. My case is not an individual case; it has raised fundamental questions concerning the contemporary dominant interpretation of the Concordat of 1933. The danger has

become apparent that in our state universities the Catholic theological faculties will become state-financed Church institutions of research and teaching and that the "Church-bound" civil office of the professors will become a Church office salaried by the state. Thereby the question is posed whether a balance between the rights and obligations of the two Concordat partners in reference to the Catholic theological faculties is maintained when the state has to bear all the burdens of such ecclesiastical measures.

7. Concerning the events of the last three months many tendentious and false things have been reported from the official Church side. Consequently I thank my colleagues Norbert Greinacher and Herbert Haag, who are editing a detailed documentation which will be published in May by Piper Verlag. This volume will document the following: the efforts of the University of Tübingen, the appeals of numberless Catholics, Catholic groups and associations, and finally also my own attempts to arrive at an understanding, all shattered above all because of the irreconcilability of specific representatives of the German episcopacy. At the same time the documentation will make clear the background, the responsibilities, and the effects of the "Küng case," which in truth is an "official Church case."

8. Despite the inner-University solution, therefore, the fundamental questions remain, and the debates will not cease: the question, now as before unanswered by Rome and the Bishops, concerning their infallibility remains. The question of a contemporary credible Christian proclamation in church and school remains. The questions of the understanding between the confessions and the mutual recognition of offices and celebrations of the Eucharist remain. The questions of the urgent tasks of reform remain: from those of birth control through mixed marriages and divorce to the ordination of women, mandatory celibacy, and the consequent catastrophic lack of priests. Above all the question to the leadership of the Catholic Church remains: Where are you leading *our* Church? On the path of John XXIII and

the Second Vatican Council into a greater Catholic breadth, humanness, and Christianness? Or on the path of the First Vatican Council and the Pius Popes back into an authoritarian Catholic ghetto? I would still like to hope that nevertheless the spirit of true evangelical catholicity will finally emerge victorious over the anti-spirit of a juridically narrowed, rigidly doctrinaire, and triumphalistic, anxiety-ridden Catholicism.

World Protest

The protest reaction to the Vatican's censuring of Küng was explosive and widespread. The torrent of newspaper articles and editorials, radio and television coverage, letters, statements, speeches, and the like in protest against the Vatican and German episcopal measures and in support of Küng all over the Western world cannot be measured. As noted before, Küng himself received over 5,000 letters of support! The dossiers of the material generated from December 18, 1979, to April 1980 occupy yards and yards of bookshelves in Küng's library. The documentation edited by Norbert Greinacher and Herbert Haag, *Der Fall Küng*, encompasses 546 pages, but by no means contains all the pertinent documentation—only the most important. Just under 300 pages of *Der Fall Küng* consist almost entirely of protests against the Vatican and the German Bishops, with very few remarks supportive of them. The protests came from a wide variety of organizations, groups, theological faculties, and individuals. Many tens of thousands of persons were involved. But beyond the material in this documentation, still another one, a 200-page documentation of supporting statements and letters from Austria, was published (Peter Karner, ed., *Der Fall Küng ein ökumenisches Problem*, Dorotheergasse 16, Vienna, 1980). Many statements were issued in America, of which only some of the more important will be reproduced below. Apparently there was no effort made to collect documentation in other countries.

I personally have seen scores of articles and editorials on the Küng affair published in 1980, in a wide variety of Italian, Spanish, Portuguese, English, French, and German-language religious journals. A systematic gathering and analyzing of all this material would be quite revealing of the attitudes of many reflective Christians in these countries. Unfortunately that work has not yet been done, and hence cannot be reported on here. However, Greinacher and Haag do reproduce in 175 pages some thirty-eight lengthy statements and articles supportive of Küng (and several neutral or negative statements), published for the most part in national or international newspapers or journals in Germany, Austria, Switzerland, Denmark, France, and the United States—that is apart from the statements by theological faculties and other groups, which fill another 115 pages. These supportive articles were often written by internationally known figures, such as: Friedrich Heer, Heinrich Fries, Yves Congar, Johannes Neumann, Jürgen Moltmann, Heinrich Ott, Wolfhart Pannenberg, Eberhard Jüngel, Josef Blank, Willem Adolph Visser't Hooft, and Andrew Greeley. Unfortunately because of space limitations their stimulating articles, and others, cannot be reproduced here.

Greinacher and Haag also provide a very brief overview of the editorials on the Küng affair in the national and international newspapers in Germany, Holland, Austria, Switzerland, France, England, Italy, and Spain. This overview, which does not deal at all with the regional newspapers of the various countries or other printed and other news media, listed some twenty-three editorials, of which only three, two from *Der Spiegel* (which traditionally attacks everyone) and one from the generally conservative *Le Figaro* of Paris, were not at least moderately supportive of Küng. Lest it be thought that Greinacher and Haag simply selected the newspapers supportive of Küng and neglected the rest, it should be noted that their overview comes from the report of the Catholic News Agency (Katholische Nachrichtenagentur, KNA, January 17, 1980).

The breadth and intensity of the protest can of course also be measured somewhat by the reaction of the Bishops—the scores of thousands of copies of their *Documentation,* the millions of their pamphlets, the nationwide "pastoral letter," news conferences, etc., all of which must have cost a million marks or more (not to mention the subsidizing by Cardinal Krol of Philadelphia of the translation of the German Bishops' *Documentation* into English —*The Küng Dialogue*).

This huge outpouring of protest and support can partly be traced to Küng's personal popularity—his books have sold hundreds of thousands of copies around the world and he has lectured many times, in many languages, in many countries over the years. These personal contacts have won him many friends, for his personality is very low-key, warm, and open. But even this widespread personal popularity cannot by itself adequately account for the magnitude of the protest. As noted above, as early as 1963, Küng had become something of a symbol of the new Catholic freedom unleashed at Vatican II. This symbol quality of Küng did not lessen in the ensuing years, but if anything increased, because of his constantly being attacked by the Church authorities and his successful fighting back.

But even beyond that, it must be recalled that although the December 18, 1979, move against Küng came as a total surprise to everyone, except those who planned and executed it (I was awakened at 4:30 A.M. on December 18 by a call from Ed Grace, the editor of *NTC News* in Rome, with the stunning news), the sense of repression and tension in the Catholic Church at that time was very strong. In the spring of 1979, the French Dominican Jacques Pohier was silenced and forbidden to say Mass because of his book *Quand je dis Dieu* (Editions du Seuil, 1978). In July 1979, the Vatican issued a condemnation of the book *Human Sexuality: New Directions in American Catholic Thought,* written by Anthony Kosnik and five other committee members of the Catholic Theological Society of America. In September 1979, Pope John Paul II told the Jesuits to be "more obedient"; a restrictive letter from Jesuit General Father Pedro Arrupe to all Jesuits resulted. Late in September 1979, John Paul II visited the United States and caused a great deal of consternation because of his many strongly worded conservative theological and disciplinary statements, particularly in the areas of sex, priestly celibacy, and women in the priesthood. In October 1979, Jesuit William Callahan was ordered from his post in Washington, D.C., because of his continued public support of the cause of women priests. Also that fall another American Jesuit, Robert Drinan, was ordered by the Pope not to run for elective office again (he had taken a legally nuanced stand on the question of abortion). Pressure had been building up against Father Edward Schille-beeckx during that summer and fall (he physically collapsed while teaching as a result), and finally on December 13–15, 1979, he was interrogated by the Doctrinal Congregation in Rome (only a year later did he receive a letter from the Vatican clearing him of the charges).

In preparation for that December 1979 hearing, thousands of signatures were gathered on petitions in Holland and elsewhere in support of Schillebeeckx. One such petition was also circulated in the United States among Catholic theologians and religious scholars, gathering hundreds of signatures to be sent to Cardinal Šeper. It stressed the need to shift from a restrictive to a dialogic mode of action on the part of Church authorities—a theme that was to appear time and again. It was as follows:

(97)
Catholic Petition to the Congregation of the Doctrine of the Faith Concerning Schillebeeckx and Methods of Procedure

Public attention has recently been drawn to the fact that a procedure against the theological writings of the Rev. Edward Schillebeeckx, O.P., has been instituted by the Congregation of the Doctrine of the Faith, and is about to culminate in a hearing in Rome, December 10–20, 1979.

Whereas, concerning Church renewal and reform, Vatican II stated that "all are led . . . wherever necessary, to under-take with vigor the task of renewal and reform," and that all

Catholics' "primary duty is to make a careful and honest appraisal of whatever needs to be renewed and done in the Catholic household itself,"[1] and,

Whereas, in working for this "continual reformation of which the Church always has need,"[2] "the search for truth, however, must be carried out in a manner that is appropriate to the dignity of the human person and his social nature, namely, by free enquiry with the help of teaching or instruction, communication and dialogue," and, that, "Truth can impose itself on the mind of man only in virtue of its own truth, which wins over the mind with both gentleness and power."[3]

Whereas, the present Pope, John Paul II, stressed the need he and his fellow bishops, and the whole Church, have for the work of theologians when he stated, "The Church needs her theologians, particularly in this time and age. . . . The Bishops of the Church . . . all need your [theologians'] work, your dedication and the fruits of your reflection. We desire to listen to you and we are eager to receive the valued assistance of your responsible scholarship,"[4] and,

Whereas, in the same statement to Catholic theologians and scholars Pope John Paul II repeated the need for fostering freedom of investigation when he said, "We will never tire of insisting on the eminent role of the university . . . a place of scientific research" which must apply "the highest standards of scientific research, constantly updating its methods and working instruments . . . in freedom of investigation,"[5] and,

Whereas, his predecessor Paul VI clearly pointed out in great detail that the most apt manner of discerning truth today is dialogue, noting among other things that "dialogue

[1] *Decree on Ecumenism,* no. 4.
[2] *Ibid.,* no. 6.
[3] *Declaration on Religious Liberty,* nos. 1–2.
[4] "Address to Catholic Theologians and Scholars at the Catholic University of America," October 7, 1979.
[5] *Ibid.*

is demanded . . . by the maturity humanity has reached this day and age,"[6] and,

Whereas, the Vatican Secretariat for Unbelievers, in likewise following this directive, officially stated that "all Christians should do their best to promote dialogue . . . as a duty of fraternal charity suited to our progressive and adult age,"[7] and carefully linked dialogue with Church renewal and freedom of investigation when it wrote, "The willingness to engage in dialogue is the measure and strength of that general renewal which must be carried out in the Church, which implies a still greater appreciation of liberty. . . . Doctrinal dialogue should be initiated with courage and sincerity, with the greatest freedom and with reverence,"[8]

Therefore, we the undersigned Catholic Theologians and religious scholars wish to express our deep concern about the function and methods of procedure of the Congregation of the Faith, not only in the case of Father Schillebeeckx, but in general.

In line with the above-cited conciliar, papal, and Vatican quotations, we believe that the function of any church leadership vis-à-vis theology should be not a negative but a positive one, and that consequently the function of the Congregation of the Doctrine of the Faith should be to *promote dialogue* among theologians of varying methodologies and approaches so that the most enlightening, helpful, and authentic expressions of theology could ultimately find acceptance.

Hence, we call upon the Congregation of the Doctrine of the Faith to eliminate from its procedures "hearings," and the like, substituting for them dialogues that would be either issue-oriented, or, if it is deemed important to focus on the work of a particular theologian, would bring together not only the theologian in question and the consultors of the Congregation of the Doctrine of the Faith, but also a worldwide selection of the best pertinent theological scholars of varying

[6] *Ecclesiam suam,* no. 79.
[7] *Humanae personae dignitatem,* August 28, 1968, no. 1.
[8] *Ibid.*

methodologies and approaches. These dialogues could well be conducted with the collaboration of the International Theological Commission, the Pontifical Biblical Commission, universities, theological faculties, and theological organizations. Thus, the best experts on the issues concerned would work until acceptable resolutions were arrived at. Such a procedure of course is by no means new; it is precisely the procedure utilized at the Second Vatican Council.

Finally, we call on the Congregation of the Doctrine of the Faith to turn the December 1979 "hearing" of Professor Schillebeeckx into just such an authentic dialogue, which instead of limiting will liberate all participants for the good of the whole Church.

EUROPE

Three days after the Schillebeeckx hearing in Rome the cloud burst over Küng, on December 18, 1979.

On the following day, December 19, a Committee for the Defense of Christian Rights in the Church was formed out of Tübingen on a German nationwide basis; it was ecumenical in makeup. The Committee issued a declaration the next day, December 20, which eventually was signed by 7,000 persons. It read as follows:

(98)

Christian rights in the Church are threatened. It is becoming ever clearer that arbitrary acts, injuries of fundamental rights, and authoritarian decisions are characterizing ecclesiastical styles of leadership. At the cost of the happiness of millions of men and women attempts are made to force through a particular understanding of the truth. That stands in clear contradiction to the liberating, bond-bursting message of Jesus Christ.

We were shocked to see how very much these inquisitorial

measures contradict the command of love and reconciliation of Jesus. Of course the Church cannot do without official proclamation. However, this proclamation is to serve the message of Jesus Christ and the faith of men and women, not, however, the self-affirmation of an elite.

We affirm that instead of realizing as Christian rights those fundamental rights of every man and woman which in exemplary fashion were won in the French Revolution, as would be appropriate to the Church's commission, the Church today is far from guaranteeing within its own area those rights which it has itself often proclaimed.

We demand therefore that there be no falling back behind the democratic fundamental rights of all men and women which were created by the Enlightenment, and in particular that there be no hindrance to freedom of opinion and freedom of conscience. We demand that there be no disciplining of critically thinking men and women, that there be no tolerating of procedures in which the authorities registering the complaint have all the rights and the charged person on the other hand has as good as none. We demand that there be no insistence upon dependency relationships which are based on authority, discipline, and obedience rather than upon collegiality and fraternity. We demand, therefore, that there be no offense against the commandment of tolerance and mutual respect.

First signers: Heinrich Albertz, Berlin; Josef Blank, Saarbrücken; Walter Dirks, Freiburg; Norbert Greinacher, Tübingen; Otto-Herbert Hajek, Stuttgart; Walter Jens, Tübingen; Ernst Käsemann, Tübingen; Johann Baptist Metz, Münster; Jürgen Moltmann, Tübingen; Rolf-Michael Schulze, in the name of "Reader Initiative *Publik*."

Greinacher and Haag printed the statements of some thirty-seven German organizations and groups in support of Küng. Three of those statements will have to suffice as a sampling here. On February 4, 1980, an open letter was published from ninety Catholic university professors (not on theological faculties) to their colleagues on the Catholic theological faculties, urging them to stand up for freedom and the other values that grew out of Vatican II and to support Küng. Ironically, it came only a day before the seven colleagues of Küng on the Tübingen Catholic Theology Faculty made their statement withdrawing their support from Küng (see above, pp. 439–44). Their statement was as follows:

(99)

Honored Colleagues!

In the name of countless Christians we Catholic academic teachers turn for help to you, which in the present situation can hardly be given by any other group of Christians:

Many men and women of our time have increasing difficulties in making the Christian faith as it is proclaimed by the official Church the basis of their lives. The change in our world of experience upon the one hand and the rigid holding to the formulations of faith which were formed by the thought of past epochs by the Church on the other hand, lead to a split of consciousness. Thus an increasing unease drives many Christians of all levels to a helpless distance from the Church and faith. Likewise for us academic teachers it is becoming ever more difficult to make understandable to our colleagues and students our attachment to the Church.

The Second Vatican Council indeed provided stimuli for an understanding and experience of the faith that was adapted to our times. However, unfortunately in recent years they have again largely been brought to a standstill. Instead of continuing further the difficult process of rethinking in common with the "laity" of varying levels of education, the official Church has in fact encouraged the polarization of "progressives" and "conservatives" feared by it through an anxious application of brakes. Verbal protestations and folklorist declarations of Catholic solidarity likewise cannot cover this up.

It must be acknowledged that a number of theologians have unmistakenly continued to work in the spirit of the Council. It is shocking, however, that these efforts often are not gratefully taken up by the ecclesiastical officials and transmitted further. Rather, they discriminate against the "intellectuals," therefore above all the theologians, and charge that they confuse "the simple ones." Therefore the latter are in need of the protection of the Church. In reality, however, the "simple ones" are kept simple through this "protection" and the thoughtful ones are restricted in that, in contradiction to the New Testament, they are tied to the "letter which binds and thus extinguishes the spirit which can enliven."

Nevertheless the hope of many laity is directed to you, the academic teachers of theology, who most of all must be recognized as competent experts by the Church leadership, especially if you stand up in common. To be sure, you must not take over the tactical style of the official Church. You must not through halfhearted "on the one hand—on the other hand" statements and involved formulations, which only the very few understand, conceal your real meaning. Speak out openly what most of you are thinking. Your statements, of course, can only then be convincing if they likewise are exemplified in the concrete situation.

The condemnation of Küng is such a situation. Küng unfortunately is not an "exceptional case." He has only aroused more attention in public than his predecessors because his books were written for a wider readership.

Put your small differences of opinion into the background. For the most part they are unavoidable and even productive. What is important here, however, is that the faulty decision of the Church leadership should become a learning process for everyone. Stand up for the freedom of research and teaching even in our Church—for everyone who thus clearly professes it, as does Küng. In the interest of the Church stand up to its leadership "face to face" as once Paul did to

Peter. Show your solidarity with the Tübingen Faculty and declare courageously:

The withdrawal of the teaching commission from Küng is not an infallible decision; it is not a responsible one, and must be repealed!

Nevertheless, the Catholic professors of theology were at work to fulfill their colleagues' request, and on February 12, 1980, they sent a letter to the President of the German Bishops' Conference, Cardinal Höffner, which by February 28, 1980, had 148 signatures. It was drafted by the faculty at Munich and the first signers were Professors Alfons Auer (Tübingen), Heinrich Fries (Munich), and Bernhard Welte (Freiburg). There is another irony in this, since Auer was one of the "Tübingen Seven." Their letter was as follows:

(100)

Very Honorable Cardinal,

Being aware of the responsibility to theology and the Church, the undersigned professors and dozents on the German Catholic theological faculties perceive it as their obligation to inform the Bishops of their deep disturbance and concern about the recent development in the relationship of the ecclesiastical officials to theology. Consequently we turn to you as the President of the German Bishops' Conference with this letter.

What fills us with the greatest concern is the coming change in the relationship of the Bishops to scholarly theology in general which has been expressed in connection with the measures taken in the Küng case and in various statements by the authorized representative of the Bishops' Conference. As the discussion in recent weeks both among the public and in the faculties makes clear, the developments threaten to lead to a crisis of trust between the teaching and proclaiming task of the Bishops and scholarly theology, which for all concerned would have profound consequences and therefore cannot be desired by anyone.

We appeal therefore to the Bishops from their side to undertake everything possible to meet the danger of such a crisis in trust. Without wishing to take a position on the theological statements which have been criticized by the Bishops, we would like to point out several viewpoints which appear to us to be of special importance for the relationship of the episcopal teaching office to theology:

1. In order to fulfill its task as a science, theology must be able to make unhindered use of the freedom to utilize all appropriate methods for the research and explanation of the faith. Of the freedom to follow the force of logic and data and to be able to follow the methods dictated by this force of logic and data there can never be too much. Its utilization can never be arbitrary. The task of the episcopal teaching office can, therefore, not be to prescribe or to recommend to theology specific methods, and to forbid others, but rather—if this should be necessary—by the power of office to indicate when an explanation resulting from this or that method cannot be viewed as a legitimate explanation of the authentic faith witnessed to in the belief of the Church and proclaimed by the Pope and Bishops.

Along with the declaration of 1979, signed by 1,360 theologians, on the "Freedom of Theology," we emphasize that "for us theologians this freedom goes hand in hand with the heavy responsibility not to jeopardize the genuine unity and the true peace of the Church and all its members." On the other hand, we must with the same Declaration confirm that we "wish to carry out our obligation to search out and speak the truth without being hampered by administrative measures and sanctions. We expect that our freedom will be respected whenever, to the best of our ability, we voice or publish our reasoned theological conviction."

2. Likewise the possibility to put forth and test hypotheses, to carry out controversies with reasons and arguments, and to correct and overcome errors through scholarly dispu-

tation—all of which belongs to the unrelinquishable freedom of theology—must be able to be claimed by theology in an unhindered fashion. The more unhindered the scholarly disputation can be, the more it will fend off subjective arbitrariness by the force of its strict argumentation and thereby serve the truth. Whoever recommends or imposes a limitation of the principle "Theologia disputat" takes from it the specific instrument of its finding the truth and causes it to fall short of that decisive step through which it had become a "science" in the thirteenth century.

Taught by the history of theology, we are convinced by the referred-to Declaration "that erroneous theological opinions cannot be disposed of through coercive measures. In our world they can be effectively corrected only by an unrestricted, objective, and scholarly discussion in which the truth will win the day by its own resources."

3. With emphasis we must point to the wide-ranging consequences which every limitation of the freedom of theology necessarily entails. These concern not only the service which theology in the explanation of the faith in contemporary times has to perform for the Church, but they affect in a special way likewise the ecumenical work and the status of theology in the university.

a. If Catholic theology no longer possesses the freedom to inquire from what is to what was, from the present to the origin in order to open up once again the lost possibilities of unity and union, the ground will be pulled out from underneath the ecumenical discussion of the theologians from the side of Catholic theology. With this, however, the ecumenical efforts of the Church in general lose their credibility; the developments to the present time would have to come to a standstill.

b. Its credibility as a science also depends on the freedom of theology in its methods and in unhindered argumentation and discussion. If this freedom comes into doubt in public, the most serious fears for the existence of the theological faculties at the state universities will be engendered. In giving up the place of theology in the university, however, the Church would be giving up an important possibility to realize the universal claim of the faith in an age which is formed by science, as is ours.

4. We acknowledge the teaching office of the Pope and the Bishops and accept the responsibility that is bound up with the teaching task of theologians; on the other hand, however, we likewise expect from the Bishops an appropriate confidence in this responsibility and a corresponding support of our work. We acknowledge that the Pope and the Bishops even in the most recent declarations have referred to the importance of theology and its justified and necessary freedom. It should, however, be possible to understand that without hesitation and without restrictions on the part of the bearers of ecclesiastical office. All the more do we regret it when measures are taken which by overstepping the proportionality of means threaten to push theology as a whole into a negative role and when these measures are justified by expressions which must awaken the appearance among the faithful that the teaching of theology is nothing other than a conglomerate of mutually contradicting subjective opinions —indeed, theology is a potential threat from which the teaching office must protect the simple faith. Theological research must not appear as something which runs counter to the necessary unity and the consent of the faith; such a placing in opposition would necessarily bring the truth claim of the faith itself along with the seeking of the truth by theology into discredit. Theology, which takes up and seeks to work out the difficult problems with which the faith today is confronted, is doing nothing other than its duty. It seeks to meet the confusion of the faithful. Therefore it needs the trust and the encouragement of all ecclesiastical office bearers and must be protected from the danger of being discredited in the eyes of the faithful.

5. As the most recent developments have shown, and as likewise the Bishops have admitted, the reform of the Roman

doctrinal procedures cannot be viewed as sufficient. We repeat, therefore, the suggestions of the above-cited Declaration and urgently request the Bishops to work further for a reform of the Roman procedures which will match the principles laid out in these suggestions. Only a procedure whose justice is clear to every person of good will is in a position appropriately to assure the credibility of the Church and theology.

Very Honored Cardinal,

The most recent developments awaken the impression that the Bishops' view of theology, despite some contrary statements, has changed enormously in comparison to the time of the Council. Likewise from Switzerland, Italy, France, and other countries we hear of great unrest over the changed style of ecclesiastical authority. It would be a disaster if this represented the beginning of a process which led back behind that which the Second Vatican Council and the decades-long responsible work of theologians had accomplished. Therefore, we plead with the German Bishops to do everything possible to roll back the consequences which have resulted from the most recent developments and to give back to theology that status without which the theologians cannot responsibly perform their work for the welfare of men and women in the Church and the world.

The Executive Committee of the Theological Council of the Diocese of Rottenburg went through an immense amount of work analyzing all the documentation they could obtain—and it was much—with the result that they made the following detailed statement in support of Küng:

(101)

The Executive Committee of the Theological Council of the Diocese of Rottenburg-Stuttgart has since the announcement of the withdrawal of the *Missio canonica* from

Professor Dr. Hans Küng intensively concerned itself with the procedures and documentation.

From this there arose a documentation which was made available to all the students of the Catholic Theology Faculty at the University of Tübingen and against whose background the majority of the Executive Committee, and those co-signers who follow, make the following statement:

1. The analysis of the background of events which led to the withdrawal of the *Missio canonica* from Professor Hans Küng allow us to view the procedure of the Doctrinal Congregation and the German Bishops' Conference as an example of today's self-understanding of the Church office: In the manner and form of the procedure of the Doctrinal Congregation inquisitorial characteristics become apparent, and the relationships between the diocesan church, national Bishops' Conference, and the curial agencies in a tragic manner are shown to be a relationship of dependence. Fraternal collaboration appears impossible. In a procedure that is to be characterized as secretive diplomacy the final steps against Hans Küng were prepared in a secret conference in Brussels by representatives of the German Bishops' Conference and the Curia.

Cardinal Ratzinger appeared in prophetic fashion to have already anticipated the measures against Küng four weeks beforehand when he denied him the right to teach the Catholic faith even before the withdrawal of the *Missio*. The victim himself was notified of the decision at the same time as it was made public, namely, at a time when the Christian communities prepared themselves for Christmas, the Feast of Peace. For the thereby prepared un-peace and uncertainty the Bishops and the curial authorities alone bear the responsibility.

2. We register outrage at the manner of working of the Congregation for the Doctrine of the Faith. In an administrative procedure it has made a decision which for Professor Küng has consequences that are like very serious penal procedures. Likewise in this procedure important legal guaran-

tees which correspond to a modern sense of justice—which despite previous manifold criticism were not contained in the order of procedure itself—were neglected.

This is especially the case in the missing right of access to documents, the court-like interrogation character of the colloquium, the keeping secret of the stages of the proceedings from the victim and from the competent local bishop, and the less than clear function of the "mandatory defender" (Relator pro auctore).

In view of the dispute between the ecclesiastical teaching office and theology as a science, the "Küng affair" points to an intensified action by the Roman doctrinal authorities against unliked theologians which raises the question: who is likely to be the next?

Likewise the massive intervention by the President of the German Bishops' Conference in concert with Rome shows that the greater independence of the local churches and their leaders which was demanded by Vatican II is ever more being lost in favor of a centralized and curial power.

3. The investigation of the *Documentation* of the German Bishops' Conference in comparison with the documentation published by Walter Jens reveals how one-sidedly and thereby irresponsibly the public has been informed about the background of the withdrawal of the *Missio canonica* by the German Bishops.

a. Indeed, with an overview of the documentation to the Küng case from the Secretariat of the German Bishops the reader has the impression that in the whole dispute only one side (namely, that of the German Bishops' Conference and the Doctrinal Congregation) has concerned itself with an objective clarification, while the other side (that of Professor Küng) has characterized itself by a stubborn holding on to its "errors." Already the selection alone from the letters of Küng, which are placed in a tendentious context—and in one case (nolens volens) a quotation is even falsified (in the *Documentation* of the German Bishops' Conference of December 18, 1979, in the overview page 5) which gives the reader the impression that Küng views himself as infallible—provides a key to the view of the editor.

b. The reader is supposed to have been given the impression that Hans Küng was the only one who ever demanded a just proceedings, although Cardinal Döpfner and many colleagues of Professor Küng had already stood up for such.

c. In addition, the impression which is given by the *Documentation* of the German Bishops' Conference—that Professor Küng has not shown himself open and ready to discuss clarifications, deepenings, expansions, and precisions of his theological positions—is false.

Our doubts about the legality of the proceedings and their credibility against Professor Küng are increased still further when we compare the reasons of the German Bishops' Conference and those of the Doctrinal Congregation for the withdrawal of the *Missio canonica*.

It is evident that in the reasons given by the German Bishops' Conference substantive theological questions are introduced which for their part were not the object of a proceedings of the Doctrinal Congregation. This raises in us the question of who in the German Bishops' Conference had an interest in connecting his own theological conceptions with the proceedings of the Doctrinal Congregation against Küng but to conceal this in public.

This concrete case and the declarations concerning it show again very clearly that the teaching office understands itself as the *only* preserver and protector of the full truth of the deposit of the faith. In the Declaration of the Doctrinal Congregation of December 18, 1979, it appears that the concepts "teaching office," "Church," and "teaching office of the Church" vary in their significance; obviously, they are in part used synonymously. Behind this there stands a restricted concept of the theology of the teaching office which is construed in the narrowest possible understanding of the Church—almost even limited to the "papal teaching office."

Theology according to this model is only a handmaiden of the teaching office and is *absolutely* bound to the hierarchical office as the source of truth and the source of external as well as internal norms. Thus it is clear why theology can be guarded over formally as well in content and why every individual judgment which is grounded in individual theological research is a private opinion which needs be erroneous (and thereby presents a breach of loyalty with the teaching office) as long as it is not held to be true by the teaching office, the sole protector of the truth.

However: this delegation model (theology exists only as delegated by the teaching office) totally limits theology as a science, that is, with freedom for research and teaching, and does not allow it critically and repeatedly and on its own theological self-responsibility to engage in efforts to find the truth and also announce its results. The question is not about the independence of theology from the Church and the teaching office, but rather about the with-for-and-in-one-another of theology and of the teaching office and the Church on the basis of dialogue.

They are, therefore, two fundamentally different starting points according to the basic question of *norms:* according to one, the truth, which must be believed, has manifested itself once and for all in the teaching office, while the other seeks to take seriously men and women in their history, their seeking and erring, their existential being, and ask what can the Christian message of Jesus Christ mean for each of these and how can the Church look out for it; it attempts to make this understandable, able to be questioned, and thereby likewise credible, in a language appropriate to the times. Regarding the teaching office in the Church the question is raised whether its representatives are in a position to perceive precisely this task. The insidious leakage of members from the Church and the increasingly difficult pastoral situation in the parishes themselves find, in our opinion, a cause not least in the fact that the teaching office is not capable of making the deposit of the faith in the Church understandable. Here the consequences of a "welfare-church" which does not take the individual believer as subject sufficiently seriously become clear.

4. The withdrawal of the *Missio canonica* from Professor Küng reminds us of our own experiences with the German Bishops' Conference and individual Ordinaries: the increasing bureaucratization and regimentation which substitutes for dialogue, the hindering of hopeful initiatives in the *oikoumene*) e.g., in the university parishes), the increasing tendency toward uniformity (see the guidelines for pastoral service), and the mistrust of engaged critical Christians which shows effects even in the recruitment procedures for ecclesiastical service.

It is not only individual cases which shock us, but rather the backward-oriented "law-and-order attitude" which strikes at the entire Church.

Of course it should not be overlooked here that there are hopeful beginnings of churchly cooperation (joint synods of the bishoprics in the Federal Republic of Germany, employment training courses of individual dioceses).

5. All this makes clear in a drastic way how far we in the Church are from what was decided upon in the Second Vatican Council and in the Common Synod of the bishoprics as a path indicator. The Second Vatican Council had defined the Church as a fraternal community and the People of God. "The entire community and every member thereof participate in the task of the Church to be bearers of the saving mission of Christ. From the common responsibility no one can exclude himself or be excluded" (Common Synod).

The procedure of the German Bishops' Conference and the Doctrinal Congregation and the image of the Church sought for in the ecclesiastical public as a business with business regulations, reduce, however, the Church to a caricature of what it really ought to be.

Therefore the actions leading to the withdrawal of the *Mis-*

sio canonica are an occasion for us to proclaim anew the liberating message of the Gospel in society and Church.

In addition to the statements of support for Küng by the Catholic Theology Faculty of Tübingen given above, and the letter drafted by the Catholic Theology Faculty of the University of Munich and signed by 148 Catholic theology professors, also given above, four other Catholic theological faculties in Germany issued public statements of support for Küng; they were Paderborn, Münster, Bonn, and Mainz. Three Protestant theological faculties in Germany also issued public statements of support for Küng: Tübingen, Marburg, and Hamburg.

But probably the most vigorous reply in Germany came from the Society of University Theologians in an open letter dated January 20, 1980. Theirs was not the language of diplomacy. Rather, it was straightforward and unvarnished. They were obviously furious and wanted to communicate that "reasoned" anger, which they did rather effectively, as follows:

(102)

The membership assembly of the AGT [Arbeitsgemeinschaft der Theologen—Society of University Theologians of West Germany] during its conference of January 18–20, 1980, concerned itself with the events surrounding Professor Küng. We consequently formed the following opinion:

1. The Congregation for the Doctrine of the Faith, the President of the German Bishops' Conference, Cardinal Höffner, and Bishop Dr. Georg Moser of the Diocese of Rottenburg-Stuttgart informed the public of the withdrawal of the *Missio canonica* from Professor Küng on December 18.

The withdrawal of the teaching commission shortly before Christmas was obviously designed to hinder effective protests and perverted the meaning of the Christian feast of love and reconciliation.

2. In the events surrounding Professor Küng it became

clear to us that the matter concerns not only the person of
Küng, but rather clearly sets forth a model procedure which
touches upon the teaching office in its relationship to theological research, reveals the manner of working of the Congregation for the Doctrine of the Faith, and provides an
insight into the connection between the local church and
curial agencies.

3. We register with outrage the manner of working of the
Congregation for the Doctrine of the Faith, which in a quite
transparent formalized administrative procedure arrived at a
decision which has extremely serious consequences for Professor Küng that are very like a penal proceedings in nature.
Despite manifold criticism, again in this proceedings important legal guarantees have been left out of consideration
which correspond to the modern sense of rights, thereby
doing injury to human rights. This is true especially concerning the lack of the right of access to documents, the manner
and meaning of the "colloquium," which has been proven to
have the character of an interrogation, the keeping secret
from the accused and the competent local bishop portions of
the proceedings, the function and manner of operating of the
"Relator pro auctore," to name only a few points.

4. We feel as especially shameful for the universal Church
the self-aggrandizing presentation of the Bishops as it is expressed in the introduction to the *Documentation* [*The Küng
Dialogue,* in English] and in the documentation itself. After
the introduction it is difficult for readers to study the documentation without prejudice and to form their own opinions,
especially also because it is not complete. (Thus, for the faithful the impression is created that with Küng one is dealing
with a stubborn man who rejects all dialogue, who believes
himself to have gathered together all truth—cf. the incorrect
citation from one of Küng's letters, enclosure 34, in the introduction to the above-named *Documentation:* "by the authority of God . . ." The claim that Küng by his theses and behavior confuses the simple Catholic is projected back onto
the Bishops themselves through this dishonest politics of in-

formation. In addition, it appears to us that the comparison of Küng with the Nazi ideologue Rosenberg by Cardinal Höffner is quite unmatchable in lack of taste.)

This manner of presentation of facts is in danger of obscuring the problematics, for example, of the colloquia with their inquisitorial characteristics and of weighting unevenly the conclusions of the proceedings against Professor Küng.

It is nevertheless clear that Professor Küng has put forth effort to engage in genuine dialogues with the Bishops, that he has had dialogues, that he has presented very nuanced positions on theologically disputed questions and that the episcopal dialogue partners persisted in a rigid discussion of formularies.

5. We are astonished at the differing bases for argumentation by the Congregation for the Doctrine of the Faith and by the German Bishops' Conference.

In distinction to the Doctrinal Congregation, the statement of the German Bishops' Conference speaks primarily of christological, mariological, and ecclesiological questions, which on the other hand were not the objects of a proper proceedings by the Doctrinal Congregation. This increases our doubts about the legality of the actions undertaken against Professor Küng and their credibility.

6. The statement of the German Bishops' Conference in their Pulpit Statement that a theologian may not place Church statements in doubt means the end of all theology and of the historical development of proclamation in the Church. The theologian will be turned into someone who simplistically explains what the authorities issue in magisterial statements. The further theological development of the heritage of the faith is blocked.

7. The question is posed in reference to the teaching office of the Church whether the responsible persons are capable of carrying out this task.

The gradually increasing drainage of members from the Church, the increasingly difficult pastoral situation in the parishes themselves, have as a cause, in our opinion, in no small measure the fact that the contemporary bearers of the teaching office are not capable of proclaiming understandably the heritage of the faith in the Church. Here the consequences of a Welfare Church, which has not taken the individual believer as a subject sufficiently seriously, are becoming apparent. We are consequently of the opinion that those leaders have through their actions in the Küng affair, that is, in the manner and way they went about the withdrawal of his *Missio canonica,* seriously endangered the peace of the community and made a constructive solution to existing serious questions in the Church more difficult.

The Roman Doctrinal Congregation and the German Bishops must bear the responsibility for the damage which through their actions they have inflicted on and in the Church.

As indicated above, Greinacher and Haag reprinted dozens of lengthy articles of support for Küng in German newspapers and journals. Let a relatively brief article serve as an example of the rest. It was written by Professor Heinrich Fries, newly retired professor of fundamental and ecumenical theology of the Catholic Theology Faculty of the University of Munich. It was published in the *Süddeutsche Zeitung* (Munich), the *Frankfurter Allgemeine Zeitung,* and *Commonweal* (New York). It should be recalled that although Küng was Fries's successor at Tübingen, Fries did contribute a critical essay in the collection edited by Rahner against Küng's *Infallible?,* and that Fries has the reputation of being a moderate liberal. It might also be mentioned that Fries likewise wrote a personal letter in Küng's behalf to the Pope, the sort of thing he had never done before. His article was as follows:

(103)
Hans Küng: A Witness of the Christian Faith

Among the reasons given for the Vatican's withdrawal of Professor Hans Küng's teaching authorization as a Catholic theologian two are particularly mentioned: that his writings and teaching "cause confusion among the faithful" and that they "depart from the full integrity of Catholic teaching."

For my part I do not wish to defend or justify all the utterances made or steps taken by Hans Küng—he is a controversial, discomforting, and provocative theologian. Nonetheless I ask myself whether the conclusions drawn were "unavoidable," and whether "there was no longer any other way out," especially since in recent times it had grown quiet around Küng.

Concerning the decision made I have the following reflections:

1. Alongside the faithful who feel themselves made uneasy by Küng, one cannot overlook the extremely large number of those who have found an authentic assistance to their faith in Küng's books, especially *On Being a Christian* and *Does God Exist?* They have been strengthened in their faith and have found a new and credible approach to its understanding and assimilation. These two books have become a genuine and precious treasure for many pastors, religion teachers, and preachers—that is especially true if one reads what is written instead of constantly looking for what is missing!

2. Through word and writing Küng reaches people in general and Christians who are situated on the fringes of the churches, who have distanced themselves from the Christian faith and who take a critical stance over against the Church —persons who hardly take notice of Church proclamations. When such people read Küng's books—how many that is is indicated by the hundreds of thousands of copies printed— they obviously do not do so in order to take final leave of their faith and Church, but rather to find a way again to re-establish contact with the reality of their faith. And has Küng not given many the courage to believe in God and to be a Christian? Has he not provided many motives and arguments for "why one should remain in the Church"?

How will all these people react to the measures taken against Küng? Will they not be confused and dismayed? Can one dismiss this question with the remark sometimes heard: let them go, good riddance! Can the Catholic Church, which since Vatican II—the greatest event in its recent history—has committed itself to the task of dialogue, encounter, and open approach to humanity, to the whole world, do such?

3. The open, discomforting, and critical questions which Küng poses—to be sure, at times aggressively and importunately—were not invented by him; he simply calls the existing problems by their names. And he is of the indisputably correct opinion that questions will not be answered by silence and prohibitions.

4. Should one be glad or irritated that, for example, Küng gave a lecture on the question of God in Peking, that his book *Does God Exist?* is translated, read, and discussed in Russia—and not to strengthen atheism, but to treat it critically and to open doors to faith? Is Küng here not performing a pastoral and missionary service—as a witness of the Christian faith?

5. Küng's interpretation of the infallibility of the Church's teaching office as it was formulated at Vatican I (1870) has been particularly criticized. I myself wrote an essay critical of Küng's interpretation in the volume edited by Karl Rahner on the problem of infallibility. Nevertheless, the following should be noted: If upon the initiative of Pope John Paul II intensive conversations with the Orthodox should be taken up, if the Pope hopes that unity with the Churches of the East will come to pass by the beginning of the next millennium, then the themes which were formulated at Vatican I will have to undergo an inquiry even more comprehensive than as formulated by Küng. For Vatican I divides the Church of the East from the Church of the West to this very day.

6. Has the Church become so narrow and anxiety-ridden in 1979 that—despite many justified criticisms—it can no longer accept the theologian Hans Küng as a theologian?

And is the same Church so prodigally rich in talent and theologians whose voice is heard throughout the whole world that it can without hesitation afford to dispense with Hans Küng?

If possible, the public outcry in Küng's native Switzerland was even more supportive of Küng. A Catholic base community in Lucerne, near Küng's home town and where he went to the Gymnasium, issued an open letter to the Swiss Bishops' Conference which by the end of February 1980 had 15,500 signatures. It was as follows:

(104)

Very Honored Bishops,

We are stunned by the decision of the official Church against Professor Hans Küng.

We are enraged by the authoritarian procedure and the misuse of power in order to silence an uncomfortable theologian by the withdrawal of the teaching commission.

We are dismayed that a Church which preaches love and peace behaves absolutely intolerantly in its decisions concerning those who think differently.

We are troubled that this Church through such machinations becomes unbelievable as an advocate of human rights.

In our protest we find ourselves bound together with all those Christians who wish that they might be free in their Church to express their opinions and feelings.

We are counting on you, the Swiss Bishops, to deliver our protest to Rome and there to intervene for the conversation of human rights in the Church.

Still another declaration was circulated in Switzerland and gained 9,162 signatures by January 25, 1980. It was sent to Cardinal Šeper, with copies to the German and Swiss Bishops' Conferences. It was as follows:

(105)

1. The undersigned have learned with dismay that the Swiss theology professor and former conciliar *peritus* Hans Küng has had his ecclesiastical commission to teach on the Catholic Theology Faculty of the University of Tübingen withdrawn by the Vatican.

2. They protest against the way and manner of this procedure. Neither the Swiss Bishops nor Hans Küng himself knew of this "night and fog operation" shortly before Christmas. To silence uncomfortable theologians by such—inquisitorial—procedures makes non-credible a Church which in the world public stands up for human rights.

3. Hans Küng offered with his theological work help for all those who wish to be responsible about and deepen their faith in contemporary times. The silencing of his tongue will impair many. Likewise the hopes which the Second Vatican Council had awakened in seeking Christians have been destroyed.

4. The procedure against Hans Küng, moreover, contributes to the creation in the Catholic Church of a climate of fear and repression which hinders every free expression of opinion.

5. All circles which were seriously concerned with the *oikoumene* and had found in Hans Küng an engaged battler for their concerns will be struck a serious blow.

6. The undersigned demand that the measures against Hans Küng be repealed.

The Association for the Concerns of the Council and Synod issued a declaration in the middle of January 1980. It was as follows:

(106)

Approximately a thousand men and women took part in the work of "Synod 72." Beyond this group there was a large number of Christians who were interested and engaged. Many see the basis of their working in the Church and their Christian co-responsibility in the texts of the Council and the Synod.

Various events and developments within the Church at the end of the seventies have led these Christians to fear that their concerns and their engagement will be disillusioned and will come to nothing. One sign of this is the many questions, statements, and events occasioned by the Küng affair.

The Association for the Concerns of the Council and Synod suggests the following viewpoints for the continued discussion in this situation:

Objectivity, yes, but without one side claiming ahead of time a monopoly on objectivity for itself.

Polarization, no, but no obscuring, but rather clearly defined positions.

Unity, yes, but without a pseudo-equality and absorption of various insights and paths to a common truth of faith.

Reconciliation, yes, but without cooptations and emotional compromises.

Responsibility for community, yes, but in the manner of a creative joint participation.

The Association for the Concerns of the Council and Synod is of the opinion that the expression of disappointed feelings and hopes provides a chance for the Church to be responsible and critical. In the future this should be utilized for the task of the Church in the world. For this it is necessary that the Church leadership seriously enter into the situation of those Christians who must live out their faith in various areas of responsibility (e.g., pastoral work, education, politics, culture). Concretely in the case of Küng the Association suggests that the debate about the continuity of truth and its conservation be intensively and honestly carried out in all areas of Church education and public work. "An objective decision can likewise in the Church in most cases be made only after a public opinion has been formed. The spirit of God can be effective in an open and public formation of opinion among consciously responsible Christians as well in the decisions of

officials" (Synod of the Bishopric of Basel, *Kirche heute,*
7.16). In initiatives to attain a new form of ecclesiastical
doctrinal procedures all the principles of justice should be observed (especially the principles of subsidiarity, appropriate
justice, and proportionality).

The Association, which constituted itself in the face of the
present situation, pursues especially the following goal: to
provide the concerns of the Council and Synod a hearing
in the eighties, to bring them into appropriate discussions,
to collaborate in their realization, and thereby to support the
Church leadership.

Support for Küng from the theology professors in Switzerland
was also very strong. Fifty Catholic theology professors and
dozents issued the following declaration:

(107)

The undersigned professors and dozents of the Swiss Catholic theological faculties are concerned in the extreme by the
decision of the Roman teaching office that Professor Hans
Küng can neither be viewed as a Catholic theologian nor
teach as one. Above all they feel that their trust in the
Church leadership has been made uncertain by the manner
and timing of the procedure. In connection with other doctrinal procedures, this case appears to them to give grounds for
a concern that free discussion in theology will be enormously
limited in the future. They do not believe that solidarity and
unity in the Church can be assured by disciplinary measures.
The hope which has grown up in the Church since the Council and the Synod for a fraternal dialogue appears to them to
be endangered. The emphasis on the obligation of Catholic
theologians to the truth of the faith as conserved by the teaching office appears to them one-sided when thereby the obligation to reflect on the pressing questions of men and women
in the Church and to sustain the vitality of the faith is forgotten. However one may evaluate his theses individually, Pro-

fessor Küng in his widely effective publications made an indisputable contribution to bringing men and women nearer again to the Church. He has fostered the ecumenical dialogue as it has otherwise been sought by the Church. If one investigates his writings from the viewpoint of the danger for the life of faith, then one must also observe them from the viewpoint of the chances they have opened for a language of the faith which is close to life and relevant to the present.

The undersigned theologians therefore request the Swiss Bishops to work so that an appeal by Professor Küng in Rome will lead to a new review of the decision.

The following declaration signed by eighty-five professors and dozents of the Protestant theological faculties of Basel, Bern, Geneva, Lausanne, Neuchâtel, and Zurich—82 percent of the entire theology faculty—was issued on January 31, 1980:

(108)

The undersigned professors and dozents of the Swiss Protestant theological faculties have noted with concern the withdrawal of the ecclesiastical teaching commission from Professor Hans Küng decreed by Rome.

Precisely because the ecumenical obligation and solidarity has become important in our theological work we cannot here remain indifferent spectators. We are all the more concerned that the procedure against Hans Küng will necessarily bring with it a regretfully negative effect on the ecumenical climate in our land. With us Hans Küng is in wide circles the best-known exponent of the ecumenical opening in the Roman Catholic Church. Consequently he has always encountered us Protestants in dialogue with a clear emphasis on his being a Catholic theologian. He has likewise often put critical and challenging questions to us from his Catholic conviction. Precisely thereby has he fructified and advanced the ecumenical dialogue in our country. The ecclesiastical teaching prohibition decreed against him threatens to cripple

the freedom and openness of theological research and ecumenical practice.

We assure Hans Küng of our ecumenical solidarity.

We place ourselves at the side of our Roman Catholic colleagues in the Swiss theological faculties in their statements
concerning the reprimand of Hans Küng. We request the
Swiss Bishops to do everything possible so that the ecumenical dialogue and ecumenical cooperation in our country will
not suffer permanent damage.

Beyond all this, Greinacher and Haag reproduced the supportive
statements of four other Swiss organizations—Swiss artists, Swiss
writers, and two different groups of Catholic seminarians.

As mentioned above, a 200-page book of letters, etc., in support of Küng from Austria alone was later published. In addition
Greinacher and Haag reported the formation of four separate
Austrian groups: the Salzburg Initiative of Christians for Truth
and Openness in the Church, the Christian Initiative for Truth
and Peace (Linz), the Christian Initiative for Dialogue and Reconciliation (Graz), and a Viennese group. All four groups
gathered signatures for the same declaration, which follows, although 1,660 persons from the Graz Initiative also sent a strong
letter of support for Küng to their bishop on June 10, 1980. The
Linz Initiative alone had gathered 2,500 signatures by February
25, 1980.

(109)

Out of care and responsibility for the Christian faith the
undersigned regret the manner of procedure of the Roman
Doctrinal Congregation against the theology professor Hans
Küng.

Professor Küng, through his writings and lectures, through
his open criticism, but also through his clear confession to
the Church, has been for many seeking and critically thinking men and women a hopeful sign that they likewise could

have a place in the Catholic Church. Through him many alienated Christians found an approach to the Christian faith.

There can be various opinions concerning the theological statements of Küng and his personal attitude toward Rome, and there should be debate about this.

"Truth is the basis of peace" (John Paul II in his Christmas message of 1979). We believe that the truth cannot be assured through Roman disciplinary measures, but rather lets itself be found in a free and intensive exchange. We view the measures against Küng as a step backward from the Council. We reject, therefore, such a manner of proceeding because it serves neither the truth nor peace.

(Contact person is Anton Weiss, Eisteichgasse 25, A-8010 Graz, Austria)

From Holland, besides various individual initiatives, a declaration of support for Küng was issued by professors from the various faculties of the Catholic University of Nijmegen—which had also recently vigorously supported one of its own theologians: Schillebeeckx. They issued the following declaration with seventy-three signatures on December 20, 1979:

(110)

The Theology Faculty does not believe it is its task continually to react publicly to the changing current questions. Now, however, since it is so soon after the affair of one of its own professors that a renowned sister Faculty is struck by the measures of the Doctrinal Congregation, silence by us could be falsely interpreted.

Therefore the undersigned feel themselves compelled to make the following declaration:

1. that they view the critical function of theology as a modest but necessary contribution to the passage of the People of God through history;

2. that they therefore do not share the view that conse-

quently their colleague Küng is not to be considered a Catholic theologian;

3. that they acknowledge that the manner in which H. Küng and the Congregation for the Doctrine of the Faith related with each other can be criticized;

4. that they see in the manner of proceeding a threat to the credibility of the Roman Catholic Church;

5. that they are of the opinion that time and energy could be better utilized and that therefore they wish to conduct theological scholarship in the future as a liberating service to the women and men of today.

In France protest and reform groups of Catholics have been in existence for some years, as well as over five hundred base communities. It was from the banding together of a number of the latter that an invitation was issued to Küng to lecture in April 1980, specifically as a "Catholic theologian," which he did. Since that time a French Committee for the Defense of the Rights of Christians in the Church was formed (contact person is Richard Walther, 68 Rue de Babylone, 75007 Paris, France). Earlier, on January 28, 1980, the members of both the Catholic and Protestant theology faculties at the University of Strasbourg issued a strong declaration in support of Küng which was signed by seventeen members of the Catholic Theology Faculty and thirteen members of the Protestant Theology Faculty. It was as follows:

(111)

Prompted by the measures against Hans Küng and the currently conducted proceedings against other Catholic theologians, we theologians of the Faculties of Catholic and of Protestant Theology of the University of Strasbourg declare the following:

1. We confirm the necessity of free and responsible theological work.

A critical reflection within the area of faith is necessary since the experience of faith is deeply woven in human culture. Precisely because the assent of faith is essentially free, and in the name of the Gospel, upon which our Churches call, we believe: This striving toward insight and critical evaluation must be able to develop itself freely. The university to which we belong appears to us as one of the privileged places for such research. There is, however, in our conviction, no intellectual freedom without responsibility. Theology is prepared to be responsible for its doctrinal opinions equally before public opinion, vis-à-vis other researchers, and in the midst of the entire Christian community. It recognizes particularly that in every Church there are legitimate agencies of order which stand in the service of a faithful confession of the faith.

2. We are disturbed by the fact that in the Catholic Church there are still certain proceedings which try to hold theological research under control. Concerning the proceedings as the Roman Doctrinal Congregation perceives them we regret especially:

   a. that the accused are denied access to their documents,
   b. that they cannot have themselves represented by a defender of their choice,
   c. that they are not granted the right to be heard in person by their judges.

We demand a change in this procedure so that every right to defense will be observed, beginning with the recently censured theologians. More generally said: Free theological critique as the regulating court of first instance is to bear complete responsibility. The local church and its shepherds are confirmed in the full exercise of their responsibility.

3. We fear that the retention of the incriminating proceedings and the piling up of restrictive measures could lead to a severe backlash in ecumenical relations. Who can believe that the Catholic Church is sincere in its intentions about dialogue with the other Churches if within its own bosom such a dialogue is not practiced? How can a Church present itself as an ecumenical partner when its attitude is characterized by mistrust and fear? It is our hope that the dialogue between

the Churches continue; we are for our part determined to
apply our talents to this end.

4. We are concerned, indeed disturbed, about the lamenta-
ble burden with which the Christian witness in the world is
weighed down by the referred-to procedures. Everywhere
freedom finds itself threatened. The ideological conflicts are
increasingly embittered. How will the Church—not only
through words, but through deeds—bear witness in the future that it is faithful to the Gospel? Can it still be believed
that it is working for the coming of a new world if within itself the value of the person is undermined and if Christians
show themselves incapable of persevering through unavoidable conflicts?

Brief note should also be taken of an article by the most prestigious of all French theologians, Yves Congar. On January 2,
1980, he published a rather lengthy article on the Küng affair.
Most of it was a review of the developments from the writing of
The Church to the most recent events (one must remember that
Congar knew Küng well from Küng's student days in Rome and
then especially from the time of the Second Vatican Council
when they both were *periti* in Rome). On a more reflective level
Congar wrote the following:

(112)

These grave insufficiencies [the complaints about *On
Being a Christian*] have stimulated sometimes exaggerated
criticisms. We are dealing here with a book which in its rich-
ness, its power, its warmth can communicate to many a presentation of Christianity, indeed, even a strengthening of the
faith, and in fact it has so communicated. A strengthening of
the faith? Yes! Not to speak of the many standing hesitantly
on the periphery who in this way are drawn into faith. It
is for them first of all that Küng has written. . . . A cardinal
once said to me in 1964 or 1965 that Paul VI had remarked
to him: " 'I am searching for,' said the Holy Father, 'young

theologians who one day could assure the following of the older ones. I thought of Hans Küng, but he has too little love!'" I would not say that he is lacking in love, either for Christ or for the Church. In fact, he loves passionately, but not in the same manner as Paul VI, and also not—if you permit me to say—in the same manner as I. Küng's love expresses itself in his goal of absolute honesty vis-à-vis history and the needs of the time. They carry his study. They move him to formulate the expectations and hopes of the grass roots and to take up the painful questions of the Reformation and modern criticism.

Church of God, my Mother, what are you doing with this difficult child, my brother?

Even in Spain, where one might not have thought to look for strong support for Küng, fifty Catholic theologians published a supportive statement in *El País* (Madrid) on December 23, 1979. They noted that they could have secured many more signatures, but that they wished to hurry into print to express their immediate solidarity with Küng. Their text was as follows:

(113)

"Professor Küng, in his writings, has departed from the integral truth of Catholic faith, and therefore he can no longer be considered a Catholic theologian or function as such in a teaching role." With these words the Declaration of the Doctrinal Congregation refers to "some major points in the theological doctrine of Professor Hans Küng." In the face of this declaration affirmed by Pope John Paul II, we the undersigned[1] wish to express the following:

1. A respectful but vigorous protest against the methods of the Roman ecclesiastical authorities is to be brought forward. Professor Küng and the Catholic Theology Faculty of the

---

[1] The timing (Christmas) and our wish *immediately* to make known our solidarity with H. Küng prevented us from obtaining still many more theologians' agreement.

University of Tübingen, where he has taught for almost twenty years, learned of this action over the radio. We believe that both of them should have been informed previously.

We are also of the opinion that Professor Küng should have been given a final opportunity for a review of his position on the disputed points and also warned as to the consequences of a continued insistence on his point of view.

It is a contradiction if the Church authorities on the one hand proclaim human rights in society and on the other hand these rights are violated within the Church itself.

2. Although we acknowledge the value of the theological works of Küng, we do not *a priori* exclude the possibility that there could be points within it which would be in need of revision. However, we believe that the natural locus in which such possible defects are to be discerned and corrected is the forum of theological research. At the same time we do not exclude the possibility that under specific circumstances the teaching office might and should express its plenipotentiary and final word. However, that should take place only after the previous exhaustion of all other possibilities: dialogue, admonition, etc.

We believe that this has not been the case with Professor Küng. We believe rather that in his theological activity he has called upon the freedom of research which is an essential element of theology.

3. We fear that this manner of proceeding against Hans Küng and other theologians who have contributed to the work and realization of the Second Vatican Council at the same time runs contrary to the spirit of this very Council.

4. In view of the above we request that the Doctrinal Congregation review the "Küng case." We associate ourselves with the suggestion from Küng himself that an international theological commission be set up for the investigation of his case. Such a commission would be the appropriate organ for casting light on the disputed doctrinal opinions. Simply to

suppress in an authoritarian manner would certainly not contribute to giving "an account of our hope," as the first letter
of Peter demands (1 Pet. 3:15).

5. Professor Küng should know that, although we do not
present a blank check vis-à-vis all the points of his theology
(which he likewise would not expect), we feel ourselves in
solidarity with him in his personal drama.

We cannot in this moment forget either that in an extraordinary manner and fashion he has contributed to making the
Christian faith understandable and acceptable for many men
and women of our time. The manner of behavior of the ecclesiastical authorities toward him has caused confusion in
not a few of the faithful who had found stimulus and support
in his work. We would also like to call attention to his contribution to the ecumenical dialogue which by the condemnation of his theology will be severely injured.

6. Finally, the Catholic teaching office should also know
that it can rely on our honest and Gospel-true loyalty. Nevertheless, we commit ourselves not to a cheap loyalty which
says yes and amen to everything (for that indeed means not
to take the teaching office seriously), but rather one which responsible men and women who are capable of making decisions exercise, who rejoice when they can say yes, and
thereto speak a friendly no when they believe they must do
so according to their conscience and in the name of the Gospel.

Support for Küng from Poland is even more surprising. For over
ten years now there has existed in Poland a Movement of the
Common Way, a group of base communities inspired by a theology
professor, Father Gustav Klapuch—who has since been removed
from his teaching post and silenced. At present there are fifty
such base communities comprising around 1,500 persons. Their
focus is renewal and human rights in the Church. Since 1974,
they have regularly published a newsletter entitled *Nasza Droga*
(*Our Way*), which has been giving thorough coverage to the cases

of Pohier, Schillebeeckx, and especially Küng. (Contact person is Jozef Biskup, ul. Marchlewskiego 29 B, 42-600 Tarnowskie Gory, Poland.)

On the international level as such there were at least two significant statements of support for Küng, one Catholic and one Protestant and Orthodox, as it were. The first came from the directors of *Concilium,* that most prestigious international Catholic theological journal, which is published in six to eight languages (German, Dutch, English, French, Spanish, Italian, and sometimes Polish and Japanese) and of which Küng is a charter member. The brief text was as follows:

(114)

We, the directors of the international theological journal *Concilium,* see no solid basis for no longer viewing our colleague Hans Küng as a Catholic theologian. We wish to urge, therefore, a revision of the judgment.

Moreover, we demand that ecclesiastical procedures finally recognize the generally accepted human rights.

The second international support statement came from the World Council of Churches in Geneva. The WCC membership, of course, includes most of the world's Protestant and Orthodox Churches (270 member Churches). Very quickly, on December 19, 1979, the day after the Roman action against Küng, a spokesperson for the WCC made the following statement:

(115)

The dispute is in essence concerned with the issue of authority in the Church, which has become the most sensitive point in ecumenical theological discussion. The action taken against Professor Küng, therefore, cannot be regarded simply as an internal affair of the Roman Catholic Church, but has immediate ecumenical repercussions.

Already in 1973, when the Sacred Congregation for the Doctrine of the Faith published a "Declaration in Defense of the Catholic Doctrine on the Church Against Certain Errors of the Present Day" (*Mysterium ecclesiae*), the General Secretary of the World Council of Churches, Dr. Philip A. Potter, said in his report to Central Committee: "I regret the publication of this Declaration which seems, in its basic intention, to limit the search for new ways of understanding and expressing the Church's faith and life in the post-Vatican II climate and in a rapidly changing world. It will now be necessary to discover how far and in what manner we can together pursue theological discussions whether bilaterally or multilaterally."

The decision against Professor Küng highlights the urgent need for the WCC, and in all likelihood for the Churches which are in official dialogue with the Roman Catholic Church, to raise this fundamental issue with the Secretariat for Promoting Christian Unity of the Roman Curia.

Still further word on the matter came from the WCC when at the meeting of their Executive Committee, February 11–16, 1980, in Strasbourg, Philip Potter made an important speech regarding the Küng affair. According to the office of the WCC in Geneva, the text is not available, but the following is a report on it as found in *Le Figaro* (Paris), February 18, 1980:

(116)

In the course of his speech Potter directed fundamental questions to the Roman Catholic Church. First Potter praised the "new Pope" and stated that he was very satisfied with his many declarations about ecumenism: "He assured me personally of his enthusiasm for the search for the unity of the Church." On the theological, social, and other levels collaboration is developing satisfactorily. However, there are indications—like the Küng affair—that there are attitudes and statements of the Roman Church which in the eyes of

Potter call forth the most severe criticism and an express reserve. Above all he emphasized the intensification of the authority of the Pope and the Bishops. In this connection he stated: "This leads to the renewal again of all the questions which go back to the Reformation and which concern also our search for office."

In reference to the conversations of the Mixed Commission between Geneva and Rome, Potter underlined: "This Committee would have to know where we are going and above all how the statements of the Secretariat for Unity are to be harmonized with the decrees of the Holy Office.

Secondly, the General Secretary brought up the following problem: How can one express and confess a common faith, how can one progress in free theological research, how can one pose questions which divide Geneva and Rome in the new context, which context is a world in anxiety? "One cannot do it," he emphasized expressly, "simply by using the documents of the Second Vatican Council. One must ask oneself whether the Second Vatican Council was a door or whether it was a border, a barrier. We have the impression that the Second Vatican Council is perceived as the end of research. This is not the ecumenical style which we know. It is not the style of a living faith in the Holy Spirit who urges us forward."

Potter closed with the fundamental question which the World Council of Churches puts to itself and to Rome in view of the continuation of the dialogue: "What is the freedom of research, and what are its limits?"

AMERICA

Ever since the anti-Americanism and the anti-Modernism of Rome from around the turn of this century, the American Catholic hierarchy has not been characterized by a sense of independence vis-à-vis Rome. Moreover, the long years of dominance by Cardinal Spellman in the nominating of new bishops during the middle decades of this century produced an atmosphere on the highest levels of the American Catholic Church structure that was not welcoming of Catholic self-criticism. Only recently has that begun to change during the years of the Apostolic Delegate Jean Jadot, who just left his Washington post in 1980—but the bishops appointed during his term of office are still relatively young. Hence, the official structures of dissent have not been highly developed in the United States—as they have been, for example, in Holland. Nevertheless, there were many strong protests forthcoming from America, from both Catholics and non-Catholics.

At 4:30 A.M. Eastern Standard Time, on December 18, 1979, the news of the Vatican action against Küng was released to the world. As mentioned above, I was awakened with the news by a call from Rome—the international telephone lines were very busy for the next several days. Soon three of us, Father Charles Curran of the Catholic University in Washington, Father David Tracy of the University of Chicago Divinity School, and I, decided that it would be important to issue a brief statement of solidarity with Küng as quickly as possible. We divided the United States—really the eastern third only, with a few California exceptions—among us and gave ourselves some nineteen hours to gather signatures from fellow Catholic theologians over the telephone. Since the statement would have to be read over the phone, it had to be short and simple. The task was further complicated by the fact that an east coast snowstorm knocked out some university switchboards, leaving large gaps in the list of those we might have called. Nevertheless, within the allotted time we gathered the signatures of seventy-five American Catholic theologians, and on December 19, the day after Rome's action, we released the statement and signatures to the world press. Our accompanying explanatory note for the press was as follows:

(117)

As the coordinating team involved in this one-sentence statement, we recognize the need for long-term study and action concerning the issues in the Küng case, including the deplorable process. Because of the shortness of time and the season of the year, no effort was made to contact a large number of Roman Catholic theologians in North America. It was our intention only to indicate that a sufficient number of recognized and committed Roman Catholic theologians affirm that Hans Küng is indeed a Roman Catholic theologian.

Charles E. Curran
Leonard Swidler
David W. Tracy

The one-sentence statement signed by the seventy-five theologians was as follows:

We as concerned and committed Roman Catholic theologians, cognizant that no one of us necessarily agrees with the opinions on particular issues of any other Roman Catholic scholar including Hans Küng, publicly affirm our recognition that Hans Küng is indeed a Roman Catholic theologian.

There of course was a flood of coverage of the affair in the news media, including the Catholic press, and within it, many editorials. Let one be a sample here of those many. It takes a moderate stance, and was published by the editors of the moderate and highly respected Jesuit weekly *America* (January 5, 1980). The beginning and end are as follows:

(118)

For anyone who loves the church, the Vatican censure of Hans Küng can only be a cause of profound sadness. In declaring that Father Küng, one of the most successful contemporary apologists of the Christian faith, could "no longer be considered a Catholic theologian or function as such in a teaching role," the Sacred Congregation for the Doctrine of the Faith presumably sought to protect the unity of the church and the integrity of its doctrine. Ironically, its action will more likely result in bitter polarization rather than unity, and confusion rather than clarity about doctrine. For the chorus of protests from theologians in Europe and North America was preoccupied with the methods by which the Congregation had judged Father Küng. The actual doctrinal points at issue between the Vatican and Father Küng received only passing attention and were obscured in the uproar. . . .

But if the Congregation thought to reduce the influence of Father Küng's ideas by such an action, it misread the circumstances that affect the communication of ideas in today's culture. Father Küng's books will continue to be read; his lectures will, if anything, be even better attended despite the fact that his academic identification at the University of Tübingen may be redefined. If his theological conclusions are inconsistent with Catholic tradition, they will be challenged and criticized by other theologians as, in fact, they have been in the past. A genuine concern for ecumenical harmony is not served by stretching theological ambiguities in every direction. In seeking to establish its authority in doctrinal matters, the Congregation would have been better advised to depend on a rigorous and detailed criticism of Father Küng's ideas rather than an official condemnation that in today's world must appear repressive, will certainly prove ineffectual and invariably invests its subject with the mantle of the intellectual martyr.

The unity of the church and the integrity of its doctrine are essential to Catholic life, but they must be promoted by methods that reveal the face of the Gospel rather than distort it.

Many articles, letters to the editor, and the like appeared in the Catholic and general press in the ensuing weeks. Again, a systematic gathering and analysis of them would doubtless be revealing, but, as before, because of space limitations, one example will have to suffice. Father Andrew Greeley is a Catholic theologian and sociologist of immense influence. He has published over 100

books of his own and writes innumerable articles, including a
newspaper column which is syndicated all over the United States.
On March 23, 1980, he published the following syndicated newspaper column:

(119)

The melancholy thing about the Hans Küng affair is that it
proves you can still be condemned in the church not for what
you say, not even for what you claim you say, but for what
people say you say; and that you can be punished not for
what you are but for what people say you are.

Thus it is asserted by the German hierarchy that Küng is a
threat to the faith of the German people—an assertion which
is utterly without proof and is almost certainly false.

It is also said that his Christology denies the divinity of
Jesus. Küng asserts that he does not intend to deny the doctrine of the council of Chalcedon at all. Nonetheless he is
condemned, even though the "Christology from below" of
Karl Rahner is at least as much a development on the teaching of that ecumenical council as is the Christology of Küng.

Moreover those who purport to defend Küng (as for example Garry Wills) in the world press agree with the German hierarchy that he is stubborn, petulant, self-promoting,
and not very bright and also agree that he does not believe in
the traditional Christian doctrine of the divinity of Jesus.

With friends like Time, Newsweek and Garry Wills, Küng
doesn't need enemies.

The real Küng and his real teachings get lost in the welter
of controversy about what he is alleged to have said and
what kind of a person he is alleged to be.

I have marveled at the ability of even scholarly commentators to misinterpret and misunderstand what Küng writes. I
think part of his great suffering now comes from the fact that
his attempt at clarification—some of them very clear indeed
—produce even more misunderstanding. I don't think he yet

realizes that the misunderstanding is deliberate and in some cases malicious.

Nor is Küng the only victim of this distortion of teaching and distortion of personality. Every major Catholic thinker who has fallen under attack in the last 150 years, it seems to me, has been denounced not for what he taught but what people distorted him to have taught—Rosinini, Lacordaire and Newman in the last century; Teilhard, LaFarge, Congar, de Lubac in this century.

If you live long enough (as have de Lubac and Congar, and as Newman did) another generation comes along and is baffled as to why you were misunderstood. If you don't live long enough . . . well, too bad for you.

Let me illustrate the process with a controversy that erupted in the United States a few years ago. A prominent Jesuit theologian accused a prominent diocesan theologian of not believing in life after death. The reason? One of the diocesan theologian's good friends and colleagues didn't believe in it, and, in his writing, he had not mentioned the subject— even though none of his writings provided a situation where the subject could logically come up.

The diocesan priest responded first privately, then publicly, that of course he believed in life after death. Somehow this wasn't quite enough. While his critic said, somewhat superciliously, that he was glad to hear it, the tone indicated that he remained skeptical.

Priests all over the country say confidently that I don't like ordinary pastoral work. I reply that I love it and that I do it when I'm in Arizona, and would do it in Chicago if I could. My response doesn't matter; the distortion has been spoken and it stands.

Hans Küng has become an inkblot, a popular, handsome, successful, charismatic figure, who can be turned into whatever distortion that the envious, the petty, the small, the sick wish to make him. And few will stand up and say, "that's not what the man said!"

Even the great Karl Rahner remains dispicably quiet when
Küng the teacher and Küng the person are distorted beyond
all charity, all justice and all reason. And many of the not-
great cheer wildly to see someone whose success they envy
and despise torn down. As a nun who was hassling Küng at
an international meeting 10 years ago said to me, "It's not
every day that someone unimportant gets a chance to put the
great Hans Küng in the corner."

She was more honest than most.

I have known Küng for a long time. He is not the man either his critics or his defenders say he is. He is, rather, gen-
tle, sensitive, conservative and deeply committed to the
church (has no one read his paper on the obligation to attend Sunday Mass?). He believes in the resurrection, in the
divinity, in all the traditional Catholic teachings.

Even on the highly controversial infallibility question he
has merely raised topics for discussion—most of which have
never been discussed since his rivals have been too busy
denouncing him to bother to listen, much less reply.

So is he or is he not a "catholic" theologian?

The Hans Küng who was condemned by the Holy office
and defended by left-handed compliments in much of the
world press is, I quite agree, not a Catholic theologian.

But that man doesn't exist.

The real Hans Küng, read objectively and in context, is
not the man who was condemned.

Finally, it all comes to what another churchman said
recently: "What can one say of the practice of combatting or
silencing those who do not share the same views by labeling
them as enemies, attributing to them hostile intentions and
using skillful and constant propaganda to brand them as aggressive?"

The man who said it was John Paul II. He said it the same
day that Küng was condemned.

I can't figure it out either.

Various petitions were drawn up in support of Küng on local
and regional bases. Again, one sample will have to suffice. It came

from the eastern Pennsylvania–southern New Jersey area, and was a typical grass-roots initiative. It gathered 169 signatures and was in the form of a letter to Cardinal Šeper, dated January 28, 1980. It read as follows:

(120)

Dear Cardinal Šeper:

We Roman Catholics of the Philadelphia, Camden, and Trenton dioceses are deeply disturbed by the recent restrictive actions of the Vatican Curia which run contrary to the whole spirit of Vatican II and the Gospel. The latest of these Vatican actions taken was the December 18, 1979, Declaration against Father Hans Küng that he can "no longer be considered a Catholic theologian or function as such in a teaching role"; it leaves us no responsible choice but to express our profound concern in the most forceful terms:

We are deeply disturbed that the Vatican action was taken not only without dialogue with Father Küng and without even minimal procedures of due process, but in fact in the greatest of secrecy so that Father Küng and the world were suddenly presented with a *fait accompli.*

We are further deeply disturbed that this secretive manner of acting, so reminiscent of the pre-Vatican II Catholicism that we all believed had been outgrown, should misleadingly be portrayed as having been carried out at the end of a years-long dialogue with Professor Küng.

In fact, since 1967, when the Vatican first began to inquire into the writings of Father Küng, he has repeatedly stated that he would go to Rome for a colloquium when at least the minimums of due process procedures were accorded him, namely that he be shown the evidence against him so that he could prepare a proper defense, that he be allowed to name his own counsel, that there be a proper right of appeal. None of these were granted him.

In fact, through the mediating efforts of Cardinal Julius Döpfner of Munich (who unfortunately died in 1976), the Vatican inquiry against Küng was officially closed on February 14, 1975.

In fact, since there has been no communication whatsoever from the Vatican Curia to Father Küng after February, 1975, the Vatican action against Küng in December, 1979, after an almost five-year silence, was taken not only without dialogue, but even precipitously, without warning or notice.

We recall that Pope Paul VI urged the use of dialogue by all today when he stated, "dialogue is demanded . . . by the maturity humanity has reached this day and age."[1]

We recall further that the Vatican Secretariat for Unbelievers in following this papal mandate wrote that "all Christians should do their best to promote dialogue . . . as a duty of fraternal charity suited to our progressive and adult age. . . .

"The willingness to engage in dialogue is the measure and strength of that general renewal which must be carried out in the Church, which implies a still greater appreciation of liberty. . . .

"Doctrinal dialogue should be initiated with courage and sincerity, with the greatest freedom and with reverence."[2]

We therefore call upon the Congregation for the Doctrine of the Faith to respond to this challenge of Pope Paul VI and of its Vatican colleagues in the spirit of Vatican II and the Gospels and employ true dialogue and exemplary due process procedures in its relations to Father Hans Küng and all other Roman Catholics.

One of the more long-range effects in America of the Küng affair was the founding of the Association for the Rights of Catholics in the Church (ARCC) in March 1980. Many Catholics felt galvanized into organizational action by the Küng affair, coming as the culmination of a long line of restrictive moves by the Vatican during 1979, as outlined above. Groups of Catholics met all

---

[1] *Ecclesiam suam,* no. 79.
[2] *Humanae personae dignitatem,* August 28, 1968, no. 1.

over the United States during January and February to discuss whether and then how to organize. On March 7–9, 1980, in Milwaukee, Wisconsin, some thirty-five delegates, representing ten U.S. metropolitan areas where local groups had discussed the launching of the national association, met and founded the organization. It was noted then that at least ten other local ARCC groups had already been organized or were in the process of being organized and that liaisons with similar national organizations in other countries, e.g., Germany, Switzerland, France, Poland, had also been developed. Since that time a National Board has been chosen and met, an executive director hired, a newsletter started, and membership greatly increased.

ARCC stated that because it had been founded to promote the rights of all Catholics in the Church, its members, like its delegates at the founding convention, included women and men, laypeople, religious and clergy—including bishops—academics and activists, and other committed Catholics who fit no such categories. One bishop wrote to one of the conveners of ARCC: "It sounds exactly like what we need these days. The aims seem worthwhile and loyal to the Church. I am writing you now to encourage you and your colleagues, and to thank you for all your hard work on behalf of renewal." ARCC's brief statement of purpose read as follows:

(121)

To bring about substantive structural change in the Catholic Church. It seeks to institutionalize a collegial understanding of Church in which decision-making is shared and accountability is realized among Catholics of every kind and condition. It affirms that there are fundamental rights which are rooted in the humanity and baptism of all Catholics. To this end the association will develop and implement a Charter for the Rights of Catholics in the Church.

The project of drawing up the Charter for the Rights of Catholics in the Church on an international basis is already well launched. A further "partial list of the early activities of ARCC" was also outlined as follows:

1. *Research* into the rights of Catholics in the Church and the procedures necessary to guarantee them.
2. *Education* to make people aware of the rights of Catholics in the Church.
3. *Advocacy* of the acknowledged rights of Catholics when such rights appear to be violated.
4. *Promotion* of procedures whereby claimants to disputed rights have full access to the means of persuasion in the Catholic Church.
5. *Provision* of a vehicle whereby the experience of "loyal dissent" in speech and action may be brought to the universal Catholic Church and be legitimized in it.

(Contact: ARCC, P.O. Box 3932, Philadelphia, PA 19146. Tel. 215-623-1702)

At its founding convention ARCC also clearly linked itself with the Küng affair when it decided to invite Küng to speak under its auspices. Küng did lecture for ARCC, in November 1980, once in Philadelphia and once in New York, under the sponsorship of National ARCC and the two local chapters.

The ecumenical storm of protest over the Vatican action against Küng bordered on the violent. It came from all types of organizations, groups, and individuals. One very broad-based group was the North American Academy of Ecumenists, which was founded in 1967, and is composed of professors, researchers, and professionals in ecumenism from Catholic, Orthodox, and Protestant Churches. All of its members have been involved in ecumenical dialogue with the Roman Catholic Church on one or many levels over the years, which fact gives their commentary considerable weight. The Executive Board of the NAAE sent the following letter to Cardinal Šeper on January 9, 1980, and released it to the press several days later:

(122)

Dear Cardinal Šcpcr:

On behalf of the Executive Board of the North American Academy of Ecumenists we write to express grave concerns in the matter of the disciplinary action taken by the Sacred Congregation for the Doctrine of the Faith against Professor Hans Küng.

As professors of ecumenical theology, as persons active in ecumenical endeavors, we know and appreciate the work of Dr. Küng. Neither we, nor our students, have found it necessary to agree with all of his positions in order to profit greatly from them. The vast majority of his readers must feel the same way. The action against this renowned Roman Catholic theologian will inhibit him and consequently many others in their service of teaching to all Christians. This is much to be regretted, for theologians are needed to serve not only as interpreters of past tradition, but also as guides for the converging way ahead.

A related matter concerns us as well. While we recognize the need for a ministry of pastoral oversight in the church, we cannot overlook unanswered questions having to do with the fairness of the procedures leading to the Congregation's action of December 18, 1979. Certainly in the rare instances where such actions may be warranted, most knowledgeable persons of good will should be able to recognize that procedures followed are impeccably fair and just.

It is our hope and prayer that through continuing dialogue the official recognition of Father Hans Küng as a Roman Catholic theologian may soon be restored.

> Respectfully yours,
> Professor William J. Boney, President
> Professor Francine Cardman, Vice President

cc: Cardinal Jan Willebrands, Archbishop Jean Jadot, Archbishop Antoine Hacault, Bishop Ernest Unterkoefler, Bishop Thomas Kelly, Professor Hans Küng

Even much earlier an interdenominational organization of academics called itself into existence out of concern for academic freedom. On December 21, 1979, it issued the following news release:

(123)

In the wake of the Vatican action against Professor Hans Küng and the threat of a move by German ecclesiastical officials to either have Professor Küng removed from his professorial chair at the Catholic Theological Faculty of the University of Tübingen or have his professorial chair and the Ecumenical Research Institute, of which he is the Director, transferred out of the Catholic Theological Faculty, a new organization was formed in America.

The new organization is called "Committee of Academics Concerned for Responsible Freedom." It is interdenominational in composition, being made up of university and college professors.

Although the organization is new and is gathering additional members, it felt it was imperative to take immediate action to try to prevent any interference in university affairs by non-university agencies, in this case the German Bishops (the University of Tübingen is a state university). To that end they sent cables to the civil officer in the state of Baden-Württemberg (in which Tübingen lies) who is in charge of all university matters, namely the *Wissenschaftsminister* (Academic Minister), the President of the University of Tübingen, and the Dean of the Catholic Theological Faculty of the University of Tübingen.

The text of the cables is as follows:

As academics we should be shocked and outraged if the Wissenschaftsminister were to take any action whatsoever against Professor Hans Küng within the context of the University of Tübingen as a result of extra-academic pressure.

Signed for the "Committee of Academics Concerned for Responsible Freedom,"
Professor T. Patrick Burke, Temple University
Professor Franklin Littell, Hebrew University
(Jerusalem)
Professor Elisabeth Fiorenza, Notre Dame University

Another ecumenical organization of religious scholars, the Society of Christian Ethics, held its annual convention early in January 1980, and passed the following resolution on January 19, 1980:

(124)

In view of the recent Vatican declaration against Professor Hans Küng and its investigation of Edward Schillebeeckx and other Catholic scholars in the United States and elsewhere, we, the Society of Christian Ethics, which is an ecumenical society of theological scholars in North America, wish to express our deep concern about these recent developments.

We acknowledge the concern of church authorities for the integrity of teaching in a pastoral setting. Nonetheless, we insist that to suppress creative and critical theological inquiry discourages theological scholarship within the church and has a chilling effect on the theological exploration necessary for the successful continuation of the ecumenical dialogue: Furthermore, to restrict creative and critical theological inquiry without following the requirements of due process offends against academic freedom, justice, and human rights.

On January 2, 1980, a group of well-known Protestant Church leaders and scholars who had been deeply involved in ecumenical dialogue with Catholics wrote a letter of protest to Cardinal Willebrands, the President of the Vatican Secretariat for Christian Unity. The makeup of the twenty-one ecumenical signers was Lutheran, Methodist (including two bishops), and Presbyterian. The letter was as follows:

(125)

Your Eminence:

We, the undersigned Protestant theologians and clergy, express to his Holiness our concern and sense of dismay over the processes of the Congregation for the Doctrine of the Faith in the cases of Fr. Hans Küng and Fr. Edward Schillebeeckx, O. P. We are not concerned to defend the theological formulations peculiar to Fr. Küng and Fr. Schillebeeckx. We are concerned that the processes of the Congregation for the Doctrine of the Faith threaten the spirit of unity for which our Lord prayed and which Vatican II revived throughout all the Christian churches who regard themselves as, in some sense, members of the holy Catholic Church. We are loath to believe that the dissolution of such frail unity we presently have is of no consequence to his Holiness.

Over the past fifteen years substantial healing has taken place among Christian churches, but recent actions of the Congregation for the Doctrine of the Faith have brought the churches perilously close to the reopening of old divisive wounds. For our part we reaffirm to his Holiness and to all Christians our commitment to the unity for which Christ prayed and for which He continues to pray. We shall therefore resist the recrudescence of old divisions and the inception of new ones.

Because his Holiness, by word and action, influences the life of the total Christian community, we humbly request that he consider the ecumenical implications of the actions taken by the Congregation for the Doctrine of the Faith, and we implore him to take actions which will signal to the whole world his recognition of the pluralism of Christian witness inherent in the church catholic.

The former Chairman of the Commission on Faith and Order of the World Council of Churches, Professor J. Robert Nelson of Boston University, who also had been the first Protestant professor of theology at the Gregorian University in Rome, was also deeply dismayed at the Vatican action and wrote on January 14, 1980, to Cardinal Willebrands the following letter:

(126)

Your Eminence,

With ardent yearning for the promoting of the unity of all Christian people, the reintegration of the unity of the Churches, and the extension of the Gospel of Our Lord Jesus Christ as the Light of the world, I ask you to accept this sincere expression of my present feeling of dismay. In the spirit on your own chosen motto, we try to speak *veritatem in caritate*.

The hopes were raised by the Second Vatican Council in the minds of diverse Christians everywhere that the Roman Catholic Church was endorsing a new freedom of spirit and openness to all the ways by which faithful and serious priests, theologians and other scholars would give an account of their faith in Jesus Christ and His Evangel. The Council has indeed imparted a new and vigorous encouragement to numerous persons, Catholics as well as Protestants and Orthodox, to be guided by the Holy Spirit into the understanding of God's saving truth. The primacy of the Holy Scriptures and the authority of the living Tradition have prevailed in this notable response of Christians to the need for bringing up-to-date their modes of thought for both teaching and proclamation.

This authentically ecumenical development has made it possible for many instances to be experienced in which the designated representatives of the various communions have found themselves converging toward agreement on some significant matters of theology and doctrine. This ecumenical process, thanks to God's direction, is continuing.

No authoritative church bodies and none of us who have participated in the ecumenical conversations are free from some blame for retarding the progress of this new and hopeful movement. Recognizing our own deficiencies of faith and wisdom, however, we must still act upon the Apostle's principle that what concerns each member or communion of the Body of Christ concerns us all.

This is why I, as an individual Christian, join my brothers and sisters of various churches and countries in stating my fervent hope that the injunction laid against the Reverend Professor Hans Küng of the University of Tübingen will be lifted. By his eminently scholarly publications, his many addresses and writings and his personal witness, Father Küng inspires countless men and women of the Oikoumene, strengthening their effectiveness for the evangelization of people who do not yet confess Jesus Christ as Lord and Saviour.

I presume to write to you because I know that your personal and official contributions to unity and mission in the ecumenical context have been, and remain, an inspiration to many. So I join others in prayer and expectation that certain leading personages of the German hierachy, the Congregation for the Doctrine of the Faith, the Secretariat for Promoting Christian Unity, and the Holy Father John Paul II will be moved to recognize the wisdom and need to find ways of sustaining the teaching ministry of Father Küng and such others who, with most serious and faithful intent, are interpreting the Divine Word of Truth for the world today.

There were of course many editorials in various Protestant and interdenominational journals about the Küng affair, all of them supportive of Küng except for very conservative organs. One example again will have to stand for the rest. It is from the broadly inter-Protestant, moderately liberal, highly respected weekly *The Christian Century*. In this case its sentiments and language were hardly "moderate." The January 2, 1980, editorial was as follows:

(127)
A Profane Act by the Sacred Congregation

So the Sacred Congregation for the Doctrine of the Faith has finally found its victim. By condemning Hans Küng, certainly the most influential theologian in the world, and by doing so with the assent of Pope Paul II, it is serving notice on all other Catholic thinkers that it has them under scrutiny.

Restraint is more becoming than rage on the part of Protestants. Their own houses are also not in order. Southern Baptists, Missouri Lutherans, and other groups have held heresy hunts of their own, with just as little regard for evangelical truth and fair play.

If there cannot be anger, let there be sadness and sympathy, not only for Küng, who can take care of himself, but also for less-well-poised Catholic scholars. As they sign up in solidarity with him, they put their good names and careers on the line. Upon his request for non-Catholic support, we offer ours, though at no personal risk. Ours comes out of regard for the man and what he represents and out of concern for the church catholic.

I

That the Sacred Congregation acted so profanely is natural. It is as instinctive for inquisitors to hold inquisitions as it is for crocodiles to eat explorers. That the pope reviewed the case and went along with it is the deeply troubling sign. It represents the loss of still another of his constituencies, and a loss of morale in an already demoralized sector of Catholicism.

Why regret the papal action? Why not think of this in the mood of Mayor Fiorella La Guardia, with his "When I make a mistake, I make a beaut!" and pass it off at that? While inquisitors are supposed to show their fangs, pastors—most notably the chief pastor, when dealing with his chief scholar

—are to be pastoral. Was John Paul? Did they meet? Dare bureaucratic professionals, who disclose nothing of their operations, be entrusted to handle such cases?

What does this action reveal about the mentality and skill of a pope whom the world was coming to love? Had he let the Sacred Congregation do its dirty work alone, he could have remained silent and kept people guessing. After all, who expects the pope to have his hand in everything? "Masterly inactivity," Cardinal James Gibbons called this approach to administration. Let there be polarities in the church. John Paul could have implied: I have my kind of truth, the official custodianship of that "deposit of faith" to which the Congregation refers, and Küng has his, which depends on examinations of texts and traditions. Why go easy on Galileo after the centuries and help create new Galileos now? Why do what so many traditionalists do—fail to see who the best friends of a tradition are? Küng is one, as the ages will reveal.

II

December 18 was a sad day for the Church and a good day for its enemies. For decades it has been possible to confound atheists, agnostics and academicians of many viewpoints by showing that people like Hans Küng could, indeed, be faith-full, hope-full and charity-filled in regard to God, to Jesus Christ and, under the Holy Spirit, to the church—*while* carrying on inquiry and asking questions about murky issues and shaky dogmatic formulations. These days the confounders are confounded, and truth goes begging for a home.

December 18 was, on short terms, a happy day for the authoritarians in Catholicism and, by bizarre alliance, for their counterparts elsewhere. By God, we got the big one, old smart-ass Küng, he of the brains and charm and following. By God, it's good that *somebody* has the brass to have standards and hound out heretics! Protestant inerrantists feel right at home with Catholic infallibilists in their enjoyment of power over truth.

Grant the inquisitors and the pope a point. Maybe Küng, in his inquiries and testings, was pushing at the edges of Catholic tradition. But did they in their treatises satisfy him or anyone that they could prove their case out of the texts and the deepest resources of argument and proof?

The condemners will not win everything, of course. Hundreds of Catholic theologians are engaged in secular employment. Many more are lay men and women, untouchable by a church that, having lost the power and spirit to persuade, reaches for the weapons of coercion. These are not the days of Galileo, and the curses of a condemning church carry no social weight. At all. The hundreds of thousands of thoughtful Catholics who are Catholic because Küng and his kind have been convincing will keep on reading him and his kind, though they may be estranged from the church of which he has become "so deeply ashamed."

Yet darkness falls over another part of the church, and the places where the lights can burn within it are fewer this month. Timid bishops, seminary rectors, Catholic university officials, and theologians themselves, not knowing whose company to keep or how far to go in pursuit of truth, will lose the kind of daring which Christianity needs today if it is to outthink the secular world on urgent issues and help the community of faith survive into a new day.

The authoritarians can find aid and comfort in the news from the end of the 1970s. They have taken much aid and comfort from news throughout the 1970s. But who is to say that the church is in better shape for their decade of repression, for the recruitment they have successfully carried on among those who seek refuge from the challenges of modernity? Who would have thought that already we would be looking back on the good old days of Pope John, he of the masterly activity for truth, and Pope Paul, he of the masterly inactivity for pastorality's sake? And who cannot but hope that the man who bears both their names might not, in the face of protest, have second thoughts instead of getting his back up, as most people predict he will?

If not, given his vigor and youth and vision of beleaguer-
ment, this could be a long rest-of-the-century for Catholicism, and a darker night for Christianity. Or shall there be,
this late in the millennium, a new Reformation, at last?

Several Protestant theological schools also registered their protests, including perhaps the most prestigious of them, Harvard Divinity School. Its protest took the form of a resolution of the Faculty, issued on December 21, 1979. The resolution was as
follows:

(128)

The Faculty of Divinity of Harvard University is charged
with "the serious, impartial, and unbiased investigation of
Christian truth." Indispensable for this task is freedom of inquiry for all participants. We share this theological responsibility with a worldwide community of scholars past and
present. We are conscious of the need for an open dialogue
among Christian theologians and with representatives of
other religious communities and other scholarly disciplines—
a dialogue which has been greatly enhanced by the Second
Vatican Council.

At Harvard Divinity School, we are involved in ever-
widening and deepening collaboration with Roman Catholic
and other schools through the Boston Theological Institute.
We participate in the training of future Roman Catholic
priests and scholars, and our Roman Catholic colleagues
share in the education of future Protestant ministers as well
as doctoral candidates of many persuasions. An enriching
feature of our community has been the inclusion of the
Charles Chauncey Stillman Professors of Roman Catholic
Studies and other Roman Catholic colleagues on our faculty.

Crucial to these new dimensions of theological inquiry is
the recognition that the universal church exceeds the bound-
aries of any historical ecclesiastical body. The growing ecu-

menical dialogue itself exercises a corrective discipline stronger and more lasting than any authorities can enforce.

Therefore, we state our deep concern about the action taken by the Sacred Congregation for the Doctrine of the Faith with respect to the contribution our colleague Hans Küng has made to theology and to the church. We fear that restriction of the scholarship and teaching of this eminent theologian will silence an important Roman Catholic voice in the ecumenical dialogue. We further fear that such actions may adversely affect the climate of present and future Roman Catholic theological work, and thus endanger the task—both Roman Catholic and ecumenical—of creatively preserving and promoting Christian truth.

McCormick Theological Seminary, a Presbyterian seminary in the Chicago area, sent a cable with the signatures of all its faculty and administrators to the Pope in protest. The text of the cable, sent in late December 1979, was as follows:

(129)

Your Holiness,

We, Faculty members of McCormick Theological Seminary, an institution of the United Presbyterian Church in the U.S.A. located in Chicago, Illinois, express our profound distress that an order has been issued, with your approval, to remove Professor Hans Küng from his university post and to forbid him to teach as a Roman Catholic theologian. According to our current information, this order has not yet been carried out. It may not be too late to limit the damage already done to the morale of Roman Catholic and other theological faculties, to your own administration, and to the world reputation of Roman Catholicism.

We call to your attention three concerns:

1. An *ecumenical* concern. Since Vatican II, we have approached the Roman Catholic Church with new expectations.

Yet, as you must know, the Papacy itself remains a major ecumenical problem. This use of Papal power threatens to
close doors to ecumenical possibilities not only with Protestants but also with the Orthodox world, for which we know
you are deeply concerned.

2. A *theological* concern. We make no judgment on the
adequacy or orthodoxy of Professor Küng's writings. Nor do
we deny that the Church has responsibility to teach the faith
clearly. But the gospel cannot be honored by silencing conscientiously held theological opinions. On the contrary, the
gospel creates a potent context for freedom of conscience
and freedom of inquiry.

3. A *human* concern. It is inconceivable to us, your Holiness, that you, nourished not only in the Church but in the
university, author of *The Acting Person,* could suppose that
Christ's cause will be aided by an act of violence against the
human spirit. Not only does this act threaten the liberty of
expression against another human being: it denies values
you yourself have articulated. It has disappointed persons of
every faith and of no faith who have looked to you as a symbol of needed spiritual values.

We call upon you to stay this action against Professor
Küng and to countenance no further actions of this kind.

At the Divinity School of the University of Chicago the approach was somewhat different. There the protest was registered
by the student body. Their statement (undated) was as follows:

(130)

We the undersigned members of the student body of the
University of Chicago Divinity School protest the disciplinary action taken by the Congregation for the Doctrine of
the Faith against the Reverend Professor Hans Küng of the
University of Tübingen. Specifically we protest the manner in
which this action was taken, as painfully dissonant with the
recent papal call to honor high standards of justice and

human rights. It is our most serious concern, as Catholics, Protestants, and Jews who are entering the community of religious and theological scholarship, that the freedom of that community of scholars not only be maintained but fostered. This is not simply an intramural issue for the Roman Catholic Church. It is an issue that involves all students and scholars of religion and theology at every level because it constitutes a threat to the multi-dimensional character of our creative thought. We feel any church that only permits one school of thought, one language, one type of formulation of its tradition effectively stifles the effort of creative theology in that tradition. It is also in keeping with the mark of catholicity in the Roman Catholic Church, as we understand it, that there be a plurality of voices in the theological community. We protest the action taken against Professor Küng as a serious threat to our community of scholarship. We consider him an important and valuable member of our community, whose contribution, as a Roman Catholic thinker, and as a Roman Catholic teacher, we desire to continue. It is with a deep sense of sorrow that we make this protest to you, and we request that it be given your serious, prayerful attention and reflection.

A number of protests were also issued from specifically denominational stances as well as the interdenominational ones above. One of these protests came from Orthodox Christian theologians, which from one perspective is surprising, and from another, not at all. It is surprising in that one thinks of the Orthodox—stereotypically—as conservative and authority-oriented, and hence not given to a protest such as this. However, the most central reason for the Vatican censure of Küng was his questioning the doctrine of papal infallibility, which is also perhaps the major difference between the Orthodox and Rome. Hence, one would expect support for Küng from this quarter. There is, therefore, a special irony in the Vatican move against Küng just after the Pope returned from a visit to the Ecumenical Patriarch in Istanbul to set up arrangements to work toward reunion between East and West.

The following letter, sent on January 3, 1980, to Cardinal Šeper, was from two prominent Greek Orthodox theologians, who, though writing in their own names only, were in fact the current and past presidents of the Orthodox Theological Society in America. The text was as follows:

(131)

Dear Cardinal Šeper:

We the undersigned Greek Orthodox theologians are members of several theological consultations and greatly concerned with the reunion of the Christian Church. Over the years we have been pleased with the progress that Greek Orthodox–Roman Catholic dialogues have made. As you know, one of the fundamental problem areas between Orthodoxy and Catholicism is that of authority. We have been encouraged by the initiatives of both Rome and Constantinople and the kind of progress that has been made in our relations. The mandates which were issued at the Second Vatican Council leading to an ever increasing spirit of dialogue, collegiality, and shared responsibility within the Roman Catholic Church have drawn our two churches ever closer together.

However, we have been viewing the recent developments within the Roman Catholic Church, particularly those stemming from your congregation, with ever growing disappointment, for they seem to us to move in a direction diametrically opposed to the earlier progress made in the spirit of Vatican II.

The latest development, namely, the public dismissal of Reverend Professor Hans Küng as no longer to be considered a Roman Catholic theologian because of his work on the question of infallibility, appeared to us to be the latest in a series of actions that were reminiscent of Vatican I Catholicism's authoritarian-oriented mode of procedure. Such a manner of procedure, it seems to us, cannot but spread a profound chill over the relations between our churches, which in recent years has grown so warm. Indeed, such a development distresses us deeply. Moreover, we are convinced that it is certainly not your wish to take any actions which would widen the distance between Christian Churches.

Hence, we wish to call this inevitable side effect to your attention in the hope that you will quickly be able to find a way to repair the serious damage that has already been done to the image of the Roman Catholic Church in the eyes of many Orthodox Christians. We hope that such action on your part would include not only the necessary attainment of a reconciliation with Rev. Hans Küng, but also the reestablishment and improvement of procedures which would be in accord with the spirit of Vatican II's decisions of collegiality, dialogue, and shared responsibility.

Respectfully yours,

(Rev.) Demetrios J. Constantelos, Ph.D.
Professor of History and Religious
Studies, Stockton State College
Stockton, NJ.
(Rev.) George C. Papademetriou, Ph.D.
St. Nicholas Greek Orthodox Church,
Lexington, MA.

The United Methodist Church, the second-largest of the American Protestant denominations, has long been deeply involved in dialogue with the Roman Catholic Church. It too was deeply disturbed by the Vatican action. Many Methodist spokespersons, including bishops, registered public protest, which was widely reported in the press. Here the editorial of the *United Methodist Reporter,* which refers to the news reports on other Methodist protests in its text, will have to represent the other statements. Although the issue of the paper in which the editorial appeared was dated January 4, 1980, it is clear that it had been written before December 30, 1979, when the "second Roman decision" was announced. The text was as follows:

(132)
Censure of Hans Küng by Vatican cause
for concern by Protestants

Events during recent years—particularly the goodwill visit
of Pope John Paul II to the United States last year—have
served to emphasize the commonality of purpose and heritage among Protestant and Roman Catholic Christians.

The recent censure of Roman Catholic theologian Hans
Küng by the Vatican's high tribunal for doctrinal matters,
however, serves to illustrate that deep-seated differences between Roman Catholics and Protestants remain, and cannot
be glossed over.

Dr. Küng is perhaps the most widely read and influential
Roman Catholic theologian among Protestants. His work has
played a prominent role in the creation of a new climate during the past two decades in which Protestants and Roman
Catholics can discuss both their differences and their common beliefs openly and with minimal hostility.

The Vatican's toleration of Dr. Küng's ceaseless examination of Roman Catholic doctrine—particularly the doctrine
of papal infallibility—has given hope to both Protestants and
Catholics who are devoted to lessening the divisions between
different parts of the Body of Christ.

With the removal by the Vatican's "Sacred Congregation
for the Doctrine of the Faith" of Father Küng's right to teach
with the Church's blessing and to be called a "Catholic theologian," we believe the Roman Catholic hierarchy has taken
a step backward which is bound to conjure up images among
Protestants of a time when the former "Holy Office" crushed
reasoned dissent, created an atmosphere of inquisitional ste-
rility, and thus cut off meaningful dialogue with non-
Catholics.

The very topics with which Dr. Küng has dealt in his writings, and for which he is now censured—papal infallibility,

concepts of the divinity of Christ, and the teaching authority of the Church—are precisely the foundational matters which must be dealt with openly and thoroughly if Roman Catholics and Protestants are ever seriously to consider ways of bridging their differences.

While we would not presume to meddle in the internal workings of the Roman Catholic Church, we believe Protestant and Catholic Christians alike have a stake in whether or not the Vatican decides to stifle critical theological inquiry.

Pope John Paul II's recent decision to suspend the high tribunal's verdict until he is able to discuss the matter personally with bishops in Germany who are Dr. Küng's immediate superiors is a hopeful sign.

We hope the Pope will see fit to moderate the Vatican's position in this matter, and that Dr. Küng will be allowed to continue to examine openly and with the approval of his Church the weighty and complex doctrinal issues to which he has devoted his professional life.

Without any doubt, the Lutheran-Catholic Consultation in the United States (since 1966) has been far and away the most fruitful theologically of all the ecumenical dialogues anywhere in the world. The Consultation meets in plenary session for several days every six months, but the various research and drafting committees often meet much more frequently in between. Their productivity in both quality and quantity in the past fifteen years has been nothing short of astounding. Hence, when all of the Lutheran participants in this Consultation, save one, who was out of the country on sabbatical, sent a letter of protest to Cardinal Šeper, it was a significant indication of how deep the wound was that resulted from the censure of Küng. Again, there was a special irony in the Vatican's acting against Küng mainly because of his work on infallibility, and very especially because in the two "censured" infallibility writings of 1979 Küng recommended the setting up of an ecumenical commission on the infallibility question. As the Lutherans indicated in their letter to Cardinal Šeper, they had already taken a major step in that direction with their thorough bilateral ecumenical study of infallibility. Their letter of January 8, 1980, was as follows:

(133)

Your Eminence:

We the undersigned Lutheran theologians, participants in the official Dialogue in the United States of America sponsored by the Lutheran World Ministries and the Bishops' Committee for Ecumenical and Interreligious Affairs, wish to register our dismay over the procedures employed by the Sacred Congregation for the Doctrine of the Faith in its recent actions regarding Edward Schillebeeckx and Hans Küng.

The particular formulations used by these theologians are not our concern in the present context, but the manner in which action has been taken is. Secretive and non-dialogical ways of exercising teaching authority (as the Congregation's are, rightly or wrongly, widely perceived as being) endanger the mutuality, trust, and openness which has characterized our dialogue with Roman Catholic theologians during the past fifteen years, and which has made possible substantial progress toward fuller unity in the understanding of our common Christian faith.

This progress is evident in the six joint reports which we have published and submitted to our respective churches, most recently on "Papal Primacy and the Universal Church" (1974), and "Teaching Authority and Infallibility in the Church" (1979). We are profoundly grateful to God for enabling us to play a part in the healing of old wounds, but we fear that the lack of even inner-Catholic dialogue in the recent action of your Congregation will hinder further advances in Lutheran–Roman Catholic relations, and even render negatory those already made.

In conclusion, we are deeply disturbed by the damage done to the ecumenical openness towards Roman Catholics which has arisen in our Churches as a consequence of the grace-filled initiative of the Second Vatican Council and of Popes John XXIII and Paul VI; and we are persuaded that different methods on the part of the Sacred Congregation for the Doctrine of the Faith could do much to sustain and increase this openness rather than dissipate it, as it now has.

Respectfully yours,
Robert W. Bertram
Eugene L. Brand
Joseph A. Burgess
Karlfried Froehlich
Eric W. Gritsch
John F. Johnson
Fred Kramer
George A. Lindbeck
John Reumann

Various protests also issued forth from the Anglican world, both within and without the United States. But the strongest by far, both in word and in action—for an imminent covenantal relationship between an Episcopal and a Roman Catholic diocese was thereby postponed indefinitely—came from the Episcopal Bishop of Newark, New Jersey, Rt. Rev. John S. Spong. Bishop Spong's statement, given at Trinity Cathedral in Newark on September 10, 1980, linked together two Vatican actions which Bishop Spong found intolerable—the first action was that of the Küng affair. The text of his statement was as follows:

(134)

It has been a difficult year for the ecumenical movement. The hope that seemed so universal when John XXIII was the head of the Roman Catholic Church now seems so battered, perhaps broken. It is a time of great sadness for Christians.

The year began with the case of Hans Küng. The Roman Catholic hierarchy decided that this world-famous theologian could no longer bear the credentials of an official Roman Catholic theologian. The issue here is not whether Dr. Küng is right or wrong on any particular theological point. It is the assumption by the Roman Catholic hierarchy that their understanding of the truth is identical with the truth. And therefore anyone who challenges, questions, or disagrees with that understanding of truth cannot help being wrong. Never did they meet Dr. Küng in the arena of debate; never did they test his scholarship against their own. Because he differed from the official line and would not submit to a closed hearing, he was judged to be wrong and was removed as an official theologian of the Roman Catholic Church.

Theology for Rome was thus revealed to be a frozen, finished enterprise. Theology, which at best is a human attempt to make rational sense out of the human experience of God, has been declared by Rome to be as unchanging as God himself. That is an incredible and frightening theological claim.

If there is no room in Rome for theological debate among Roman Catholics, if the infallibility of the papacy or of official theological positions cannot be challenged, then let us be honest and say there is no room for such debate and discussion between Protestants and Catholics unless we enjoy participating in time-consuming and meaningless games. If this is, in fact, the position of the Roman Catholic Church, then their only possible reason for talking with people who disagree is to convert them. That is not a proper basis for ecumenical discussion, but the Küng affair suggests that this is the way things are. Consequently it has destroyed any realistic hope that I possessed that there can be fruitful ecumenical dialogue with the Roman Catholic Church today.

If that point was not clear in the Hans Küng episode, it has been newly emphasized and accented by the most recent action of the American Catholic Bishops' Conference. With the approval of the Vatican, the Bishops declared that dissident Anglican clergy would be received into the Roman Catholic Church under certain conditions including reordination.

Let me say first that I have no objection to Anglican

priests becoming Roman Catholic priests or Roman Catholic priests becoming Anglican priests. That has happened with regularity on an individual and private basis since the time of the Reformation. At this moment three former Roman Catholic priests are in Anglican Orders and are working effectively in the Episcopal Diocese of Newark. Secondly, I am pleased at any wedge that can be opened in the Roman Catholic Church to allow a married priesthood. Perhaps the presence of former Episcopal clergy who are married functioning as priests of the Roman Catholic Church will be a leavening and positive influence that will lead to a change in the issue of mandatory celibacy to which Rome seems at present to be committed.

But the action that was taken by the Roman Catholic Church was an official public action. It was not a private or individual matter. It was an unprecedented involvement by a sister communion in the internal affairs of the Episcopal Church. The impact would be similar if an official body of the Episcopal Church were to enter a Roman Catholic debate by issuing a public invitation to enter the Anglican Communion to Roman Catholic priests who favor the ordination of women or to Roman Catholic lay persons who favor the use of birth control devices. The Episcopal Church might even hold out additional incentives such as allowing certain Roman Catholic rites and traditions to be continued. Clearly such an action would not lend itself to trust or to the integrity of an ecumenical dialogue.

Beyond that, this action was taken by the Roman Catholic Church unilaterally. The Episcopal Church was not officially contacted. Our Presiding Bishop was informed of that decision; he was not consulted about it. The Rt. Rev. Arthur Vogel, Bishop of West Missouri and the only American Episcopal bishop on the International Anglican/Roman Catholic Consultation, expressed great surprise at the decision. The Anglican/Roman Catholic Consultation met the second week in September to deal with the effects, not to debate or discuss the possibility. That kind of insensitive action indicates that

ecumenicity is not a major concern of the Roman Catholic
Church, despite rhetoric to the contrary.

The announcement that Anglican clergy who desire to
make this transition would have to be reordained was a reas-
sertion of the ancient and generally discredited claim by
Rome that Anglican Orders are not recognized as valid.
There is little historic debate today among Anglican or
Roman Catholic scholars about the issue of valid orders in
both churches. The Anglican/Roman Catholic Consultation
has come to the very edge of mutual recognition. However,
in the recent action none of this careful, scholarly work was
taken into consideration. This was rather a heavy-handed,
pre-Vatican II type action that comes with all the marks of
medieval ecclesiastical arrogance.

Finally, it was an action which many of the women priests
and supporters of the rights of women to be ordained to the
priesthood within the Episcopal Church found personally in-
sulting. Since 1964, the Episcopal Church has been involved
in a decision-making process in regard to the ordination of
women. The Lambeth Conference of the Anglican bishops of
the world has affirmed this expansion of our priestly ministry. In 1976 the General Convention of the Episcopal
Church, meeting in Minneapolis, authorized the ordination of
women. Any change this significant creates tension and
sometimes causes minor schism or splintering. The Roman
Catholic Church has its Bishop Lefebvre and should understand that quite well. Change always takes time to be absorbed and to become normative. That absorption process
was well underway when this clumsy intervention into the
Episcopal tension was introduced by the Roman Catholic action.

If the Episcopal Church must fight our sister Roman communion in order to affirm the full role of women in the life of
the Church, then sadly we will do so. If, as some believe, the
Roman Catholic Church is saying that the price of continued
ecumenical dialogue and further ecumenical relations is the
cessation by the Episcopal Church of the ordination of

women, then let me be very specific and say the price of continued ecumenical dialogue with the Roman Catholic Church has at this moment become too high.

I will take my stand proudly at the side of our women priests and on behalf of a sexual wholeness in ministry long before I would mourn the loss of an ecumenical dialogue with a church that seems to me in the area of human sexuality to be marching firmly into the nineteenth century. I will not be a party to the continuing sexist oppression of women under the guise of pious phrases or under the appeal to "sacred tradition," even in the name of the ecumenical movement. Sexism in the Roman Catholic Church is a painfully obvious and present phenomenon. It is seen not only in the negativity toward the ordination of women, but also in the requirement of celibacy for priesthood, in the attitude toward birth control. The Pope stated only this week that birth control was "anti-Christian" and "against civilization."

The Diocese of Newark, the Archdiocese of Newark, and the Diocese of Paterson have for some years been working toward a covenant relationship. Further meetings on this endeavor are scheduled for next January. It is my feeling that in the light of this recent action by the Roman Catholic Church the continuation of conversations aimed at a covenant relationship might be interpreted as a violation of the integrity of the Episcopal Church or as an insult to or compromise of our women priests. For this reason with great sadness I am notifying the Archbishop of Newark and the Bishop of Paterson that I will postpone further conversations on this vital matter until actions reveal that the ecumenical climate is more conducive to significant progress and real results.

I do not take this action or say these words lightly, but honesty demands that they be said clearly and publicly.

John S. Spong
Bishop of Newark

Aftermath

Küng normally had anywhere from 100 to 200 students in his lecture classes at Tübingen. But after December 18, 1979, the hall, which seated 300, filled up and the lectures were piped into another lecture hall of 300 seats. He was given leave during the summer semester of 1980 (April 15–July 15), and in the fall began to lecture again under the new arrangement, outside the Catholic Theology Faculty. He was scheduled to give weekly lectures open to the whole University. One might have thought that after the excitement of the previous winter had subsided, especially since Küng was absent during the intervening semester, his lectures would no longer have drawn the oversized crowds of 600. In fact, he consistently drew crowds of 1,000! And this went on week after week. One must also bear in mind that in the German university system there is absolutely no obligation on students to attend lectures, whether they register for them or not. Moreover, since Küng would no longer be examining students—except for the relatively small number writing dissertations under him—the motivation of having to know the material of the examining professor also did not operate to bring students to his lectures. The fact that his lecture course—on ecumenical theology—focused on many current problems, including the contemporary Catholic Church and also infallibility (!), probably also contributed to his drawing power. In any case, the University decided in the winter of 1981 to have Küng give another University-wide lecture course during the summer semester 1981.

A similar enthusiasm for Küng's lectures was also shown throughout the United States when he came on a whirlwind lecture tour from November 5 to 16, 1980, including San Francisco, Los Angeles, Dallas (where he lectured several times before the huge annual convention of the American Academy of Religion–Society of Biblical Literature), Atlanta, Nashville, Boston, New Haven, New York, and Philadelphia. His crowds consistently ran into the thousands. For example, on the morning of November 16, at the end of his grueling tour, after lecturing and giving interviews from 10 A.M. to 1 A.M. the previous day in Philadelphia, he was up early to be driven to New York to preach at the Sunday-morning service in Riverside Church (Presbyterian). The church, which holds 3,000, had people standing in the aisles to hear Küng preach for forty-five minutes on the "Sonship of God"; afterward he spent two hours speaking to hundreds of people individually (in English, German, French, Spanish, or Italian). That was followed by a CBS nationwide television interview, lunch, and then a rush down to St. Joseph's Catholic Church in Greenwich Village to concelebrate Mass with the Catholic clergy there and again to preach for fifty minutes. The church, much smaller, held only 700. When it was full the overflow was put into the church basement, and the overflow from that into the school cafeteria, and sound was piped in, all told, to something more than 1,300 persons. That celebration was co-sponsored by the Association for the Rights of Catholics in the Church (ARCC). Again Küng spoke with people individually, until at the last minute he was driven to the airport for a 7 P.M. flight to London—he arrived at 6:52. The timing was crucial because a large press conference was awaiting him at the London end of the flight, after which he was driven up to Cambridge University for an afternoon lecture in the University Chapel.

Clearly, Küng had a wide and deep response.

Further support of a different sort and from a different source, and a very important one, came in the form of a declaration of

the Society of Catholic Dogmatic and Fundamental Theologians
on the relationship of the teaching office and theology. The declaration was passed almost unanimously by the membership meeting of the Society in Freising (outside of Munich) on January 3,
1981, to be sent to the Presidents of the German, Austrian, Swiss,
and Berlin Bishops' Conferences, as well as the Prefect of the
Vatican Doctrinal Congregation. A comparison between the 1981
declaration and the 1968 declaration of freedom for theology by
1,360 theologians from fifty-three countries (which basically had
been drafted by Küng) will show very great similarities. There
were a few additions which reflected events and demands since
1968; for example, Küng's post-1968 demand that an appeal system be provided turns up in the 1981 declaration. Without mentioning any names, it clearly was a direct and sharp criticism of the
German Bishops and the Doctrinal Congregation in their handling of the Küng affair. The text was as follows:

(135)

1. The Society of Catholic Dogmatic and Fundamental
Theologians is convinced that Catholic theology as a science
of faith is possible in the Church only on the foundation and
under the norm of the Church's faith—and this includes
community with the teaching office. Precisely because today
the concern is to make the Gospel, which the teaching office
and theology must serve, present within the context of new
questions and new cultures in credible and reasoned ways,
the bishops and the theologians can each carry out their own
responsibilities only in loyal collaboration.

2. Theology can perform its service in and for the Church
only in freedom. The freedom which is grounded in the Gospel itself includes a responsibility for unity and peace in the
Church. However, precisely for the sake of this service in the
Church, theology must be able freely to carry out research
and freely to discuss the results of its research. It must put
forward theses and hypotheses whose truth can be determined only in the discussion. It must take new methods into

service and thereby reckon with the autonomy of the different disciplines. With this there can and must arise on the foundation of the one faith of the Church various schools and directions. One-sided theses and developments can most effectively be corrected by unhindered, objective, scholarly discussion.

3. Conflicts between the Church's teaching office and individual theologians are always possible and at times for the sake of the truth perhaps even necessary. With this, overstepping of bounds can occur on both sides. Thus it can be the right and duty of a theologian to admonish and criticize a representative of the teaching office if he expresses himself in a theologically improper way or intervenes inappropriately in the area of theology. On the other side the Church teaching office has the right and duty to call a theologian to a reckoning if he in the opinion of the Church's teaching office leaves or distorts the foundation of Catholic doctrine of the faith and thereby causes confusion in the Church's community of faith. Such disputes must be carried out on both sides in the spirit of justice and fraternity, objectivity, and without personal denigration. Public polemics injure both sides and do not serve the building up of the Church.

4. It is Catholic doctrine that the final decision in doctrinal conflicts lies with the competent agency of the Church's teaching office and that its decision may make a claim to be respected even when it cannot be put forth with ultimate bindingness, and therefore can fundamentally err. Since, however, the truth wishes to convince through itself, it is expected from the Church's teaching office that it will put forth such decisions in an argued manner, and thereby trust more in the power of the truth and the force of the arguments than in administrative measures—which do not rid the world of open questions, but can deliver damaging blows to the credibility of the Church.

5. In keeping with the rule in Matthew 18: 15–18, doctrinal proceedings and disciplinary measures can only be a last resort when inner-theological discussion, personal dialogue,

and public admonishment have remained fruitless and otherwise serious injury to the Church's community of the faith is
threatened. In every case such disciplinary measures will be
carried out only after an orderly proceedings, which is in
keeping with the present-day sense of justice and the Christian ethos. That includes above all the following:

> (1) That the theologian concerned will be granted a just
> hearing before the opening of the proceedings, and before
> the closing issuance of judgment;
> (2) That the subject of the proceedings be only the writ-
> ings of author himself or the public statements acknow-
> ledged by him, not, however, unauthorized reports, or
> indeed denunciations;
> (3) That the theologian be granted access to all the
> documents pertinent to the proceedings and that he have
> the opportunity of making a written or oral statement on
> them;
> (4) That the theologian concerned can with free choice
> specify a defender (discussion adviser), who has the right
> to participate in the colloquium within the proceedings;
> (5) That an appeal from a passed judgment can be
> made to a higher court, and therefore such proceedings
> as a rule should be conducted on the level of the local
> church or the competent Bishops' Conference first, and
> only then in an appeals proceedings in the Roman
> Congregation for the Doctrine of the Faith.

In order to avoid every appearance of bias the Church's
teaching office should utilize as theological consultors and
evaluators only recognized experts, and if the question to be
handled is sufficiently weighty, theologians of the various ec-
clesiastically recognized schools and directions and the
widest possible cultural and national circles should be employed. In this the ancient tradition of obtaining evaluations
from theological faculties, or making use of the counsel and
mediation of theological societies and similar institutions,
can be helpful.

The Society of Dogmatic and Fundamental Theologians is convinced that the currently valid order of procedure of the Congregation for the Doctrine of the Faith is—from the perspective of the credibility of the Church and for the sake of peace in the Church—in urgent need of a swift revision.

6. The Society of Catholic Dogmatic and Fundamental Theologians requests of the Bishops a trusting and fruitful collaboration, which during the Second Vatican Council, to the good of the Church and its credibility in the world, was practiced, but which in the post-conciliar phase has been burdened by both sides. While respecting the differing responsibilities of bishops and theologians, this includes among other things regular contacts and consultations. The Society and its members on their side declare themselves prepared for such a loyal collaboration in the service of the truth of the Gospel. They were confirmed in this readiness by the address of Pope John Paul II to scientists in Cologne and theologians in Alttöting (on November 15 and 18, 1980).

The alleged trigger for the December 18, 1979, Vatican action against Küng was the writing of the introduction to August Hasler's book *How the Pope Became Infallible* in 1979. This high-level popularized version of the very dense, highly scholarly earlier two-volume work by Hasler argued that Vatican I was really not a "free" council, and hence . . . The book was translated into English and was published early in 1981 by Doubleday. Further, a paperback edition of 75,000 copies was issued in German in 1981 also. The infallibility question obviously was not going to go away.

Hasler, although only a relatively young man of forty-three, knew in early summer 1980 that he was dying of cancer. On June 21, 1980, while on his deathbed in a Munich hospital, Hasler collaborated with his colleague in Catholic Church history, Professor Georg Denzler of the History Faculty at the University of Bamberg, in writing an open letter to the Pope about the problem of infallibility. Hasler died on July 1, 1980, and the letter was widely published—posthumously. It was as follows:

(136)

Holy Father!

On May 15, 1980, you sent a letter to the German Bishops' Conference in which you confirmed in laudatory fashion the decision of the Congregation for the Doctrine of the Faith which was supposed authoritatively and definitively to have closed the discussion on papal infallibility, going on for over a decade. You did this mindful of your heavy responsibility for the security of the faith. Although in "the hierarchy of truth revealed by God and professed by the Church" you place the doctrine of infallibility at a lower level of value, you nevertheless are convinced that "it is, in a certain way, the key to the very certainty in professing and proclaiming the faith for the life and behavior of believers. When this fundamental base is weakened or destroyed the most elementary truths of our faith suddenly begin to collapse." As understandable as this concern of yours is, we must nevertheless in all clarity point out to you that in no way have you answered those questions which for a very long time have been raised in an ever more pressing manner and which disturb an ever increasing number of Catholics.

1. *How can the dogma of the infallibility of the papal teaching office be grounded in the Bible and the Tradition of the Church?*

Already at the First Vatican Council (1869–70) an unusually large and qualified minority of 140 bishops were confronted with a conflict of conscience because of the data from the Bible and Tradition. They opposed already at that time the arguments put forth for papal infallibility and they could not, with the best of will, see how the new dogma could be integrated with the history of the Church. Further research has further intensified this problem.

2. *How can the decision of the First Vatican Council be viewed as valid when at that time it came into existence against a better insight and with manifold force?*

As long as these two questions are not satisfactorily answered, the infallibility debate will not be laid to rest. Therefore, Holy Father, we find it extremely regrettable that you have not made the slightest attempt openly to address the real problems which press upon many Christians today. Further, you have not seen it worth the effort to look into the often made suggestion [e.g., Lutheran-Catholic Consultation (U.S.); Hans Küng in his recent introduction to Hasler's book *How the Pope Became Infallible*] to have an ecumenical, interdisciplinary, international commission impartially investigate this complex of problems.

It is difficult to grasp how by your course of action you wish to defend the truth, which in your letter you count among the fundamental rights of the human person. How does this fit with your attempt to cut off discussion and research in theology and history without having provided even meager sketchy arguments on the subject itself? Troubled, we ask ourselves, why Catholic theology at all, when its representatives are ever again warned "to remain loyal to the doctrine of the Church" and not publish research results which are different, out of concern for the prevailing dogma and the teaching office of the Church, which alone can make decisions? Likewise you very unjustly praise the German Bishops' Conference for its "attention and good will," whereas it also, in what touches on the dogma of infallibility, proceeded without a word about the biblical and historical substantive questions.

It fills us with profound concern that you have so little understanding for and place so little value on historical truth, in the face of which, however, Pope Leo XIII claimed the Church need not fear. How can you, for example, maintain that Jesus had to grant to Peter and his followers infallibility "because humanity is fallible"? We cannot find in the Bible that Jesus outfitted the papacy with infallibility. Likewise your calling upon Bishop Irenaeus (died around A.D. 202) is unjustified, for he in no way understood the Roman Church as the sole norm for all other Christians, but rather much more expressly attributed to other Churches of Apostolic origin this same function as well as to Rome.

Your claim to defend the truth is further made non-credible by the fact that you do not act in the area closest to you, i.e., to see to it that finally the manifold hindrances which plague research into Vatican Council I are eliminated. Now as before the archives of the most important curial offices of that period remain closed.

Holy Father, in your letter you declare your intention to work for a renewed Church in the sense of the Second Vatican Council. When, however, you cite texts of this Council you always search out passages which emphasize the unchanged elements. You thereby give those Catholics who have difficulties in and with the modern world, especially in the area of science, absolutely no help. Here also the truth question stands at the center. How can a Church appear credible and reform itself when it is so concerned with the structures of power—you of course have a preference for the word "service"—and so little with the triumph of divine truth?

Time and again you assert that you wish to work for the unity of all Christians. That all, however, remains mere lip service as long as you are not prepared to lay hold of the main problems of Vatican I. The dogmatic definitions of this Council constitute the only major obstacle to the reunion of Christians. Only recently, on April 28, 1980, Roman Catholic and Russian Orthodox theologians, after a fruitful dialogue in Odessa, issued a joint concluding document in which they named among the differences which would be difficult to overcome "the dogmatic formulation of the First Vatican Council concerning the primacy and the infallibility of the Bishop of Rome."

Precisely in connection with ecumenism you have repeatedly spoken of how necessary and important dialogue is. However, whoever listens more carefully recognizes quickly that you do not intend any real dialogue. For you exclude

596 KÜNG IN CONFLICT

every modification of your own position and perceive no possibility of following the arguments of the other side with the result that your own view might be placed in question.

In conclusion we wish to assure you that this letter is written out of a sincere concern for a free development in Church and society. Therefore, we urgently request that you unhesitatingly take up all the questions which today are connected with papal infallibility and collaborate effectively in seeing to it that these questions are objectively studied and clarified.

Bamberg—Munich, June 21, 1980

> Dr. Theol. Georg Denzler
> Prof. of Church History
>   Bamberg University
> Dr. Theol. Dr. Phil. August B. Hasler
> Habilitand for Modern History,
> University of Munich

On May 22, 1980, Pope John Paul II sent a letter, dated May 15, to the German Bishops' Conference specifically about the Küng affair. It was a congratulatory letter—congratulating the Bishops, that is. Some saw it as an attempt to shore up the flagging reputation of the German Bishops. In any case, it contained a number of rather startling passages. In the first section the Pope praises the German Bishops' Conference for working so "collegially" with the Vatican on the move against Küng. Of course, this "collegiality"—which did not include the main, indeed, the only legal "decision-maker" in the matter, the local bishop, Georg Moser—was precisely what had caused such an outcry of foul play among so many Catholics. To describe as praiseworthy and virtuous what much of the world perceived as shameful and cowardly was indeed grasping the horns of the dilemma frontally.

A second startling passage dealt with infallibility. That of course was the key issue between Küng and the Vatican. Küng's inquiry all along had been: Can one really hold to the doctrine of infallibility in the face of all the outlined difficulties? If so, please give evidence and reasons why. Küng's complaint was that all the

Vatican writing on the matter simply repeated previous affirmations and never even attempted to give arguments and evidence why the affirmations should be accepted, other than external authority. In this letter the matter of infallibility is again taken up at some length. But the heart of the treatment is simply a series of rhetorical questions asking whether it is possible for the Church not to have the gift of infallibility. What is so startling about this approach is that it is of course immediately apparent to every reasonably reflective person that naturally the Church need not have such a characteristic. Every student of medieval history knows that it was not until the thirteenth century that the doctrine of papal infallibility was expounded—only to be roundly condemned by Pope John XXII. The concept that was long traditional in the Church at that time, and also long, long afterwards, was that of indefectibility—which Küng had been restressing. At least in the recent past the various Vatican documents on infallibility had insisted on its acceptance because Church authority had committed itself to it previously—*quod scripsit, scripsit*. But here the Pope, or whoever wrote the document, abandoned the relative security of the argument from authority—shamed out of it by Küng?—for the absolutely indefensible position of the rhetorical question—*a petitio principii*.

A third startling, even breathtaking, passage is the section dealing with dialogue. Dialogue, specifically interreligious dialogue, has been officially and unofficially mandated and practiced by Catholics for almost two decades now. There has been wide experience, reflection, and writing on the subject. Anyone at all conversant with these knows that what makes such dialogue possible now—and it is something new under the sun, for it did not exist until perhaps a hundred years ago at the earliest, if then—is the "relativizing" of the human perception of statements about truth. In the last hundred years the wide acceptance of the findings of historicism, sociology of knowledge, and language analysis has made critical Western people see all statements about reality as more and more "relational," related to the time and culture, the sociological class and circumstances, and the language of the speaker. This perception of the relational character of all statements is a *sine qua non* of authentic dialogue, for it assumes that no one person or group can, by the very nature of finite knowledge and the statements of it, know everything about a topic. Rather than being certain about having the full "truth" about a matter, such critical persons claim that one is certain that it is impossible ever to have the full "truth" about something expressed by one person or group. Even the Vatican Declaration *Mysterium ecclesiae,* 1973 (see above, pp. 83–84), concedes this point straightforwardly, and even vigorously. And yet, the writer of the Pope's letter to the German Bishops speaks about certainty in faith ahead of time being the only possible stance from which to enter into authentic dialogue. One comes to debate mainly to teach the opponent, but one comes to dialogue to learn for oneself. If one, however, has complete certainty ahead of time, one cannot genuinely enter into dialogue—only covert debate.

The letter also has some interestingly "soft" things to say about Küng at the end. It was these, understood *in optimam partem,* that Küng used to respond.

The Pope's letter was as follows:

(137)

Venerable and dear brothers in the episcopate.

1. The substantial documentation which you have published in relation to certain theological affirmations of Professor Hans Küng shows how much attention and good will have been employed to clarify this important and difficult problem. Both the pastoral letter read in churches Jan. 13, 1980, and the detailed "Declaration" published recently express the pastoral and magisterial responsibility conforming to the character of your office and of your episcopal mission.

I wish, in anticipation of the coming feast of Pentecost, to confirm you in your mission as pastors in the spirit of love and divine truth and also to thank you for all the concern you have shown regarding the above-mentioned problem and the cooperation you have given to the Apostolic See, in particular, to the Congregation for the Doctrine of the Faith, whose duty—always essential for the life of the Church—seems to be in our times particularly burdened with responsibility and difficulty.

The motu proprio *Integrae servandae,* which during the Second Vatican Council outlined the duties and the procedure of the above-named congregation, emphasizes the necessity of cooperation with the episcopate and thus, exactly corresponds to the principle of collegiality reaffirmed by the Council. Such cooperation, in the case in question, was practiced in a particularly intense manner.

There are many reasons for which the Church of our times must demonstrate itself more than ever as a Church of knowledge and effective collegiality among its bishops and pastors. In such a Church one can also verify more fully that which St. Irenaeus said about the Roman See of Peter, describing it as the center of the ecclesial community, which must gather and unite the individual local churches and all the faithful (cf. *Adversus Haereses:* pp. 7, 848).

Equally the modern Church must be—more than ever—the Church of authentic dialogue, which Pope Paul VI pointed out in the fundamental encyclical at the beginning of his pontificate. *Ecclesiam suam.* The interchange which this involves must lead to a meeting in truth and in justice. In dialogue the Church seeks to understand humanity better and thus its own mission. The Church brings to it the knowledge and truth which are communicated to it in faith.

It is not contradictory to the essence of this dialogue, however, that the Church, in this, is not only what it seeks and receives but also that which it has received based on certainty, which in such a colloquium still becomes augmented and deepened but never abandoned. On the contrary: It would be contrary to the essence of dialogue if the Church would wish in this dialogue to suspend its convictions and turn its back on the knowledge which already has been given to it.

Furthermore, that dialogue which the bishops conduct with

a theologian, who in the name of the Church and because of
his charge teaches the faith of the Church, has a particular
character. This is subject to other conditions, in relation to
those which are conducted with persons of different convictions in the common search for a meeting point. The first
thing to clarify here is that the one who teaches at the charge
of the Church corresponds also in act and wants to agree to
this charge.

Regarding the teaching charge of Professor Küng, one
must put forward the following questions: Does a theologian
who does not integrally accept the doctrine of the Church still
have the right to teach in the name of the Church and on a
basis of the special mission which is received? Can he still
want to do so, if several dogmas of the Church are in contrast with his personal convictions? And then, can the
Church—in this case the responsible body—in such circumstances continue to oblige the theologian to do it despite everything?

The decision of the Congregation for the Doctrine of the
Faith, taken in common accord with the German Bishops'
Conference, is the result of the honest and responsible reply
to these questions. At the base of these questions and this
concrete reply, one finds a fundamental right of the human
person, that is, the right to truth which must be protected
and defended.

Certainly Professor Küng has declared with insistence that
he wishes to be and remains a Catholic theologian. In his
works, however, he manifests clearly that he does not consider several authentic doctrines of the Church as definitively
decided and binding on himself and on his theology. Based
on his personal convictions, he is no longer able to work in
the sense of the mission which he received from the bishop in
the name of the Church.

The Catholic theologian, as any scientist, has the right to
free analysis and research in his own field: obviously, in a
manner which corresponds to the nature itself of the Catholic
theologian. When, however, it is a question of the oral and

written expression of results of that research and reflection, it is necessary to respect in a particular way the principle formulated by the Synod of Bishops in 1967 with the expression "paedagogia fidei" (pedagogy of the faith).

It can be advantageous and right to point out the rights of theology. However, it is necessary, at the same time, to take into rightful account also its particular responsibilities. One must not forget either the right or the duty of the teaching office in deciding what conforms to the doctrine of the Church on faith and morals and what does not. The verification, the approval or the denial of a doctrine, lies within the competency of the prophetic mission of the Church.

2. Several questions and several aspects connected with the discussions of Professor Küng are of a fundamental character and of general importance for the actual period of post-conciliar reform. I would like, therefore, to deal with them a little more amply in the following section.

In the generation to which we belong the Church has made enormous efforts to better understand its nature and the mission entrusted by Christ in relation to humanity and the world, especially the modern world. It has done it through the historic service of the Second Vatican Council. We believe that Christ was present in the assembly of bishops, that he worked in them by means of the Holy Spirit, promised to the apostles at the eve of his passion, when he spoke of the "spirit of truth" which would teach them every truth and which would remind them of all that they had heard from Christ himself (cf. John 14:17–26). From the work of the Council was born the program of renewal of the Church from within, a program of wide and courageous range, joined with a deepened awareness of the true mission of the Church, which by its nature is missionary.

Although the post-conciliar period was not free from difficulty (as had already occurred in the history of the Church), we believe that Christ is present in it—the same Christ who even to the apostles, at times, made storms on the lake, which seemed to bring them to shipwreck. After nightly

fishing, during which they had caught nothing, he transformed this failure into an unexpected abundance of fish,
when they cast their nets on the word of the Lord (cf. Luke
5:4–5). If the Church wants to be faithful to its mission in
the stage of its history, undoubtedly difficult and decisive, it
can only do it by putting itself within hearing distance of the
word of God, that is listening to the "word of the Spirit," as
it came to the Church through tradition and, directly,
through the teaching office of the last Council.

In order to follow such work—arduous and "humanly"
very difficult—a special faith in Christ and his Gospel is necessary, because only he is "the way." Therefore, only by
maintaining fidelity to established signs, preserving the continuity of the way, followed by the Church for 2,000 years,
can we be certain that we will achieve for ourselves that
power from on high which Christ himself promised the apostles and the Church which attests to his presence "until the
end of the world" (Matthew 28:20).

If there is, therefore, something essential and fundamental
in the daily life of service in the Church, it is the particular
orientation of souls and hearts towards the fullness of the
mystery of Christ, redeemer of humanity and of the world,
and at the same time, fidelity to the image of the nature and
mission of the Church, as, after so many historic experiences,
was presented by the Second Vatican Council. According to
the express doctrine of that Council, "every renewal of the
Church essentially consists in an increase of fidelity to its
own calling" (*Unitatis redintegratio,* n. 6). Every attempt to
replace the image of the Church, which comes from its nature and mission, with another, inevitably leads us away from
the sources of light and strength of the spirit, of whom we
have a particularly great need today. We must not delude
ourselves that another model of the Church—more "laicized"
—can respond in a more adequate way to the demands of a
greater presence of the Church in the world and to its greater
awareness of the problems of humanity. Such can only be a

Church deeply rooted in Christ, in the sources of his faith, hope and charity.

The Church must be, moreover, very humble and at the same time secure in remaining in the same truth, in the same doctrine of faith and morals which it received from the Christ, who in this sphere gave it the gift of a specific "infallibility." Vatican II inherited from the First Vatican Council the doctrine of tradition in this regard, and it confirmed it and presented it in a more complete context, that is in the context of the mission of the Church, which has a prophetic character, thanks to its participation in the prophetic mission of Christ himself. In this context and in strict connection with "the way of faith," in which all the faithful participate, this "infallibility" has a character of gift and of service.

If anyone understands it differently, he moves away from the authentic vision of faith and, even if perhaps unconsciously, but in a real way, separates the Church from him who, as the bridegroom, "loved" it and gave himself for it. Endowing the Church with all that is indispensable to fulfill the mission which Christ entrusted to it, could he possibly have deprived it of the certainty of professed and proclaimed truth? Could he possibly deprive of this gift especially those who, after Peter and the apostles, inherited a particular pastoral and magisterial responsibility before all the community of believers? Exactly because humanity is fallible, Christ—wanting to preserve the Church in truth—could not leave its pastors-bishops and especially Peter and his successors, without that particular gift, which is the assurance of infallibility in the teaching of the truths of the faith and the principles of morals.

Therefore, we profess infallibility, which is a gift of Christ given to the Church. And we cannot not profess it, if we believe in the love with which Christ loved his Church and continuously loves it.

We believe in the infallibility of the Church not out of respect for any human being but for Christ himself. We are

convinced, in fact, that even for him who participates in a
special way in the infallibility of the Church, it is essentially
and exclusively a condition of service, which he must exercise in the Church. In fact, in no case, and so much less in
the Church, can "power" be understood and exercised if not
as service. The example of the Teacher is decisive here.

We must, on the other hand, harbor deep fear, if in the
Church itself the faith in this gift of Christ is put in doubt. In
such a case, the roots from which the certainty of truth professed and proclaimed in it would be cut off at the same
time. Although the truth on infallibility of the Church can
justly seem a less central truth and of minor order in the hierarchy of truth revealed by God and professed by the
Church, nevertheless it is, in a certain way, the key to the
very certainty in professing and proclaiming the faith for the
life and behavior of believers. When this fundamental base is
weakened or destroyed the most elementary truths of our
faith suddenly begin to collapse.

It is a question, therefore, of an important problem in the
present post-conciliar period. When in fact the Church must
undertake the work of renewal, it is necessary that it have a
particular certainty of faith, through which, renewing itself
according to the doctrine of the Second Vatican Council, it
remains in the same truth which it had received from Christ.
Only thus can one be sure that Christ is present in one's own
boat and guides it firmly even through the most threatening
storms.

3. Anyone who participates in the history of our century
and is not unfamiliar with the various trials which the
Church lives in its midst, in the march of these first post-
conciliar years, is conscious of these tempests. The Church
must confront these storms and cannot be affected by uncertainty in faith and by relativism of truth and morals. Only a
Church deeply consolidated in its faith can be a Church of
authentic dialogue. Dialogue requires, in fact, a particular
maturity in proclaimed and professed truth. Only such maturity, that is certainty in faith, is able to oppose the radical ne-

gations of our time, even when they are aided by various means of propaganda and pressure. Only such a mature faith can become an effective advocate of true religious liberty, liberty of conscience and all the rights of humanity.

The program of the Second Vatican Council is courageous; therefore, it asks in its fulfillment a particular confidence in the Spirit who has spoken (Acts 2:7) and requires a fundamental faith in the power of Christ. This confidence and this faith, as a measure of our times, must be great as that of the apostles, who after the ascension of Jesus, "devoted themselves to constant prayer . . . with Mary" (Acts 1:14) in the Upper Room of Jerusalem.

Undoubtedly such faith in the power of Christ also calls for the ecumenical work of Christian unity, undertaken by the Second Vatican Council, if we intend it as was presented by the Council in the decree *Unitatis redintegratio* (Decree on Ecumenism). It is significant that this document does not speak of "compromise," but of meeting in an ever more mature fullness of Christian truth: "The manner and order in which Catholic belief is expressed should in no way become an obstacle to dialogue with our brethren. It is, of course, essential that doctrine be clearly presented in its entirety. Nothing is so foreign to the spirit of ecumenism as a false conciliatory approach which harms the purity of Catholic doctrine and obscures its assured genuine meaning" (n. 11; cf. n. 4).

Therefore, from the ecumenical point of view of the union of Christians, one cannot in any way pretend that the Church renounces certain truths professed by it. It would be contrary to the way the Council indicated. If that Council, to achieve such an end, affirms that "Catholic faith must be explained with more profundity and exactness," it is indicating also the duty of theologians. Most significant is that section of the decree *Unitatis redintegratio* which deals directly with Catholic theologians, emphasizing that "in searching together with separated brethren into the divine mysteries," they must remain "faithful to the doctrine of the Church" (n 11). Previously, I already pointed to the "hierarchy" or order or truths of Catholic doctrine, of which theologians must be reminded, particularly "when comparing doctrines." The Council evokes such a hierarchy, given that "they vary in their relation to the foundation of the Christian faith" (*ibid.*).

In such a way ecumenism, this great inheritance of the Council, can become a more mature reality, that is only on the road of a greater commitment of the Church, inspired by certainty of faith and by a faith in the power of Christ, which, since the beginning, the pioneers of this work have distinguished themselves.

4. Venerable and dear brothers of the German Bishops' Conference!

One can love the Church only when one loves one's brothers: each and every one in particular. Therefore, this letter which I write to you in relation to recent events of Professor Hans Küng is also dictated by love for our brother.

To him, I wish again to repeat that which was expressed already in other circumstances: We continue to nurture the hope that a meeting in the truth proclaimed and professed by the Church can be achieved, that he can be again called "Catholic theologian." This title presupposes necessarily the authentic faith of the Church and the readiness to serve its mission in a manner clearly defined and verified throughout the centuries.

Love requires that we seek a meeting in truth with every person. Therefore, we do not cease to implore God for such a meeting in a particular way with this man, our brother, who as Catholic theologian, which he would like to be and remain, must share with us a particular responsibility for the truth professed and proclaimed by the Church. Such a prayer is, in a certain sense, the fundamental word of love towards humanity, towards neighbor, since through it we find him in God himself who, as the unique source of love, is at the same time in the Holy Spirit the light of our hearts and our consciences. It is also the first and deepest expression of that concern of the Church, in which its pastors especially must participate.

In this communion of prayer and common pastoral concern, I entreat for you at the coming feast of Pentecost the abundance of gifts of the divine Spirit and I greet you in love of Christ with my special apostolic blessing.

From the Vatican, May 15, feast of the Ascension of Christ, in the year 1980, second of the pontificate. Ioannes Paulus PP II.

Although Küng's legal position at the University had been resolved in a way that was relatively satisfactory to him, his profound commitment to working for renewal of the Catholic Church would not let him be content to be a "quasi-outsider" in Catholic theology. He is committed to regaining his *Missio canonica*. As a step toward that goal he wrote a personal letter to Pope John Paul II on August 25, 1980.

In his letter, which was handwritten, Küng said that in reading and rereading the Pope's letter to the German Bishops he was particularly touched by the Pope's words that his letter was "dictated by love for our brother" Küng and that he asked God for "a meeting in the truth . . . in a particular way with this man, our brother, who as Catholic theologian, which he would like to be and remain, must share with us a particular responsibility for the truth professed and proclaimed by the Church." Küng expressed deep gratitude for those sentiments, and went on to indicate that it was precisely that responsibility for the truth that has continued to shape his work since December 18, 1979. He explained, however, that the increasing anxieties and problems within Catholicism, with other Christian Churches, and between theologians and Church authorities since that time have led him increasingly to feel the need for a reconciliation between himself and the Church authorities.

Küng noted that the Pope's letter was understood by many as a move on his part toward a rapprochement that could result in a conversation between the two of them—Küng wished to understand the letter in the same way. Küng remarked that even from the beginning of John Paul II's pontificate he, Küng, had expressed a desire for a personal meeting with the Pope (cf. Küng's letter to John Paul II, pp. 370–77), which, even though it would not solve all problems, would nevertheless be an important gesture of dialogue and show concretely that even with the most grave differences of opinion Christ's love ruled supreme and that harmful polarizations could be avoided.

To date the letter has not been answered.

A Theologian-Historian's Evaluation

In the foregoing pages I have attempted for the most part to play the role of the "objective" historian, selecting what seemed to be the most important documents and providing their context so that the reader could follow the events at first hand and judge the developments accordingly. Having accomplished that task—I hope within the acceptable minimums of historical "objectivity," given the inevitable subjectivity of all historiography, even in the choice of problems and the selection of documents—I would like now very briefly to step beyond the first role of the historian. Having absorbed the previous hundreds of pages of documents (and one "absorbs" in a very intimate way when one translates), and many more hundreds of pages of documents not here reproduced, plus having read almost all of the writings of Küng and having known and worked with him for over a score of years, it would be appropriate for me to give an evaluation of the relationship between Küng and Catholic Church authorities.

One way the question might be put is: Why does Küng get into trouble with the Vatican when other Catholic theologians do not? There are several components in an answer to that question. First of all, it should be remembered that it is just not so that other Catholic theologians do not have difficulties with the Vatican. We have seen above that in 1979 alone Pohier, Schillebeeckx, and

Kosnick *et al.* ran into severe public difficulties, to which list of well-known theologians can be added the names of Piet Schoonenberg, Leonardo Boff, and Charles Curran, who likewise are under Vatican investigation, plus many others of lesser fame. In terms of ongoing, years-long difficulties with Rome and/or their national hierarchy, Schillebeeckx, Schoonenberg, and Curran have post-Vatican II records that come close to rivaling Küng's.

Probably the most important reason why Küng does get into difficulties with Church authorities is that he takes the historical-critical method seriously and carries its results over into his theological reflections. He of course is by far not the only Catholic theologian to do so, but he does it with a consistency that is not matched by all. And where it is, and other necessary factors are present, as, for example, in the case of Schillebeeckx, the resultant problems are much the same. As discussed above, Küng's method of doing theology is fundamentally historical, and hence dynamic, unafraid of the idea of change. This world view is completely at odds with the traditional, static one. As Thomas Kuhn has shown in the history of science, the shift from one "paradigm" by which reality is understood to a new one is always fraught with resistance and turbulence before the new paradigm is accepted—one thinks pre-eminently of the agonies of Copernicus, Kepler, and Galileo in moving from the geocentric to the heliocentric paradigm. Given the acceleration of change in the contemporary world, one hopes that Küng will be functioning as Copernicus, Kepler, and Galileo and beyond all rolled into one.

Another reason for Küng's difficulties is his total honesty. For him that is a virtue that cannot be displaced by other considerations—he says as much in the whole book entitled *Truthfulness: The Future of the Church.* A number of other Catholic theologians are aware of the results of historical studies, but at certain critical points "fudge" their application to Christian doctrine. In many cases it is a matter of having a fundamentally different ecclesiology; they start out with what the Church has traditionally taught on some matter through some authoritative expression, e.g., a conciliar or papal document, and assume that it cannot be faulted, not "essentially," although they will nowadays allow for "development." The difficulties come when the "development" moves from, e.g., Gregory XVI and Pius IX's solemn condemnations of religious freedom to Vatican II's solemn approbation of religious freedom. Küng, and others, would say that in such instances one cannot meaningfully, honestly, speak about "development," but one would have to admit the possibility of error in at least one of the two contradictory positions (the former position is obviously his choice). Such probity precipitates papal problems.

Even the above matters would not have gotten Küng into so much difficulty if it were not for the fact that he, deliberately and as the result of great effort, writes in such an understandable manner about problems that many contemporary men and women have. As Cardinal Volk put it: "The trouble with your book is that it is too plausible." The result is that Küng is extremely widely read, and *therefore* the Church authorities are concerned about him; he has influence and his world view is displacing theirs in the minds and actions of an increasing number of Catholics. This factor is an extremely important one in explaining Küng's difficulties with authorities. I wrote a book entitled *Freedom in the Church* in 1969, which expressed many of the same views on infallibility and other issues as did Küng before and after. But I have never had any difficulties with Church authorities—reason: only a few thousand copies of the book were sold, hence no influence, and therefore no challenge to the authorities' static world view. Only the combination of the above elements can explain Küng's constant conflicts.

A second question I would like to reflect on briefly is that of the legality, the properness, the justice of the action taken against Küng, particularly the Vatican–German Bishops' Conference action of December 18, 1979. It must of course at the outset be stated that the *modus operandi* of the Doctrinal Congregation after Vatican II has changed rather significantly, certainly from the time of Galileo, and also from the time of the anti-Modernism heresy hunt earlier this century. However, it still falls far short of the minimally accepted canons of justice and legal procedure in contemporary Western civilization. Surely it is cause not of pride but of shame if the "pagans" are more sensitive to justice than the leadership of the Catholic Church. In a joint declaration 1,360 Catholic theologians from all over the world made this point—along with concrete suggestions for remedies—back in 1968. Knowledge of human nature and the sociological laws that govern all institutions "explain" why the Catholic leadership has not yet been sufficiently shamed into effective remedies, but that insensitivity to justice is nevertheless the cause of profound shame for numberless Catholics before the secular world—especially in view of the experience of their "founder" Jesus with justice from the various authorities of his time (mainly Roman then too!).

It appears completely clear to me that the Vatican move against Küng on December 18, 1979, violated not only a basic sense of justice but also the Doctrinal Congregation's own order of procedure. Küng pointed this out several times in the above documents. If the Vatican in fact thought that the two small writings of 1979 dealing with infallibility constituted a really serious matter (difficult as it may be to convince oneself that they could be sincere in professing such an attitude), the obvious move they had to make before they could issue a sentence was to initiate a new proceedings against the writings in question. The same is even more true of their summary condemnatory treatment of Küng's Christology and Mariology, neither of which items had ever been the subject of any proceedings or, as far as one knows, even investigation by Rome at all. Such treatment by the Vatican —to say nothing of the German Bishops' Conference—was obviously a gross violation of due process. A clear proof of the shocking quality of this violation by the complicitous, secret action of the Doctrinal Congregation and the leadership of the German Bishops' Conference is the stunned and at first strongly resistant reaction by Bishop Moser when he was informed at the secret meeting in Brussels of the—under the circumstances, one really has to say—"plot" against Küng, even to the point of freely writing about it later (see above, pp. 402–4).

As noted above in the documentation section, the change in personnel in three instances dramatically altered Küng's relationship to the Church authorities in Germany and in Rome. The first was the replacement of the moderate Paul VI by the conservative, and actively so, John Paul II (with the brief pontificate of John Paul I in between). The second and third were the replacement of the moderately conservative, but open and friendly, Cardinal Döpfner by the conservative, and not friendly to Küng, Ratzinger as the Cardinal Archbishop of Munich and the very conservative, and aggressively hostile to Küng, Höffner, Cardinal Archbishop of Cologne, as the President of the German Bishops' Conference. It was really the combination of the first and the third that precipitated the December 18, 1979 action.

For the historian of the Catholic Church in modern times there are some rather scary resemblances to the situation in Europe in the 1830s. In 1830, Gregory XVI became Pope—a very conservative one—after a pontificate by his predecessor of only a few months. In Cologne, Archbishop Droste-Vischering—a very conservative prelate—took over from his liberal predecessor, Archbishop Spiegel, in the 1830s. In 1835, Rome condemned the work of Hermes, the foremost Catholic theologian of the period, who was trying to express Catholic thought in the categories of the time (he had died in 1831). After 1837, Archbishop Droste-Vischering mounted an aggressive campaign in conjunction with Rome to have all the disciples of Hermes, who were theology professors at various universities, removed from their post. It worked. That was the beginning of the so-called "Catholic" or "Churchly" movement that went from one repression to another, eventually blotting out almost all the advances made in theology and practice of the previous decades (much of Germany, centering on Tübingen, in the first third of the nineteenth century, boasted a full-fledged pre-Vatican II Vatican II-Catholicism—see Leonard Swidler, *Aufklärung Catholicism 1750–1850*, Missoula: Scholars Press, 1978). The restrictive pontificate of Gregory XVI was followed by the reactionary pontificate of Pius IX, culminating in the declaration of papal infallibility at Vatican I in 1870. There is no need to draw out the parallels, except to note that Höffner's predecessor as the Archbishop of Cologne was the liberal Cardinal Frings (he led the "revolt of the Cardinals" against the Curia at the beginning of Vatican II). One hopes that the extraordinary parallels do not continue.

Index

LEONARD SWIDLER is professor of Catholic thought and interreligious dialogue at Temple University (Philadelphia), where
he is also editor of the *Journal of Ecumenical Studies,* which he
co-founded in 1963. After having taken a Ph.D. in history from
the University of Wisconsin (1961) and an S.T.L. in Catholic
theology from the University of Tübingen (1959), he has written,
edited, or translated some twenty books and is the author of scores
of articles.